W9-AEB-479

Contemporary Strategy Analysis

To Sue

Contemporary Strategy Analysis

Fifth Edition

Robert M. Grant

Blackwell
Publishing

© 1991, 1995, 1998, 2002, 2005 by Robert M. Grant

BLACKWELL PUBLISHING
350 Main Street, Malden, MA 02148-5020, USA
108 Cowley Road, Oxford OX4 1JF, UK
550 Swanston Street, Carlton, Victoria 3053, Australia

The right of Robert M. Grant to be identified as the Author of this Work has been asserted in accordance with the UK Copyright, Designs, and Patents Act 1988.

First edition published 1991 by Blackwell Publishers Ltd
Second edition published 1995 by Blackwell Publishers Ltd
Third edition published 1998 by Blackwell Publishers Ltd
Fourth edition published 2002 by Blackwell Publishers Ltd
Fifth edition published 2005 by Blackwell Publishing Ltd

Library of Congress Cataloging-in-Publication Data

Grant, Robert M., 1948–
    Contemporary strategy analysis / Robert M. Grant. – 5th ed.
        p.   cm.
    Includes bibliographical references and index.
    ISBN 1-4051-1998-5 (hardcover : alk. paper) – ISBN 1-4051-1999-3 (pbk. : alk. paper)
1. Strategic planning. I. Title.

    HD30.28.G72 2005
    658.4′012–dc22

                                                            2004007696

A catalogue record for this title is available from the British Library.

Set in 10/12pt Galliard
by Graphicraft Limited, Hong Kong
Printed and bound in the United Kingdom
by TJ International, Padstow, Cornwall

The publisher's policy is to use permanent paper from mills that operate a sustainable forestry policy, and which has been manufactured from pulp processed using acid-free and elementary chlorine-free practices. Furthermore, the publisher ensures that the text paper and cover board used have met acceptable environmental accreditation standards.

For further information on
Blackwell Publishing, visit our website:
www.blackwellpublishing.com

Contents

Preface

The purpose of *Contemporary Strategy Analysis* is to equip managers and students of management with the core concepts, frameworks, and techniques of strategic management which will allow them to make better decisions both for their companies and themselves. To achieve this I have written a book that endeavors to be both rigorous and relevant.

The approach is analytical. If strategic management is all about managing to achieve superior performance, then the essential tasks of strategy are to identify the sources of profit available to the business, and to formulate and implement a strategy that exploits these sources of profit. The result is a book that is simultaneously theoretical and practical. It is theoretical to the extent that it concentrates upon the fundamental factors that determine business success. It is practical to the extent that acquiring deep insight into the determinants of business success is the basis for developing strategies that work.

This fifth edition of the book reflects the impact of two key forces reshaping today's business environment: competition and turbulence. Innovation, entrepreneurship, and the dissolution of national and industry boundaries all increase the intensity of competition. As a result, the quest for competitive advantage becomes critical for survival. My primary goal for the fifth edition has been to sharpen and develop the analysis of competitive advantage through a stronger focus upon the need to identify, develop, and exploit the resources and capabilities of the enterprise. The new edition gives increased prominence to the tools of knowledge management, to the development of new organizational capabilities, and the ownership of standards.

As the rate of change of the business environment continues to accelerate – driven by technology, deregulation, changing customer preferences, and volatile exchange rates and commodity prices – the implications for strategic management are far reaching. At the most basic level, strategy making extends beyond questions of resource deployment and market positioning to address fundamental questions such as: What is our business? What are we trying to achieve? What is our identity as an organization? Managing under conditions of rapid change also requires new approaches to strategy analysis. In this edition I explore the analysis of real options, patterns of industry evolution, the sources of strategic innovation, and the implications of complexity theory.

This new edition of the book comes in the wake of a series of traumatic events in the business environment – the bursting of the dot.com bubble, the collapse of the technology-led stock market boom of 1995–2001, and the turbulent and tragic international developments since September 2001. The harsh realities of this first decade of the twenty-first century have dispelled the hubris and "irrational exuberance" that characterized the end of the 1990s. The outcome has been a reaffirmation of the fundamental principles of strategy, notably the need to base business strategies upon careful analysis of customer choice, competition, and the internal strengths and weaknesses of firms.

Recent years have also seen clear reaction against the materialism and massive appropriations of corporate wealth by corproate executives. The rising awareness of ethics, sustainability, and corporate social responsibility does not invalidate the view of strategy as a quest for profit, but it demonstrates that the pursuit of profit requires alignment between the goals of business enterprises and long-term interests of society and the natural world.

Finally, this new edition of *Contempory Strategy Analysis* reaffirms the co-dependence of strategy formulation and strategy implementation. Unlike some other strategy texts, I do not split the book into separate sections for strategy formulation and strategy implementation. I offer an integrated approach to strategy formulation and implementation in the belief that these cannot be treated in isolation from one another. A strategy that is formulated without regard to its implementation is likely to be fatally flawed. At the same time, it is through their implementation that strategies adapt and emerge. Hence, I introduce organizational design as part of the basic toolkit of strategy analysis (Part II of the book). Subsequent chapters that explore different types of strategy and different business contexts provide an integrated treatment of strategy formulation and strategy implementation. At the same time, I set limits as to how far down the path of strategy implementation it is sensible to travel. Ultimately, strategy implementation takes us into the functional areas of the business – finance, marketing, operations, human resource management, and information systems. I leave these functions to their own specialists.

There is very little in this book that is original – I have plundered mercilessly the ideas, theories, and evidence of fellow scholars. My greatest debts are to my colleagues and students at the business schools where this book has been developed and tested – Georgetown University, City University, UCLA, California Polytechnic, Bocconi University, and the University of British Columbia. This edition has also benefited from feedback and suggestions from professors and students in other schools where *Contempory Strategy Analysis* is used. I am grateful to all of you. I continue to learn and look forward to sharing that learning with you.

Robert M. Grant
Washington DC
April 2004

I
Introduction

1

The Concept of Strategy

Strategy is the great work of the organization. In situations of life or death, it is the Tao of survival or extinction. Its study cannot be neglected.
—Sun Tzu, The Art of War

OUTLINE

INTRODUCTION AND OBJECTIVES

Strategy is about winning. This chapter explains what strategy is and investigates its role in success – both for organizations and individuals. Although our primary concern will be business, we shall also note the critical importance of strategy in other fields of human endeavor, including warfare, entertainment, politics, and sport. We will distinguish strategy from planning. Strategy is not a detailed plan or program of instructions; it is a unifying theme that gives coherence and direction to the actions and decisions of an individual or an organization.

We shall go on to examine the role of analysis in strategy formulation. If strategy is purely a matter of intuition and experience, then there is little point in studying this book – the only way to learn is to go and do. The key premise that underlies this book is that there are concepts, frameworks, and techniques that are immensely useful in formulating and implementing effective strategies.

By the time you have completed this chapter, you will be able to:

■ Appreciate the contribution that strategy can make to successful performance, both for individuals and for organizations.

■ Understand the basic analytical framework that underlies this book where the two fundamental components of strategy analysis are the analysis of the external environment (primarily industry analysis) and the analysis of the internal environment (primarily the analysis of the firm's resources and capabilities).

■ Understand the major trends in the development of business strategy over the past 40 years.

■ Recognize the multiple roles that strategic management plays within organizations.

Since the purpose of strategy is to help us to win, we start by looking at the role of strategy in success.

THE ROLE OF STRATEGY IN SUCCESS

Strategy Capsules 1.1, 1.2, and 1.3 outline examples of success in three very different arenas: Madonna in popular entertainment, General Giap and the North Vietnamese armed forces in warfare, and the Williams sisters in tennis. Can the success of these diverse individuals and the organizations they led be attributed to any common factors?

For none of these three examples can success be attributed to overwhelmingly superior resources:

- Madonna possesses vitality, intelligence, and tremendous energy, but lacks outstanding talents as a vocalist, musician, actress, or any other of the principal vocations within popular entertainment.

- The military, human, and economic resources of the Vietnamese communists were dwarfed by those of the United States and South Vietnam. Yet, with the evacuation of US military and diplomatic personnel from Saigon in 1975, the world's most powerful nation was humiliated by one of the world's poorest.

- Masterminding the incredible success of Venus and Serena Williams on the world tennis circuit during 2000–03 was manager, coach and father, Richard Williams. Brought up in an impoverished, single-parent family, Williams had no prior experience of either coaching or playing tennis.

Nor can their success be attributed either exclusively or primarily to luck. For all three, lucky breaks provided opportunities at critical junctures. None, however, was the beneficiary of a consistent run of good fortune. More important than luck was the ability to recognize opportunities when they appeared and to have the clarity of direction and the flexibility necessary to exploit these opportunities.

My contention is that the key common ingredient in all these success stories was the presence of a soundly formulated and effectively implemented *strategy*. These strategies did not exist as a plan; in several cases the strategy was not even made explicit. Yet, in all three, we can observe a consistency of direction based on a clear understanding of the "game" being played and a keen awareness of how to maneuver into a position of advantage.

1. Underpinning Madonna's two decades as a superstar has been a strategy built upon dedication, opportunism, periodic reinvention of image and product offerings, and a well-coordinated multimarket presence.

2. The victory of the Vietnamese communist forces over the French and then the Americans is a classic example of how a sound strategy pursued with total commitment over a long period can succeed against vastly superior resources. The key was Giap's strategy of a protracted war of limited engagement. With American forces constrained by domestic and international opinion from using their full military might, the strategy was unbeatable once it began to sap the willingness of the US government to persevere with a costly, unpopular foreign war.

STRATEGY CAPSULE 1.1 Madonna

Summer 2003 saw little sign of any slowdown in the career of 44-year-old Madonna Louise Veronica Ciccone. During May, her tenth album, *American Life*, topped the Billboard charts. A deal with GAP to promote their clothing also involved Gap distributing Madonna's first children's book, *The English Roses.* Meanwhile, at her music and film production company, Maverick, her list of projects and stable of recording artists continued to grow. Twenty years after her first hit album, Madonna was still the world's highest earning female entertainer and one of the best-known women on the planet.

In the summer of 1978, aged 19, Madonna arrived in New York with $35 to her name. After five years of struggle, she landed a recording contract. *Madonna* (1983) ultimately sold 10 million copies worldwide, while *Like a Virgin* (1984) topped 12 million copies. Between 1985 and 1990, six further albums, three world tours, and five movie roles had established Madonna with an image and persona that transcended any single field of entertainment: she was rock singer, actor, author, and pinup. Yet, she was more than this – as her web site proclaims, she is "icon, artist, provocateur, diva, and mogul." She has also made a great deal of money.

What is the basis of Madonna's incredible and lasting success? Certainly not outstanding natural talent. As a vocalist, musician, dancer, songwriter, or actress, Madonna's talents seem modest. Few would regard her as an outstanding beauty.

She possesses relentless drive. Her wide range of activities – records, concerts, music videos, movies, books, and charity events – belies a remarkable dedication to a single goal: the quest for superstar status. For close to 20 years, Madonna has worked incessantly to establish, maintain, and renew her popular appeal. She is widely regarded as a workaholic who survives on little sleep and rarely takes vacations: "I am a very disciplined person. I sleep a certain number of hours each night, then I like to get up and get on with it. All that means that I am in charge of everything that comes out."

She has drawn heavily on the talents of others: writers, musicians, choreographers, and designers. Many of her personal relationships have been stepping stones to career transitions. Her transition from dance to music was assisted by relationships, first, with musician Steve Bray, then with disc jockey John Benitex. Her entry into Hollywood was accompanied by marriage to Sean Penn and an affair with Warren Beatty. Most striking has been her continuous reinvention of her image. From street-kid look of the early 1980s, to hard-core sexuality of the 90s, and spiritual image that accompanied motherhood, Madonna's fans have been treated with multiple reincarnations. As Jeff Katzenberg of Dreamworks observed: "She has always had a vision of exactly who she is, whether performer or businesswoman, and she has been strong enough to balance it all. Every time she comes up with a new look it is successful. When it happens once, OK, maybe it's luck, but twice is a coincidence, and three times it's got to be a remarkable talent. And Madonna's on her fifth or sixth time."

She was quick to learn the ropes both in Tin Pan Alley and in Hollywood. Like Evita Perón, whom Madonna portrayed in *Evita*, Madonna has combined determination, ambition, social astuteness, and mastery of the strategic use of sex. As a self-publicist she is without equal. In using sex as a marketing tool, she has courted controversy through nudity, pornographic imagery, suggestions of sexual deviance, and the juxtaposition of sexual and religious themes. But she is also astute at walking the fine line between the shocking and the unacceptable. In recent years Madonna has devoted increasing time to nurturing the talents of others, mainly through her recording, film production, and management company, Maverick Inc., a joint venture with Time Warner. Her protégés included Mirwais, William Orbit, Donna De Lory, and the Deftones, and the comedian Ali G: "I've met these people along the way in my career and I want to take them everywhere I go. I want to incorporate them into my little factory of ideas. I also come into contact with a lot of young talent that I feel entrepreneurial about."

3. The Williams sisters' domination of women's tennis was the fulfillment of a strategy formulated by their father, Richard Williams, even before the two girls were born. The strategy was built upon systematic development of playing skills and physical strength, the fostering of drive and psychological resilience, and establishing a family environment that provided competition, discipline, and support.

We can go further. What do these examples tell us about the characteristics of a strategy that are conducive to success? In all three stories, four common factors stand out (see Figure 1.1):

1. *Goals that are simple, consistent, and long term.* All three individuals displayed a single-minded commitment to a clearly recognized goal that was pursued steadfastly over a substantial part of their lifetime.
    ■ Madonna's career featured a relentless drive for stardom in which other dimensions of her life were either subordinated to or absorbed within her career goals.
    ■ North Vietnamese efforts were unified and focused on the ultimate goal of reuniting Vietnam under communist rule and expelling a foreign army from Vietnamese soil. By contrast, US efforts in Vietnam were bedeviled by confused objectives. Was the United States supporting an ally, stabilizing Southeast Asia, engaging in a proxy war against the Soviet Union, or pursuing an ideological struggle against world communism?

FIGURE 1.1 Common elements in successful strategies

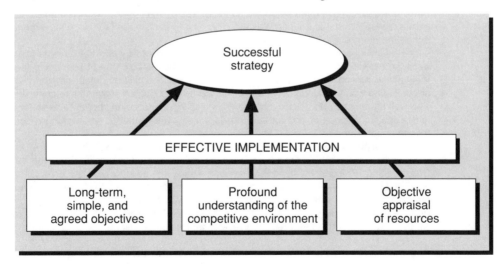

STRATEGY CAPSULE 1.2   General Giap and the Vietnam Wars, 1948–75

> As far as logistics and tactics were concerned, we succeeded in everything we set out
> to do. At the height of the war the army was able to move almost a million soldiers a
> year in and out of Vietnam, feed them, clothe them, house them, supply them with arms
> and ammunition and generally sustain them better than any army had ever been sus-
> tained in the field . . . On the battlefield itself, the army was unbeatable. In engagement
> after engagement the forces of the Vietcong and the North Vietnamese Army were thrown
> back with terrible losses. Yet, in the end, it was North Vietnam, not the United States
> that emerged victorious. How could we have succeeded so well yet failed so miserably?[1]

Despite having the largest army in Southeast Asia, North Vietnam was no match for South
Vietnam so long as the South was backed by the world's most powerful military and industrial
nation. South Vietnam and its United States ally were defeated not by superior resources but
by a superior strategy. North Vietnam achieved what Sun Tzu claimed was the highest form
of victory: the enemy gave up.

The prime mover in the formulation of North Vietnam's military strategy was General Vo Nguyen
Giap. In 1944, Giap became head of the Vietminh guerrilla forces. He was commander-in-chief
of the North Vietnamese Army until 1974 and Minister of Defense until 1980. Giap's strategy
was based on Mao Tse Tung's three-phase theory of revolutionary war: first, passive resistance during which political support is mobilized; second, guerrilla warfare aimed at weakening
the enemy and building military strength; finally, general counteroffensive. In 1954, Giap's brilliant victory over the French at Dien Bien Phu fully vindicated the strategy. Against South Vietnam
and its US ally, the approach was similar.

> Our strategy was . . . to wage a long-lasting battle . . . Only a long-term war could
> enable us to utilize to the maximum our political trump cards, to overcome our material
> handicap, and to transform our weakness into strength. To maintain and increase our
> forces was the principle to which we adhered, contenting ourselves with attacking when
> success was certain, refusing to give battle likely to incur losses.[2]

The strategy built on the one resource where the communists had overwhelming superiority: their will to fight. As Prime Minister Pham Van Dong explained: "The United States is the
most powerful nation on earth. But Americans do not like long, inconclusive wars . . . We can
outlast them and we can win in the end."[3] Limited military engagement and the charade of the
Paris peace talks helped the North Vietnamese prolong the conflict, while diplomatic efforts to
isolate the United States from its Western allies and to sustain the US peace movement accelerated the crumbling of American will to win.

The effectiveness of the US military response was limited by two key uncertainties: what
were the objectives and who was the enemy? Was the US role one of supporting the South
Vietnamese regime, fighting Vietcong terrorism, inflicting a military defeat on North Vietnam,
or combating world communism? Lack of unanimity over goals translated into confusion as to
who was the enemy and whether the war was military or political in scope. Diversity of opinion
and a shifting balance of political and public opinion were fatal for establishing a consistent
long-term strategy.

The consistency and strength of North Vietnam's strategy allowed it to survive errors in
implementation. Giap was premature in launching his general offensive. Both the 1968 Tet
Offensive and 1972 Easter Offensive were beaten back with heavy losses. By 1974, Giap recognized that the Watergate scandal had so weakened the US presidency that an effective American
response to a new communist offensive was unlikely. On April 29, 1975, Operation Frequent
Wind began evacuating all remaining Americans from South Vietnam, and the next morning
North Vietnamese troops entered the Presidential Palace in Saigon.

Sources: [1] Col. Harry G. Summers Jr., *On Strategy* (Novato, CA: Presidio Press, 1982): 1;
[2] Vo Nguyen Giap, *Selected Writings* (Hanoi: Foreign Language Publishing House, 1977);
[3] J. Cameron, *Here Is Your Enemy* (New York: Holt, Rinehart, Winston, 1966).

■ Richard Williams is a remarkable example of focused parenting – unlike parents who set goals for their children, Williams had children in order to fulfill a specific goal.

2. *Profound understanding of the competitive environment.* All three individuals designed their strategies around a deep and insightful appreciation of the arena in which they were competing.

■ Fundamental to Madonna's continuing success has been a shrewd understanding of the ingredients of stardom and the basis of popular appeal. This extends from the basic marketing principle that "sex sells" to recognition of the need to manage gatekeepers of the critical media distribution channels. Her periodic reincarnations reflect an acute awareness of changing attitudes, styles, and social norms.

■ Giap understood his enemy and the battlefield conditions where he would engage them. Most important was appreciation of the political predicament of US presidents in their need for popular support in waging a foreign war.

■ Richard Williams is an astute observer of the world of professional tennis in terms of recognizing both the physical and mental qualities of world-ranked players.

3. *Objective appraisal of resources.* All three strategies were effective in exploiting internal strengths, while protecting areas of weakness.

■ By positioning herself as a "star," Madonna exploited her abilities to develop and project her image, to self-promote, and to exploit emerging trends, while avoiding being judged simply as a rock singer or an actress. Her live performances rely heavily on a large team of highly qualified dancers, musicians, vocalists, choreographers, and technicians, thus compensating for any weaknesses in her own performing capabilities.

■ Giap's strategy was carefully designed to protect against his army's deficiencies in arms and equipment, while exploiting the commitment and loyalty of his troops.

■ In grooming Venus and Serena for tennis greatness, Richard Williams has taken careful account of their different physical characteristics as well as their separate vulnerabilities and psychological needs.

4. *Effective implementation.* Without effective implementation, the best-laid strategies are of little use. Critical to the success of Madonna, Giap, and Williams was their effectiveness as leaders in terms of capacity to reach decisions, energy in implementing them, and effectiveness in instilling loyalty and commitment among subordinates. All three built organizations that allowed effective marshaling of resources and capabilities, and quick responses to changes in the competitive environment.

These observations about the role of strategy in success can be made in relation to most fields of human endeavor. Whether we look at warfare, chess, politics, sport, or business, the success of individuals and organizations is seldom the outcome of

STRATEGY CAPSULE 1.3   Williams & Daughters

Between 2000 and 2003, Venus and Serena Williams dominated women's tennis. The Williams v. Williams Wimbledon final of 2000 inaugurated an era of sibling dominance: in 2002 and 2003, both Wimbledon and the US Open featured all-Williams finals. The sisters were even more remarkable given their race and socio-economic background. Black tennis champions are rare, where the typical breeding grounds of world-class players tend to be suburbs and country clubs rather than the inner city.

The architect of the sisters' success in professional tennis was father, Richard Williams. Born in Shreveport, Louisiana to an impoverished single mother, Williams was determined to better himself. By the mid-1970s, he ran a small security business and lived with his wife and four children in Compton, Los Angeles. His vision is now part of sporting mythology:

> Once upon a time a poor black man (his name is Richard) and his wife (her name is Oracene) got married and settled down in South Central L.A. One day Richard is idly watching tennis on TV when prize money figures are displayed. He turns to Oracene and says, "Honey, let's have two kids. They'll be daughters, and I'll raise them to be tennis superstars and millionaires. Life will be good." Oracene, a little more practical than her husband, says, "Richard, you've never owned a tennis racquet. I know dammed well you've never played tennis." But Richard says, "Not to worry baby. How hard can it be? You hit a little ball into a big green square."

Venus Williams was born on June 17, 1980; Serena followed her 14 months later. Surrounding himself with tennis books and videos, Richard Williams began planning the girls' development. "There was a plan from two years before Venus was actually born as to how I would raise my kids with the help of my wife – their education, their food and most of all their tennis. I'm the master planner, no-one is going to outplan me." At the age of four, Venus began tennis lessons in the public courts coached by Richard. In the following year, Serena joined them. Richard's approach to coaching was both comprehensive and unorthodox:

- He bought used tennis balls for 10 cents each. He reasoned that poorly bouncing balls would require his girls to be faster across court.

- Wondering why men's tennis services were so much stronger than women's, he hypothesized that girls are not so used to throwing things as boys. On this basis, he encouraged Venus and Serena to throw their tennis racquet as far as they could.

- He had the sisters working on a punchbag to develop the girls' strength, hand-eye coordination, and footwork.

- He made the girls use baseball bats to return tennis balls – "it develops accuracy and swing."

- During laborious training sessions the girls would work on improving their accuracy by hitting balls repeatedly at fixed markers.

Above all, Father Williams worked on developing commitment, attitude, and psychological resilience. He was dedicated to developing his daughters as winners – "They are champions in art, in education, in designing their clothes, in helping underprivileged kids – as well as champions in tennis." He would place large signs around the house and garden: "Venus, you must take control of your future!" "Venus, when you fail, you fail alone!" "Serena, you must learn to

---

STRATEGY CAPSULE 1.3 *(cont'd)*

---

listen." He was well aware of the dangers of early burnout. While focusing on tennis, he encouraged his girls to participate in track, basketball, ice-skating and, most of all, their schoolwork. In 1991, he pulled both girls out of the national junior circuit – the usual path to stardom for young tennis players – in order to alleviate outside pressure on them.

He trained them too in other aspects of championship tennis. When they were 4 and 5, he bought a video camera and began media training them. As soon as they became professional, they became involved in clothes design, sponsorship, and public service activities. By the time Venus won her first US Open title at the age of 17, the girls were well prepared for the role of tennis champions.

Sources: Douglas S. Looney, "Venus Rising," *Christian Science Monitor*, May 22, 1998; Terry Jervis, *Raising Tennis Aces: The Williams Story* (DVD distributed by Xenon Pictures, 2002).

---

a purely random process. Nor is superiority in initial endowments of skills and resources typically the determining factor. Strategies that build on the basic four elements almost always play an influential role.

Look at the "high achievers" in any competitive area. Whether we review the 44 American presidents, the CEOs of the Fortune 500, or our own circles of friends and acquaintances, it is apparent that those who have achieved outstanding success in their careers are seldom those who possessed the greatest innate abilities. Success has gone to those who managed their careers most effectively – typically by combining the four strategic factors. They are goal focused; their career goals have taken primacy over the multitude of life's other goals – friendship, love, leisure, knowledge, spiritual fulfillment – which the majority of us spend most of our lives juggling and reconciling. They know the environments within which they play and tend to be fast learners in terms of understanding the keys to advancement. They know themselves in terms of both strengths and weaknesses. And they implement their career strategies with commitment, consistency, and determination. Similar points have been made by management guru, Peter Drucker, in his advice on how to be the CEO of our own careers.[1]

While focusing on a few, clearly delineated career goals is conducive to outstanding career success, such success may be matched by dismal failure in other areas of life. Many people who have reached the pinnacles of their careers have led lives scarred by poor relationships with friends and families and stunted personal development. These include Howard Hughes and John Paul Getty in business, Richard Nixon and Joseph Stalin in politics, Marilyn Monroe and Elvis Presley in entertainment, Joe Louis and O. J. Simpson in sport, and Bobby Fischer in chess. Fulfillment in our personal lives is likely to require broad-based lifetime strategies.[2]

These same ingredients of successful strategies – clear goals, understanding the competitive environment, resource appraisal, and effective implementation – form the key components of our analysis of business strategy. These principles are not new. Over 2,000 years ago, Sun Tzu wrote:

Know the other and know yourself:
Triumph without peril.
Know Nature and know the Situation:
Triumph completely.[3]

THE BASIC FRAMEWORK FOR STRATEGY ANALYSIS

The same four principles that are critical to the design of successful strategies form the analytical foundations on which this book is based. Our framework views strategy as forming a link between the firm and its external environment (see Figure 1.2). The firm embodies three sets of key characteristics:

- Its goals and values.

- Its resources and capabilities.

- Its organizational structure and systems.

The external environment of the firm comprises the whole range of economic, social, political, and technological factors that influence a firm's decisions and its

FIGURE 1.2 The basic framework: strategy as a link between the firm and its environment

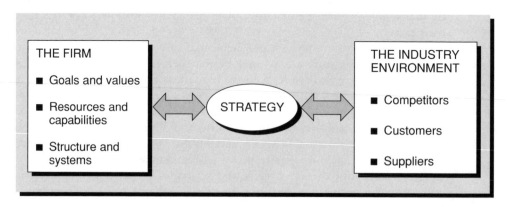

performance. However, for most strategy decisions, the core of the firm's external environment is its *industry*, which is defined by its relationships with customers, competitors, and suppliers.

The task of business strategy, then, is to determine how the firm will deploy its resources within its environment and so satisfy its long-term goals, and how to organize itself to implement that strategy.

What's Wrong With SWOT?

Distinguishing between the external and the internal environment of the firm is common to most approaches to strategy analysis. The best known and most widely used of these approaches is the "SWOT" framework which classifies the various influences on a firm's strategy into four categories: Strengths, Weaknesses, Opportunities, and Threats. The first two – strengths and weaknesses – relate to the internal environment; the last two – opportunities and threats – relate to the external environment.

Which is better, a two-way distinction between internal and external influences or the four-way SWOT taxonomy? The key issue is whether it is sensible and worthwhile to classify internal factors into strengths and weaknesses and external factors into opportunities and threats. In practice, such distinctions are difficult:

- Is BMW's German home base a strength or a weakness for BMW? Its German origins are fundamental for its reputation for engineering excellence and the skills of its German based engineers and technicians are essential to its claim to be the "world's ultimate driving machine." At the same time, Germany is a high cost country with an inflexible labor market and is subject to a plethora of European Union regulations. Hence, BMW's German home base is both a strength and a weakness.

- Is the opening of Iraq's oil sector a threat or an opportunity to American petroleum majors such as Exxon Mobil and ChevronTexaco? Iraq offers opportunities for profitable investment. At the same time, its potential to massively expand its supplies of crude represents a threat to world oil prices.

The lesson here is that an arbitrary classification of external factors into opportunities and threats, and internal factors into strengths and weaknesses, is less important than a careful identification of these external and internal factors followed by an appraisal of their implications. My approach to strategy analysis favors a simple two-way classification of *internal* and *external* factors. What will characterize our strategic appraisal will be the rigor and depth of our analysis of these factors, rather than a superficial categorization into strengths or weaknesses, and opportunities or threats.

Strategic Fit

Fundamental to this view of strategy as a link between the firm and its external environment is the notion of *strategic fit*. For a strategy to be successful, it must be consistent with the characteristics of the firm's external environment, and with the characteristics of the firm's internal environment – its goals and values, resources and capabilities, and structure and systems. As we shall see, the failure of many companies is caused by lack of consistency with either the internal or external environment. The difficulties experienced by Marks & Spencer, the British retail giant, since 1998 were primarily the result of lack of fit between strategy and the needs of the external environment. Overseas, M&S was applying strategies that had succeeded at home in very different market circumstances. In Britain, M&S had failed to respond to shifting consumer preferences and new approaches to sourcing and supply chain management. In other cases, many companies have failed to align their strategies to their internal resources and capabilities – the downfall of telecom companies such as WorldCom and Global Crossing and multimedia conglomerates such as Vivendi Universal and Kirsch Group was due primarily to strategies that overextended the companies beyond the limits of their financial resources and management capabilities.

A BRIEF HISTORY OF BUSINESS STRATEGY

Origins and Military Antecedents

Enterprises need business strategies for much the same reasons that armies need military strategies – to give direction and purpose, to deploy resources in the most effective manner, and to coordinate the decisions made by different individuals. Indeed, the concepts and theories of business strategy have their antecedents in military strategy. The term *strategy* derives from the Greek word *strategia*, meaning "generalship," itself formed from *stratos*, meaning "army," and *-ag*, "to lead."[4] However, the concept of strategy did not originate with the Greeks. Sun Tzu's classic *The Art of War*, written about 500 BC, is regarded as the first treatise on strategy.[5]

Military strategy and business strategy share a number of common concepts and principles, the most basic being the distinction between strategy and tactics. *Strategy* is the overall plan for deploying resources to establish a favorable position; a *tactic* is a scheme for a specific action. Whereas tactics are concerned with the maneuvers necessary to win battles, strategy is concerned with winning the war. Strategic decisions, whether in military or business spheres, share three common characteristics:

- They are important.

- They involve a significant commitment of resources.

- They are not easily reversible.

Many of the principles of military strategy have been applied to business situations. These include the relative strengths of offensive and defensive strategies; the merits of outflanking over frontal assault; the roles of graduated responses to aggress-ive initiatives; the benefits of surprise; and the potential for deception, envelopment, escalation, and attrition.[6] At the same time, the differences between business com-petition and military conflict must be recognized. The objective of war is (usually) to defeat the enemy. The purpose of business rivalry is seldom so aggressive: most business enterprises limit their competitive ambitions, seeking coexistence rather than the destruction of competitors.

The tendency for the principles of military and business strategy to develop along separate paths indicates the absence of a general theory of strategy. The publication of Von Neumann and Morgenstern's *Theory of Games* in 1944 gave rise to the hope that a general theory of competitive behavior would emerge. During the subsequent six decades, game theory has revolutionized the study of competitive interaction, not just in business but politics, military conflict, and international relations as well.[7] Nevertheless, as we shall see in Chapter 4, despite offering striking insights into com-petition and bargaining, game theory has yet to fulfill its potential as a practical and broadly applicable approach to formulating business strategies.[8]

From Corporate Planning to Strategic Management

The evolution of business strategy has been driven more by the practical needs of business than by the development of theory. During the 1950s and 1960s, senior executives were experiencing increasing difficulty in coordinating decisions and maintaining control in companies that were growing in size and complexity. Financial budgeting provided the basic framework for annual financial planning, while discounted cash-flow (DCF) approaches to capital budgeting provided a new approach to appraising individual investment projects. Corporate planning was devised as a framework for co-ordinating individual capital investment decisions and planning the long-term development of the firm. The foundation of the new cor-porate planning was macroeconomic forecasts of major economic aggregates, which were then disaggregated into forecasts for the firm's individual markets and specific products. The typical format was a five-year corporate planning document that set goals and objectives, forecast key economic trends (including market demand, the company's market share, revenue, costs, and margins), established priorities for dif-ferent products and business areas of the firm, and allocated capital expenditures. The diffusion of corporate planning was accelerated by a flood of articles and books addressing this new science.[9] By 1963, SRI found that the majority of the largest US companies had set up corporate planning departments.[10] Strategy Capsule 1.4 provides an example of such formalized corporate planning.

A major emphasis of corporate planning during the 1960s and early 1970s was planning diversification – expansion into new business sectors, often through acquisi-tion. Igor Ansoff, one of the founding figures of the new discipline of corporate strategy, went as far as to define strategy in terms of diversification decisions:

> Strategic decisions are primarily concerned with external rather than internal problems of the firm and specifically with the selection of the product-mix that the firm will pro-duce and the markets to which it will sell.[11]

STRATEGY CAPSULE 1.4 Business Models and Business Strategies

Few business buzzwords survived the internet bust of 2000. One term that did earn a permanent place in the strategy lexicon is *business model*. The central question that venture capitalists posed every would-be "netpreneur" was: "What is your business model?"

Is *business model* simply an alternative term for *business strategy*? If so, what is the distinction and in what ways can the concept of a business model assist us in our strategy analysis?

At its root, a business model is the concept behind a business in terms of its underlying economic logic: What is the basis on which profit is made in this business? This is dependent upon the ability of the business to create value for customers that exceeds the costs entailed in providing the good or service.

Business models are particularly relevant in relation to new business concepts – new products, new services, or fundamentally new approaches to producing or delivering existing products or services. The key question facing every would-be entrepreneur is: "Is this an undiscovered opportunity, or is this simply a bad idea that others have already rejected?"

American Express's invention of the traveler's check is a classic example of the development of an attractive and robust business model. The traveler's check offered multiple streams of profit:

- It offered convenience for travelers – for which they would be willing to pay a charge.

- It offered increased business to merchants accepting travelers' checks – for which they would be willing to pay a commission.

- It offered interest returns to American Express, on the basis that the checks are paid for by the traveler some time before American Express needs to reimburse the merchant who takes the checks as payment.

- Some checks are never cashed.

Evaluating a business model involves two tests. First, the narrative test: Does the story make sense? Second, the numbers test: Can the business cover its costs and yield a viable return on capital? Many internet startups failed because they didn't provide services that anyone was willing to pay for. Others failed because the numbers didn't add up. Webvan's costs in setting up warehouses and distribution meant that it was very difficult to earn a profit in distributing low-margin products like groceries.

A business model is not the same as a strategy. Business models are concerned only with the underlying business concept – they don't take account of competition. When a number of firms adopt a similar business model, the critical determinant of success is which firm will be most successful in deploying its unique attributes in order to create a competitive advantage. Few of the world's most successful companies have achieved their success on the basis of new business models – most have utilized established business models but with superior strategies. Sam Walton imitated the discount store model established by Kmart and others – however, he did so with a customer focus, a passion for cost efficiency, and a recognition of the potential of small-town America that soon put Wal-Mart at the head of the pack.

Source: Joan Magretta, Why Business Models Matter, *Harvard Business Review* (May 2002): 86–92.

The rush to establish departments of corporate planning was part of a wider enthusiasm among both companies and governments for "scientific" techniques of decision making, including cost–benefit analysis, discounted cash flow (DCF) appraisal, linear programming, econometric forecasting, and macroeconomic demand management. Many economists and social commentators argued that scientific decision-making and rational planning by corporations and governments were superior to the haphazard workings of the market economy.[12]

During the 1970s, circumstances changed. Not only did diversification fail to deliver the anticipated synergies, but also the oil shocks of 1974 and 1979 ushered in a new era of macroeconomic instability, combined with increased international competition from resurgent Japanese, European, and Southeast Asian firms. Faced with a more turbulent business environment, firms could no longer plan their investments, new product introductions, and personnel requirements three to five years ahead, simply because they couldn't forecast that far into the future.

The result was a shift in emphasis from *planning* to *strategy making*, where the focus was less on the detailed management of companies' growth paths than on positioning the company in markets and in relation to competitors in order to maximize the potential for profit. This transition from *corporate planning* to what became termed *strategic management* was associated with increasing focus on competition as the central characteristic of the business environment and competitive advantage as the primary goal of strategy. As Bruce Henderson, founder of the Boston Consulting Group, observed:

> Strategy is a deliberate search for a plan of action that will develop a business's competitive advantage and compound it. For any company, the search is an iterative process that begins with a recognition of where you are now and what you have now. Your most dangerous competitors are those that are most like you. The differences between you and your competitors are the basis of your advantage. If you are in business and are self-supporting, you already have some kind of advantage, no matter how small or subtle . . . The objective is to enlarge the scope of your advantage, which can only happen at someone else's expense.[13]

This shift of attention toward strategy as a quest for performance focused attention on the sources of profitability. During the late 1970s and into the 1980s, the emphasis was upon sources of profit within firms' external environments. Michael Porter of Harvard Business School pioneered the application of industrial organization economics to analyzing the determinants of firm profitability.[14] Other researchers focused upon how profits were distributed between the different firms in an industry. The Boston Consulting Group pioneered a series of studies into the impact of market share and learning upon costs and profits.[15] These two lines of inquiry – the determinants of industry profitability and determinants of profitability differences within industries – provided the basis of the empirical analysis undertaken by the Strategic Planning Institute's PIMS (Profit Impact of Market Strategy) project.[16]

By the 1990s, the focal point for strategy analysis shifted from the sources of profit in the external environment to the sources of profit within the firm. Increasingly the resources and capabilities of the firm became regarded as the main source of competitive advantage and the primary basis for formulating strategy.[17] This emphasis on what has been called the *resource-based view of the firm* has represented a substantial shift in thinking about strategy. Industry analysis encourages firms to seek out attractive markets and favorable strategy positions. The result was substantial imitation of strategies between firms. The primacy now given to internal resources and capabilities has done the reverse: firms increasingly look to what differentiates them from their competitors and design strategies that exploit these differences in order to establish unique positions of competitive advantage. Michael Porter, answering the question, "What is strategy?" makes the point: "Competitive strategy is about being different. It means deliberately choosing a different set of activities to deliver a unique mix of value."[18]

The emphasis on exploiting distinctive resources and capabilities resulted in firm strategies moving in the opposite direction to the 1970s and early 1980s. Instead of expanding through diversification and vertical integration, firms moved towards increasing specialization – divesting non-core businesses and outsourcing those activities where they did not possess superior competence. Such narrowing of firm scope encouraged a move towards greater inter-firm collaboration through alliances and joint ventures. The term *co-opetition* has been used to describe the recent recognition that strategy is as much about cooperation as it is competition.[19]

The technology boom of the late 1990s encouraged a major flourishing of new thinking about business strategy – even though much of it did not survive the technology bust of 2000–2002. Rapidly declining costs of communication and information processing fostered new thinking about the networked economy and dynamics of standards wars,[20] the impact of "disruptive technologies,"[21] the central role of knowledge,[22] and the phenomenon of winner-take-all markets.[23] The rapid pace of change in technology-based markets stimulated interest in applying option theory and complexity science to strategy making.[24] Most important has been interest in strategic innovation. When industries were changing rapidly and unpredictably, what novel approaches to making money and establishing competitive advantage could be invented?[25] A key aspect of this quest has been interest in new business models – fundamentally new approaches to accessing sources of value (see Strategy Capsule 1.5). Table 1.1 summarizes the development of strategic management over time.

The Meaning of Strategy

In the light of this review, what can we conclude about the meaning of the term *strategy*? At its most general level, strategy is concerned with planning how an organization or an individual will achieve its goals. As soon as we move beyond general notions of strategy to more precise definition, then these depend upon the type of arena within which strategy is being deployed. In warfare, strategy is about achieving military victory over the enemy, in politics it is about managing power and electoral support to attain and hold on to office; in business it is about ensuring the survival and prosperity of the firm.

TABLE 1.1 The Evolution of Strategic Management

PERIOD	1950s	1960s–EARLY 1970s	LATE 1970s–MID 1980s	LATE 1980s–1990s	2000s
Dominant Theme	Budgetary planning and control	Corporate planning	Positioning	Competitive advantage	Strategic and organizational innovation
Main Issues	Financial control	Planning growth, especially diversification and portfolio planning	Selecting industries and markets Positioning for market leadership	Focusing strategy around sources of competitive advantage New business development	Reconciling size with flexibility and responsiveness
Principal Concepts and Techniques	Financial budgeting Investment planning Project appraisal	Medium- and long-term forecasting Corporate planning techniques Synergy	Industry analysis Segmentation Experience curves PIMS analysis SBUs Portfolio planning	Resources and capabilities Shareholder value Knowledge management Information technology	Cooperative strategies Competing for standards Complexity and self-organization Corporate social responsibility
Organizational Implications	Systems of operational and capital budgeting become key mechanisms of coordination and control	Creation of corporate planning departments and long-term planning processes Mergers and acquisitions	Multidivisional and multinational structures Greater industry and market selectivity	Restructuring and reengineering Refocusing Outsourcing E-business	Alliances and networks New models of leadership Informal structures Less reliance on *direction*, more on *emergence*

STRATEGY CAPSULE 1.5 Corporate Planning in a Large US Steel Company, 1965

The first step in developing long-range plans was to forecast the product demand for future years. After calculating the tonnage needed in each sales district to provide the "target" fraction of the total forecast demand, the optimal production level for each area was determined. A computer program that incorporated the projected demand, existing production capacity, freight costs etc., was used for this purpose.

When the optimum production rate in each area was found, the additional facilities needed to produce the desired tonnage were specified. Then the capital costs for the necessary equipment, buildings, and layout were estimated by the Chief Engineer of the corporation and various district engineers. Alternative plans for achieving company goals were also developed for some areas, and investment proposals were formulated after considering the amount of available capital and the company debt policy. The Vice President who was responsible for long-range planning recommended certain plans to the President, and after the top executives and the Board of Directors reviewed alternative plans, they made the necessary decisions about future activities.

Source: Harold W. Henry, *Long Range Planning Processes in 45 Industrial Companies* (Englewood Cliffs, NJ: Prentice-Hall, 1967): 65.

The nature of strategy also depends upon the stability and predictability of the environment in which strategies are applied. As we have noted, in the stable business environment of the 1960s, strategy was associated with detailed plans. In the turbulent business conditions of the recent decades, strategy became much more about the overall direction of the enterprise. As a result, in their strategic planning, companies have put greater emphasis on mission, vision, business principles, and performance targets and less upon specific actions. This shift in emphasis from plans to overall direction of the enterprise does not imply any downgrading of the role of strategy. Certainly, greater volatility puts a premium on flexibility, responsiveness, and opportunism. Yet, in these circumstances, strategy becomes more rather than less important. To cope with turbulence – in particular, to screen the huge array of opportunities that appear and to ensure a coherent approach to the various forces buffeting the firm – a sense of identity and direction is critical. Bain & Company has pointed to the importance of *strategic principles* – "a memorable and actionable phrase that distills the essence of a company's corporate strategy."[26] This notion of strategy as direction and principles takes us back to our three introductory examples. Madonna, General Giap, and Richard Williams did not possess plans in any formal sense; however, we can discern principles and guidelines that give consistency to the stream of decisions that each made over a period of decades.

As a result, there is little consensus as to the definition of strategy, either in its generic sense or applied to business. Table 1.2 offers a selection of definitions. Typically, business strategy is defined in terms of its content – in particular, the kinds of choices that are seen as paramount. Some writers define strategy primarily in relation to external market positioning. Thus, Costas Markides defines strategy in terms of choice of market position, which is determined by the answers to three questions:

TABLE 1.2   Some Definitions of Strategy

- Strategy: a plan, method, or series of actions designed to achieve a specific goal or effect.
  —*Wordsmyth Dictionary*

- Lost Boy: "Injuns! Let's go get 'em!"
  John Darling: "Hold on a minute. First we must have a strategy."
  Lost Boy: "Uhh? What's a *strategy*?"
  John Darling: "It's, er . . . it's a plan of attack."
  —Walt Disney's *Peter Pan*

- The determination of the long-run goals and objectives of an enterprise, and the adoption of courses of action and the allocation of resources necessary for carrying out these goals.
  —Alfred Chandler, *Strategy and Structure* (Cambridge, MA: MIT Press, 1962)

- A strategy is the pattern or plan that integrates an organization's major goals, policies and action sequences into a cohesive whole. A well-formulated strategy helps marshal and allocate an organization's resources into a unique and viable posture based upon its relative internal competencies and shortcomings, anticipated changes in the environment, and contingent moves by intelligent opponents.
  —James Brian Quinn, *Strategies for Change: Logical Incrementalism* (Homewood, IL: Irwin, 1980)

- Strategy is the pattern of objectives, purposes, or goals and the major policies and plans for achieving these goals, stated in such a way as to define what business the company is in or is to be in and the kind of company it is or is to be.
  —Kenneth Andrews, *The Concept of Corporate Strategy* (Homewood, IL: Irwin, 1971)

- What business strategy is all about is, in a word, *competitive advantage* . . . The sole purpose of strategic planning is to enable a company to gain, as efficiently as possible, a sustainable edge over its competitors. Corporate strategy thus implies an attempt to alter a company's strength relative to that of its competitors in the most efficient way.
  —Kenichi Ohmae, *The Mind of the Strategist* (Harmondsworth: Penguin Books, 1983)

"Who should I target as customers?
What products or services do I offer them?
How should I do this?"[27]

Jay Barney defines strategy in terms of a firm's deployment of its internal resources:

"Strategy is a pattern of resource allocation that enables firms to maintain or improve their performance."[28]

Among all the different definitions of strategy, there is one basic commonality – strategy is about *choice*. These key strategic choices revolve around two fundamental choices:

- *Where* to compete?

- *How* to compete?

As we shall see below, the answers to these questions also define the two principal levels of firm strategy – *corporate strategy* and *business strategy*.

CORPORATE AND BUSINESS STRATEGY

The goal of strategy is to ensure the survival and prosperity of the firm. This requires that the firm earns a return on its capital that exceeds the cost of its capital. What determines the ability of the firm to earn such a rate of return? There are two routes. First, the firm may locate in an industry where favorable conditions result in the industry earning a rate of return above the competitive level. Second, the firm may attain a position of advantage *vis-à-vis* its competitors within an industry, allowing it to earn a return in excess of the industry average (see Figure 1.3).

These two sources of superior performance define the two basic levels of strategy within an enterprise:

- *Corporate strategy* defines the scope of the firm in terms of the industries and markets in which it competes. Corporate strategy decisions include investment in diversification, vertical integration, acquisitions, and new ventures; the allocation of resources between the different businesses of the firm; and divestments.

- *Business strategy* is concerned with how the firm competes within a particular industry or market. If the firm is to prosper within an industry, it must establish a competitive advantage over its rivals. Hence, this area of strategy is also referred to as *competitive strategy*.

Using different terminology, Jay Bourgeois has referred to corporate strategy as the task of *domain selection* and business strategy as the task of *domain navigation.*[29]

FIGURE 1.3 The sources of superior profitability

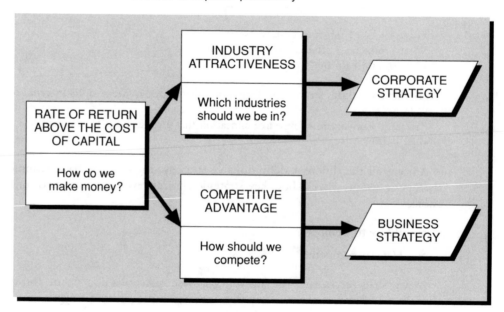

FIGURE 1.4 Levels of strategy and organizational structure

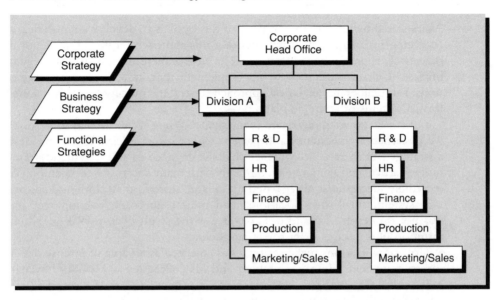

The distinction between corporate and business strategy and their connection to the two basic sources of profitability may be expressed in even simpler terms. The purpose and the content of a firm's strategy are defined by the answer to a single question: "How can the firm make money?" This question can be elaborated into two further questions: "What business or businesses should we be in?" And, within each business: "How should we compete?" The answer to the first question describes the corporate strategy of the company; the answer to the second describes the primary themes of business (or competitive) strategy.

The distinction between corporate strategy and business strategy corresponds to the organization structure of most large companies. Corporate strategy is the responsibility of the top management team and the corporate strategy staff. Business strategy is the responsibility of divisional management (see Figure 1.4).

In practice, the picture is a little more complicated. Most large, multibusiness companies are organized not only into major divisions, but these divisions are sub-divided into individual business units. In addition, companies are organized by functions as well as by business sector. Business strategies are elaborated and implemented through *functional strategies* in terms of production, R&D, marketing, human resources, and finance.

As an integrated approach to firm strategy, this book deals with both business and corporate strategy. However, my primary emphasis will be business strategy. This is because the critical requirement for a company's success is its ability to establish competitive advantage. Hence, issues of business strategy precede those of corporate strategy. At the same time, these two dimensions of strategy are closely linked: the scope of a firm's business has implications for the sources of competitive advantage, and the nature of a firm's competitive advantage determines the range of businesses it can be successful in.

HOW STRATEGY IS MADE: *DESIGN* VERSUS *EMERGENCE*

As indicated by its title, the purpose of this book is to develop an analytical approach to strategic management. Implementing this approach requires that senior managers objectively appraise the enterprise and its environment, formulate a strategy that maximizes the chances for success, and implement that strategy. Among large organizations, this deliberate, analytical approach to strategy making typically occurs through formal systems of strategic planning.

But is this how strategies are really made? When we examined Madonna's career, we discerned a consistency and pattern to her career decisions that we described as a strategy, yet there is no evidence that she engaged in any systematic strategic planning or articulated her strategy. Similarly with many successful companies, Wal-Mart's incredibly successful strategy based upon large store formats, hub-and-spoke distribution system, small-town locations, and unique approach to employee motivation was not the result of grand design – it was the result of Sam Walton's hunches and intuition plus a series of historical accidents.

How organizations make strategy has emerged as an area of intense debate within the strategy field. Henry Mintzberg and his colleagues at McGill University distinguish *intended*, *realized*, and *emergent* strategies. *Intended strategy* is strategy as conceived of by the top management team. Even here, rationality is limited and the intended strategy is the result of a process of negotiation, bargaining, and compromise, involving many individuals and groups within the organization. However, *realized strategy* – the actual strategy that is implemented – is only partly related to that which was intended (Mintzberg suggests only 10–30 percent of intended strategy is realized). The primary determinant of realized strategy is what Mintzberg terms *emergent strategy* – the decisions that emerge from the complex processes in which individual managers interpret the intended strategy and adapt to changing external circumstances.[30]

Analysis of Honda's successful entry into the US motorcycle market has provided a battleground for the debate between those who view strategy making as primarily a rational, analytical process of deliberate planning (the *design school*) and those that envisage strategy as emerging from a complex process of organizational decision making (the *emergence* or *learning school*) of strategy.[31] According to the Boston Consulting Group, Honda pursued a rational, analytic approach to designing a strategy based upon exploiting economies of experience and scale to establish unassailable cost leadership in the world motorcycle industry.[32] However, subsequent interviews with the Honda managers in charge of US market entry revealed a different story: a haphazard approach to entry, with little analysis and no clear plan.[33] The massive success of the 50cc Supercub was as great a surprise to the Honda managers as to anyone. As Mintzberg observes: "Brilliant as its strategy may have looked after the fact, Honda's managers made almost every conceivable mistake until the market finally hit them over the head with the right formula."[34]

Henry Mintzberg's critique over analytical approaches to strategy design goes further. Not only is rational design an inaccurate account of how strategies are actually formulated, it is a poor way of making strategy. "The notion that strategy is something that should happen way up there, far removed from the details of running an organization on a daily basis, is one of the great fallacies of conventional strategic management."[35] At the basis of this fallacy is that it fails to allow for learning though a continuous interaction between strategy formulation and strategy implementation in which strategy is constantly being adjusted and revised in light of experience.

Although the debate between the two schools continues,[36] it is increasingly apparent that the central issue is not "Which school is right?" but, "How can the two views complement one another to give us a richer understanding of strategy making?" Let us explore these complementarities in relation to the factual question of how strategies are made and the normative question of how strategies should be made.

- *How is strategy made?* For most organizations, strategy making is a combination of design and emergence. The deliberate design of strategy (through formal processes such as board meetings and strategic planning) has been characterized as a primarily top-down process. Emergence has been viewed as the result of multiple decisions at many levels, particularly within middle management, and has been viewed as a bottom-up process. These processes may interact in interesting ways. At Intel the key historic decision to abandon memory chips and concentrate upon microprocessors was the result of a host of decentralized decisions taken at divisional and plant level that were subsequently acknowledged by top management and promulgated into strategy.[37] In practice, both design and emergence occur at all levels of the organization. The strategic planning systems of large companies involve top management passing directives and guidelines down the organization and the businesses passing their draft plans up to corporate. Similarly, emergence occurs throughout the organization – opportunism by CEOs is probably the single most important reason why realized strategies deviate from intended strategies. What we can say for sure is that the role of emergence relative to design increases as the business environment becomes increasingly volatile and unpredictable. Organizations that inhabit relatively stable environments – the Roman Catholic Church and national postal services – can plan their strategies in some detail. Organizations whose environments cannot be forecast with any degree of certainty – a gang of car thieves or a construction company located in the Gaza Strip – can only establish a few strategic principles and guidelines, the rest must emerge as circumstances unfold.

- *What's the best way to make strategy?* Mintzberg's advocacy of strategy making as an iterative process involving experimentation and feedback is not necessarily an argument against the rational, systematic design of strategy. The critical issues are, first, determining the balance of design and emergence and, second, how to guide the process of emergence. The strategic planning systems of most companies involve a combination of design and emergence. Thus, corporate headquarters sets guidelines in the form of mission statements, business principles, performance targets, and capital expenditure budgets.

However, within the strategic plans that are decided, divisional and business unit managers have considerable freedom to adjust, adapt, and experiment. I have described this type of strategic planning process as one of "planned emergence."[38] The view that strategic management in a turbulent environment is to be achieved through a combination of rational, top-down planning and decentralized emergence is supported by the findings of complexity theory. Rapid adaptation to changing environmental conditions is typically achieved through seemingly chaotic processes of decentralized responses where the overall effectiveness of this adaptation is maintained through moderate levels of adaptive tension and simple rules that foster coordination. Bill McKelvey argues that Jack Welch's management of General Electric embodied simple directives ("Be number 1 or number 2 in your sector," "Simplicity . . . Self-confidence," "Achieve six-sigma quality") together with strong performance incentives, which corresponds closely to the implications of complexity thinking.[39] We shall explore the implications of complexity theory more fully in Chapter 17.

My approach in this book is to emphasize and outline analytic approaches to strategy formulation. This is not because I wish to downplay the role of skill, intuition, emotion, and creativity – these qualities are essential ingredients of successful strategies. Nevertheless, whether strategy formulation is formal or informal, whether strategies are deliberate or emergent, there can be little doubt as to the importance of systematic analysis as a vital input into the strategy process. Without analysis, the process of strategy formulation, particularly at the senior management level, is likely to be chaotic, with no basis for comparing and evaluating alternatives. Moreover, critical decisions become susceptible to power battles, to the whims and preferences of individual managers, to contemporary fads, and to wishful thinking. Concepts, theories, and analytic frameworks are not substitutes for experience, commitment, and creativity; their key role is to provide frameworks for organizing discussion, processing information and opinions, and assisting communication and consensus. They may even stimulate rather than repress creativity and innovation.

Central to the rational approach to strategy analysis is the idea that we can systematically analyze the reasons for business success and failure and apply this learning to formulating business strategies. The key lesson to be drawn from the attacks by Mintzberg and others on strategic planning, is not that strategic planning should be abandoned, but that the processes and tools of strategy making need to be improved. If we downplay the role of systematic analysis and emphasize intuition and emotion, there is a danger that we enter a world of new-age mysticism in which there is no clear basis for reasoned choices and in which disorder threatens the progressive accumulation of knowledge and understanding.

The goal of this book is to promote analysis that is sound, relevant, and applicable. If strategy analysis does not take account of experiential learning, the practicalities of implementation, and the potential for emergence and self-organization – then it is poor analysis. Strategy formulation must involve intuition, reflection, and the interaction between thought and action. However, the deployment of sound analysis can support the development of intuition and promote creativity. Analysis can also facilitate the organizational processes through which strategy is formulated through providing a common conceptual language and frameworks that can clarify points of similarity and difference between alternative ideas.

THE DIFFERENT ROLES OF STRATEGIC MANAGEMENT WITHIN THE FIRM

Once we begin to consider the *process* of strategy making within organizations, it becomes apparent that strategic management fulfills multiple roles. Among these, three key managerial purposes stand out.

Strategy as Decision Support

At the outset of this chapter, we identified strategy as a key element in success. But why is this so? Strategy, I have argued, is a pattern or theme that gives coherence to the decisions of an individual or organization. But why can't individuals or organizations make optimal decisions in the absence of such a unifying theme? Consider the 1997 "man-versus-computer" chess epic in which Gary Kasparov was defeated by IBM's "Deep Blue." Deep Blue did not need strategy. Because of its phenomenal memory capacity and computing power, it could identify its optimal moves based on a huge decision tree that computed the implications of every possible move. Kasparov, in contrast, was subject to the cognitive limitations that constrain all human beings. To the extent that decision makers are limited by *bounded rationality* – though rational by intent, humans are limited in their search and information-processing capacity – strategy in the form of guidelines and decision criteria can enhance the quality and consistency of strategic decision-making.[40]

When we move from individuals to organizations, the problem of optimizing decisions becomes much greater and it becomes impossible to consider the implications of every permutation of decision choices. In these circumstances, strategic principles such as Wal-Mart's "Low prices, every day," or Southwest Airlines' "Meet customers' short-haul travel needs at fares competitive with the cost of automobile travel," can simplify decision making by *constraining* the range of decision alternatives considered, and by acting as a *heuristic* – a rule of thumb that reduces the search required to find an acceptable solution to a decision problem.

Strategy not only simplifies decision making, the creation of a strategy process also results in better decision making, first, by allowing the knowledge of different individuals to be pooled, second, by facilitating the application of analytic tools. The tools and frameworks of industry analysis, resource analysis and performance appraisal that you will become familiar with in the next few chapters of this book will result in your designing better strategies that will result in better decisions, and improved performance.

Strategy as a Coordinating Device

Strategy making, we have observed, is an emergent process involving decision making by all members of the organization. The greatest challenge facing any organization with multiple members is how to achieve coordination of individual actions. Strategy can promote coordination in several ways. First, it is a communication device. Statements of strategy are a powerful means through which the CEO can communicate the identity, goals, and competitive stance of the company to all organizational members. However, communication alone is not enough to achieve coordination. For cooperation to be effective, buy-in is essential from the different functions, levels and interest groups within an organization. One role of the strategic planning process is to provide a forum in which views are exchanged and consensus developed. Once a strategy has been agreed, the strategic planning process typically involves a set of goals and commitments that are then monitored over the strategic planning period. The growing role of the strategic planning processes of large companies as mechanisms for coordination is evident in the shift of strategic planning responsibilities from corporate planning professionals to line managers, and from corporate to business levels.[41]

Strategy as Target

Strategy is forward looking. It is concerned not only with how the firm will compete now, but also what the firm will become in the future. Many organizations articulate this idea of becoming in a *vision statement*. The purpose of a forward looking view of what the company will become is not just to establish a direction to guide the formulation of strategy, but also to set aspirations for the company that can motive the members of the organization. Hamel and Prahalad argue that a critical ingredient in the strategies of outstandingly successful companies is what they term "strategic intent" – an obsession with achieving leadership within the field of endeavor.[42] Examples of strategic intent include the goal of the Apollo program "To put a man on the moon by the end of the decade," McDonald's pronouncement that "Our vision is to dominate the global food service industry," and Coca-Cola's "Project Infinity" (see Strategy Capsule 1.6). Jim Collins and Jerry Porras make a similar point: US companies that have been sector leaders for 50 years or more – Merck, Walt Disney, 3M, IBM, and Ford – have all generated commitment and drive through setting "Big, Hairy, Ambitious Goals."[43] Sir Brian Pitman, chairman of Lloyds TSB, Britain's most profitable retail bank, argues:

> A big benefit to be derived from setting ambitious goals is that the status quo is never enough. The challenge itself brings forth new ideas and new excitement. It encourages out-of-the-box thinking.[44]

Hamel and Prahalad extend their argument further. In a dynamic environment, the conventional approach to strategy formulation, which emphasizes the fit between internal resources and external opportunities, may be insufficient to drive long-run competitiveness. Critical to the success of upstart companies – such as CNN

STRATEGY CAPSULE 1.6 Coca-Cola's Project Infinity

Coca-Cola has 43 percent of the US market for carbonated soft drinks. In the United States Coca-Cola products are sold through 2 million stores, 450,000 restaurants, and 1.4 million vending machines. A dominant player with limited growth prospects? Not according to Chairman Roberto Goizueta, who calculated Coca-Cola's market share as 3 percent. Why the discrepancy? Goizueta identifies the relevant market as the human race's total consumption of fluids. The purpose of Project Infinity is to galvanize the company into exploiting its infinite opportunities for market growth.

How will this ambitious goal be translated into sales? Rather than looking at Coke's overall share of the US and world market, the company will break down its market share data to identify discrepancies in market share between countries, localities, and specific outlets. In Bismarck, North Dakota, consumption per person averages 566 eight-ounce servings each year; in nearby Jamestown, consumption is only 314. In Memphis, Tennessee, consumption per head is 50 percent higher than in nearby Hot Springs, Arkansas.

Standing in a shopping center in Atlanta, Jack Stahl, head of Coke's US operations, can see a grocery store, three restaurants, and three vending machines, all of which sell Coke. Saturated market? No, a "microcosm of opportunity," says Stahl. "Nearby apartment buildings and office complexes could support more vending machines. I bet 150 people come into that hair salon each day – why shouldn't it sell Coke?"

Source: "A Coke and a Perm?," *Wall Street Journal*, May 8, 1997: A1.

in television, Apple in computers, Yamaha in pianos, and Southwest Airlines and Virgin Atlantic in air travel – was a mismatch between resources and aspirations, in which unreasonable ambition became the driving force for innovation, risk taking, and continuous improvement. Strategy, according to Hamel and Prahalad, should be less about fit and resource allocation, and more about *stretch* and *resource leverage*.[45] What we seem to be observing here is conflict between a firm's resource strength and the commitment and the intensity with which it implements its strategy. Resource scarcity may engender ambition, innovation, and a "success-against-the-odds" culture, while resource abundance may engender complacency and sloth.

THE ROLE OF ANALYSIS IN STRATEGY FORMULATION

This discussion, first, of strategy as an emergent process and, second, of the role of strategy in coordination, communication, and motivation raises some important issues about the types of analysis that are relevant to strategic management. Ever since two leading Harvard management professors identified "modern management techniques" as instrumental in American firms' declining international competitiveness,[46] analytical approaches to management have been castigated for being static, conservative, risk averse, inflexible, short term, and detrimental to innovation.

The purpose of this book is not to defend conventional approaches to business strategy analysis, but to do better. Management's approach to strategy must be dynamic, flexible, and innovative. It must recognize the powerful role that values and goals play in organizations, and the importance of the strategy process in facilitating communication and coordination. It must recognize the importance of intuition, tacit knowledge, and learning-by-doing in complementing more "scientific" analysis.

Strategic management is still a young field. It lacks an agreed, internally consistent, empirically validated body of theory and draws widely from economics, psychology, sociology and biology on an *ad hoc* basis. Unlike the more technically oriented managerial disciplines – finance, operations research, and production management – strategy analysis does not generate solutions to problems. It does not yield scheduling algorithms or identify which investment proposal had the highest net present value. The strategic questions that companies face – like those that individuals face (Shall I marry? Shall I go into investment banking or consumer goods marketing?) – are simply too complex to be programmed.

The purpose of strategy analysis is not to provide answers but to help us understand the issues. Most of the analytic techniques introduced in this book are frameworks that allow us to identify, classify, and understand the principal factors relevant to strategic decisions. Such frameworks are invaluable in allowing us to come to terms with the complexities of strategy decisions. In some instances, the most useful contribution may be in assisting us to make a start on the problem. By guiding us to the questions we need to answer, and by providing a framework for organizing the information gathered, we are in a superior position to a manager who relies exclusively on experience and intuition. Finally, analytic frameworks and techniques can improve our flexibility as managers. The analysis in this book is general in its applicability; it is not specific to particular industries, companies, or situations. Hence, it can help increase our confidence and effectiveness in understanding and responding to new situations and new circumstances. By encouraging depth of understanding in fundamental issues concerning competitive advantage, customer needs, organizational capabilities, and the basis of competition, the concepts, frameworks, and techniques in this book will encourage rather than constrain innovation, flexibility, and opportunism.

SUMMARY

This chapter has covered a great deal of ground – I hope that you are not suffering from indigestion. If you are feeling a little overwhelmed, not to worry: we shall be returning to most of the themes and issues raised in this chapter in the subsequent chapters of the book.

The next stage is to delve further into the basic strategy framework shown in Figure 1.2. Each element of this framework – goals and values, the industry environment, resources and capabilities, and structure and systems – comprise the basic components of strategy analysis. Part II of the book will devote a separate chapter to each. (In the case of industry analysis – two chapters.) We then deploy these tools in the analysis of competitive advantage (Part III), in the formulation and implementation of business strategies in different industry contexts (Part IV), and then in the development of corporate strategy (Part V). Figure 1.5 shows the framework for the book.

FIGURE 1.5 The structure of the book

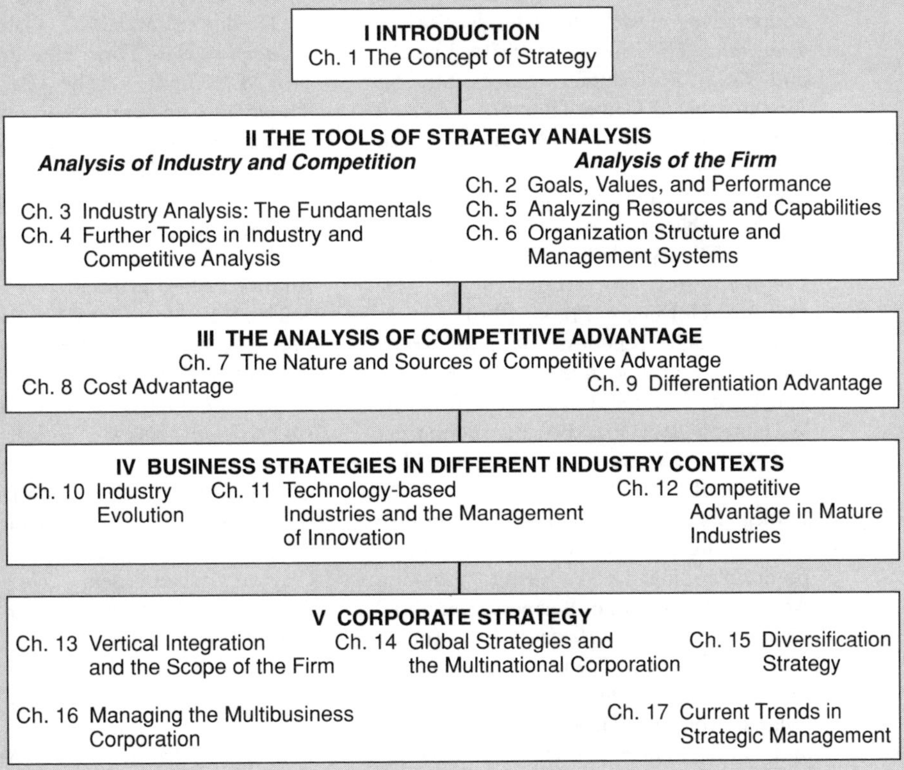

```
                    I INTRODUCTION
                 Ch. 1 The Concept of Strategy

              II THE TOOLS OF STRATEGY ANALYSIS
   Analysis of Industry and Competition          Analysis of the Firm
                                          Ch. 2 Goals, Values, and Performance
   Ch. 3 Industry Analysis: The Fundamentals   Ch. 5 Analyzing Resources and Capabilities
   Ch. 4 Further Topics in Industry and         Ch. 6 Organization Structure and
          Competitive Analysis                          Management Systems

              III THE ANALYSIS OF COMPETITIVE ADVANTAGE
          Ch. 7 The Nature and Sources of Competitive Advantage
   Ch. 8 Cost Advantage                          Ch. 9 Differentiation Advantage

       IV BUSINESS STRATEGIES IN DIFFERENT INDUSTRY CONTEXTS
   Ch. 10 Industry    Ch. 11 Technology-based         Ch. 12 Competitive
          Evolution          Industries and the Management      Advantage in Mature
                             of Innovation                      Industries

                    V CORPORATE STRATEGY
   Ch. 13 Vertical Integration    Ch. 14 Global Strategies and   Ch. 15 Diversification
          and the Scope of the Firm    the Multinational Corporation      Strategy

   Ch. 16 Managing the Multibusiness          Ch. 17 Current Trends in
          Corporation                                Strategic Management
```

NOTES

1 Peter F. Drucker, "Managing Oneself," *Harvard Business Review* (March–April 1999): 65–74.

2 Stephen Covey (*The Seven Habits of Highly Effective People*, Simon & Schuster, 1989) advises us to start at the end – to visualize our own funerals and imagine what we would like the funeral speakers to say about us and our lives. He then recommends that we go on to develop lifetime mission statements based upon the multiple roles that each of us occupies in life.

3 Sun Tzu, *The Art of Strategy: A New Translation of Sun Tzu's Classic "The Art of War,"* trans. R. L. Wing (New York: Doubleday, 1988).

4 Roger Evered, "So What Is Strategy?" *Long Range Planning* 16, no. 3 (June 1983): 57–72.

5 Sun Tzu, op. cit.

6 On the links between military and business strategy, see Roger Evered, op. cit.; Nigel Campbell, "Lanchester Market Structures: A Japanese Approach to the Analysis of Business Competition," *Strategic Management Journal* 7 (1986): 189–200; Eric Clemons and Jason Santamaria, "Maneuver Warfare," *Harvard Business Review* (April 2002): 46–53. For a review of the concepts and principles of military strategy, see B. H. Liddell Hart, *Strategy* (New York: Praeger, 1968).

[7] On the contribution of game theory to business strategy analysis, see Franklin M. Fisher, "Games Economists Play: A Noncooperative View," *RAND Journal of Economics* 20 (Spring 1989): 113–24; and Colin F. Camerer, "Does Strategy Research Need Game Theory?," *Strategic Management Journal* 12, Special Issue (Winter 1991): 137–52.

[8] For practical and accessible introductions to the application of game theory, see Thomas C. Schelling, *The Strategy of Conflict*, 2nd edn (Cambridge, MA: Harvard University Press, 1980); A. K. Dixit and B. J. Nalebuff, *Thinking Strategically: The Competitive Edge in Business, Politics, and Everyday Life* (New York: W. W. Norton, 1991); and A. Brandenburger and B. J. Nalebuff, *Co-opetition* (New York: Doubleday, 1996).

[9] During the late 1950s, *Harvard Business Review* featured a number of articles on corporate planning: D. W. Ewing, "Looking Around: Long-range Business Planning" (*Harvard Business Review*, July–August 1956): 135–46; B. Payne, "Steps in Long-range Planning," *Harvard Business Review* (March–April 1957): 95–101; W. J. Platt and N. R. Maines, "Pretest Your Long-range Plans," *Harvard Business Review* (January–February 1959): 119–27; H. E. Wrap, "Organization for Long-range Planning," *Harvard Business Review* (January–February 1957): 37–47.

[10] Frank F. Gilmore, *Formulation and Advocacy of Business Policy*, rev. edn (Ithaca, NY: Cornell University Press, 1970): 16.

[11] Igor Ansoff, *Corporate Strategy* (London: Penguin, 1985): 18.

[12] J. K. Galbraith (*New Industrial State*, London: Penguin, 1968) predicted that planning by large corporations and governments would supersede markets in allocating resources.

[13] Bruce D. Henderson, "The Origin of Strategy," *Harvard Business Review* (November–December 1989): 139–43.

[14] Michael E. Porter, *Competitive Strategy* (New York: Free Press, 1980).

[15] Boston Consulting Group, *Perspectives on Experience* (Boston: Boston Consulting Group, 1978).

[16] R. D. Buzzell and B. T. Gale, *The PIMS Principles* (New York: Free Press, 1987).

[17] R. M. Grant, "The Resource-based Theory of Competitive Advantage: Implications for Strategy Formulation," *California Management Review* 33 (Spring 1991): 114–35; D. J. Collis and C. Montgomery, "Competing on Resources: Strategy in the 1990s," *Harvard Business Review* (July–August 1995): 119–28.

[18] Michael E. Porter, "What is Strategy?," *Harvard Business Review* (November–December 1996): 64.

[19] A. Brandenburger and B. J. Nalebuff, *Co-opetition* (New York: Doubleday, 1996).

[20] Carl Shapiro and Hal R. Varian, *Information Rules* (Boston: Harvard Business School Press, 1998).

[21] Clayton Christensen, *The Innovator's Dilemma* (Boston: Harvard Business School Press, 1997).

[22] Nick Bontis and Chun Wei Choo (eds.), *The Strategic Management of Intellectual Capital and Organizational Knowledge: A Collection of Readings* (New York: Oxford University Press, 2002).

[23] Robert H. Frank and Philip J. Cook, *The Winner-Take-All Society* (New York: Penguin, 1997).

[24] On option theory and strategy see: T. Copeland and V. Antikarov, *Real Options: A Practitioner's Guide* (Texere, 2001); E. S. Schwartz and L. Trigeorgis, *Real Options and Investment under Uncertainty: Classical Readings and Recent Contributions* (Cambridge: MIT Press, 2001). On complexity and strategy, see S. Brown and K. Eisenhardt, *Competing on the Edge: Strategy as Structured Chaos* (Boston: Harvard Business School Press, 1998) and P. Anderson, "Complexity Theory and Organization Science," *Organization Science* 10 (May–June 1999): 243–57.

[25] Gary Hamel, *Leading the Revolution* (Boston: Harvard Business School Press, 2000).

26 Orit Gadiesh and James Gilbert, "Transforming Corner-office Strategy into Front-line Action," *Harvard Business Review* (May 2001): 73–80.

27 Constantinos C. Markides, *All the Right Moves: A Guide to Crafting Breakthrough Strategy* (Boston: Harvard Business School Press, 2000): 1.

28 Jay B. Barney, *Gaining and Sustaining Competitive Advantage* (Reading, MA: Addison-Wesley, 1997).

29 L. J. Bourgeois, "Strategy and the Environment: A Conceptual Integration," *Academy of Management Review* 5 (1980): 25–39.

30 See Henry Mintzberg, "Patterns of Strategy Formulation," *Management Science* 24 (1978): 934–48; "Of Strategies: Deliberate and Emergent," *Strategic Management Journal* 6 (1985): 257–72; and *Mintzberg on Management: Inside Our Strange World of Organizations* (New York: Free Press, 1988).

31 The two views of Honda are captured in two Harvard cases: *Honda [A]* (Boston: Harvard Business School, Case 384049, 1989) and *Honda [B]* (Boston: Harvard Business School, Case 384050, 1989).

32 Boston Consulting Group, *Strategy Alternatives for the British Motorcycle Industry* (London: Her Majesty's Stationery Office, 1975).

33 Richard T. Pascale, "Perspective on Strategy: The Real Story Behind Honda's Success," *California Management Review* 26, no. 3 (Spring 1984): 47–72.

34 Henry Mintzberg, "Crafting Strategy," *Harvard Business Review* 65 (July–August 1987): 70.

35 Henry Mintzberg, "The Rise and Fall of Strategic Planning," *Harvard Business Review* (January–February 1994): 107–14.

36 For further debate of the Honda case, see: Henry Mintzberg, Richard T. Pascale, M. Goold, and Richard P. Rumelt, "The Honda Effect Revisited," *California Management Review* 38 (Summer 1996): 78–117.

37 R. A. Burgelman and A. Grove, "Strategic Dissonance," *California Management Review* 38 (Winter 1996): 8–28.

38 "Strategic Planning in a Turbulent Environment: Evidence from the Oil and Gas Majors," *Strategic Management Journal* 14 (June 2003): 491–517.

39 Bill McKelvey, "Energising Order-Creating Networks of Distributed Intelligence: Improving the Corporate Brain," *International Journal of Innovation Management* 5(2) (June 2001).

40 The concept of bounded rationality was developed by Herb Simon and James March: J. G. March and H. A. Simon, *Organizations* (New York: Wiley, 1956); J. G. March, "Bounded Rationality, Ambiguity and the Engineering of Choice," *Bell Journal of Economics* 9 (1978): 587–608.

41 These trends are evident from several recent studies of strategic planning in large companies: R. M. Grant, "Strategic Planning in a Turbulent Environment: Evidence from the Oil Majors," *Strategic Management Journal* 24 (June 2003): 491–518; and I. Wilson, "Strategic Planning Isn't Dead – It Changed," *Long Range Planning* 27, no. 4 (1994).

42 Gary Hamel and C. K. Prahalad, "Strategic Intent," *Harvard Business Review* (May–June 1989): 63–77.

43 J. C. Collins and J. I. Porras, *Built to Last: Successful Habits of Visionary Companies* (New York: HarperCollins, 1995).

44 Sir Brian Pitman, "In My Opinion," *Management Today* (June 2000): 14.

45 Gary Hamel and C. K. Prahalad, "Strategy as Stretch and Leverage," *Harvard Business Review* (March–April 1993): 75–84.

46 W. J. Abernathy and R. H. Hayes, "Managing Our Way to Economic Decline," *Harvard Business Review* (July–August 1980): 67–77.

II
The Tools of Strategy Analysis

2

Goals, Values, and Performance

The strategic aim of a business is to earn a return on capital, and if in any particular case the return in the long run is not satisfactory, then the deficiency should be corrected or the activity abandoned for a more favorable one.

—Alfred P. Sloan Jr.,
My Years with General Motors

OUTLINE

Introduction and Objectives

Our framework for strategy analysis (Figure 1.2) comprises four components: the firm's goals and values, its resources and capabilities, its structure and management systems, and its industry environment. Hence, strategy may be viewed as the way in which the firm deploys its resources and capabilities within its business environment in order to achieve its goals. Our review of the four components of strategy analysis begins with goals and values, and – by extension – we consider the performance of the firm in attaining its goals.

Firms possess multiple goals. A firm's choices of goals and the ways in which its goals are pursued are influenced by the firm's values. However, in this chapter we make a bold and simple assumption – that the primary goal of the firm is to maximize profit over the long term. This assumption of profit maximization underlies the analysis of the book as a whole. Business strategy, we have already noted is fundamentally a quest for profit. Hence, most of the frameworks and techniques of strategy analysis that the book introduces are concerned with identifying and exploiting the sources of profitability open to the firm.

However, in pursuing profitability as their primary strategic goal, firms face a fundamental dilemma: businesses that have been most outstandingly successful in generating profits for their owners have typically been enterprises whose driving ambitions have been goals other than profit. As we shall see, while profit is the life-blood of the organization, it is not a goal that is particularly successful in unifying, edifying or capturing the imaginations of organizational members. Linking a sense of mission to the pursuit of profit represents one of the greatest challenges of strategic management.

By the time you have completed this chapter you will be able to:

- Appreciate the arguments that have been made for shareholder versus stakeholder approaches to the goals of the firm.

- Recognize the relationship between profit maximization and value maximization.

- Diagnose a company's performance problems in a systematic, strategic manner.

- Translate the overall goals of long-term profit maximization into meaningful performance targets that can be measured and monitored.

- Understand the linkages between financial analysis and strategic analysis – and appreciate how qualitative strategic analysis can complement quantitative financial analysis.

- Comprehend the role of values, mission, and vision in formulating and implementing strategy.

STRATEGY AS A QUEST FOR VALUE

Business is about creating value. Value can be created in two ways: by production and by commerce. Production creates value by physically transforming products that are less valued by consumers into products that are more valued by consumers – turning clay into coffee mugs, for example. Commerce creates value, not by physically transforming products, by repositioning them in space and time. Trade involves transferring products from individuals and places where they are less valued to individuals and locations where they are more valued. Similarly, speculation involves transferring products from a point in time where the product is valued less to a point in time where it is valued more. Thus, the essence of commerce is creating value through arbitrage across time and space.[1]

The difference between the value of a firm's output and the cost of its material inputs is its *value added*. Value added is equal to the sum of all the income paid to the suppliers of factors of production. Thus:

$$\text{Value Added} = \text{Sales revenue from output } less \text{ Cost of material inputs}$$
$$= \text{Wages/Salaries} + \text{Interest} + \text{Rent} + \text{Royalties/License fees}$$
$$+ \text{Taxes} + \text{Dividends} + \text{Retained profit}$$

In Whose Interest? Shareholders vs. Stakeholders

The value created by firms is distributed among different parties: employees (wages and salaries), lenders (interest), landlords (rent), government (taxes), and owners (profit). Firms also create value for their customers to the extent that the satisfaction customers gain exceeds the price they pay (i.e., they derive *consumer surplus*). It is tempting, therefore, to think of the business enterprise as operating for the benefit of multiple constituencies. This view of the business enterprise as a coalition of interest groups where top management's role to balance these different – often conflicting – interests is referred to as the *stakeholder* approach to the firm.[2]

The notion of the corporation balancing the interests of multiple stakeholders has a long tradition, especially in Asia and continental Europe. By contrast, English-speaking countries have promoted *shareholder capitalism* in preference to *stakeholder capitalism*. These differences are reflected in international differences in companies' legal obligations. In the US, Canada, the UK, and Australia, company boards are required to act in the interests of shareholders. By contrast, French boards are required to pursue the national interest, Dutch boards are required to ensure the continuity of the enterprise, and German supervisory boards are constituted to include representatives of both shareholders and employees.

Whether companies should operate exclusively in the interests of their owners or should also pursue the goals of other stakeholders is an ongoing debate. During the late 1990s, shareholder capitalism was in the ascendant – driven by the superiority of the US economy in generating innovation, entrepreneurship, productivity growth, and job creation. In the comparatively sluggish German and Japanese economies, capital market pressures forced many companies to increase shareholder focus often accompanied by radical restructuring. However, the catastrophic failure of some of the most prominent advocates of shareholder value creation – Enron and WorldCom in particular – and widespread distaste over the excessive top management remuneration resulting from efforts to align managers' interests with those of shareholders has greatly undermined the case for shareholder capitalism.

The responsibilities of business to employees, customers, society, and the natural environment remain central ethical and social issues. Nevertheless, in order to make progress in developing an analytical approach to designing successful strategies, I shall avoid these issues by adopting a simplifying assumption. The simple assumption that underlies the approach to strategy outlined in this book is that companies operate in the interests of their owners by seeking to maximize profits over the long term. Why do I make this assumption and how do I justify it? Let me point to four key considerations:

1. *Competition.* Competition erodes profitability. As competition increases, the interests of different stakeholders converge around the goal of survival. Survival requires that, over the long term, the firm earns a rate of profit that covers its cost of capital. Among 2,717 companies included in the Russell 3000 index, Stern Stewart calculated that well over half were earning negative economic profit, i.e. they were not covering their cost of capital.[3] Across many sectors of industry, the heat of international competition is such that few companies have the luxury of pursuing goals that diverge substantially from profit maximization. In the fiercely competitive automobile industry, the key issue for companies such as Fiat, Ford, and Renault is not whether they should pursue the interests of shareholders or a broader group of stakeholders, but whether they can survive the vicious competition and depressed margins of the automobile sector. If a company cannot – over the long term – earn a return on its capital that covers its cost of capital, it will be unable to attract the finance needed to replace its assets.

2. *The market for corporate control.* Management teams that do not serve the interests of shareholders will be replaced by teams that do. The past 20 years have seen a more active "market for corporate control" in which companies that have failed to maximize the profit potential of their assets have been acquired by companies (and investment groups) that do. In recent years, private investment groups – Hicks, Muse, Tate & Furst, and Texas Pacific – have been very active in acquiring underperforming public companies. External pressure on top management to operate in the shareholder interest has also come through more active institutional shareholders. A large pension fund, California Public Employees' Retirement System, has been especially prominent in pressuring the boards of directors of companies that have failed to generate satisfactory shareholder return. Shareholder pressure is evident in the insecurity of chief executives. During the late 1990s, the proportion of Fortune 500 corporations that replaced their CEOs for reasons other than routine retirement increased sharply.[4]

3. *Convergence of stakeholder interests.* Even beyond the common interest of all stakeholders in the survival of the firm, there is likely to be more community of interests than conflict of interests among different stakeholders. The quest for profits over the long term is likely to require that a company gains loyalty and commitment from its employees, builds trusting relationships with suppliers and customers, and gains confidence and support from governments and communities. The evidence from research is that companies that adhere to strong ethical principles, that support sustainable development, and engage in corporate philanthropy are also those that are the most capable in building capabilities, adapting to new external circumstances, and – ultimately – delivering the strongest financial performance.[5]

4. *Simplicity.* Finally, a compelling reason for assuming that firms exist to make profit is the need for simplification in order to permit systematic analysis. The key problem of a stakeholder approach is the need to cope with multiple goals with specified tradeoffs between goals. The result is vastly increased complexity.[6] Virtually all the major tools of business decision making, from pricing rules to discounted cash flow analysis, are rooted in the assumption of profit maximization – or at minimum, the assumption that more profit is better than less.

Accepting that company strategies are directed primarily toward the goal of making profit doesn't mean that we have to accept that profit is the sole motivation driving business enterprises and their strategies. As we noted in the last chapter when discussing strategic intent, the forces driving the architects of some of the world's greatest enterprises – Henry Ford at Ford Motor Company, Bill Gates at Microsoft, and Akio Morita at Sony – are seldom financial. The dominant drivers tend to be creativity, the desire to make a difference in the world, the fulfillment of a vision. Nevertheless, even when enterprises and their leaders have motives that transcend mere money making, achieving these high-minded goals will only be possible through enterprises that are commercially successful and commercial success requires the adoption of profit-oriented strategies. Consider the founding of Apple Computer by entrepreneur-visionaries Steve Jobs and Steve Wozniak. Their goal was to change the world through creating a computer that would become proficient within a very short time. Jobs and Wozniak's failure to realize their vision was not the result of a faulty vision, but of a faulty strategy. Apple lost out to IBM and Microsoft because its strategy did not take sufficient account of the sources of competitive advantage in the personal computer industry.

What Is Profit?

Thus far, we have referred to firms' quest for profit in loose terms. It is time to look more carefully at what we mean by profit and how it relates to shareholder value.

Profit is the surplus of revenues over costs available for distribution to the owners of the firm. But, if profit maximization is to be a realistic goal, the firm must know what profit is and how to measure it. Otherwise, instructing managers to maximize

TABLE 2.1 Performance of Leading US Companies Using Different Profitability Measures (2002 data)

COMPANY	NET INCOME ($M)[1]	RETURN ON SALES (%)[2]	RETURN ON EQUITY (%)[3]	RETURN ON CAPITAL EMPLOYED (%)[4]	ECONOMIC VALUE ADDED ($M)[5]	MARKET VALUE ADDED ($M)[6]	RETURN TO SHAREHOLDERS (%)[7]
Citigroup	15,276	15.2	17.6	13.1	2,964	68,078	(24.1)
General Electric	14,118	10.7	22.2	14.7	5,983	222,767	(37.8)
Exxon Mobil	11,460	6.3	15.4	6.6	(2,175)	85,108	(8.9)
Altria	11,102	17.9	57.0	15.1	6,696	28,230	(6.8)
Bank of America	9,249	20.2	18.4	10.7	341	20,427	14.5
Pfizer	9,126	25.9	45.7	7.0	(2,779)	52,683	(22.1)
Wal-Mart	8,039	3.3	20.5	13.0	2,928	207,346	(11.8)
Microsoft	7,829	27.6	15.0	22.0	2,201	212,340	(22.0)
Merck	7,149	13.8	31.3	19.1	3,872	107,076	(26.0)
American International	5,519	8.1	9.3	7.6	(1,249)	40,845	(26.9)

Notes:
[1] Net after-tax profits.
[2] Net income as a percentage of sales revenues.
[3] Net income as a percentage of (year end) shareholders' equity.
[4] (Post tax net profit + Interest on debt)/(Average shareholders' equity + Average debt)
[5] Post-tax net operating profits *less* cost of capital
[6] Total market value (equity + debt) *less* total investment in assets by investors.
[7] (Dividend in 2002 + Change in share price during 2002)/Share price at beginning of 2002.
Sources: *Fortune*, April 14, 2003; Stern Stewart & Company.

profit creates uncertainty and latitude for individual interpretation. What is the firm to maximize: total profit, margin on sales, return on equity, return on invested capital, or what? Over what time period? With what kind of adjustment for risk? And what is profit anyway – accounting profit, cash flow, or economic profit? The ambiguity is apparent once we consider the profit performance of companies. Table 2.1 shows that any ranking of companies by performance depends critically on how profitability is measured. There are several uncertainties that need to be resolved:

- Does profit maximization mean maximizing total profit or rate of profit? If the latter, are we concerned with profit as a ratio to sales (return on sales), total assets (return on assets), or shareholders' equity (return on equity)? As an objective, each will lead to perverse results. The instruction to "maximize total profit" is likely to encourage investment in activities that are profitable but where the return falls below the cost of capital. Maximizing the rate of profit encourages the firm to divest assets to the point where it is reduced to a rump of a few exceptionally profitable activities.

- Over what time period is profitability being maximized? The specification of time period is critical. Once top management becomes committed to maximizing quarterly earnings, there is a danger that long-term profitability may be undermined through cutting investment in fixed assets and R&D.

■ How is profit to be measured? Accounting profit is defined by the accounting principles under which a company's financial statements are drawn up. Not only does a company's profit vary according to the accounting rules of its country of domicile, but a company has considerable discretion with regard to which items it expenses and which it capitalizes, the depreciation schedule it chooses, how it values its assets, and how it deals with unusual items.[7] In the aftermath of accounting scandals at Enron, Ahold, and other companies, and earnings restatements at blue-chip companies such as General Electric, the credibility of accounting profit as a meaningful performance indicator is shredded.

From Accounting Profit to Economic Profit

A major problem of accounting profit is that it combines two types of returns: the *normal return to capital* that rewards investors for the use of their capital; and *economic profit*, which is the pure surplus available after all inputs (including capital) have been paid for. One approach to a purer and more reliable measure of profit is to distinguish these two elements and to focus on economic profit as a measure of performance. To distinguish pure or economic profit from accounting profit, economists and business strategists often refer to economic profit as *rent* or *economic rent*.

The most widely used measure of economic profit is Economic Value Added (EVA), devised and popularized by the New York consulting company Stern Stewart & Company.[8] EVA is measured as Net Operating Profit After Tax (NOPAT) less Weighted Average Cost of Capital (WACC). Thus, for Anheuser-Busch, EVA was calculated as follows:

	Operating Profit	$1,756m
less	Taxes	$617m
less	Cost of Capital	$904m
=	Economic Value Added	$235m

where cost of capital was calculated as:

■ Cost of equity 14.3 percent.

■ Cost of debt (adjusted for the tax deductibility of interest payments) 5.2 percent.

■ Weighted average cost of capital 11.3 percent.

■ Total capital employed $8.0 billion.[9]

The advantages of economic profit over accounting profit lie both in setting performance targets for companies and business units and in evaluating performance achieved. As a target, economic profit overcomes the problems associated with instructing managers either to maximize accounting earnings (which encourages firms to overinvest through accepting projects that generate returns at less than the cost of capital) or to maximize rate of return on capital (which encourages underinvestment and the divestment of profitable assets). Thus, maximizing economic profit is consistent with maximizing shareholder value. In evaluating profit performance, economic profit has the virtue of imposing a tighter financial discipline than does accounting profit, by clarifying the fact that businesses earning less than their cost of capital are really making a loss. James Meenan, chief financial officer of AT&T, reported:

> The effect of adopting EVA on AT&T's businesses is staggering. "Good" is no longer a positive operating earnings. It's only when you beat the cost of capital.[10]

Using EVA rather than accounting returns has provided a dramatically tighter discipline on capital-intensive companies, which had previously failed to take full account of the cost of their capital employed. Varity Corporation provides one example (see Strategy Capsule 2.1). At Coca-Cola, former CEO, Robert Goizueta, claimed that using EVA enabled Coca-Cola to "shed far-flung businesses, squeeze more Coke syrup from fewer plants, and generally build a hoard of value."[11]

STRATEGY CAPSULE 2.1   Varity Corporation's Deployment of EVA

Varity makes auto components and diesel engines. It was created out of the ruins of the farm-machinery giant, Massey-Ferguson. Chairman and CEO Victor Rice outlined the firm's use of EVA:

> EVA permeates every level at Varity from the boardroom to the shop floor. My bonus as well as all senior managers' bonuses are determined solely by whether Varity achieves its EVA target . . . We believe that this approach enables us to directly align management and shareholder interests . . . Here are some of the specific ways we've applied EVA:

- Varity's EVA was negative $150 million in 1992. We set a five-year target to reach positive EVA in annual increments using a pre-tax cost of capital of 20 percent. By 1995 we were approaching 80 percent of our target.

- EVA caused us to take a closer look at our capital structure. Recognizing the higher cost of equity versus debt we embarked on a stock buyback program.

- EVA identifies operations and projects that earn more than the cost of capital. EVA analysis confirmed our decision to build new manufacturing facilities for our Kelsey-Hayes antilock brake business.

- We use the EVA model to evaluate potential joint ventures. We determined that a joint venture between our UK Perkins diesel-engine business and Ishikawajima-Shibaura in Japan would generate returns in excess of cost of capital.

- As part of our annual strategic planning process we use EVA analysis to quantify business initiatives such as expansion in new markets and acquisitions.

- EVA provides a means of determining whether the sale of businesses or assets is in the best interests of shareholders.

- Almost every business process in our 80 plants and offices is influenced by EVA. For example, improvements in cycle times and inventory turns reduce capital needs and, in turn, create value.

STRATEGY CAPSULE 2.1 *(cont'd)*

- Using incentives to create a positive return on capital, EVA encourages managers to behave as if they are shareholders. We link employee bonuses directly to EVA improvement . . . All 4,000 Perkins employees, including union members, are tied to an EVA-based compensation plan.

Source: Victor Rice, "Why EVA Works for Varity," *Chief Executive*, September 1996.

Linking Profit to Enterprise Value

The owners of a firm are interested in profits since it is the returns that accrue to them. Once we consider multiple periods of time, then profit maximization means maximizing the net present value of profits over the lifetime of the firm.

In the case of publicly listed companies, owners do not receive profits directly; they receive dividends paid out of profits. So, are shareholders interested in maximizing dividends? Not really, since most companies pay only a fraction of net profits in dividends and many, especially in the technology sector, pay none at all. Shareholders are interested in *total shareholder return*, which comprises dividends plus the change in the market value of the shares. Since share price appreciation comprises by far the greater part of shareholder return, we can assume that shareholders' primary objective is maximizing the stock market value of their company.

How is this determined? Essentially, the value of the firm is calculated in the same way as for any other asset: it is the net present value (NPV) of the cash flows to that asset. Hence, the value of an enterprise is the NPV of its cash flows. This means that shareholder value maximization uses the same discounted cash flow (DCF) methodology that applies to the analysis of investment projects. Most strategy analysis focuses upon *total enterprise value* – the market value of all the firm's securities (including debt securities) – rather than shareholder value only. This is because of the difficulties of distinguishing debt from equity – preference shares, convertible debt, and junk bonds have the characteristics of both debt and equity.[12] Hence, we can calculate the NPV of the firm as a whole in the same way that we calculate the NPV of an individual project. Thus, the value of an enterprise (V) is the sum of its free cash flows (C) in each year t, discounted at the enterprise's cost of capital (r).[13] The relevant cost of capital is the weighted average cost of capital (r_{e+d}) that averages the cost of equity (r_e) and the cost of debt (r_d):

$$V = \sum_t \frac{C_t}{(1 + r_{e+d})^t}$$

where *free cash flow* (C) is measured as:

Net Operating Profit *plus* Depreciation *less* Taxes *less* Investment
in Fixed and Working Capital.

Thus, to maximize its value, a firm seeks to maximize its future net cash flows (its *free cash flow*) while also managing its finances in order to minimize its cost of capital.

What are the implications of this value-maximizing approach for our concept of profit maximization? To begin with, it implies that *cash flow* rather than *accounting profit* is the relevant performance measure. In practice, valuing companies by discounting economic profit gives the same result as by discounting net cash flows. The difference is in the treatment of the capital consumed by the business. The cash flow approach deducts capital at the time when the capital expenditure is made; the EVA approach follows the accounting convention of charging capital as it is consumed (through charging depreciation). In principle, a full DCF approach is the most satisfactory approach to valuing companies. In practice, however, a DCF approach involves problems of forecasting cash flows many years ahead in that many profitable companies are likely to have negative cash flows for the whole of their growth phase. The preference of many financial analysts for cash-based accounting is based upon the fact that cash flows are less easily manipulated by company managers for cosmetic purposes than are accounting profits. The greater purity of cash over profit comes at a cost – the problem of having to estimate cash flows further into the future in order to get meaningful estimates of enterprise value.

The case for using economic profit as a performance measure rests mainly on simplicity and practicality. First, since managers are more familiar with accounting-based measures of profitability than with cash flows, it may be easier to wean managers off accounting profit on to economic profit than on to cash flow. Second, economic profit provides a useful measure for assessing a firm's performance in a single year, whereas free cash flow does not.[14]

Applying DCF Analysis to Valuing Companies, Businesses, and Strategies

The biggest difficulty in using DCF analysis to value companies and business units is forecasting cash flows sufficiently far into the future. Given the level of uncertainty affecting most businesses, even one-year forecasts of profits and cash flows may be difficult. To estimate future cash flows we may need to make assumptions. For example in a stable, growth business (the sole dairy in an expanding village) it may be reasonable to assume that the current year's cash flow (C_0) will grow at a constant rate (g) to infinity. In this case, the above equation becomes:

$$V = \frac{C_0}{(r_{e+d} - g)^t}$$

A slightly more sophisticated approach is to forecast free cash flow over the medium term – say five years – then to calculate a horizon value (H) based either on the book value of the firm at that time or on some more arbitrary forecast of cash flows beyond the medium term:

$$V = C_0 + \frac{C_1}{(1 + r)^1} + \frac{C_2}{(1 + r)^2} + \frac{C_3}{(1 + r)^3} + \frac{C_4}{(1 + r)^4} + \frac{H_4}{(1 + r)^4}$$

The same approach used to value companies and business units can be applied to evaluating alternative strategies. Thus, for a business unit, or for a whole company, different strategy options can be appraised by forecasting the cash flows to the business (or company) under each strategy and then selecting the strategy that produces the highest NPV.[15] Since the early 1990s, companies have increasingly integrated value analysis into their strategic planning processes. At PepsiCo, for example, value maximization provides the basis on which strategic plans are formulated, divisional and business unit targets are set, and performance is monitored. A key merit of value maximization is its consistency. The same DCF methodology is used to value individual projects, individual business units, alternative business strategies, and the company as a whole.

Applying enterprise value analysis to appraising business strategies involves several steps:

- Identify strategy alternatives (the simplest approach is to compare the current strategy with the preferred alternative strategy).

- Estimate the cash flows associated with each strategy.

- Estimate the implications of each strategy for the cost of capital – according to the risk characteristics of different strategies and their financing implications, different strategies will be associated with a different cost of capital.

- Select the strategy that generates the highest net present value.

Though in principle simple, applying DCF analysis to strategy selection runs into major practical difficulties. The central problem is forecasting cash flows. A strategy that is implemented today is likely to influence a company's cash flows over its entire life. Given the volatility and unpredictability of the business conditions facing most companies, making any reasonable forecast of the costs and revenues resulting from a particular strategy is exceedingly difficult. But even if we ignore the problems associated with forecasting an uncertain future, the feasibility of linking a strategy with specific cash flow outcomes is doubtful. As we discussed in the first chapter, a strategy is not a detailed plan, it is a direction and a set of guidelines. As such, a strategy will be consistent with a range of specific outcomes in terms of product introductions, output levels, prices, and investments in new plant. Once we recognize that strategy is about reconciling flexibility with direction in an uncertain environment, there are two key implications as far as strategy analysis is concerned: first, it may be better to view strategy as a portfolio of options rather than a portfolio of investment projects; second, qualitative approaches to strategy analysis may be more useful than quantitative ones. We take up each of these themes in next two sub-sections.

STRATEGY AND REAL OPTIONS

The simple idea that there is value to having the option to do something has important implications for how we value firms. In recent years, the principles of option pricing have been extended from financial securities to investment projects and business enterprises. The resulting field of *real option analysis* has emerged as one of the most important developments in financial theory over the past decade, with far-reaching implications for strategy analysis. The technical details of valuing real options are complex. However, the underlying principles are intuitive. Let me outline the basic ideas of real options theory and what they mean for strategy analysis.

During the late 1990s, many western oil majors were exploring for oil and gas projects in the energy-rich but infrastructure-poor former soviet republic of Kazakhstan. These investments faced multiple risks – the risks of not finding oil, the unknown future price of oil, the political and economic uncertainties of the region, and doubts over the construction of a pipeline to take oil and gas to world markets. Given the costs and risks, the DCF returns to investments in developing Kazak oil and gas fields looked unattractive. Yet, by 2002 Eni, ChevronTexaco, BP, British Gas and several other companies were making multimillion-dollar investments in exploration and production.

The key is that none of the companies were committing to a decade-long series of investments in the full chain of activities from seismic analysis to pipelines construction. The companies had invested in initial phases of oil and gas development where the decision to engage in the next stage depended upon the outcome of the current stage. Each of these project phases could be regarded as acquiring an option on investing in the next phase of the project. At the end of each phase the decision was made whether to invest in the subsequent phase, to wait, or to abandon the project.

In a world of uncertainty, where investments, once made, are irreversible, flexibility is valuable. Instead of committing to an entire project, there is virtue in breaking the project into a number of phases, where the decision of whether and how to embark on the next phase can be made in the light of prevailing circumstances and the learning gained from the previous stage of the project. Most large companies have a *phases and gates* approach to product development in which the development process is split into distinct phases, at the end of which the project is reassessed before being allowed through the "gate." Such a phased approach creates option values. Option value arises from the potential to amend the project during the development process or even abandon it. One of the key buzz-words of the e-commerce boom of 1998–2000 was "scalability" – the potential to scale up or replicate a project or business model should the initial version be successful. Again, such scalability is a source of option value.

Calculating Option Value

The principles of option valuation were developed by Fischer Black and Myron Scholes[16] and Robert Merton.[17] The *Black-Scholes option-pricing model* provides a formula for pricing financial options. The value of securities options was shown to depend on six variables: the price of the security, the exercise price of the option, uncertainty, the

FIGURE 2.1 The six levels of financial and real options

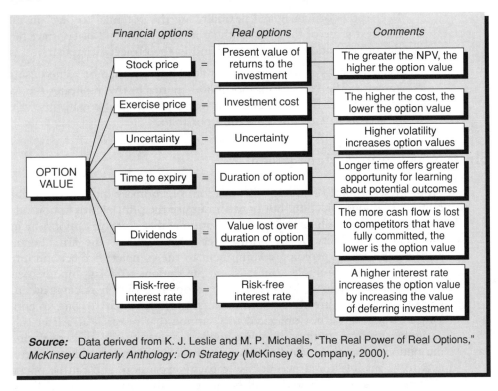

Source: Data derived from K. J. Leslie and M. P. Michaels, "The Real Power of Real Options," *McKinsey Quarterly Anthology: On Strategy* (McKinsey & Company, 2000).

time to expiry, dividend payments, and the risk-free rate of interest.[18] Subsequent research showed that the same formula could be extended to value *real options* – capital investments that embodied a series of go/no go choices.[19] Figure 2.1 shows how the same factors that determine the value of a financial option also determine the value of a real option.

Calculating real option values is complex: modeling uncertainty and incorporating the range of managerial options at different stages of a project typically soon immerses the analyst in complex mathematics. However, the basic process is logical and straightforward. McKinsey & Company outline a four-stage process:

1. Apply a standard DCF analysis to the project without taking account of any flexibility options.

2. Model uncertainty in the project using event trees. Thus, if the project is exploiting oil reserves under the Caspian Sea in Azerbaijan, the key uncertainties would be the chances of finding oil within the exploration lease; the amount and quality of the oil found; the cost of developing the field; the chances of a pipeline being built to the Black Sea or across Iran; the price of crude oil; and the levels of taxes imposed by the Azerbaijan government. Under different outcomes for each of these uncertainties, DCF values can be calculated.

3. Identify the key managerial decisions that can be made at different points of the project's development so as to convert the event tree into a decision tree. Key aspects of managerial flexibility are the potential to defer investment in the next stage of the project, the potential to expand or contract the scale of the project, and the ability to abandon the project altogether.

4. The total project with managerial flexibility can then be valued using what is known as the "replicating portfolio" approach: this replicates the cash flows of the project by a portfolio of priced securities and equates the value of the project to that of the replicating portfolio.[20]

Strategy as Options Management

From the viewpoint of strategy formulation, our primary interest is not the technicalities of options valuation, but how we can use the principles of option valuation to create shareholder value. The key observation is that creating options, by increasing the strategic flexibility of the firm, increases the value of the firm. For individual projects, this means avoiding commitment to the complete project and introducing decision points at multiple stages, where the options to delay, modify, or abandon the project are retained. Merck, an early adopter of option pricing, noted, "When you make an initial investment in a research project, you are paying an entry fee for a right, but you are not obligated to continue that research at a later stage."[21] In designing projects, options thinking implies comparing the costs of flexibility with the options value that such flexibility creates. New plants that allow different products to be manufactured permit easy capacity expansion, and can be operated with different types of raw material will be more valuable than more specialized plants.

Options thinking has also been influential in relation to collaborative relationships between firms. The increased propensity for firms to form joint ventures and strategic alliances when entering new markets and exploring new technologies can be attributed, in part, to the desire to create options in relation to these opportunities. Thus, General Motors' network of strategic alliances with other automakers includes Fiat, Suzuki, and Daewoo. These alliances create options for closer involvement with these partners. Thus, with Suzuki, GM has invested in several joint-venture plants; it had the option of acquiring Daewoo in 2000, but decided not to exercise this option.[22]

BUILDING PRINCIPLES OF VALUE CREATION INTO STRATEGY ANALYSIS

Our discussion so far has established the following:

- For the purposes of strategy formulation, profit maximization is a reasonable assumption. In a multiperiod setting, profit maximization means the maximization of enterprise value.

- Measuring profit is difficult – free cash flow and economic profit are better indicators of the firm's value creation efforts than accounting net income.

■ Discounted cash flow approaches to valuing companies, business units, projects, and strategies will tend to underestimate their value where significant option values are present.

■ Assessing the extent to which a particular strategy creates value for the firm is difficult. Both the techniques we have introduced are troublesome in practice. DCF approaches to value creation are problematic because of the difficulties of estimating cash flows far into the future. Real option approaches to estimating the value created by a strategy are problematic because of the complexity and information requirements of real option valuation.

Given the problems associated with operationalizing value maximization, it is hardly surprising that companies tend to persist with familiar approaches to performance measurement that rely upon accepted accounting principles. While financial purists decry the use of accounting-based measures of performance, in practice the differences between cash flow, economic profit, and accounting profit indicators of performance evaluation are narrower than is often recognized. The longer the period of time under consideration, the greater the convergence between different measures. The specific measure of profit selected is less important than awareness of the limitations and biases inherent in the chosen measure. John Kay has shown that, under certain circumstances, accounting measures of profit approximate economic profit.[23] Over the life of the firm, the net present value of net cash flows from operations, economic profit based on historic cost accounting profit, economic profit based on replacement cost measures, and excess returns to shareholders are the same.[24]

Given the difficulties of forecasting cash flows far into the future, most approaches to implementing value maximization tend to resort to profitability measures that utilize the accounting data generated by firms as part of their financial reporting and relating to fairly short time periods. Those who decry the use of accounting profit must temper their enthusiasm for EVA and cash flow with the recognition that these "purer" indicators of performance begin with accounting-based measures of operating profit. It is notable that McKinsey & Company's approach to maximizing company value begins with DCF analysis, yet when it comes to estimating the value of a business or appraising past performance, the McKinsey methodology relies heavily on accounting-based measures – notably return on invested capital (defined as net operating income after tax as a percentage of net operating assets).[25]

For the purposes of formulating value-creating strategies, the key financial analysis to be performed is, first, appraising the current performance of the business; second, analyzing the potential for a new strategy to improve performance; third, setting performance targets for the managers responsible for implementing the strategy. Let us look at some practical approaches for undertaking these tasks.

Appraising Current Performance

The first stage of any strategy formulation exercise usually involves appraising the current performance of the organization and diagnosing the sources of any performance problems. To this extent, good strategic practice emulates good medical practice – diagnosis precedes prescription.

If, as we have argued, the primary strategic goal of a firm is to maximize its present value, then appraising performance is difficult. Given that the net present value of the firm is the discounted value of future cash flows, the problem is that we have little idea of what these might be. In the case of public companies, the stock market value represents an external valuation of the firm, however, we cannot easily use stock market valuation to indicate whether the current valuation is below its potential or whether the valuation would be higher with an alternative strategy.

As a result, most approaches to assessing the performance of a firm look less at the future stream of cash flows and more at current and past financial performance measures typically based upon accounting profitability.

Return on invested capital (or, equivalently, return on capital employed) remains the predominant measure of the past performance of companies and individual businesses. By comparing the rate of return to the cost of capital, we can determine the extent to which the business is earning economic profit. However, for the purposes of strategy formulation, we need to go further. If profit performance is unsatisfactory, we need to diagnose the sources of poor performance so that management can take corrective action. Such diagnosis requires that we disaggregate overall return on capital into its constituent elements in order to identify the fundamental "value drivers." However, to establish whether particular ratios are "good" or "bad," we need some benchmark for comparison. Useful comparisons are the same company's performance ratios in earlier years or the same ratios for comparable companies.

Using the "Du Pont formula," we can disaggregate return on capital into sales margin and capital turnover. But we can go further: as Figure 2.2 shows, sales margin and capital productivity can be further disaggregated into their constituent items. This analysis allows us to identify the sources of poor performance in terms of specific activities.

Strategy Capsule 2.2 investigates Hewlett-Packard's anemic financial performance by comparing it to the industry's top performer, Dell. By disaggregating overall return on capital employed we can begin to pinpoint the sources of HP's low profitability. If we then combine the financial data with qualitative data on HP's strategy, its operations, the organizational issues it has faced, and the conditions in the world market for microcomputers and imaging products – we can begin to formulate hypotheses as to why HP has performed poorly. This can then provide the basis for identifying corrective measures.

Evaluating Alternative Strategies

A probing diagnosis of a firm's current performance – as outlined above – provides a useful starting point. We need to establish how well or badly a firm is performing and then diagnose the sources of good or bad performance. If a firm is making losses or is performing worse than its major competitors, then the main priority for strategy is to attack the primary sources of deficient performance. If current performance

FIGURE 2.2 Disaggregating return on capital employed

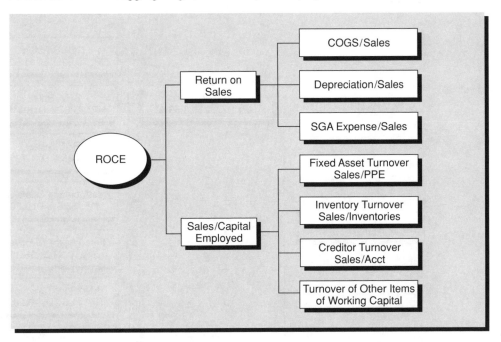

STRATEGY CAPSULE 2.2   Diagnosing Performance: Why is Hewlett-Packard's Profitability So Much Lower than Dell's?

HP's return on capital employed has been vastly inferior to that of Dell: while Dell is one of the most profitable companies in the technology sector, HP barely broke even during the spring and early summer of 2003. Disaggregating into sales margin and capital productivity shows that HP is disadvantaged in both. However, further disaggregation is more revealing. In particular:

- HP's cost of goods is lower in relation to sales than Dell – or equivalently, HP's gross margin is higher than Dell. This suggests that Dell has no particular advantage in costs of purchased components and that HP is more vertically-integrated than Dell (it undertakes more of its own manufacturing).

- HP's costs of sales and administration are about twice those of Dell in relation to sales.

- HP is substantially more R&D intensive than Dell.

- Dell's asset productivity is vastly superior to that of HP. Dell is almost three times as productive in terms of fixed assets (property, plant and equipment) and a staggering nine times as efficient in terms of inventory turnover. These indicators point to the vastly greater efficiency of Dell's system of direct sales with products built-to-order as compared to HP's more conventional manufacturing and distribution system.

STRATEGY CAPSULE 2.2 *(cont'd)*

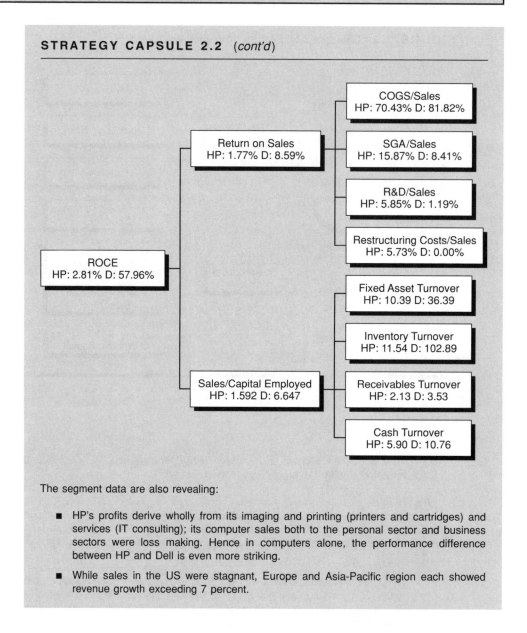

The segment data are also revealing:

■ HP's profits derive wholly from its imaging and printing (printers and cartridges) and services (IT consulting); its computer sales both to the personal sector and business sectors were loss making. Hence in computers alone, the performance difference between HP and Dell is even more striking.

■ While sales in the US were stagnant, Europe and Asia-Pacific region each showed revenue growth exceeding 7 percent.

is so bad that the survival of the enterprise is in question, then strategy must adopt a short-term orientation and focus, at least initially, on staunching cash flow drain.

Even if a firm is performing well, it is not enough to conclude that the present strategy is working well and should therefore be continued. The world of business is one of constant change, and the role of strategy is to assist the firm to adapt to changing market and competitive conditions. Hence, even for outstandingly successful companies such as Wal-Mart, Dell, Nokia, Altria, and Toyota, the challenge is to devise new strategies that can enable the firm to perform better than it would if it had stuck with its previous winning formula. But, as we have already noted, we cannot simply test out alternative strategies by calculating which one will yield the greatest net present value of the firm. The problems of estimating future cash flows are simply too daunting. In practice, therefore, strategy formulation requires more qualitative tools of strategic analysis. We may not be able to forecast the cash flows that might result from HP pruning its product line, adopting new technologies, or repositioning its products in the market, but we can analyze the industry trends, product market conditions, and sources of competitive advantage that are likely to determine HP's future profit streams and then make soundly based judgments about which strategy offers the best prospects.

Setting Performance Targets

As discussed in Chapter 1, an important role for strategic planning systems is to drive corporate performance through setting performance aspirations then monitoring assessing results against targets. To be effective in motivating organizational members, this type of performance management needs to be implemented through a company-wide system. While the overall corporate performance goal is to increase long-run profits with a view to maximizing the value of the firm, such a goal is meaningless outside the top echelon of management. Corporate targets need to be translated into more specific goals that are meaningful for managers further down the organization. The key is to match performance targets to the variables over which different managers exert some control. Thus, for the CEO, it may make sense to set the overall goal of maximizing enterprise value. For the chief operating officer and divisional heads, it makes more sense to set more specific financial goals (such as maximizing ROCE on existing assets and investing in projects whose rate of return exceeds the cost of capital). For functional, departmental, and unit managers, more specific operating targets are preferable. Thus, in a retailing company, store managers might be given targets with regard to sales per square foot and gross margins. Warehouse managers might be required to achieve target levels of inventory turns. Purchasing managers might be required to reduce the cost of goods purchased as a percentage of sales revenue. The chief financial officer might be required to minimize average cost of capital and reduce cash balances.

The same procedure that we used to disaggregate return on capital for appraising past performance can be used to set performance targets appropriate to different levels and functions within the organization. Figure 2.3 uses the same breakout of the drivers of return on capital as Figure 2.2. The difference is that Figure 2.3 provides a basis for identifying the financial and operating ratios appropriate to managers at the different levels and in the different functions of the company.

Balanced Scorecards

The problem with any system of performance management is that the performance goals are long term (e.g. maximizing profits over the lifetime of the company)

FIGURE 2.3 Linking value drivers to performance

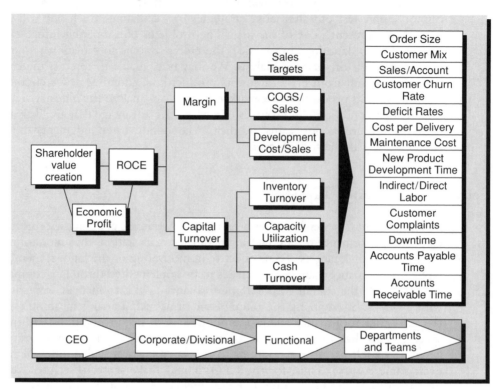

but to act as an effective control system, performance targets need to be monitored over the short term. The problem with the above financially based approach of disaggregating profitability into its constituent ratios is that the short-term pursuit of financial targets is unlikely to result in long-term profit maximization. One solution to this dilemma is to link the overall corporate goal of value maximization to strategic and operational targets to ensure that the pursuit of financial goals is not at the expense of the longer term strategic position of the company. The most widely-used method for doing this is the *balanced scorecard* developed by Robert Kaplan and David Norton.[26] The balanced scorecard methodology provides an integrated framework for balancing financial and strategic goals, and extending these balanced performance measures down the organization to individual business units and departments. The performance measures combine the answers to four questions:

1. *How do we look to shareholders?* The financial perspective is composed of measures such as cash flow, sales and income growth, and return on equity.

2. *How do customers see us?* The customer perspective comprises measures such as goals for new products, on-time delivery, and defect and failure levels.

3. *What must we excel at?* The internal business perspective relates to internal business processes such as productivity, employee skills, cycle time, yield rates, and quality and cost measures.

4. *Can we continue to improve and create value?* The innovation and learning perspective includes measures related to new product development cycle times, technological leadership, and rates of improvement.

By balancing a set of strategic and financial goals, the scorecard methodology allows the strategy of the business to be linked with the creation of shareholder value while providing a set of measurable targets to guide this process. Thus, at machinery and chemicals conglomerate FMC, Kaplan and Norton report:

> Strategists came up with 5 and 10-year plans, controllers with one-year budgets and near-term forecasts. Little interplay occurred between the two groups. But the score-card now bridges the two. The financial perspective builds on the traditional function performed by controllers. The other three perspectives make the division's long-term strategic objectives measurable.[27]

Mobil Corporation's North American Marketing and Refining business (NAM&R) was a pioneer of the balanced scorecard during the 1990s. Faced with pressures of unsatisfactory profit performance, the business adopted the scorecard methodology as a means of linking strategy with financial performance goals and translating these into operating objectives tailored to the specific performance requirements of individual business units and functional departments. The scorecard provided a mechanism for "cascading down" divisional strategy into specific operating goals. The result was an integrated system where scorecards provided the measurements by which the performance of each unit and department was appraised and against which performance-related pay bonuses were determined.[28] Figure 2.4 shows NAM&R's scorecard.

VALUES, MISSION, AND VISION

There is more to business than making money. Profit maximization (enterprise value maximization, to be more precise) provides the foundation for strategy analysis, yet it is not the goal that inspired Henry Ford to build a business that profoundly changed twentieth-century lifestyles; nor is it the one that causes Bill Gates to continue working at Microsoft rather than retiring to enjoy his billions of dollars of personal wealth; nor does making money for shareholders provide motivation or direction to the thousands of employees of both companies. Most successful companies are fired with a sense of purpose that extends well beyond the desire for wealth. Dennis Bakke, founder of the international power company AES, argues:

> Profits are to business as breathing is to life. Breathing is essential to life, but is not the purpose for living. Similarly, profits are essential for the existence of the corporation, but they are not the reason for its existence.

FIGURE 2.4 Balanced scorecard for Mobil North American Marketing and Refining

		Strategic Objectives	Strategic Measures
Financially Strong	Financial	F1 Return on Capital Employed F2 Cash Flow F3 Profitability F4 Lowest Cost F5 Profitable Growth F6 Manage Risk	■ ROCE ■ Cash Flow ■ Net Margin ■ Full cost per gallon delivered to customer ■ Volume growth rate vs. industry ■ Risk index
Delight the Consumer	Customer	C1 Continually delight the targeted consumer	■ Share of segment in key markets ■ Mystery shopper rating
Win–Win Relationship	Customer	C2 Improve dealer/distributor profitability	■ Dealer/distributor margin on gasoline ■ Dealer/distributor survey
Safe and Reliable	Internal	I1 Marketing 1. Innovative products and services 2. Dealer/distributor quality	■ Non-gasoline revenue and margin per square foot ■ Dealer/distributor acceptance rate of new programs ■ Dealer/distributor quality ratings
	Internal	I2 Manufacturing 1. Lower manufacturing costs 2. Improve hardware and performance	■ ROCE on refinery ■ Total expenses (per gallon) vs. competition ■ Profitability index ■ Yield index
Competitive Supplier	Internal	I3 Supply, Trading, Logistics 1. Reducing delivered cost 2. Trading organization 3. Inventory management	Delivered cost per gallon vs. competitors ■ Trading margin ■ Inventory level compared to plan and to output rate
Good Neighbor	Internal	I4 Improve health, safety, and environmental performance	■ Number of incidents ■ Days away from work
On Spec On time	Internal	I5 Quality	■ Quality index
Motivated and Prepared	Learning and growth	L1 Organization involvement L2 Core competencies and skills L3 Access to strategic information	■ Employee survey ■ Strategic competitive availability ■ Strategic information availability

There are three concepts – all closely related – that are extremely useful in helping companies think about their identity, their purpose, and the fundamental elements of their strategy. These are *values*, *mission*, and *vision*.

The Role of Values

When justifying the adoption of profit maximization as the primary goal of business, I advanced the argument that adhering to firm values is typically consistent with the pursuit of profit. However, this polite dismissal of the role of values fails to acknowledge their critical role in strategic management. All companies possess broader organizational values that are integral to their sense of who they are, what they represent, what they want to achieve, and how they intend to achieve it. These values constrain, augment, and may even transcend the fundamental requirement of profitability. Values such as providing opportunities for employees' development and self-realization, pursuing unmatched product quality, creating a safe working environment, and working for the improvement of the natural environment may constrain the pursuit of profitability, but they also play a vital role in building strategic intent and forming consensus and commitment within the organization. For example:

- The Royal Dutch/Shell Group has long been committed to a set of business principles based on core values of honesty, integrity, and respect for people, and the promotion of trust, openness, teamwork, professionalism, and pride. Shell argues that its values "mean we take pride in what we do . . . gives us clarity when making decisions, unifies and motivates staff, and allows society to measure our performance beyond the generation of wealth."

- At Body Shop, the enthusiasm and loyalty of customers and the zeal of employees and franchisees are nourished by the principles of environmental and social responsibility espoused by the founder Anita Roddick.

- The ability of McDonald's to sell 60 billion hamburgers in 86 countries and to generate vast profits for itself and its franchisees cannot be explained exclusively by a profit-driven strategy of low costs, standardization, and marketing. McDonald's is sustained by values that transcend social class and national culture and are enshrined in the principles of "quality, consistency, cleanliness, and value."

Thus, the paradox of Milton Friedman's dictum that "the one and only one social responsibility of business [is] to increase its profits . . ." is that dedication to profit is unlikely to provide the motivation needed to ensure the success of the business. The evidence from a number of studies suggests that linking strategy to the broader pursuit of social and moral purpose may facilitate rather than impede profit performance over the long term. The values a firm embraces can assist in building relationships between the firm and others with whom it does business, can help build employee commitment and loyalty, and may offer the basis for differentiation. If human beings are concerned not just with material reward but with pursuing meaning in their lives, organizations that can help instill a sense of purpose will have an advantage over those that do not.[29] The CEO of jeans-maker Levi Strauss & Co. argues that, in a volatile business environment where decision making must be diffused, corporate values become even more important: ". . . the controls have to be conceptual . . . It's the ideas of a business that are controlling, not some manager in authority."[30]

The Role of Vision and Mission

On their own, neither the goal of profit (or shareholder value) maximization nor the values which guide a company's behavior, play much role in defining its strategy. The starting point for strategy is some underlying idea of why the business exists. Jim Collins and Jerry Porras argue that core values must be complemented by *core purpose* – the organization's most fundamental reason for being.[31] Thus, Walt Disney's core purpose is to make people happy, not to make movies or build theme parks. Core values together with core purpose combine to form an organization's *core ideology* – which "defines an organization's timeless character" and is "the glue that holds the organization together." Core ideology forms one major element of a company's vision that represents the unchanging heart of a company's strategy. Core ideology tells us what a company is, but not where it is going, hence, the other essential component of vision is a view of the company's future development (in Collins and Porras' terminology, an *envisioned future*). Such a future view needs to be articulated. One way is through a vivid description of the future intention, for example, Henry Ford's statement that he would:

> . . . build a motor car for the great multitude . . . It will be so low in price that no man making good wages will be unable to own one and to enjoy with his family the blessing of hours of pleasure in God's great open spaces . . . When I'm through, everyone will be able to afford one, and everyone will have one.

Alternatively, the future may be envisioned in terms of specific goals – what Collins and Porras describe as "Big, Hairy, Ambitious Goals" (or *BHAGs*). These are the equivalent to what we described in Chapter 1 as *strategic intent*. "There is a difference," they claim, "between merely having a goal and being committed to a huge, daunting challenge – such as climbing Mount Everest. A true BHAG is clear and compelling, serves as a unifying focal point of effort, and acts as a catalyst for team spirit."[32] Thus:

- In 1915, City Bank, which later became Citigroup, set out to "Become the most powerful, the most serviceable, the most far-reaching world financial institution that has ever been seen."

- In the 1940s, Stanford University established the goal of being "the Harvard of the West."

STRATEGY CAPSULE 2.3   The Pitfalls of Pursuing Shareholder Value:
Boeing

Boeing was one of the most financially successful members of the Dow Jones Industrial Index between 1960 and 1990. Yet, financial goals or financial controls had little role in Boeing's management over this period. CEO Bill Allen was interested in building great planes and leading the world market with them: "Boeing is always reaching out for tomorrow. This can only be accomplished by people who live, breathe, eat and sleep what they are doing." Allen bet the company on the 747, yet when asked by non-executive director Crawford Greenwalt for financial projections on the project, Allen was utterly vague. "My God," muttered Greenwalt, "these guys don't even know what the return on investment will be on this thing."

The change came in the mid-1990s when Boeing acquired McDonnell Douglas and a new management team of Harry Stonecipher and Phil Condit took over. Mr. Condit proudly talked of taking the company into "a value-based environment where unit cost, return on investment, shareholder return are the measures by which you'll be judged."

The result was lack of investment in major new civil aviation projects and diversification into defense and satellites. Under Condit, Boeing relinquished market leadership in passenger aircraft to Airbus, while faltering as a defense contractor due partly to ethical lapses by key executives. When Condit resigned on December 1, 2003, Boeing's stock price was 20 percent lower than when he was appointed.

Source: Adapted from John Kay, "Forget how the Crow Flies," *Financial Times Magazine* (January 17, 2004): 17–27.

■ In the early 1950s, Sony set out to "Become the company most known for changing the worldwide poor quality image associated with Japanese products."

One of the great paradoxes of strategic management is that many of the companies that have been most successful at earning profits and creating shareholder value have been companies that eschewed such goals in favor of corporate purposes that were oriented towards technical achievement, customer satisfaction, or social change. Conversely, many of the companies that have been most resolutely focused upon profitability and shareholder have suffered dismal financial performance. Boeing offers a telling example of this paradox (see Strategy Capsule 2.3).

Bennis and Nanus argue that the development and articulation of vision is a central task of leaders:

> To choose a direction, a leader must first have developed a mental image of a possible and desirable future state of the organization . . . which we call a vision. A vision articulates a view of a realistic, credible, attractive future for the organization . . . With a vision, the leader provides an all-important bridge from the present to the future.[33]

A distinction is sometimes made between vision statements and *mission statements*. A vision statement is an articulation of what the company wishes to become or where it seeks to go. A mission statement is more a statement of corporate purpose, and often defines the area of business in which it competes. Some companies have separate statements of mission and vision (see Strategy Capsule 2.4).

STRATEGY CAPSULE 2.4   Statements of Mission and Vision:
The Chevron Way

Mission: We are an international company providing energy and chemical products vital to the growth of the world's economies. Our mission is to create superior value for our stockholders, our customers, and our employees.

Vision: Our vision is to be Better than the Best, which means:

- Employees are proud of their success as a team;
- Customers, suppliers, and government prefer us;
- Competitors respect us;
- Communities welcome us;
- Investors are eager to invest in us.

Our primary objective is to exceed the financial performance of our strongest competitors. Our goal is to be No. 1 among our competitors in total Stockholder Return. We will balance long-term growth and short-term results in the pursuit of this objective.
  Our approach to the business is based on:

- Committed team values
- Total quality management
- Protecting People and the Environment

  We will be guided by the *Strategic Intents* in our Corporate Strategic Plan and will measure progress with the *Vision Metrics*. These include:

■ Superior Stockholder Return	Metric:	Total Stockholder Return
■ Superior Financial Performance	Metrics:	Return on Capital Employed Earnings Growth
■ Delighted Customers	Metric:	Customer Satisfaction
■ Competitive Operating Advantage	Metric:	Operating Expense per Barrel
■ Public Favorability	Metric:	Public Favorability Index
■ Committed Team Performance	Metrics:	Worldwide Employee Survey Results Safety

Source: Chevron Corporation Annual Reports

SUMMARY

Chapter 1 established that strategy is about success and provided a framework for viewing strategy as a link between the firm and its industry environment. This chapter has explored the first component of that framework – the goals, values, and performance of the firm. The key assumption in this chapter is that the firm operates in the interests of its owners through maximizing their returns (profits), which implies maximizing the net present value of the firm. At the same time, we must not be too restrictive in our focus upon profitability and wealth creation: as I note in discussion of values, vision, and mission, strategy is also about creating purpose and unifying the energy and creativity of organizational members in pursuing that purpose.

However, if the ultimate goal is to create value for the firm (whether total enterprise value or shareholder value) then the role of strategy analysis is to identify and exploit the sources of this value. I have shown that we can combine both financial analysis and strategic analysis to discover how value is created (and where it is being destroyed). Financial analysis – particularly through the disaggregation of corporate-wide profitability ratios (such as ROCE) can be revealing, but ultimately we also need strategic analysis to unravel the drivers of industry profitability and competitive advantage. Following McKinsey & Company, we can view the determination of overall company performance as a multi-stage procedure (see Figure 2.5).

FIGURE 2.5 A comprehensive value metrics framework

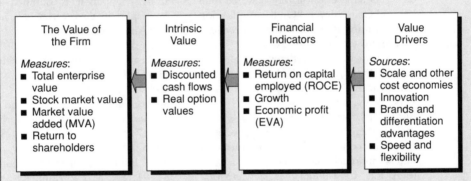

Source: Adapted from T. Copeland, T. Koller, and J. Murrin, *Valuation*, 3rd edn (New York: Wiley, 2000).

The challenge ahead is to develop our understanding of these drivers of profitability and value. Let us begin with the industry environment of the firm.

NOTES

[1] In this chapter, I use the term "value" in two distinct senses. Here I am referring to *economic value*, which is worth as measured in monetary units. We shall also be discussing *values* as moral principles or standards of behavior.

[2] T. Donaldson and L. E. Preston, "The stakeholder theory of the corporation," *Academy of Management Review* 20 (1995): 65–91.

[3] Stern Stewart & Co. Russell 3000 Annual Ranking Data, 2003.

4 Margarethe Wiersema, "Holes at the Top: Why CEO Firings Backfire," *Harvard Business Review* (December 2002): 66–78.

5 Stuart L. Hart and Mark B. Milstein, "Global Sustainability and the Creative Destruction of Industries," *Sloan Management Review* 41 (Fall 1999): 23–33.

6 See Kenneth R. MacCrimmon, "An Overview of Multiple Objective Decision Making," in J. L. Cochrane and M. Zeleny (eds), *Multiple Criteria Decision Making* (Columbia, SC: University of South Carolina Press, 1973).

7 For discussion of the problems of accounting-based measures of profitability, see F. M. Fisher and J. J. McGowan, "On the Misuse of Accounting Rates of Return to Infer Monopoly Profit," *American Economic Review* 73 (1983): 82–7. For a more conciliatory view, see John Kay and Colin Meyer, "On the Application of Accounting Rates of Return," *Economic Journal* 96 (1986): 199–207.

8 Go to www.sternstewart.com. See also: G. Bennett Stewart III and Al Ehrbar, *EVA: The Real Key to Creating Wealth* (New York: Wiley, 1999).

9 Although I focus on Stern Stewart's EVA analysis, there is nothing new or proprietary about the concept of economic profit. A similar approach has been proposed by John Kay in *Foundations of Corporate Success: How Corporate Strategies Add Value* (Oxford: Oxford University Press, 1993). Kay uses the term *added value*, which is defined as "the difference between the (comprehensively accounted) value of a firm's output and the (comprehensively accounted) cost of the firm's inputs" (19).

10 Shawn Tully, "EVA: The Real Key to Creating Wealth," *Fortune* (September 20, 1993): 42.

11 Shawn Tully, "America's Greatest Wealth Creators," *Fortune* (November 8, 2000): 68.

12 T. Copeland, T. Koller, and J. Murrin, *Valuation: Measuring and Managing the Value of Companies*, 3rd edn (New York: Wiley, 2000): Chapter 8 also note that, as compared with enterprise value, share-holder value (using the "Equity DCF Model") "provides less information about the sources of value creation and is not as useful in identifying value-creation opportunities" (151).

13 Note that the cost of equity can be calculated using the Capital Asset Pricing Model: Firm X's cost of equity = the risk-free rate of interest + a risk premium. The risk premium is the excess of the stock market rate of return over the risk-free rate multiplied by Firm X's beta coefficient (its measure of *systematic risk*). See Copeland, Koller, and Murrin (op. cit.): 214–17.

14 As Copeland, Koller, and Murrin (op. cit.: 143) note: "Management could easily improve free cash flow in a single year at the expense of long-term value creation simply by delaying investments."

15 This "shareholder value" approach to strategy appraisal is outlined by Alfred Rappaport in *Creating Shareholder Value: The New Standard for Business Performance* (New York: Free Press, 1986); "Selecting Strategies That Create Shareholder Value," *Harvard Business Review* (May–June 1981): 139–49; "Linking Competitive Strategy and Shareholder Value Analysis," *Journal of Business Strategy* (Spring 1987): 58–67; and "CFOs and Strategists: Forging a Common Framework," *Harvard Business Review* (May–June 1992): 84–91. See also Enrique R. Arzac, "Do Your Business Units Create Shareholder Value?," *Harvard Business Review* (January–February 1986): 121–6.

16 F. Black and M. Scholes, "The Pricing of Options and Corporate Liabilities," *Journal of Political Economy* 81 (1993): 637–54.

17 R. C. Merton, "The Theory of Rational Option Pricing," *Bell Journal of Economics and Management Science* 4 (1973): 141–83.

18 After receiving the Nobel Prize for economics in 1995, Scholes and Merton went on to put their theories to work – with John Merriweather, they formed Long-Term Capital Management, a hedge fund. Their sophisticated computer models could not cope with the simultaneous shocks

of the Southeast Asian financial crisis and Russian bond default of 1998. The collapse of LTCM brought the global financial system to the brink of collapse.

19 A. Dixit and R. Pindyck, *Investment under Uncertainty* (Princeton, NJ: Princeton University Press, 1994); A. Dixit and R. Pindyck, "The Options Approach to Capital Investment," *Harvard Business Review* (May–June 1995): 105–15; Stewart C. Myers, "Finance Theory and Financial Strategy," *Interfaces* 14 (January–February 1984): 134–6.

20 See Copeland, Koller, and Murrin, op. cit.: 406–19.

21 Nancy Nichols, "Scientific Management at Merck: An Interview with CFO Judy Lewent," *Harvard Business Review* (January–February 1994): 89–105.

22 The application of option theory to strategic management is discussed by Bruce Kogut and Nalin Kulatilaka, "Options Thinking and Platform Investments: Investing in Opportunity," *California Management Review* (Winter 1994): 52–69; Rita G. McGrath, "A Real Options Logic for Initiating Technology Positioning Investments," *Academy of Management Review* 22 (1997): 974–96; Rita G. McGrath, W. Furrier, and A. Mendel, "Real Options as Engines of Choice and Heterogeneity," *Academy of Management Review* 29 (1) (2004).

23 John A. Kay, "Accountants, Too, Could Be Happy in a Golden Age: The Accountant's Rate of Profit and the Internal Rate of Return," *Oxford Economic Papers* 28 (1976): 447–60; and John A. Kay and Colin Meyer, "On the Application of Accounting Rates of Return," *Economic Journal* 96 (1986): 199–207.

24 John A. Kay, *Foundations of Corporate Success: How Business Strategies Create Value* (Oxford: Oxford University Press, 1993): 207.

25 Copeland, Koller, and Murrin, op. cit.: Chapters 9 and 11.

26 The methodology is outlined in a number of books and articles by R. S. Kaplan and D. P. Norton. See "The Balanced Scorecard: Measures That Drive Performance," *Harvard Business Review* (January–February 1992); *Balanced Scorecard: Translating Strategy into Action* (Boston: Harvard Business School Press, 1996); "Using the Balanced Scorecard as a Strategic Management System," *Harvard Business Review* (January–February 1996).

27 R. Kaplan and D. Norton, "Putting the Balanced Scorecard to Work," *Harvard Business Review* (September–October 1993): 147.

28 R. Kaplan and D. Norton, *The Strategy-focused Organization* (Boston: Harvard Business School Press, 2001): Chapter 2, "How Mobil Became a Strategy-focused Organization."

29 Abraham Maslow, "A Theory of Human Motivation," *Psychological Review* 50 (1943): 370–96, postulated that human beings have a hierarchy of needs, the highest being that of "self-actualization:" the realization of one's distinctive psychological potential that goes beyond economic and social fulfillment.

30 Robert Howard, "Values Make the Company: An Interview with Robert Haas," *Harvard Business Review* (September–October 1990): 133–43.

31 James Collins and Jerry Porras, "Building Your Company's Vision," *Harvard Business Review* (September–October 1996): 65–77.

32 Ibid.: 73.

33 W. Bennis and B. Nanus, *Leaders: The Strategies for Taking Charge* (New York: Harper and Row, 1985); quoted by G. Saloner, A. Shepard, and J. Poldolny, *Strategic Management* (New York: Wiley, 2000): 27.

3

Industry Analysis: The Fundamentals

When a management with a reputation for brilliance tackles a business with a reputation for poor fundamental economics, it is the reputation of the business that remains intact.

—**Warren Buffett, Chairman, Berkshire Hathaway**

The reinsurance business has the defect of being too attractive-looking to new entrants for its own good and will therefore always tend to be the opposite of, say, the old business of gathering and rendering dead horses that always tended to contain few and prosperous participants.

—**Charles T. Munger, Chairman, Wesco Financial Corp.**

OUTLINE

INTRODUCTION AND OBJECTIVES

In this chapter and the next we explore the external environment of the firm. In Chapter 1 we observed that profound understanding of the competitive environment is a critical ingredient of a successful strategy. We further noted that business strategy is essentially a quest for profit. The primary task for this chapter is to identify the sources of profit in the external environment. The firm's proximate environment is its industry environment; hence the focus of our environmental analysis will be industry analysis.

Industry analysis is relevant both to corporate-level and business-level strategy.

- Corporate strategy is concerned with deciding which industries the firm should be engaged in and how it should allocate its resources among them. Such decisions require assessment of the attractiveness of different industries in terms of their profit potential. The main objective of this chapter is to understand how the competitive structure of an industry determines its profitability.

- Business strategy is concerned with establishing competitive advantage. By analyzing customer needs and preferences and the ways in which firms compete to serve customers we identify the general sources of competitive advantage in an industry – what we call *key success factors*.

By the time you have completed this chapter you will be able to:

- Identify the main structural features of an industry that influence competition and profitability.

- Use industry analysis to explain why in some industries competition is more intense and profitability lower than in other industries.

- Use evidence on structural trends within industries to forecast changes in competition and profitability in the future.

- Develop strategies to influence industry structure in order to improve industry profitability.

- Analyze competition and customer requirements in order to identify opportunities for competitive advantage within an industry (*key success factors*).

FROM ENVIRONMENTAL ANALYSIS TO INDUSTRY ANALYSIS

The business environment of the firm consists of all the external influences that affect its decisions and performance. Given the vast number and range of external influences, how can managers hope to monitor, let alone analyze, environmental conditions? The starting point is some kind of system or framework for organizing information. For example, environmental influences can be classified by *source* (e.g. into political, economic, social, and technological factors ("PEST analysis")) or by *proximity* (the "micro-environment" or "task environment" can be distinguished from the wider influences that form the "macro-environment").[1] Though systematic, continuous scanning of the whole range of external influences might seem desirable, such extensive environmental analysis is unlikely to be cost effective and creates information overload.

The prerequisite for effective environmental analysis is to distinguish the vital from the merely important. To do this, let's return to first principles. For the firm to make profit it must create value for customers. Hence, it must understand its customers. Second, in creating value, the firm acquires goods and services from suppliers. Hence, it must understand its suppliers and how to form business relationships with them. Third, the ability to generate profitability from value-creating activity depends on the intensity of competition among firms that vie for the same value-creating opportunities. Hence, the firm must understand competition. Thus, the core of the firm's business environment is formed by its relationships with three sets of players: customers, suppliers, and competitors. This is its industry environment.

This is not to say that macro-level factors such as general economic trends, changes in demographic structure, or social and political trends are unimportant to strategy analysis. These factors may be critical determinants of the threats and opportunities a company will face in the future. The key issue is how these more general environmental factors affect the firm's industry environment (Figure 3.1). Consider the threat of global warming. For most companies this is not an important strategic issue (at least, not for the next few hundred years). For the producers of automobiles, however, the implications of global warming for taxes on gasoline and restrictions on

FIGURE 3.1   From environmental analysis to industry analysis

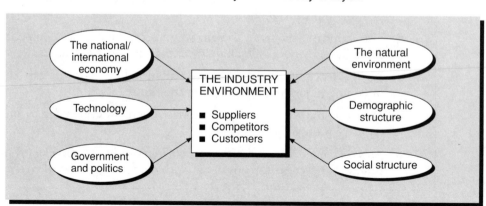

burning fossil fuels mean that global warming is a vital issue. However, to analyze the strategic implications of global warming, the automobile manufacturers need to trace its implications for their industry environment:

- What will be the impact on demand? Will consumers favor more fuel-efficient cars, or will there be a shift from gasoline-powered to electrically powered vehicles?

- Will there be substitution of public transportation for private transportation?

- Will there be new entry by manufacturers of electric vehicles into the car industry?

- Will the heavy R&D costs associated with adapting cars to the new environmental challenge cause the industry to consolidate?

THE DETERMINANTS OF INDUSTRY PROFIT: DEMAND AND COMPETITION

If the purpose of strategy is to help a company to survive and make money, the starting point for industry analysis is a simple question: What determines the level of profit in an industry?

As already noted, business is about the creation of value for the customer either by production (transforming inputs into outputs) or commerce (arbitrage). Value is created when the price the customer is willing to pay for a product exceeds the costs incurred by the firm. But value creation does not translate directly into profit. The surplus of value over cost is distributed between customers and producers by the forces of competition. The stronger is competition among producers, the more of the surplus is received by customers in *consumer surplus* (the difference between the price they actually pay and the maximum price they would have been willing to pay) and the less is the surplus received by producers (as *producer surplus* or *economic rent*). A single supplier of bottled water at an all-night rave can charge a price that fully exploits the dancers' thirst. If there are many suppliers of bottled water, then, in the absence of collusion, competition causes the price of bottled water to fall toward the cost of supplying it.

The surplus earned by producers over and above the minimum costs of production is not entirely captured in profits. Where an industry has powerful suppliers – monopolistic suppliers of components or employees united by a strong labor union – a substantial part of the surplus may be appropriated by these suppliers (the profits of suppliers or premium wages of union members).

The profits earned by the firms in an industry are thus determined by three factors:

- The value of the product to customers.

- The intensity of competition.

- The bargaining power of the producers relative to their suppliers.

Industry analysis brings all three factors into a single analytic framework.

ANALYZING INDUSTRY ATTRACTIVENESS

Tables 3.1 and 3.2 show the profitability of different US industries. Some industries (such as tobacco, pharmaceuticals, and medical equipment) consistently earn high rates of profit; others (such as iron and steel, nonferrous metals, airlines, and basic building materials) have failed to cover their cost of capital. The basic premise that underlies industry analysis is that the level of industry profitability is neither random nor the result of entirely industry-specific influences – it is determined by the systematic influences of the industry's structure. The US pharmaceutical industry and the US steel industry not only supply very different products, they also have very different structures, which make one highly profitable and the other a nightmare of

TABLE 3.1   The Profitability of US Industries, 1999–2002

INDUSTRY	MEDIAN ROE 1999–2002 (%)	INDUSTRY	MEDIAN ROE 1999–2002 (%)
Pharmaceuticals	26.8	Trucking, Truck Leasing	10.8
Tobacco	22.0	Energy	10.8
Household and Personal Products	20.5	General Merchandisers	10.5
		Utilities: Gas and Electric	10.5
Food Consumer Products	22.8	Food and Drug Stores	10.3
Diversified Financials	18.5	Industrial and Farm Equipment	10.0
Medical Products and Equipment	18.8	Wholesalers: Food and Grocery	10.0
Beverages	17.3	Motor Vehicles and Parts	9.8
Securities	16.5	Home Equipment, Furnishings	9.5
Scientific, Photographic, and Control Equipment	16.3	Railroads	9.0
Saving Institutions	16.0	Mail, Package, and Freight Delivery	8.8
Commercial Banks	15.8	Pipelines	8.5
Food Services	15.5	Hotels, Casinos, Resorts	8.0
Engineering, Construction	14.3	Insurance: Life and Health	7.6
Publishing, Printing	14.3	Real Estate	7.3
Petroleum Refining	14.3	Building Materials, Glass	7.0
Apparel	13.5	Temporary Help	6.5
Computer Software	13.5	Metals	6.0
Mining, Crude-Oil Production	13.5	Semiconductors and Other Electronic Components	5.8
Computer and Data Services	13.3		
Furniture	13.3	Insurance: Property and Casualty	5.3
Electronics, Electrical Equipment	12.8	Food Production	5.3
Chemicals	12.8	Telecommunications	3.5
Specialty Retailers	12.3	Forest and Paper Products	3.5
Automotive Retailing and Services	11.8	Network and Other Communications Equipment	(4.0)
Computers, Office Equipment	11.5	Airlines	(34.8)
Healthcare	11.0		

Source: Fortune 1000 by Industry.

TABLE 3.2 The Profitability of US Industries Measured by EVA and Return on Assets, 1986–97

INDUSTRY	EVA/CE[1] (%)	ROA[2] (%)	INDUSTRY	EVA/CE (%)	ROA (%)
Tobacco	9.4	14.4	Broadcasting and Publishing	(1.5)	6.0
Computer Software and Services	5.9	10.4	Cars and Trucks	(1.5)	2.2
Entertainment	4.4	8.4	Healthcare Services	(1.7)	3.3
Personnel-Supply Services	4.0	–	Machine Tools and Hand Tools	(1.7)	6.0
Personal Care	2.8	8.0	Appliances and Home Furnishings	(1.9)	3.2
Medical Products	2.7	9.5	Transportation Services	(2.0)	3.2
Food Processing	2.5	8.5	Printing and Advertising	(2.0)	2.3
Food Retailing	2.5	6.5	Telephone Equipment and Services	(2.1)	7.0
IT Consulting Services	2.1	6.5	Plastics and Products	(2.6)	5.3
Apparel	1.1	10.7	General Engineering	(3.0)	5.2
Games and Toys	0.8	–	Computers and Peripherals	(3.1)	3.1
Packaging	0.8	5.0	Electrical Products	(3.3)	4.6
Drugs and Research	0.7	7.6	Aerospace and Defense	(3.3)	4.8
Chemicals	0.3	8.0	Railroads	(3.4)	3.8
Beverages	0.2	5.6	Hotels and Motels	(3.6)	–
Eating Places	0.1	6.9	Machinery	(4.1)	–
Car Parts and Equipment	(0.0)	4.6	Instruments	(4.2)	5.1
Textiles	(0.1)	7.4	Airlines	(4.2)	1.0
Fashion Retailing	(0.4)	9.3	Construction and Engineering	(4.6)	–
Food Distribution	(0.6)	–	Oil and Gas	(4.6)	2.5
Building Materials	(0.6)	5.6	Steel	(6.4)	2.3
Drug Distribution	(0.7)	5.5	Cable Television	(7.2)	(3.3)
Metals	(1.0)	–	Electronics	(9.2)	3.5
Telephone Companies	(1.2)	4.6	Petroleum Services	(9.8)	(0.6)
Discount Retailing	(1.2)	6.4	**Average**	**(1.1)**	**5.6**
Semiconductors and Components	(1.3)	6.0			
Paper and Products	(1.5)	5.2			

Notes:
[1] EVA/CE measures the ratio of Economic Value Added (as estimated by Stern Stewart) to capital employed for the companies in each industry.
[2] ROA measures the percentage of net income to total assets for each industry.
Source: G. Hawawini, V. Subramanian, and P. Verdin, "Is Firms' Profitability Driven by Industry or Firm-Specific Factors? A New Look at the Evidence," *Strategic Management Journal* 24 (January 2003): 1–16. Reproduced by permission of John Wiley & Sons Limited.

price competition and weak margins. The pharmaceutical industry produces highly differentiated products with price-insensitive consumers and each new product receives monopoly privileges in the form of 17-year patents. The steel industry produces a commodity product with declining demand, strong substitute competition, massive overcapacity, and is squeezed on one side by powerful customers and on the other by strong labor unions. Conversely, the US steel industry and the US airline industry supply very different products, but they share a number of similarities

STRATEGY CAPSULE 3.1 Chewing Tobacco, Sausage Skins, and Slot Machines: In Praise of Niche Markets

UST Inc. (formerly US Tobacco) has been the most profitable company in the S&P500 over the past 10 years with return on equity frequently topping 100%. Even in 2002, when an antitrust litigation resulted in a $1.2 billion charge against earnings, UST succeeded in earning a return on capital employed of 38%. What's the secret of UST's success? It's simple – it controls 78% of the US market for "smokeless tobacco" (chewing tobacco and snuff), with brands such as Skoal, Copenhagen, Long Cut, and Red Seal. Despite its association with a bygone era of cowboys and rural poverty, chewing tobacco has been a growth market over the past two decades with a surprisingly large number of young consumers. UST's long-established brands, its distribution through tens of thousands of small retail outlets, and the unwillingness of major tobacco companies to enter this market (due to the poor image and social unacceptability of the product) have made UST's market position unassailable. Federal controls on the advertising of smokeless tobacco products have buttressed UST's market position by making it more difficult for would-be entrants to establish their brands.

Devro plc is based in the Scottish village of Moodiesburn. It supplies collagen sausage skins ("casings") worldwide. "From the British 'Banger' to the Chinese Lap Cheong, from the French Merguez to the South American Chourizo, Devro has a casing to suit all product types." Although badly hit by scares over "mad cow" disease and foot-and-mouth disease, Devro's 60% of the world market for collagen casings including 94% of the UK market, 83% of the Australian market and 40% of the US market has allowed it to ride the difficult market conditions of the late 1990s.

United Game Technology (UGT) is the world's dominant manufacturer of slot machines for casinos and other locations where gambling is permitted. With a continuous flow of new gaming machines – 2002 product launches included Elvira: Mistress of the Dark, Hundred Play Draw Poker, and Ms Little Green Men – UGT's US market share exceeded 70%, and it established market leadership in a number of European countries, including the UK. With leadership in mechanical and electronic gaming technologies, a raft of patents, and close relations with the casino companies supported by its policy of leasing rather than selling machines, UGT market leadership appeared unchallengeable. During 1999 to 2002, UGT earned an average return on equity of 61%.

Sources: www.ustinc.com, www.devro.plc.uk, www.igt.com.

of industry structure which result in both earning dismal rates of profit. Some of the most attractive industries are those which supply a niche product – the limited markets for such products often mean dominance by just one or two companies (see Strategy Capsule 3.1).

The underlying theory of how industry structure drives competitive behavior and determines industry profitability is provided by industrial organization (IO) economics. The two reference points are the *theory of monopoly* and the *theory of perfect competition*, which form two ends of the spectrum of industry structures. A single firm protected by barriers to the entry of new firms forms a monopoly in which it can appropriate in profit the full amount of the value it creates. By contrast, many firms supplying an identical product with no restrictions on entry or exit constitute perfect competition: the rate of profit falls to a level that just covers firms' cost of capital. In the real world, industries fall between these two extremes. The US market

TABLE 3.3 The Spectrum of Industry Structures

	Perfect Competition	Oligopoly	Duopoly	Monopoly
Concentration	Many firms	A few firms	Two firms	One firm
Entry and Exit Barriers	No barriers	Significant barriers		High barriers
Product Differentiation	Homogeneous product (Commodity)	Potential for product differentiation		
Information Availability	No impediments to information flow	Imperfect availability of information		

for chewing tobacco is close to being a monopoly; the Chicago grain markets are close to being perfectly competitive. Most manufacturing industries and many service industries tend to be *oligopolies*: they are dominated by a small number of major companies. Table 3.3 identifies some key points on the spectrum. By examining the principal structural features and their interactions for any particular industry, it is possible to predict the type of competitive behavior likely to emerge and the resulting level of profitability.

Porter's Five Forces of Competition Framework

Table 3.3 identifies four structural variables influencing competition and profitability. In practice, there are many features of an industry that determine the intensity of competition and the level of profitability. A helpful, widely used framework for classifying and analyzing these factors is the one developed by Michael Porter of Harvard Business School.[2] Porter's Five Forces of Competition framework views the profitability of an industry (as indicated by its rate of return on capital relative to its cost of capital) as determined by five sources of competitive pressure. These five forces of competition include three sources of "horizontal" competition: competition from substitutes, competition from entrants, and competition from established rivals; and two sources of "vertical" competition: the bargaining power of suppliers and buyers (see Figure 3.2).

The strength of each of these competitive forces is determined by a number of key structural variables, as shown in Figure 3.3.

Competition from Substitutes

The price customers are willing to pay for a product depends, in part, on the availability of substitute products. The absence of close substitutes for a product, as in

FIGURE 3.2 Porter's Five Forces of Competition framework

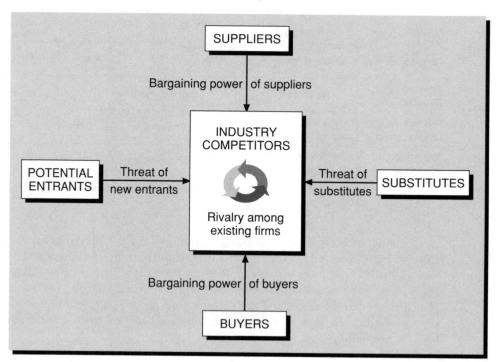

the case of gasoline or cigarettes, means that consumers are comparatively insensitive to price (i.e., demand is inelastic with respect to price). The existence of close substitutes means that customers will switch to substitutes in response to price increases for the product (i.e., demand is elastic with respect to price). E-commerce has provided a new source of substitute competition that has proved devastating for a number of established businesses. The travel agency industry in Europe and North America has been pushed to the brink of ruin by the growth of on-line reservations systems operated by specialists such as Expedia and Travelocity and by the airlines directly.

The extent to which substitutes limit prices and profits depends on the propensity of buyers to substitute between alternatives. This, in turn, is dependent on their price–performance characteristics. If city-center to city-center travel between Washington and New York is 50 minutes quicker by air than by train and the average traveler values time at $30 an hour, the implication is that the train will be competitive at fares of $25 below those charged by the airlines. The more complex the needs being fulfilled by the product and the more difficult it is to discern performance differences, the lower the extent of substitution by customers on the basis of price differences. The failure of low-priced imitations of leading perfumes to establish significant market share reflects, in part, consumers' difficulty in recognizing the performance characteristics of different fragrances.

FIGURE 3.3 The structural determinants of the Five Forces of Competition

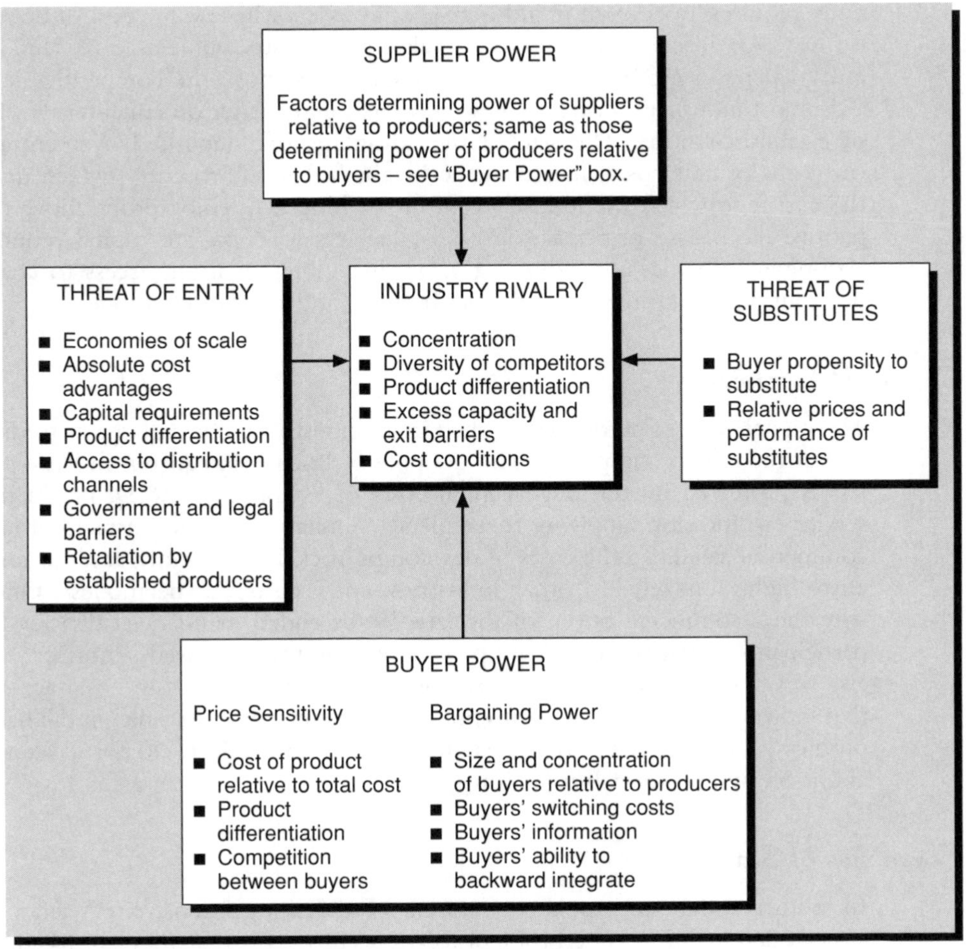

SUPPLIER POWER

Factors determining power of suppliers relative to producers; same as those determining power of producers relative to buyers – see "Buyer Power" box.

THREAT OF ENTRY

- Economies of scale
- Absolute cost advantages
- Capital requirements
- Product differentiation
- Access to distribution channels
- Government and legal barriers
- Retaliation by established producers

INDUSTRY RIVALRY

- Concentration
- Diversity of competitors
- Product differentiation
- Excess capacity and exit barriers
- Cost conditions

THREAT OF SUBSTITUTES

- Buyer propensity to substitute
- Relative prices and performance of substitutes

BUYER POWER

Price Sensitivity

- Cost of product relative to total cost
- Product differentiation
- Competition between buyers

Bargaining Power

- Size and concentration of buyers relative to producers
- Buyers' switching costs
- Buyers' information
- Buyers' ability to backward integrate

Threat of Entry

If an industry earns a return on capital in excess of its cost of capital, that industry acts as a magnet to firms outside the industry. Unless the entry of new firms is barred, the rate of profit will fall toward its competitive level. The US bagel industry, for example, faced a flood of new entrants in 1996, which caused a sharp diminution of profit prospects.[3] The threat of entry rather than actual entry may be sufficient to ensure that established firms constrain their prices to the competitive level. Only American Airlines offers a direct service between Dallas-Fort Worth and Santa Barbara, California, for example. Yet, American may be unwilling to exploit its monopoly position if other airlines can easily extend their routes to cover the same two cities. An industry where no barriers to entry or exit exist is *contestable*: prices and profits tend towards the competitive level, regardless of the number of firms within the industry.[4] Contestability depends on the absence of sunk costs. Sunk costs exist where entry requires investment in industry-specific assets whose value cannot be recovered on exit. An absence of sunk costs makes an industry vulnerable to "hit-and-run" entry whenever established firms raise their prices above the competitive level.

In most industries, however, new entrants cannot enter on equal terms with those of established firms. The size of the advantage of established over entrant firms (in terms of unit costs) measures the height of barriers to entry, which determines the extent to which the industry can, in the long run, enjoy profit above the competitive level. The principal sources of barriers to entry are capital requirements, economies of scale, cost advantages, product differentiation, access to channels of distribution, governmental and legal barriers, and retaliation.

Capital Requirements

The capital costs of getting established in an industry can be so large as to discourage all but the largest companies. The duopoly of Boeing and Airbus in large passenger jets is protected by the huge capital costs of establishing R&D, production, and service facilities for supplying these planes. Similary with the business of launching commercial satellites: the costs of developing rockets and launch facilities make new entry highly unlikely. In other industries, entry costs can be modest. One reason why the e-commerce boom of the late 1990s ended in financial disaster for most participants is that the initial setup costs of new internet-based ventures were typically very low. Across the service sector more generally, startup costs are still such that individual, self-financing entrepreneurs can enter. For example, in the hamburger business, franchise costs for a restaurant are around $350,000 for a Wendy's and about $1 million for a Burger King.[5]

Economies of Scale

In industries that are capital or research or advertising intensive, efficiency requires large-scale operation. The problem for new entrants is that they are faced with the choice of either entering on a small scale and accepting high unit costs, or entering on a large scale and running the risk of underutilized capacity while they build up sales volume. In automobiles, it is generally reckoned that to be a low-cost producer, sales of over four million vehicles a year are necessary. These economies of scale have deterred entry into the industry so that the only new entrants in recent decades have been state-supported companies (e.g., Proton of Malaysia and Maruti of India) or companies that gambled that low input costs would offset their scale inefficiency (e.g., Samsung and Ssangyong of Korea, both of which were in acute difficulty by 2000). The main source of scale economies is new product development costs. Thus, developing and launching a new model of car typically costs over $1.5 billion. Similarly in passenger jets, the $20 billion required to develop Airbus's proposed A380 superjumbo means that sales of over 800 planes are necessary to break even. Once Airbus had committed to the project, then Boeing was effectively excluded from the superjumbo segment of the market.

Absolute Cost Advantages

Apart from economies of scale, established firms may have a cost advantage over entrants simply because they entered earlier. Absolute cost advantages often result from the acquisition of low-cost sources of raw materials. Saudi Aramco's access to the world's biggest and most accessible oil reserves give it an unassailable cost advantage over Shell, Exxon Mobil, and the other western majors whose production costs per barrel are at least three times those of Saudi Aramco. Absolute cost advantages may also result from economies of learning. Sharp's cost advantage in flat screen TVs results from its early entry into this market and its ability to move down the learning curve faster than Sony or Philips.

Product Differentiation

In an industry where products are differentiated, established firms possess the advantages of brand recognition and customer loyalty. The percentage of US consumers loyal to a single brand varies from under 30 percent in batteries, canned vegetables, and garbage bags, up to 61 percent in toothpaste, 65 percent in mayonnaise, and 71 percent in cigarettes.[6] New entrants to such markets must spend disproportionately heavily on advertising and promotion to gain levels of brand awareness and brand goodwill similar to that of established companies. One study found that, compared to early entrants, late entrants into consumer goods markets incurred additional advertising and promotional costs amounting to 2.12 percent of sales revenue.[7] Alternatively, the new entrant can accept a niche position in the market or can seek to compete by cutting price.

Access to Channels of Distribution

Whereas lack of brand awareness among consumers acts as a barrier to entry to new suppliers of consumer goods, a more immediate barrier for the new company is likely to be gaining distribution. Limited capacity within distribution channels (e.g., shelf space), risk aversion by retailers, and the fixed costs associated with carrying an additional product result in retailers being reluctant to carry a new manufacturer's product. The battle for supermarket shelf space between the major food processors (typically involving lump-sum payments to retail chains in order to reserve shelf space) means that new entrants scarcely get a look in.

Governmental and Legal Barriers

Some economists (notably those of the Chicago School) claim that the only effective barriers to entry are those created by government. In taxicabs, banking, telecommunications, and broadcasting, entry usually requires the granting of a license by a public authority. From medieval times to the present day, companies and favored individuals have benefited from governments granting them an exclusive right to ply a particular trade or offer a particular service. In knowledge-intensive industries, patents, copyrights, and other legally protected forms of intellectual property are major barriers to entry. Xerox Corporation's monopolization of the plain-paper copier industry until the late 1970s was protected by a wall of over 2,000 patents relating to its xerography process. Regulatory requirements and environmental and safety standards often put new entrants at a disadvantage to established firms, because compliance costs tend to weigh more heavily on newcomers.

Retaliation

Barriers to entry also depend on the entrants' expectations as to possible retaliation by established firms. Retaliation against a new entrant may take the form of aggressive price-cutting, increased advertising, sales promotion, or litigation. The major airlines have a long history of retaliation against low-cost entrants. Southwest and other budget airlines have alleged that selective price cuts by American and other major airlines amounted to predatory pricing designed to prevent its entry into new routes.[8] To avoid retaliation by incumbents, new entrants may seek initial small scale entry into less visible market segments. When Toyota, Nissan, and Honda first entered the US auto market, they targeted the small car segments partly because this was a segment that had been written off by the Detroit Big Three as inherently unprofitable.[9]

The Effectiveness of Barriers to Entry

Empirical research shows industries protected by high entry barriers tend to earn above average rates of profit[10] and that capital requirements and advertising are particularly important impediments to entry to sources of increased profitability.[11]

Whether barriers to entry are effective in deterring potential entrants depends on the resources and capabilities that potential entrants possess. Barriers that are effective against new companies may be ineffective against established firms that are diversifying from other industries. George Yip found no evidence that entry barriers deterred new entry.[12] Some entrants possessed resources that allowed them to surmount barriers and compete against incumbent firms using similar strategies. Thus, Mars used its strong position in confectionery to enter the ice cream market, while Virgin has used its brand name to enter a wide range of industries from airlines to telecommunications. Other companies circumvented entry barriers by adopting innovative strategies. During the late 1990s, a host of established consumer products companies from banks to bookstores faced new competition from e-commerce startups that used the internet to by-pass conventional distribution channels.

Rivalry between Established Competitors

For most industries, the major determinant of the overall state of competition and the general level of profitability is competition among the firms within the industry. In some industries, firms compete aggressively – sometimes to the extent that prices are pushed below the level of costs and industry-wide losses are incurred. In others, price competition is muted and rivalry focuses on advertising, innovation, and other nonprice dimensions. Six factors play an important role in determining the nature and intensity of competition between established firms: concentration, the diversity of competitors, product differentiation, excess capacity, exit barriers, and cost conditions.

Concentration

Seller concentration refers to the number and size distribution of firms competing within a market. It is most commonly measured by the concentration ratio: the combined market share of the leading producers. For example, the four-firm concentration ratio (*CR4*) is the market share of the four largest producers. A market dominated by a single firm (e.g., Microsoft in PC operating systems, or UST in the US smokeless tobacco market) displays little competition and the dominant firm can exercise considerable discretion over the prices it charges. Where a market is dominated by a small group of leading companies (an oligopoly), price competition may also be restrained, either by outright collusion, or more commonly through "parallelism" of pricing decisions.[13] Thus, in markets dominated by two companies, such as alkaline batteries (Duracell and Eveready), color film (Kodak and Fuji), and soft drinks (Coke and Pepsi), prices tend to be similar and competition focuses on advertising, promotion, and product development. As the number of firms supplying a market increases, coordination of prices becomes more difficult, and the likelihood that one firm will initiate price-cutting increases. However, despite the common observation that the elimination of a competitor typically reduces price competition, while the entry of a new competitor typically stimulates it, systematic evidence of the impact of seller concentration on profitability is surprisingly weak. Richard Schmalensee concluded that: "The relation, if any, between seller concentration and profitability is weak statistically and the estimated effect is usually small."[14]

Diversity of Competitors

The extent to which a group of firms can avoid price competition in favor of collusive pricing practices depends upon how similar they are in terms of origins, objectives, costs, and strategies. The cozy atmosphere of the US auto industry prior to the advent of import competition was greatly assisted by the similarities of the companies in terms of cost structures, strategies, and top management mindsets. The intense competition that affects the car markets of Europe and North America is partly due to the different national origins, costs, strategies, and management styles of the competing firms. Similarly, the key challenge faced by OPEC is agreeing and enforcing output quotas among member countries that are sharply different in terms of objectives, production costs, politics, and religion.

Product Differentiation

The more similar the offerings among rival firms, the more willing customers are to substitute and the greater the incentive for firms to cut prices to increase sales. Where the products of rival firms are virtually indistinguishable, the product is a commodity and price is the sole basis for competition. Commodity industries such as agriculture, mining, and petrochemicals tend to be plagued by price wars and low profits. By contrast, in industries where products are highly differentiated (perfumes, pharmaceuticals, restaurants, management consulting services), price competition tends to be weak, even though there may be many firms competing.

Excess Capacity and Exit Barriers

Why does industry profitability tend to fall so drastically during periods of recession? The key is the balance between demand and capacity. Unused capacity encourages firms to offer price cuts to attract new business in order to spread fixed costs over a greater sales volume. Excess capacity may be cyclical (e.g. the boom–bust cycle in the semiconductor industry); it may also be part of a structural problem resulting from overinvestment and declining demand. In these latter situations, the key issue is whether excess capacity will leave the industry. *Barriers to exit* are costs associated with capacity leaving an industry. Where resources are durable and specialized, and where employees are entitled to job protection, barriers to exit may be substantial.[15] Exit barriers in the European oil refining industry resulting from the high costs of dismantling refineries, environmental cleanup, and employee layoffs have resulted in a continuing overhang of excess capacity that has kept profits at a very low level. Conversely, rapid demand growth creates capacity shortages that boost margins. During the latter half of 2003, for instance, bulk cargo shipping rates increased fourfold as a result of increased Chinese demand for iron ore. On average, companies in growing industries earn higher profits than companies in slow growing or declining industries (see Figure 3.4).

FIGURE 3.4 The impact of growth on profitability

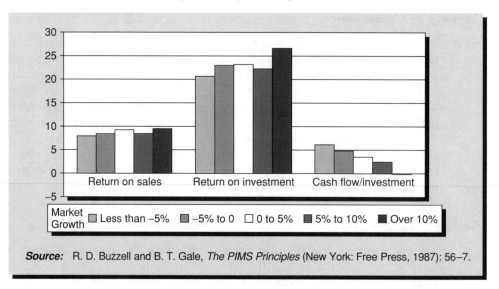

Source: R. D. Buzzell and B. T. Gale, *The PIMS Principles* (New York: Free Press, 1987): 56–7.

Cost Conditions: Scale Economies and the Ratio of Fixed to Variable Costs

When excess capacity causes price competition, how low will prices go? The key factor is cost structure. Where fixed costs are high relative to variable costs, firms will take on marginal business at any price that covers variable costs. The consequences for profitability can be disastrous. Between 2001 and 2003, the total losses of the US airline industry exceeded the cumulative profits earned during the entire previous history of the industry. The willingness of airlines to offer heavily discounted tickets on flights with low bookings reflects the very low variable costs of filling empty seats. The devastating impact of excess capacity on profitability in petrochemicals, tires, steel, and semiconductors is a result of high fixed costs in these businesses and the willingness of firms to accept additional business at any price that covers variable costs.

Scale economies may also encourage companies to compete aggressively on price in order to gain the cost benefits of greater volume. If scale efficiency in the auto industry means producing four million cars a year, a level that is achieved by only six of the nineteen international auto companies, the outcome is a battle for market share as each firm tries to achieve critical mass.[16]

Bargaining Power of Buyers

The firms in an industry operate in two types of markets: in the markets for inputs and the markets for outputs. In input markets firms purchase raw materials, components, and financial and labor services. In the markets for outputs firms sell their goods and services to customers (who may be distributors, consumers, or other manufacturers). In both markets the transactions create value for both buyers and sellers. How this value is shared between them in terms of profitability depends on their relative economic power. Let us deal first with output markets. The strength of buying power that firms face from their customers depends on two sets of factors: buyers' price sensitivity and relative bargaining power.

Buyers' Price Sensitivity

The extent to which buyers are sensitive to the prices charged by the firms in an industry depends on four main factors:

■ The greater the importance of an item as a proportion of total cost, the more sensitive buyers will be about the price they pay. Beverage manufacturers are highly sensitive to the costs of metal cans because this is one of their largest single cost items. Conversely, most companies are not sensitive to the fees charged by their auditors, since auditing costs are such a small proportion of overall company expenses.

■ The less differentiated the products of the supplying industry, the more willing the buyer is to switch suppliers on the basis of price. The manufacturers of T-shirts, light bulbs, and blank videotapes have much more to fear from Wal-Mart's buying power than have the suppliers of perfumes.

■ The more intense the competition among buyers, the greater their eagerness for price reductions from their sellers. As competition in the world automobile industry has intensified, so component suppliers are subject to greater pressures for lower prices, higher quality, and faster delivery.

■ The greater the importance of the industry's product to the quality of the buyer's product or service, the less sensitive are buyers to the prices they are charged. The buying power of personal computer manufacturers relative to the manufacturers of microprocessors (Intel, Motorola, Advanced Micro Devices) is limited by the critical importance of these components to the functionality of their product.

Relative Bargaining Power

Bargaining power rests, ultimately, on refusal to deal with the other party. The balance of power between the two parties to a transaction depends on the credibility and effectiveness with which each makes this threat. The key issue is the relative cost that each party sustains as a result of the transaction not being consummated. A second issue is each party's expertise in leveraging its position through gamesmanship. Several factors influence the bargaining power of buyers relative to that of sellers:

■ *Size and concentration of buyers relative to suppliers.* The smaller the number of buyers and the bigger their purchases, the greater the cost of losing one. Because of their size, health maintenance organizations (HMOs) can purchase health care from hospitals and doctors at much lower cost than can individual patients.

■ *Buyers' information.* The better informed buyers are about suppliers and their prices and costs, the better they are able to bargain. Doctors and lawyers do not normally display the prices they charge, nor do traders in the bazaars of Tangier and Istanbul. Keeping customers ignorant of relative prices is an effective constraint on their buying power. But knowing prices is of little value if the quality of the product is unknown. In the markets for haircuts, interior design, and management consulting, the ability of buyers to bargain over price is limited by uncertainty over the precise attributes of the product they are buying.

■ *Ability to integrate vertically.* In refusing to deal with the other party, the alternative to finding another supplier or buyer is to do it yourself. Large food-processing companies such as Heinz and Campbell Soup have reduced their dependence on the manufacturers of metal cans by manufacturing their own. The leading retail chains have increasingly displaced their suppliers' brands with their own-brand products. Backward integration need not necessarily occur – a credible threat may suffice.

TABLE 3.4   The Impact of Unionization on Profitability

| | PERCENTAGE OF EMPLOYEES UNIONIZED | | | | |
	none	1 to 35%	35 to 60%	60 to 75%	over 75%
ROI (%)	25	24	23	18	19
ROS (%)	10.8	9.0	9.0	7.9	7.9

Source: R. D. Buzzell and B. T. Gale, *The PIMS Principles: Linking Strategy to Performance* (New York: Free Press, 1987): 67. © 1987 by the Free Press, a division of Simon Schuster Adult Publishing Group. All rights reserved.

Empirical evidence points to the tendency for buyer concentration to depress prices and profits in supplying industries.[17] PIMS data show that the larger the average size of customers' purchases and the larger the proportion of customers' total purchases the item represents, the lower the profitability of supplying firms.[18]

Bargaining Power of Suppliers

Analysis of the determinants of relative power between the producers in an industry and their suppliers is precisely analogous to analysis of the relationship between producers and their buyers. The only difference is that it is now the firms in the industry that are the buyers and the producers of inputs that are the suppliers. The key issues are the ease with which the firms in the industry can switch between different input suppliers and the relative bargaining power of each party.

Because raw materials, semi-finished products, and components are often commodities supplied by small companies to large manufacturing companies, their suppliers usually lack bargaining power. Hence, commodity suppliers often seek to boost their bargaining power through cartelization (e.g., OPEC, the International Coffee Organization, and farmers' marketing cooperatives). A similar logic explains labor unions. Conversely, the suppliers of complex, technically sophisticated components may be able to exert considerable bargaining paper. The supplier power of Intel in microprocessors, Microsoft in operating systems, Sharp in flat screens, and Seagate in disk drives has been a powerful factor depressing the profitability of the PC manufacturers. Forward integration by suppliers into a customer industry increases their supplier power and depresses profitability in the customer industry.[19]

Labor unions are important sources of supplier power. Where an industry has a high percentage of its employees unionized – as in steel, airlines and automobiles – profitability is reduced (see Table 3.4).

APPLYING INDUSTRY ANALYSIS

Once we understand how industry structure drives competition, which, in turn, determines industry profitability, we can apply this analysis, first to forecasting industry profitability in the future, and second to devising strategies for changing industry structure.

Describing Industry Structure

The first stage of industry analysis is to identify the key elements of the industry's structure. In principle, this is a simple task. It requires identifying who are the main players – the producers, the customers, the suppliers, and the producers of substitute goods – then examining some of the key structural characteristics of each of these groups that will determine competition and bargaining power.

In most manufacturing industries the identity of the different groups of player is usually straightforward, in other industries – particularly in service industries – building a picture of the industry may be more difficult. Consider the television industry. There are a number of different types of player and establishing which are buyers, which are sellers, and where the industry boundaries lie is not simple. In terms of industry definition, do we consider all forms of TV distribution or identify separate industries for broadcast TV, cable TV, and satellite TV? In terms of identifying buyers and sellers, we see that there the industry has quite a complex value chain with the producers of the individual shows, networks that put together program schedules, and local broadcasting and cable companies that undertake final distribution. For the distribution companies there are two buyers – viewers and advertisers. Some companies are vertically integrated across several stages of the value chain – thus, networks such as Fox and NBC not only create and distribute program schedules, they are also backward integrated into producing some TV shows and they are forward integrated into local distribution through ownership of local TV stations.

Sorting out the different players and their relationships therefore involves some critical issues of industry definition. Which activities within the value chain do we include the industry? What are the horizontal boundaries of the industry in terms of both products and geographical scope? We shall return to some of these issues of industry definition in a subsequent section.

Forecasting Industry Profitability

We can use industry analysis to understand why profitability has been low in mining for metals and high in medical equipment but, ultimately, our interest in industry analysis is not to explain the past, but to predict the future. Investment decisions made today will commit resources to an industry for a decade or more – hence, it is critical that we are able to predict what industry profitability is likely to be in the future. Current profitability tends to be a poor indicator of future profitability. However, if an industry's profitability is determined by its structure of an industry, then we can use observations of the structural trends in an industry to forecast the likely changes in competition and profitability. Given that changes in industry structure tend to be long term and are the result of changes in customer buying behavior, changes in technology, and the strategies being implemented by the firms in the industry, we can use our current observations to identify emerging structural trends.

To predict the future profitability of an industry, our analysis proceeds in three stages:

1. Examine how the industry's current and recent levels of competition and profitability are a consequence of the industry's present structure.

2. Identify the trends that are changing the industry's structure. Is the industry consolidating? Are new players seeking to enter? Are the industry's products becoming more differentiated or more commoditized? Does it look as though additions to industry capacity will outstrip the industry's growth of demand?

3. Identify how these structural changes will affect the Five Forces of Competition and resulting profitability of the industry. Compared with the present, does it seem as though the changes in industry structure will cause competition to intensify or to weaken? Rarely do all the structural changes move competition in a consistent direction – typically, some factors will cause competition to increase, others will cause competition to moderate. Hence, determining the overall impact on profitability is likely to be a matter of judgment.

Strategy Capsule 3.2 discusses the profitability prediction in relation to the US casino industry.

Since the late 1990s, industry profitability in most of the world's major industrial nations has been declining – indeed, some studies suggest that profitability, in real terms, has been on a downward long-term trend for the past four decades. Increasing international competition appears to be a major contributor to deteriorating profitability. For a brief period of the late 1990s, there was a widespread belief that – in the US at least – the technology boom and the productivity gains associated with it might have reversed this trend, even at the point where the standard approaches to industry analysis might need to be abandoned or at least rewritten. The downturn of 2000–2002, and the bursting of the internet bubble in particular, have restored faith in the notion that the so-called "New Economy" did not require any rewriting of the principles of industry and competitive analysis. In retrospect, it appears fairly obvious that the impact of digital technologies was primarily to intensify competition and erode industry profits (see Strategy Capsule 3.3).

Strategies to Alter Industry Structure

Understanding how the structural characteristics of an industry determine the intensity of competition and the level of profitability provides a basis for identifying opportunities for changing industry structure in order to alleviate competitive pressures. The first issue is to identify the key structural features of an industry that are responsible for depressing profitability. The second is to consider which of these structural features are amenable to change through appropriate strategic initiatives. For example:

■ In the European and North American oil refining industry, most firms have earned returns well below their cost of capital due to multiple competitors, excess capacity, and commodity products. In response, the oil majors have consolidated to reduce rivalry and facilitate capacity rationalization. In Europe,

STRATEGY CAPSULE 3.2 Prospects for the US Casino Industry

The late 1990s and early 2000s saw rapid development of the US casino gambling industry. The perception of the industry as a gold mine was shared not just by the existing casino operators, but also by municipalities, states, and entertainment companies. The result was unprecedented expansion.

In terms of new entry, casino gambling expanded well beyond its traditional centers in Las Vegas, Nevada, and Atlantic City, NJ. The municipalities and state governments saw gambling as offering new tax revenue sources and economic development opportunities. The result was the introduction of riverboat casinos and the licensing of casinos in Mississippi and seven other states (in addition to Nevada and New Jersey). The 1988 Indian Gaming Regulatory Act opened the way for casinos on Indian reservations. By 2002 there were over 100 casinos on Indian reservations across 17 states. One of the biggest was Foxwood's, owned by the Mashantucket Pequot tribe in Ledyard, CT. During 2000, the relaxation of gambling restrictions on the Indian reservations in California encouraged a new wave of casino projects.

For the major casino companies, rivalry to build the "biggest and best" hotel/casino complexes in Las Vegas and Atlantic City became increasingly intense. Between 1996 and 2000, the number of hotel rooms at Las Vegas casinos doubled. New "mega-casinos" in Vegas included the $390 million Luxor, the $450 million Treasure Island, the $1 billion MGM Grand resort, the $1.6 billion Bellagio, the $1.4 billion New York, and the 6000-room, $1.5 billion Venetian Hotel. Personal rivalry between Donald Trump and Mirage Resorts' Steve Wynn helped fuel capacity expansion in Atlantic City, where the impact of excess capacity was exacerbated by the high fixed costs of operating casinos.

Competition between casino companies involved ever more ambitious differentiation. The new casinos in Las Vegas broke fresh ground in spectacle, entertainment, theming, and sheer scale. Price competition was also evident in terms of subsidized travel packages, free rooms and other perks for "high rollers."

Growing substitute competition included an increasing number of state lotteries, offshore gambling on cruiseships, the installation of slot machines at horsetracks, and, most significantly, the growth of internet gambling.

Increasing competition encouraged rapid industry consolidation. By 2003, three major players dominated the industry: MGM Mirage, Park Place (which combined the casino interests of Hilton Hotels and Starwood Hotels), and Harrah's Entertainment.

The impact of new entry, excess capacity, and substitute competition upon industry margins depends on the extent to which new supply will create its own demand and the ability of the industry leaders to keep their instincts for aggressive competition under control. During the 1990s increased demand for gambling was able to absorb the rapid increase in casino capacity and the growth in alternative gambling media. Total US gambling revenues rose from $124 billion in 1982, to $304 billion in 1991, $509 billion in 1996, and over $700 billion in 1999. Nevertheless, as the data below show, industry profitability remained low.

Company	Return on equity (%), 1998–2002
MGM Mirage	7.8
Park Place Entertainment	9.4
Harrah's Entertainment	12.2
Mandalay Resorts Group	12.6
Trump Hotels and Casinos	4.2

The critical issue for the period 2004–2008 was whether the demand for casino gambling would continue to grow at a pace that would take up the new casino capacity under construction, or whether new casino capacity, new gambling locations, and new forms of gambling would cause increasingly aggressive competition to destroy the industry's profitability.

Sources: www.ft.com; Shawn Tully, "The New King of Casinos," *Fortune*, September 18, 2000: 156–68.

STRATEGY CAPSULE 3.3 Competition in the New Economy

The development and diffusion of information and communications technologies (ICT) spawned the growth of many new industries – wireless telephony, satellite TV, and a host of e-commerce businesses – and transformed many established businesses from bookselling to financial services. The resulting boom in productivity, spawning of new investment, and the shift from an industrial-based to knowledge-based economy encouraged the belief that the advanced industrialized economies were entering a "New Economy" where the economic laws that had governed the "Old Economy" would not necessarily apply.

Certainly, many features of the knowledge-based economy based upon digital technologies were different – in particular the increasing returns associated with the information and knowledge.* However, in terms of *profitability*, the implications of the virtual, information-based economy looked less favorable. Let us consider specifically the implications of the internet for competition and profitability within industries. By applying the good-old Five Forces framework, Michael Porter showed that – rather than usher in a new era of opportunity and profitability, most of the implications of internet technology for existing industries were profoundly negative in terms of profitability. Thus, whether we are considering stockbroking, bookselling, banking, or educational services, the advent of the internet has typically resulted in increased rivalry among competitors, reduced barriers to entry, and enhanced the power of buyers. While the advent of the internet during the 1990s made available a wide range of e-commerce opportunities, the harsh reality is that where we look at established industries such as retailing or financial services, or new industries such as internet service provision or electronic markets, the main impact of the internet has been to intensify competition and erode industry attractiveness. The bursting of the dot.com bubble in 2000–2001 seems to be the inevitable result of the stock market catching up with strategic reality.

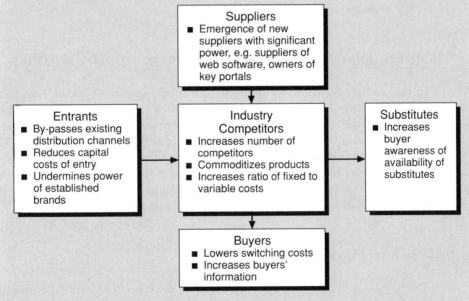

Note:
* Paul Romer, "Increasing Returns and Long-run Growth," *Journal of Political Economy* 54 (1986): 897–908; Paul Romer, "The Soft Revolution," *Journal of Applied Corporate Finance* (Summer 1998).
Source: Adapted from M. E. Porter, "Strategy and the Internet," *Harvard Business Review* (March 2001): 63–77.

BP and Mobil merged their downstream activities and, in the US, Shell and Texaco formed a downstream joint venture. In the subsequent wave of mega mergers, BP acquired Amoco, then Arco. Exxon merged with Mobil and Chevron with Texaco. The merger of Total, Fina, and Elf created a super-major that dominated the oil products markets of France and the Low Countries.

■   Excess capacity has also been a major problem in the European petrochemicals industry. Through a series of bilateral plant exchanges, each company has sought to build a leading position within a particular product area.[20]

■   In the US airline industry, the major airlines have sought to offset an unfavorable industry structure by a number of strategies. In the absence of significant product differentiation, the airlines have used frequent-flier schemes as a means of recreating customer loyalty. Through hub-and-spoke route systems, the companies have achieved dominance of particular airports: American at Dallas-Fort Worth, US Airways at Charlotte NC, and Northwest at Detroit and Memphis. Mergers and alliances have reduced the numbers of competitors on many routes.

■   Building entry barriers is a vital strategy for preserving high profitability in the long run. A primary goal of the American Medical Association has been to maintain the incomes of its members by controlling the numbers of doctors trained in the United States and imposing barriers to the entry of doctors from overseas.

DEFINING INDUSTRIES: WHERE TO DRAW THE BOUNDARIES

In our earlier discussion of the structure of the television broadcasting industry, I noted that a key challenge in industry analysis is defining the relevant industry. The Standard Industrial Classification (SIC) offers an official guide, but this provides limited practical assistance. Suppose Jaguar, a subsidiary of Ford Motor Company, is assessing its future prospects. In forecasting the profitability of its industry, should Jaguar consider itself part of the "motor vehicles and equipment" industry (SIC 371), the automobile industry (SIC 3712), or the luxury car industry? Should it view its industry as national (UK), regional (Europe), or global?

Industries and Markets

The first issue is clarifying what we mean by the term "industry." Economists define an industry as a group of firms that supplies a market. Hence, a close correspondence exists between markets and industries. So, what's the difference between analyzing industry structure and analyzing market structure? The principal difference is that industry analysis – notably Five Forces analysis – looks at industry profitability being determined by competition in two markets: product markets and input markets.

Everyday usage makes a bigger distinction between industries and markets. Typically, industry is identified with relatively broad sectors, while markets refer to specific products. Thus, the firms within the packaging industry compete in many distinct product markets – glass containers, steel cans, aluminum cans, paper cartons, plastic containers, and so on. The distinction between the economist's approach to industry and everyday usage of the term also relates to geographical boundaries. From an economist's viewpoint, the US automobile industry would denote all companies supplying the US auto market – irrespective of the location. In everyday usage, the term "US auto industry" typically refers to auto manufacturers located within the US, and is often restricted to US-owned automakers (which now includes primarily Ford and General Motors).

For the purposes of industry analysis, we need to adopt the economist's approach to identifying and defining industries. Thus, our starting point is the market – which are the group of firms that compete to supply a particular service? The result may be that, for the purposes of industry analysis, we may wish to disregard conventional concepts of industry. For example, if we are examining competition within the banking industry, it is likely that we would want to regard banking as comprising a number of industries – banks supply a number of distinct services and competition in each product market comprises different sets of firms. Most basic is the distinction between retail banking and investment banking. Even within retail banking we can distinguish different industry groups. For example, credit cards and consumer lending are closely related products, but they involve distinct product offerings and different groups of competing firms.

Given the conventional view of industries as broad economic sectors, Shiv Mathur and Alfred Kenyon argue that, in order to focus on the realities of competition, it is best to abandon the concept of industry in favor of a micro-level approach that begins with customers choosing between rival offerings. Strategy Capsule 3.4 outlines their approach.

STRATEGY CAPSULE 3.4 Mathur and Kenyon's Approach to Competitive Analysis

---

Mathur and Kenyon argue that our conventional concept of industry is fundamentally flawed. In order to analyze competition, we must begin with customer choice. Customers do not choose a product or a company, their unit of choice is the single offering. Competitive strategy is the "positioning of a single offering vis-à-vis a unique set of potential customers and competitors." Thus:

- Land Rover's Discovery and Defender models are separate offerings because they compete for different groups with different preferences and with different competing offerings from other companies. To the extent that customer preferences and the range of competitors are different in France from Canada or Malaysia, then we can regard each model in each country as a separate offering competing in a separate market.

- London's Dorchester Hotel comprises a number of separate offerings: luxury hotel accommodation, restaurant services, cocktail bar drinks, and various personal services and retail products. The customers for these may be much the same, but each will have a separate set of competitors.

STRATEGY CAPSULE 3.4 *(cont'd)*

The result is a micro approach to analyzing markets and competitive strategy that contrasts sharply with that associated with Michael Porter. Not only are offerings much more narrowly defined than products, but each offering has its own unique market.

Should we abandon our more aggregated industry analysis in favor of the meticulously micro analysis advocated by Mathur and Kenyon? The critical consideration is the type of question that we want our competitive analysis to answer. For decisions relating to marketing strategy – including product design, pricing, advertising, distribution, and entry into specific market segments – analysis of competition between narrowly defined offerings in relation to specific customers and customer groups is likely to be particularly revealing.

The case for retaining a more broadly-based approach to industry analysis rests on the objective of understanding and predicting medium-term profit trends (periods of over one year). Here the conventional Five Forces analysis of fairly broadly-defined industries has two virtues. First, it allows us to consider competition in two markets simultaneously – the market for outputs and markets for inputs. Second, it takes account of supply-side substitution. Even though Ford's different brands – Land Rover, Jaguar, Volvo and Lincoln – compete for different customers with different sets of competitors, they utilize many common components and can (with some reequipping) be produced at different Ford plants. Other car manufacturers can similarly switch production capacity between their different models. Hence, although heavily segmented, we can conceive of the automobile industry as a single industry subject to some common trends that will influence profitability similarly throughout the many different market segments.

Source: Shiv Mathur and Alfred Kenyon, *Creating Value: Successful Business Strategies* (Oxford: Butterworth-Heinemann, 2002).

Defining Markets: Substitution in Demand and Supply

I have argued that the key to defining industry boundaries is identifying the relevant market. By focusing on the relevant market, we do not lose sight of the critical relationship among firms within an industry: competition. But how do we define markets?

A market's boundaries are defined by substitutability. There are two dimensions to this – substitutability on the demand side and the supply side. Let us consider once more the market within which Jaguar competes. Starting with the demand side, if customers are unwilling to substitute trucks for cars on the basis of price differences, Jaguar's market should be viewed as automobiles rather than all motor vehicles. Again, if customers are only willing to substitute between Jaguars and other makes of luxury cars, then Jaguar's relevant market is luxury cars rather than the automobile market as a whole.

But this fails to take account of substitutability on the supply side. If manufacturers find it easy to switch their production from luxury cars to family sedans to sports cars and the like, such supply-side substitutability would suggest that Jaguar is competing within the broader automobile market. The ability of Toyota, Nissan, and Honda to penetrate the luxury car market suggests that supply-side substitutability between mass-market autos and specialty autos is moderately high. Similarly, the automobile industry is frequently defined to include vans and light trucks, since these can be manufactured at the same plants as automobiles (often using the same platforms and engines). So too with "major appliance" manufacturers. They tend to be classified as a single industry, not because consumers are willing to substitute between refrigerators and dishwashers, but because the manufacturers can use the same manufacturing plants and distribution channels for different appliances.

The same considerations apply to the geographical boundaries of markets. Should Jaguar view itself as competing in a single global market or in a series of separate national or regional markets? The criterion here again is substitutability. If customers are willing and able to substitute cars available on different national markets, or if manufacturers are willing and able to divert their output among different countries to take account of differences in margins, then a market is global. The key test of the geographical boundaries of a market is price: if price differences for the same product between different locations tend to be eroded by demand-side and supply-side substitution, then these locations lie within a single market.

In practice, drawing the boundaries of markets and industries is a matter of judgment that depends upon the purposes and context of the analysis. If Ford is considering the pricing and market positioning of its Jaguar cars, it must take a micro-level approach that defines markets around each model, in each country, and in relation to different categories of customer (e.g., distinguishing between sales to car rental companies and sales to individual consumers). In considering decisions over investments in fuel cell technology, the location of engine plants, and which new products to develop over the next five years, Ford will view Jaguar as one part of its auto and light truck business and will define its market as global and extending across its full range of models. The longer term the decisions are that it is considering, the more broadly it will wish to consider its markets, since substitutability is higher in the long run than in the short term.

Second, the precise delineation of the boundaries of a market or industry is seldom critical to the outcome of our analysis so long as we remain wary of external influences. The market in which an offering competes is a continuum rather than a bounded space. Thus, we may view the competitive market of Disneyland, Anaheim as a set of concentric circles. Closest is Universal Studios Tour. Slightly more distant competitors are Sea World and Six Flags. Further still might be a trip to Las Vegas, or a skiing weekend. Beyond these would be the broader entertainment market that might include cinemas, the beach, or playing video games.

For the purposes of applying the Five Forces framework, industry definition is not critical. We define an industry "box" within which industry rivals compete, but because we include competitive forces outside the industry box – notably entrants and substitutes – the precise boundaries of the industry box are not greatly important. Whether we view Harley-Davidson as competing in the "retro" segment of the heavyweight motorcycle industry, in the heavyweight motorcycle industry, or in the motorcycle industry as a whole is not critical to the outcome of our analysis. Even if we define Harley's market narrowly, we can still take into account competition from Triumph and Ducati as substitute competition. Indeed, we might want to consider competition from more distant substitutes – sports cars, motorized water craft, and participation in "extreme sports."

FROM INDUSTRY ATTRACTIVENESS TO COMPETITIVE ADVANTAGE: IDENTIFYING KEY SUCCESS FACTORS

The Five Forces framework allows us to determine an industry's potential for profit. But how is industry profit shared between the different firms competing in that industry? As we have noted in our discussion of industry dynamics, competition between industry participants is ultimately a battle for competitive advantage in which firms rival one another to attract customers and maneuver for positional advantage. The purpose of this section is to look explicitly at the sources of competitive advantage within an industry. In subsequent chapters, we develop a more comprehensive analysis of competitive advantage. Our goal here is to identify those factors within the firm's market environment that determine its ability to survive and prosper – its *key success factors*.[21] In Strategy Capsule 3.5, Kenichi Ohmae of McKinsey's Tokyo office discusses key success factors in forestry and their link with strategy.

STRATEGY CAPSULE 3.5 Probing for Key Success Factors

As a consultant faced with an unfamiliar business or industry, I make a point of first asking the specialists in the business, "What is the secret of success in this industry?" Needless to say, I seldom get an immediate answer, and so I pursue the inquiry by asking other questions from a variety of angles in order to establish as quickly as possible some reasonable hypotheses as to key factors for success. In the course of these interviews it usually becomes quite obvious what analyses will be required in order to prove or disprove these hypotheses. By first identifying the probable key factors for success and then screening them by proof or disproof, it is often possible for the strategist to penetrate very quickly to the core of a problem.

Traveling in the United States last year, I found myself on one occasion sitting in a plane next to a director of one of the biggest lumber companies in the country. Thinking I might learn something useful in the course of the five-hour flight, I asked him, "What are the key factors for success in the lumber industry?" To my surprise, his reply was immediate: "Owning large forests and maximizing the yield from them." The first of these key factors is a relatively simple matter: purchase of forest land. But his second point required further explanation. Accordingly, my next question was: "What variable or variables do you control in order to maximize the yield from a given tract?"

He replied: "The rate of tree growth is the key variable. As a rule, two factors promote growth: the amount of sunshine and the amount of water. Our company doesn't have many forests with enough of both. In Arizona and Utah, for example, we get more than enough sunshine but too little water, and so tree growth is very low. Now, if we could give the trees in those states enough water, they'd be ready in less than fifteen years instead of the thirty it takes now. The most important project we have in hand at the moment is aimed at finding out how to do this."

Impressed that this director knew how to work out a key factor strategy for his business, I offered my own contribution: "Then under the opposite conditions, where there is plenty of water but too little sunshine – for example, around the lower reaches of the Columbia River – the key factors should be fertilizers to speed up the growth and the choice of tree varieties that don't need so much sunshine."

Having established in a few minutes the general framework of what we were going to talk about, I spent the rest of the long flight very profitably hearing from him in detail how each of these factors was being applied.

Source: Kenichi Ohmae, *The Mind of the Strategist* (Harmondsworth: Penguin, 1982): 85.

Like Ohmae, our approach to identifying key success factors is straightforward and common sense. To survive and prosper in an industry, a firm must meet two criteria: first, it must supply what customers want to buy; second, it must survive competition. Hence, we may start by asking two questions:

- What do our customers want?
- What does the firm need to do to survive competition?

To answer the first question we need to look more closely at customers of the industry and to view them not so much as a source of bargaining power and hence as a threat to profitability, but more as the basic rationale for the existence of the industry and as the underlying source of profit. This implies that the firm must identify who its customers are, what are their needs, and how they choose between competing offerings. Once we have identified the basis of customers' preference, this is merely the starting point for a chain of analysis. For example, if consumers' choice of supermarkets is based primarily on which charges the lowest prices and if the ability to charge low prices depends on low costs, the key issues concern the determinants of costs among supermarkets.

The second question requires that the firm examines the basis of competition in the industry. How intense is competition and what are its key dimensions? Thus, in the luxury car market, consumers select primarily on the basis of prestige, design, quality, and exclusiveness. However, these qualities are an insufficient basis for success. In this intensely competitive market, survival requires a strong financial position (to finance new product development) and costs that are sufficiently low to allow a company to cover its cost of capital.

A basic framework for identifying key success factors is presented in Figure 3.5. Application of the framework to identify key success factors in three industries is outlined in Table 3.5.

FIGURE 3.5   Identifying key success factors

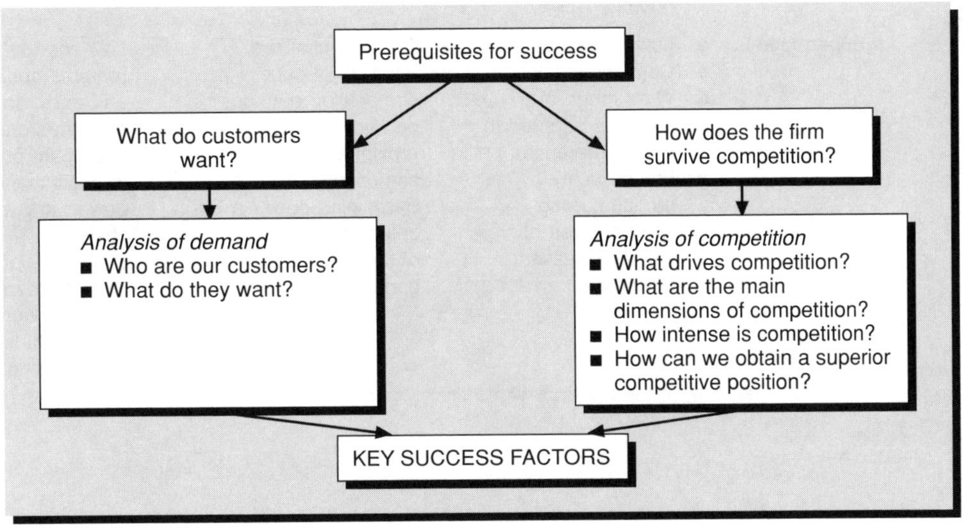

TABLE 3.5 Identifying Key Success Factors: Steel, Fashion Clothing, and Supermarkets

	WHAT DO CUSTOMERS WANT? (Analysis of demand)	HOW DO FIRMS SURVIVE COMPETITION? (Analysis of competition)	KEY SUCCESS FACTORS
Steel	■ Low price. ■ Product consistency. ■ Reliability of supply. ■ Specific technical specifications for special steels.	■ Commodity products, excess capacity, high fixed costs, excess capacity, exit barriers, and substitute competition mean intense price competition and cyclical profitability. ■ Cost efficiency and strong financial resources essential.	■ Conventional sources of cost efficiency include: large-scale plants, low-cost location, rapid adjustment of capacity to output. ■ Alternatively, high technology, small scale plants can achieve low costs through flexibility and high productivity. ■ Differentiation through technical specifications and service quality.
Fashion clothing	■ Wide variety of customer preferences relating to garment type, style, quality, color. ■ Customers willing to pay price premium for brand, stylishness, exclusivity, and quality. ■ Mass market highly price sensitive.	■ Low barriers to entry and exit, low seller concentration, and buying power of retail chains imply intense competition. ■ Differentiation can yield substantial price premium, but imitation is rapid.	■ Need to combine effective differentiation with low costs. ■ Key differentiation variables are speed of response to changing high fashions, style, reputation and quality. ■ Cost efficiency requires manufacture in low wage countries.
Supermarkets	■ Low prices. ■ Convenient location. ■ Wide range of products adapted to local preferences. ■ Fresh/quality produce; good service; ease of parking; pleasant ambience.	■ Markets localized. ■ Intensity of price competition depends on number and proximity of competitors. ■ Bargaining power a critical determinant of cost of bought-in goods.	■ Low-cost operation requires operational efficiency, scale-efficient stores, large aggregate purchases to maximize buying power, low wage costs. ■ Differentiation requires large stores (to allow wide product range), convenient location, easy parking.

Key success factors can also be identified through the direct modeling of profitability. In the same way that our Five Forces analysis models the determinants of industry-level profitability, we can also attempt to model firm-level profitability in terms of identifying the key factors that drive a firm's relative profitability within an industry. In Chapter 2, we made some progress on this front. By disaggregating a firm's return on capital employed into individual operating factors and ratios, we can pinpoint the most important determinants of firm success (see Figure 2.2). In many industries, these primary drivers of firm-level profitability are well known and widely used as performance targets. Strategy Capsule 3.6 gives a well-known

---

STRATEGY CAPSULE 3.6 Identifying Key Success Factors by Modeling Profitability: Airlines

---

Profitability, as measured by operating income per available seat-mile (ASM), is determined by three factors: yield which is total operating revenues divided by the number of revenue passenger miles (RPM); load factor which is the ratio between RPMs and ASMs; and unit cost which is total operating expenses divided by ASMs. Thus:

$$\frac{\text{Income}}{\text{ASMs}} = \frac{\text{Revenue}}{\text{RPMs}} \times \frac{\text{RPMs}}{\text{ASMs}} \text{ less } \frac{\text{Expenses}}{\text{ASMs}}$$

Some of the primary determinants of each of these measures are the following:

- Revenue/RPMs
  - Intensity of competition on routes flown.
  - Effective yield management to permit quick price adjustment to changing market conditions.
  - Ability to attract business customers.
  - Superior customer service.

- Load factors
  - Competitiveness of prices.
  - Efficiency of route planning (e.g., through hub-and-spoke systems).
  - Building customer loyalty through quality of service, frequent-flier programs.
  - Matching airplane size to demand for individual flights.

- Expenses/ASMs
  - Wage rates and benefit levels.
  - Fuel efficiency of aircraft.
  - Productivity of employees (determined partly by their job flexibility).
  - Load factors.
  - Level of administrative cost.

In their battle for survival, the airlines have sought to optimize as many of these factors as possible in order to improve their profitability. To enhance revenue, several airlines have withdrawn from their most intensely competitive routes, others have sought to achieve a fare premium over the cut-price airlines through superior punctuality, convenience, comfort, and services. To improve load factors, companies have become more flexible in their pricing and in allocating different planes to different routes. Most notably, companies have sought to cut costs by increasing employee productivity, reducing overhead, sharing services with other airlines, and reducing salaries and benefits.

FIGURE 3.6 Identifying key success factors through analyzing profit drivers: the case of retailing

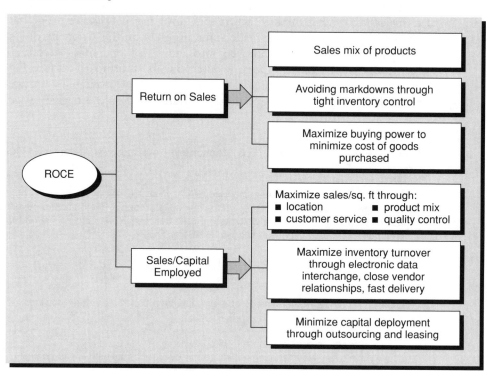

profitability formula used in the airline industry, then identifies the factors that drive the profitability ratios. More generally, the approach introduced in Chapter 2 to dis-aggregate return on capital into its component ratios can be extended to identify the specific operational and strategic drivers of superior profitability. Figure 3.6 applies this analysis to identifying success factors in retailing.

The value of success factors in formulating strategy has been scorned by some strategy scholars. Pankaj Ghemawat observes that the "whole idea of identifying a success factor and then chasing it seems to have something in common with the ill-considered medieval hunt for the philosopher's stone, a substance that would transmute everything it touched into gold."[22] The objective here in identifying key success factors is less ambitious. There is no universal blueprint for a successful strategy and, even in individual industries, there is no "generic strategy" that can guarantee superior profitability. However, each market is different in terms of what motivates customers and how competition works. Understanding these aspects of the industry environment is a prerequisite for an effective business strategy. Never-theless, this does not imply that firms within an industry adopt common strategies. Since every firm comprises a unique set of resources and capabilities, even when an industry is subject to common success factors (e.g. low costs), firms will select unique strategies to link their resources and capabilities to industry success factors.

SUMMARY

In Chapter 1, we established that profound understanding of the competitive environment is a critical ingredient of a successful strategy. In this chapter, we have developed a systematic approach to analyzing a firm's industry environment in order to evaluate that industry's profit potential and to identify the sources of competitive advantage. The centerpiece of our approach is Porter's Five Forces of Competition framework, which links the structure of an industry to the competitive intensity within it and to the profitability that it realizes. Although every industry is unique, competition and profitability are the result of the systematic influences of the structure of that industry. The Porter framework provides a simple, yet powerful organizing framework for classifying the relevant features of an industry's structure and predicting their implications for competitive behavior. The framework is particularly useful for predicting industry profitability and for identifying how the firm can influence industry structure in order to improve industry profitability.

As with most of the tools for strategy analysis that we shall consider in this book, the Porter Five Forces framework is easy to comprehend. While its basis is a substantial body of microeconomic theory, the relationships it posits are straightforward and consistent with commonsense. However, the real learning about industry analysis, and about the Porter framework in particular, derives from its *application*. It is only when we apply the Porter framework to analyzing competition and diagnosing the causes of high or low profitability in an industry that we are forced to confront the complexities and subtleties of the model. What industry (or industries) does a company compete in? Where do the industry's boundaries lie? How wide a range of substitutes do we consider? How do excess capacity, cost structures, and exit barriers interact with one another?

I urge you to put the tools of industry analysis to work – not just in your strategic management coursework, but also in your interpretation of everyday business events. Why are the telecom equipment makers having such a tough time currently? What will be the impact of direct internet-based IPOs (such as Google's) on competition and profitability within investment banking? Is your cousin's plan to leave her law firm and run an antique stall in London's Portobello Road such a good idea given the competitive forces within this market?

Through practical applications of the Porter framework, we shall also become aware of its limitations. In the next chapter we shall consider some of these limitations and look to ways in which we can extend and augment our analysis with additional concepts, tools, and frameworks.

NOTES

1 For a review of macro-environmental ("PEST") analysis, see V. K. Narayanan and L. Fahey, "Macroenvironmental Analysis: Understanding the Environment Outside the Industry," in L. Fahey and R. M. Randall (eds.), *The Portable MBA in Strategy*, 2nd edn (New York: Wiley, 2001): 189–214.

2 Michael E. Porter, *Competitive Strategy: Techniques for Analyzing Industries and Competitors* (New York: Free Press, 1980): Chapter 1. For a summary, see his article, "How Competitive Forces Shape Strategy," *Harvard Business Review* 57 (March–April 1979): 86–93.

3 The *Wall Street Journal* ("For Bagel Chains, Investment May Be Money in the Hole," December 30, 1997: B8) reported that the influx of new bagel chains, including Einstein/Noah Bagel Corp., Manhattan Bagel, BAB Holdings (Big Apple Bagels), Uncle B's Bakery, Bruegger's Bagel, Big City Bagels, and a host of others, resulted in widespread losses as prices were cut and margins fell.

4 W. J. Baumol, J. C. Panzar, and R. D. Willig, *Contestable Markets and the Theory of Industry Structure* (New York: Harcourt Brace Jovanovitch, 1982). See also Michael Spence, "Contestable Markets and the Theory of Industry Structure: A Review Article," *Journal of Economic Literature* 21 (September 1983): 981–90.

5 "Annual Franchise 500," *Entrepreneur* (January 2001).

6 "Brand Loyalty Is Rarely Blind Loyalty," *Wall Street Journal* (October 19, 1989): B1.

7 Robert D. Buzzell and Paul W. Farris, "Marketing Costs in Consumer Goods Industries," in Hans Thorelli (ed.), *Strategy + Structure = Performance* (Bloomington, IN: Indiana University Press, 1977): 128–9.

8 In October 1999, the Dept. of Justice alleged that American Airlines was using unfair means in attempting to monopolize air traffic out of Dallas-Fort Worth. (http://www.aeroworldnet.com/1tw05179.htm).

9 Marvin Lieberman ("Excess Capacity as a Barrier to Entry," *Journal of Industrial Economics* 35, June 1987: 607–27) argues that, to be credible, the threat of retaliation needs to be supported by incumbents holding excess capacity giving them the potential to flood the market.

10 See for example: J. S. Bain, *Barriers to New Competition* (Cambridge, MA: Harvard University Press, 1956) and H. M. Mann, "Seller Concentration, Entry Barriers, and Rates of Return in Thirty Industries," *Review of Economics and Statistics* 48 (1966): 296–307.

11 W. S. Comanor and T. A. Wilson, *Advertising and Market Power* (Cambridge: Harvard University Press, 1974); and L. Weiss, "Quantitative Studies in Industrial Organization," in M. Intriligator (ed.), *Frontiers of Quantitative Economics* (Amsterdam: North Holland, 1971).

12 George S. Yip, "Gateways to Entry," *Harvard Business Review* 60 (September–October 1982): 85–93.

13 F. M. Scherer and D. R. Ross, *Industrial Market Structure and Economic Performance*, 3rd edn (Boston: Houghton Mifflin, 1990); R. M. Grant, "Pricing Behavior in the UK Wholesale Market for Petrol. A 'Structure-Conduct Analysis'," *Journal of Industrial Economics* 30 (March 1982).

14 Richard Schmalensee, "Inter-Industry Studies of Structure and Performance," in Richard Schmalensee and Robert D. Willig, *Handbook of Industrial Organization*, 2nd edn (Amsterdam: North Holland, 1988): 976. For evidence on the impact of concentration in banking, airlines, and railroads, see D. W. Carlton and J. M. Perloff, *Modern Industrial Organization* (Glenview, IL: Scott, Foresman, 1990): 383–5.

15 The problems caused by excess capacity and exit barriers are discussed in Charles Baden Fuller (ed.), *Strategic Management of Excess Capacity* (Oxford: Basil Blackwell, 1990).

16 R. M. Grant, "Daimler Chrysler and the World Automobile Industry," in R. M.

Grant, *Cases in Contemporary Strategy Analysis*, 3rd edn (Oxford: Blackwell, 2002).

17 S. H. Lustgarten, "The Impact of Buyer Concentration in Manufacturing Industries," *Review of Economics and Statistics* 57 (1975): 125–32; and Robert M. Grant, "Manufacturer–Retailer Relations: The Shifting Balance of Power," in G. Johnson (ed.), *Business Strategy and Retailing* (Chichester: John Wiley, 1987).

18 Robert D. Buzzell and Bradley T. Gale, *The PIMS Principles: Linking Strategy to Performance* (New York: Free Press, 1987): 64–5.

19 Ibid.

20 Joe Bower, *When Markets Quake* (Boston: Harvard Business School Press, 1986).

21 The term was coined by Chuck Hofer and Dan Schendel, *Strategy Formulation: Analytical Concepts* (St. Paul: West Publishing, 1977): 77, who defined key success factors as "those variables that management can influence through its decisions and that can affect significantly the overall competitive positions of the firms in an industry . . . Within any particular industry they are derived from the interaction of two sets of variables, namely, the economic and technological characteristics of the industry . . . and the competitive weapons on which the various firms in the industry have built their strategies."

22 Pankaj Ghemawat, *Commitment: The Dynamic of Strategy* (New York: Free Press, 1991): 11.

4

Further Topics in Industry and Competitive Analysis

INTRODUCTION AND OBJECTIVES

The framework of industry analysis outlined in the previous chapter (the Porter model in particular) offers a systematic and widely applicable approach to describing industry structure, predicting industry profitability, designing strategies to influence industry structure, and identifying key success factors. At the same time, our view of industry and competition has been a simplified one. Consider the following:

- The only relationships between products that we have considered are substitute relations. Many products – both goods and services – have complementary relationships with one another. What do complementary relationships imply for competitive analysis and the potential for profit?

- In many sectors, industry structure may be much less stable than envisaged by the Porter model. Rather than structure determining competition in some predictable way, competition – particularly technological competition – may reshape industry structure very rapidly. Look at the pace of change in the recorded music industry, in mobile telephone handsets, or in television broadcasting over the past few years.

- We have not explored the dynamic rivalry that characterizes business competition in the real world. Pepsi-Cola's competitive environment is determined more by the strategy and marketing tactics of Coca-Cola than by the structure of the world soft drinks industry. Similarly, Reuter's competitive environment is dominated by the competitive strategy of Bloomberg, as is Boeing's by Airbus Industrie. To understand competition as a dynamic, personalized process we shall draw upon the tools of game theory and competitor analysis.

- We need to analyze competition and profitability not just at the industry level, but within specific segments too. American Airlines competes in the world airline industry. However, each route comprises a different market with a different set of competitors. Between New York and Paris, American's closest competitor is Air France, but between New York and Montreal it is Air Canada. To take account of the internal heterogeneity of industries and the fact that the companies within an industry may compete within a number of distinct markets, we shall disaggregate industries both horizontally and vertically.

This chapter will extend the analysis of industry and competition to address the above topics. In doing so, you will acquire the following capabilities:

- To analyze the impact of goods and services that are *complements* to those supplied by a firm, and to identify the potential for the firm to make profit through managing relationships with the suppliers of complements.

- To recognize the implications of game theory for competitive analysis, in particular, the potential gains to cooperative strategies and the use of threats, commitments, signaling, deterrence, and preemption to gain and sustain competitive advantage.

- To use competitor analysis to predict the competitive moves rivals are likely to initiate and likely responses by rivals to our own competitive initiatives.

- To segment an industry into its constituent markets, to appraise the relative attractiveness of different segments, and identify differences in key success factors among them.

- To classify the firms within an industry into strategic groups based on similarities in their strategies.

EXTENDING THE FIVE FORCES FRAMEWORK

Does Industry Matter?

Porter's Five Forces of Competition has been the subject of constant criticism. Some have attacked its theoretical foundations, arguing that the structure–conduct–performance approach to industrial organization that underlies it lacks rigor (especially when compared with the logical and mathematical robustness of game theory). The main defense of industry analysis is that it is useful in allowing us to understand competition and to predict changes in profitability on the basis of changes in industry structure.

A more serious attack is that, irrespective of its theoretical rigor, in reality a firm's industry environment is a relatively minor determinant of that firm's profitability. A series of studies measuring the proportion of interfirm differences in profitability attributable to industry factors has produced very different results (see Table 4.1). Despite major differences in the findings of different studies, a common conclusion emerges very clearly: industry factors account for a minority of interfirm differences in profitability (less than 20 percent in all the studies).

These sobering findings have several implications. First, they point to the need to understand more deeply the determinants of competitive behavior between companies and the extent to which it has implications for industry level profitability. We need to reconsider the relationship between industry structure and competition and explore more rigorous and sophisticated approaches to analyzing competition – game theory in particular. Second, we need to disaggregate broad industry groupings and

TABLE 4.1 What determines interfirm differences in profitability? The role of industry

	PERCENTAGE OF VARIANCE IN FIRMS' RETURN ON ASSETS EXPLAINED BY:		
	INDUSTRY EFFECTS	FIRM-SPECIFIC EFFECTS	UNEXPLAINED VARIANCE
Schmalensee (1985)	19.6%	0.6%	80.4%
Rumelt (1991)	4.0%	44.2%	44.8%
McGahan & Porter (1997)	18.7%	31.7%	48.4%
Hawawini et al. (2003)	8.1%	35.8%	52.0%

Sources: R. Schmalensee "Do markets differ much?" *American Economic Review*, 75 (1985): 341–51; R. P. Rumelt "Does industry matter much?" *Strategic Management Journal* 12 (1991): 167–85; A. M. McGahan and M. E. Porter "How much does industry matter, really?" *Strategic Management Journal* 18 (1997): 15–30; G. Hawawini, V. Subramanian, and P. Verdin, "Is Firms' Profitability Driven by Industry or Firm-Specific Factors? A New Look at the Evidence," *Strategic Management Journal* 24 (January 2003): 1–16.

examine competition at the level of particular segments and strategic groupings of firms. Let us begin by considering the possibilities of extending the Porter framework.

Complements: A Missing Force in the Porter Model?

The Porter framework identifies the suppliers of substitute goods and services as one of the forces of competition that reduces the profit available to the firms within an industry. However, economic theory identifies two types of relationship between different products: substitutes and complements. While the presence of substitutes reduces the value of a product, complements increase value. The availability of ink cartridges for my printer transforms its value to me.

The suppliers of complementary products (*complementors*) play an important role in most firms' competitive environment. To introduce complements into competitive analysis, Brandenburger and Nalebuff have developed a framework they call the *value net*.[1] Apart from the presence of complementors, the model differs from the Porter Five Forces framework by lumping together industry rivals, potential entrants, and suppliers of substitutes into the single category of "competitors" (see Figure 4.1). Given that we have already gained practice in applying the Porter framework, the simplest way to take account of the role of complements is to add a sixth force to Porter's framework (see Figure 4.2).

Whatever way we introduce complements and complementors into our competitive analysis, the key issue is analyzing their impact. Where products are close complements, they have little value to customers individually – customers value the whole system. But how is the value shared between the producers of the different complementary products? Bargaining power and its deployment are the key. During the early 1990s, Nintendo video game consoles earned it huge profits. Although most of the revenue and consumer value was in the software – mostly supplied

FIGURE 4.1 The value net

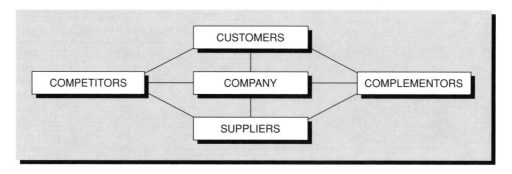

FIGURE 4.2 Five Forces, or Six?

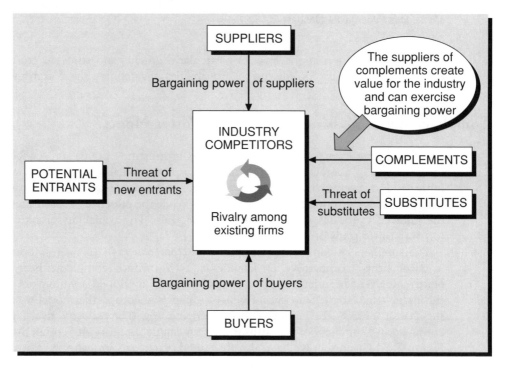

by independent developers – Nintendo was able to appropriate most of the profit potential of the entire system. Nintendo's strategic genius was in the management of its relationships with games developers. Nintendo established a dominant relationship with games developers by controlling its operating system, by issuing developer licenses to many producers of games software developers, and by maintaining tight control over the manufacture and distribution of games cartridges (from which Nintendo earned a hefty royalty).[2]

In PCs, power has been on the side of the software suppliers – Microsoft in particular. IBM's adoption of open architecture meant that Microsoft Windows became a proprietary standard, while PCs were gradually reduced to commodity status.

Where two products are complements to one another, profit will accrue to the supplier that builds the stronger market position and reduces the value contributed by the other. How is this done? The key is to achieve monopolization, differentiation, and shortage of supply in one's own product, while encouraging competition, commoditization, and excess capacity in the production of the complementary product. IBM is attempting to shift the balance of power between hardware and software producers through its promotion of Linux and other open-source software programs. By pressing to differentiate its hardware products while commoditizing software, it can reduce the power of Microsoft and garner a bigger share of the profit returns from systems of hardware and software.[3]

Dynamic Competition: Creative Destruction and Hypercompetition

The notion that industry structure is relatively stable and determines competitive behavior in a predictable way ignores the dynamic forces of innovation and entrepreneurship. Joseph Schumpeter viewed competition as a "perennial gale of creative destruction" through which favorable industry structures – monopoly in particular – contain the seeds of their own destruction by attracting incursions from new and established firms deploying innovatory strategies and innovatory products to unseat incumbents.[4]

This view of Schumpeter (and the "Austrian school" of economics) that competition is a dynamic process of rivalry that constantly reformulates industry structure suggests that it may be more appropriate to view structure as the outcome of competitive behavior rather than vice-versa.[5] The key consideration is the speed of structural change in the industry – if the pace of structure transformation is rapid, a Porter Five Forces approach has limited usefulness in predicting competition and profitability.

Most empirical studies of changes over time in industry structure and profitability show Schumpeter's process of "creative destruction" to be more of a breeze than a gale. In established industries, entry occurs so slowly that profits are undermined only gradually,[6] while changes in industrial concentration tend to be slow.[7] As one survey observed: "the picture of the competitive process . . . is, to say the least, sluggish in the extreme."[8] Overall, the studies show a fairly consistent picture of the rate of change of profitability and structure. Both at the firm and the industry level, profits tend to be highly persistent in the long run.[9]

However, some industries show clear evidence of "creative destruction." Jeffrey Williams defines "Schumpeterian industries" as those subject to rapid product innovation with relatively steep experience curves – they include semiconductors, consumer electronics, and computers.[10] Indeed, the number of sectors subject to these dynamic, unstable conditions seems to be growing. Rich D'Aveni uses the term *hypercompetition* to describe industry environments characterized by intense and rapid competitive moves where competitors must move quickly to build advantages and erode the advantages of their rivals.[11] Hypercompetitive behavior involves continuously generating new competitive advantages and destroying, obsoleting, or neutralizing the opponent's competitive advantage, thereby disrupting the status quo of the marketplace by creating disequilibrium. Central to the concept of hypercompetition is the idea that competitive advantage is transitory. If advantages are not sustainable, the only route to sustained superior performance is through continually recreating and renewing competitive advantage. We shall return to this issue in Chapter 7 when we consider competitive advantage in greater depth.

THE CONTRIBUTION OF GAME THEORY

Central to the criticisms of Porter's Five Forces as a static framework is its failure to take full account of competitive interactions among firms. In Chapter 1, we noted that the essence of strategic competition is the interaction among players, such that the decisions made by any one player are dependent on the actual and anticipated decisions of the other players. By relegating competition to a mediating variable that links industry structure with profitability, the Five Forces analysis offers little insight into firms' choices of whether to compete or cooperate; sequential competitive moves; and the role of threats, promises, and commitments. Over the past quarter century game theory has revolutionized microeconomics and has made huge contributions to other fields of competitive analysis from politics and international relations to sociology and psychology. Game theory offers two especially valuable contributions to strategic management:

1. *It permits the framing of strategic decisions.* Apart from any theoretical value of the theory of games, game theory provides a structure, a set of concepts, and a terminology that allows us to describe a competitive situation in terms of:
   - identity of the players;
   - specification of each player's options;
   - specification of the payoffs from every combination of options;
   - the sequencing of decisions using game trees.

   This permits us to understand the structure of the competitive situation and facilitates a systematic, rational approach to decision making.

2. *It can predict the outcome of competitive situations and identify optimal strategic choices.* Through the insight it offers into situations of competition and bargaining, game theory can predict the equilibrium outcomes of competitive situations and the consequences of strategic moves by any one player. Game theory provides penetrating insights into central issues of strategy that go well beyond pure intuition. Simple game models (e.g. "Prisoners' Dilemma") predict cooperative versus competitive outcomes, whereas more complex games permit analysis of the effects of reputation,[12] deterrence,[13]

information,[14] and commitment[15] – especially within the context of multiperiod games. Particularly important for practicing managers, game theory can indicate strategies for improving the structure and outcome of the game through manipulating the payoffs to the different players.

Despite exploding interest and rapid development of game theory during the 1980s, its influence on strategic management practice remained limited until the 1990s. Since then, practical applications of game theory have grown as a result of a number of practical guides to the application of game theory's tools and insights.[16] Game theory has provided illuminating insights into a wide variety of situations, including the Cuban missile crisis of 1962,[17] President Reagan's 1981 tax cut,[18] rivalry between Boeing and Airbus Industrie,[19] the problems of OPEC in agreeing to production cuts, the competitive impact of Philip Morris's "Marlboro Monday" price cut,[20] decisions over investments in new production capacity,[21] and auctions of airwave spectrum.[22]

Cooperation

One of the greatest benefits of game theory is its ability to view business interactions as comprising both competition and cooperation. A key deficiency of the Five Forces framework is in viewing inter-firm relations as exclusively competitive in nature. The central message of Adam Brandenburger and Barry Nalebuff's book *Co-opetition* is recognizing the competitive/cooperative duality of business relationships.[23] Whereas Coca-Cola's relationship with Pepsi-Cola is essentially competitive, that between Intel and Microsoft is primarily complementary. Thus:

- A player is your complementor if customers value your product more when they have the other player's product than when they have your product alone.

- A player is your competitor if customers value your product less when they have the other player's product than when they have your product alone.

However, there is no simple dichotomy between competition and cooperation: a player may occupy multiple roles. The battle to supply the operating system for the next generation of wireless phones pits Microsoft against the Symbian consortium. Samsung is a member of Symbian, but also is an important licensee of Microsoft's Smartphone operating system. Exxon and Shell have been bitter rivals for over a century in both upstream and downstream markets. At the same time, Exxon and Shell cooperate in a number of joint ventures including NAM, the Dutch gas company; Infinium, a manufacturer of lubricant additives; and the California Fuel Cell Partnership. The desire of competitors to cluster together – antique dealers in London's Bermondsey Market and movie studios in Hollywood – points to the complementary relations among competitors in growing the size of their market and developing its infrastructure. Similarly, with customers and suppliers, though in creating value, they are also rivals in sharing that value.

In many business relationships, competition results in a more inferior outcome for the players than would cooperation. The classic Prisoners' Dilemma game is one where a pair of suspects to a crime are arrested and each is offered an incentive to "grass" on the other. The dominant strategy is for each to implicate the other, even though, if both had remained silent, there would have been insufficient evidence for a conviction and the pair would have avoided conviction. Examples of Prisoners' Dilemmas include:

- A price war between evenly matched competitors that results in no change in market share and only lower profits all round.

- Competitive bidding between rival art collectors at an auction of old masters.

- Bargaining between a buyer and seller for a product whose quality cannot be discerned prior to purchase (e.g., a used car). The seller has an incentive to offer low quality; the buyer has an incentive to offer a low price in the likelihood that quality will be poor. The equilibrium is a low-priced, low-quality product, though both parties would benefit from a better-quality, higher-price product.

How can such Prisoners' Dilemmas be resolved? One answer is to change a one-period game (single transaction) into a repeated game. In the case of the supplier–buyer relationship, moving from a spot transaction to a long-term vendor relationship gives the supplier the incentive to offer a better-quality product and the buyer to offer a price that offers the seller a satisfactory return. In the case of price competition, markets dominated by two or three suppliers tend to converge toward patterns of price leadership where price competition is avoided.

A second solution is to change the payoffs in the game. The Mafia has been successful in changing the payoffs in the classic Prisoners' Dilemma game such that confessing and implicating accomplices is no longer a dominant strategy. It achieves this by imposing draconian reprisals on those who break the code of silence.

Deterrence

One way of changing a game's equilibrium through adjusting its payoffs is through *deterrence*. The principle behind deterrence is to impose costs on the other players for actions that we deem to be undesirable. By establishing the certainty that deserters would be shot, the British army provided a strong incentive to its troops to participate in advances on heavily fortified German trenches during World War I.

The key to the effectiveness of any deterrent is that it must be credible. The problem here is that if administering the deterrent is costly or unpleasant for the threatening party, the deterrent is not credible. Incumbents in a market may threaten a would-be entrant with aggressive price cuts. However, the entrant may rationalize that, once it has entered the market, it is no longer in the incumbent firm's best interest to engage in a costly price war. The key then is for the incumbent to make a credible commitment to price cutting. One example would be a clause in customer commitments that it will match any price cuts offered by a rival. Thus, a retailer's price guarantee that it will make a refund to any customer able to purchase an equivalent item at a lower cost is in effect providing a deterrent to any competitor cutting its prices. Firms may deliberately invest in excess capacity to discourage new entry. Alcoa expanded its capacity to warn off potential entrants into the US aluminum industry (*United States versus Alcoa*, 1945). Conversely, in both compact disks and X-ray scanners, the reluctance of the dominant firms (Philips in CDs, EMI in CT scanners) to invest heavily in new capacity to meet growing demand allowed the entry of a wave of newcomers.[24] However, Marvin Lieberman has cast doubt on the effectiveness of excess capacity in deterring new entry.[25]

Deterrence has provided a central theme in defense strategy. The nuclear arms race between the US and the then Soviet Union was based on the logic of "mutual assured destruction" – the certainty of retaliation against any nuclear attack risked the destruction of the entire human race. However, the ability for deterrence to produce a stable, peaceful equilibrium depends on the capacity for rival parties to be deterred. The mounting violence in Israel and Palestine during 2000–2004 results, in part, from the failure of tit-for-tat retaliation to deter further aggression.

Commitment

For deterrence to be effective it must be credible, which means being backed by some kind of commitment. Commitment is an interesting strategy since it is seemingly irrational – it involves the elimination of strategic options. When Hernan Cortes destroyed his ships on arrival in Mexico in 1519, he achieved, first, motivation for his men to conquer the Aztec empire, and second, a signal to Montezuma that any Aztec aggression could not lead to Spanish withdrawal. Airbus's investments in advertising, research, and supply contracts during 2000–2002 for its A380 superjumbo was to signal its commitment both to airlines and to Boeing, so that the airlines would be encouraged to place orders, and Boeing would be discouraged from developing a rival plane.

These commitments to aggressive competition have been described as "hard commitments." A company may also make commitments to avoid aggressive competition, what are called "soft commitments."[26] The airlines' frequent-flier programs are a commitment by the airlines to redeem miles flown with free tickets. They also signal to other airlines a shift of competition away from price competition and carry the message that the airline is less vulnerable to a rival's price cuts. How these different types of commitment affect the profitability of the firm making the commitment depends on the type of game being played. Where companies compete on price, game theory shows that they tend to match one another's price changes.[27] Hence, under price adjustments, hard commitments (e.g., a commitment to cut price) tend to have a negative profit impact and soft commitments (e.g., a commitment to raise prices) have a positive impact. Conversely, where companies compete on output, game theory shows that increases in output by one firm results in output reductions by the other.[28] Hence, under quantity adjustments, a hard commitment (e.g., a commitment to build new plants) will tend to have a positive effect on the committing firm's profitability, since it will tend to be met by other firms reducing their output.[29]

Changing the Structure of the Game

There are many ways in which a player can change the structure of the game it is playing. A company may seek to change the structure of the industry within which it is competing in order to increase the profit potential of the industry or to appropriate a greater share of the profit available. Thus, establishing alliances and agreements with competitors can increase the value of the game by increasing the size of the market and building joint strength against possible entrants. There may be many opportunities for converting win–lose (or even lose–lose) games into win–win games. A cooperative solution was found to Norfolk Southern's competition with CSX for control of Conrail, for example. The 1997 bidding war was terminated when CSX and Norfolk Southern agreed to cooperate in acquiring and dismembering Conrail.

In some cases, it may be advantageous for a firm to create competition for itself. When Intel developed its 8086 microprocessor, it gave up its potential monopoly by offering second-sourcing licenses to AMD and IBM. Although Intel was creating competition for itself, it was also encouraging the adoption of the 8086 chip by computer manufacturers (including IBM) who were concerned about overdependence on Intel. Once Intel had established its technology as the industry standard, it developed its family of 286, 386, 486, and Pentium processors and became much more restrictive over licensing.

Signaling

How a competitor will react to a company's strategic initiative depends on how the competitor perceives the initiative. The term *signaling* is used to describe the selective communication of information to competitors (or customers) designed to influence their perception and hence to provoke or avoid certain types of reaction.[30] The use of diversionary attacks and misinformation is well developed in military warfare. In 1944, Allied deception was so good that even during the D-Day landings in Normandy, the Germans believed that the main invasion would occur near Calais. The principal role of signaling is to deter competitors. But, as noted in discussing deterrence, information on its own is not enough: signals need to be credible. Thus, Allied misinformation concerning the invasion of Europe included the marshaling of a phantom army designed to convince the German high command that the Normandy invasion was merely a diversionary mission.

The credibility of threats is critically dependent on the company's reputation.[31] Even though carrying out threats against rivals is costly and depresses short-term profitability, exercising such threats can build a reputation for aggressiveness that deters competitors in the future. The benefits of building a reputation for aggressiveness may be particularly great for diversified companies where reputation can be transferred from one market to another.[32] Hence, Procter & Gamble's protracted market share wars in disposable diapers and household detergents have established a reputation for toughness that protects it from competitive attacks in other markets. Other companies whose aggressive quest for market share has gained them reputations as "killer competitors" include Gillette in razor blades, Anheuser-Busch in beer, and Emerson Electric in sink disposal units. Faced with such formidable and unrelenting rivals, smaller competitors have typically retreated to niches or given up the fight altogether.

Signaling may also be used to maintain cooperative pricing among firms. In the UK retail market for gasoline, the initiation of a price increase is normally preceded by a period of consensus building, during which the price leader tests the water by press releases that comment upon "the unsatisfactory level of margins in the industry," the "need to recoup recent cost increases," and the likelihood that "a price increase will become necessary in the near future."[33]

Is Game Theory Useful?

The value of game theory to strategic management has generated lively debate. For economists this seems paradoxical, since to them game theory *is* the theory of strategy. As one of my economist friends explained to me: "The essence of strategic thinking is to anticipate your competitor's moves in advance. Studying your competitor's likely reaction dramatically improves your ability to choose a strategy that will be successful."

In analyzing these patterns of action and reaction, the great virtue of game theory is its rigor. In microeconomics, the game theory revolution of the past quarter-century has established the analysis of markets and firm behavior on a much more secure theoretical foundation. However, the price of mathematical rigor has been limited applicability to real world situations. Game theory provides clear prediction in highly stylized situations involving few external variables and highly restrictive assumptions. The result is a mathematically sophisticated body of theory that suffers from unrealistic assumptions, lack of generality, and an analysis of dynamic situations through a sequence of static equilibriums.[34] When applied to more complex (and more realistic) situations, game theory frequently results in either no equilibrium or multiple equilibriums, and outcomes that are highly sensitive to small changes in the assumptions. In general, game theory has not developed to the point where it permits us to model real business situations in a level of detail that can generate precise predictions.

In terms of empirical application, game theory has done a much better job of explaining the past than of predicting the future. In diagnosing Nintendo's domination of the video games industry in the 1980s, Monsanto's efforts to prolong NutraSweet's market leadership beyond the expiration of its patents, or Airbus's wresting of market leadership from Boeing, game theory provides penetrating insight into the competitive situation and deep understanding of the rationale behind the strategies deployed. However, in predicting outcomes and designing strategies, game theory has been much less impressive.

Practical applications of game theory have also been underwhelming in their success. To allocate licenses for wireless telecommunication, the US Federal Communications Commission employed leading game theorists to design its digital wireless spectrum auctions during 1995–7. The outcome was a disaster – licenses for some cities were sold for $1 and allegations of collusion among bidders were widespread.[35]

So, where can game theory assist business managers? As with all our theories and frameworks, game theory is useful not because it gives us answers, but because it can help us understand business situations. Game theory provides a set of tools that allows us to structure our view of competitive interaction. If we identify the players in a game, identify the decision choices available to each player, specify the performance implications of each combination of decisions, and predict how each player is likely to react to the decision choices of the other, then we have made huge progress in understanding the dynamics of competition. Most importantly, by describing the structure of the game we are playing, we have a basis for suggesting ways of changing the game and thinking through the likely outcomes of such changes.

Although game theory continues its rapid development, it is nevertheless far from providing the central theoretical foundation for strategic management. Though we draw on game theory in several places in this book, particularly in exploring the interaction between firms in markets dominated by a handful of major competitors, our emphasis in strategy formulation will be less on achieving advantage through influencing the behavior of competitors and much more on transforming competitive games through building positions of unilateral competitive advantage. The competitive market situations with which we shall be dealing will, for the most part, be different from those considered by game theory. Game theory typically deals with competitive situations with closely matched players where each has a similar range of strategic options (typically relating to price changes, advertising budgets, capacity decisions, and new product introductions). The outcome of these games is highly dependent on order of moves, signals, bluffs, and threats. Our emphasis in strategy analysis will be less on the similarities between firms and their strategic options than on their differences. The key to competitive advantage and superior performance will be exploiting uniqueness.

COMPETITOR ANALYSIS

We have argued that in highly concentrated industries, the key characteristics of a company's external environment are determined by the behavior of a few rivals – possibly a single firm. In household detergents, Unilever's industry environment is dominated by the strategy of Procter & Gamble. The same is true in soft drinks (Coke and Pepsi), jet engines (GE, United Technologies, and Rolls-Royce), and business news periodicals (*Business Week*, *Fortune*, and *Forbes*). Similar circumstances exist in more local markets. For the owner of the Shell gas station in the English village of Coalpit Heath, the dominant feature of the local gasoline market is the competitive behavior of the Texaco station across the road. Game theory provides a theoretical apparatus for analyzing competitive interaction between small numbers of rivals but, for everyday business situations, game theory's formal models are not readily applicable. Given the limitations of game theory, I will outline an approach to predicting competitor behavior that draws upon the characteristics and observed behavior of specific firms. Let us examine how we can acquire information about competitors and then use this information to predict their behavior.

Competitor Intelligence

Competitor intelligence involves the systematic collection and analysis of public information about rivals for informing decision making. It has three main purposes:

- To forecast competitors' future strategies and decisions.

- To predict competitors' likely reactions to a firm's strategic initiatives.

- To determine how competitors' behavior can be influenced to make it more favorable.

For all three purposes, the key requirement is to understand competitors in order to predict their choices of strategy and tactics and their reactions to environmental changes and our own competitive moves. To understand competitors, it is important to be informed about them. Competitor intelligence is a growth field, with a flood of recent books,[36] a dedicated journal,[37] a host of specialist consulting firms, and professional associations.[38] Among the one-fifth of large US corporations estimated to have set up competitor intelligence units, *Business Week* reports that Anne Selgas, Eastman Kodak's director of competitive intelligence, reads particularly widely:

> [She] regularly reads an extensive list of publications that even she considers a tad bizarre. Her favorite is the *Transylvania Times*, a semi-weekly out of tiny Brevard in North Carolina's Transylvania County. A medical film rival – Sterling Diagnostic Imaging Inc. – has a plant there, and Selgas says the paper has lots of hiring and layoff news that helps her understand what's going on.[39]

The distinction between legitimate competitor intelligence and illegal industrial espionage is blurred. The boundaries between public and private information are not always clear. The application of trade secrets law to the information carried by an employee moving between firms is murky. Several well publicized cases of information theft have underlined the dangers. These have included General Motors' litigation against Volkswagen over information theft involving former GM manager Jose Ignacio Lopez and Boeing's indictment for stealing documents from Lockheed Martin to help it win a multi-billion dollar federal missiles contract.[40]

FIGURE 4.3 A framework for competitor analysis

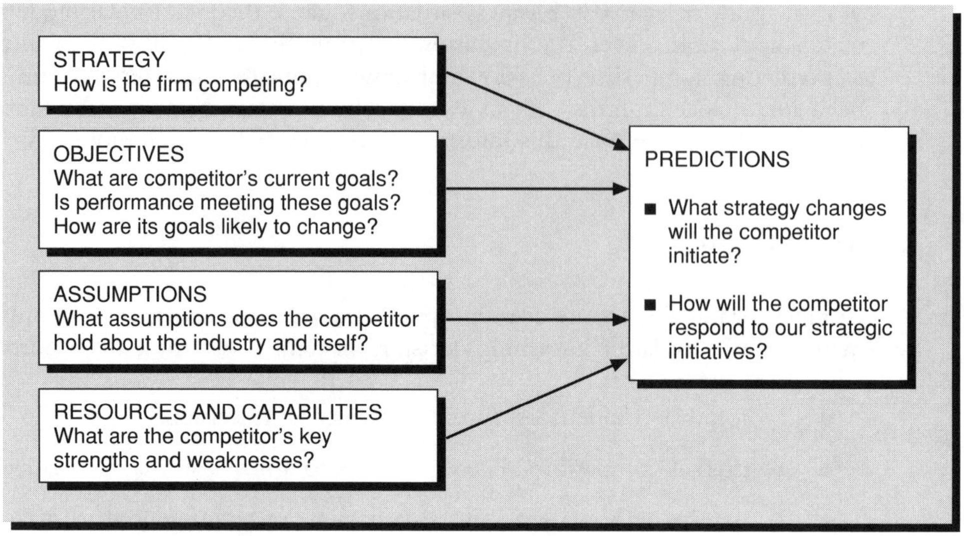

A Framework for Predicting Competitor Behavior

Competitor intelligence is not simply about collecting information. The problem is likely to be too much rather than too little information. The key is a systematic approach that makes clear what information is required and for what purposes it will be used. The objective is to *understand* one's rival. A characteristic of great generals from Hannibal to Patton has been their ability to go beyond military intelligence and to "get inside the heads" of their opposing commanders. Michael Porter proposes a four-part framework for predicting competitor behavior (see Figure 4.3).

1. Competitor's Current Strategy

To predict how a rival will behave in the future, we must understand how that rival is competing at present. In the absence of forces for change, it is reasonable to assume that a company will compete in the future in much the same way as it competes at the present. A company's strategy may be identified on the basis of what it says and what it does. These two are not necessarily the same. As we noted in Chapter 1, a company's statements of strategy intentions (e.g., in its annual reports – especially the chairman's letter to shareholders – and in presentations to financial analysts) may deviate from its realized strategy as indicated by its capital expenditures, its new product launches, its R&D initiatives, and its HR decisions. Thus, in building a picture of a company's strategy, the key is to link the content of top management communication (with investors, the media, and financial analysts) with the evidence of strategic actions – particularly those that involve commitment of resources. For both sources of information, company web sites are invaluable.

2. Competitor's Objectives

To forecast how a competitor might change its strategy, we must identify the goals it pursues. A key issue is whether a company is driven by financial goals or market goals. A company whose primary goal is attaining market share is likely to be much more aggressive a competitor than one that is mainly interested in profitability. The decline of the US automobile and consumer electronics industries in the face of Japanese competition has been attributed to the willingness of domestic companies to cede market share in an attempt to maintain short-term profitability.[41] By comparison, companies like Procter & Gamble and Coca-Cola are obsessed with market share and tend to react aggressively when rivals step on their turf. The scariest competitors are those that are not subject to profit disciplines at all. The cyclical behavior of world markets for sugar, copper, and coffee owes much to the behavior of state-owned enterprises which, when faced with low world prices, tend to increase their exports in a vain attempt to preserve the foreign exchange revenues for their governments.

The level of current performance in relation to the competitor's objectives is important in determining the likelihood of strategy change. The more a company is satisfied with present performance, the more likely it is to continue with its present strategy. If, on the other hand, the competitor's performance is falling well short of target, the likelihood of radical strategic change, possibly accompanied by a change in top management, is increased.

3. Competitor's Assumptions about the Industry

A competitor's strategic decisions are conditioned by its perceptions of itself and the outside world. The perceptions are guided by its assumptions concerning the industry and business in general. Both are likely to reflect the beliefs that senior managers hold about their industry and the success factors within it. Evidence suggests that not only do these systems of belief tend to be stable over time, they also tend to converge among the firms within an industry. These industry-wide beliefs about the determinants of success have been described by J.-C. Spender as "industry recipes."[42]

Industry recipes may engender "blindspots" that limit the capacity of a firm – even an entire industry – to respond to an external threat. During the 1960s, the Big Three US automobile manufacturers firmly believed that small cars were unprofitable. This belief was partly a product of their own cost allocation procedures. The result was a willingness to yield the fastest-growing segment of the US automobile market to imports. The complacency of British and US motorcycle manufacturers in the face of Japanese competition reflects similar beliefs (see Strategy Capsule 4.1).

4. Competitor's Resources and Capabilities

Evaluating the likelihood and seriousness of a competitor's potential challenge requires assessing the strength of that competitor's resources and capabilities. What are the competitor's financial resources, brand strength, operational capabilities, and management skills? If our rival has a massive cash pile, it would be unwise for our

STRATEGY CAPSULE 4.1 Motorcycle Myopia

During the 1960s, BSA was the leading motorcycle manufacturer in Britain, while Harley-Davidson was the leader in the US. During the 1960s, both markets experienced increased import penetration from Japan, but given the emphasis by Honda, Suzuki, and Yamaha on smaller motorcycles, the Japanese challenge was largely discounted.

Eric Turner, chairman of BSA Ltd. (manufacturer of Triumph and BSA motorcycles), commented in 1965:

> The success of Honda, Suzuki, and Yamaha has been jolly good for us. People start out by buying one of the low-priced Japanese jobs. They get to enjoy the fun and exhilaration of the open road and they frequently end up buying one of our more powerful and expensive machines.

Similar complacency was expressed by William Davidson, president of Harley-Davidson:

> Basically, we do not believe in the lightweight market. We believe that motorcycles are sports vehicles, not transportation vehicles. Even if a man says he bought a motorcycle for transportation, it's generally for leisure time use. The lightweight motorcycle is only supplemental. Back around World War I, a number of companies came out with lightweight bikes. We came out with one ourselves. We came out with another in 1947 and it just didn't go anywhere. We have seen what happens to these small sizes.

By the end of the 1970s, BSA and Triumph had ceased production and Harley-Davidson was barely surviving. The world motorcycle industry, including the large bike segments, was dominated by the Japanese.

Sources: *Advertising Age* (December 27, 1965); *Forbes* (September 15, 1966); Richard T. Pascale, *Honda A* (Harvard Business School, Case 9-384-049, 1983).

company to unleash a possible price war by initiating price cuts. Conversely, if we direct our competitive initiative towards our rivals' weaknesses, it may be difficult for them to respond. Richard Branson's Virgin Group has launched a host of entrepreneurial new ventures, typically in markets dominated by a powerful incumbent – British Airways in airlines, EMI in music, Vodaphone in wireless telecommunications. Branson's strategy has been to adopt innovative forms of differentiation that are difficult for established incumbents to respond to.

Applying the Results of Competitor Analysis

For the purpose of strategy formulation, competitor analysis is useful in predicting how a rival is likely to behave and influencing its behavior. To predict a competitor's behavior, our first question is: "What competitive initiatives is the firm likely to take?" This requires that we carefully identify current forces that are likely to provoke a change in strategy. These may be external – a shift in consumer preferences or input costs – or internal – a failure to achieve current performance targets or dissension among top management. Whatever the sources, a careful identification of current strategy and goals and the company's assumptions about the industry and its capabilities provides a sound basis on which to forecast the direction of change.

Second, we may wish to forecast a competitor's likely reactions to our own initiatives. The same four components of competitor analysis profile can assist us in this. Consider, for example, the "burger wars" that followed Burger King's attacks on McDonald's using price cuts, its Big King competitor to the Big Mac, and its "new fries." How would McDonald's respond?

- McDonald's current strategy was similar to that of Burger King – both sought worldwide leadership on the global fast food market through low cost production of a standardized menu based on burgers, fries, and soft drinks.

- McDonald's was committed to a combination of revenue growth and profitability objectives. By the late 1990s, volume growth was slowing – especially in the US. McDonald's was acutely sensitive to any loss of market share.

- McDonald's strategy had been founded on a central belief in *value* – in terms of competitive behavior this converted into a willingness to cut price in order to boost volume growth.

- In terms of resources and capabilities, McDonald's represented a formidable competitor. It was financially strong, possessed worldwide reach, and its management team was committed to the company's principles and mission.

The analysis points to the likelihood that any competitive initiative by Burger King would be likely to trigger an aggressive response from McDonald's. This was indeed the case and during 1997–2001 the burger market of America (and some other countries too) was rocked by the continuing battle between Burger King and McDonald's.[43]

SEGMENTATION ANALYSIS[44]

The Uses of Segmentation

In the previous chapter I noted the difficulty of drawing industry boundaries and the need to define industries both broadly and narrowly according to the types of question we are seeking to answer. For initial strategic analysis we typically define industries broadly: automobiles, computer software, airlines, and investment banking. However, once we get down to a more detailed analysis of competition, we need to focus upon markets that are drawn more narrowly in terms of both products and geography. This process of disaggregating industries into specific markets we call *segmentation*.

Segmentation is particularly important if competition varies across the different submarkets within an industry such that some are more attractive than others. A company can avoid some of the problems of an unattractive industry by judicious segment selection. Consider Dell Computer, in the intensely competitive personal computer industry. One of the ways in which Dell has maintained its margins is by continuously shifting towards higher margin products, customer groups, and geographical areas. During 1999–2003, Dell shifted resources from desktop PCs to servers, storage systems, and laptops; and from the more mature markets of North America and Europe to the growth markets of the Asia-Pacific region. Its direct distribution model allows highly detailed segmentation analysis – it can analyze probability at the level of the individual customer. "We cut the market and then cut it again, looking for the most profitable customers to serve," says vice chairman Kevin Rollins.[45]

Key success factors also differ by segment. In the restaurant industry, the requirements for success are almost totally different between the fast-food segment and luxury restaurants. The result is that within a single industry, very different companies with very different strategies coexist.

Stages in Segmentation Analysis

The purpose of segmentation analysis is to identify attractive segments, to select strategies for different segments, and to determine how many segments to serve. The analysis proceeds in five stages (see Strategy Capsule 4.2 for a summary and application).

1. Identify Key Segmentation Variables

The first stage of segmentation analysis is to determine the basis of segmentation. Segmentation decisions essentially are choices about which customers to serve and what to offer them, hence segmentation variables relate to the characteristics of customers and the product (see Figure 4.4). The most appropriate segmentation variables are those that partition the market most distinctly in terms of limited substitutability among both customers (demand-side substitutability) and producers (supply-side substitutability). Distinct market segments tend to be recognizable from price differentials. Thus, in the auto industry, color is probably not a good segmentation variable (white and red Honda Accords sell at much the same price); size is a better segmentation variable (full-size cars sell at a price premium over subcompact cars).

Typically, segmentation analysis generates far too many segmentation variables. For our analysis to be manageable, we need to reduce these to two or three. To do this we need to:

- Identify the most *strategically significant* segmentation variables. Which variables are most important in creating meaningful divisions in a market?

- Combine segmentation variables that are closely correlated. Thus, in the restaurant industry, price level, service level (waiter service/self-service), cuisine (fast-food/full meals), and alcohol license (wine served/soft drinks only) are likely to be closely related. We could use a single variable, restaurant type, with three categories – full-service restaurants, cafés, and fast-food outlets – as a proxy for all of these variables.

FIGURE 4.4   The basis for segmentation: the characteristics of buyers and products

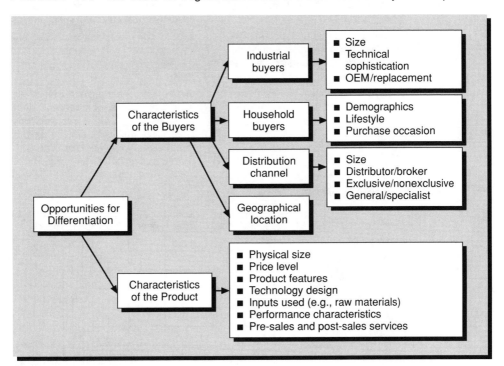

2. Construct a Segmentation Matrix

Once the segmentation variables have been selected and discrete categories determined for each, the individual segments may be identified using a two- or three-dimensional matrix. Thus, the European metal container industry might be analyzed in a three-dimensional segmentation matrix (see Strategy Capsule 4.2), whereas the world automobile industry might be segmented simply by vehicle type and geographical region (see Strategy Capsule 4.3).

3. Analyze Segment Attractiveness

Profitability within an industry segment is determined by the same structural forces that determine profitability within an industry as a whole. As a result, Porter's Five Forces of Competition framework is equally effective in relation to a segment as to an entire industry. Strategy Capsule 4.3 points to some implications of a Five Forces analysis for certain segments of the world automobile industry.

There are, however, a few differences. First, when analyzing the pressure of competition from substitute products, we are concerned not only with substitutes from other industries, but, more importantly, substitutes from other segments within the same industry. Second, when considering entry into the segment, the main source of entrants is likely to be producers established in other segments within the same

STRATEGY CAPSULE 4.2 Segmenting the European Metal Can Industry

1. Identify Key Segmentation Variables and Categories

- Identify possible segmentation variables

  Raw material, can design, can size, customer size, customer's industry, location

- Reduce the number of segmentation variables: Which are most significant? Which are closely correlated and can be combined?

  Type of can, customer industry, customer location

- Identify discrete categories for each segmentation variable.

  Type of can: steel 3-piece, steel 2-piece, aluminum 2-piece, general cans, composite cans, aerosols. Type of customer: food processing, fruit juice, petfood, soft drink, toiletries, beer, oil. Location: France, Germany, Spain/Portugal, Italy, UK, Benelux/Netherlands.

2. Construct a Segmentation Matrix

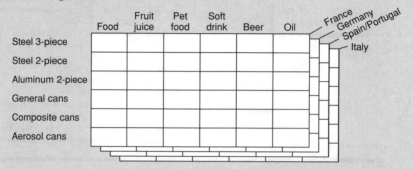

3. Analyze Segment Attractiveness

Apply Five Forces analysis to individual segments. For example, the market for aluminum 2-piece cans to soft drink canners in Italy may be analyzed as follows:

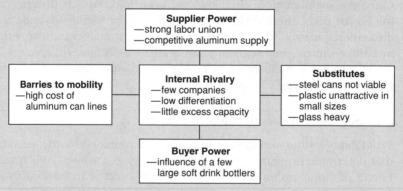

4. Identify Key Success Factors in Each Segment

Within each segment, how do customers choose, and what is needed to survive competition?

5. Analyze Attractions of Broad versus Narrow Segment Scope

- What is the potential to share costs and transfer skills across segments?
- How similar are key success factors between segments?
- Are there benefits of segment specialization?

STRATEGY CAPSULE 4.3 Segmenting the World Automobile Market

A global automobile producer such as Ford or Toyota might segment the world auto market by product type and geography. A first-cut segmentation might be along the following lines:

		REGIONS					
		North America	Western Europe	Eastern Europe	Asia	Latin America	Australasia	Africa
P R O D U C T S	Luxury cars							
	Full-size sedans							
	Mid-size sedans							
	Small sedans							
	Station wagons							
	Minivans							
	Sports cars							
	Sport-utility							
	Pickup trucks							

To identify segments with the best profit prospects for the future, we need to understand why, in the past, some segments have been more profitable than others. For example, during the 1990s:

■ The North American market for small sedans was unprofitable due to many competitors (all the world's major auto producers were represented), lack of clear product differentiation, and customers' price sensitivity.

■ The North American/European markets for passenger minivans have been highly profitable segments due to strong demand relative to capacity, and comparatively few participants. Chrysler's survival during the 1980s was primarily owing to its strong position within this segment. The influx of companies into minivans was eroding margins by the late 1990s.

■ The luxury car segment is traditionally a high-margin segment due to few players, high product differentiation, and price insensitivity of buyers. However, margins in the 1990s were low: the small size of the segment made it difficult to spread the fixed costs of new model development; the new entry by Honda (Acura), Toyota (Lexus), and Nissan (Infiniti) and the acquisition of Jaguar by Ford increased competition.

Once we understand the factors that determined segment profitability in the past, we can predict segment profitability in the future.

industry. The barriers that protect a segment from firms located in other segments are called *barriers to mobility* to distinguish them from the *barriers to entry* that protect the industry as a whole.[46] When barriers to mobility are low, then the superior returns of high profit segments tend to be quickly eroded. Thus, the high margins earned on sports utility vehicles during the mid-1990s were competed away once most of the world's main auto producers had entered the segment.

Segmentation analysis can also be useful in identifying unexploited opportunities in an industry. For example, a segmentation matrix of the restaurant industry in a town or locality might reveal a number of empty segments. Companies that have built successful strategies by concentrating upon unoccupied segments include Wal-Mart (discount stores in small towns), Enterprise Rent-A-Car (suburban locations), and Edward Jones (full-service brokerage for small investors in smaller cities). The interesting question is whether "white spaces" on the segmentation matrix represent unexploited opportunities or absence of viable demand.

4. Identify the Segment's Key Success Factors

Differences in competitive structure and in customer preferences between segments result in different key success factors. By analyzing buyers' purchase criteria and the basis of competition within individual segments, we can identify key success factors for individual segments. For example, the US bicycle market can be segmented on the basis of the age group of the customer (infants, children, youths, adults), price, branding, and distribution channel. Combining and categorizing these segmentation variables results in four major segments, each with different key success factors (see Figure 4.5).

FIGURE 4.5   Segmentation and key success factors: the US bicycle market

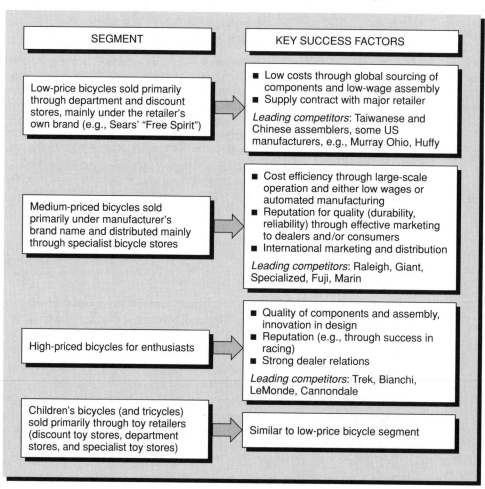

5. Select Segment Scope

Finally, a firm needs to decide whether it wishes to be a segment specialist, or compete across multiple segments. The advantages of a broad over a narrow segment focus depend on two main factors: similarity of key success factors and the presence of shared costs. If key success factors are different across segments, a firm will need to deploy distinct strategies and may have difficulties in drawing upon the same capabilities. Harley-Davidson's attempt to compete in sports motorcycles through its Buell brand has met limited success.

The ability to share costs across different segments has been a major factor in automobiles where very few specialist manufacturers survive and most of the world's main car makers offer a full range of vehicles allowing them to share costs through common platforms and components. The analysis of a company's optimal segment range is similar to the analysis of diversification versus specialization. We shall return to this issue in Chapter 15.

Vertical Segmentation: Profit Pools

Segmentation is usually horizontal – markets are disaggregated according to products, geography, and customer groups. An industry can also be segmented vertically by identifying different value chain activities. Bain & Company show that profitability varies greatly between different vertical activities and proposes *profit pool mapping* as a technique for analyzing the vertical structure of profitability.[47] For example, in the US automobile industry, downstream activities such as finance, leasing, insurance, and service and repair are much more profitable than manufacturing (see Figure 4.6). During 2000–2003, almost all of Ford and GM's profits were derived from the financial services they offered to dealers and car buyers.

To map an industry's profit pool, Bain & Company identifies four steps:

1. *Defining the pool's boundaries.* What is the range of value-adding activities that your business sector encompasses? The Bain consultants argue that it may be desirable to look beyond conventional industry boundaries.

2. *Estimating the pool's overall size.* Total industry profit may be available from industry reports or by applying the average margin earned by a sample of companies to an estimate of industry total revenues.

3. *Estimating profit for each value chain activity in the pool.* Here is the key challenge. It requires gathering data from companies that are "pure players" – specialized in the single value chain activity – and disaggregating data for "mixed players" – those performing multiple activities.

4. *Checking and reconciling the calculations.* Comparing the aggregation of profits in each activity (stage 3) with the total for the industry (stage 2) provides opportunities for reconciling differences and refining the estimates.

FIGURE 4.6 The US auto industry profit pool

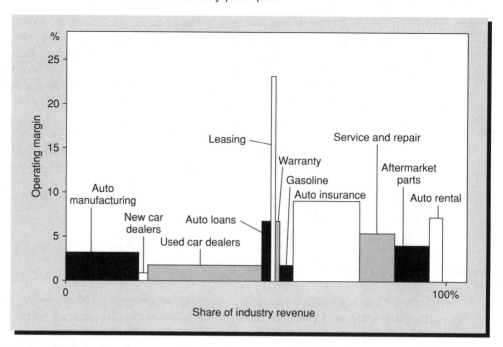

STRATEGIC GROUPS

Whereas segmentation analysis concentrates on the characteristics of markets as the basis for disaggregating industries, strategic group analysis segments an industry on the basis of the strategies of the member firms. A strategic group is "the group of firms in an industry following the same or a similar strategy along the strategic dimensions."[48] These strategic dimensions might include product range, geographical breadth, choice of distribution channels, level of product quality, degree of vertical integration, choice of technology, and so on. By selecting the most important strategic dimensions and locating each firm in the industry along them, it is possible to identify groups of companies that have adopted more or less similar approaches to competing within the industry. Figure 4.7 identifies strategic groups within the world automobile industry; Figure 4.8 shows strategic groups within the oil industry.[49]

Strategic group analysis developed out of initial work on the domestic appliance[50] and brewing industries.[51] Most of the empirical research into strategic groups has been concerned with analyzing differences in profitability among firms.[52] The basic argument is that mobility barriers between strategic groups permit some groups of firms to be persistently more profitable than other groups. In general, the proposition that profitability differences *within* strategic groups are less than differences *between* strategic groups has not received robust empirical support.[53] The inconsistency of empirical findings may reflect the fact that the members of a strategic group, though

FIGURE 4.7   Strategic groups within the world automobile industry

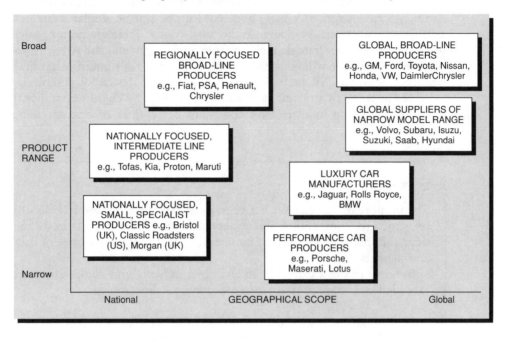

FIGURE 4.8   Strategic groups within the world petroleum industry

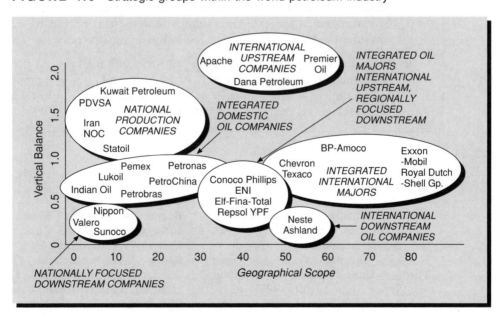

pursuing similar strategies, are not necessarily in competition with one another. For example, within the European airline industry, budget airlines such as EasyJet, AirOne, Virgin Express, Volare, and Sky Europe pursue similar strategies, but do not, for the most part, compete on the same routes. Strategic group analysis is very useful in identifying strategic niches within an industry and the strategic positioning of different firms; it is less useful as a tool for analyzing interfirm profitability differences.[54] This view of strategic groups is a valuable device for describing industry structure in terms of strategic positioning supported by cognitive studies that show managers within an industry have consistent perceptions of firm groupings within the industry.[55]

SUMMARY

The purpose of this chapter has been to go beyond the basic analysis of industry structure, competition and profitability presented in Chapter 3, and consider the interactive nature of competition and the complexities of industries and markets.

In terms of our capabilities in analyzing industry and competition, we have extended our strategy tool kit in a number of directions:

- We have recognized the potential for complementary products to add value and noted the importance of developing strategies that can exploit this source of value.

- We have noted the importance of competitive interactions between close rivals and learned a structured approach to analyzing competitors and predicting their behavior. At a more sophisticated theoretical level, we have recognized some of the findings of game theory that we can use to understand competition and develop winning strategies.

- We examined the microstructure of industries and markets and the value of segmentation analysis, profit pool analysis, and strategic group analysis in understanding industries at a more detailed level and in selecting an advantageous strategic position within an industry.

NOTES

[1] Adam Brandenburger and Barry Nalebuff, *Co-opetition* (New York: Doubleday, 1996).

[2] See Adam Brandenburger and Barry Nalebuff, "The Right Game: Use Game Theory to Shape Strategy," *Harvard Business Review* (July–August 1995): 63–4; and A. Brandenburger, J. Kou, and M.

Burnett, *Power Play (A): Nintendo in 8-bit Video Games* (Harvard Business School Case #9-795-103, 1995).

[3] Carliss Baldwin, Siobhan O'Mahony, and James Quinn, *IBM and Linux (A)* (Harvard Business School Case # 903-083, 2003).

4 J. A. Schumpeter, *The Theory of Economic Development* (Cambridge, MA: Harvard University Press, 1934).

5 See Robert Jacobson, "The Austrian School of Strategy," *Academy of Management Review* 17 (1992): 782–807; and Greg Young, Ken Smith, and Curtis Grimm, "Austrian and Industrial Organization Perspectives on Firm-Level Competitive Activity and Performance," *Organization Science* 7 (May–June 1996): 243–54.

6 R. T. Masson and J. Shaanan, "Stochastic Dynamic Limit Pricing: An Empirical Test," *Review of Economics and Statistics* 64 (1982): 413–22; R. T. Masson and J. Shaanan, "Optimal Pricing and Threat of Entry: Canadian Evidence," *International Journal of Industrial Organization* 5 (1987).

7 Richard Caves and Michael E. Porter, "The Dynamics of Changing Seller Concentration," *Journal of Industrial Economics* 19 (1980): 1–15; P. Hart and R. Clarke, *Concentration in British Industry* (Cambridge: Cambridge University Press, 1980).

8 P. A. Geroski and R. T. Masson, "Dynamic Market Models in Industrial Organization," *International Journal of Industrial Organization* 5 (1987): 1–13.

9 Dennis C. Mueller, *Profits in the Long Run* (Cambridge: Cambridge University Press, 1986).

10 Jeffrey R. Williams, "The Productivity Base of Industries," working paper (Carnegie-Mellon Graduate School of Industrial Administration, 1994) and *Renewable Advantage: Crafting Strategy through Economic Time* (New York: Free Press, 1999).

11 Richard D'Aveni, *Hypercompetition: Managing the Dynamics of Strategic Maneuvering* (New York: Free Press, 1994): 217–18.

12 Keith Weigelt and Colin F. Camerer, "Reputation and Corporate Strategy: A Review of Recent Theory and Applications," *Strategic Management Journal* 9 (1988): 137–42.

13 A. K. Dixit, "The Role of Investment in Entry Deterrence," *Economic Journal* 90 (1980): 95–106.

14 P. Milgrom and J. Roberts, "Informational Asymmetries, Strategic Behavior and Industrial Organization," *American Economic Review* 77, no. 2 (May 1987): 184–9; J. Tirole, *The Theory of Industrial Organization* (Cambridge, MA: MIT Press, 1988).

15 Pankaj Ghemawat, *Commitment: The Dynamic of Strategy* (New York: Free Press, 1991).

16 There are several outstanding introductions to the principles and applications of game theory: Thomas C. Schelling, *The Strategy of Conflict*, 2nd edn (Cambridge: Harvard University Press, 1980); A. K. Dixit and B. J. Nalebuff, *Thinking Strategically: The Competitive Edge in Business, Politics, and Everyday Life* (New York: W. W. Norton, 1991); and John McMillan, *Games, Strategies, and Managers* (New York: Oxford University Press, 1992).

17 Graham Allison, *Essence of Decision: Explaining the Cuban Missile Crisis* (Boston: Little, Brown, 1971).

18 A. K. Dixit and B. J. Nalebuff, op. cit.: 131–5.

19 M. Lynn, *Birds of Prey: Boeing Vs. Airbus, A Battle for the Skies* (New York: Four Walls Eight Windows, 1997).

20 "Business War Games Attract Big Warriors," *Wall Street Journal* (December 22, 1994): B1.

21 Michael E. Porter and A. M. Spence, "The Capacity Expansion Process in a Growing Oligopoly: The Case of Corn Wet Milling," in J. McCall (ed.), *The Economics of Information and Uncertainty* (Chicago: University of Chicago Press, 1982).

22 "The Price is Right," *Economist* (July 29, 2000): 34; "Game Theory in Action: Designing the US Airwaves Auction," *Financial Times* Mastering Strategy Supplement (October 11, 1999): 4.

23 Adam Brandenburger and Barry Nalebuff, op. cit.

24 A. M. McGahan, "The Incentive not to Invest: Capacity Commitments in the Compact Disk Introduction," in R. A. Burgelman and R. S. Rosenbloom (eds),

Research on Technological Innovation Management and Policy, vol. 5 (Greenwich, CT: JAI Press, 1994). EMI and the CT Scanner [A] and [B] (Harvard Business School, 1993), reprinted in R. M. Grant and K. E. Neupert, *Cases in Contemporary Strategy Analysis* (Oxford: Blackwell): Chapter 10.

25 Marvin B. Lieberman, "Excess Capacity as a Barrier to Entry: An Empirical Appraisal," *Journal of Industrial Economics* 35 (1987): 607–27.

26 J. Chevalier, "When It Can Be Good to Burn Your Boats," *Financial Times* Mastering Strategy Supplement (October 25, 1999): 2–3.

27 Games where price is the primary decision variable are called Bertrand models after the nineteenth-century French economist Joseph Bertrand.

28 Games where quantity is the primary decision variable are called Cournot models after the nineteenth-century French economist Augustin Cournot.

29 Fiona Scott Morton, "Strategic Complements and Substitutes," *Financial Times* Mastering Strategy Supplement (November 8, 1999): 10–13.

30 For a review of research on competitive signaling, see O. Heil and T. S. Robertson, "Toward a Theory of Competitive Market Signaling: A Research Agenda," *Strategic Management Journal* 12 (1991): 403–18.

31 For a survey of the strategic role of reputation, see Keith Weigelt and Colin Camerer, "Reputation and Corporate Strategy: A Review of Recent Theory and Applications," *Strategic Management Journal* 9 (1988): 443–54.

32 P. Milgrom and J. Roberts, "Predation, Reputation, and Entry Deterrence," *Journal of Economic Theory* 27 (1982): 280–312.

33 R. M. Grant, "Pricing Behavior in the UK Wholesale Market for Petrol," *Journal of Industrial Economics* 30 (1982): 271–92.

34 There are numerous critiques of the usefulness of game theory. F. M. Fisher, "The Games Economists Play: A Noncooperative View," *Rand Journal of Economics* 20 (Spring 1989): 113–24, points to the ability of game theory to predict almost any equilibrium solution. Colin Camerer describes this as the "Pandora's Box Problem," see C. F. Camerer, "Does Strategy Research Need Game Theory?," *Strategic Management Journal*, special issue, 12 (Winter 1991): 137–52. Steve Postrel illustrates this problem by developing a game theory model to explain the rationality of bank presidents setting fire to their trousers; see S. Postrel, "Burning Your Britches Behind You: Can Policy Scholars Bank on Game Theory," *Strategic Management Journal*, special issue, 12 (Winter 1991): 153–5. Michael E. Porter, "Toward a Dynamic Theory of Strategy," *Strategic Management Journal*, special issue, 12 (Winter 1991): 95–117, notes that game theory "stops short of a dynamic theory of strategy . . . these models explore the dynamics of a largely static world."

35 "Learning to Play the Game," *Economist* (May 17, 1997): 93.

36 Larry Kahaner, *Competitive Intelligence: How to Gather, Analyze, and Use Information to Move Your Business to the Top* (Carmichael, CA: Touchstone Books, 1998); Michelle and Curtis Cook, *Competitive Intelligence* (London: Kogan Page, 2000); J. E. Prescott and S. H. Miller, *Proven Strategies in Competitive Intelligence: Lessons from the Trenches* (Wiley: New York, 2001).

37 *Competitive Intelligence Review* (New York: John Wiley).

38 The Society of Competitive Intelligence Professionals (www.scip.org) and the Canadian Institute for Competitive Intelligence (www.cici-icic.ca).

39 "They Snoop to Conquer," *Business Week* (October 28, 1996): 172–6.

40 D. W. Simon, "Prosecution of IP Theft Increases," *The National Law Journal* (August 11, 2003), www.foley.com.

41 M. Dertouzos, R. Lester, and R. Solow, *Made in America: Regaining the Productive Edge* (Cambridge, MA: MIT Press, 1989).

42 J.-C. Spender, *Industry Recipes: The Nature and Sources of Managerial Judgement*

(Oxford: Basil Blackwell, 1989). How social interaction promotes convergence of perceptions and beliefs is discussed by Anne Huff, "Industry Influences on Strategy Reformulation," *Strategic Management Journal* 3 (1982): 119–31.

[43] What's Eating McDonald's: the Competition, for Starters," *Fortune* (October 13, 1997).

[44] This section draws heavily on M. E. Porter, *Competitive Advantage* (New York: Free Press, 1985): Chapter 7.

[45] O. Gadiesh and J. L. Gilbert, "Profit Pools: A Fresh Look at Strategy," *Harvard Business Review* (May–June 1998): 146.

[46] Richard E. Caves and Michael E. Porter, "From Entry Barriers to Mobility Barriers: Conjectural Decisions and Contrived Deterrence to New Competition," *Quarterly Journal of Economics* 91 (1977): 241–62.

[47] O. Gadiesh and J. L. Gilbert, "Profit Pools: A Fresh Look at Strategy," *Harvard Business Review* (May–June 1998): 139–47; O. Gadiesh and J. L. Gilbert, "How to Map Your Industry's Profit Pools," *Harvard Business Review* (May–June 1998): 149–62.

[48] Michael E. Porter, *Competitive Strategy* (New York: Free Press, 1980): 129.

[49] For further discussion of strategic groups and their role in strategy analysis, see John McGee and Howard Thomas, "Strategic Groups: Theory, Research, and Taxonomy," *Strategic Management Journal* 7 (1986): 141–60.

[50] Michael Hunt, Competition in the Major Home Appliance Industry, doctoral dissertation (Harvard University, 1973); and Michael E. Porter, "Structure Within Industries and Companies' Performance," *Review of Economics and Statistics* 61 (1979): 214–27.

[51] K. Hatten, D. Schendel, and A. Cooper, "A Strategic Model of the US Brewing Industry," *Academy of Management Journal* 21 (1978): 592–610.

[52] Karel Cool and Dan Schendel, "Strategic Group Formation and Performance: The Case of the US Pharmaceutical Industry," *Management Science* 33 (1987): 1102–24; A. Feigenbaum and H. Thomas, "Strategic Groups and Performance: The US Insurance Industry," *Strategic Management Journal* 11 (1990): 197–215.

[53] K. Cool and I. Dierickx, "Rivalry, Strategic Groups, and Firm Profitability," *Strategic Management Journal* 14 (1993): 47–59.

[54] Ken Smith, Curtis Grimm, and Stefan Wally, "Strategic Groups and Rivalrous Firm Behavior: Toward a Reconciliation," *Strategic Management Journal* 18 (1997): 149–57.

[55] R. K. Reger and A. S. Huff, "Strategic Groups: Cognitive Perspective," *Strategic Management Journal* 14 (1993): 103–24.

5

Analyzing Resources and Capabilities

Analysts have tended to define assets too narrowly, identifying only those that can be measured, such as plant and equipment. Yet the intangible assets, such as a particular technology, accumulated consumer information, brand name, reputation, and corporate culture, are invaluable to the firm's competitive power. In fact, these invisible assets are often the only real source of competitive edge that can be sustained over time.

—**Hiroyuki Itami, Mobilizing Invisible Assets**

You've gotta do what you do well.
—**Lucino Noto, formerVice Chairman, Exxon Mobil**

OUTLINE

INTRODUCTION AND OBJECTIVES

In Chapter 1, I noted that the focus of strategy thinking has been shifted from the external environment towards its internal environment. In this chapter, we will make the same transition. In looking within the firm, we will concentrate our attention on the resources and capabilities that firms possess. In doing so, we shall build the foundations for our analysis of competitive advantage (which began in Chapter 3 with the discussion of key success factors).

By the time you have completed this chapter you will be able to:

■ Appreciate the role of a firm's resources and capabilities as a basis for formulating strategy.

■ Identify and appraise the resources and capabilities of a firm.

■ Evaluate the potential for a firm's resources and capabilities to confer sustainable competitive advantage.

■ Use the results of resource and capability analysis to formulate strategies that exploit internal strengths while defending against internal weaknesses.

■ Identify the means through which a firm can develop its resources and capabilities.

We begin by explaining why a company's resources and capabilities are so important to its strategy.

FIGURE 5.1   Analyzing resources and capabilities: the interface between strategy and the firm

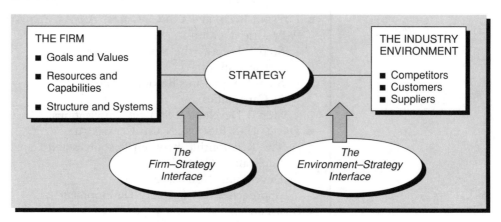

THE ROLE OF RESOURCES AND CAPABILITIES IN STRATEGY FORMULATION

Strategy is concerned with matching a firm's resources and capabilities to the opportunities that arise in the external environment. So far, the emphasis of the book has been the identification of profit opportunities in the external environment of the firm. With this chapter, our emphasis shifts from the interface between strategy and the external environment towards the interface between strategy and the internal environment of the firm – more specifically, with the resources and capabilities of the firm (see Figure 5.1).

The comparatively recent interest of business strategy in resources and capabilities contrasts with the central role that resource analysis has always played in military strategy. International diplomacy up until the collapse of the Soviet Union has been based upon the resource-based notion of *balance of power*. The outcomes of most major wars have been determined by resource superiority. The unease among the German High Command over Hitler's military strategy during World War II was based on the realization that Germany lacked the resources to wage simultaneous wars on the Eastern, Western, and North African fronts as well as in the sky and at sea. Military historian Liddell Hart argues that the fundamental principle of military strategy is "concentration of strength against weakness."[1]

Basing Strategy on Resources and Capabilities

During the 1990s, ideas concerning the role of resources and capabilities as the principal basis for firm strategy and the primary source of profitability coalesced into what has become known as the *resource-based view of the firm*.[2] Central to this "resource-based view" is the idea that the firm is essentially a pool of resources and capabilities, and that these resources and capabilities are the primary determinants of its strategy and performance.

To understand why the resource-based view has had a major impact on strategy thinking, let us go back to the starting point for strategy formulation, which is typically some statement of the firm's identity and purpose (often expressed in a mission statement). Identity tends to be defined by the answer to the question: "What is our business?" Traditionally, firms have defined their businesses in terms of the market they serve: "Who are our customers?" and "Which of their needs are we seeking to serve?" However, in a world where customer preferences are volatile and the identity of customers and the technologies for serving them are changing, a market-focused strategy may not provide the stability and constancy of direction needed to guide strategy over the long term. When the external environment is in a state of flux, the firm itself, in terms of its bundle of resources and capabilities, may be a much more stable basis on which to define its identity. Thus, defining the firm in terms of what it is capable of doing may offer a more durable basis for strategy than a definition based upon the needs that the business seeks to satisfy.[3]

Ted Levitt's solution to the problem of external change was that companies should define their markets broadly (in terms of underlying customer needs) rather than narrowly (in terms of specific products): railroad companies should have seen themselves as being in the transportation business, not the railroad business.[4] However, such broadening of the target market is of little value if the company cannot develop the capabilities required to serve customer requirements across a wide front. Although railroad companies diversified into airlines, shipping, and trucking, their performance in these markets was generally poor. The railroad companies often did better by diversifying into real-estate development, pipelines, telecommunications, and oil and gas exploration – businesses where their resources and capabilities could be more readily deployed.

Seeking to serve broadly defined customer needs has often led companies into difficulty:

- Efforts by Merrill Lynch, American Express, and Sears Roebuck to "serve the full range of financial needs of our customers" by diversifying across stock-broking, retail banking, investment banking, insurance, and real-estate brokerage gave rise to serious problems and resulted in disappointing profitability.[5]

- Allegis Corporation's attempt to "serve the needs of the traveler" through combining United Airlines, Hertz car rental, and Westin Hotels was a costly failure.

By contrast, several companies whose strategies have been based on developing and exploiting clearly defined internal capabilities have successfully adjusted to and exploited external change:

- Honda's strategy since its founding in 1948 has been built around its expertise in the development and manufacture of engines; this capability has successfully carried it from motorcycles to a number of gasoline-engined products (see Figure 5.2).

FIGURE 5.2 Honda Motor Company: product development milestones

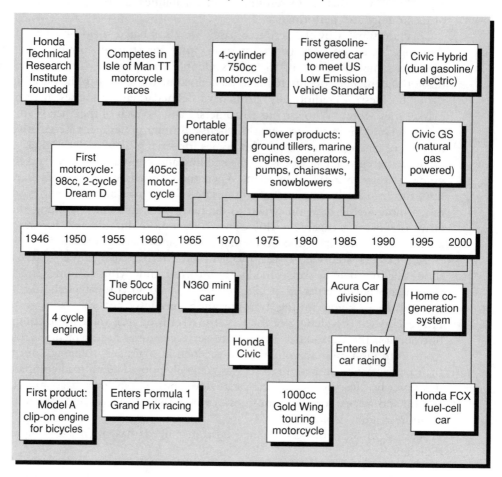

- 3M Corporation has expanded from sandpaper, into adhesive tapes, audiotapes and videotapes, road signs, medical products, and floppy disks. Its product list comprises over 30,000 separate products. Is it a conglomerate? Certainly not, claims 3M. Its vast product range rests on a foundation of key technologies relating to adhesives and thin-film coatings, and its remarkable ability to manage the development and marketing of new products (see Figure 5.3).

In general, the greater the rate of change in a firm's external environment, the more likely it is that internal resources and capabilities will provide a secure foundation for long-term strategy. In fast-moving, technology-based industries, new companies are built around specific technological capabilities. The markets where these capabilities are applied are a secondary consideration. Motorola, the Texas-based supplier of wireless telecommunications equipment, semiconductors, and direct satellite

FIGURE 5.3 The evolution of capabilities and products: 3M

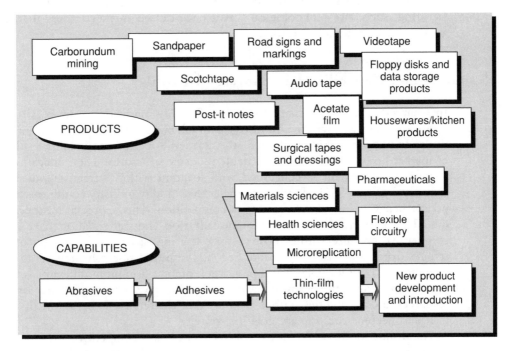

communications, has undergone many transformations, from being a leading provider of TVs and car radios to its current focus on telecom equipment. Yet, underlying these transformations has been a consistent focus on wireless electronics.

When a company faces the imminent obsolescence of its core product, should its strategy focus upon continuing to serve fundamental customer needs or upon deploying its resources and capabilities in other markets?

- When Olivetti, the Italian typewriter manufacturer, faced the displacement of typewriters by microcomputers during the 1980s, it sought to maintain its focus on serving the word processing needs of businesses by expanding into PCs. The venture was a costly failure.[6] By contrast, Remington, another leading typewriter manufacturer, moved into products that required similar technical and manufacturing skills: electric shavers and other personal care appliances.[7]

- Eastman Kodak's dominance of the world market for photographic products based upon chemical imaging has been threatened by digital imaging. Over the past 20 years, Kodak has invested billions of dollars developing digital technologies and digital imaging products. Yet profits and market leadership in digital imaging remain elusive for Kodak. Might Kodak have been better off sticking with its chemical know-how and developing its interests in specialty chemicals, pharmaceuticals, and healthcare?[8]

The difficulties experienced by established firms in adjusting to technological change within their own markets are well documented – in typesetting and in disk-drive manufacturing, successive technological waves have caused market leaders to falter and allowed new entrants to prosper.[9]

Resources and Capabilities as Sources of Profit

In Chapter 1, we noted that superior profitability might derive from two sources: location within an attractive industry, and achieving a competitive advantage over rivals. Industry analysis emphasizes the former: superior profitability is the result of market power conferred by favorable industry structures. The implication is that strategic management is concerned with locating within attractive industries and industry segments, and adopting strategies that modify industry conditions and competitor behavior in order to moderate competition. This approach has been undermined by two factors. First, internationalization and deregulation have increased competitive pressure within most sectors, few industries (or segments) offer cozy refuges from vigorous competition. Second, empirical research suggests that industry factors account for only a small proportion of inter-firm profit differentials.[10] Hence, establishing competitive advantage through the development and deployment of resources and capabilities, rather than seeking shelter from the storm of competition, has become the primary goal for strategy.

The distinction between industry attractiveness and competitive advantage (based on superior resources) as sources of a firm's profitability correspond to economists' distinction between different types of profit (or *rent*). The profits arising from market power are referred to as *monopoly rents*; those arising from superior resources are *Ricardian rents*, after the nineteenth-century British economist David Ricardo. Ricardo showed that, even when the market for wheat was competitive, fertile land would yield high returns. Ricardian rent is the return earned by a scare resource over and above the cost of bringing it into production.[11]

In practice, distinguishing between profit arising from market power and profit arising from resource superiority is less clear in practice than in principle. A closer look at Porter's Five Forces framework suggests that industry attractiveness derives ultimately from the ownership of resources. Barriers to entry, for example, are the result of patents, brands, distribution channels, learning, or some other resource possessed by incumbent firms. Similarly, the lack of rivalry resulting from the dominance of a single firm (monopoly) or a few firms (oligopoly) is usually based upon the concentrated ownership of key resources such as technology, manufacturing facilities, or distribution facilities.

The resource-based approach has had a profound impact on companies' strategy formulation. When the primary concern of strategy was industry selection and positioning, companies tended to adopt similar strategies. The resource-based view, by contrast, emphasizes the uniqueness of each company and suggests that the key to profitability is not through doing the *same* as other firms, but rather through exploiting *differences*. Establishing competitive advantage involves formulating and implementing a strategy that exploits the uniqueness of a firm's portfolio of resources and capabilities. Thus, although Southwest Airlines, Wal-Mart, and Nucor all pursue strategies of cost leadership, each does so through the deployment of unique combinations of resources and capabilities and through distinctive strategies and organizational systems. Competitors can learn from their success, but attempts to replicate their strategies are likely to flounder since replicating these companies' strategies requires replicating resource combinations that are the result of unique histories and circumstances.

The remainder of this chapter outlines a resource-based approach to strategy formulation. Fundamental to this approach is recognizing that a firm must seek a thorough and profound understanding of its resources and capabilities. Such understanding provides a basis for:

1. Selecting a strategy that exploits an organization's key strengths. Mariah Carey's disastrous 2001–2002 was the result of her straying from her core competences (see Strategy Capsule 5.1). Walt Disney's turnaround under Michael Eisner's leadership was the result of exploiting its underlying resources more effectively (see Strategy Capsule 5.2).

2. Developing the firm's resources and capabilities. Resource analysis is not just about deploying existing resources, it is also concerned with filling resource gaps and building capability for the future. Toyota, Microsoft, Johnson & Johnson, and British Petroleum are all companies whose long-term success owes much to their commitment to nurturing talent, developing technologies,

---

STRATEGY CAPSULE 5.1 Focusing Strategy around Core Capabilities: Lyor Cohen on Mariah Carey

2001 was a disastrous year for Mariah Carey. Her first movie, *Glitter*, was a flop, the soundtrack was Carey's most poorly received album in a decade, her $80 million recording contract was dropped by EMI, and she suffered a nervous breakdown.

Lyor Cohen, the aggressive, workaholic chief executive of Island Def Jam records was quick to spot an opportunity:

> "I cold-called her on the day of her release from EMI and I said, I think you are an unbelievable artist and you should hold your head up high," says Cohen. "What I said stuck on her and she ended up signing with us."

His strategic analysis of Carey's situation was concise:

> "I said to her, what's your competitive advantage? A great voice, of course. And what else? You write every one of your songs – you're a great writer. So why did you stray from your competitive advantage? If you have this magnificent voice and you write such compelling songs, why are you dressing like that, why are you using all these collaborations [with other artists and other songwriters]? Why? It's like driving a Ferrari in first – you won't see what that Ferrari will do until you get into sixth gear."

Cohen signed Carey in May 2002. Under Universal Music's Island Def Jam Records, Carey returned to her core strengths: her versatile voice, song writing talents, and ballad style.

STRATEGY CAPSULE 5.2 Resource Utilization: Revival at Walt Disney

When Michael Eisner arrived at Walt Disney Productions in 1984 to take over as president, the company was in its fourth consecutive year of declining net income and its share price had fallen to a level that was attracting predators. Between 1984 and 1988, Disney's sales revenue increased from $1.66 billion to $3.75 billion, net income from $98 million to $570 million, and the stock market's valuation of the company from $1.8 billion to $10.3 billion. Yet, during Eisner's first three years at Disney, there was no major shift of strategy. All Disney's major initiatives of the 1980s – the Epcot Center, Tokyo Disneyland, Touchstone Films, the Disney Channel, and the acquisition of Arvida Corporation – had been launched by the previous management.

The key to the Disney turnaround was the mobilization of Disney's considerable resource base. Prominent among Disney's underutilized resources were 28,000 acres of land in Florida. With the help of the Arvida Corporation, a land development company acquired in 1984, Disney began hotel, resort, and residential development of these landholdings. New attractions were added to the Epcot Center, and a new theme park, the Disney-MGM Studio Tour, was added. Disney World expanded beyond theme parks into resort vacations, the convention business, and residential housing.

In exploiting its huge film library, Disney went far beyond its usual practice of periodic re-releases of its classic movies. It introduced videocassette sales of Disney movies and licensed packages of movies to TV networks. A single package of films licensed to a European TV network raised $21 million. The huge investments in the Disney theme parks were more effectively exploited through heavier marketing effort and increased admission charges. Encouraged by the success of Tokyo Disneyland, Disney embarked on further international duplication of its US theme parks with Euro Disneyland just outside Paris, France.

The most ambitious feature of the turnaround was Disney's regeneration as a movie studio. As well as maintaining the company's commitment to high-quality family movies (and cartoons in particular), Eisner began a massive expansion of its Touchstone label, which had been established in 1983 with the objectives of putting Disney's film studios to fuller use and establishing the company in the teenage and adult markets. To achieve fuller utilization, Disney Studios quickly doubled the number of movies in production. Simultaneously, it engaged in aggressive recruiting of leading producers, directors, filmmakers, actors, and scriptwriters. In 1988, it became America's leading studio in terms of box office receipts. Studio production was further boosted by Disney's increasing TV presence, both through the Disney Channel and programs for network TV.

Above all, the new management team was exploiting Disney's most powerful and enduring asset: the affection of millions of people of different nations and different generations for the Disney name and the Disney characters.

and building capabilities that allow adaptability to their changing business environments.

Our starting point is to identify and assess the resources and capabilities available to the firm.

THE RESOURCES OF THE FIRM

It is important to distinguish between the resources and the capabilities of the firm: resources are the productive assets owned by the firm; capabilities are what the firm

FIGURE 5.4   The links among resources, capabilities, and competitive advantage

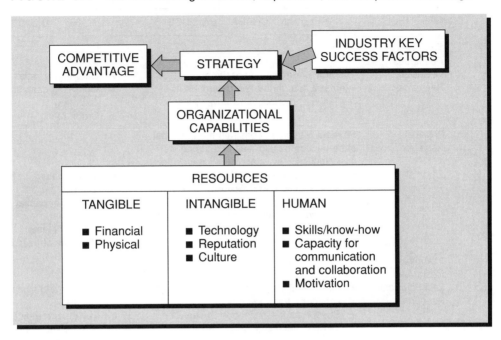

can do. Individual resources do not confer competitive advantage, they must work together to create *organizational capability*. It is capability that is the essence of superior performance. Figure 5.4 shows the relationship among resources, capabilities, and competitive advantage.

Drawing up an inventory of a firm's resources can be surprisingly difficult. No such document exists within the accounting or management information systems of most corporations. The corporate balance sheet provides a limited view of a firm's resources – it comprises mainly financial and physical resources. To take a wider view of a firm's resources it is helpful to identify three principal types of resource: tangible, intangible, and human resources. Table 5.1 specifies some of the components of each category.

Tangible Resources

Tangible resources are the easiest to identify and evaluate: financial resources and physical assets are identified and valued in the firm's financial statements. Yet, balance sheets are renowned for their propensity to obscure strategically relevant information, and to under or over value assets. Historic cost valuation can provide little indication of an asset's market value. Disney's movie library had a balance sheet value of $2.49 billion on September 30, 1999. But this valuation was based on production cost less amortization – Disney's classic animated movies were almost certainly ascribed no balance sheet value, despite their continuing potential to generate revenue.

TABLE 5.1 Classifying and Assessing the Firm's Resources

RESOURCE	RELEVANT CHARACTERISTICS	KEY INDICATORS
Tangible Resources Financial Resources	The firm's borrowing capacity and its internal funds generation determine its resilience and capacity for investment	■ Debt/equity ratio ■ Operating cash flow/free cash flow ■ Credit rating
Physical Resources	Physical resources constrain the firm's set of production possibilities and impact its cost position. Key characteristics include: ■ The size, location, technical sophistication, and flexibility of plant and equipment ■ Location and alternative uses for land and buildings ■ Reserves of raw materials	■ Market values of fixed assets ■ Vintage of capital equipment ■ Scale of plants ■ Flexibility of fixed assets
Intangible Resources Technological Resources	■ Intellectual property: patent portfolio, copyright, trade secrets ■ Resources for innovation: research facilities, technical and scientific employees	■ Number and significance of patents ■ Revenue from licensing patents and copyrights ■ R&D staff as a percent of total employment ■ Number and location of research facilities
Reputation	■ Reputation with customers through the ownership of brands and trademarks; established relationships with customers; the reputation of the firm's products and services for quality and reliability ■ The reputation of the company with suppliers, government, and the community	■ Brand recognition ■ Brand equity ■ Percent of repeat buying ■ Objective measures of comparative product performance (e.g., Consumers' Association ratings, J. D. Power ratings) ■ Surveys of corporate reputation (e.g. *Fortune*)
Human Resources	■ The education, training and experiences of employees determine the skills available to the firm ■ The adaptability of employees contributes to the strategic flexibility of the firm. The social and collaborative skills of employees determine the capacity of the firm to transform human resources into organizational capabilities ■ The commitment and loyalty of employees determine the capacity of the firm to attain and maintain competitive advantage	■ Educational, technical, and professional qualifications of employees ■ Compensation relative to industry ■ Percentage of days lost through stoppages and industrial disputes ■ Absentee rates ■ Employee turnover rate

However, our goal of resource analysis is not simply to value a company's assets; it is to understand this potential for creating competitive advantage. Information that British Airways possesses tangible fixed assets with a book value of £9.5 billion is of little use in assessing their strategic value. To assess British Airways' ability to compete effectively in the world airline industry we need to know about the composition of these assets, the location of land and buildings, the types of plane and their age, and so on.

Once we have fuller information on a company's tangible resources we explore how we can create additional value from them. This requires that we address two key questions:

1. *What opportunities exist for economizing on their use?* It may be possible to use fewer resources to support the same level of business, or to use the existing resources to support a larger volume of business. In the case of British Airways, there may be opportunities for consolidating administrative offices and engineering and service facilities. Improved inventory control may allow economies in inventories of parts and fuel. Better control of cash and receivables permits a business to operate with lower levels of cash and liquid financial resources.

2. *What are the possibilities for employing existing assets more profitably?* Could British Airways generate better returns on some of its planes by redeploying them into cargo carrying? Should BA seek to redeploy its assets from Europe and the North Atlantic to Asia-Pacific? Might its European network generate greater returns if it was reconstituted as a budget airline? Railroad companies have become adept at using their rail networks to route gas pipelines and fiber-optic telecommunication cables.

Intangible Resources

For most companies, intangible resources contribute much more than do tangible resources to total asset value. Yet, in relation to company financial statements, intangible resources remain largely invisible – particularly in the US where R&D is expensed and intellectual property is typically undervalued. The exclusion or undervaluation of intangible resources from company balance sheets is a major reason for the large and growing divergence between companies' balance sheet valuations ("book values") and their stock market valuations (see Table 5.2). Among the most important of these undervalued or unvalued intangible resources are brand names. Table 5.3 shows companies owning brands valued at $20 billion or more.

Brand names and other trademarks are a form of *reputational asset*: their value is in the confidence they instill in customers. This value is reflected in the price premium that customers are willing to pay for the branded product over that for an unbranded or unknown brand. Brand value (or "brand equity") can be estimated by taking the price premium attributable to a brand, multiplying it by the brand's annual sales volume, then calculating the present value of this revenue stream. The

TABLE 5.2 Large Corporations* with the Highest Ratio of Share Price to Book Value per Share

COMPANY	MARKET-TO-BOOK RATIO	INDUSTRY	COUNTRY
1 Accenture	27.6	Consulting	US
2 Gillette	17.9	Personal care	US
3 Anheuser Busch	16.8	Brewing	US
4 Gap	17.0	Retailing	US
5 Kellogg	16.0	Food	US
6 Dell Computer	15.9	Computers	US
7 Oracle	12.2	Software	US
8 GlaxoSmithKline	11.0	Drugs	UK
9 Hennes & Mauritz	10.5	Retailing	Sweden
10 SAP	10.1	Software	Germany
11 SCM	10.0	Computers	US
12 Pfizer	9.9	Drugs	US
13 Unilever	9.6	Consumer goods	UK-Neth
14 Coca-Cola	9.3	Soft drinks	US
15 Sysco	9.1	Food services	US
16 Forest Labs	8.5	Drugs	US
17 EBay	8.2	E-business	US
18 Pepsico	8.0	Soft drinks	US
19 Medtronic	7.9	Medical equipment	US
20 3M	7.8	Diversified	US
21 Procter & Gamble	7.8	Consumer goods	US
22 France Telecom	7.6	Telecom	France
23 Smith & Nephew	6.7	Drugs	UK
24 Johnson & Johnson	6.7	Drugs	US

*   Companies among top 300 in the world by market capitalization with highest market-to-equity ratio in May 2003.
Source: *Business Week* "Global 1000" for 2003.

brand valuations in Table 5.3 involve estimating the operating profits for each brand (after taxation and a capital charge), estimating the proportion of net operating income attributable to the brand, then capitalizing these returns. The value of a company's brands can be increased by extending the product/market scope over which the company markets those brands. Philip Morris is an expert at internationalizing its brand franchises. Harley-Davidson's brand strength has not only permitted the company to obtain a price premium of about 40 percent above that of comparable motorcycles, but also to license its name to the manufacturers of clothing, coffee mugs, cigarettes, and restaurants.

Reputation may be attached to a company as well as to its brands. Charles Fombrun argues that a company's prosperity and survival depends upon the support it can attract from employees, customers, investors, and governments.[12] Company reputation is a valuable resource, not just in relation to customers, but also in relation to employees, suppliers (including financial institutions), and governments. In 2003, the Harris-Fombrun survey showed Johnson & Johnson followed by Harley-Davidson and Coca-Cola to have the highest "reputation quotients."[13]

TABLE 5.3   The World's Most Valuable Brands, 2003

RANK	BRAND	BRAND VALUE IN 2003, $ BILLION	CHANGE FROM 2002	COUNTRY OF ORIGIN
1	Coca-Cola	70.45	+1%	USA
2	Microsoft	65.17	+2%	USA
3	IBM	51.76	+1%	USA
4	GE	42.34	+2%	USA
5	Intel	31.11	+1%	USA
6	Nokia	29.44	−2%	Finland
7	Disney	28.03	−4%	USA
8	McDonald's	24.69	−6%	USA
9	Marlboro	2218	−8%	USA
10	Mercedes	21.31	+2%	Germany
11	Toyota	20.78	+7%	Japan
12	Hewlett-Packard	19.86	+18%	USA
13	Citibank	18.57	+3%	USA
14	Ford	17.07	−16%	USA
15	American Express	16.29	+3%	USA
16	Gillette	15.98	+7%	USA
17	Cisco	15.57	−3%	USA
18	Honda	15.63	+4%	Japan
19	BMW	15.11	+5%	Germany
20	Sony	13.15	−5%	Japan

Note: Brand values are calculated as the net present value of future earning generated by the brand. From the income generated by the company (or division), Interbrand deducts the cost of owning the tangible resources, then subtracts the earnings generated by other intangibles. Finally, Interbrand calculates brand strength based upon the brand's market leadership, its stability, and its ability to cross geographical and cultural borders. Brand strength is used as an indicator of the riskiness of future brand earnings which is added into the discount rate at which future brand earnings are discounted.
Source: Interbrand.

   Like reputation, technology is an intangible asset whose value is not evident from most companies' balance sheets. Intellectual property – patents, copyrights, trade secrets, and trademarks – comprise technological and artistic resources where ownership is defined in law. Over the past 20 years, companies have become more attentive to the value of their intellectual property. Texas Instruments was one of the first companies to begin managing its patent portfolio in order to maximize its licensing revenues. For some companies, their ownership of intellectual property is a key source of their market value. Examples include: Qualcomm's patents relating to CDMA digital wireless telephony and Unisys's patent covering the LZW data compression algorithm.

Human Resources

Human resources are the *productive services* that human beings offer to the firm in terms of their skills, knowledge, and reasoning and decision-making abilities. Human resources do not appear on corporate balance sheets for the simple reason that people cannot be owned: companies contract with their employees to purchase their time and expertise. Identifying and appraising the stock of human resources within a firm is complex and difficult. Human resources are appraised at the time of recruitment, where qualifications and experience are used as indicators of performance potential, and in employment, typically through annual performance reviews.

Companies are continually seeking more effective methods to assess the performance abilities and performance potential of their employees (and potential employees). Over the past decade, human resource appraisal has become far more systematic and sophisticated. Organizations are relying less on formal qualifications and more on flexibility, learning potential, and the ability to work collaboratively in teams. Many have established assessment centers specifically for the purpose of providing comprehensive, quantitative assessments of the skills and attributes of individual employees. *Competency modeling* involves identifying the set of skills, content knowledge, attitudes, and values associated with superior performers within a particular job category, then assessing each employee against that profile.[14] The results of such competency assessments can then be used to identify training needs, make selections for hiring or promotion, and determine compensation. The technique was pioneered by David McClelland of Harvard University and developed subsequently by McBer & Co. and the Hay Group.[15] A central feature of competency modeling is the emphasis it gives not just to technical and professional abilities, but also to the psychological and social aptitudes so critical in linking technical and professional abilities to overall job performance. Recent interest in *emotional intelligence* reflects growing recognition of the importance of social and emotional skills and values.[16]

The ability of employees to harmonize their efforts and integrate their separate skills depends not only on their interpersonal skills but also the organizational context. This organizational context as it affects internal collaboration is determined by a key intangible resource: the *culture* of the organization. The term *organizational culture* is notoriously ill defined. It relates to an organization's values, traditions, and social norms. Building on the observations of Peters and Waterman that "firms with sustained superior financial performance typically are characterized by a strong set of core managerial values that define the ways they conduct business," Jay Barney identifies organizational culture as a firm resource of great strategic importance that is potentially very valuable.[17]

ORGANIZATIONAL CAPABILITIES

Resources are not very productive on their own. A brain surgeon is close to useless without a radiologist, anesthetist, nurses, surgical instruments, imaging equipment, and a host of other resources. To perform a task, a team of resources must work together. We use the term *organizational capability* to refer to a firm's capacity to undertake a particular productive activity. Just as an individual may be capable of playing the violin, ice skating, and speaking Mandarin, so an organization may possess the capabilities needed to manufacture widgets, distribute them throughout Latin America, and hedge the resulting foreign exchange exposure. The literature uses the terms *capability* and *competence* interchangeably.[18]

Our primary interest is in those capabilities that can provide a basis for competitive advantage. Selznick used *distinctive competence* to describe those things that an organization does particularly well relative to its competitors.[19] Hamel and Prahalad coined the term *core competences* to distinguish those capabilities fundamental to a firm's performance and strategy.[20] Core competences, according to Hamel and Prahalad, are those that:

■ Make a disproportionate contribution to ultimate customer value, or to the efficiency with which that value is delivered, and

■ Provide a basis for entering new markets.[21]

Prahalad and Hamel criticize US companies for emphasizing product management over competence management. They compare the strategic development of Sony and RCA in consumer electronics. Both companies were failures in the home video market. RCA introduced its videodisk system, Sony its Betamax videotape system. For RCA, the failure of its first product marked the end of its venture into home video systems and heralded a progressive retreat from the consumer electronics industry. RCA was acquired by GE, which then sold off the combined consumer electronics division to Thomson of France. Sony, on the other hand, acknowledged the failure of Betamax, but continued to develop its capabilities in video technology. This continuous development and upgrading of its video capabilities resulted in a string of successful video products from camcorders and digital cameras to the PlayStation game console.

A strategic focus on capabilities rather than products is also observable in Canon's development. Canon's technological capabilities lie in the integration of microelectronics, fine optics, and precision engineering. Figure 5.5 shows how these technologies are common to most of Canon's product introductions during the late 1980s.

Classifying Capabilities: Functions and Value Chain Activities

To identify a firm's capabilities, we need to have some basis for classifying and disaggregating its activities. Two approaches are commonly used:

1. A *functional analysis* identifies organizational capabilities in relation to each of the principal functional areas of the firm. Table 5.4 classifies the principal functions of the firm and identifies organizational capabilities pertaining to each function.

2. A *value chain analysis* separates the activities of the firm into a sequential chain. Michael Porter's representation of the value chain distinguishes between *primary activities* (those involved with the transformation of inputs and interface with the customer) and *support activities* (see Figure 5.6). Porter's generic value chain identifies a few broadly defined activities that can be disaggregated to provide a more detailed identification of the firm's activities (and the capabilities that correspond to each activity). Thus, marketing might include market research, test marketing, advertising, promotion, pricing, and dealer relations.[22]

FIGURE 5.5 Canon: products and capabilities

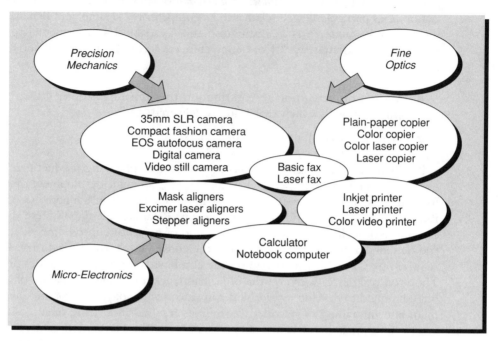

FIGURE 5.6 Porter's value chain

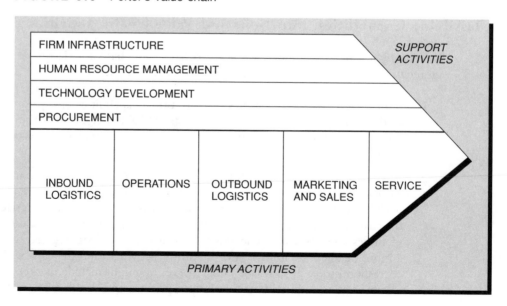

TABLE 5.4 A Functional Classification of Organizational Capabilities

FUNCTIONAL AREA	CAPABILITY	EXEMPLARS
CORPORATE FUNCTIONS	■ Financial control ■ Strategic management of multiple businesses ■ Strategic innovation ■ Multidivisional coordination ■ Acquisition management ■ International management	ExxonMobil, PepsiCo General Electric, Procter & Gamble British Petroleum Unilever, Shell ConAgra, Cisco Systems Shell, Citigroup
MANAGEMENT INFORMATION	■ Comprehensive, integrated MIS network linked to managerial decision making	Wal-Mart, Capital One, Dell Computer
RESEARCH & DEVELOPMENT	■ Research ■ Innovative new product development ■ Fast-cycle new product development	IBM, Merck Sony, 3M Canon
OPERATIONS	■ Efficiency in volume manufacturing ■ Continuous improvements in operations ■ Flexibility and speed of response	Briggs & Stratton, YKK Toyota, Harley-Davidson Zara, Four Seasons Hotels
PRODUCT DESIGN	■ Design capability	Nokia, Apple Computer
MARKETING	■ Brand management ■ Promoting reputation for quality ■ Responsiveness to market trends	P&G, Altria Johnson & Johnson, MTV, L'Oreal
SALES AND DISTRIBUTION	■ Effective sales promotion and execution ■ Efficiency and speed of order processing ■ Speed of distribution ■ Quality and effectiveness of customer service	PepsiCo, Pfizer L. L. Bean, Dell Computer Amazon.com, Zara Singapore Airlines, Caterpillar

The Architecture of Capability

Although the concept of an organization possessing the capability (or competence) to perform certain activities is straightforward, understanding the structure and determinants of capability is much more complex. Why is 3M so good at developing new products for a variety of home, office, and medical needs? How is Wal-Mart able to combine relentless cost focus and high levels of flexibility and adaptability? Why is Toyota so superior to either Ford or GM in developing new models of car and launching them globally? We can hypothesize about the answers to these questions, but the fact remains: We don't really know how organizational capabilities are created, how they are performed, and why some companies perform a capability to a much higher standard than another. To begin to understand organizational capabilities, let us look at their structure.

Capability as Routine

Organizational capability requires the expertise of various individuals to be integrated with capital equipment, technology, and other resources. But how does this integration occur? Virtually all productive activities involve teams of people undertaking closely coordinated actions without significant direction or verbal communication. Richard Nelson and Sidney Winter have used the term *organizational routines* to refer to these regular and predictable patterns of activity made up of a sequence of coordinated actions by individuals.[23] Such routines form the basis of most organizational capabilities. At the manufacturing level, a series of routines governs the passage of raw materials and components through the production process to the factory gate. Sales, ordering, distribution, and customer service activities are similarly organized through a number of standardized, complementary routines. Even top management activity includes routines: monitoring business unit performance, capital budgeting, and strategic planning.

Routines are to the organization what skills are to the individual. Just as the individual's skills are carried out semi-automatically, without conscious coordination, so organizational routines are based on firm-level tacit knowledge and the mutual understandings of team members. Typically, how routines work cannot be fully articulated by any member of the team (including the manager or team leader).

Just as individual skills become rusty when not exercised, so it is difficult for organizations to retain coordinated responses to contingencies that arise only rarely. Hence, there may be a tradeoff between efficiency and flexibility. A limited repertoire of routines can be performed highly efficiently with near-perfect coordination. The same organization may find it extremely difficult to respond to novel situations.[24]

Routinization is an essential step in translating directions and operating practices into capabilities. In every McDonald's hamburger restaurant, operating manuals provide precise directions for the conduct of every activity undertaken, from the placing of the pickle on the burger to the maintenance of the milk-shake machine. In practice, the operating manuals are seldom referred to in the course of day-to-day operations – through continuous repetition and employees' on-the-job and off-the-job training, tasks become routinized.

The Hierarchy of Capabilities

Whether we approach capabilities from a functional or value chain approach, it is evident that broad functions or value chain activities can be disaggregated into more specialist capabilities performed by smaller teams of resources. What we observe is a hierarchy of capabilities where more general, broadly defined capabilities are formed from the integration of more specialized capabilities. For example:

- A hospital's capability in treating heart disease depends on its integration of capabilities pertaining to a patient's diagnosis, cardiovascular surgery, pre- and post-operative care, as well as capabilities relating to various administrative and support functions.

- Toyota's manufacturing capability – its system of "lean production" – is a highly complex organizational capability requiring the integration of a large number of more specific capabilities relating to the manufacture of particular components and subassemblies, supply-chain management, production scheduling, assembly processes, quality control procedures, systems for managing innovation and continuous improvement, and inventory control mechanisms.

FIGURE 5.7   The hierarchical nature of capabilities: a manufacturer of PBXs

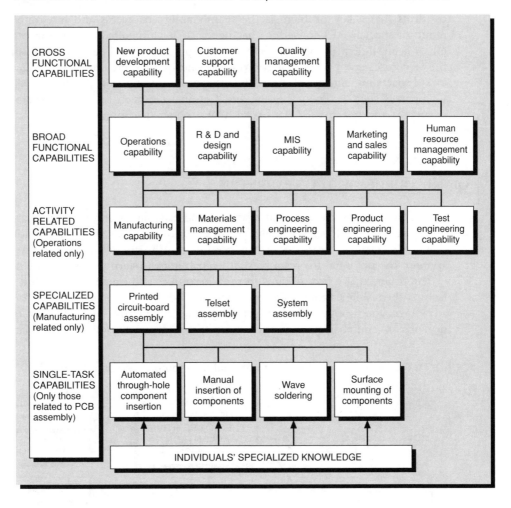

Functional capabilities comprise many specialized capabilities relating to individual tasks. At a higher level of integration are capabilities that require cross-functional integration. Thus, new product development capability requires the integration of R&D, marketing, manufacturing, finance, and strategic planning.[25] Figure 5.7 offers a partial view of the hierarchy of capabilities of a telecom equipment maker.

Higher-level capabilities involve the integration of lower-level capabilities, but this integration is not easy. Functional capabilities cannot be integrated directly, but only through integrating the knowledge of individual functional specialists. This is precisely why higher-level capabilities are so difficult to perform. New product development requires the integration of a wide diversity of specialized knowledge and skill, yet communication constraints mean that the number of individuals who can be directly involved in the process is limited. A common solution has been the creation of cross-functional product development teams. Though setting up such teams would appear to be a straightforward task, research into new product development confirms that a key problem is the team's ability to access and integrate the vast range of specialized knowledge that needs to be imbedded within the product. A major achievement of Japanese industrial corporations has been the establishment of the structures and patterns of coordination needed to integrate knowledge across a broad spectrum, and greatly to reduce the cycle time for new product development. Companies such as Toyota, Sony, and Canon have been leaders in developing the structures and systems for fast-paced new product development.

APPRAISING THE PROFIT-EARNING POTENTIAL OF RESOURCES AND CAPABILITIES

So far, we have established what resources and capabilities are, how they can provide a long-term focus for a company's strategy, and how we can go about identifying them. However, if the focus of this book is the pursuit of profit, we also need to appraise the potential for resources and capabilities to earn profits for the company.

The profits that a firm obtains from its resources and capabilities depend on three factors: their abilities to *establish* a competitive advantage, to *sustain* that competitive advantage, and to *appropriate* the returns to that competitive advantage. Each of these depends on a number of resource characteristics. Figure 5.8 shows the key relationships.

FIGURE 5.8 The rent-earning potential of resources and capabilities

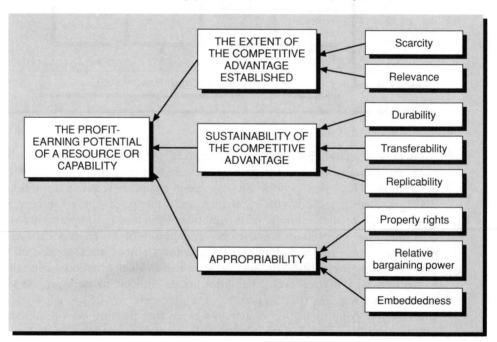

Establishing Competitive Advantage

For a resource or capability to establish a competitive advantage, two conditions must be present:

1. *Scarcity.* If a resource or capability is widely available within the industry, then it may be essential to compete, but it will not be a sufficient basis for competitive advantage. In oil and gas exploration, new technologies such as directional drilling and 3-D seismic analysis are critical to reducing the costs of finding new reserves. However, these technologies are widely available from oilfield service and IT companies. As a result, such technologies are "needed to play," but they are not sufficient to win.

2. *Relevance.* A resource or capability must be relevant to the key success factors in the market. British coal mines produced some wonderful brass bands. Unfortunately, these bands did little to assist the mines in meeting competition from cheap imported coal and North Sea gas. As retail banking shifts toward automated teller machines and online transactions, so the retail branch networks of the banks have become less relevant for customer service. Thus, resources and capabilities are valuable only if they can be linked to one or more of the key success factors within an industry: they must assist the firm in creating value for its customers, or in surviving competition.

Sustaining Competitive Advantage

The profits earned from resources and capabilities depend not just on their ability to establish competitive advantage, but also on how long that advantage can be sustained. This depends on whether resources and capabilities are *durable* and whether rivals can *imitate* the competitive advantage they offer. Resources and capabilities are imitable if they are *transferable* or *replicable*.

Durability

Some resources are more durable than others and, hence, are a more secure basis for competitive advantage. The increasing pace of technological change is shortening the useful life span of most resources including capital equipment and proprietary technologies. Reputation, on the other hand, can show remarkable resilience to the passage of time. Brands such as Heinz sauces, Kellogg's' cereals, Campbell's soup, Hoover vacuum cleaners, Singer sewing machines, and Coca-Cola have been market leaders for periods of a century or more. Corporate reputation is similarly long-lived – unless tarnished by misdeeds or ineptitude.

Transferability

The simplest means of acquiring the resources and capabilities necessary for imitating another firm's strategy is to buy them. If rivals can acquire the resources required to imitate the strategy of a successful company, that company's competitive advantage will be short lived. The ability to buy a resource or capability depends on its transferability – the extent to which it is mobile between companies. Some resources, such as finance, raw materials, components, machines produced by equipment suppliers, and employees with standardized skills (such as short-order cooks and auditors), are transferable and can be bought and sold with little difficulty. Some resources are not easily transferred – either they are entirely firm specific, or their value depreciates on transfer.[26]

Sources of immobility include:

- Geographical immobility of natural resources, large items of capital equipment, and some types of employees may make it difficult for firms to acquire these resources without relocating themselves.

- Imperfect information concerning the quality and productivity of resources creates considerable risks for firms seeking to acquire those resources. Such imperfections are especially important in relation to human resources. People are exceptionally heterogeneous and their performance is highly context specific, particularly within team-based production.[27] Sellers of resources have better information about the characteristics of the resources on offer than potential buyers – this creates a "lemons problem" for firms seeking to acquire resources.[28] Jay Barney has shown that different valuations of resources by firms can result in their being either underpriced or overpriced, giving rise to differences in profitability between firms.[29]

- Complementarity between resources means that the detachment of a resource from its "home team" causes it to lose productivity and value. Thus, if brand reputation is associated with the company that created it, a change in ownership of the brand erodes its value. The acquisition of Harrods department store by the Al Fayed brothers raised concerns over the possible detriment of foreign ownership to Harrods' reputation as the quintessential English department store. Managers, like sports stars, may be unable to replicate their former performance with a new team.

- Organizational capabilities, because they are based on teams of resources, are less mobile than individual resources. Even if the whole team can be transferred (in investment banking it has been commonplace for whole teams of analysts or M&A bankers to defect from one bank to another), the dependence of the team on a wider network of relationships and corporate culture may pose difficulties for recreating the capability in the new company.

Replicability

If a firm cannot buy a resource or capability, it must build it. In financial services, innovations such as interest rate swaps, stripped bonds, electricity futures, weather options, and most other derivatives can similarly be imitated easily by competitors. Unlike mechanical or chemical innovations, few financial innovations can be patented. In retailing, competitive advantages that derive from store layout, point-of-sale technology, charge cards, and extended opening hours can be copied easily by competitors.

Less easily replicable are capabilities based on complex organizational routines. Federal Express's national, next-day delivery service and Nucor's system for steel manufacturing that combines efficiency with flexibility are complex capabilities based on unique corporate cultures. Some capabilities appear simple but prove difficult to replicate. Just-in-time scheduling and quality circles are relatively simple techniques used effectively by Japanese companies. Although neither require advanced manufacturing technologies or sophisticated information systems, their dependence on high levels of collaboration through communication and trust meant that many American and European firms had difficulty implementing them.

Even where replication is possible, incumbent firms may benefit from the fact that resources and capabilities that have been accumulated over a long period are often less costly and more productive than the same assets that have been accumulated quickly by would-be imitators. Dierickx and Cool identify several sources of incumbent advantage from accumulated stocks of resources and capabilities:

- *Asset mass efficiencies* occur where a strong initial position in technology, distribution channels, or reputation facilitates the subsequent accumulation of these resources.

- *Time compression diseconomies* are the additional costs incurred by imitators when attempting to accumulate rapidly a resource or capability. Thus, "crash programs" of R&D and "blitz" advertising campaigns tend to be less productive than similar expenditures made over a longer period.[30]

Appropriating the Returns to Competitive Advantage

Who gains the returns generated by a resource or capability? We should normally expect that such returns accrue to the owner of that resource or capability. However, ownership is not always clear-cut. The boundary between the human capital owned by the employee and the know-how of the company is particularly difficult to define. When General Motors' cost-cutting whiz José Ignacio Lopez de Arriortua and his team left GM for Volkswagen in March 1993, were they transferring their individual knowledge and expertise, or were they stealing GM's trade secrets?[31] Charles Ferguson claims that when engineers and managers leave an IT company to form their own business startup, this is not simply high-tech entrepreneurship, it is really the exploitation of corporate knowledge for private gain.[32] Acquisitions of knowledge-intensive companies are always risky because of the possibility that key employees may exit (see Strategy Capsule 5.3). The prevalence of partnerships (rather than joint-stock companies) in professional service industries (lawyers, accountants, and management consultants) reflects the desire for a closer linkage between a business and its key human assets.

The less clearly defined are property rights in resources and capabilities, the greater the importance of relative bargaining power in determining the division of

STRATEGY CAPSULE 5.3 When Your Competitive Advantage Walks Out the Door: Gucci

On September 10, 2001, French retailer Pinault Printemps Redoute (PPR) agreed to acquire 67% of Gucci Group – the Italian-based fashion house and luxury goods maker. PPR subsequently offered to acquire the outstanding shareholding of Gucci at a price of $85.52 a share. On November 4, 2003 the managers and shareholders of the two companies were stunned to learn that Chairman Domenico De Sole and Vice Chairman Tom Ford would be leaving Gucci in April 2004.

The duo had masterminded Gucci's transformation from a chaotic, near-bankrupt family firm with an over-licensed brand into a close rival to LVMH – the luxury goods powerhouse. As creative director, Tom Ford had established Gucci as the hottest label around, through fashion shows that were practically rock shows, associations with famous faces, and hiring young designers such as Stella McCartney and Alexander McQueen. De Sole's astute leadership had established careful planning and financial discipline, which built Gucci's global presence (especially in Asia).

How great a blow was De Sole and Ford's departure to the parent PPR? In principle, a new CEO and new head of design could be hired. In practice, talent of the ilk of De Sole and Ford was a rare commodity. Especially rare was the combination of a designer and a CEO who could work together with the harmony and shared vision of De Sole and Ford. And what would be the impact on the Gucci brand? Gucci (and its sister brand Yves Saint Laurent) had become almost synonymous with Tom Ford. Of greatest concern was that De Sole and Ford might set up a new fashion house that would go into competition with Gucci.

The stock market's reaction was ominous. On November 3, 2003 Gucci's share price was $86.10; on November 6 it had fallen to $84.60, however, in the absence of PPR's guarantee to acquire their shares at $85.52, analysts estimated that Gucci would be trading at around $74. The implication is that Gucci was worth $1.2 billion less without De Sole and Ford than with them.

Source: Adapted from articles in the *Financial Times* during November 5–8, 2003.

returns between the firm and its individual members. In the case of team-based organizational capabilities, this balance of power between the firm and an individual employee depends crucially on the relationship between individuals' skills and organizational routines. The more deeply embedded are individual skills and knowledge within organizational routines, and the more they depend on corporate systems and reputation, the weaker the employee is relative to the firm.

Conversely, the closer an organizational capability is identified with the expertise of individual employees, and the more effective those employees are at deploying their bargaining power, the better able employees are to appropriate rents. If the individual employee's contribution to productivity is clearly identifiable, if the employee is mobile, and if the employee's skills offer similar productivity to other firms, the employee is in a strong position to appropriate a substantial proportion of his or her contribution to the firm's value added. If the improvements in team performance, game attendance, and TV ratings that Kevin Garnett brings to the Minnesota Timberwolves would work for any basketball team, then it is likely that the $100 million contract that Garnett signed in October 2003 fully exploits the value he brings. Similarly, the $200 million paid in transfer fees by Real Madrid for soccer stars Zinedine Zidane, Luis Figo, Ronaldo, and David Beckham seem likely to leave little value to be appropriated by Real Madrid. In recent years investment banks and consulting companies have emphasized the team-based nature of their capabilities. In downplaying the role of individual expertise, they can improve their firm's potential for appropriating the returns to their capabilities.

PUTTING RESOURCE AND CAPABILITY ANALYSIS TO WORK: A PRACTICAL GUIDE

While acknowledging the importance of resources and capabilities as sources of superior performance, few companies have made much progress in applying systematically the principles of resource and capability analysis. Let me offer a simple, step-by-step approach to how a company can appraise its resources and capabilities and then use the appraisal to guide strategy formulation.

Step 1 Identify the Key Resources and Capabilities

Drawing up an initial list of key resources and capabilities can be done from both the demand side and the supply side. On the demand side, we can begin with key success factors (see Chapter 3). What factors determine why some firms in an industry are more successful than others and on what resources and capabilities are these success factors based? Suppose we are evaluating the resources and capabilities of Volkswagen AG, the German-based automobile manufacturer. From the demand side we would start with its success factors in the world automobile industry: low-cost production, attractively designed new models embodying the latest technologies, and the financial strength to weather the cyclicality and heavy investment requirements of the industry. What capabilities and resources do these key success factors imply? They would include manufacturing capabilities, new product development capability, effective supply chain management, global distribution, brand strength, scale-efficient plants with up-to-date capital equipment, a strong balance sheet, and so on. To organize and categorize these various resources and capabilities, it is helpful to switch our attention to the supply side and look at the company's value chain. What is the chain of activities in which the company is engaged, from new product development to purchasing, to supply chain management, to component manufacture, assembly, and right the way through to dealership support and after-sales service? We can then look at the capabilities at each stage of the chain and the resources that underpin these capabilities.

Step 2 Appraising Resources and Capabilities

Resources and capabilities need to be appraised against two key criteria. First is their *importance*: Which resources and capabilities are most important in conferring sustainable competitive advantage? Second, where are our strengths and weaknesses as compared with competitors?

Assessing Importance

The temptation in assessing which resources and capabilities are most important is to concentrate on customer choice criteria. What we must bear in mind, however, is that our ultimate objective is not to attract customers, but to make superior profit through establishing a sustainable competitive advantage. For this purpose we need to look beyond customer choice to the underlying strategic characteristics of resources and capabilities. To do this we need to look at the set of appraisal criteria outlined in the previous section on "Appraising the Profit-Earning Potential of Resources and Capabilities." In the case of Volkswagen, and the auto industry generally, many resources and capabilities are essential to compete in the business, but several of them are not scarce (for example, total quality management capability and technologically advanced assembly plants have become widely diffused within the industry), while others (such as IT capability and design capability) are outsourced to external providers – either way, they are "needed to play" but not "needed to win." On the other hand, resources such as brand strength and a global distribution network, and capabilities such as fast-cycle new product development and global logistics capability, cannot be easily acquired or internally developed – they are critical to establishing and sustaining advantage.

Assessing Relative Strengths

Objectively appraising the comparative strengths and weaknesses of a company's resources and capabilities relative to competitors is difficult. In assessing their own competencies, organizations frequently fall victim to past glories, hopes for the future, and their own wishful thinking. The tendency toward hubris among companies – and their senior managers – means that business success often sows the seeds of its own destruction.[33] Among the failed industrial companies in both America and Britain are many whose former success blinded them to their stagnating capabilities and declining competitiveness:

- Sheffield, England, once supplied cutlery and silverware to the world. Its stubborn belief in its superior production skills and product quality contributed to its near extinction in the face of foreign competition.[34]

- Lack of domestic competition and easy access to sources of coal and iron ore encouraged complacency and chauvinism among US steelmakers concerning their technological prowess and the superior quality of American steel. Neglect of new process technology and customers' preferences resulted in a rapid decline in the face of competition from imports and domestic minimills.[35]

Firms may be unaware of the capabilities they possess. In the mid-1950s, Richard and Maurice McDonald owned a single hamburger restaurant in San Bernardino,

California. It was Ray Kroc, then a milkshake salesman, who recognized the merits of the McDonalds' approach to fast-food and the potential for replicating their system.[36] The Starbucks chain of coffee houses has a remarkably similar history. It was a visiting housewares salesman, Howard Schultz, who saw the potential of the original Seattle shop and eventually acquired it.

To identify and appraise a company's capabilities, managers must look broadly, deeply, and from different perspectives. A starting point is internal discussion and review. Focus groups comprising managers from an organization can be valuable in sharing insights and evidence and building consensus regarding their organization's resource and capability profile. The evidence of history can offer powerful insights: in reviewing the projects and initiatives where the company has performed well and those where it has performed poorly, do any patterns appear?

Finally, in order to move the analysis from the subjective to the objective level, *benchmarking* is a powerful tool for quantitative assessment of performance relative to that of competitors. Benchmarking is "the process of identifying, understanding, and adapting outstanding practices from organizations anywhere in the world to help your organization improve its performance."[37] Before a company's own practices can be improved, it is necessary to assess their performance. In terms of capability assessment, benchmarking offers a systematic framework and methodology for identifying particular functions and processes and then for comparing their performance with other companies. As McKinsey & Co. has shown, performance difference between top-performing and average-performing companies in most activities tends to be wide.[38] Benchmarking has played a key role in capability upgrading at many companies. For example:

- Xerox's revitalization during the 1980s owed much to detailed comparisons that showed the massive superiority of Japanese competitors in cost efficiency, quality, and new product development. Every department was encouraged to look globally to identify best-in-class companies against which to benchmark. For inventory control and customer responsiveness, Xerox benchmarked L. L. Bean, the direct-mail clothing company.

- Bank of America's vice chairman, Martin Sheen, commented, "We have worked a lot with the Royal Bank of Canada on benchmarking because our sizes and philosophies are comparable and we're not direct competitors. We have had some particularly good exchanges with them on processes. We can also benchmark through the Research Board against an array of competitors reported in a disguised fashion. What these do is to highlight anomalies. You can't get down to a unit cost or systems task level. But if a comparable company has 22 people and we have 60, we can sit down and try to figure out what's going on."

Ultimately, appraising resources and capabilities is not about data, it's about insight and understanding. Every organization has some activity where it excels or has the potential to excel. For Federal Express, it is a system that guarantees next-day delivery anywhere within the United States. For BMW it is the ability to integrate world-class engineering with design excellence and highly effective marketing. For McDonald's, it is the ability to supply millions of hamburgers from thousands of outlets through-out the world, with remarkable uniformity of quality, customer service, and hygiene. For General Electric, it is a system of corporate management that reconciles co-ordination, innovation, flexibility, and financial discipline in one of the world's largest and most diversified corporations. All these companies are examples of highly suc-cessful enterprises. One reason why they are successful is that they have recognized what they can do well and have based their strategies on it. For poor-performing companies, the problem is not necessarily an absence of distinctive capabilities, but a failure to recognize what they are and to deploy them effectively.

Bringing Together Importance and Relative Strength

Putting together the two criteria – importance and relative strength – allows us to highlight a company's key strengths and key weaknesses. Consider, for example, Volkswagen AG. Table 5.5 provides a partial (and hypothetical) identification and appraisal of VW's resources and capabilities during the late 1990s in relation to the two criteria of importance and relative strength outlined above. Figure 5.9 then brings the two criteria together into a single display. Dividing this display into four quad-rants allows us to identify those resources and capabilities that we may regard as key strengths and those that we may identify as key weaknesses. For example, our assess-ment suggests that plant and equipment, engineering capability, manufacturing capability, and supply chain management are key strengths of VW, while distribu-tion (a relatively weak presence in the US and Japan), new product development (no consistent record of fast-cycle development of market-winning new models), and financial management are key weaknesses.

FIGURE 5.9 Appraising VW's resources and capabilities (hypothetical)

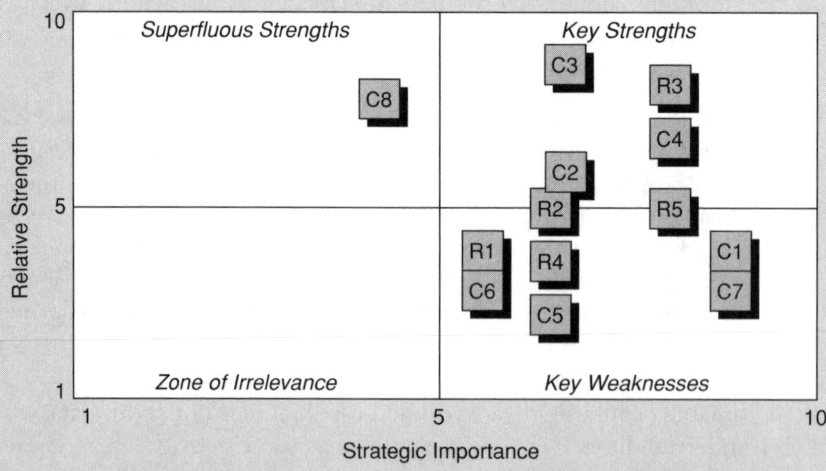

Note: The table is based upon the ratings of resources and capabilities in Table 5.5.

TABLE 5.5 Appraising VW's Resources and Capabilities

	IMPORTANCE[1]	VW'S RELATIVE STRENGTH[2]	COMMENTS
RESOURCES			
R1. Finance	6	4	VW's capital investments exceed operating cash flows. Debt/equity ratio is high relative to other major auto companies
R2. Technology	7	5	Despite technical strengths, VW is not a leader in automotive technology
R3. Plant and equipment	8	8	Has invested heavily in upgrading plants
R4. Location	7	4	Plants in key low-cost, growth markets (China, Mexico, Brazil), but German manufacturing base is very high cost
R5. Distribution (dealership network)	8	5	Geographically extensive distribution with special strength in emerging markets. Historically weak position within the US
CAPABILITIES			
C1. Product development	9	4	Traditionally weak at VW. Major hits are few: Beetle (introduced 1938), Golf (1974), Passat (1974), Vanagon (1979). Despite recent upgrading and proliferation of new models, product development still weak compared to Toyota
C2. Purchasing	7	5	Traditionally weak – strengthened by senior hires from Opel and elsewhere
C3. Engineering	7	9	The core technical strength of VW
C4. Manufacturing	8	7	Problems of inflexibility, and indifferent quality largely resolved during 1990s
C5. Financial management	6	3	Has traditionally lacked a strong financial orientation
C6. R&D	6	4	A comparative strength of VW, but becoming less important as technology shifts increasingly to suppliers
C7. Marketing and sales	9	4	Despite traditional weakness in recognizing and meeting customer needs in different national markets, VW has increased its sensitivity to the market, improved brand management, and managed its advertising and promotion with increasing dexterity
C8. Government relations	4	8	Important in emerging markets

[1] Both scales range from 1 to 10 (1 = very low, 10 = very high).
[2] VW's resources and capabilities are compared against those of GM, Ford, Toyota, Honda, Chrysler, Nissan, Honda, Fiat, and PSA, where 5 represents parity. The ratings are based upon the author's subjective judgement.

Step 3 Developing Strategy Implications

Our key focus is on the two right-hand quadrants of Figure 5.9. How do we exploit our key strengths most effectively? What do we do about our key weaknesses in terms of both upgrading them and reducing our vulnerability to them? Finally, what about our "inconsequential" strengths? Are these really superfluous, or are there ways in which we can deploy them to greater effect?

Exploiting Key Strengths

Having identified resources and capabilities that are important and where our company is strong relative to competitors, the key task is to formulate our strategy to ensure that these resources are deployed to the greatest effect. If engineering and manufacturing capabilities are key strengths of Volkswagen, then it may wish to maintain a stronger presence in component manufacture and assembly than some of its rivals, who are increasingly outsourcing manufacturing activities. If VW is well positioned in the potential growth markets of China, Eastern Europe, and Latin America, exploiting this strength may require developing models that will appeal to these markets.

To the extent that different companies within an industry have different capability profiles, this implies differentiation of strategies within the industry. If Toyota's most distinctive capability is its fast-cycle new product development, the implication is that it will compete through technological and design leadership – bringing in new models with the latest designs and technologies quickly. By contrast, if Hyundai's primary strength is its low-cost manufacturing that derives from its South Korean location, its strategy should rely less on innovative new models and more on exploiting the cost advantages associated with their Korean location: this will favor internationalization strategies based on exporting from the home base.

IBM's revival under the leadership of Lou Gerstner is an interesting case of transformational strategy that built on IBM's core strengths. During the late 1990s, IBM shifted its strategy to concentrate on two areas of business: services (notably IT consulting) and technology development (including components). This strategy represents a return to IBM's traditional core capabilities:

- Customer service – IBM's mainframe business was built not just on leading-edge products, such as the 360 range of computers, but also, and just as important, on IBM's unparalleled service network that was committed to solving the problems of its business customers.

- Basic technology – for several decades IBM has possessed the biggest patent portfolio of any IT company.

Managing Key Weaknesses

What does a company do about its key weaknesses? The immediate response is to think of how it can fill these resource gaps: investing in those resources and capabilities where a company is at a disadvantage to its principal competitors. We shall appraise and look at how companies can extend existing capabilities and develop new capabilities in the next section. For the time being, let us acknowledge that converting weakness into strength is likely to be a long-term task for most organizations and that, in the short to medium term, a company is likely to be stuck with the resources and capabilities that it inherits from the previous period.

When faced with clear weaknesses in certain functions or value chain activities, outsourcing may be a satisfactory solution. Thus, in the automobile industry, companies have become increasingly selective in the activities they perform internally. During the 1930s, Ford was almost completely vertically integrated. At its massive River Rouge plant, coal and iron ore entered at one end, completed cars exited at the other. By 2003, Ford had outsourced most component manufacture, much of its design work was being undertaken by independent design studios, and services ranging from IT to security were being provided by third parties. In athletic shoes and clothing, Nike undertakes product design, marketing, and overall "systems integration," but manufacturing, logistics, and many other functions are contracted out. We shall consider the vertical scope of the firm at greater depth in Chapter 13.

How can a company adapt its strategy to defend against key weaknesses, or even to turn a weakness into a competitive advantage? Consider Harley-Davidson. With sales of 300,000 bikes a year (compared with 4 million at Honda), Harley is too small to compete on technology and the development of innovative new products. How has it dealt with this problem? It has made a virtue out of its outmoded technology and traditional designs. The fact that Harley-Davidson bikes embody otherwise obsolete push-rod engines and designs that have not changed substantially since the 1950s has become central to the retro-look appeal of the "hog."

What about Superfluous Strengths?

What about those resources and capabilities where a company has particular strengths, but these don't appear to be important sources of sustainable competitive advantage? One response may be to lower the level of investment from these resources and capabilities. If a retail bank has a strong, but increasingly underutilized, branch network, this may be an opportunity to prune its real estate assets and invest in IT approaches to customer services.

However, in the same way that companies can turn apparent weaknesses into competitive strengths, so it is possible to develop innovative strategies that turn apparently inconsequential strengths into valuable resources and capabilities. Edward Jones' network of brokerage offices and 8,000-strong sales force looked increasingly irrelevant in an era when brokerage transactions were increasingly going on-line. However, by emphasizing personal service, the trustworthiness of its brokers, and its traditional, conservative investment virtues, Edward Jones has continued to build market share.

Consider too my own institution, Georgetown University's McDonough School of Business. A unique characteristic of the school is its Jesuit heritage, a resource that one might think would be difficult to regard as an important source of competitive advantage in the fiercely competitive MBA market. Yet, to the extent that a fundamental principle of Jesuit education is developing the whole person and that success as a manager is not just about what you know but also about who you are, Georgetown's Jesuit tradition can provide a key differentiating factor through the MBA program's emphasis on developing the values, integrity, and emotional intelligence necessary to be a successful business leader.

DEVELOPING RESOURCES AND CAPABILITIES

Conventional approaches to developing resources and capabilities have emphasized *gap analysis* – identifying discrepancies between the current position and the desired future position, then adopting policies to fill those gaps. Such approaches are of limited value. In the case of resources, investing in areas of weakness – whether it is proprietary technology or manufacturing facilities – can be very expensive and, because of the complex complementarities between different resources, such investments may deliver limited returns. In the case of capabilities, because we know little about their operation or their microstructure, developing them is a complex and hazardous endeavor.

The Relationship between Resources and Capabilities

Possibly the most difficult problem in developing capabilities is that we know little about the linkage between resources and capabilities. In most sports, the relationship between the skills of the individual players and team performance is weak. Across all sports there are examples of highly paid, star-studded professional teams who perform poorly and champion teams conspicuous by the absence of superstar players. In European football (soccer), some of the most expensive teams of the past 10 years (Chelsea, Inter-Milan, and Lazio) have under-performed compared with teams built on far more modest expenditures (see Strategy Capsule 5.4).

Among business firms, we observe the same phenomenon. The firms that demonstrate the most outstanding capabilities are not necessarily those with the greatest resource endowments:

- In automobiles, GM has four times the output of Honda and four times the R&D expenditure, yet it is Honda, not GM, that is world leader in power train technology.

STRATEGY CAPSULE 5.4 Star Players and Team Performance in European Soccer

---

Since the early 1990s, expenditures by leading clubs on acquiring players have rocketed. Prior to 1994, no player had been transferred between clubs at a fee exceeding $20 million. After 1999, transfer fees for top players regularly exceeded $50 million. The table below shows the three best performing teams in Italy, Spain and the UK over the period 1998–99 to 2002–03 and their expenditures on transfer fees.

STRATEGY CAPSULE 5.4 *(cont'd)*

BEST PERFORMING TEAMS 1998–2003	EXPENDITURES ON KEY PLAYERS
Valencia (Spain)	Pablo Aimar ($20.4m), Ruben Baraja ($12m)
Real Madrid (Spain)	Zinedine Zidane ($68m), Luis Figo ($55m), Ronaldo ($43m), Nicolas Anelka ($36m), David Beckham ($26m)
Deportivo La Coruna (Spain)	Sergio Gonzales ($16m), Alberto Luque ($15m)
Juventus (Italy)	Gianluigi Buffon ($49m), Pavel Nedved ($38m), Lilian Thuram ($33m), David Trezeguet ($21m), Marco de Viao ($10m)
AC Milan (Italy)	Rui Costa ($42m), Alessandro Nesta ($30m), Andriy Shevchenko ($24m), Andrea Pirlo ($16m), Kaka ($9m)
Parma (Italy)	Hidetoshi Nakata ($30m), Sdrian Mutu ($9m)
Manchester United (England)	Rio Ferdinand ($45m), Juan Veron ($42m), Ruud van Nistelrooy ($30m), Cristiano Ronaldo ($18m), Fabien Bartez ($12m), Diego Forlan ($10m), Kleberson ($9m), Mikael Silvestre ($6m)
Arsenal (England)	Sylvain Wiltord ($20m), Thierry Henry ($16m), Dennis Bergkamp ($12m), Nwankwo Kanu ($7m), Gilberto Silva ($7m), Patrick Vieira ($6m)
Liverpool (England)	Emile Heskey ($16m), El Hadji Diouf ($15m), Dietmar Hamann ($12m), Chris Kerkland ($8m), Harry Kewell ($8m), Salif Diao ($8m)

Despite the heavy expenditures by many of these teams on players, it is notable that only four of the nine teams feature among the top three heaviest spenders on players during 1997–2003 in each country:

BIGGEST SPENDING TEAMS 1997–2003	EXPENDITURES ON KEY PLAYERS
Real Madrid (Spain)	See above
Barcelona (Spain)	Marc Overmars ($33m), Ronaldhino ($32m), Rivaldo ($24m), Javier Saviola ($24m), Patrick Kluivert ($18m), Dani ($15m), Ricardo Quaresma ($6m)
Real Betis (Spain)	Denilsonm de Oliviera ($33m), Marcos Assuncao ($7m), Fernando Fernandez ($3m)
Lazio (Italy)	Hernan Crespo ($54m), Gaizka Mendieta ($45m), Claudio Lopez ($33m), Christian Vieri ($30m), Juan Veron ($27m), Jaap Stam ($25m), Stefani Fiore ($22m), Giuliano Giannichedda ($22m), Simone Inzaghi ($18m), Fabio Liverani ($12m), Bernardo Corradi ($12m)
Inter Milan (Italy)	Christian Vieri ($48m), Ronaldo ($27m), Francesco Toldo ($27m), Hernan Crespo ($25m), Fabio Cannavaro ($25m)
Juventus (Italy)	See above
Chelsea (England)	Damien Duff ($26m), Hernan Crespo ($25m), Claude Makelele ($25m), Adrian Mutu ($24m), Jimmy-Flod Hassdelbaink ($23m), Juan Veron ($19m), Jesper Gronkjaer ($12m), Emmanuele Petit ($12m), Geremi ($11m), Wayne Bridge ($11m), Joe Cole ($10m), William Gallas ($10m), Mario Stanic ($9m), Marcel Desailly ($7m)
Manchester United	See above
Arsenal	See above

- In consumer electronics, Sony has had a smaller research budget than Philips for the past three decades, yet Sony has introduced many more successful innovations than Philips.

- In telecom equipment it was the upstart Cisco rather than the telecom equipment giants such as Lucent, Nortel Networks, and Alcatel that established leadership in the new world of package switching.

According to Hamel and Prahalad, it is not the size of a firm's resource base that is the primary determinant of capability, but the firm's ability to *leverage* its resources. Resources can be leveraged in the following ways:

- *Concentrating resources* through the processes of *converging* resources on a few clearly defined and consistent goals; *focusing* the efforts of each group, department, and business unit on individual priorities in a sequential fashion; and *targeting* those activities that have the biggest impact on customers' perceived value.

- *Accumulating resources* through *mining experience* in order to achieve faster learning, and *borrowing* from other firms – accessing their resources and capabilities through alliances, outsourcing arrangements, and the like.

- *Complementing resources* involves increasing their effectiveness through linking them with complementary resources and capabilities. This may involve *blending* product design capabilities with the marketing capabilities needed to communicate these to the market, and *balancing* to ensure that limited resources and capabilities in one area do not hold back the effectiveness of resources and capabilities in another.

- *Conserving resources* involves utilizing resources and capabilities to the fullest by *recycling* them through different products, markets, and product generations; and *co-opting* resources through collaborative arrangements with other companies.[39]

Replicating Capabilities

Growing capabilities requires that the firm replicates them internally.[40] Some of the world's most successful corporations are those that have been able to replicate their capabilities in different product and geographical markets. Ray Kroc's genius was to take the original McDonald's formula and replicate it thousands of times over in building a global chain of hamburger restaurants. Other leading service companies – Marriott, BankOne, Club Med, eBay – have built large and successful programs on the principle that once a capability has been developed, its replication in another location can be achieved at a low cost.

If routines develop learning-by-doing, and the knowledge that underpins them is tacit, replication is far from easy. Replication requires *systematization* of the knowledge that underlies the capability – typically through the formulation of standard operating procedures. Thus, McDonald's has distilled its business system into operating procedures and training manuals that govern the operation and maintenance of every aspect of its restaurants. In most cases, however, it is not possible to fully articulate how the capabilities operate – the knowledge upon which capabilities are based is too tacit and too diffused among different individuals to be fully articulated. In such circumstances, argue Gabriel Szulanski and Sid Winter, the best approach is to replicate exactly. Thus, when Intel builds new fabrication plants, it follows a policy called *Copy Exactly!*, where the minutest details of the lead plant are replicated.[41]

Developing New Capabilities

Creating certain resources – a brand or an overseas distribution network – may be difficult, costly, and take considerable time, but at least the extent of the challenge can be understood. Creating organizational capabilities poses a much higher level of difficulty. If capabilities are based on routines that develop through practice and learning, what can the firm do to establish such routines within a limited time period? We know that capabilities involve teams of resources working together, but, even with the tools of business process mapping, we typically have sketchy understanding of how people, machines, technology, and organizational culture fit together to achieve a particular level of performance. In the same way that we can only speculate about what makes Tiger Woods the greatest golfer of our time, we are unable fully to diagnose how Dell achieves its brilliance at logistics management or how Electronic Arts has been able to develop video games that continue to set new standards in complexity, sophistication, and player involvement.

Capability as a Result of Early Experiences

Organizational capability is clearly *path dependent* – a company's capabilities today are the result of its history. More importantly, this history will constrain what capabilities that the company can perform in the future. To understand the origin of a company's capabilities, a useful starting point is to study the circumstances that existed and events that occurred at the time of the company's founding and early development. How did Wal-Mart develop its super-efficient system of warehousing and distribution? This system was not the result of careful planning and design, but of initial conditions: because of its rural locations, the company was unable to get reliable distribution from its suppliers, and so it established its own distribution system. How does one explain Wal-Mart's amazing commitment to cost efficiency? Its management systems are undoubtedly important, but ultimately it is Wal-Mart's origins in small-town Arkansas and the values and personality of its founder, Sam Walton, that sustains its obsession with efficiency and cost cutting.

Consider too the world's largest oil and gas majors (see Table 5.6). Despite long histories of competing together in the same markets, with near-identical products, and similar strategies, the majors display very different capability profiles. Exxon and the Royal Dutch/Shell Group have shared parallel development for over a century yet have very different capability profiles. Exxon is known for its financial manage-

TABLE 5.6 Distinctive Capabilities as a Consequence of Childhood Experiences: The Oil Majors

COMPANY	DISTINCTIVE CAPABILITY	EARLY HISTORY
Exxon	Financial management	Exxon's predecessor, Standard Oil (NJ), was the holding company for Rockefeller's Standard Oil Trust
Royal Dutch/Shell Group	Coordinating a decentralized global network of 200+ operating companies	Shell Transport & Trading headquartered in London and founded to sell Russian oil in China and the Far East. Royal Dutch Petroleum headquartered in The Hague; founded to exploit Indonesian reserves
BP	"Elephant hunting"	Discovered huge Persian reserves, went on to find Forties field (North Sea) and Prudhoe Bay (Alaska)
ENI	Deal making in politicized environments	The Enrico Mattei legacy; the challenge of managing government relations in post-war Italy
Mobil	Lubricants	Vacuum Oil Co. founded in 1866 to supply patented petroleum lubricants

ment capabilities exercised through rigorous investment controls and emphasis on cost efficiency. Shell is known for its decentralized, international management capabilities, in particular its adaptability to a wide variety of national environments. These differences can be traced back to the companies' nineteenth-century origins. Exxon (then Standard Oil New Jersey) was part of Rockefeller's Standard Oil Trust, where it played a key holding company role with responsibilities for the financial management of other parts of the Standard Oil empire. Shell was established to sell Russian oil in China and the Far East, while Royal Dutch was established to exploit Indonesian oil reserves. With head offices thousands of miles away in Europe, it is little wonder that the group developed a decentralized, adaptable management style.

Organizational Capability: Rigid or Dynamic?

These long periods over which capabilities develop have important implications for firms' capacity for change. The more highly developed a firm's organizational capabilities are, the narrower their repertoire and the more difficult it is for the firm to adapt them to new circumstances. Dorothy Leonard-Barton argued that core capabilities are simultaneously *core rigidities* – they inhibit firms' ability to access and develop new capabilities.[42] Nevertheless, some companies appear to have the capacity to continually upgrade, extend, and reconfigure their organizational capabilities. David Teece and his colleagues have referred to *dynamic capabilities* as the "firm's ability to integrate, build, and reconfigure internal and external competences to address rapidly changing environments."[43] The mere fact that some firms in technologically fast-moving environments are capable of adapting and prospering over periods of several decades – 3M, Hewlett-Packard, Canon, Siemens, to mention a few – points to the existence of higher-order capabilities that permit the reconfiguration, adaptation, and creation of functional and technical capabilities.[44]

Yet, such dynamic capabilities are far from common. For most companies it appears that highly developed capabilities in existing products and technologies create barriers to acquiring capabilities in new products and new technologies. When responding to radical change within an industry, or in exploiting entirely new business opportunities, new firms are often at an advantage to established firms. Whereas new firms are faced with the challenge of acquiring entirely new capabilities, established firms are faced with the dual challenges of acquiring new capabilities and dismantling existing obsolete capabilities.

In most new industries, the most successful firms tend to be startups rather than established firms. In personal computers, it was newcomers such as Dell, Acer, Compaq, and Gateway that emerged as most successful during the 1990s. Among established firms, relatively few (IBM, Hewlett-Packard, and Toshiba) went on to significant success. Many others (e.g., Xerox, GE, Texas Instruments, AT&T, and Olivetti) fell by the wayside. In established industries, *disruptive* or *architectural* change has often been associated with new entrants or peripheral firms overturning established market leaders.[45]

Approaches to Capability Development

So, how do companies go about developing new capabilities? Let us review five approaches commonly utilized.

1. Mergers and Acquisitions

If new capabilities can only be developed over long periods, then acquiring a company that has already developed the desired capability can short-circuit the tortuous process of capability development. In technologically fast-moving environments, established firms typically use acquisitions as a means of acquiring specific technical capabilities – Cisco Systems and Microsoft have each benefited substantially from such acquisitions. Microsoft's adaptation to the internet era was based largely upon acquiring capabilities through acquisition. These included Vermeer Technologies (1996), eShop (1997), LinkAge Software (1997), Hotmail (1998), NetGames (2000), Great Plains Software (2001), Navision (2002), and many, many more.

However, using acquisitions as a means of extending a company's capability base involves major risks. On its own, acquisition does not achieve the intended goal. Once the acquisition has been made, the acquiring company must find a way to integrate the acquiree's capabilities with its own. Herein lies the main difficulty with most mergers and acquisitions:

- Compaq Computer's attempt to build competitive advantage in the corporate sector by adding DEC's sales and customer service capabilities to its own technology and product development capacities was a dismal failure.[46]

- AT&T's attempt to merge its telecommunications expertise with the computer skills of NCR was an even greater disaster. After years of fruitless attempts at managing the convergence of telecommunications and computing, AT&T eventually spun off NCR.

- A key objective of the merger between Daimler-Benz and Chrysler was to combine Daimler's engineering and technological strengths with Chrysler's design flair and fast-cycle product development capability in mass-market cars. Despite careful planning and massive efforts to promote integration, differences in corporate and national culture have posed massive barriers to knowledge transfer and organizational integration.[47]

2. Strategic Alliances

Given the high cost of acquiring companies, alliances offer a more targeted and cost effective means to acquire or access another company's capabilities. A *strategic alliance* is a cooperative relationship between firms involving the sharing of resources in pursuit of common goals. Strategic alliances comprise a wide variety of collaborative relationships, which include joint research, technology-sharing arrangements, shared manufacturing, joint marketing and/or distribution arrangements, and vertical partnerships, to mention but a few. Alliances may involve formal agreements or they may be entirely informal; they may or may not involve ownership links. Alliances offer an opportunity to *access* another firm's capabilities – many outsourcing arrangements tend to take the form of stable, long-term strategic alliances. Other alliances are for the purpose of *acquiring* the partner's capabilities through organizational learning.[48] When General Motors formed its NUMMI joint venture with Toyota, its motive was to learn Toyota's "lean" approach to manufacturing.[49] Where both alliance partners are trying to acquire one another's capabilities, the result may well be a "competition for competence" that ultimately destabilizes the relationship.[50]

3. Incubating Capabilities

A critical problem in developing new capabilities is that the organizational structure, management systems, and behavioral norms that support existing capabilities may be unsuitable for new capabilities. To resolve this problem, companies may need to develop new capabilities in organizationally separate units. For example:

- IBM developed its prototype personal computer at its Entry Level Systems unit led by IBM veteran Bill Lowe. The unit was located in Florida, over a thousand miles away from IBM's corporate headquarters in New York. The isolation of the unit and the protection and support it received from IBM's CEO, John Opel, were critical in allowing the PC development team to create a product design and business system that were totally different from those that characterized IBM's mainframe business.[51]

- Brown & Root, the engineering services company, developed world-beating capabilities in logistics management and emergency-response services that support a business with revenues of over $500 million. This development took place in a "protected and stimulating environment in which the new competences were able to flourish. The environment was bounded not by fire walls, but by a one-way membrane that allowed the incubator to beg, borrow, or steal people and practices from the main business, while not being bound by its rules."[52]

- The pioneering online financial services company Egg was established by its London-based parent, Prudential Insurance, in the Midlands towns of Dudley and Derby – well away from the London headquarters.

These incubator arrangements combine two key advantages: the new unit can establish the flexibility and autonomy of a startup, while drawing on the established resources and capabilities of the parent. However, the challenge occurs when the established organization needs to bring the new capability back into the company. During the 1970s and '80s, Xerox's Palo Alto Research Center did more than any other company to develop the technologies that formed the basis of the microcomputer revolution. However, it was much easier for these technologies to flow to nearby competitors – Hewlett-Packard, Apple, Microsoft, and Sun Microsystems – than it was for them to be absorbed by Xerox's east coast establishment. GM's Saturn has had a similar experience. The Tennessee-based subsidiary achieved its objective of developing new manufacturing and marketing capabilities, but, as yet, these seem to have had little impact on the parent organization.[53]

4. Product Sequencing

If we do not fully comprehend the structure of organizational capabilities or the mechanisms through which they operate, it is difficult to manage their creation and development. In such circumstances, an indirect approach to capability developing is advisable. If we cannot design new capabilities from scratch, but if we know what types of capabilities are required for different products, then by *pushing* the development of particular products we can *pull* the development of the capabilities that those products require. For such an approach to be successful it must be systematic and incremental. Developing complex capabilities over a significant period of time requires a sequencing of products where each stage of the sequence has specific capability development goals.[54]

The development of products and capabilities at 3M illustrates a co-evolutionary process (see Figure 5.3). An even more striking example is the rapid emergence of Hyundai as a leading international supplier of automobiles between its entry into the auto industry in 1986, and its emergence as a world-class competitor by the mid-1990s (see Figure 5.10).[55]

This parallel development of a firm's product portfolio and its base of resources and capabilities is referred to by Hiroyuki Itami as *dynamic resource fit*.[56] There is a two-way relationship between products and resources: resources are needed to

FIGURE 5.10 Product sequencing to build capabilities: Hyundai Motor, 1968–1995

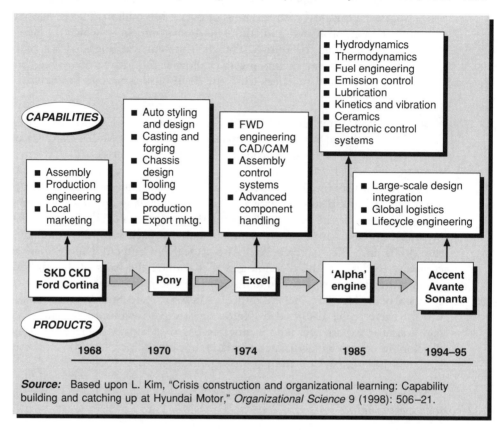

Source: Based upon L. Kim, "Crisis construction and organizational learning: Capability building and catching up at Hyundai Motor," *Organizational Science* 9 (1998): 506–21.

produce the products, but in the course of production skills, technology and know-how are generated. Matsushita followed this principle of parallel and sequential development of products and resources in its international expansion strategy. In a new foreign country, Matsushita begins with technically unsophisticated products such as batteries, then moves on to the production of products requiring more complex manufacturing and marketing capabilities:

> In every country batteries are a necessity, so they sell well. As long as we bring a few advanced automated pieces of equipment for the processes vital to final product quality, even unskilled labor can produce good products. As they work on this rather simple product, the workers get trained, and this increased skill level then permits us to gradually expand production to items with increasingly higher technology levels, first radios, then televisions.[57]

5. Managing the Process

We have observed how commitment to ambitious performance goals can create the driving force for the continual development of a firm's capabilities. Gary Hamel and C. K. Prahalad emphasize that *strategic intent, resource leverage and stretch*, and the drive to "create the future" are more important in building sustainable competitive advantage than initial resource advantages.[58] Michael Porter also emphasizes the need for companies to continually upgrade their resources and capabilities in order to sustain competitive advantage.[59]

Recent research into organizational capabilities offers the prospect that, by better understanding the emergence, structure and development of organizational capability we can identify the potential for these processes to be more effectively managed.[60]

SUMMARY

We have shifted the focus of our attention from the external to the internal environment of the firm. This internal environment comprises many features of the firm, but for the purposes of strategy analysis, the key issue is what the firm *can do*. This means looking at the resources of the firm and the way resources are brought together to create organizational capabilities. Our main interest is in identifying those resources and capabilities that have the potential to establish sustainable competitive advantage for the company. A systematic appraisal of a company's resources and capabilities then provides the basis for reconsidering strategy. How can the firm deploy its strengths to maximum advantage? How can it minimize its vulnerability to its weaknesses? How can it develop and extend its capabilities to meet the challenges of the future? Figure 5.11 provides a simplified view of the approach to resource analysis developed in this chapter.

FIGURE 5.11 Summary: a framework for analyzing resources and capabilities

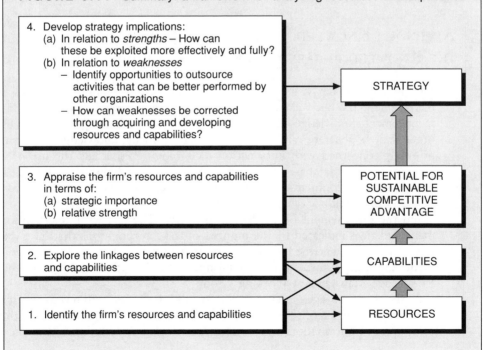

Despite the progress that has been made in the last ten years in our understanding of resources and capabilities, there is much that remains unresolved. We know little about the microstructures of organizational capabilities and how they are established and develop. Can firms develop entirely new capabilities, or must top management accept that distinctive capabilities are the result of experience-based learning over long periods of time through processes that are poorly understood? If that is the case, strategy must be concerned with exploiting, preserving, and developing the firm's existing pool of resources and capabilities, rather than trying to change them. We have much to learn in this area.

Although much of the discussion has been heavy on concepts and theory, the issues are practical. The management systems of most firms devote meticulous attention to the physical and financial assets that are valued on the balance sheet, much less attention has been paid to the critical intangible and human resources of the firm, and even less to the identification and appraisal of organizational capability. Most firms are now aware of the importance of their resources and capabilities, but the techniques of identifying, assessing, and developing them are woefully underdeveloped.

Because the resources and capabilities of the firm form the foundation for building competitive advantage, we shall return again and again to the concepts of this chapter. Our next port of call is the structures and systems through which the firm deploys its resources, builds and exercises its capabilities, and implements its strategy.

APPENDIX: KNOWLEDGE MANAGEMENT AND THE KNOWLEDGE-BASED VIEW OF THE FIRM

During the past ten years our thinking about resources and capabilities and their management has been extended and reshaped by a surge of interest in knowledge management. Knowledge management refers to processes and practices through which organizations generate value from knowledge. Initially, knowledge management was primarily concerned with information technology – especially the use of intranets, groupware, and databases for storing, analyzing, and disseminating information. Subsequent developments in knowledge management have been concerned less with data and more with organizational learning – especially the transfer of best practices – and the management of intellectual property. The level of interest in knowledge management is indicated by the number of large corporations that have created the position of chief knowledge officer, the spawning of a host of knowledge management consulting firms, and the establishment by the US government of the Federal Knowledge Management Working Group.

At the academic level, interest in the role of knowledge within organizations represents the confluence of several research streams including resource-based theory, the economics of information, epistemology, evolutionary economics, and the management of technology. The outcome has been a *knowledge-based view of the firm* that considers the firm as a set of knowledge assets with the purpose of deploying these assets to create value.

Is knowledge management a major breakthrough in management practice or mere fad? A growing body of evidence points to the ability of knowledge management to generate substantial gains in performance. At the same time many of its manifestations are highly dubious. *The Wall Street Journal* reports that Saatchi & Saatchi's director of knowledge management is "absorbing everything under the sun," including the implications of breakthrough products such as Japanese pantyhose "embedded with millions of microcapsules of vitamin C and seaweed extract that burst when worn to provide extra nourishment for the limbs."[61] Lucy Kellaway of the *Financial Times* notes that beyond the simple truth that "companies that are good at sharing information have an advantage over companies that are not. . . . The subject [of knowledge management] has attracted more needless obfuscation and wooly thinking by academics and consultants than any other."[62]

My approach is to regard knowledge management and the knowledge-based view of the firm as important extensions of our analysis of resources and capabilities. In terms of resources, knowledge is acknowledged to be the overwhelming important productive resource; indeed, the value of people and machines lies primarily in the fact that they embody knowledge. From the strategic viewpoint, knowledge is a particularly interesting resource: many types of knowledge are scarce, much of it is difficult to transfer, and complex forms of knowledge may be very difficult to replicate. Capabilities may be viewed as the manifestation of the knowledge of the organization. The tools of knowledge management can illuminate the architecture of organizational capability and indicate how capability can be created, developed, maintained, and replicated.

Types of Knowledge

The single most useful contribution of knowledge management is the recognition that different types of knowledge have very different characteristics. A key distinction is between *knowing how* and *knowing about*. *Know-how* is primarily *tacit* in nature – it involves skills that are expressed through their performance (riding a bicycle, playing the piano). *Knowing about* is primarily *explicit* – it comprises facts, theories, and sets of instructions. The primary difference between tacit and explicit knowledge lies in their transferability. Explicit knowledge is revealed by its communication: it can be transferred across individuals, across space, and across time. This ease of communication means that explicit knowledge – information especially – has the characteristics of a *public good*: once created, it can be replicated among innumerable users at very low marginal cost (IT has driven these costs to near zero for most types of information). Tacit knowledge, on the other hand, cannot be codified; it can only be observed through its application and acquired through practice, hence its transfer between people is slow, costly, and uncertain.

This distinction has major implications for strategy. If explicit knowledge can be transferred so easily, it is seldom the foundation of sustainable competitive advantage.

Because explicit knowledge leaks so quickly to competitors, it is only secure when it is protected, either by intellectual property (patents, copyrights, trade secrets) or by secrecy ("The formula for Coca-Cola will be kept in a safe in the vault of our Atlanta headquarters guarded by armed Coca-Cola executives"). The challenge of tacit knowledge is the opposite: if Ms. Jenkins is an incredibly successful salesperson, how can the skills embedded in her brain be transferred to the rest of the salesforce of Acme Delights? For consulting companies, the distinction between tacit ("personalized") and explicit ("systematized") knowledge defines their business model and is a central determinant of their strategy.[63]

The tacit/explicit distinction has important implications for the distribution of decision-making authority within the company. If the knowledge relevant to decisions is explicit, it can be easily transferred and assembled in one place, hence permitting centralized decision making (treasury activities within companies are typically centralized). If knowledge is primarily tacit, it cannot be transferred and decision making needs to be located among the people where the knowledge lies. If each salesperson's knowledge of how to make sales is based on their intuition and their understanding of their customers' idiosyncrasies, such knowledge cannot be easily transferred to their sales managers. It follows that decisions about their working hours and selling tactics should be made by them, not by the sales manager.

Types of Knowledge Process

A second component of knowledge management is understanding the processes through which knowledge is developed and applied. Two categories of knowledge processes can be identified: those that are concerned with increasing the stock of knowledge available to the organization, and those that are concerned with the application of the organization's knowledge. J.-C. Spender refers to the former as *knowledge generation* and the latter as *knowledge application*. James March's distinction between *exploration* and *exploitation* recognizes a similar dichotomy.[64] Within these two broad areas we can identify a number of different knowledge processes, each of which has been associated with particular techniques and approaches to knowledge management (see Figure 5.12).

The best-developed and most widely applied techniques of knowledge management have focused on some of the most basic aspects of knowledge application and exploitation. For example:

- In the area of *knowledge identification*, companies are increasingly assembling and systematizing information on their knowledge assets. These include assessments and reviews of patent portfolios and providing personnel data that allows each employee to identify the skills and experience of other employees in the organization. A key aspect of such knowledge identification is the recognition of knowledge that is being generated within the organization so that it can subsequently be stored for future use. Such knowledge identification is especially important in project-based organizations to ensure that knowledge developed in one project is not lost to the organization. Systematic post-project

FIGURE 5.12   Knowledge processes within the organization

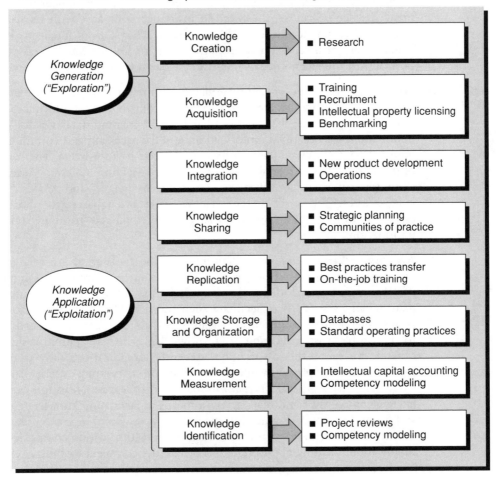

reviews are a central theme in the US Army's "lessons learned" procedure. At the Army's National Training Center, the results of practice maneuvers and simulated battles are quickly identified, then distilled into tactical guidelines and recommended procedures by the Center for Army Lessons Learned. A similar systematized learning process is applied to identifying knowledge generated from actual operation. During the military intervention in Bosnia in 1995, the results of every operation were forwarded to the Center for Lessons Learned to be collected and codified. Resulting lessons learned were distributed to active units every 72 hours.[65] By the late 1990s, virtually every major management consulting firm had introduced a system whereby the learnings of each consulting project had to be identified, written up, and submitted to a common database.

- *Knowledge measurement* involves the difficult task of applying metrics to the organization's stock of knowledge and its utilization. The pioneer of measurement has been Skandia, the Swedish insurance company, with its system of intellectual capital accounting.[66] Dow Chemical's system of intellectual capital management also relies on quantitative tools to link its intellectual property portfolio to the shareholder value using a balanced scorecard approach.

- For knowledge to be efficiently utilized within the organization, *knowledge storage and organization* are critical. The key contribution of information technology to knowledge management has been in creating databases for storing information, for organizing information, and for accessing and communicating information, to facilitate the transfer of and access to knowledge. The backbone of the Booz-Allen & Hamilton's "Knowledge-On-Line" system,[67] Accenture's (formerly Andersen Consulting) "Knowledge Xchange," and AMS's "Knowledge Express"[68] is an IT system that comprises a database, groupware (such as Lotus Notes), and an intranet that permits employees to input and access information.

- *Knowledge sharing and replication* involves the transfer of knowledge from one part of the organization (or from one person) to be replicated in another part (or by another individual). A central function of IT-based knowledge management systems is to facilitate such transfer. However, tacit knowledge is not amenable to codification within an IT system. The traditional answer to the problem of replicating tacit knowledge is to use apprenticeships and other forms of on-the-job training. Recently, organizations have discovered the important role played by informal networks in transferring experiential knowledge. These self-organizing *communities of practice* are increasingly being deliberately established and managed as a means of facilitating knowledge sharing and group learning.[69] Replicating capabilities poses an even greater challenge. Gabriel Szulanski shows that transferring best practices within companies is not simply about creating appropriate incentives; the complexity of the knowledge involved constitutes the most significant barrier.[70]

- *Knowledge integration* represents one of the greatest challenges to any company. Producing most goods and services requires bringing together the knowledge of multiple individuals. The essential task of almost all organizational processes is integrating individual knowledge in an effective and efficient manner. For example, a strategic planning system may be seen as a vehicle for integrating the different knowledge bases of managers at different levels of the organization and from different functions in order to create the best strategy for the company. Similarly with new product development: the key is to integrate the knowledge of many technical experts and across a range of functions. A wide body of evidence points to the effectiveness of project teams in integrating knowledge.[71]

Within knowledge generation, it is possible to distinguish between the internal creation of knowledge (*knowledge creation*) and the search to identify and absorb existing knowledge from outside the organization (*knowledge acquisition*). The mechanisms through which knowledge is acquired from outside the organization are typically well known: hiring skilled employees, acquiring companies or their knowledge resources, benchmarking companies that are recognized as "best-in-class" for certain practices, and learning through alliances and joint ventures. Creativity remains a key challenge for most companies. While most studies of creativity emphasize the role of the individual and the types of environment conducive to individual creativity, Dorothy Leonard has explored the role of groups and group processes in stimulating innovation.[72]

Knowledge Conversion

In practice, knowledge generation and application are not distinct. For example, the application of existing knowledge creates opportunities for learning that increase the stock of knowledge.[73] Nonaka's theory of knowledge creation identifies the processes of *knowledge conversion* – between tacit and explicit and between individual and organizational knowledge – as central to the organization's building of its knowledge base.[74] The conversion of knowledge between the different knowledge types

FIGURE 5.13   Nonaka's spiral of knowledge creation

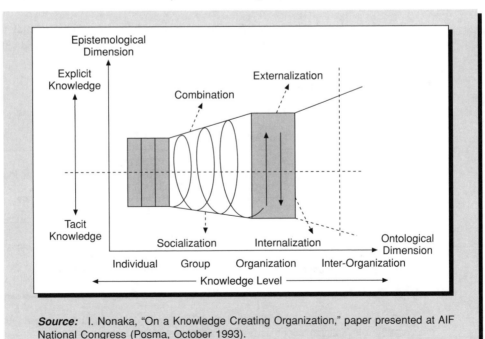

Source: I. Nonaka, "On a Knowledge Creating Organization," paper presented at AIF National Congress (Posma, October 1993).

(the "epistemological dimension") and knowledge levels (the "ontological dimension") forms a knowledge spiral in which the stock of knowledge broadens and deepens (see Figure 5.13). Nonaka specifies four types of knowledge conversion (see Figure 5.14).

Converting tacit into explicit knowledge is critical to companies that wish to replicate their capabilities. Several companies have created huge amounts of value from systematizing tacit knowledge and then replicating it in multiple locations:

- Henry Ford's Model T was initially produced on a small scale by skilled metal workers one car at a time. Ford's assembly-line mass-production technology systematized that tacit knowledge, built it into machines and a business process, and replicated it in Ford plants throughout the world. With the knowledge built into the system, the workers no longer needed to be highly skilled, so Ford's plants were staffed by semi-skilled workers.

- When Ray Kroc discovered the McDonald brothers' hamburger stand in Riversdale, California, he quickly recognized the potential for systematizing their operation and fast-service, assembly-line meals, not just in a single location but in many McDonald's outlets. McDonald's knowledge is systematized and replicated through operating manuals, videos, and training programs. It allows its thousands of worldwide outlets to produce fast food to exacting standards by a labor force that, for the most part, possesses very limited culinary skills.

The Knowledge-based View of the Firm

The *knowledge-based view of the firm* is an approach to firm analysis that views the business enterprise as an institution for generating and applying knowledge. It is based

FIGURE 5.14 Nonaka's knowledge conversion matrix

	Tacit Knowledge	*TO*	Explicit Knowledge
Tacit Knowledge *FROM*	SOCIALIZATION Sharing of tacit knowledge among individuals and from the organization to the individual		EXTERNALIZATION The articulation and systematization of tacit into explicit knowledge. Use of metaphor to communicate tacit concepts
Explicit Knowledge	INTERNALIZATION Instructions and principles are converted into intuition and routines		COMBINATION A key role of information systems is to combine different units of information and other forms of explicit knowledge

Source: I. Nonaka, "On the Knowledge Creating Organization," paper presented at the AIF National Congress (Posma, October 1991).

upon a set of ideas about the knowledge processes within the firm. Most importantly, it recognizes that the processes of knowledge generation and knowledge application require different organizational arrangements. Efficiency in creating and storing knowledge requires that individuals specialize in particular types of knowledge. Yet, production requires the integration of many different types of knowledge. Hence, the fundamental challenge of business organizations is to reconcile these two processes.[75] Despite the emphasis of much of the knowledge management literature on *organizational learning*, the danger of learning is that it can easily undermine the efficiencies of specialization. Thus, the challenge for composer Richard Rodgers and lyricist Oscar Hammerstein was how to collaborate effectively in order to write musicals such as *South Pacific*, *The King and I*, and the *Sound of Music*, while preserving their distinctly specialized skills.

How can knowledge be integrated in ways that preserve the efficiencies of specialization? Among the processes that have been suggested are *rules*, whereby specialists translate their knowledge into rules and directives to guide the practices and behavior of others, and *routines*, whereby different specialists establish ways of interacting that allow each to input their knowledge into a combined process. For knowledge integration to work efficiently, there needs to be some degree of *common knowledge* that permits different specialists to collaborate and interact. This common knowledge comprises elements such as a common language to support communication and a common culture to support compatible behaviors and cognitive processes. By recognizing the specific features of different knowledge processes, it is possible to recognize the type of organizational structure and systems needed to support each knowledge process. Awareness of these complexities of processing knowledge offers a view of the business enterprise that is richer and more sophisticated than economic theories of the firm that focus on transaction costs or efficient incentive structures. Thus, Bruce Kogut and Udo Zander argue that firms are:

> . . . social communities in which individual and social expertise is transferred into economically-useful products and services by the application of a set of higher-order organizing principles. Firms exist because they provide a social community of voluntaristic action structured by organizing principles that are not reducible to individuals.[76]

Conclusion

At the academic level, the analysis of the characteristics of knowledge and the processes through which the firm creates value from knowledge has the potential to develop our understanding of fundamental aspects of the role of firms and the nature of management – including the structure and creation of organizational capability.

In terms of practical techniques of knowledge management, considerable advances have been made. The key contribution is in closing the gap between the sophisticated tools of financial and operational analysis to which tangible assets have been subject (including the full panoply of financial accounting), and the gross neglect to which most intangible assets have been subject. While plant, equipment, inventories, and financial assets have long been subject to careful scrutiny and detailed valuation, it is only recently that attempts have been made even to value brands and intellectual property (patents, copyrights, trademarks, and the like). Meanwhile, more intangible – yet even more critical – assets such as capabilities and corporate reputation have received very little systematic attention.

The field of knowledge management is vast. It could be argued that, since all management is involved with managing the knowledge embodied within human beings, machines, and business systems, knowledge management covers virtually the whole field of management. In this situation, the value of knowledge management is not merely a set of techniques for improving the efficiency with which knowledge is developed and exploited within the firm, it is also a perspective that can broaden our understanding of the firm and its management.

Given the scope of knowledge management and the vast range of tools, techniques, and frameworks that have been developed, where does a company begin to incorporate knowledge management within its management systems? The starting point, we suggest, is to identify the linkage between knowledge and the basis through which the firm creates value. This can then highlight the key processes through which knowledge is generated and applied. Consider the following examples:

- For Dow Chemical, the core of its value creation is in generating intellectual property – patents and trade secrets – in the form of new chemical products and processes, and exploiting them through worldwide manufacturing, marketing, and sales. Dow's "Intellectual Capital Management" places its central emphasis on the company's patent portfolio and links its intellectual property to a broad range of intellectual capital variables and processes and ultimately to the company's total value.[77]

- For McKinsey & Co., the key to competitive advantage and creating value for clients is to continually build on the knowledge it generates from client assignments, and to systematize and conceptualize that knowledge base. Building the knowledge base first requires a structure for allowing specialization. This was achieved through the creation of practices organized by industry group (e.g., consumer goods, financial institutions, energy, basic materials, government) and by function (e.g., strategy, organization, IT, operations). Second, it requires that knowledge generated from each project is captured, systematized, and made available for subsequent client projects.[78]

- For McDonald's restaurants, knowledge management is primarily concerned with implementing the McDonald's system. This is a detailed set of operating practices that extend from the company's values down to the placing of a pickle on the bun of a Big Mac and the procedure for servicing a McDonald's milkshake machine. The essence of the McDonald's system is the systematization of knowledge into a detailed set of rules that are followed in every McDonald's outlet. These explicit operating practices are internalized within employees' cognition and behavior through rigorous attention to training, both in formal training programs at Hamburger University, and in training at individual restaurants.

The design of every knowledge process must take account of the characteristics of the knowledge being deployed. The fundamental distinction here is between explicit and tacit knowledge. Take a simple example of the transfer of best practice between the different fabrication plants of a multinational semiconductor plant. If the knowledge is explicit, then such knowledge can be disseminated in the form of reports, or directives requiring every plant to adopt a new standard operating procedure. If the knowledge is tacit – it is the result of the experience or intuition of a single plant manager – the task is more difficult. Transferring the best practice is likely to require either visits by other plant managers to the innovating plant, or for the innovating plant manager to adopt a consulting role and visit other plants in the group for the purpose of teaching employees there.

It is in the area of managing tacit knowledge (which includes, typically, the major part of the knowledge relevant to organizational capability) where the major challenges and opportunities in knowledge management lie. Information technology has made huge strides in the storage, analysis, and systematization of explicit knowledge. However, the greater part of organizational learning is experience based and intuitive. Identifying this knowledge, and transferring it to other parts of the organization in order to utilize it more effectively, remains a fundamental management challenge.

NOTES

1 B. H. Liddell Hart, *Strategy* (New York: Praeger, 1954): 365.

2 The "resource-based view" is described in J. B. Barney, "Firm Resources and Sustained Competitive Advantage," *Journal of Management* 17 (1991): 99–120; J. Mahoney and J. R. Pandian, "The Resource-Based View within the Conversation of Strategic Management," *Strategic Management Journal* 13 (1992): 363–80; M. A. Peterlaf, "The Cornerstones of Competitive Advantage: A Resource-Based View," *Strategic Management Journal* 14 (1993): 179–92; David Collis and Cynthia Montgomery, "Competing on Resources: Strategy in the 1990s," *Harvard Business Review* (July–August 1995): 119–28.

3 J. B. Quinn emphasizes the need for companies to focus their strategies around the activities of their key internal strengths in *Intelligent Enterprise* (New York: Free Press, 1992).

4 Theodore Levitt, "Marketing Myopia," *Harvard Business Review* (July–August 1960): 24–47.

5 Robert M. Grant, "Diversification in Financial Services: Why Are the Benefits So Elusive?," in A. Campbell and K. Luchs (eds), *Strategic Synergy* (London: Heinemann, 1994).

6 "Olivetti: On the Ropes," *Economist* (May 20, 1995): 60–1; "Olivetti Reinvents Itself Once More," *Wall Street Journal* (February 22, 1999): A.1.

7 www.remington-products.com.

8 "Eastman Kodak: Meeting the Digital Challenge," in R. M. Grant and K. E. Neupert, *Cases in Contemporary Strategy Analysis* 3rd edn (Oxford, Blackwell, 2003).

9 M. Tripsas, "Unraveling the Process of Creative Destruction: Complementary Assets and Incumbent Survival in the Typesetter Industry," *Strategic Management Journal* 18, Summer Special Issue (1997): 119–42; J. Bower and C. M. Christensen, "Disruptive Technologies: Catching the Wave," *Harvard Business Review* (January–February 1995): 43–53.

10 See Table 4.1 in the previous chapter.

[11] For a discussion of different types and sources of profit, see Jeff W. Trailer, "On the Theory of Rent and the Mechanics of Profitability," working paper #00-1 (Pennsylvania State University, Erie, 2000).

[12] C. Fombrun, "The Value to be Found in Corporate Reputation," *Financial Times* Mastering Management Series, December 4, 2000: 8–10.

[13] www.harrisinteractive.com.

[14] Edward Lawler, "From Job-Based to Competency-Based Organizations," *Journal of Organizational Behavior* 15 (1994): 3–15.

[15] See Lyle Spencer, David McClelland, and S. Spencer, *Competency Assessment Methods: History and State of the Art* (Hay/McBer Research Group, 1994); Kathryn Cofsky, "Critical Keys to Competency-Based Pay," *Compensation and Benefits Review* (November–December 1993): 46–52; Lyle Spencer and Sigune Spencer, *Competence At Work: Models for Superior Performance* (New York, Wiley: 1993).

[16] D. Goleman, *Emotional Intelligence* (New York: Bantam, 1995).

[17] Jay Barney, "Organizational Culture: Can It Be a Source of Sustained Competitive Advantage?," *Academy of Management Review* 11 (1986): 656–65.

[18] While some attempts have been made to differentiate the two, Gary Hamel and C. K. Prahalad argue, in *Harvard Business Review* (May–June 1992): 164–5, that "the distinction between competencies and capabilities is purely semantic."

[19] P. Selznick, *Leadership in Administration: A Sociological Interpretation* (New York: Harper & Row, 1957).

[20] C. K. Prahalad and Gary Hamel, "The Core Competences of the Corporation," *Harvard Business Review* (May–June 1990): 79–91.

[21] Gary Hamel and C. K. Prahalad, letter, *Harvard Business Review* (May–June 1992): 164–5.

[22] Porter's value chain is the main framework of his *Competitive Advantage* (New York: Free Press, 1984). McKinsey & Company refers to the firm's value chain as its "business system." See: C. F. Bates, P. Chatterjee, F. W. Gluck, D. Gogel, and A. Puri, "The Business System: A New Tool for Strategy Formulation and Cost Analysis," in *McKinsey on Strategy* (Boston: McKinsey & Company, 2000).

[23] R. R. Nelson and S. G. Winter, *An Evolutionary Theory of Economic Change* (Cambridge, MA: Belknap, 1982).

[24] In the restaurant industry, specialists survived better than generalists except where the environment was highly variable, in which case generalists displayed greater adaptability (John Freeman and Michael Hannan, "Niche Width and the Dynamics of Organizational Populations," *American Journal of Sociology* 88, 1984: 1116–45).

[25] For an illuminating description of the integration of functional and technical capabilities to develop new automobiles, see K. B. Clark and T. Fujimoto, *Product Development Performance* (New York: Free Press, 1991).

[26] This concept of resources being specific to the firm is developed in Richard Caves' discussion of "specific assets" (see "International Corporations: The Industrial Economics of Foreign Investment," *Economica* 38, 1971: 1–27). This differs from Oliver Williamson's use of the same term, which refers to assets that are specific to a particular transaction, not a particular firm (see *The Economic Institutions of Capitalism*, New York: Free Press, 1985: 52–6).

[27] A. A. Alchian and H. Demsetz, "Production, Information Costs, and Economic Organization," *American Economic Review* 62 (1972): 777–95.

[28] G. Akerlof, "The Market for Lemons: Qualitative Uncertainty and the Market Mechanism," *Quarterly Journal of Economics* 84 (1970): 488–500.

[29] J. B. Barney, "Strategic Factor Markets: Expectations, Luck and Business Strategy," *Management Science* 32 (October 1986): 1231–41.

[30] Ingemar Dierickx and Karel Cool, "Asset Stock Accumulation and Sustainability of Competitive Advantage," *Management Science* 35 (1989): 1504–13.

31 "Court orders VW to stop recruiting Opel executives," *Financial Times* (April 3, 1993): 7.

32 Charles Ferguson, "International Competition, Strategic Behavior, and Government Policy in Information Technology Industries," Ph.D. thesis (MIT, 1987). For a critique, see George Gilder, "The Revitalization of Everything: The Law of the Microcosm," *Harvard Business Review* (March–April 1988): 49–61. For a rejoinder, see Charles Ferguson, "From the People Who Brought You Voodoo Economics," *Harvard Business Review* (May–June 1988).

33 Danny Miller, *The Icarus Paradox: How Exceptional Companies Bring About Their Own Downfall* (New York: HarperBusiness, 1990).

34 Robert M. Grant, "Business Strategy and Strategy Change in a Hostile Environment: Failure and Success Among British Cutlery Producers," in Andrew Pettigrew (ed.), *The Management of Strategic Change* (Oxford: Basil Blackwell, 1987).

35 Paul R. Lawrence and Davis Dyer, *Renewing American Industry* (New York: Free Press, 1983): 60–83.

36 www.mcdonalds.com.

37 Benchnet: The Benchmarking Exchange (http://66.124.245.130/).

38 S. Walleck, D. O'Halloran, and C. Leader, "Benchmarking World-Class Performance," *McKinsey Quarterly* 1 (1991).

39 Gary Hamel and C. K. Prahalad, *Competing for the Future* (Boston: Harvard Business School Press, 1994).

40 Sid Winter, "The Four Rs of Profitability: Rents, Resources, Routines, and Replication," in Cynthia Montgomery (ed.), *Resource-Based and Evolutionary Theories of the Firm* (Boston: Kluwer, 1995): 147–78.

41 Gabriel Szulanski and Sidney Winter, "Getting it Right the Second Time," *Harvard Business Review* (January 2002): 62–9. See also their "Replication as Strategy," *Organization Science* 12 (June 2001): 730–43.

42 Dorothy Leonard-Barton, "Core Capabilities and Core Rigidities," *Strategic Management Journal*, Summer Special Issue (1992): 111–26.

43 D. J. Teece, G. Pisano, and A. Shuen, "Dynamic Capabilities and Strategic Management," *Strategic Management Journal* 18 (1997): 509–33. The nature of dynamic capability is further explored in K. M. Eisenhardt and J. A. Martin, "Dynamic Capabilities: What Are They?," *Strategic Management Journal* 21 (2000): 1105–21 and Henk Volberda, *Building the Flexible Firm* (Oxford: Oxford University Press, 1998).

44 Henk Volberda argues that flexibility is feasible with appropriate management approaches (*Building the Flexible Firm*, Oxford: Oxford University Press, 1998). Martha Feldman and Brian Pentland offer a theory of organizational routines that is consistent with adaptation and variety of outcomes ("Reconceptualizing Organizational Routines as a Source of Flexibility and Change," *Administrative Science Quarterly* 48 (March 2003)).

45 A number of studies have explored the failure of established firms to survive radical innovation. See, for example, R. M. Henderson and K. B. Clark, "Architectural Innovation: The Reconfiguration of Existing Product Technologies and Failure of Established Firms," *Administrative Science Quarterly* 35 (1990): 9–30; Clay Christensen, "The Rigid Disk Drive Industry: A History of Commercial and Technological Turbulence," *Business History Review* 67 (1993): 531–88; M. Tripsas, "Unravelling the Process of Creative Destruction: Complementary Assets and Incumbent Survival in the Typesetter Industry," *Strategic Management Journal* 18 (Summer Special Issue, 1997): 119–42; A. Henderson, "Firm Strategy and Age Dependence: A Contingent View of the Liabilities of Newness, Adolescence and Obsolescence," *Administrative Science Quarterly* 44 (1999): 281–314; S. Karim and W. Mitchell, "Path-Dependent and Path-Breaking Change: Reconfiguring Business Resources Following Acquisitions in the US Medical Sector, 1978–1995,"

Strategic Management Journal 21 (2000): 1016–81.

46 "Merger Brief: The Digital Dilemma," *Economist* (July 22, 2000): 55–6.

47 "Merger Brief: The Daimler Chrysler Emulsion," *Economist* (July 29, 2000): 57–8.

48 See, for example, Marjorie Lyles, "Learning Among Joint-venture Sophisticated Firms," *Management International Review* 28, Special Issue (1988): 85–98; A. Mody, "Learning Through Alliances," *Journal of Economic Behavior and Organization* 20 (1993): 151–70; D. C. Mowery, J. E. Oxley, and B. S. Silverman, "Strategic Alliances and Interfirm Knowledge Transfer," *Strategic Management Journal* 17, Winter Special Issue (1996): 77–93; A. C. Inkpen and M. M. Crossan, "Believing Is Seeing: Joint Ventures and Organizational Learning," *Journal of Management Studies* 32 (1995): 595–618.

49 Joseph A. Badaracco, *The Knowledge Link: How Firms Compete Through Strategic Alliances* (Boston: Harvard Business School Press, 1991).

50 G. Hamel, "Competition for Competence and Inter-partner Learning within International Strategic Alliances," *Strategic Management Journal* 12, Summer Special Issue (1991): 83–103.

51 Tait Elder, "Lessons from Xerox and IBM," *Harvard Business Review* (July–August 1989): 66–71.

52 Kevin Coyne, Stephen Hall, and Patricia Clifford, "Is Your Core Competence a Mirage?," *McKinsey Quarterly* no. 1 (1997): 40–54.

53 Jack O'Toole, *Forming the Future: Lessons from the Saturn Corporation* (New York: Harper, 1996).

54 Connie E. Helfat and Ruth S. Raubitschek, "Product Sequencing: Co-evolution of Knowledge, Capabilities and Products," *Strategic Management Journal* 21 (2000): 961–79.

55 L. Kim, "Crisis Construction and Organizational Learning: Capability Building and Catching-up at Hyundai Motor," *Organizational Science* 9 (1998): 506–21.

56 Hiroyuki Itami, *Mobilizing Invisible Assets* (Boston: Harvard University Press, 1987): 125.

57 A. Takahashi, *What I Learned from Konosuke Matsushita* (Tokyo: Jitsugyo no Nihonsha, 1980); in Japanese, quoted by Itami, op. cit.: 25.

58 Gary Hamel and C. K. Prahalad, "Strategic Intent," *Harvard Business Review* (May–June, 1989): 45–52; Gary Hamel and C. K. Prahalad, "Strategy and Stretch and Leverage," *Harvard Business Review* (March–April, 1993): 53–62; Gary Hamel and C. K. Prahalad, *Competing for the Future* (Boston: Harvard Business School Press, 1994).

59 Michael E. Porter, "Toward a Dynamic Theory of Strategy," *Strategic Management Journal*, Winter Special Issue (1991): 111.

60 See, in particular, Sid Winter, "The Satisficing Principle in Capability Development," *Strategic Management Review* 21 (2000): 981–96; Giovanni Dagnino, "Bridging the Strategy Gap: Firm Strategy and Co-evolution of Capability Space and Opportunity Space," University of Catania Discussion Paper, 2002.

61 "Saatchi's 'Manager of Knowledge' Keeps Track of What's Trendy," *Wall Street Journal* (February 28, 1997): B.16.

62 Lucy Kellaway column, *Financial Times* (June 23, 1999): 13.

63 M. Hansen, N. Nohria, and T. Tierney, "What's Your Strategy for Managing Knowledge?," *Harvard Business Review* (March 1999): 106–16.

64 J.-C. Spender, "Limits to Learning from the West," *The International Executive* 34 (September/October 1992): 389–410; J. G. March, "Exploration and Exploitation in Organizational Learning," *Organization Science* 2 (1991): 71–87.

65 "Lessons Learned: Army Devises System to Decide What Does and What Does Not Work," *Wall Street Journal* (May 23, 1997): A1 and A10.

66 L. Edvinsson and S. Malone, *Intellectual Capital: Realizing Your Company's True Value by Finding its Hidden Brainpower* (New York: Harper Business, 1997);

D. Marchand and J. Roos, "Skandia AFS: Measuring and Visualizing Intellectual Capital," Case GM 624 (Lausanne: IMD, 1996).

67 "Cultivating Capabilities to Innovate: Booz-Allen & Hamilton," Case 9-698-027 (Boston: Harvard Business School, 1997).

68 "American Management Systems: The Knowledge Centers," Case 9-697-068 (Boston: Harvard Business School, 1997).

69 E. C. Wenger and W. M. Snyder, "Communities of Practice: The Organizational Frontier," *Harvard Business Review* (January–February 2000).

70 G. Szulanski, "Exploring Internal Stickiness: Impediments to the Transfer of Best Practices within the Firm," *Strategic Management Journal* 17, Winter Special Issue (1996): 27–44.

71 See, for example, K. B. Clark and T. Fujimoto, *Product Development Performance* (New York: Free Press, 1991); and K. Imai, I. Nonaka, and H. Takeuchi, "Managing the New Product Development Process: How Japanese Companies Learn and Unlearn," in K. Clark, R. Hayes, and C. Lorenz (eds), *The Uneasy Alliance* (Boston: Harvard Business School Press, 1985).

72 D. Leonard and S. Sensiper, "The Role of Tacit Knowledge in Group Innovation," *California Management Review* 40 (Spring 1998): 112–32; Dorothy Leonard, *The Wellsprings of Knowledge* (Boston: Harvard Business School Press, 1996).

73 Peter McNamara, "Managing the Tension Between Knowledge Exploration and Exploitation: The Case of UK Biotechnology," Ph.D. thesis (City University Business School, London, 2000).

74 I. Nonaka and H. Takeuchi, *The Knowledge-Creating Company* (Oxford: Oxford University Press, 1995).

75 See, for example, H. Demsetz, "The Theory of the Firm Revisited," in *The Nature of the Firm* (New York: Oxford University Press, 1991): 159–78; and R. M. Grant, "Toward a Knowledge-based Theory of the Firm," *Strategic Management Journal* 17, Winter Special Issue (1996): 109–22.

76 B. Kogut and U. Zander, "Knowledge of the Firm, Combinative Capabilities, and the Replication of Technology," *Organization Science* 3 (1992): 389.

77 G. Petrash, "Dow's Journey to a Knowledge Value Management Culture," *European Management Journal* 14 (August 1996): 365–73.

78 "McKinsey & Company: Managing Knowledge and Learning," Case Number 9-396-357 (Boston: Harvard Business School, 1996).

6

Organization Structure and Management Systems

Ultimately, there may be no long-term sustainable advantage other than the ability to organize and manage.

—*Jay Galbraith and Ed Lawler*

OUTLINE

INTRODUCTION AND OBJECTIVES

"Great strategy; lousy implementation," is an epithet applied to massive organizational failures from King Darius's defeat by the Athenians at the Battle of Marathon to Jean-Marie Messier's attempt to turn Vivendi into an international multimedia giant. The idea that the formulation of strategy can be separated from its implementation has become institutionalized by the numerous strategic management texts that devote separate sections to strategy formulation and strategy implementation.

This supposed division between formulation and implementation is fiction. At the most obvious level, formulating a strategy without taking into account the conditions under which it will be implemented will result in a poorly designed strategy. A fundamental flaw in the corporate planning systems of 25 years ago was separating strategy formulation – the task of corporate executives and strategic planners – from its implementation by divisional heads and middle managers. The adage "Structure follows Strategy" acknowledges this sequential approach to strategy making.

The comment, "Great strategy; lousy implementation," gives unjustified credit to the strategist. If the strategy has been designed without taking account of the organization's capacity for implementation, it's a lousy strategy. From an analytical perspective, the tools of strategy formulation draw heavily upon the principles of organization that are usually associated with "strategy implementation." For example, in the previous chapter we show how a firm's capabilities depend upon its organization – how individuals coordinate with one another. If capabilities are the primary basis of the firm's strategy, and if capabilities are a product of the structure that coordinates teams of resources to work together, then it might be argued that *strategy follows structure*. The key point, however, is not whether strategy or structure takes precedence, but the recognition that the two are closely interdependent.[1] Consider, for example, Benetton, with its closely coordinated network of local suppliers and worldwide network of franchised retailers; or General Electric, with its 17 business groups coordinated and controlled by its corporate headquarters; or Amway, with its pyramid of commission-based, independent distributors. These companies reinforce Tom Peters' dictum that "Strategy *is* Structure."

Having established that how companies organize themselves is fundamental to their strategy and their performance, the goal of this chapter is to introduce the key concepts and ideas necessary to understand and design companies' structures and systems. The approach is concise and selective. I do not intend to offer a potted overview of organizational theory. My aim is to introduce some basic principles of organizational design and to apply these to key aspects of firm structure. The principles outlined here will be further developed in later chapters when we consider strategies within particular business contexts. For example, Chapter 11 considers the organizational conditions conducive to innovation; Chapter 12 considers organization and organizational change within mature industries; Chapter 13 discusses vertical structures and outsourcing; Chapter 14 examines the structure and management systems of the multinational corporation; and Chapter 16 deals with organizing the multidivisional company.

By the time you have completed this chapter you will be able to:

- Recognize the key organizational innovations that have shaped the evolution of the modern corporation.

- Understand the basic principles that determine the structural characteristics of complex human organizations.

- Apply the principles of organizational design to recommend the types of organizational structure suited to particular tasks and particular business environments.

- Understand the role of information systems, strategic planning, financial control, and human resource management in the coordination and control of corporations.

- Appreciate the forces that are causing companies to seek new organizational structures and management systems.

THE EVOLUTION OF THE CORPORATION

Firms and Markets

Most of the world's production of goods and services is undertaken by corporations – enterprises with a legal identity that is distinct from the individuals that own the enterprise. The main exceptions include agriculture and crafts in the developing world, where family-based production predominates, and services such as defense, policing, and education that are usually provided by government organizations.

This has not always been so. Until the nineteenth century, the only large corporations were colonial trading companies such as the Dutch East India Company, Hudson's Bay Company, and the United Africa Company. As late as the 1840s, the largest enterprises in the US in terms of numbers of workers were agricultural plantations.[2] Most manufacturing was organized through networks of self-employed, home-based workers. The English woolen industry consisted of home-based spinners who purchased raw wool (on credit) from a merchant to whom they sold the yarn; the merchant resold the yarn to home-based weavers from whom he purchased cloth. This "putting-out" system survived until the introduction of powered looms, when weavers relocated to factories. With factory-based production it was more efficient for weavers to work as employees than independent contractors.

The shifting boundary between firms and markets is a central feature of economic organization. In the capitalist economy, production is organized in two ways: in *markets* – by the price mechanism – and in *firms* – by managerial direction. The relative roles of firms and markets are determined by efficiency: if the *administrative costs* of firms are less than the *transaction costs* of markets (as occurred in the English textile industry after the introduction of the factory system), transactions will tend to be organized within firms rather than across markets. We shall revisit the *transaction cost theory* when we consider vertical integration in Chapter 13.

Line and Staff Structure

Initially, most companies were small. Lack of transportation limited each firm's market to its immediate vicinity, while lack of communication prevented the firm from operating in multiple locations. The railroad and the telegraph changed all that. While new forms of transportation and communication created the opportunity for companies to grow, developments in organizational structure and management techniques gave firms the capacity to grow. The railroad companies themselves were the first to realize the potential of the new transportation and communications technologies to establish the first administrative hierarchies in American business using *line and staff* structures, with line operations organized around separate geographical divisions and head offices organized in functional staff departments.

The Multidivisional Corporation

This emergence of the modern corporation with multiple operating units and a head office organized by function was the first of the two "critical transformations" identified by Alfred Chandler.[3] The second was the emergence during the 1920s of the divisionalized corporation, which, over time, replaced both the centralized, functional structures that characterized most industrial corporations and the loosely knit, holding companies that had been created by the wave of mergers at the beginning of the twentieth century. The pioneers were Du Pont, which adopted a product division structure to replace its functional structure in 1920, and General Motors, which arrived at a similar structure but from a quite different starting point.

■ At Du Pont, increasing size and a widening product range strained the functional structure and top management became overloaded. As Alfred Chandler observed:

> . . . the operations of the enterprise became too complex and the problems of coordination, appraisal and policy formulation too intricate for a small number of top officers to handle both long-run, entrepreneurial and short-run, operational administrative activities.[4]

The solution devised by Pierre Du Pont was to decentralize: ten product divisions were created, each with their own sales, R&D and support activities. The corporate head office headed by an Executive Committee took responsibility for coordination, strategy, and resource allocation.[5]

■ General Motors, which had grown by acquisition into a loose holding company, adopted a similar structure as a solution to the problems of weak financial control and a confused product line. The new structure (shown in Figure 6.1) was based on two principles: the chief executive of each division was fully responsible for the operation and performance of that division, while

FIGURE 6.1 General Motors Corporation: organizational structure, 1921

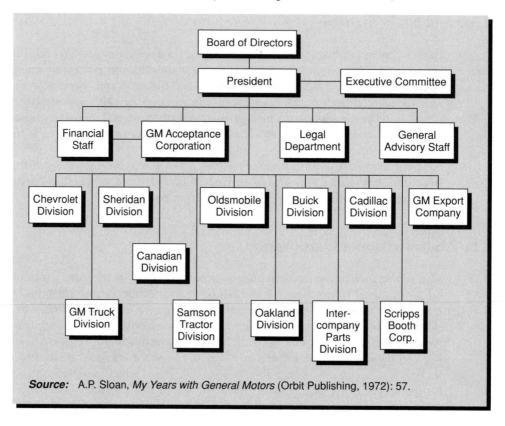

Source: A.P. Sloan, *My Years with General Motors* (Orbit Publishing, 1972): 57.

TABLE 6.1 The Evolution of the Modern Industrial Corporation

ENVIRONMENTAL INFLUENCES	STRATEGIC CHANGES	ORGANIZATIONAL CONSEQUENCES
Early nineteenth century Local markets. Transport and communication slow. Labor-intensive production.	Firms small, specialized, and focused on local market.	No complex administrative or accounting systems. No middle management.
Late nineteenth century Railroads, telegraph, and mechanization permit large-scale production and distribution.	Geographical expansion: national distribution, large-scale production. Broadening of product lines. Forward integration.	Emergence of functional organization structures with top management providing coordination. Development of accounting and control systems. Line and staff distinction.
Early twentieth century Excess capacity in distribution systems, increased availability of finance. Desire for growth.	Product diversification.	Increased difficulties of cross-functional coordination; top management overload. Functional structure replaced by multidivisional structure: operational management at the division level, strategic management at corporate head office.

the general office, headed by the president, was responsible for the development and control of the corporation as a whole, including:

- monitoring return on invested capital within the divisions;
- coordinating the divisions (including establishing terms for interdivisional transactions);
- establishing a product policy.[6]

The primary feature of the divisionalized corporation was the separation of operating responsibilities, which were vested in general managers at the divisional level, from strategic responsibilities, which were located at the head office. The divisionalized corporation reconciled central coordination with the efficiencies and responsiveness of operational decentralization.

Table 6.1 summarizes the principal developments in the evolution of the modern corporation during the past two centuries.

THE PRINCIPLES OF ORGANIZATIONAL DESIGN

According to Henry Mintzberg:

Every organized human activity – from making pots to placing a man on the moon – gives rise to two fundamental and opposing requirements: the division of labor into various tasks, and the coordination of these tasks to accomplish the activity. The structure of the organization can be defined simply as the ways in which labor is divided into distinct tasks and coordination is achieved among these tasks.[7]

We begin with these two fundamental organizational requirements: *division of labor* (or *specialization*) and *coordination*.

Specialization and Division of Labor

Firms exist because they are efficient institutions for the organization of economic activities, particularly the production of goods and services. The fundamental source of efficiency in production is *specialization*, especially the *division of labor* into separate tasks. The classic statement on the gains due to specialization is Adam Smith's description of pin manufacture:

> One man draws out the wire, another straightens it, a third cuts it, a fourth points it, a fifth grinds it at the top for receiving the head; to make the head requires two or three distinct operations; to put it on is a peculiar business, to whiten the pins is another; it is even a trade by itself to put them into the papers.[8]

Smith's pin makers produced about 4,800 pins per person each day. "But if they had all wrought separately and independently, and without any of them having been educated to this peculiar business, they certainly could not each have made 20, perhaps not one pin, in a day." Similarly, Henry Ford experienced huge productivity gains by installing moving assembly lines and assigning individuals to highly specific production tasks. Between the end of 1912 and early 1914, the time taken to assemble a Model T fell from 106 hours to just over six hours. More generally, the difference in human productivity between modern industrial society and primitive subsistence society is the result of the efficiency gains from individuals specializing.

But specialization comes at a cost. The more a production process is divided between different specialists, the greater are the costs of coordination. The more volatile and unstable the external environment, the greater the number of decisions that need to be made and the higher are coordination costs. Hence, the more stable is the environment, the greater is the optimal division of labor. This is true both for firms and for entire societies. Civilizations are built on increased division of labor, which is only possible through stability. As Bosnia, Liberia, and the Congo have demonstrated so tragically, once chaos reigns, societies regress toward subsistence mode where each family unit must be self-sufficient.

The Coordination Problem

No matter how great the specialist skills possessed by individuals, unless these individuals can coordinate their efforts, production doesn't happen. The current challenge for every coach of a national soccer team is how to coordinate the efforts of a group of talented individuals within a limited time before the next World Cup finals.

Conversely, the exceptional performance of organizations such as Wal-Mart, the Cirque du Soleil, and Lance Armstrong and his US Postal Service cycling team are primarily the result of superb coordination between organizational members. How do individuals within organizations coordinate their efforts? Let us look at the operation of four different coordination mechanisms:

- *Price.* In the market, coordination is achieved through the *price mechanism.* Price mechanisms also exist within firms. Different departments and divisions may trade on an arm's-length basis, where internal prices (*transfer prices*) are either negotiated or set by corporate headquarters.

- *Rules and directives.* The key feature of corporations and other formal organizations is the existence of employment contracts. Unlike self-employed workers, who negotiate market contracts for individual tasks, employees enter general employment contracts where (within certain limits) they agree to perform a range of duties as required by their employer. Authority is exercised by means of general rules ("Employees will report for work not later than 8.30 a.m.") and specific directives ("Miss Moneypenny, show Mr. Bond his new cigarette case with 3G digital communication and concealed death ray").

- *Mutual adjustment.* The simplest form of coordination involves the mutual adjustment of individuals engaged in related tasks. In soccer or doubles tennis, each player coordinates with fellow team members without any authoritative relationship among them. Such mutual adjustment occurs in leaderless teams and work groups.

- *Routines.* Where activities are performed recurrently, coordination based on mutual adjustment and rules becomes institutionalized within organizational routines. As we noted in the previous chapter, these "regular and predictable sequences of coordinated actions by individuals" are the foundation of organizational capability. If organizations are to perform complex activities at extreme levels of efficiency and reliability, coordination by rules, directives or mutual adjustment is not enough – coordination must become embedded in routines.

The relative roles of these different coordination devices depend on the types of activity being performed and the intensity of collaboration required. Price mechanisms work well in situations of "arm's-length" coordination. For example, in coordinating production and sales, it may be sufficient to offer sales personnel simple price incentives such as higher commission rates on those products where inventories are high. Rules tend to work well for activities where standardized outcomes are required and the decision-making abilities of the operatives involved may be limited – most quality control procedures involve the application of simple rules. Routines form the basis for coordination in most activities where close interdependence exists between individuals, whether a basic production task (supplying customers at Starbucks) or a more complex activity (performing a heart by-pass operation or implementing a systems integration project for a multinational corporation).

The Cooperation Problem: Incentives and Control

The discussion of coordination has dealt only with the technical problem of integrating the actions of different individuals. However, coordination problems are not entirely solved by implementing coordination mechanisms, there is also the problem of different organizational members having conflicting goals. This is referred to as the *cooperation problem*. Overcoming goal conflict requires creating incentives and controls.

The economics literature analyzes goal misalignment in terms of *agency problems*. An *agency relationship* exists when one party (the principal) contracts with another party (the agent) to act on behalf of the principal. The problem of such a relationship is ensuring that the agent acts in the principal's interest. Within the firm, attention has focused on the agency problem that exists between owners (shareholders) and professional managers. The problem of ensuring that managers operate companies to maximize shareholder wealth is at the center of the corporate governance debate. During the 1990s, changes in top management remuneration – in particular the increasing emphasis given to stock options – were intended to align the interests of managers with those of shareholders.[9] What became apparent in a series of corporate scandals that included Enron, WorldCom, Royal Ahold, and Parmalat is that CEO incentives encouraged them to manipulate reported earnings rather than to work for long-term profitability.[10]

Agency problems exist throughout the hierarchy. For individual employees, systems of incentives, monitoring, and appraisal are designed to encourage pursuit of organizational objectives and overcome employees' tendency either to do their own thing or simply to shirk. The organization structure and its related cultures may itself create problems. Either unintentionally or by design, organizational units create their own subgoals that do not align with one another. The classic conflicts are between different functions: sales wishes to please customers, production wishes to maximize output, R&D wants to introduce mind-blowing new products, while finance worries about profit and loss.

Several mechanisms are available to management for achieving goal alignment within organizations:

- *Control mechanisms* typically operate on the basis of managers supervising groups of subordinates. Managerial supervision involves monitoring behavior and performance, while subordinates are obliged to seek approval for actions that lie outside their area of authority. Such hierarchical supervision and control rests on both positive and negative incentives. Positive incentives are typically the reward of promotion up the hierarchy in return for compliance; negative incentives are dismissal and demotion for failing to acquiesce to rules and directives.

- *Financial incentives* are designed to reward performance. Such incentives extend from piece-rates for production workers to stock options and profit bonuses for executives. Such performance-related incentives have two main benefits: first, they are *high powered* – they relate rewards directly to output –

and second, they economize on the need for costly monitoring and supervision of employees. The problems of pay-for-performance arise where employees work in teams or on activities where output is difficult to measure. Linking pay to individual performance may discourage collaboration.

■ *Shared values.* Some organizations are able to achieve high levels of cooperation and low levels of goal conflict without extensive control mechanisms and without performance-related incentives. Churches, charities, choral groups, indeed most voluntary organizations fall into this category. The reason is the commonality of goals between organizational members. In a series of landmark studies from Peters and Waterman's *In Search of Excellence* to Collins and Porras's *Built to Last*, the presence of shared core values has distinguished companies that have been successful over the long term.[11] The role of culture as a control mechanism that is an alternative to bureaucratic control or the price mechanism is central to Bill Ouchi's concept of *clan control.*[12] The role of corporate culture in encouraging conformity to organizational goals has long been recognized among Japanese corporations. However, in western companies too – in Wal-Mart, Four Seasons Hotels, Amway, and the Shell Group – the presence of shared values and principles encourages the alignment of individual and corporate goals without necessarily undermining the individuality of organizational members. Such control saves on monitoring costs: self-control and informal monitoring by co-workers substitute for managerial supervision and financial incentives. Similar observations can be made about companies driven by a common technological vision. At Apple Computer in the 1980s, the belief that Apple was leading a computer revolution that would transform and democratize society permitted intense cooperation with very little formal control. As one cynic noted: "What's the difference between Apple and the Boy Scouts? In the Boy Scouts, the kids have adult supervision!"

We shall return to these issues of incentives and control when we consider the management systems of companies.

HIERARCHY IN ORGANIZATIONAL DESIGN

How have companies addressed these basic needs for specialization, coordination, and cooperation? The traditional approach to large-scale organization has been to create *hierarchy*. Despite the negative associations that currently attach to hierarchy, I shall argue that hierarchical structures are essential for creating efficient and flexible coordination in complex organizations. The critical issue is not whether or not to organize by hierarchy – there is little alternative – but how the hierarchy should be structured and how the different parts of it should relate to one another. Hierarchies come in many forms. Traditionally, hierarchy is associated with bureaucratic approaches to management control. However, hierarchical structures may also be organized along *organic* lines. The past decade has seen important changes in how companies structure and manage hierarchical structures.

Hierarchy as Coordination: Modularity

Hierarchy is fundamental to the structure of all organizations; indeed, according to Herbert Simon, hierarchy is present in virtually all complex systems. If a hierarchy is defined as a system composed of interrelated subsystems, examples of hierarchy include:

- The human body, which is composed of a hierarchy of cells, organs, and sub-systems such as the respiratory system, nervous system, digestive system, and so on.

- Physical systems are composed at the macro level of planets, stars, and galaxies, and at the micro level of subatomic particles, atoms, and molecules.

- Social systems consist of individuals, families, communities, tribes or socio-economic groups, and nations.

- A book consists of letters, words, sentences, paragraphs, and chapters.

Note that this is a broader concept of hierarchy than that encountered in most discussions of organization design, where hierarchy is identified with *administrative hierarchy*, in which organizational members are arranged in superior–subordinate relationships and authority flows downward from the top.

Viewed in this broad context of subsystems and component units, there are two key advantages to hierarchical structures:

1. *Economizing on coordination.* As we have noted, the gains from specializa-tion come at the cost of coordination. Suppose there are five programmers designing a piece of customized computer software. If they are structured as a "self-organized team," where coordination is by mutual adjustment (see Figure 6.2a), ten bilateral interactions must be managed. Alternatively, suppose

FIGURE 6.2   How hierarchy economizes on coordination

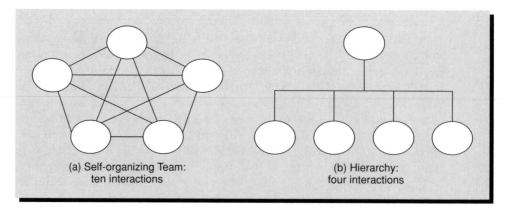

(a) Self-organizing Team:
ten interactions

(b) Hierarchy:
four interactions

the programmer with the biggest feet is selected to be supervisor. In this simple hierarchy (Figure 6.2b), there are only four relationships to be managed. Of course, this says nothing about the quality of the coordination: if the programmers' work is highly interdependent, hierarchical relationships may not allow for the richness of communication and collaboration that a team structure would permit. As an organization increases in size and complexity, so the communication-economizing benefits of hierarchically arranged modules increase:

> By breaking up a complex system into discrete pieces – which can then communicate with one another through standard interfaces within a standardized architecture – one can eliminate what would otherwise be an unmanageable spaghetti tangle of interconnections.[13]

2. *Adaptability*. Hierarchical, modular systems are able to evolve more rapidly than unitary systems that are not organized into subsystems. Such adaptability requires some degree of *decomposability*: the ability of each component subsystem to operate with some measure of independence from the other subsystems. Modular systems that allow significant independence for each module are referred to as *loosely coupled*.[14] In developing a new model of automobile, a modular structure permits different subassemblies (engine, brakes, steering, electricals, etc.) to be developed by separate teams that do not need constant communication and coordination with the designers of every other unit.[15] Once developed, defects can be corrected by replacing a single subunit – the engine, the gearbox, or the exhaust system – without having to scrap the entire car. Similar advantages exist for modular organizations. In a divisionalized firm, such as GE, decisions can be made in GE's jet engines business that do not require prior coordination with GE's other main business areas. Similarly, GE can acquire a new business (e.g. Vivendi-Universal entertainment) or dispose of an existing subsidiary (e.g., Genworth Financial, its life and mortgage insurance business) without requiring organizational changes throughout the company.[16]

The efficiency and flexibility advantages of modularity and hierarchical communication are evident in Nelson Mandela's restructuring of the ANC (see Strategy Capsule 6.1). Let's look more closely at administrative hierarchies associated with *bureaucratic* or *mechanistic* organizational forms.

Hierarchy as a Control: Bureaucracy

I have shown that hierarchy is an efficient solution to the problem of *coordination* in organizing complex tasks. To the extent that hierarchy is also a device for exercising control, it is also one solution to the problem of *cooperation* in organizations. The *administrative hierarchy*, in which power is located at the apex of the hierarchy and delegated downward, has been the basic design for large organizations since early

STRATEGY CAPSULE 6.1 Hierarchical Structures: The 1952 Mandela Plan for the ANC

Along with many others, I had become convinced that the government intended to declare the ANC (African National Congress) and the SAIC (South African Indian Congress) illegal organizations, just as it had done with the Communist Party. It seemed inevitable that the state would attempt to put us out of business as a legal organization. With this in mind, I approached the National Executive with the idea that we must come up with a contingency plan . . . They instructed me to draw up a plan that would enable the organization to operate from underground. This strategy came to be known as the Mandela-Plan, or simply, M-Plan.

The idea was to set up organizational machinery that would allow the ANC to take decisions at the highest level, which could then be swiftly transmitted to the organization as a whole without calling a meeting. In other words, it would allow the organization to continue to function and enable leaders who were banned to continue to lead. The M-Plan was designed to allow the organization to recruit new members, respond to local and national problems and maintain regular contact between the membership and the underground leadership.

I worked on it for a number of months and came up with a system that was broad enough to adapt itself to local conditions and not fetter individual initiative, but detailed enough to facilitate order. The smallest unit was the cell, which in urban townships consisted of roughly ten houses on a street. A cell steward would be in charge of each of these units. If a street had more than ten houses, a street steward would take charge and the cell stewards would report to him. A group of streets formed a zone directed by a chief steward, who was in turn responsible to the secretariat of the local branch of the ANC. The secretariat was a subcommittee of the branch executive, which reported to the provincial secretary. My notion was that every cell and street steward would know every person and family in his area, so that he would be trusted by his people and know whom to trust. The cell steward arranged meetings, organized political classes, and collected dues. He was the linchpin of the plan.

The plan was accepted and was implemented immediately. Word went out to the branches to begin to prepare for this covert restructuring . . . As part of the M-Plan, the ANC introduced an elementary course of political lectures for its members throughout the country. These lectures were meant not only to educate but to hold the organization together. They were given in secret by branch leaders. Those members in attendance would in turn give the same lectures to others in their homes and communities.

Source: Nelson Mandela, *Long Walk to Freedom* (London: Little, Brown, 1994): 134–5.

Chinese civilization. Administrative hierarchies operate as *bureaucracies.* According to Max Weber, writing at the end of the nineteenth century, bureaucracy is based upon the following principles:

1. *Specialization* through a "systematic division of labor" with clear job definitions and individual authority limited to the sphere of work responsibilities.

2. *Hierarchical structure* with "each lower office under the control and supervision of a higher one."

3. *Coordination and control* through rules and standard operating procedures.

4. *Standardized employment rules and norms.*

5. *Separation of management and ownership.*

6. *Separation of jobs and people*, where the organization is defined by positions and their associated responsibilities and authority, not by individuals; there is no ownership of the position by the individual.

7. *Rational-legal authority* based on "belief in the legality of enacted rules and the right of those elevated to authority under such rules to issue commands."

8. *Formalization* in writing of "administrative acts, decisions, and rules."[17]

The bureaucratic form of organization is highly formalized, eliminating most of the features that characterize human societies and human behavior: cooperation, innovation, personality, variation, and emotion. For this reason, Burns and Stalker describe bureaucratic organizations as *mechanistic*,[18] while Mintzberg calls them *machine bureaucracies*.[19]

Mechanistic and Organic Forms

For much of the twentieth century, the bureaucratic model dominated thinking about organizational structure. This was partly because of Weber's clear articulation of the principles of bureaucracy and partly because most large organizations – the military and civil service in particular – embodied these principles. However, as management thinking developed after the Second World War, interest grew in alternatives to bureaucracy.

During the 1950s and 1960s, the *human relations school* recognized that cooperation and coordination within organizations was about social relationships as well as bureaucratic principles. Empirical research among Scottish engineering companies by Burns and Stalker found that firms could be classified according to the extent that they relied upon bureaucracy or upon less formalized social interaction. They identified two organizational forms:

- *Mechanistic* forms that were characterized by bureaucracy, and

- *Organic* forms that were a less formalized organizational type where coordination relied upon mutual adjustment, jobs were less narrowly defined, and patterns of interaction were flexible and multidirectional.

Table 6.2 contrasts key characteristics of the two forms.

The relative merits of bureaucratic relative organic structures depend on the activities undertaken and the surrounding environment. Where an organization is supplying standardized goods or services (beverage cans, blood tests, or haircuts for army inductees) using well-understood processes, in an environment where change is slow and predictable, the bureaucratic model with its standard operating procedures and high levels of specialization offers substantial efficiency advantages. The problems occur when the bureaucratic model has to produce heterogeneous outputs from heterogeneous inputs, using poorly understood technologies, in an environment where change requires constant adjustment. Here, the bureaucracy fails because greater organizational flexibility is required.

TABLE 6.2 Mechanistic vs. Organic Organizational Forms

FEATURE	MECHANISTIC	ORGANIC
Task definition	Rigid and highly specialized	Flexible and less narrowly defined
Coordination and control	Rules and directives vertically imposed	Mutual adjustment, common culture
Communication	Vertical	Vertical and horizontal
Knowledge	Centralized	Dispersed
Commitment and loyalty	To immediate superior	To the organization and its goals
Environmental context	Stable with low technological uncertainty	Unstable with significant technological uncertainty and ambiguity

Source: Adapted from Richard Butler, *Designing Organizations: A Decision-Making Perspective* (London: Routledge, 1991): 76.

But even when faced with variability in the outside environment, firms may attempt to retain the advantages of bureaucracy by trying to control variation. McDonald's business system is highly mechanistic, relying heavily upon standardized, formalized working practices that are carefully documented in the company's operating procedures. Making this system work requires that McDonald's carefully controls its inputs to reduce variation: potatoes are carefully selected for size and shape, managers are carefully selected and trained, consumer tastes and expectations are carefully managed through advertising and promotion.

Within companies, the organization of different functions and departments depends upon these same variables. Stable, standardized activities such as payroll, treasury, taxation, customer support, and purchasing activities tend to operate well when organized along bureaucratic principles; research, new product development, marketing, and strategic planning require more organic modes of organization.

Rethinking Hierarchy

Hierarchical organizations add layers as they get bigger. Thus, with a fixed span of control of three, a firm with four employees (including the CEO) is organized into two layers, five to 13 employees requires three layers, from 14 to 41 employees requires four layers, and 42 to 122 employees requires five layers. (Sketch this for yourself.) If the hierarchy is run as a bureaucracy with centralized power, growth implies an increasing ratio of managers to operatives, slower decision making, and increased loss of control.[20]

In a stable environment with limited decision-making pressure on top management, such ponderousness is of little consequence. However, in a fast-paced business environment, the slow movement of information up the hierarchy and decisions down the hierarchy can be fatal. As business has become increasingly turbulent, so administrative hierarchy organized along bureaucratic principles have become increasingly unpopular.

However, the movement to reform and restructure corporate hierarchies does not amount to a rejection of hierarchy as an organizing principle. So long as there are benefits from the division of labor, hierarchy is inevitable.[21] The critical issue is to reorganize hierarchies in order to increase responsiveness to external change. The organizational changes that have occurred in giant corporations such as Unilever, British Petroleum, and General Electric have retained the basic multidivisional structures of the companies, but reduced the number of hierarchical layers, decentralized decision making, shrunk headquarters staffs, emphasized horizontal rather than vertical communication, and shifted the emphasis of control from *supervision* to *accountability*.[22]

While the dominant trend among large corporations has been towards increased decentralization, some companies appear to oscillate between phases of decentralization and centralization. Thus, British Petroleum engaged in radical decentralization during 1994–96, but by 2000–2002 was re-centralizing decision making and control. Nickerson and Zenger argue that this type of "structural modulation" in a company's formal structure is effective in achieving an optimal balance between centralization and decentralization within the organization.[23]

APPLYING THE PRINCIPLES OF ORGANIZATIONAL DESIGN

We have established that the fundamental problem of organization is reconciling specialization with coordination and cooperation. The basic solution to organizing complex organizations – whether they are business enterprises, religious orders, political associations, or criminal organizations – is hierarchy. The essence of hierarchy is creating specialized units coordinated and controlled by a superior unit. But this does not take us very far. On what basis should specialized units be defined? How should decision-making authority be allocated? And what kind of relationships should there be between different organizational units?

In this section, we will tackle the first two of these questions: the basis of grouping and the allocation of decision-making power. In the next section, we identify some typical organizational structures found in business enterprises. Then, in the following section we shall look at structuring relations between units – the operation and design of management systems.

Defining Organizational Units

In creating a hierarchical structure, on what basis are individuals assigned to organizational units within the firm? This issue is fundamental and complex. Multinational, multiproduct companies are continually grappling with the issue of whether they should be structured around product divisions, country subsidiaries, or functional departments, and periodically they undergo the disruption of changing from one to another. Some of the principal bases for grouping employees are common tasks, products, geography, and process:

- *Tasks.* Organizational units can be created around common tasks. This usually means grouping together employees who do the same job – thus, a firm might create a machine shop, a maintenance department, a secretarial pool, and a sales office.

- *Products.* Where a company offers multiple products, these can provide a basis for structure. Magazine publishing companies tend to be organized with a separate editorial group publishing each title. In a department store, departments are defined by products: kitchen goods, bedding, lingerie, and so on.

- *Geography.* Where a company serves multiple local markets, organizational units can be defined around these localities. Wal-Mart is organized by individual stores, groups of stores within an area, and groups of areas within a region. The Roman Catholic church is organized into parishes, dioceses, and archdioceses.

- *Process.* A process is a sequence of interlinked activities. An organization may be viewed as a set of processes: the product development process, the manufacturing process, the sales and distribution process, and so on. A process may correspond closely with an individual product, or a process may be dominated by a single task. Functional organizations tend to combine task-based and process-based grouping.

Organizing on the Basis of Coordination Intensity

On what basis should people be grouped into units within an organization? The fundamental issue is achieving the coordination necessary to integrate the efforts of different individuals. This implies grouping individuals according to the intensity of their coordination needs. Those individuals whose tasks require the most intensive coordination should work within the same organizational unit.

- In a geographically dispersed organization where communication across distance is difficult, the organization must be built upon local units. The ANC is an example (see Strategy Capsule 6.1).

- Where an organization is not particularly diversified in relation to products and does not need to be differentiated by location, but possesses strong functional specializations, then a grouping around functional tasks is appropriate. For example, British Airways is organized primarily around functions: flight operations, engineering, marketing, sales, customer service, human resources, information, and finance.

- Where a company is diversified over many products and these products are substantially different in terms of technology and markets, then organization around product groups will permit the most effective coordination. Virtually all diversified companies – General Electric, 3M, Sony, Siemens, and Unilever – are organized by product divisions.

The principle of organizing according to intensity of coordination requirements together with the principle of decentralizing through loose coupling is the basis for Oliver Williamson's concept of *hierarchical decomposition*. At the operating level (where decision making is high frequency), organization units are created where the interactions are strong. At the strategic level (where decision making is low frequency), a separate organization unit is created to exercise coordination and direction. Hence:

> The hierarchical decomposition principle can be stated as follows: Internal organization should be designated in such a way as to effect quasi-independence between the parts, the high frequency dynamics (operating activities) and low frequency dynamics (strategic planning) should be clearly distinguished, and incentives should be aligned within and between components so as to promote both local and global effectiveness.[24]

To organize according to coordination needs requires understanding the nature of interdependence within an organization. James Thompson distinguished three levels of interdependence: *pooled interdependence* (the loosest), where individuals operate independently but depend upon one another's performance; *sequential interdependence*, where the output of one individual is the input of the other; and *reciprocal interdependence* (the most intense), where individuals are mutually dependent. Thompson argued that organizational design needed to begin with creating organizational units where interdependence was the most intense.[25]

Changes in technology, strategy, and the environment result in changes in interdependencies that require companies to change the basis on which they define their structure. For example, as trade and communication between countries has become easier and consumer preferences between countries have become more homogeneous, multinational corporations have shifted from geographically based structures to worldwide product divisions.

Other Factors Influencing the Definition of Organizational Units

Coordination requirements are not the only consideration in deciding how to group together employees and activities within the firm. Additional factors that influence the efficiency of different organizational arrangements include:

■ *Economies of scale.* There may be advantages in grouping together activities where scale economies are present. Thus, it may be desirable to group together research activities even if there is little coordination among different research projects, simply to exploit scale economies in specialized facilities and technical personnel.

■ *Economies of utilization.* It may also be possible to exploit efficiencies from grouping together similar activities that result from fuller utilization of employees. Even though there may be little need for individual maintenance engineers to coordinate with one another, establishing a single maintenance department permits maintenance personnel to be utilized more fully than assigning a maintenance engineer to each manufacturing cell.

- *Learning.* If establishing competitive advantage requires building distinctive capabilities, firms must be structured to maximize learning. Typically, it was assumed that learning was best achieved by grouping together individuals doing similar jobs – creating a manufacturing engineering department, a quality control department, and a finance function. More recently, it has been observed that the specialized functional and discipline-based knowledge may be less important than *architectural knowledge* – knowing how to link together specialized knowledge from different fields. This implies the creation of multifunctional work groups comprising experts from different knowledge bases.

- *Standardization of control systems.* Tasks may be grouped together in order to achieve economies in standardized control mechanisms. An advantage of the typing pool and the sales department was that employees doing near-identical jobs could be subject to the same system of monitoring, performance measurement, training, and behavioral norms. In the Appendix to Chapter 5, we drew a distinction between knowledge-generating – or *exploration* – activities and knowledge-application – or *exploitation* – activities. Exploration activities are likely to require looser, more organic structures and systems, while exploitation activities are likely to require more mechanistic approaches. Reconciling such different management systems within the same company is easier if creative activities such as research and new product development are separate organizational units from the more routine activities such as manufacturing and accounting.[26]

ALTERNATIVE STRUCTURAL FORMS

On the basis of these alternative approaches to grouping tasks and activities, we can identify three basic organizational forms: the functional structure, the multidivisional structure, and the matrix structure.

The Functional Structure

Single-business firms tend to be organized along functional lines. Grouping together functionally similar tasks is conducive to exploiting scale economies, promoting learning and capability building, and deploying standardized control systems. Since cross-functional integration occurs at the top of the organization, functional structures are conducive to a high degree of centralized control by the CEO and top management team.

However, even for single-product firms, functional structures are subject to the problems of cooperation and coordination. Different functional departments develop their own goals, values, vocabularies, and behavioral norms which make cross-functional integration difficult. As the size of the firm increases, the pressure on top management to achieve effective integration increases. Because the different functions of the firm tend to be *tightly coupled* rather than *loosely coupled*, there is limited scope for decentralization. In particular, it is very difficult to operate individual functions as semi-autonomous profit centers.

The real problems arise when the firm grows its range of products and businesses. As we noted with Du Pont during the early twentieth century, once a company expands its product range, cross-functional coordination within each product area becomes critical. Thus, when IBM entered the personal computer business, it could not graft the new business onto its existing functional structure. To coordinate between designers, hardware engineers, software engineers, marketers, and others, IBM established its PC division as a standalone operation (see p. 168).

Although the long-term trend among very large companies has been for product-based, divisionalized companies to replace functionally organized companies, the trend is not entirely one way. As companies mature, the need for strong centralized control and effective functional coordination sometimes takes precedence over tight cross-functional integration at the product level. Apple Computer and General Motors are such examples.

- When John Scully became CEO of Apple in 1984, the company was organized by product groups: Apple II, Apple III, Lisa, and Macintosh. These product divisions achieved highly effective coordination among hardware engineers, software engineers, production managers, and marketing personnel. The problem was that there was little integration across products: each product was completely incompatible with the others, and the structure failed to exploit scale economies within functions. Scully's response was to reorganize Apple along functional lines in order to gain control, reduce costs, and achieve a more coherent product strategy.

- General Motors, pioneer of the multidivisional structure, has adopted a more functional structure. As its strategic priorities have shifted from differentiation and segmentation toward cost efficiency, it has maintained its brand names (Cadillac, Oldsmobile, Chevrolet, Buick), but merged the separate divisions into a more functionally-based structure to exploit scale economies and faster technical transfer (see Figure 6.3 and compare it with Figure 6.1).

The Multidivisional Structure

We have seen how the product-based, multidivisional structure emerged during the twentieth century in response to the coordination problems caused by diversification. The key advantage of divisionalized structures (whether product based or geographically based) is the potential for decentralized decision making. The multidivisional structure is the classic example of a loose-coupled, modular organization where business-level strategies and operating decisions can be made at the divisional level, while the corporate headquarters concentrates upon corporate planning, budgeting, and providing common services.

FIGURE 6.3 General Motors Corporation: organizational structure, 1997

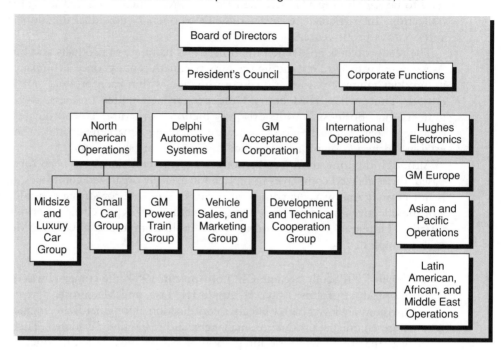

Central to the efficiency advantages of the multidivisional corporation is the ability to apply a common set of corporate management tools to a range of different businesses. At ITT, Harold Geneen's system of "managing by the numbers" allowed him to cope with over 50 divisional heads reporting directly to him. At British Petroleum, John Browne's system of "performance contracts" allows direct reporting by over 20 "strategic performance units." Divisional autonomy also fosters the development of top management leadership capability among business-level leaders – an important factor in CEO succession.

The large, divisionalized corporation is typically organized into three levels: the corporate center, the divisions, and individual business units, each representing a distinct business for which financial accounts can be drawn up and strategies formulated. Figure 6.4 shows General Electric's organizational structure at the corporate and divisional levels.

Some multidivisional companies are hybrids – some divisions are defined by products, others by geography. Figure 6.5 shows Mobil Corporation's divisional structure prior to its merger with Exxon. Some of Mobil's "business groups" were product based (e.g., Mobil Chemical Company; Supply, Trading and Transportation), some were defined by region (e.g., South America, Asia/Pacific); others combined the two (e.g., North American Exploration and Production). Other divisions were functionally defined (e.g., Mobil Technology Company).

In Chapter 16, we shall look in greater detail at the organization of the multibusiness corporation.

FIGURE 6.4 General Electric: organizational structure, 2002

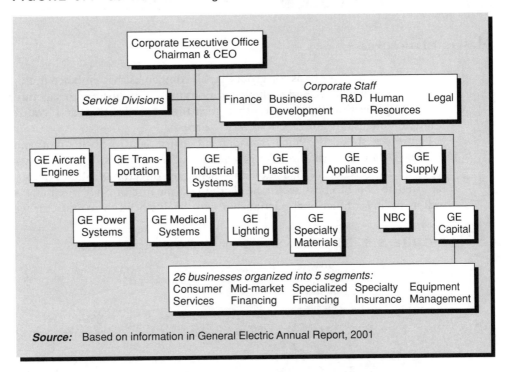

Source: Based on information in General Electric Annual Report, 2001

FIGURE 6.5 Mobil Corporation: organizational structure, 1998

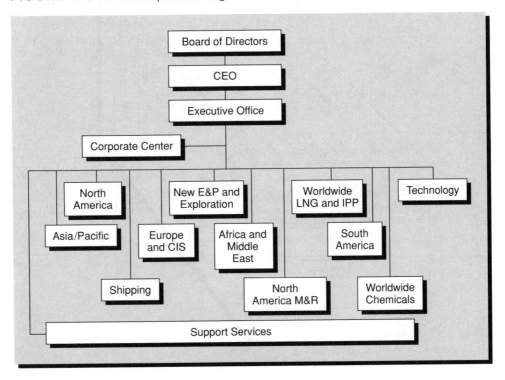

Matrix Structures

Whatever the primary basis for grouping, all companies that embrace multiple products, multiple functions, and multiple locations must coordinate across all three dimensions. Organizational structures that formalize coordination and control across multiple dimensions are called *matrix structures.*

Figure 6.6 shows the Shell management matrix (up to Shell's reorganization in 1996). Within this structure, the general manager of Shell's Berre refinery in France reported to his country manager, the managing director of Shell France, but also reported to the business sector head, the coordinator of Shell's refining sector, as well as having a functional relationship with Shell's head of manufacturing.

FIGURE 6.6 Royal Dutch/Shell Group: pre-1996 matrix structure

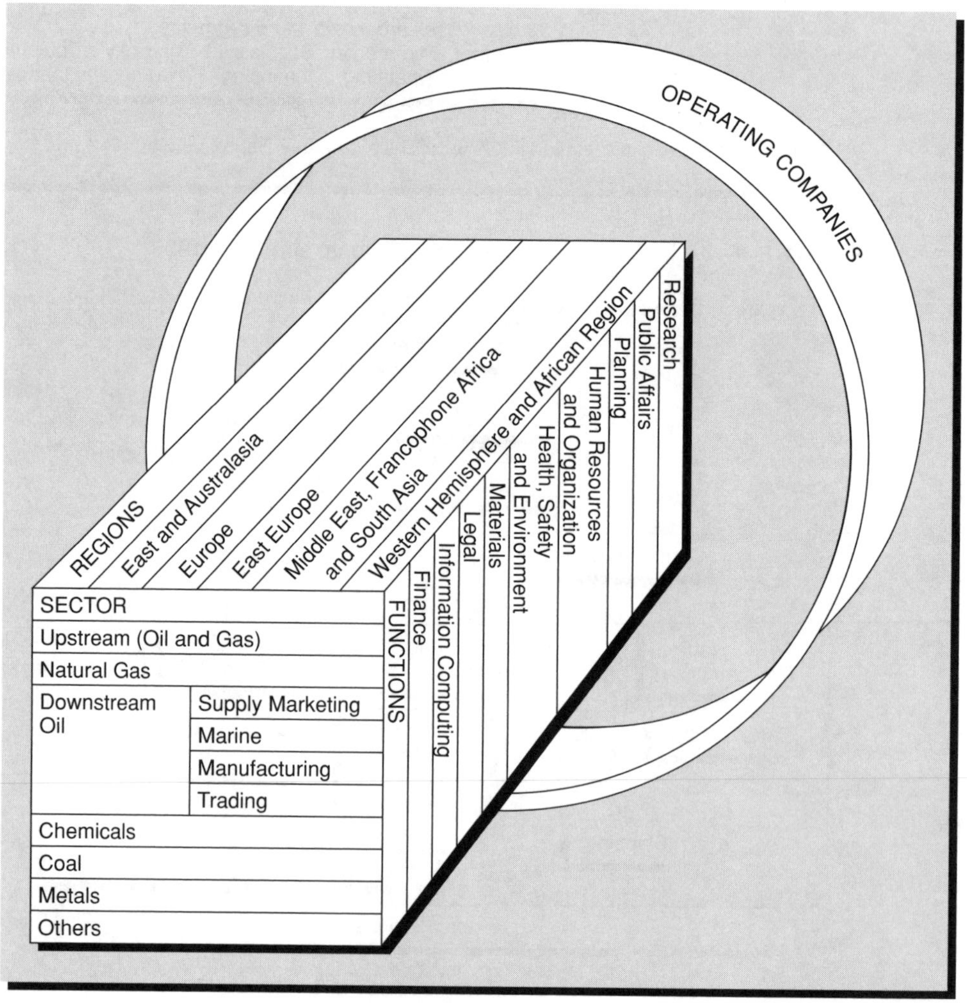

During the 1960s and 1970s, many companies adopted matrix structures as a means of reconciling the coordination needs of businesses, functions, and geographical areas. To achieve superior coordination, the matrix structure sacrifices *unity of command* – one of Henri Fayol's fundamental principles of effective management.[27] While diffusing coordination and control, in all matrix organizations one dimension tends to be dominant in terms of budgetary authority, personnel appraisal, and strategy formulation. In the Shell matrix the geographical dimension, as represented by country heads and regional coordinators, exerted primary authority.

In recent years, most large corporations have been dismantling or reorganizing their matrix structures. The problem of the matrix organization is not that it attempts to coordinate across multiple dimensions – in complex organizations such coordination is essential. The problem is that matrix structures overformalize such relationships, resulting in excessive corporate staffs and over-complex systems that slow decision making and dull entrepreneurial initiative. Shell abandoned its matrix in 1995–6 in favor of a structure based upon four business sectors: Exploration and Production, Oil Products, Chemicals, and Gas and Power. During 2001 and 2002, the Swiss-Swedish engineering giant ABB abandoned its much-lauded matrix structure in the face of plunging profitability and mounting debt. In both cases, the matrix structures were barriers to cost efficiency and central control. While all large, complex organizations need to coordinate within products, functions, and geographical areas, they do not necessarily need *formal* structures for this. The trend has been to focus formal systems of coordination and control on one dimension, then allow the other dimensions of coordination to be mainly informal.[28]

Nonhierarchical Coordination Structures

Recognition of the rigidities and costs associated with hierarchical, authority-based approaches to coordination has encouraged companies to experiment with alternatives to administrative hierarchies. A variety of organizational forms has appeared, including team-based organizations, project-based organizations, adhocracies, cluster designs, shamrock organizations, honeycomb organizations, inside-out doughnuts, and networks. Let's look at a few of these more closely.

■ *Team-based and project-based organizations.* Project-based organizations exist in sectors such as construction, consulting, and engineering services, where business activities take the form of specific projects of limited duration. Because every project is different, and every project goes through a changing sequence of activities, projects need to be undertaken by closely interacting teams, where each team exists only for the life of the project. Such teams have long existed in the construction industry, oil exploration, and other industries where the work forms highly differentiated projects of a limited duration. As technological and product life cycles shorten, so more and more businesses are becoming project-like in nature. In these environments, formality gives way to flexible coordination based upon routines, problem solving, and mutual adjustment.

■ *Adhocracies.* The flexibility, lack of formal structure, and reliance upon spontaneous coordination evident in team-based organizations, has encouraged Henry Mintzberg to describe these extremely organic organizational forms as *adhocracies*.[29] Adhocracies consist of experts who collaborate in nonroutine modes, typically in multifunctional project teams. Adhocracies tend to exist within knowledge-intensive activities such as new product development groups, research organizations, and consulting firms. Each specialist is valued for his or her expertise and there is little exercise of authority. Adhocracies work well with activities that involve problem solving and nonroutine operations.

■ *Self-organizing groups.* As management thinking has become more influenced by biology than by physics and engineering, so interest has grown in the self-organizing characteristics of biological organisms such as flocks of birds, beehives, and ants' nests. According to Stuart Kaufman, self-organization is a common feature of complex systems involving a haphazard quest for order in the face of potential chaos. Even before the influence of complexity theory on management,[30] some companies were experimenting with self-management. AES, the Virginia-based independent power producer, deployed a system of management it described as the "honeycomb." The principal elements of the honeycomb management philosophy are:
  – no employee handbooks, manuals, or rules (except safety);
  – no operating, maintenance, or technical departments;
  – no shift supervisors or maintenance supervisors;
  – no staff, except financial;
  – no "turf."[31]

■ *Virtual networks.* When horizontal coordination is supported by the tools of modern information and technological coordination, the question arises as to whether institutions such as firms with legal identities and employment contracts are really essential in order to manage productive tasks. In recent years there has been a growing interest in networks – both networks of firms (such as the small firm networks that comprise much of Italy's packaging and clothing industries), and networks of individuals.[32] Open source software communities such as those that have created the Linux operating system and Apache web server software are particularly interesting (and successful) examples of virtual networks. They involve thousands of volunteers spread throughout the world who collaborate electronically without employment contracts or financial reward.[33]

These different organizational forms share several common characteristics:

1. *A focus on coordination rather than control.* In contrast to the "command-and-control" hierarchy, these structures focus almost wholly upon achieving coordination. Financial incentives, culture, and social controls take the place of hierarchical control.

2. *Reliance on coordination by mutual adjustment.* Central to all nonhierarchical structures is their dependence on voluntaristic coordination through bilateral and multilateral adjustment. The capacity for coordination through mutual adjustment has been greatly enhanced by information technology.

3. *Individuals in multiple organizational roles.* Reconciling complex patterns of coordination with high levels of flexibility and responsiveness is difficult if job designs and organizational structures are rigidly defined. Adhocracies and team-based organizations feature individuals switching their organizational roles and occupying multiple roles simultaneously. For example, for most of the 1990s, AES had no finance function, no HR function, no safety or environmental affairs functions, and no public relations department. These functions were performed by teams of operatives and line managers.

MANAGEMENT SYSTEMS FOR COORDINATION AND CONTROL

The relationship between management systems and organizational structure is similar to that between the skeleton and bodily systems in the human body. The skeleton provides the framework; the respiratory system, digestive system, and nervous system are the means by which the body operates. Computer networks offer another analogy: the hardware provides the structure and the software provides the systems that make the network operational.

Management systems provide the mechanisms of communication, decision making, and control that allow companies to solve the problems of achieving both coordination and cooperation. Four management systems are of primary importance: the information systems, the strategic planning systems, the financial systems, and the human resource management systems.

Information Systems

Information is fundamental to the operation of all management systems. As the work of Chandler and other business historians has shown, the development of the telegraph, telephone, and computer had a huge impact on the practice of management and the size and structure of the firm. Accounting systems are key components of firms' information systems. They collect, organize, and communicate financial information to top management and other parts of the organization.

Administrative hierarchies are founded on vertical information flows: the upward flow of information to the manager and the downward flow of instructions. The trend towards decentralization and informality in organizations rests upon two key aspects of increased information availability: *information feedback* to the individual on job performance, which has made self-monitoring possible, and *information networking*, which has allowed individuals to coordinate their activities voluntarily without hierarchical supervision. A central element of total quality management has been recognition that regular, real-time, performance feedback to employees permits them to take responsibility for quality control, reducing or eliminating the need for supervisors and quality controllers. During the past decade, corporate intranets, web-based information systems, and groupware have transformed organizations' capacity for decentralized coordination.

Strategic Planning Systems

Small enterprises can operate successfully without an explicit strategy. The firm's strategy may exist only in the head of the founder and, unless the founder needs to write a business plan in order to attract outside financing, the strategy may never be articulated. Corporations with an established management structure tend to have some form of strategic planning process, though in single-business companies the strategy process may be informal and irregular. Larger companies, especially those with multiple businesses, have more systematic strategic planning processes, the outcome of which is a documented corporate plan that integrates the business plans of the individual divisions.

Whether formal or informal, systematic or ad hoc, documented or not, the strategy formulation process is an important vehicle for achieving coordination within a company. As discussed in Chapter 1, the strategy process occupies multiple roles within the firm. It is a process for improving decision making by encouraging systematic analysis and bringing together the knowledge from different parts of the company. It is a coordination device that ensures consistency between the decisions being made at different levels and in different parts of the organization. It is a way of stimulating performance though building commitment around vision, mission, and long-term targets.

The system through which strategy is formulated varies considerably from company to company. Even after the entrepreneurial startup has grown into a large company, strategy making may remain the preserve of the chief executive. Functional managers may provide key inputs such as financial projections and market analysis, but the key elements of strategy – goals, new business developments, capital investment, and key competitive initiatives – are often decided by the chief executive.[34] At MCI Communications during the 1980s, strategic planning was the responsibility of the chairman and CEO: "We do it strictly top-down at MCI."[35] The first director of strategic planning was warned: "If you ever write a strategic plan, you will be fired!"

The more systematized strategic planning processes typical of large companies with separate divisions or business units traditionally follow an annual cycle. Strategic plans tend to be for three to five years and combine top-down initiatives (indications of performance expectations and identification of key strategic initiatives) and bottom-up business plans (proposed strategies and financial forecasts for individual divisions and business units). After discussion between the corporate level and the individual businesses, the business plans are amended and agreed and integrated into an overall corporate plan that is presented to and agreed by the board of directors. Figure 6.7 shows a typical strategic planning cycle.

FIGURE 6.7 The generic strategic planning cycle

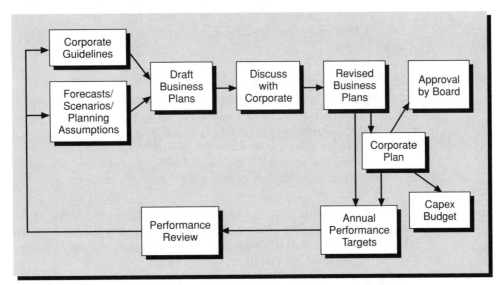

The resulting strategic plan typically comprises the following elements:

- *A statement of the goals* the company seeks to achieve over the planning period with regard to both financial targets (e.g., targets for revenue growth, cost reduction, operating profit, return on capital employed, return to shareholders) and strategic goals (e.g., market share, new products, overseas market penetration, and new business development). For example, the December 2000 strategy announcement by the Royal Dutch/Shell Group established an ROCE target of 15 percent and growth of hydrocarbon output of 5 percent a year.[36]

- *A set of assumptions or forecasts* about key developments in the external environment to which the company must respond. For example, Shell's plans formulated in 2000 were based on an assumed oil price of $14 a barrel (despite the fact that prevailing oil prices at the time were close to $30 a barrel).

- *A qualitative statement* of how the shape of the business will be changing in relation to geographical and segment emphasis, and the basis on which the company will be establishing and extending its competitive advantage. For example, Shell's 2000 strategy emphasized upstream investment and building on existing strengths in the Asia-Pacific region, especially in power, liquefied natural gas, and gas-to-liquids conversion.

- *Specific action steps* with regard to decisions and projects, supported by a set of mileposts stating what is to be achieved by specific dates. For example, Shell's strategy mileposts included reducing costs in chemicals by $650 million by the end of 2001, and introducing differentiated fuels in 40 countries by the same time.

- *A set of financial projections*, including a capital expenditure budget and outline operating budgets. For example, Shell's December 2000 strategy statement set a capital expenditure budget of $10–12 billion per year, a debt/equity ratio of 25 to 38 percent within five years, and cuts in annual operating costs of $5 billion.

Although directed toward making decisions that are documented in written strategic plans, the important elements of strategic planning are the *strategy process*: the dialog through which knowledge is shared and ideas communicated, the establishment of consensus, and the commitment to action and results.

Increasing turbulence in the business environment has caused strategic planning processes to become less formalized and more flexible. For example, among the world's largest petroleum majors, the key changes have been as follows:

- Strategic planning became more heavily focused on performance targets, especially on financial goals such as profitability and shareholder return. The result has been a shift of emphasis from longer-term strategic planning toward shorter-term financial planning.

- Companies recognized the impossibility of forecasting the future and based their strategies less on medium- and long-term economic and market forecasts of the future and more on more general issues of strategic direction (in the form of vision, mission, and strategic intent) and alternative views of the future (e.g., using scenario analysis).

- Strategic planning shifted from a *control perspective*, in which senior management used the strategic planning mechanisms as a means of controlling decisions and resource deployments by divisions and business units and departments, toward more of a *coordination perspective*, in which the strategy process emphasized dialog involving knowledge sharing and consensus building. As a result, the process became increasingly informal and put less emphasis on written documents.

- A diminishing role for strategic planning staff as responsibility for strategic decisions and the strategy-making process become located among senior managers.[37]

Financial Planning and Control Systems

Financial planning and control systems relate to budgeting activities and financial targets. If profitability is the primary goal of the firm, then financial systems are inevitably the primary mechanism through which top management seeks to control performance. At the center of financial planning is the *budgetary process*. This involves setting and monitoring financial estimates with regard to income and expenditure over a specified time period, both for the firm as a whole and for divisions and sub-units. Budgets play multiple, somewhat ambiguous roles. They are in part an estimate of incomes and expenditures for the future, in part a target of required financial performance in terms of revenues and profits, and in part a set of authorizations for expenditure up to specified budgetary limits. Two types of budget are set: the capital expenditure budget and the operating budget.

The Capital Expenditure Budget

Capital expenditure budgets are established through both top-down and bottom-up processes. From the top down, strategic plans establish annual capital expenditure budgets for the planning period both for the company as a whole and for individual divisions. From the bottom up, capital expenditures are determined by the approval of individual capital expenditure projects. Companies have standardized processes for evaluating and approving projects. Requests for funding are prepared according to a standardized methodology, typically based on a forecast of cash flows discounted at the relevant cost of capital (adjusted for project risk). The extent to which the project's returns are sensitive to key environmental uncertainties is also estimated. Capital expenditure approvals take place at different levels of a company according to their size. Projects up to $5 million might be approved by a business unit head, projects up to $25 million might be approved by divisional top management, larger projects might need to be approved by the top management committee, while the biggest projects require approval by the board of directors.

The Operating Budget

The *operating budget* is a pro forma profit and loss statement for the company as a whole and for individual divisions and business units for the upcoming year. It is usually divided into quarters and months to permit continual monitoring and the early identification of variances. The operating budget is part forecast and part target. It is set within the context of the performance targets established by the strategic plan. Thus, Shell's performance targets for 2003 and 2004 included an ROCE of 13 to 15 percent and a reduction in operating costs of $5 billion.[38] Each business typically prepares an operating budget for the following year that is then discussed with the top management committee and, if acceptable, approved. At the end of the financial year, business-level divisional managers are called upon to account for the performance over the past year.

Human Resource Management Systems

Ultimately, achieving coordination and cooperation within an organization is about managing people. Ultimately, strategic and financial plans are dependent upon influencing the ways in which people within the organization behave. To support strategic and financial plans, companies need systems for setting goals, creating incentives and monitoring performance at the level of the individual employee. The central role for human resource management is establishing an incentive system that supports the implementation of strategic plans and performance targets through aligning employee and company goals. The general problem, we have noted, is one of agency: How can a company induce employees to do what it wants?

The problem is exacerbated by the imprecision of employment contracts. Unlike most contracts, employment contracts are vague about employee performance expectations. The employer has the right to assign the employee to a particular category of tasks for a certain number of hours per week, but the amount of work to be performed and the quality of that work are unspecified. Employment contracts give the right to the employer to terminate the contract for unsatisfactory performance by the employee, but the threat of termination is an inadequate incentive: it imposes costs on the employer and only requires the employee to perform better than a new hire would. Moreover, the employer has imperfect information as to employees' work performance – in team production, individual output is not separately observable.[39]

The firm can ensure the employee's compliance with organizational goals using direct supervision of the type that administrative hierarchies are designed to do. The weaknesses of such administrative supervision are, first, there is little incentive for performance in excess of minimum requirements, second, supervision imposes costs, and third, the system presupposes that the supervisor has the knowledge required to direct the employee effectively.

The key to promoting more effective cooperation is for more sophisticated incentives than the threat of dismissal. The principal incentives available to the firm for promoting cooperation are compensation and promotion. The key to designing compensation systems is to link pay either to the inputs required for effective job performance (hours of work, punctuality, effort, numbers of customers visited) or to outputs. The simplest form of output-linked pay is piecework (paying for each unit of output produced) or commission (paying a percentage of the revenue generated).

Relating pay to individual performance is suitable for tasks performed individually. However, firms exist primarily to permit complex coordination among individuals; encouraging such collaboration requires linking pay to team or departmental performance. Where broad-based, enterprise-wide collaboration is required, there may be little alternative to linking pay to company performance through some form of profit sharing.

Corporate Culture as a Control Mechanism

We have already noted how shared values can align the goals of different stakeholders within the organization. More generally, we can view the culture of the organization as a mechanism for achieving coordination and control. *Corporate culture* comprises the beliefs, values, and behavioral norms of the company, which influence how employees think and behave.[40] It is manifest in symbols, ceremonies, social practices, rites, vocabulary, and dress. It is embedded within national cultures, and incorporates elements of social and professional cultures. As a result, a corporate culture may be far from homogeneous: very different cultures may be evident in the research lab, on the factory floor, and within the accounting department. To this extent, culture is not necessarily an integrating device – it can contribute to divisiveness.

Culture can play an important role in facilitating both cooperation and coordination. In large, decentralized corporations such as Royal Dutch/Shell, Accenture, and Matsushita, strong corporate cultures create a sense of identity among employees that facilitates communication and the building of organizational routines, even across national boundaries. The unifying influence of corporate culture is likely to be especially helpful in assisting coordination through mutual adjustment in large cross-functional teams of the type required for new product development. One of the advantages of culture as a coordinating device is that it permits substantial flexibility in the types of interactions it can support.

The extent to which corporate culture assists coordination depends on the characteristics of the culture. Salomon Brothers (now part of Citigroup) was renowned for its individualistic, internally competitive culture; this was effective in motivating drive and individual effort, but did little to facilitate cooperation. The British Broadcasting Corporation has a strong culture that reflects internal politicization, professional values, internal suspicion, and a dedication to the public good, but without a strong sense of customer focus.[41] However, culture is far from being a flexible management tool. Cultures take a long time to develop and cannot easily be changed. As the external environment changes, a highly effective culture may become dysfunctional. The Los Angeles Police Department's culture of professionalism and militarism, which made it one of the most admired and effective police forces in America, later contributed to problems of isolation and unresponsiveness to community needs.[42]

Integrating Different Control Mechanisms

The past ten years have seen substantial progress in integrating different control systems. As strategy has become more and more focused on creating shareholder value, so financial planning has become more closely integrated with strategic planning. Performance management systems have also done much to link strategic and financial planning with human resource management – especially in terms of goal setting and performance appraisal. The central aspect of the "metrics" movement within management is the ability not just to establish quantitative goals for individual employees and groups, but to create mechanisms for measuring and reporting the attainment of these targets. The balanced scorecard system outlined in Chapter 2 is but one approach to this linking of employee goals to company-wide goals.

SUMMARY

The internal structure and systems of the firm are not simply a matter of "strategy implementation," which can be separated from the hard analytics of strategy formulation. Not only is strategy implementation inseparable from strategy formulation, but issues of structure and systems are central to the fundamental issues of competitive advantage and strategy choice – the existence of organizational capability in particular.

Despite the importance of these issues, this chapter provides only a brief introduction to some of the key issues in organization design. Subsequent chapters develop many of the themes more fully in relation to particular areas of strategy and particular business contexts. Nevertheless, our progress is limited by the weakness of theory in this area. Organization theory is an exceptionally rich field that still lacks adequate integration of its component disciplines: sociology, psychology, organizational economics, systems theory, population ecology, and organizational evolution. While business enterprises continue to experiment with new organizational forms, we business school academics are still struggling to articulate general principles of organizational design.

The chapters that follow will have more to say on the organizational structures and management systems appropriate to different strategies and different business contexts. In the final chapter (Chapter 17) we shall explore some of the new trends and new ideas that are reshaping our thinking about organizational design.

Notes

1 The complementarity of strategy, structure, and management systems is emphasized in R. Whittington, A. Pettigrew, S. Peck, E. Fenton, and M. Conyon, "Change and Complementarities in the New Competitive Landscape," *Organization Science* 10 (1999): 583–96.

2 Alfred D. Chandler, *The Visible Hand: The Managerial Revolution in American Business* (Cambridge, MA: MIT Press, 1977): Chapter 2.

3 Alfred D. Chandler, *Strategy and Structure* (Cambridge: MIT Press, 1962); Chandler, *The Visible Hand*, op. cit.

4 Chandler, *Strategy and Structure*, op. cit.: 382–3.

5 http://heritage.dupont.com/floater/fl_management/floater.shtml.

6 Alfred P. Sloan, *My Years at General Motors* (London: Sidgwick & Jackson, 1963): 42–56.

7 Henry Mintzberg, *Structure in Fives: Designing Effective Organizations* (Englewood Cliffs: Prentice-Hall, 1993): 2.

8 Adam Smith, *The Wealth of Nations* (London: Dent, 1910): 5.

9 *Long Range Planning* (Special Issue on Corporate Governance, 2000).

10 "What's Wrong with Executive Compensation": A Roundtable Moderated by Charles Elson, *Harvard Business Review* (January 2003): 5–12.

11 T. Peters and R. Waterman, *In Search of Excellence* (New York: Harper & Row, 1982); James Collins and Jerry Porras, *Built to Last: Successful Habits of Visionary Companies* (New York: Harper Business, 1997).

12 William G. Ouchi, *Theory Z* (Reading, MA: Addison-Wesley, 1981).

13 R. N. Langlois, "Modularity in Technology and Organization," *Journal of Economic Behavior and Organization* 49 (September 2002): 19–37

14 J. D. Orton and K. E. Weick, "Loosely Coupled Systems: A Reconceptualization," *Academy of Management Review* 15 (1990): 203–23.

15 M. Sako and F. Murray, "Modular Strategies in Car and Computers," *Financial Times*, Mastering Strategy Part 11 (December 6, 1999): 4–7.

[16] Modularity in organizations is explored in a number of articles. See R. Sanchez and J. T. Mahoney, "Modularity, Flexibility, and Knowledge Management in Product and Organizational Design," *Strategic Management Journal* 17, Winter Special Issue (1996): 63–76; M. A. Schilling, "Toward a General Modular Systems Theory and its Application to Interfirm Product Modularity," *Academy of Management Review* 25 (2000): 312–34; C. Baldwin and K. Clark, "Managing in an Age of Modularity," *Harvard Business Review* (September–October 1997): 84–93.

[17] The quotes in this section are from Max Weber, *Economy and Society: An Outline of Interpretive Sociology* (Berkeley: University of California Press, 1968).

[18] T. Burns and G. M. Stalker, *The Management of Innovation* (London: Tavistock Institute, 1961).

[19] Henry Mintzberg, op. cit.: Chapter 9.

[20] The control loss phenomenon in hierarchies is analyzed in O. E. Williamson, "Hierarchical Control and Optimal Firm Size," *Journal of Political Economy* 75 (1967): 123–38.

[21] H. J. Leavitt, "Why Hierarchies Thrive," *Harvard Business Review* (March 2003): 97–102.

[22] R. Whittington and A. Pettigrew, "New Notions of Organizational Fit," *Financial Times*, Mastering Strategy Part 10 (November 29, 1999): 8–10.

[23] J. Nickerson and T. Zenger, "Being Efficiently Fickle: A Dynamic Theory of Organizational Choice," *Organization Science* 13 (September–October 2002): 547–67.

[24] O. E. Williamson, "The Modern Corporation: Origins, Evolution, Attributes," *Journal of Economic Literature* 19 (1981): 1537–68.

[25] J. D. Thompson, *Organizations in Action* (New York: McGraw-Hill, 1967). The nature of interdependence in organizational processes is revisited in T. W. Malone, K. Crowston, J. Lee, and B. Pentland, "Tools for Inventing Organizations: Toward a Handbook of Organizational Processes," *Management Science* 45 (March 1999): 489–504.

[26] The need for organizations to differentiate management and organization between different functional departments and product units is discussed in P. R. Lawrence and J. W. Lorsch, *Organization and Environment* (Boston: Harvard Business School Press, 1986).

[27] Henri Fayol, *General and Industrial Management* (London: Pitman, 1949, first published 1916).

[28] C. A. Bartlett and S. Ghoshal, "Matrix Management: Not a Structure, a Frame of Mind," *Harvard Business Review* (July–August 1990): 138–45.

[29] Henry Mintzberg, op. cit.: Chapter 12.

[30] S. Kaufman, *At Home in the Universe* (New York: Oxford University Press, 1996); P. Anderson, "Complexity Theory and Organization Science," *Organization Science* 10 (1999): 216–32.

[31] "AES Honeycomb (A)," Case 9-395-132 (Boston: Harvard Business School, 1995): 9.

[32] United Nations Industrial Development Organization, *The Italian Experience of Industrial Districts* (http://www.unido.org/en/doc/4310); Alessandro Lomi and Alessandro Grandi, "The Network Structure of Interfirm Relationships in the Southern Italian Mechanical Industry," in Mark Ebers (ed.), *The Formation of Inter-Organizational Networks* (Oxford: OUP, 1999).

[33] K. Crowston and B. Scozzi, "Open Source Software Projects as Virtual Organizations," *IEE Proceedings Software*, vol. 149 (2002): 3–17.

[34] William C. Finnie, *Hands-On Strategy: The Guide to Crafting Your Company's Strategy* (New York: John Wiley, 1994).

[35] Quote by CEO, Orville Wright in 1989. See "MCI Communications: Planning for the 1990s," Case 9-190-136 (Boston: Harvard Business School, 1990): 1.

[36] Information on Royal Dutch/Shell Group is from December 18, 2000 strategy presentation. See www.shell.com.

[37] R. M. Grant, "Strategic Planning in a Turbulent Environment: Evidence from the Oil Majors," *Strategic Management Journal* 24 (2003): 491–518. Similar findings have been reported by the American Productivity and Quality Center among "best practice companies" (*Strategic Planning: Final Report*, Houston: APQC, 1996).

[38] Royal Dutch/Shell Group of Companies, *2002 4th Quarter Results & Strategy Update Presentation* (February 6, 2003).

[39] A. Alchian and H. Demsetz, "Production, Information Costs, and Economic Organization," *American Economic Review* 62 (1972): 777–97.

[40] E. H. Schein, "Organizational Culture," *American Psychologist* 45 (1990): 109–19.

[41] Tom Burns, *The BBC: Public Institution and Private World* (London: Macmillan, 1977).

[42] "LAPD: Storming the Rampart," *Economist* (December 2, 2000): 72.

III

The Analysis of Competitive Advantage

7

The Nature and Sources of Competitive Advantage

One Saturday afternoon in downtown Chicago, Milton Friedman, the famous free-market economist, was shopping with his wife.

"Look, Milton!" exclaimed Mrs. Friedman. "There's a $20 bill on the sidewalk!"

"Don't be foolish, my dear," replied the Nobel laureate. "If that was a $20 bill, someone would have picked it up by now."

—economist's anecdote of doubtful authenticity

OUTLINE

INTRODUCTION AND OBJECTIVES

In this chapter, we draw together the different elements of competitive advantage that we have analyzed in prior chapters. Chapter 1 noted that a firm can earn a rate of profit in excess of its cost of capital either by locating in an attractive industry or by establishing a competitive advantage over its rivals. Of these two sources of superior profitability, competitive advantage is the more important. As competition has intensified across almost all industries, very few industry environments can guarantee secure returns; hence, the primary goal of a strategy is to establish a position of competitive advantage for the firm. Kenichi Ohmae goes as far as to define strategy as the quest for competitive advantage (see Table 1.1).

Chapters 3 and 5 provided the two primary components of our analysis of competitive advantage. The last part of Chapter 3 analyzed the external sources of competitive advantage: key success factors are the general requirements for satisfying customer needs and surviving competition within a market. Chapter 5 analyzed the internal sources of competitive advantage: the potential offered by the firm's resources and capabilities for establishing and sustaining competitive advantage.

This chapter looks more deeply at competitive advantage. We focus on the relationship between competitive advantage and the competitive process. Competition provides the incentive for establishing advantage and is the means by which advantage is eroded. Only by understanding the characteristics of competition in a market can we identify the opportunities for competitive advantage.

By the time you have completed this chapter you will be able to:

■ Identify the circumstances in which a firm can create a competitive advantage over a rival.

■ Understand how responsiveness and innovation can create competitive advantage.

■ Predict the potential for competition to erode competitive advantage through imitation.

- ■ Recognize the role of resource conditions in creating imperfections in the competitive process and, therefore, opportunities for competitive advantage.

- ■ Distinguish the two primary types of competitive advantage: cost advantage and differentiation advantage.

- ■ Apply this analysis to assess the potential for a business strategy to establish and sustain competitive advantage given the characteristics of the industry setting.

THE EMERGENCE OF COMPETITIVE ADVANTAGE

To understand how competitive advantage emerges, we must first understand what competitive advantage is. Most of us can recognize competitive advantage when we see it: Dell Computer has a competitive advantage in the supply of personal computers, Wal-Mart has a competitive advantage in discount retailing, Toyota has a competitive advantage in making cars. Defining competitive advantage is troublesome. At a basic level we can define it as follows:

> When two or more firms compete within the same market, one firm possesses a competitive advantage over its rivals when it earns (or has the potential to earn) a persistently higher rate of profit.

The problem here is that, if we identify competitive advantage with superior profitability, why do we need the concept of competitive advantage at all? The key difference is that competitive advantage may not be revealed in higher profitability – a firm may forgo current profit in favor of investment in market share, technology, customer loyalty, or executive perks.[1]

External Sources of Change

Differences in profitability between competing firms are a disequilibrium phenomenon – hence, competitive advantage emerges when change occurs. The source of the change may be external or internal to the industry: Figure 7.1 illustrates several sources. For an external change to create competitive advantage, the change must have differential effects on companies because of their different resources and capabilities or strategic positioning. For example, during 1996–8, Chrysler was the most profitable of the world's major car companies, primarily a result of its successful minivan and Jeep models. However, between the latter half of 2000 and the end of 2002 Chrysler (now a division of DaimlerChrysler) racked up losses of $4 billion – the result of slumping margins on minivans and SUVs, the strength of the US dollar, and the tripling of oil prices. Conversely, these same factors tended to strengthen competitiveness and profitability at Renault and Peugeot.

FIGURE 7.1 The emergence of competitive advantage

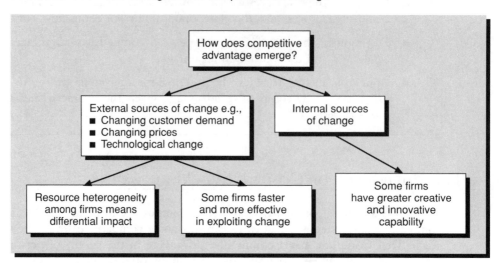

The extent to which external change creates competitive advantage and disadvantage depends on the magnitude of the change and the extent of firms' strategic differences. The more turbulent an industry's environment, the greater the number of sources of change, and the greater the differences in firms' resources and capabilities, the greater the dispersion of profitability within the industry. In the world tobacco industry, the external environment is comparatively stable and the leading firms pursue similar strategies with similar resources and capabilities. The result is that competitive advantages, as reflected in inter-firm profit differentials, tend to be small. The toy industry, on the other hand, experiences rapid and unpredictable changes in demand, technology, and fashion. The leading companies pursue different strategies and have different resources and capabilities. As a result, profitability differences are wide and variable over time.

Competitive Advantage from Responsiveness to Change

The impact of external change on competitive advantage also depends upon firms' ability to respond to change. Any external change creates opportunities for profit. The ability to identify and respond to opportunity lies in the core management capability that we call *entrepreneurship*.[2] To the extent that external opportunities are fleeting or subject to first-mover advantage, speed of response is critical to exploiting business opportunity. An unexpected rain shower creates an upsurge in the demand for umbrellas. Those street vendors who are quickest to position themselves outside a busy railroad station will benefit most.

As markets become increasingly turbulent, so responsiveness to external change has become increasingly important as a source of competitive advantage.

■ Wal-Mart's ability consistently to outperform Kmart and other discount retailers is based on a business system that responds quickly and effectively to changes in demand. Wal-Mart's distribution and purchasing are driven by point-of-sale data resulting in low inventories, few stockouts, and few forced markdowns. However, at the heart of Wal-Mart's fast-response capability is the encouragement and rewarding of initiative at all levels of the company.[3]

■ The highly successful textile industry of the Prato region of northern Italy is based on a business model pioneered by Massimo Menichetti in the early 1970s. The Prato model of small, specialized textile and clothing companies competing and cooperating through highly flexible, closely integrated networks is uniquely suited to the fast-paced business environment of fashion clothing.[4]

Responsiveness also involves anticipating changes in the basis of competitive advantage. As an industry moves through its life cycle, as customer requirements change, and as patterns of competition shift, so companies must adjust their strategies and their capabilities to take account of shifting key success factors. Monsanto showed considerable foresight in building its competitive position to outlive the expiration in 1992 of its patents on its artificial sweetener, NutraSweet. In addition to heavy promotion of the NutraSweet brand name and its "swirl" logo, Monsanto invested in scale-efficient production facilities, signed long-term exclusive supply contracts with key customers (such as Coca-Cola), and used trade secrets to protect its production know-how.[5]

Responsiveness to the opportunities provided by external change requires one key resource – information – and one key capability – flexibility. Information is necessary to identify and anticipate external changes. This requires environmental scanning. As the pace of change has accelerated, firms are less dependent on conventional analysis of economic and market research data and more dependent on "early warning systems" through direct relationships with customers, suppliers, and competitors. The faster a company can respond in real time to changing market circumstances, the less it needs to forecast the future. Short cycle times are a key requirement for fast response capability:

■ Dell Computer is a master of speed and agility. A custom order placed at 9 a.m. on Monday can be on a delivery truck by 9 p.m. Tuesday. This permits Dell to customize each computer to the customer's specifications and to operate with under 10 days' inventory, which not only cuts costs but permits Dell to adjust rapidly to fluctuations in market demand and upgrade its products by quickly taking advantage of technical advances in components. Dell's tightly coordinated supply chain allows some components and accessories to be shipped directly to the customer without being touched by Dell – UPS collects computers from Dell's Austin plant and monitors from Sony's plant in Mexico, matches them and delivers both simultaneously to the customer.[6]

■ The Zara chain of retail clothing stores owned by the Spanish company, Inditex, has a tightly integrated vertical structure that cuts the time between a garment's design and retail delivery to under three weeks – the industry

TABLE 7.1 New Product Development Performance by US, Japanese, and European Auto Producers

	JAPANESE VOLUME PRODUCER	US VOLUME PRODUCER	EUROPEAN VOLUME PRODUCER	EUROPEAN HIGH-END SPECIALIST
Average lead time (months)	42.6	61.9	57.6	71.5
Engineering hours (in millions)	1.2	3.5	3.4	3.4
Total product quality index	58	41	41	84

Source: Kim B. Clark and Takahiro Fujimoto, *Product Development Performance* (Boston: Harvard Business School Press, 1991): 73.

norm is six to nine months. This allows Zara to identify emerging fashion trends and launch new styles on the market far quicker than its mass-market competitors.[7]

The central role of speed in competitive advantage has been recognized for well over a decade. In 1988, George Stalk of the Boston Consulting Group argued that speed through time-based manufacturing, time-based sales and distribution, and time-based innovation is the primary competitive advantage of many leading-edge Japanese companies.[8] The premise that speed is the only real source of advantage in today's economy was the primary rationale behind the founding of *Fast Company* magazine in 1995. In automobiles, speed of new product development is a major advantage of Japanese companies (see Table 7.1). However, only with the advent of the internet, real-time electronic data exchange, and business process reengineering have companies been able to reduce cycle times drastically through radical changes in operations, strategy, and organization.

Competitive Advantage from Innovation: "New Game" Strategies

The changes that create competitive advantage may be internal as well as external. Internal change is generated by innovation. Innovation not only creates competitive advantage, it provides a basis for overturning the competitive advantage of other firms. Schumpeter's view of the competitive process as "a gale of creative destruction" involved market leadership being eroded not by imitation but by innovation. Innovation is typically thought of in its technical sense: the new products or processes that embody new ideas and new knowledge. In a business, however, innovation includes new approaches to doing business – *strategic innovation*. Strategic innovations (including the development of new business concepts) tend to be more important than product innovations in generating outstanding business performance (see Strategy Capsule 7.1).

What is the nature of these innovatory business concepts? Some involve creating value for customers from novel experiences, products, or product delivery or bund-

STRATEGY CAPSULE 7.1   Gary Hamel on the Quest for New
Business Models

In *Leading the Revolution*, Gary Hamel, chairman of the consulting firm Strategos and visiting professor at London Business School, argues that the age of continuity is over and we have now entered the age of revolution where the value of incumbency is being eroded and those companies that embrace discontinuous change will be the winners. The revolutionaries will win through innovatory business concepts embodied in new business models:

> In the new economy, the unit of analysis for innovation is not a product or a technology – it's a business concept. The building blocks of a business concept and a business model are the same – a business model is simply a business concept that has been put into practice. Business concept innovation is the capacity to imagine dramatically different business concepts or dramatically new ways of differentiating existing business concepts. Business concept innovation is thus the key to creating new wealth. Competition within a broad domain – be it financial services, communications, entertainment, publishing, education, energy, or any other field – takes place not between products or companies, but between business models.

Source: G. Hamel, *Leading the Revolution* (Boston: Harvard Business School Press, 2000).

ling. The competition in the retail sector is driven by a constant quest for new retail concepts and formats:

- In department stores, Nordstrom redefined the shopping experience through augmented customer service.

- In bookstores, Barnes and Noble have a retail environment that is conducive to browsing, relaxing, and social interaction. It offers spaciousness, a wide selection of books, and Starbucks coffee.

- Sephora, subsidiary of the French-based luxury products firm LVMH, has redefined the retailing of cosmetics. With 490 stores in Europe and North America at the beginning of 2004, it "seeks to defy the traditional *selling methodology* to give you what you want – Freedom, Beauty and Pleasure." For example, "Freedom comes to you in a hands-on, self-service shopping environment. Feel free to touch, smell and experience each and every product . . . You are also free to choose the level of assistance you desire, from individual experience and reflection, to detailed expert advice."[9]

Other new business models have been built around redesigned processes and novel organizational designs:

- In the US steel industry, Nucor achieved unrivaled productivity and flexibility by combining new process technologies, flat and flexible organizational structures, and innovative management systems. Since 1997, it has been the biggest steel producer in the US.

- Wal-Mart's position as the world's biggest and most successful retailer owes much to a business model based on new process technology and novel approaches to organization. Wal-Mart's supply chain, features a hub-and-spoke distribution system, innovatory techniques such as cross-docking, and the use of IT and communication to allow point-of-sale data to drive decision making across the whole value chain.

- Southwest Airlines' point-to-point, no-frills airline service using a single type of plane and flexible, non-union employees has made it the only consistently profitable airline in North America and the model for budget airlines throughout the world.

- Nike built its large and successful businesses on a business system that totally reconfigured the traditional shoe-manufacturing value chain. To begin with, Nike does not manufacture shoes – indeed, it manufactures little of anything. It designs, markets, and distributes shoes, but its primary activity is the coordination of a vast and complex global network involving design and market research (primarily in the US), the production (under contract) of components (primarily in Korea and Taiwan), and the contract assembly of shoes (in China, Philippines, India, Thailand, and other low-wage countries).

- EBay and Amazon.com, the world's most successful e-commerce startups, established themselves in the ranks of the world's 100 most valuable companies (in terms of market capitalization) through creating a whole new type of business.

How do we go about formulating innovative strategies? Are new approaches to competing and delivering superior value the result of pure creativity, or are there analyses and ways of thinking that can lead us in the right direction? The management literature suggests several approaches:

1. McKinsey & Co. has argued that innovative business concepts (what it calls "new game" strategies) typically involve reconfiguring the industry value chain. By reconstructing and rearranging the value chain, a company can change the "rules of the game" so as to capitalize on its distinctive competencies, catch competitors off guard, and erect barriers to protect the advantage created. McKinsey cites Savin in the North American market for plain-paper copiers as an example of the potency of new game strategies in challenging Xerox's seemingly impregnable competitive position (see Strategy Capsule 7.2).

2. Charles Baden Fuller and John Stopford argue that strategic innovation often involves delivering unprecedented customer satisfaction through combining performance dimensions that were previously viewed as conflicting. For example, Toyota's "lean production system" combines low cost, high quality, and innovative product differentiation. Richardson, a Sheffield-based cutlery manufacturer, uses process technology, innovatory design, and an entrepreneurial culture to supply kitchen knives that combine low price, sharpness, durability, and attractive designs.[10]

STRATEGY CAPSULE 7.2   Reconfiguring the Value Chain for New Game Strategies: Savin and Xerox

For most of the 1970s, Xerox possessed a near monopoly position in the North American market for plain-paper copiers. Xerox's dominance rested, first, upon the wall of patents that the company had built over several decades and, second, on the scale economies and reputation that its market dominance conferred. The first company to compete effectively with Xerox during the late 1970s was Savin. The basis of Savin's challenge was an approach that sought not to imitate Xerox's success but to compete in an entirely different manner.

Savin developed and patented a new low-cost technology. Its product design permitted the use of standardized parts that could be sourced in volume from Japan. Assembly was also undertaken in Japan. The result was a product whose cost was about half that of Xerox's. To avoid the costs of leasing and the need for a costly direct sales force, Savin distributed through existing office equipment dealers.

The principal differences between the approach of Savin and that of Xerox can be seen by comparing the main activities of the companies:

VALUE CHAIN ACTIVITY	XEROX	SAVIN
Technology and design	Dry xerography High copy speed Many features	Liquid toner Low copy speed Few features and options
Manufacture	Most manufacturing (including components) in house	Machines sourced from Ricoh in Japan
Product range	Wide range of machines	Narrow range of machines for different volumes and uses
Marketing	Machines leased to customers	Machines sold to customers
Distribution	Direct sales force	Distribution through dealers
Service	Directly operated service organization	Service by dealers and independent service engineers

Source: Roberto Buaron, "New-Game Strategies," *McKinsey Staff Paper* (March 1980); reprinted in *On Strategy* (McKinsey Quarterly Anthologies, 2000): 34–6.

3.   E-commerce – the conduct of transactions through electronic communication media – offers particular opportunities both for reconfiguring value chains and creating new combinations of value characteristics. The primary impact of the internet on conventional value chains has been *disintermediation* – the elimination of intermediaries such as wholesalers, retailers, and publishers. Direct reservations and ticket sales through airlines' own websites has saved them millions of dollars of sales commissions. The ability for musicians to directly sell digital recordings through their websites offers a fundamental challenge to the existing record companies.

4.   In his recent writings, Gary Hamel argues that strategic innovation is not some one-time-only event. If companies are to develop true resilience in turbulent markets they must engage in the continual reinvention of the

company's business model. This requires that top management values and fosters variety, frees up resources for new strategic initiatives, embraces paradox, and develops sense-and-respond systems that offer spontaneous responses to changing circumstances.[11] Whether such permanent revolution is either feasible or desirable is debatable. Joyce, Nohria, and Robertson's study of the key factors that differentiated between successful and unsuccessful companies emphasized the importance of stable strategies "... be clear about what your strategy is and consistently communicate it to customers, employees, and shareholders. It begins with a simple, focused value proposition that is rooted in deep, certain knowledge about your company's target customers and a realistic appraisal of your own capacities."[12]

SUSTAINING COMPETITIVE ADVANTAGE

Once established, competitive advantage is subject to erosion by competition. The speed with which competitive advantage is undermined depends on the ability of competitors to challenge either by imitation or innovation. Imitation is the most direct form of competition; thus, for competitive advantage to be sustained over time, barriers to imitation must exist. Rumelt uses the term *isolating mechanisms* to describe "barriers that limit the *ex post* equilibration of rents among individual firms."[13] The more effective these isolating mechanisms are, the longer competitive advantage can be sustained against the onslaught of rivals. Empirical studies show that the process through which competition destroys the competitive advantage of industry leaders is slow. Even over periods of a decade and more, inter-firm profit differentials tend to persist, with little change in the identities of the leaders and the laggards.[14]

To identify the sources of isolating mechanisms, we need to examine the process of competitive imitation. For one firm successfully to imitate the strategy of another, it must meet four conditions:

- *Identification.* The firm must be able to identify that a rival possesses a competitive advantage.

- *Incentive.* Having identified that a rival possesses a competitive advantage (as shown by above-average profitability), the firm must believe that by investing in imitation, it too can earn superior returns.

- *Diagnosis.* The firm must be able to diagnose the features of its rival's strategy that give rise to the competitive advantage.

- *Resource acquisition.* The firm must be able to acquire through transfer or replication the resources and capabilities necessary for imitating the strategy of the advantaged firm.

Figure 7.2 illustrates these stages and the types of isolating mechanism that exist at each stage.

FIGURE 7.2 Sustaining competitive advantage: types of isolating mechanism

REQUIREMENT FOR IMITATION	ISOLATING MECHANISM
Identification	—*Obscure* superior performance
Incentives for imitation	—*Deterrence*: signal aggressive intentions to imitators —*Preemption*: exploit all available investment opportunities
Diagnosis	—Rely on multiple sources of competitive advantage to create "*causal ambiguity*"
Resource acquisition	—Base competitive advantage on resources and capabilities that are *immobile* and *difficult to replicate*

Identification: Obscuring Superior Performance

A simple barrier to imitation is to obscure the firm's superior profitability. In the 1948 movie classic *The Treasure of the Sierra Madre*, Humphrey Bogart and his partners went to great lengths to obscure their find from other gold prospectors.[15] The Mongolian Gold Rush of 2002–2003 also featured secretive behavior as companies with good initial test results sought to acquire exploration rights on nearby properties.[16]

Avoiding competition through avoiding disclosure of a firm's profits is much easier for a private than a public company. For Mars Ltd., the nondisclosure of financial results may help the firm in protecting its highly profitable pet food and confectionery businesses.

The desire to avoid competition may be so strong as to cause companies to forgo short-run profits. The *theory of limit pricing*, in its simplest form, postulates that a firm in a strong market position sets prices at a level that just fails to attract entrants.[17]

Deterrence and Preemption

A firm may avoid competition by undermining the incentives for imitation. If a firm can persuade rivals that imitation will be unprofitable, it may be able to avoid competitive challenges. In Chapter 4 we discussed strategies of deterrence and the role of signaling and commitment in supporting them.[18]

As we have seen, reputation is critically important in making threats credible. Brandenburger and Nalebuff argue that in the aspartame market, NutraSweet's aggressive price war against the Holland Sweetener Company deterred other would-be entrants.[19]

A firm can also deter imitation by preemption – occupying existing and potential strategic niches in order to reduce the range of investment opportunities open to the challenger. Preemption can take many forms:

- Proliferation of product varieties by a market leader can leave new entrants and smaller rivals with few opportunities for establishing a market niche. Between 1950 and 1972, for example, the six leading suppliers of breakfast cereals introduced 80 new brands into the US market.[20]

- Large investments in production capacity ahead of the growth of market demand also preempt market opportunities for rivals. Monsanto's heavy investment in plants for producing NutraSweet ahead of its patent expiration was a clear threat to would-be producers of generic aspartame.

- Patent proliferation can protect technology-based advantage by limiting competitors' technical opportunities. In 1974, Xerox's dominant market position was protected by a wall of over 2,000 patents, most of which were not used. When IBM introduced its first copier in 1970, Xerox sued it for infringing 22 of these patents.[21]

The ability to sustain competitive advantage through preemption depends on the presence of two imperfections of the competitive process. First, the market must be small relative to the minimum efficient scale of production, such that only a very small number of competitors is viable. Second, there must be first-mover advantage that gives an incumbent preferential access to information and other resources, putting rivals at a disadvantage.

Diagnosing Competitive Advantage: "Causal Ambiguity" and "Uncertain Imitability"

If a firm is to imitate the competitive advantage of another, it must understand the basis of its rival's success. In most industries, there is a serious identification problem in linking superior performance to the resources and capabilities that generate that performance. Consider the remarkable success of Wal-Mart in discount retailing. It is easy for Kmart to point to the differences between Wal-Mart and itself. As one Wal-Mart executive commented: "Retailing is an open book. There are no secrets. Our competitors can walk into our stores and see what we sell, how we sell it, and for how much." The difficult task is to identify which differences are critical to the profitability differential between the two retailers. Is it Wal-Mart's store locations (typically in small towns with little direct competition)? Its tightly integrated logistics of purchasing, warehousing, and distribution? Its unique management system? The information system that supports Wal-Mart's logistics and decision-making practices? Or is it the culture that combines rural American values of thrift, simplicity, and hard work, with company traditions of family-like unity, customer attentiveness, and entrepreneurial drive?

The problem for Kmart and other wannabe Wal-Marts is what Lippman and Rumelt refer to as *causal ambiguity*.[22] The more multidimensional a firm's competitive advantage and the more each dimension of competitive advantage is based on complex bundles of organizational capabilities rather than individual resources, the more difficult it is for a competitor to diagnose the determinants of success. The outcome of causal ambiguity is *uncertain imitability*: where there is ambiguity associated with the causes of a competitor's success, any attempt to imitate that strategy is subject to uncertain success.

Acquiring Resources and Capabilities

Having diagnosed the sources of an incumbent's competitive advantage, the imitator can mount a competitive challenge only by assembling the resources and capabilities necessary for imitation. As we saw in Chapter 5, a firm can acquire resources and capabilities in two ways: it can buy them or it can build them. The period over which a competitive advantage can be sustained depends critically on the time it takes to acquire and mobilize the resources and capabilities needed to mount a competitive challenge.

There is little to add here to the discussion of transferability and replicability in Chapter 5. The ability to buy resources and capabilities from outside factor markets depends on their transferability between firms. Even if resources are mobile, the market for a resource may be subject to transaction costs – costs of buying and selling arising from search costs, negotiation costs, contract enforcement costs, and transportation costs. Transaction costs are greater for highly differentiated (or "idiosyncratic") resources.[23]

The alternative to buying a resource or capability is to create it through internal investment. As we noted in Chapter 5, where capabilities are based on organizational routines, accumulating the coordination and learning required for their efficient operation can take considerable time. Even in the case of "turn-key" plants, developing operational capability can be problematic. Michael Polanyi observed:

> I have myself watched in Hungary a new imported machine for blowing electric lamp bulbs, the exact counterpart of which was operating successfully in Germany, failing for a whole year to produce a single flawless bulb.[24]

Businesses that require the integration of a number of complex, team-based routines may take years to reach the standards set by industry leaders. GM's attempt to transfer Toyota-style, team-based production from its NUMMI joint venture at Fremont, California, to the GM Van Nuys plant 400 miles to the south involved complex problems of learning and adjustment that remained unsolved two years after the program had begun.[25]

Conversely, where a competitive advantage does not require the application of complex, firm-specific resources, imitation is likely to be easy and fast. In financial services, many new products such as money market checking accounts, brokerage accounts with checking services, stripped bonds, interest rate swaps, and various financial derivatives typically require resources and capabilities that are widely distributed among banks. Hence, imitation of financial innovations is swift. The rapid decline of Filofax, the British manufacturer (and originator) of personal organizers, similarly reflected the ease of replicating its product.[26]

First-mover Advantage

A firm's ability to acquire the resources and capabilities needed to challenge an incumbent firm depends on the extent and the sources of first-mover advantage in the market. The idea of first-mover advantage is that the initial occupant of a strategic position or niche gains access to resources and capabilities that a follower cannot match. The simplest form of first-mover advantage is a patent or copyright. By establishing a patent or copyright, the first mover possesses a technology, product, or design from which a follower is legally excluded. Early occupancy of a strategic niche can offer other resource advantages. The ability of advantaged firms to acquire superior resources and capabilities confirms the adage that "success breeds success."

- Where the resources required for competing are scarce, e.g., store locations in a new shopping mall or highly specialized employees, first movers can simply preempt these scarce resources.

- Initial competitive advantage offers a profit flow that permits the firm to invest in extending and upgrading its resource base. Pilkington's revolutionary float glass process – the manufacture of flat glass by floating molten glass on a bath of molten tin – was a competitive advantage whose life was limited to the term of the patent. However, the company used its profits and income from patent licenses to invest heavily in new plants, expand multinationally by acquiring overseas competitors, and finance R&D into fiber-optics and other new uses of glass.

- The first mover in a market establishes a reputation with suppliers, distributors, and customers that cannot be initially matched by the follower.

- Where an industry tends towards a common technical standard, the first mover may have an advantage in setting that standard.

- The first mover can build a cost advantage by moving down the industry learning curve faster than followers.[27]

We shall return to the issue of first-mover versus follower advantages when we consider competitive advantage in emerging and technology-based industries (Chapter 11).

COMPETITIVE ADVANTAGE IN DIFFERENT MARKET SETTINGS

Profiting from competitive advantage requires that the firm first establishes a competitive advantage, and then sustains its advantage for long enough to reap its rewards. To identify opportunities for establishing and sustaining competitive advantage requires understanding the characteristics of the competitive process in specific markets. For competitive advantage to exist, there must be some imperfection of competition. To identify and understand these imperfections in the competitive process, we need to recognize the types of resources and capabilities necessary to compete and the circumstances of their availability.

Our initial discussion of the nature of business in Chapter 1 identified two types of value-creating activity: trading and production. Trading involves arbitrage across space (trade) and time (speculation). Production involves the physical transformation of inputs into outputs. These different types of business activity correspond to different market types: trading markets and production markets (see Figure 7.3). We begin with a discussion of a special type of trading market: an efficient market.

Efficient Markets: The Absence of Competitive Advantage

In Chapter 3, we introduced the concept of perfect competition. Perfect competition exists where there are many buyers and sellers, no product differentiation, no barriers to entry or exit, and free flow of information. In equilibrium, all firms earn the competitive rate of profit, which equals the cost of capital. The closest real-world examples of perfect competition are financial and commodity markets (for example, the markets for securities, foreign exchange, and grain futures). These markets are sometimes described as *efficient*. An *efficient market* is one in which prices reflect all available information. Because prices adjust instantaneously to newly available information, no market trader can expect to earn more than any other. Any differences in *ex post* returns reflect either different levels of risk selected by different traders or purely random factors (luck). Because all available information is reflected in current prices, no trading rules based on historical price data or any other available information can offer excess returns: it is not possible to "beat the market" on any consistent basis. In other words, competitive advantage is absent.

The absence of competitive advantage in efficient markets can be linked to resource availability. If financial markets are efficient, it is because only two types of resource are required to participate – finance and information. If both are equally available to all traders, there is no basis for one to gain competitive advantage over another.

Competitive Advantage in Trading Markets

In order for competitive advantage to exist, imperfections (or "inefficiencies") must be introduced into the competitive process. Focusing on the relatively simple case of trading markets, let us introduce different sources of imperfection to the

FIGURE 7.3   Competitive advantage in different industry settings: trading and production

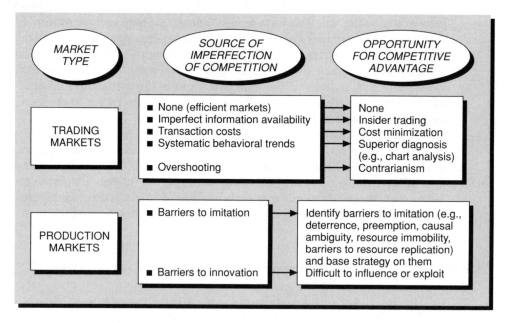

competitive process, showing how these imperfections create opportunities for competitive advantage, and how the imperfections relate to the conditions of resource availability.

Imperfect Availability of Information

Financial markets (and most other trading markets) depart from the conditions for efficiency because of imperfect availability of information. Competitive advantage, therefore, depends on superior access to information. The most likely source of superior information is privileged access to private information. Trading on the basis of such information normally falls within the restrictions on "insider trading." Though insider information creates advantage, such competitive advantage tends to be of short duration. Once a market participant begins acting on the basis of insider information, other operators are alerted to the existence of the information. Even though they may not know its content, they are able to imitate the behavior of the market leader. A commonly followed strategy in stock markets is to detect and follow insider transactions by senior company executives.

Transaction Costs

If markets are efficient except for the presence of transaction costs, then competitive advantage accrues to the traders with the lowest transaction costs. In stock markets, low transaction costs are attained by traders who economize on research and market analysis and achieve efficient portfolio diversification. Studies of mutual fund performance show that "Net of all management fees, the average managed investment fund performed worse than a completely unmanaged buy-and-hold strategy on a risk-adjusted basis. Further, the amount by which the funds fell short of the unmanaged strategy was, on average, about the same as the management cost of the funds."[28] Because of their lower costs, market index funds outperform managed funds. During the 1990s, actively managed mutual funds underperformed the S&P 500 by 3.4 percent per year and the Wilshire 5000 Index by 2.4 percent per year. The differential is mainly due to managed funds' transaction costs, which averaged 1.3 percent per annum.[29]

Systematic Behavioral Trends

If the current prices in a market fully reflect all available information, then price movements are caused by the arrival of new information and follow a random walk.[30] If, however, other factors influence price movements, there is scope for a strategy that uses an understanding of how prices really do move. Some stock market anomalies are well documented, notably the "small firm effect," the "January effect," and "weekend effects."[31] More generally, there is evidence that prices in financial markets follow systematic patterns that are the result of "market psychology," the trends and turning points of which can be established from past data. Chart analysis uses hypotheses concerning the relationship between past and future price movements for forecasting. Standard chartist tools include Elliott wave theory, Gann theories, momentum indicators, and patterns such as "support and resistance levels," "head and shoulders," "double tops," "flags," and "candlesticks." Despite mixed evidence on the success of chart analysis in financial markets,[32] systematic behavioral trends do occur in most markets, which implies that competitive advantage is gained by traders with superior skill in diagnosing such behavior.

Overshooting

One well-documented behavioral aberration is the propensity of market participants to overreact to new information, with the result that prices overshoot.[33] Such overreaction is typically the result of imitative behavior resulting in the creation of bandwagon effects. On the assumption that overshooting is temporary and is eventually offset by an opposite movement back to equilibrium, then advantage can be gained through a contrarian strategy: doing the opposite of the mass-market participants. Warren Buffett, the billionaire chairman of Berkshire Hathaway, is a declared contrarian: "The best time to buy assets may be when it is hardest to raise money," he notes. Prince Alwaleed bin Talal bin Abdulaziz Alsaud is a prominent "bottom-fisher" who acquires large stakes in temporarily depressed companies such as Citigroup, Canary Wharf, EuroDisney, Apple Computer, and Amazon.com.[34]

Competitive Advantage in Production Markets

The transitory nature of competitive advantage in trading markets is a result of the characteristics of the resources required to compete: finance and information. Finance is a relatively homogeneous resource that is widely available. Information, although highly differentiated, is transferable easily and at very low cost; hence, the competitive advantage it offers tends to be fleeting.

Production markets are quite different. Production activities require complex combinations of resources and capabilities, and these resources and capabilities are highly differentiated. The result, as we have noted, is that each producer possesses a unique combination of resources and capabilities. The greater the heterogeneity of firms' endowments of resources and capabilities, the greater the potential for competitive advantage. In the US steel industry, the entry of the minimills between 1970 and 1996 (Nucor, Chaparral, Birmingham Steel, and North Star) and restructuring by the integrated steel companies (e.g. USX and Bethlehem) increased the diversity of firms competing and widened the profit differentials between them.[35]

Differences in resource endowments among firms also have an important impact on the process by which competitive advantage is eroded. Where firms possess very similar bundles of resources and capabilities, imitation of the competitive advantage of the incumbent firm is most likely. Where resource bundles are highly differentiated, competition is likely to be less direct. Using different resources and capability, a firm may substitute a rival's competitive advantage.[36] For example:

- Canon substituted for Xerox's technical service capability in copiers by developing high-reliability copiers that needed little service.[37]

- Online discount brokers have used the internet to substitute for networks of retail offices of established brokerage companies, such as Merrill Lynch and Charles Schwab, and online research to substitute for the established brokers' research departments.[38]

Since substitute competition can come from many directions – alternative resources, technological innovations, new business models – it is difficult to counter. The key is to persuade potential competitors that substitution is unlikely to be profitable. This can be achieved through committing the firm to continuous improvement, locking in customers and suppliers, and market deterrence.[39]

Industry Conditions Conducive to Emergence and Sustaining of Competitive Advantage

In analyzing the potential for creating and sustaining advantage in production markets, I have focused upon the role of interfirm differences in resources. However, the characteristics of the industry also play a role in determining the means by which competitive advantage emerges and is eroded.

Thus, the opportunities for establishing competitive advantage in production markets depend upon the number and diversity of the sources of change in the business environment. Industries subject to a wide range of unpredictable external changes offer a multiplicity of opportunities for competitive advantage. Consider the wireless telecommunication services. The industry is subject to a vast array of dynamic forces – regulatory change, technological change, changing customer preferences, to mention but a few. All of these forces offer opportunities for competitive advantage. The complexity of the industry also determines the variety of opportunities for competitive advantage: complex products such as IT consulting offer greater scope than cement.

The extent to which competitive advantage is eroded through imitation will also depend on the characteristics of the industry. For example:

■ *Information complexity.* The more difficult it is to diagnose the basis of the success of advantaged firms, the more difficult it is to imitate their success. Industries where competitive advantage is based on complex, multilayered capabilities tend to have more sustainable competitive advantages. In movie production, the long-established leadership of studios such as Paramount, Columbia (Sony), Universal, Fox, and Disney may reflect the difficult-to-diagnose secrets of producing "blockbuster" movies, even though the individual resources (scripts, actors, technicians, and directors) can be hired from the market.

■ *Opportunities for deterrence and preemption.* Industries where the market is small (relative to the minimum efficient scale of production), essential resources are scarce or tightly held, or economies of learning are important, allow first movers to establish and sustain competitive advantage by preemption and deterrence.

■ *Difficulties of resource acquisition.* Finally, industries differ according to the availability of strategically important resources. In the bicycle messenger business in London or New York, competitive advantage is easily eroded because the key resources (cyclists, wireless communication, and marketing) are easily acquired. The securities underwriting business (whether for IPOs or corporate bond issues) offers more sustainable advantages because the key resources and capabilities (market expertise, reputation, relationships, retail distribution links, and massive financial reserves) tend to be difficult to assemble. The difficulties of assembling the resources and capabilities needed to challenge the advantages of incumbents increase to the extent that initial resource advantages are cumulative. The ability of successful companies such as Microsoft, Sony, and Procter & Gamble to attract the most talented new graduates is such an advantage.

TYPES OF COMPETITIVE ADVANTAGE: COST AND DIFFERENTIATION

A firm can achieve a higher rate of profit (or potential profit) over a rival in one of two ways: either it can supply an identical product or service at a lower cost, or it can supply a product or service that is differentiated in such a way that the customer

FIGURE 7.4 Sources of competitive advantage

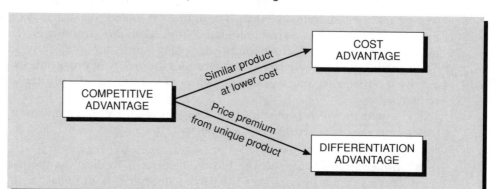

is willing to pay a price premium that exceeds the additional cost of the differentiation. In the former case, the firm possesses a cost advantage; in the latter, a differentiation advantage. In pursuing cost advantage, the goal of the firm is to become the cost leader in its industry or industry segment. Cost leadership requires that the firm "must find and exploit all sources of cost advantage . . . [and] . . . sell a standard, no-frills product."[40] Differentiation by a firm from its competitors is achieved "when it provides something unique that is valuable to buyers beyond simply offering a low price."[41] Figure 7.4 illustrates these two types of advantage.

The two sources of competitive advantage define two fundamentally different approaches to business strategy. A firm that is competing on low cost is distinguishable from a firm that competes through differentiation in terms of market positioning, resource and capabilities, and organizational characteristics. Table 7.2 outlines some of the principal features of cost and differentiation strategies.

By combining the two types of competitive advantage with the firm's choice of scope – broad market versus narrow segment – Michael Porter has defined three generic strategies: cost leadership, differentiation, and focus (see Figure 7.5). Porter views cost leadership and differentiation as mutually exclusive strategies. A firm that attempts to pursue both is "stuck in the middle":

> The firm stuck in the middle is almost guaranteed low profitability. It either loses the high volume customers who demand low prices or must bid away its profits to get this business from the low-cost firms. Yet it also loses high-margin business – the cream – to the firms who are focused on high-margin targets or have achieved differentiation overall. The firm that is stuck in the middle also probably suffers from a blurred corporate culture and a conflicting set of organizational arrangements and motivation system.[42]

In practice, few firms are faced with such stark alternatives. Differentiation is not simply an issue of "to differentiate or not to differentiate." All firms must make decisions as to which customer requirements to focus on, and where to position their product or service in the market. A cost leadership strategy typically implies a

TABLE 7.2   Features of Cost Leadership and Differentiation Strategies

GENERIC STRATEGY	KEY STRATEGY ELEMENTS	RESOURCE AND ORGANIZATIONAL REQUIREMENTS
Cost leadership	Scale-efficient plants Design for manufacture Control of overheads and R&D Process innovation Outsourcing (especially overseas) Avoidance of marginal customer accounts	Access to capital Process engineering skills Frequent reports Tight cost control Specialization of jobs and functions Incentives linked to quantitative targets
Differentiation	Emphasis on branding advertising, design, service, quality, and new product development	Marketing abilities Product engineering skills Cross-functional coordination Creativity Research capability Incentives linked to qualitative performance targets

FIGURE 7.5   Porter's generic strategies

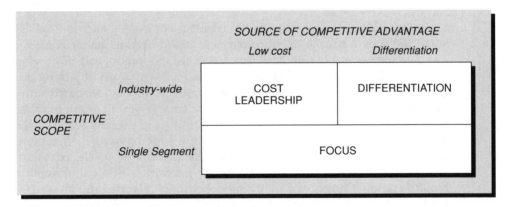

narrow-line, limited-feature, standardized offering. However, such a positioning does not necessarily imply that the product or service is an undifferentiated commodity. In the case of IKEA furniture and Southwest Airlines a low-price, no-frills offering is also associated with clear market positioning and a unique brand image. The VW Beetle shows that a low-cost, utilitarian, mass-market product can achieve cult status. At the same time, firms that pursue differentiation strategies cannot be oblivious to cost.

In most industries, market leadership is held by a firm that maximizes customer appeal by reconciling effective differentiation with low cost – Toyota, Dell, and Canon are classic examples. In many industries, the cost leader is not the market leader but is a smaller competitor with minimal overheads, nonunion labor, and cheaply acquired assets. In oil refining, the cost leaders tend to be independent refining companies rather than integrated giants such as Exxon Mobil or Shell. In car rental, the cost leader is more likely to be Rent-A-Wreck (a division of Bundy American Corporation) rather than Hertz or Avis.

Reconciling differentiation with low cost has been one of the greatest strategic challenges of the 1990s. Common to the success of Japanese companies in consumer goods industries such as cars, motorcycles, consumer electronics, and musical instruments has been the ability to reconcile low costs with high quality and technological progressiveness. The total quality management methods that they adopted exploded the myth that there is a tradeoff between high quality and low cost. Numerous studies show that innovations in manufacturing technology and manufacturing management result in simultaneous increases in productivity and quality.[43] Achieving higher quality in terms of fewer defects and greater product reliability frequently involves simpler product design, fewer component suppliers that are more closely monitored, and fewer service calls and product recalls – all of which save cost. Tom Peters observes an interesting asymmetry:

> Cost reduction campaigns do not often lead to improved quality; and, except for those that involve large reductions in personnel, they don't usually result in long-term lower costs either. On the other hand, effective quality programs yield not only improved quality but lasting cost reductions as well.[44]

Having conquered the cost/quality tradeoff, companies such as Honda, Toyota, Sony, and Canon have gone on to reconcile world-beating manufacturing efficiency and outstanding quality with flexibility, fast-paced innovation, and effective marketing.

Market leaders can use differentiation strategies as a means of putting pressure on smaller rivals. There tend to be substantial scale economies associated with advertising and new product development. The more large companies can push their smaller rivals into competing on advertising, innovation, and product features, the greater will be the cost advantages experienced by the large companies. Accenture's heavy emphasis on media advertising put considerable pressure on smaller consulting and IT services that do not possess the scale for such activities. In the motorcycle industry, Honda's product strategy of annual model changes increased the pressure on manufacturers who lacked the sales volume to justify such heavy fixed costs of new models.[45]

SUMMARY

Making money in business requires establishing and sustaining competitive advantage. Both these conditions for profitability demand profound insight into the nature and process of competition within a market. Competitive advantage depends critically on the presence of some imperfection in the competitive process – under perfect competition, profits are transitory. Our analysis of the imperfections of the competitive process has drawn us back to the resources and capabilities that are required to compete in different markets and to pursue different strategies. Sustaining competitive advantage depends on the existence of isolating mechanisms: barriers to rivals' imitation of successful strategies. The greater the difficulty that rivals face in accessing the resources and capabilities needed to imitate or substitute the competitive advantage of the incumbent firm, the greater the sustainability of that firm's competitive advantage. Hence, one outcome of our analysis is to reinforce the argument made in Chapter 5: the characteristics of a firm's resources and capability are fundamental to its strategy and its performance in decision making and long-term success.

In the next two chapters, we analyze the two primary dimensions of competitive advantage: cost advantage and differentiation advantage. In both of these areas we emphasize the importance of a deep understanding of both the firm and its industry environment. To this end, it is useful to disaggregate the firm into a series of separate but interlinked activities. A useful and versatile framework for this purpose is the value chain, which is an insightful tool for understanding the sources of competitive advantage in an industry, for assessing the competitive position of a particular firm, and for suggesting opportunities to enhance a firm's competitiveness.

NOTES

[1] Richard Rumelt argues that competitive advantage is derived from resource scarcity, and hence is a property of resources rather than firms ("What in the World is Competitive Advantage," Policy Working Paper 2003-105, Anderson School, UCLA, August 2003). However, to the extent that resources are deployed in heterogeneous bundles and complex complementarities exist between them, competitive advantage can accrue to firms even in the absence of scarcity among individual resources.

[2] Richard Rumelt, "Theory, Strategy and Entrepreneurship," in David J. Teece (ed.), *The Competitive Challenge: Strategies for Industrial Innovation and Renewal* (Cambridge, MA: Ballinger, 1987): 137, defines entrepreneurship as "the creation of new businesses." Here, we define entrepreneurship more broadly to also include the adaptation of an existing business to create and exploit a new business opportunity.

[3] Bob Ortega, *In Sam We Trust: The Untold Story of Sam Walton and How Wal-Mart is Devouring America* (New York: Times Books, 2000).

[4] H. Voss, "Virtual Organization," *Strategy and Leadership* 24 (July–August, 1996): 12–24. The Italian model of small firm networks has been documented and analyzed by Gianni Lorenzoni. See G. Lorenzoni and Charles Baden Fuller, "Creating a Strategic Center to Manage a Web of Partners," *California Management Review* 37 no. 3 (1995): 146–63; G. Lorenzoni, "Organizational Architecture, Inter-Firm Relationships and Entrepreneurial Profile: Findings from a Set of SME," *Frontiers of Entrepreneurship Research* (Boston: Babson College: 1993).

[5] "Bitter Competition: *The Holland Sweetener Co. vs. NutraSweet* (A)," Case No. 9-794-079 (Boston: Harvard Business School: 1998). See also David J. Teece, "Profiting from Technological Innovation: Implications for Integration, Collaboration, Licensing, and Public Policy," in David J. Teece (ed.), op. cit.

[6] Joan Magretta, "The Power of Virtual Integration: An Interview with Dell Computer's Michael Dell," *Harvard Business Review* (March–April 1998): 73–84.

[7] D. Arnold and D. A. Gullerma, "Zara," (Harvard Business School Case Study, March 12, 2003).

[8] George Stalk Jr., "Time – The Next Source of Competitive Advantage," *Harvard Business Review* (July–August 1988): 41–51.

[9] www.sephora.com.

[10] Charles Baden Fuller and John M. Stopford, *Rejuvenating the Mature Business* (London and New York: Routledge, 1992).

[11] Gary Hamel and Lisa Valikangas, "The Quest for Resilience," *Harvard Business Review* (September 2003): 62–75.

[12] William F. Joyce, Nitin Nohria, and Bruce Robertson, *What Really Works: The 4+2 Formula for Sustained Business Success* (New York: HarperBusiness, 2003); Nitin Nohria, William F. Joyce, and Bruce Robertson, "What Really Works," *Harvard Business Review* (June 2003).

[13] Richard P. Rumelt, "Toward a Strategic Theory of the Firm," in R. Lamb (ed.), *Competitive Strategic Management* (Englewood Cliffs, NJ: Prentice-Hall, 1984): 556–70.

[14] See John Cubbin and Paul Geroski, "The Convergence of Profits in the Long Run: Interfirm and Interindustry Comparisons," *Journal of Industrial Economics* 35 (1987): 427–42; Robert Jacobsen, "The Persistence of Abnormal Returns," *Strategic Management Journal* 9 (1988): 415–30; and Dennis C. Mueller, "Persistent Profits among Large Corporations," in Lacy Glenn Thomas (ed.), *The Economics of Strategic Planning* (Lexington, MA: Lexington Books, 1986): 31–61.

[15] The film was based on the book, by B. Traven, *The Treasure of the Sierra Madre* (New York: Knopf, 1947).

[16] "The Great Mongolian Gold Rush," *Fortune Investors Guide 2004* (December 2003).

[17] S. Martin, *Advanced Industrial Economics*, 2nd edn (Oxford: Blackwell Publishers, 2001): Chapter 8.

[18] Thomas C. Schelling, *The Strategy of Conflict*, 2nd edn (Cambridge: Harvard University Press, 1980): 35–41.

[19] Adam Brandenburger and Barry Nalebuff, *Co-opetition* (New York: Doubleday, 1996): 72–80.

[20] Richard Schmalensee, "Entry Deterrence in the Ready-to-Eat Breakfast Cereal Industry," *Bell Journal of Economics* 9 (1978): 305–27.

[21] Monopolies and Mergers Commission, *Indirect Electrostatic Reprographic Equipment* (London: Her Majesty's Stationery Office, 1976): 37, 56.

[22] S. A. Lippman and Richard P. Rumelt, "Uncertain Imitability: An Analysis of Interfirm Differences in Efficiency under Competition," *Bell Journal of Economics* 13 (1982): 418–38. The analysis of causal ambiguity has been further developed by Richard Reed and Robert DeFillippi, "Causal Ambiguity, Barriers to Imitation, and Sustainable Competitive Advantage," *Academy of Management Review* 15 (1990): 88–102.

[23] See O. E. Williamson, "Transaction Cost Economics: The Governance of Contractual Relations," *Journal of Law and Economics* 19 (1979): 153–6.

[24] M. Polanyi, *Personal Knowledge: Toward a Post-Critical Philosophy*, 2nd edn (Chicago: University of Chicago Press, 1962): 52.

[25] C. Brown and M. Reich, "When Does Union–Management Cooperation Work? A Look at NUMMI and GM-Van Nuys," *California Management Review* 31 (Summer 1989): 26–44.

[26] "Faded Fad," *Economist* (September 30, 1989): 68.

[27] For an analysis of first-mover advantage, see Marvin Lieberman and David Montgomery, "First-Mover Advantages," *Strategic Management Journal* 9 (1988): 41–58; and Marvin Lieberman and David Montgomery, "First-Mover (Dis)Advantages: Retrospective and Link with the Resource-based View," *Strategic Management Journal* 19 (1998): 1111–25.

[28] Frank J. Finn, "Evaluation of the Internal Processes of Managed Investment Funds," *Contemporary Studies in Economic and Financial Analysis*, vol. 44 (Greenwich, CT: JAI Press, 1984): 6.

29 http://www.fool.com/mutualfunds/ indexfunds/indexfunds01.htm.

30 Eugene F. Fama, "Efficient Capital Markets: A Review of Theory and Empirical Work," *Journal of Business* 35 (1970): 383–417.

31 Simon Keane, "The Efficient Market Hypothesis on Trial," *Financial Analysts Journal* (March–April 1986): 58–63.

32 H. Allen and M. Taylor, "Charts, Noise, and Fundamentals in the London Foreign Exchange Market," *Economic Journal*, conference supplement, 100 (1990): 49–59.

33 For empirical evidence, see Werner De Bondt and Richard Thaler, "Does the Stock Market Overreact?," *Journal of Finance* 42 (1985): 793–805.

34 "Prince Alwaleed: The Anti-Buffett?" *Forbes* (November 2002): 50–2.

35 "Why Steel Is Looking Sexy," *Business Week* (April 4, 1994): 106–8.

36 Jay Barney, "Firm Resources and Sustained Competitive Advantage," *Journal of Management* 17 (1991): 99–120.

37 S. K. McEvily, S. Das, and K. McCabe, "Avoiding Competence Substitution Through Knowledge Sharing," *Academy of Management Review* 25 (2000): 294–311.

38 Anjali Bakhru and Ann Brown, "Online Broking Strategies: Merrill Lynch, Charles Schwab, and E-Trade" in R. M. Grant and K. E. Neupert, *Cases in Contemporary Strategy Analysis*, 3rd edn (Oxford: Blackwell Publishing, 2003): 175–94.

39 McEvily, Das, and McCabe, op. cit.

40 Michael E. Porter, *Competitive Advantage* (New York: Free Press, 1985): 13.

41 Ibid.: 120.

42 Michael E. Porter, *Competitive Strategy* (New York: Free Press, 1980): 42.

43 See, for example, Jack R. Meredith, "Strategic Advantages of the Factory of the Future," *California Management Review* (Winter 1989): 129–45.

44 Tom Peters, *Thriving on Chaos* (New York: Knopf, 1987): 80.

45 The potential for differentiation to assist the attainment of cost leadership is analyzed by Charles Hill, "Differentiation versus Low Cost: A Contingency Framework," *Academy of Management Review* 13 (1988): 401–12.

8

Cost Advantage

SEARS MOTOR BUGGY: $395
For car complete with rubber tires, Timken roller bearing axles, top, storm front, three oil-burning lamps, horn, and one gallon of lubricating oil. Nothing to buy but gasoline.

. . . We found there was a maker of automobile frames that was making 75 percent of all the frames used in automobile construction in the United States. We found on account of the volume of business that this concern could make frames cheaper for automobile manufacturers than the manufacturers could make them themselves. We went to this frame maker and asked him to make frames for the Sears Motor Buggy and then to name us prices for those frames in large quantities. And so on throughout the whole construction of the Sears Motor Buggy. You will find every piece and every part has been given the most careful study; you will find that the Sears Motor Buggy is made of the best possible material; it is constructed to take the place of the top buggy; it is built in our own factory, under the direct supervision of our own expert, a man who has had fifteen years of automobile experience, a man who has for the past three years worked with us to develop exactly the right car for the people at a price within the reach of all.

—*Extract from an advertisement in the Sears Roebuck & Co. catalog, 1909: 1150*

OUTLINE

- INTRODUCTION AND OBJECTIVES
- ECONOMIES OF EXPERIENCE
    The Experience Curve
    Strategy Implications: The Role of Market Share
- THE SOURCES OF COST ADVANTAGE
    Economies of Scale

INTRODUCTION AND OBJECTIVES

Historically, strategic management emphasized cost advantage as the primary basis for competitive advantage in an industry. This focus on cost reflected the traditional emphasis by economists on price as the principal medium of competition – competing on price depends on cost efficiency. It also reflected the strategy preoccupations of large industrial corporations. For much of the twentieth century, the strategies of large corporations were driven by the quest for economies of scale and scope through investments in mass production and mass distribution. During the past two decades, cost efficiency remained a priority, but the focus shifted toward cost cutting through restructuring, downsizing, outsourcing, "lean production," and the quest for dynamic rather than static sources of cost efficiency.

For some industries, cost advantage is the predominant basis for competitive advantage: in commodities there is limited opportunity for competing on dimensions other than cost. But even where competition focuses on product differentiation, intensifying competition has resulted in cost efficiency becoming a prerequisite for profitability. Some of the most dramatic examples of companies and industries being transformed through the pursuit of cost efficiency are in sectors where competition has increased sharply due to deregulation, such as airlines, telecommunications, banking, and electrical power generation.

By the time you have completed this chapter, you will be able to:

■ Identify the determinants of relative cost within the industry or activity ("cost drivers").

■ Assess a firm's cost position relative to its competitors and identify the factors responsible for cost differentials.

■ Recommend cost-reduction measures.

The analysis in this chapter is oriented around these objectives. In pursuing these objectives, we shall examine techniques for:

- Identifying the basic sources of cost advantage in an industry.

- Appraising the cost position of a firm within its industry by disaggregating the firm into its separate activities.

- Using the analysis of costs and relative cost position as a basis for recommending strategies for enhancing cost competitiveness.

ECONOMIES OF EXPERIENCE

The study of cost advantage holds a special place in the development of strategy analysis. In 1968 the Boston Consulting Group (BCG) published *Perspectives in Experience*. The study documented the relationship between cost and accumulated experience – the experience curve – and demonstrated its implications for strategy. The experience curve became one of the best-known and most influential concepts in the history of strategic management.

The Experience Curve

The experience curve has its basis in the systematic reduction in the time taken to build airplanes and Liberty ships during World War II.[1] The concept of economies of learning was generalized by BCG to encompass not just direct labor hours, but the behavior of all added costs with cumulative production. In a series of studies, ranging from bottle caps and refrigerators to long-distance calls and insurance policies, BCG observed a remarkable regularity in the reductions in costs (and prices) that accompanied increased production. Doubling of cumulative production typically reduced unit costs by 20 to 30 percent. BCG summarized its observations in its "Law of Experience:"

> The unit cost of value added to a standard product declines by a constant percentage (typically between 20 and 30 percent) each time cumulative output doubles.

"Unit cost of value added" is total cost per unit of production less the cost per unit of production of bought-in components and materials. If suppliers of components and materials are subject to similar cost reductions as volume increases, then "unit cost" may be substituted for "unit cost of value added" in the definition.

Figure 8.1 shows a typical experience curve. In logarithmic form, the curve becomes a straight line. The size of the experience effect is measured by the proportion by which costs are reduced with subsequent doublings of aggregate production. The relationship between unit cost and production volume may be expressed as follows:

FIGURE 8.1 The experience curve

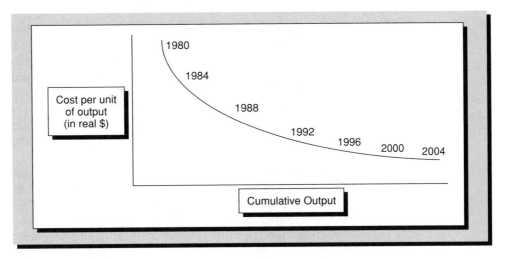

FIGURE 8.2 Examples of experience curves (logarithmic scales)

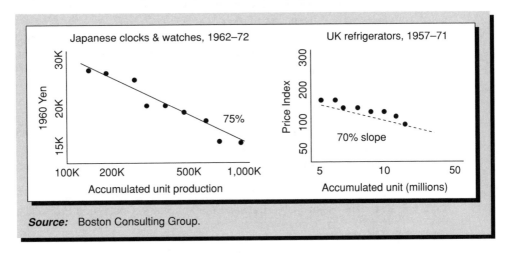

Source: Boston Consulting Group.

$$C_n = C_1 \cdot n^{-a}$$

where C_1 is the cost of the first unit of production
           C_n is the cost of the nth unit of production
           n is the cumulative volume of production
           a is the elasticity of cost with regard to output.

Experience curves may be drawn for both industries and individual firms. Figure 8.2 shows examples of experience curves estimated by the Boston Consulting Group.

Strategy Implications: The Role of Market Share

The significance of the experience curve lies in its implications for business strategy. If a firm can expand its output more than its competitors, it can move down the experience curve more rapidly than its rivals and can open up a widening cost differential. The implication drawn by BCG was that a firm's primary strategic goal should be market share. A firm's increase in cumulative output compared to a competitor's depends on their relative market shares. If Airbus holds 60 percent of the world market for large commercial jet aircraft and Boeing holds 40 percent, Airbus will reduce its costs at one-and-a-half times the rate of Boeing (other factors being equal).[2]

To benefit from the cost savings from moving down the experience curve, firms should price, not on the basis of current costs, but on the basis of anticipated costs – *penetration pricing* rather than *full-cost pricing*. In its study of the British motorcycle industry, BCG observed that British motorcycle manufacturers adopted cost-plus pricing, whereas Honda priced to meet market share objectives. Honda's assumption was that once sufficient sales volume had been achieved, costs would fall to a level that offered a satisfactory profit margin.[3] The quest for experience-based economies also points to the advantages of maximizing volume by offering a broad rather than a narrow product range and expanding internationally rather than restricting sales to the domestic market.[4]

Empirical studies confirm the positive relationship between profitability and market share.[5] As Table 8.1 shows, high market share is associated with lower costs of investment, receivables, purchases, marketing expenses, and R&D. The result is higher profit margins. Nevertheless, these findings do not necessarily mean that pursuing market share necessarily leads to higher profits. Consider the following:

- *Association is not causation.* Does market share confer superior profit, or do profitable firms use their profits to build market share? The most plausible explanation is that profitability and market share are the joint outcome of some

TABLE 8.1 The Relationship Between Market Share, Costs, and Profitability

MARKET SHARE RANK

	#1	#2	#3	#4	#5 OR BELOW
Investment/Sales	6.3	52.1	52.5	51.4	54.9
Receivables/Sales	14.7	14.7	14.7	14.8	15.3
Inventory/Sales	18.5	19.6	20.5	20.6	22.3
Purchases/Sales	41.8	43.4	45.8	48.8	51.3
Marketing/Sales	8.9	9.5	9.5	9.3	9.2
R&D/Sales	2.1	2.3	1.9	1.8	1.9
Relative Quality (%)	69.0	51.0	47.0	45.0	43.0
Relative Price (%)	105.7	103.8	103.4	103.2	103.0
Pretax Profit/Sales	12.7	9.1	7.1	5.5	4.5

Source: R. D. Buzzell and B. T. Gale, *The PIMS Principles* (New York: Free Press, 1987): 75.

underlying factor – superior efficiency, better customer service, or an innovative product.[6]

■ *The unprofitability of pursuing market share.* Even if firms with high market shares have cost advantages resulting in superior profitability, this does not necessarily imply that pursuing market share will increase profitability. If the relationship between market share and profitability is widely known and if all firms have the opportunity of competing for market share, then the competition for market share will erode any superior profitability resulting from increased market share.[7]

■ *The fallacy of composition.* Pursuing experience economies through pricing for market share may be successful for the individual firm; it can be fatal when attempted by several competitors. During the 1970s, US and European producers of steel, petrochemicals, ships, and synthetic fibers followed the lead of their Japanese competitors by investing heavily in large-scale efficient plants while cutting margins in anticipation of lower costs. Overinvestment and aggressive pricing resulted in losses that continued for a decade or more.

THE SOURCES OF COST ADVANTAGE

The key to cost analysis is to go beyond mechanistic and purely empirical approaches such as the experience curve and probe into the factors that determine a firm's cost position. The experience curve combines four sources of cost reduction: economies of scale, economies of learning, improved process technology and process design, and improved product design. To these we can add three more factors that influence a firm's relative cost position: capacity utilization, the cost of inputs, and residual efficiency. The determinants of a firm's unit costs (cost per unit of output) we term *cost drivers* (see Figure 8.3).

The relative importance of these different cost drivers varies across industries, across firms within an industry, and across the different activities within a firm. By examining each of these different cost drivers, in relation to a particular firm we can do the following:

■ Analyze a firm's cost position relative to its competitors and diagnose the sources of inefficiency.

■ Make recommendations as to how a firm can improve its cost efficiency.

Let's examine the nature and the role of each of these cost drivers.

Economies of Scale

The predominance of large corporations in most manufacturing and service industries is a consequence of economies of scale. Economies of scale exist wherever proportionate increases in the amounts of inputs employed in a production process

FIGURE 8.3 The drivers of cost advantage

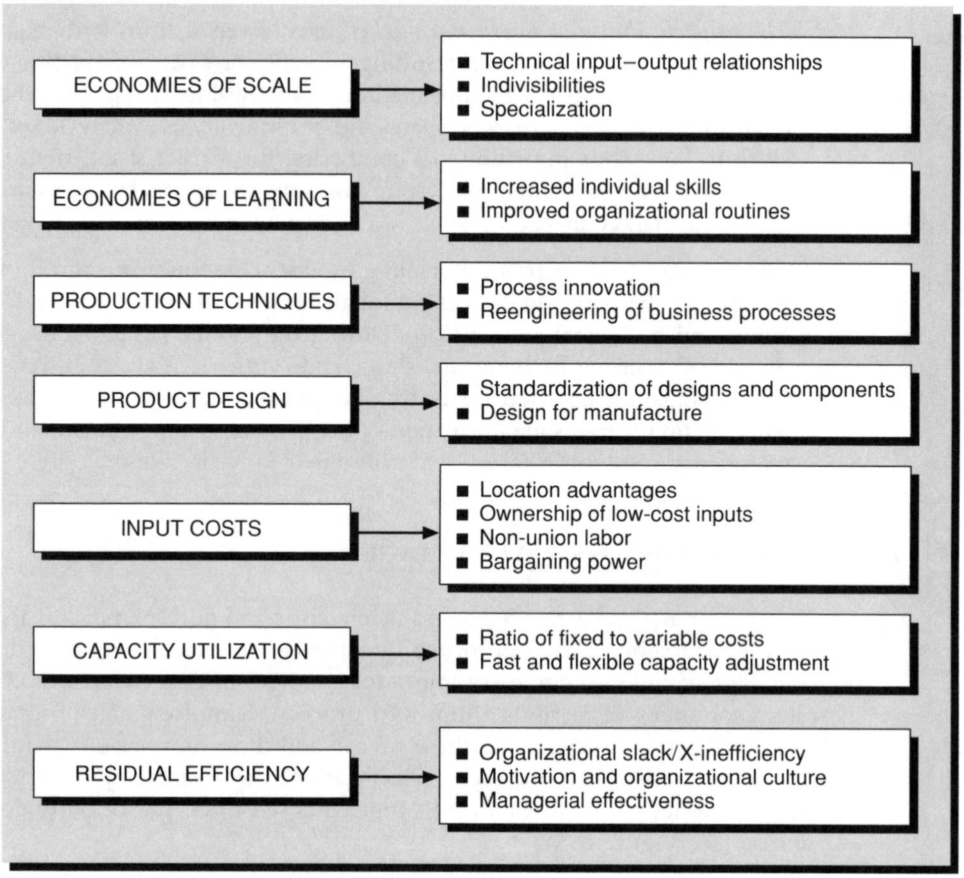

ECONOMIES OF SCALE	→	■ Technical input–output relationships ■ Indivisibilities ■ Specialization
ECONOMIES OF LEARNING	→	■ Increased individual skills ■ Improved organizational routines
PRODUCTION TECHNIQUES	→	■ Process innovation ■ Reengineering of business processes
PRODUCT DESIGN	→	■ Standardization of designs and components ■ Design for manufacture
INPUT COSTS	→	■ Location advantages ■ Ownership of low-cost inputs ■ Non-union labor ■ Bargaining power
CAPACITY UTILIZATION	→	■ Ratio of fixed to variable costs ■ Fast and flexible capacity adjustment
RESIDUAL EFFICIENCY	→	■ Organizational slack/X-inefficiency ■ Motivation and organizational culture ■ Managerial effectiveness

result in lower unit costs. Economies of scale have been conventionally associated with manufacturing. Figure 8.4 shows a typical relationship between unit cost and plant capacity. The point at which most scale economies are exploited is the Minimum Efficiency Plant Size (MEPS). Scale economies are also important in non-manufacturing operations such as purchasing, R&D, distribution, and advertising.

Scale economies arise from three principal sources:

1. *Technical input–output relationships.* In many activities, increases in output do not require proportionate increases in input. A 10,000-barrel oil storage tank does not cost five times the cost of a 2,000-barrel tank. Similar volume-related economies exist in ships, trucks, and steel and petrochemical plants.

2. *Indivisibilities.* Many resources and activities are "lumpy" – they are unavailable in small sizes. Hence, they offer economies of scale, as firms are able to

FIGURE 8.4 The long-run average cost curve for a plant

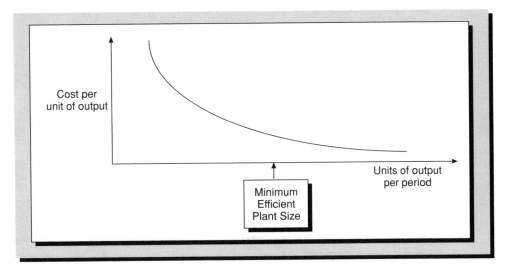

spread the costs of these items over larger volumes of output. A national TV advertising campaign or a research program into fuel cell technology will cost much the same whether it is being undertaken by Toyota or Daihatsu. However, the costs as a percentage of sales will be much lower for Toyota because it has almost 20 times the sales of Daihatsu.

3. *Specialization.* Increased scale permits greater task specialization that is manifest in greater *division of labor*. Mass production – whether in Adam Smith's pin factory or Henry Ford's auto plants (see Chapter 6) – involves breaking down the production process into separate tasks performed by specialized workers using specialized equipment. Specialization promotes learning, avoids time loss from switching activities, and assists in mechanization and automation. Similar economies are important in knowledge-intensive industries such as investment banking, management consulting, and design engineering, where large firms are able to offer specialized expertise across a broad range of know-how.

Scale Economies and Industry Concentration

Scale economies are the single most important determinant of an industry's level of concentration (the proportion of industry output accounted for by the largest firms). However, the critical scale advantages of large companies are seldom in production. In packaged consumer goods – cigarettes, household detergents, beer, and soft drinks – economies of scale in marketing are the key factor causing world markets to be dominated by a few giant companies. Advertising is a key indivisibility. Levi Strauss's 2002 60-second TV commercial made by Bartha Bogle Hegarty cost over $5 million to produce, while the fall 2003 advertising campaign for HP Compaq's consumer

FIGURE 8.5 Economies of scale in advertising: US soft drinks

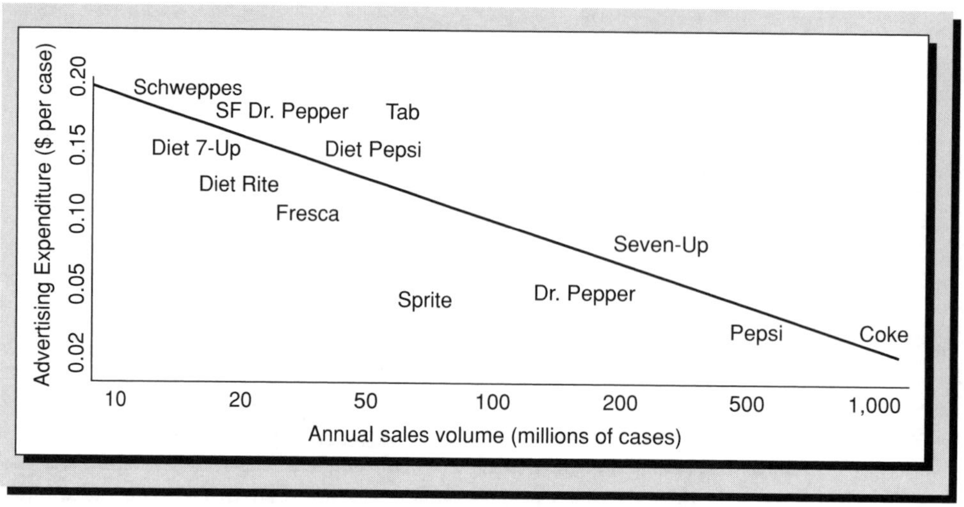

TABLE 8.2 The Development Cost (Including Plant and Tooling) of New Automobile Models

MODEL	ESTIMATED DEVELOPMENT COST
Ford Mondeo/Contour	$6 billion
GM Saturn	$5 billion
Ford Taurus (1996 model)	$2.8 billion
Ford Escort (new model, 1996)	$2 billion
Renault Clio (1999 model)	$1.3 billion
Chrysler Neon	$1.3 billion
Honda Accord (1997 model)	$0.6 billion
BMW Mini	$0.5 billion
Rolls Royce Phantom (2003 model)	$0.3 billion

Source: R. M. Grant, "DaimlerChrysler and the World Automobile Industry," in Grant and Neupert (eds), *Cases in Contemporary Strategy Analysis*, 3rd edn (Oxford: Blackwell Publishing, 2003).

products was budgeted at $300 million. Figure 8.5 shows the relationship between sales volume and average advertising costs for different brands of soft drinks.

Consolidation in the world car industry has been driven by the huge costs associated with new model development (see Table 8.2). Small and medium-sized auto companies have been acquired by larger rivals simply because they lacked the necessary volume over which to amortize the costs of developing new models. Thus, VW acquired Skoda, Seat, and Rolls Royce, while Ford acquired Jaguar, Mazda, Land Rover, and Volvo. To survive, smaller auto producers must license technology and designs from their bigger competitors.[8]

Costs of product development explain the consolidation of large passenger aircraft production into just two companies: Boeing and Airbus. Boeing's traditional cost leadership was based on its amortization of development costs over very long runs: 1,400 747s were built between 1970 and 2003. The $15 billion development cost of the Airbus A380 Superjumbo will require sales of up to 400 planes to reach break even.

The desire to exploit scale economies has also been a key driver behind global expansion. During the 1970s, Japanese companies such as Honda in motorcycles, Toyota in cars, Matsushita in consumer electronics, and Canon in cameras used global strategies to establish positions of cost leadership that seemed impregnable (at least, until the yen began appreciating substantially). In recent years, globalization has extended to the services sector – principally because of scale economies in knowledge and organizational capability. Investment backing is dominated by a few "bulge bracket" banks and the food service industry by two multinational companies – Compass and Sodexho. In hotels, international players such as Marriott and Accord continue to gain ground.

Limits to Scale Economies

Despite the prevalence of scale economies, small and medium-sized companies continue to survive and prosper in competition with much bigger rivals. In the automobile industry, the most profitable companies in recent years have been medium-sized producers such as Peugeot, Renault, and BMW. In US and European banking, smaller banks have consistently been more profitable on average than the big boys. The efficiency advantages of scale are offset by three factors:

- *Product differentiation*. Where customer preferences are differentiated, firms may find that the price premium of targeting a single segment with a differentiated product outweighs the higher cost of small-volume production. General Motors' rise to market leadership over Ford during the late 1920s is a classic example of a multi-model differentiation strategy triumphing over a single-model, scale-economy strategy.

- *Flexibility*. Scale-efficient production is likely to involve highly specialized labor and equipment, which tends to be inflexible. In a fast-changing environment, large plants and large firms do not adjust as quickly as smaller units to fluctuations in demand, prices, and customer preferences.[9]

- *Problems of motivation and coordination*. Large units tend to be more complex and more difficult to manage than smaller units. Common to some of the world's largest plants, from Crown Cork & Seal's original Philadelphia can and bottle cap plant[10] to VW's Wolfsburg Halle 54,[11] has been failure to reach maximum efficiency due to problems of strained labor relations, increased supervision costs, waste of materials, and low levels of employee motivation.

Economies of Learning

The principal source of experience-based cost reduction is learning by organization members. Repetition develops both individual skills and organizational routines. In 1943 it took 40,000 labor-hours to build a Convair B-24 bomber. By 1945 it took only 8,000 hours.[12] The more complex a process or product, the greater the potential for learning. Learning curves are exceptionally steep in semiconductor fabrication. When IBM introduced 0.18 micron, copper-interconnector chips, yields increased from zero to over 50 percent within the first two months. LCD flat screens are notoriously difficult to manufacture – a single defective chip may render an entire screen useless. The dominant position of Sharp and Samsung in flat screens is primarily a result of volume-based learning resulting in exceptionally high yields.[13] Learning occurs both at the individual level through improvements in dexterity and problem solving, and at the group level through the development and refinement of organizational routines.

Process Technology and Process Design

For most goods and services, alternative process technologies exist. A process is technically superior to another when, for each unit of output, it uses less of one input without using more of any other input. Where a production method uses more of some inputs but less of others, then cost efficiency depends on the relative prices of the inputs. Hence, in the US, cost-efficient manufacture of mobile phones is highly automated; in China, cost-efficient manufacture of mobile phones involves labor-intensive assembly.

New process technology may radically reduce costs. Pilkington's float glass process gave it (and its licensees) an unassailable cost advantage in glass production. Ford's moving assembly line reduced the time taken to assemble a Model T from 106 hours to six hours between 1912 and 1913. The automobile was transformed from a rich man's luxury to a mass-market necessity.

When process innovation is embodied in new capital equipment, diffusion is likely to be rapid. Those firms that are expanding the most rapidly and have the highest rates of net investment will tend to establish cost leadership over their slower-growing rivals. However, the full benefits of new processes typically require system-wide changes in job design, employee incentives, product design, organizational structure, and management controls.[14] Between 1979 and 1986, General Motors spent $40 billion on new process technology with the goal of becoming the world's most efficient manufacturer of automobiles. Yet, in the absence of fundamental changes in organization and management, the productivity gains were meager. Cadillac's state-of-the-art Hamtramck plant in Detroit was a nightmare of inefficiency, line stoppages, and robots run amok. After a tour of the plant, Toyota chairman Eiji Toyoda told a colleague, "It would have been embarrassing to comment on it."[15] By contrast, the success of Toyota, Nucor, Dell Computer, McDonald's, and Wal-Mart in establishing cost leadership through superior processes is the result of these companies adapting organization and human resource management to the requirements of new process technologies. The superiority of Japanese companies in flexible manufacturing systems reflects the adaptation of their management processes to the requirements of the new technology.[16]

Indeed, the greatest productivity gains from process innovation typically are the result of organizational improvements rather than technological innovation and new hardware:

- Toyota's system of lean production combines JIT, TQM, continuous improvement (*kaisan*), teamworking, job flexibility, and supplier partnerships.[17]

- Harley-Davidson's gains in productivity during the late 1980s and early 1990s resulted from reorganizing its production processes, human resource management, and control systems, but with limited investment in automation and new manufacturing hardware.[18]

- In retailing, organizational innovations such as from the chain stores during the 1930s (developed by A&P) and discount stores (pioneered by Wal-Mart and Kmart) during the 1960s resulted in huge gains in productivity.

Business Process Reengineering

During the 1990s, recognition that the redesign of operational processes could achieve substantial efficiency gains stimulated a surge of interest in a new management tool called *business process reengineering* (BPR). "Reengineering gurus" Michael Hammer and James Champy defined BPR as:

> the fundamental rethinking and radical redesign of business processes to achieve dramatic improvements in critical contemporary measures of performance, such as cost, quality, service, and speed.[19]

The reengineering movement was based on the recognition that production processes involve complex interactions among many individuals and that these processes evolve over time with little conscious or consistent direction. Redesigning business processes in a logical way can fundamentally increase their efficiency. With information technology, the temptation is to automate existing processes – "paving over cowpaths," as Michael Hammer calls it.[20] The key is to detach from the way in which a process is currently organized and to begin with the question: "If we were starting afresh, how would we design this process?" Although lacking any general theory or design framework, Hammer and Champy point to the existence of a set of "commonalities, recurring themes, or characteristics" that can guide BPR. These include:

- Combining several jobs into one.

- Allowing workers to make decisions.

- Performing the steps of a process in a natural order.

- Recognizing that processes have multiple versions and designing processes to take account of different situations.

- Performing processes where it makes the most sense, e.g., if the accounting department needs pencils, it is probably cheaper for such a small order to be purchased directly from the office equipment store along the block than to be ordered via the firm's purchasing department.

- Reducing checks and controls to the point where they make economic sense.

- Minimizing reconciliation.

- Appointing a case manager to provide a single point of contact at the interface between processes.

- Reconciling centralization with decentralization in process design, e.g., via a shared database, decentralized decisions can be made while permitting overall coordination simply through information sharing.

BPR has been attributed with achieving major gains in efficiency, quality, and speed (see Strategy Capsule 8.1). At the same time, many reengineering initiatives have produced disappointing results. One of the major realizations to emerge from BPR exercises is that most production and administrative processes are exceedingly complex. To redesign a process one must first understand it. Process mapping exercises reveal that even seemingly simple business processes, such as the procurement of office supplies, involve complex and sophisticated systems of interactions among a number of organizational members. Reengineering without a complete understanding of the process is hazardous.

Product Design

Design-for-manufacture – designing products for ease of production rather than simply for functionality and esthetics – can offer substantial cost savings, especially when linked to the introduction of new process technology.

- Volkswagen has cut new-product development costs and component costs by redesigning its 30+ different models around just four different platforms. The VW Beetle, Audi TT, Golf, and Audi A3, together with several Seat and Skoda models, all share a single platform.

- The IBM "Proprinter," one of the most successful computer printers of the 1980s, owed its low costs (and reliability) to an innovative design that:
  - reduced the number of parts from 150, found in the typical PC printer, to 60;
  - designed the printer in layers so that robots could build it from the bottom up;

STRATEGY CAPSULE 8.1 Process Reengineering at IBM Credit

IBM Credit provides credit to customers of IBM for the purchase of IBM hardware and software. Under the old system, five stages were involved:

1. The IBM salesperson telephoned a request for financing. The request was logged on a piece of paper.

2. The request was sent to the Credit Department where it was logged onto a computer and the customer's creditworthiness was checked. The results of the credit check were written on a form and passed to the Business Practices Department.

3. There the standard loan covenant would be modified to meet the terms of customer loan.

4. The request was passed to the pricer who determined the appropriate interest rate.

5. The clerical group took all the information and prepared a quote letter, which was sent to the salesperson.

Because the process took an average of six days, it resulted in a number of lost sales and delayed the sales staff in finalizing deals. After many efforts to improve the process, two managers undertook an experiment. They took a financing request and walked it around through all five steps. The process took 90 minutes!

On this basis, a fundamental redesign of the credit approval process was achieved. The change was replacing the specialists (credit checkers, pricers, and so on) with generalists who undertook all five processes. Only where the request was nonstandard or unusually complex were specialists called in. The basic problem was that the system had been designed for the most complex credit requests that IBM received, whereas in the vast majority of cases no specialist judgment was called for – simply clerical work involving looking up credit ratings, plugging numbers into standard formulae, etc.

The result was that credit requests are processed in four hours compared to six days, total employees were reduced slightly, while the total number of deals increased one hundred times.

Source: Adapted from M. Hammer and J. Champy, *Reengineering the Corporation: A Manifesto for Business Revolution* (New York: HarperBusiness, 1993): 36–9.

- eliminated all screws, springs, and other fasteners that required human insertion and adjustment and replaced them with molded plastic components that clipped together.[21]

■ Service offerings too can be designed for ease and efficiency of production. Motel 6, cost leader in US budget motels, carefully designs its product to keep operating costs low. Its motels occupy low-cost, out-of-town locations, it uses standard motel designs, it avoids facilities such as pools and restaurants, and it designs rooms to facilitate easy cleaning and low maintenance.

Capacity Utilization

Over the short and medium term, plant capacity is more or less fixed, and variations in output are associated with variations in capacity utilization. During periods of low demand, plant capacity is underutilized. This raises unit costs because fixed costs must be spread over fewer units of production. In businesses where virtually all costs are fixed (e.g., airlines, theme parks), profitability is highly sensitive to shortfalls in demand. During periods of peak demand, output may be pushed beyond the normal full-capacity operation. As Boeing discovered in 1997, pushing output beyond capacity operation increases unit costs due to overtime pay, premiums for night and week-end shifts, increased defects, and higher maintenance costs.

In declining industries, the ability speedily to adjust capacity to the current level of demand can be a major source of cost advantage. During the 1980s and early 1990s, British Steel was Europe's most profitable steel producer partly because it reduced capacity faster than its rivals. The key to such adjustment, however, is the ability to distinguish *cyclical* overcapacity – common to all cyclical industries, from semiconductors and construction to hotels and railroads – from the *structural* over-capacity that affects steel, oil refining, automobiles, and the US hospital industry.[22] However, structural overcapacity is not associated only with declining industries. In many emerging, e-commerce industries (including online stockbroking, online auctions, and internet service providers), competition to exploit scale economies and attain market leadership has resulted in capacity far outstripping demand.

Input Costs

When the firms in an industry purchase their inputs in the same competitive input markets, we can expect every firm to pay the same price for identical inputs. In most industries, however, differences in the costs incurred by different firms for similar inputs can be an important source of overall cost advantage. There are several common sources of lower input costs:

- *Locational differences in input prices.* The prices of inputs may vary between locations, the most important being differences in wage rates from one country to another. In the US, software engineers earned an average of $75,000 in 2003. In India the average is $20,000. In less-skilled occupations, differentials are much wider: in textiles, average hourly rates of pay were $11.32 in the US in 2000 and 22 cents in India.[23] Labor-intensive manufacturing – clothing, footwear, hand tools, and toys – have migrated from the first world to the third world.

- *Ownership of low-cost sources of supply.* In raw material-intensive industries, ownership or access to low-cost sources can offer crucial cost advantage. The exploration and production cost of crude oil for the three "supermajors" (Exxon Mobil, Royal Dutch/Shell, and BP) was $8.6 per barrel in 2001. For Saudi Aramco it was $1.50.

- *Non-union labor.* Where employment costs account for a major part of total costs, cost leaders are often the firms that have avoided unionization. In the US airline industry, budget carrier Jet Blue's labor costs were 25.5 percent of revenues compared to 46.8 percent for United. Senior pilots at United earned salaries in excess of $300,000, almost double those of Jet Blue, while union restrictions also resulted in them flying many fewer hours.

■ *Bargaining power.* Where bought-in products are a major cost item, differences in buying power among the firms in an industry can be an important source of cost advantage.[24] Wal-Mart's UK entry (with its acquisition of Asda) was greeted with dismay by British retailers – they recognized that Wal-Mart would be able to use its massive bargaining power to extract additional discounts from Asda's suppliers, which it could use to fuel aggressive price competition.

Residual Efficiency

In many industries, the basic cost drivers – scale, technology, product and process design, input costs, and capacity utilization – fail to provide a complete explanation for why one firm in an industry has lower unit costs than a competitor. Even after taking all these cost drivers into account, unit cost differences between firms remain. These residual efficiencies relate to the extent to which the firm approaches its efficiency frontier of optimal operation. Residual efficiency depends on the firm's ability to eliminate "organizational slack"[25] or "X-inefficiency"[26] – surplus costs that keep the firm from maximum efficiency operation. These costs are often referred to as "organizational fat" and build up unconsciously as a result of employees – both in management and on the shop floor – maintaining some margin of slack in preference to the rigors of operating at maximum efficiency.

Eliminating excess costs is difficult. It may take a shock to a company's very survival to provide the impetus for rooting out institutionalized inefficiencies. When faced with bankruptcy or a precipitous fall in profitability, companies can demonstrate a remarkable capacity for paring costs. For example, as part of the rescue of Nissan Motor by Renault, the ensuing cost cutting implemented by turn-around CEO Carlos Ghosn cut Nissan's operating costs by 20 percent during his first year.[27]

In the absence of a threat to survival, high levels of residual efficiency are typically the result of an organizational culture and management style that are intolerant toward all manifestations of unnecessary costs. At Wal-Mart, for example, parsimony and frugality are virtues that take on a near-religious significance.

Using the Value Chain to Analyze Costs

To analyze costs and make recommendations for building cost advantage, the company or even the business unit is too big a level for us to work at. As we saw in Chapter 5, every business may be viewed as a chain of activities. In most value chains each activity has a distinct cost structure determined by different cost drivers. Analyzing costs requires disaggregating the firm's value chain in order to identify:

- The relative importance of each activity with respect to total cost.

- The cost drivers for each activity and the comparative efficiency with which the firm performs each activity.

- How costs in one activity influence costs in another.

- Which activities should be undertaken within the firm and which activities should be outsourced.

The Principal Stages of Value Chain Analysis

A value chain analysis of a firm's cost position comprises the following stages:

1. *Disaggregate the firm into separate activities.* Determining the appropriate value chain activities is a matter of judgment. It requires understanding the chain of processes involved in the transformation of inputs into output and its delivery to the customer. Very often, the firm's own divisional and departmental structure is a useful guide. Key considerations are:
   - the separateness of one activity from another;
   - the importance of an activity;
   - the dissimilarity of activities in terms of cost drivers;
   - the extent to which there are differences in the way competitors perform the particular activity.

2. *Establish the relative importance of different activities in the total cost of the product.* Our analysis needs to focus on the activities that are the major sources of cost. In disaggregating costs, Michael Porter suggests the detailed assignment of operating costs and assets to each value activity. Though the adoption of activity-based costing has made such cost data more available, detailed cost allocation can be a major exercise.[28] Even without such detailed cost data, it is usually possible to identify the critical activities, establish which activities are performed relatively efficiently or inefficiently, identify cost drivers, and offer recommendations.

3. *Compare costs by activity.* To establish which activities the firm performs relatively efficiently and which it does not, benchmark unit costs for each activity against those of competitors.

4. *Identify cost drivers.* For each activity, what factors determine the level of cost relative to other firms? For some activities, cost drivers are evident simply from the nature of the activity and the composition of costs. For capital-intensive activities such as the operation of a body press in an auto plant, the principal factors are likely to be capital equipment costs, weekly production volume, and downtime between changes of dies. For labor-intensive assembly activities, critical issues are wage rates, speed of work, and defect rates.

5. *Identify linkages.* The costs of one activity may be determined, in part, by the way in which other activities are performed. Xerox discovered that its high

service costs relative to competitors reflected the complexity of design of its copiers, which required 30 different interrelated adjustments. The careful tracing of defects that appear at one stage of a production process to their source in an earlier stage is a key element of total quality management. In recent years, the optimization of activities throughout the value chain has become a major source of cost reduction, and speed enhancement has become a key challenge for computer-integrated manufacturing. SAP of Germany is a leading supplier of the integration of activities within the firm, whereas Manugistics, i2 Technologies, and several other companies compete for leadership in the market for supply chain management software.

6. *Identify opportunities for reducing costs.* By identifying areas of comparative inefficiency and the cost drivers for each, opportunities for cost reduction become evident. For example:

    ■ If scale economies are a key cost driver, can volume be increased? One feature of Caterpillar's cost-reduction strategy was to broaden its model range and OEM (original equipment manufacture) sales of diesel engines to exploit scale economies, R&D, component manufacturing, and dealer support over a larger sales volume.

    ■ Where wage costs are the issue, can wages be reduced either directly or by relocating production?

    ■ If a certain activity cannot be performed efficiently within the firm, can the activity be contracted out, or can the component or service be bought in? Outsourcing in the auto industry has extended to the point where at VW's Brazilian plant, external suppliers not only supply components and subassemblies, they are also responsible for installing them on VW's assembly line. Outsourcing of information technology functions has fueled the growth of EDS, Accenture, and other suppliers of IT services.

Figure 8.6 shows how the application of the value chain to automobile manufacture can yield suggestions for possible cost reductions.

Managing Cost Cutting

As the level of competition in most markets continues, so companies are continually being forced to seek new opportunities for cost reduction. The pressure for cost reduction is strongest in those industries where price competition is fiercest due to commodity products, excess capacity, and many competitors – steel, airlines, and chemicals are classic examples. However, pressures for cost cutting are also being felt in technology-based growth industries. In telecommunications, falling prices and excess capacity are forcing leading players such as AT&T, British Telecom, and Verizon to radically reduce their cost base. In e-commerce, the survivors among online brokers, ISPs, and online retailers were those that cut overheads to the bone. In the aftermath of the Asia crisis of 1997–8, the diversified corporations of Japan, Korea,

FIGURE 8.6 Using the value chain in cost analysis: an automobile manufacturer

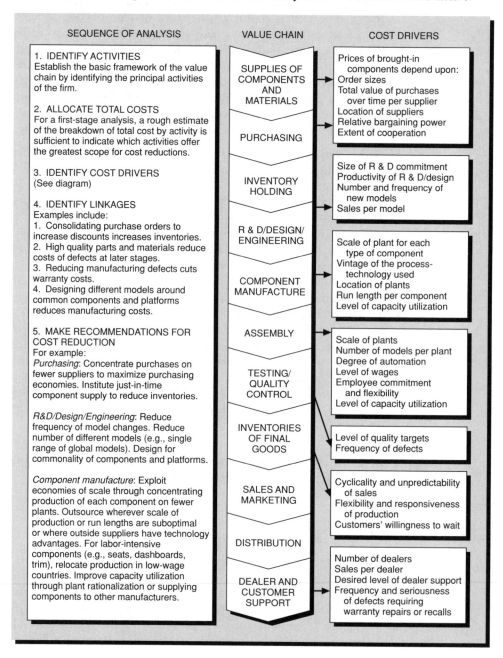

SEQUENCE OF ANALYSIS

1. IDENTIFY ACTIVITIES
Establish the basic framework of the value chain by identifying the principal activities of the firm.

2. ALLOCATE TOTAL COSTS
For a first-stage analysis, a rough estimate of the breakdown of total cost by activity is sufficient to indicate which activities offer the greatest scope for cost reductions.

3. IDENTIFY COST DRIVERS
(See diagram)

4. IDENTIFY LINKAGES
Examples include:
1. Consolidating purchase orders to increase discounts increases inventories.
2. High quality parts and materials reduce costs of defects at later stages.
3. Reducing manufacturing defects cuts warranty costs.
4. Designing different models around common components and platforms reduces manufacturing costs.

5. MAKE RECOMMENDATIONS FOR COST REDUCTION
For example:
Purchasing: Concentrate purchases on fewer suppliers to maximize purchasing economies. Institute just-in-time component supply to reduce inventories.

R&D/Design/Engineering: Reduce frequency of model changes. Reduce number of different models (e.g., single range of global models). Design for commonality of components and platforms.

Component manufacture: Exploit economies of scale through concentrating production of each component on fewer plants. Outsource wherever scale of production or run lengths are suboptimal or where outside suppliers have technology advantages. For labor-intensive components (e.g., seats, dashboards, trim), relocate production in low-wage countries. Improve capacity utilization through plant rationalization or supplying components to other manufacturers.

VALUE CHAIN

SUPPLIES OF COMPONENTS AND MATERIALS

PURCHASING

INVENTORY HOLDING

R & D/DESIGN/ ENGINEERING

COMPONENT MANUFACTURE

ASSEMBLY

TESTING/ QUALITY CONTROL

INVENTORIES OF FINAL GOODS

SALES AND MARKETING

DISTRIBUTION

DEALER AND CUSTOMER SUPPORT

COST DRIVERS

Prices of brought-in components depend upon:
Order sizes
Total value of purchases over time per supplier
Location of suppliers
Relative bargaining power
Extent of cooperation

Size of R & D commitment
Productivity of R & D/design
Number and frequency of new models
Sales per model

Scale of plant for each type of component
Vintage of the process-technology used
Location of plants
Run length per component
Level of capacity utilization

Scale of plants
Number of models per plant
Degree of automation
Level of wages
Employee commitment and flexibility
Level of capacity utilization

Level of quality targets
Frequency of defects

Cyclicality and unpredictability of sales
Flexibility and responsiveness of production
Customers' willingness to wait

Number of dealers
Sales per dealer
Desired level of dealer support
Frequency and seriousness of defects requiring warranty repairs or recalls

and Southeast Asia are engaged in the same type of restructuring and cost cutting that their western counterparts went through during the 1980s and 1990s.

The approach to cost analysis outlined above – identifying cost drivers and exploring their impact on the different activities of the business – is a useful diagnostic tool, but tells us little about how companies actually implement cost-cutting measures. The experience of cost reduction by companies over the past two decades points to two important lessons in managing for cost efficiency: first, the role of dynamic approaches to cost efficiency; second, the potential for integrated approaches to restructuring and cost reduction.

Dynamic Aspects of Cost Efficiency

One of the dangers of the analytic approach to cost analysis outlined above is its static nature. The operations management experts at Harvard Business School point out that the critical advantage of Japanese over American companies in manufacturing industries such as automobiles, consumer electronics, and construction equipment was Japanese companies' emphasis on dynamic efficiency through continuous improvement (*kaizen*).[29] The total quality movement of the 1980s encouraged western corporations to adopt a continuous improvement approach to operations management that had important implications for cost management. The emphasis of TQM on the rigorous analysis of production activities, simplification of processes, training, and empowerment of shop-floor workers resulted in reducing the costs of defects and rework, supervision and maintenance, inventories and work in progress, while stimulating process innovation.[30]

Radical Cost Surgery

For underperforming companies, incremental efficiency increases are unlikely to be sufficient, and radical, short-term initiatives to achieve major cost reductions may be needed to boost financial performance and regain investor confidence. Such radical cost reduction is likely to be part of a wider program of organizational change involving committing to shareholder wealth maximization, divesting poorly performing assets, refocusing around core strengths, and organizational changes to eliminate inefficiencies and increase accountability and speed of decision making. The term *corporate restructuring* refers to these dramatic, simultaneous changes in strategy, structure, and management systems adopted by mature corporations during the 1980s and 1990s as they sought to adjust to an environment of competition, instability, and shareholder activism. The cost-reduction measures involved include:

- Plant closures to improve capacity utilization and eliminate obsolete technology.

- Outsourcing of components and services wherever internal suppliers are less cost efficient than external suppliers.

- Reductions in employment.

■ Increasing managerial efficiency through "delayering" to reduce administrative overhead, and the application of rigorous financial targets and control to provide incentives for aggressive cost reduction.

Because of the urgency of cost reduction and the need to avoid extensive negotiation and compromise, restructuring and radical cost reduction typically involve a recentralization of power into the hands of the CEO with direct, top-down decision making and implementation. In some cases, restructuring plans may be drawn up outside the existing management structure through creating and empowering a high-level task force.

SUMMARY

Cost efficiency may no longer be a guarantee of profitability in today's fast-changing markets, but in almost all industries it is a prerequisite for success. In industries where competition has always been primarily price based – steel, textiles, and mortgage loans – increased intensity of competition requires relentless cost-reduction efforts. In industries where price competition was once muted – airlines, banking, and electrical power – firms have been forced to reconcile the pursuit of innovation, differentiation, and service quality with vigorous cost reduction.

The foundation for a cost-reduction strategy must be an understanding of the determinants of a company's costs. The principal message of this chapter is the need to look behind cost accounting data and beyond simplistic approaches to the determinants of cost efficiency, and to analyze the factors that drive relative unit costs in each of the firm's activities in a systematic and comprehensive manner.

Increasingly, approaches to cost efficiency are less about incremental efficiencies, and more about fundamentally rethinking the activities undertaken by the firm and the ways in which it organizes them. By focusing on those activities in which the firm possesses a cost advantage and outsourcing others, and by extensively reengineering manufacturing and administrative processes, firms have succeeded in achieving dramatic reductions in operating costs.

Given multiple drivers of relative cost, cost management implies multiple initiatives at different organizational levels. Careful analysis of existing activities relative to competitors can pinpoint cost-reduction opportunities by lowering input costs, accessing scale economies, and better utilizing capacity. At the same time, the firm must seek opportunities for innovation and process redesign in order to exploit new sources of dynamic efficiency.

NOTES

1 Louis E. Yelle, "The Learning Curve: Historical Review and Comprehensive Survey," *Decision Sciences* 10 (1979): 302–28.

2 For an analysis of the effect of market share on profit under differently sloped experience curves, see David Ross, "Learning to Dominate," *Journal of Industrial Economics* 34 (1986): 337–53.

3 Boston Consulting Group, *Strategy Alternatives for the British Motorcycle Industry* (London: Her Majesty's Stationery Office, 1975).

4 Charles Baden Fuller, "The Implications of the Learning Curve for Firm Strategy and Public Policy," *Applied Economics* 15 (1983): 541–51.

5 Robert D. Buzzell, Bradley T. Gale, and Ralph Sultan, "Market Share – A Key to Profitability," *Harvard Business Review* (January–February 1975); Robert D. Buzzell and Fredrick Wiersema, "Successful Share-Building Strategies," *Harvard Business Review* (January–February 1981); Robert Jacobsen and David Aaker, "Is Market Share All That It's Cracked up to Be?," *Journal of Marketing* 49 (Fall 1985): 11–22.

6 Richard Rumelt and Robin Wensley, using PIMS data, found the relationship between market share and profitability to be the result of both being joint outcomes of a risky competitive process. "In Search of the Market Share Effect," Paper MGL-63 (Graduate School of Management, UCLA, 1981).

7 Robin Wensley, "PIMS and BCG: New Horizons or False Dawn?," *Strategic Management Journal* 3 (1982): 147–58.

8 To be more precise, the economies of amortizing product development costs are *economies of volume* rather than *economies of scale*. The product development cost per unit depends on the total volume of production over the life of the model.

9 This argument was first made by David Schwartzman, "Uncertainty and the Size of the Firm," *Economica* (August 1963).

10 Joe Bower, "Crown Cork & Seal and the Metal Container Industry," Case 9-373-077 (Boston: Harvard Business School, 1984).

11 Maryann Keller, *Collision* (New York: Doubleday, 1993): 173–7.

12 Leonard Rapping, "Learning and World War II Production Functions," *Review of Economics and Statistics* (February 1965): 81–6. See also Kim B. Clark and Robert H. Hayes, "Recapturing America's Manufacturing Heritage," *California Management Review* (Summer 1988): 25.

13 "Exploiting the Flat Screen Frenzy," Forbes.com (December 12, 2003, http://www.forbes.com/business/manufacturing/2003/12/12/cz_bf_1211tv.html); "Japan Watches Display Market Go Flat," RedHerring.com (January 10, 2001).

14 Robert H. Hayes and Ramchandran Jaikumar, "Manufacturing's Crisis: New Technologies, Obsolete Organizations," *Harvard Business Review* (September–October 1988): 85; and Robert M. Grant, A. B. Shani, R. Krishnan, and R. Baer, "Appropriate Manufacturing Technology: A Strategic Approach," *Sloan Management Review* 33, no. 1 (Fall 1991): 43–54.

15 Maryann Keller, op. cit.: 169–71.

16 Ramchandran Jaikumar, "Postindustrial Manufacturing," *Harvard Business Review* (November–December 1986): 69–76.

17 James Womack and Dan T. Jones, "From Lean Production to Lean Enterprise," *Harvard Business Review* (March–April 1994); James Womack and Dan T. Jones, "Beyond Toyota: How to Root Out Waste and Pursue Perfection," *Harvard Business Review* (September–October 1996).

18 Robert M. Grant, "Harley-Davidson Inc., January 2001," in R. M. Grant and K. E. Neupert (eds), *Cases in Contemporary Strategy Analysis*, 3rd edn (Oxford: Blackwell, 2003).

19 Michael Hammer and James Champy, *Reengineering the Corporation: A Manifesto*

for Business Revolution (New York: HarperBusiness, 1993): 32. See also Michael Hammer, *Beyond Reengineering: How the Processed Centered Organization Is Changing our Work and our Lives* (New York: HarperBusiness, 1996).

20 Michael Hammer, "Reengineering Work: Don't Automate, Obliterate," *Harvard Business Review* (July–August 1990).

21 Ralph E. Gomory, "From the Ladder of Science to the Product Development Cycle," *Harvard Business Review* (November–December 1989): 103.

22 Jim Billington, "Listening to Overcapacity – Lessons from the Auto and Health Care Industries," *Harvard Management Update* (Boston: Harvard Business School, 1998, Reprint # U98068).

23 International Labor Organization (http://www.ilo.org/public/english/bureau/stat/).

24 See Robert M. Grant, "Manufacturer-Retailer Relations: The Shifting Balance of Power," in G. Johnson (ed.), *Retailing and Business Strategy* (New York: John Wiley, 1987).

25 R. Cyert and J. March, *A Behavioral Theory of the Firm* (Englewood Cliffs, NJ: Prentice-Hall, 1963).

26 H. Leibenstein, "Allocative Efficiency Versus X-Efficiency," *American Economic Review* 54 (June 1966).

27 "Nissan on the Road to Recovery," *Financial Times* (October 4, 2000): 17.

28 On activity-based costing, see Robert S. Kaplan and Robin Cooper, *Cost and Effect: Using Integrated Cost Systems to Drive Profitability and Performance* (Boston: Harvard Business School Press, 1997); Jim Billington, "The ABCs of ABC: Activity-based Costing and Management," *Harvard Management Update* (Boston: Harvard Business School Publishing, May 1999).

29 Robert H. Hayes, Steven C. Wheelwright, and Kim B. Clark, *Dynamic Manufacturing: Creating the Learning Organization* (New York: Free Press, 1988).

30 David A. Garvin, *Managing Quality: The Strategic and Competitive Edge* (New York: Free Press, 1988).

9

Differentiation
Advantage

If the three keys to selling real estate are location, location, location, then the three keys of selling consumer products are differentiation, differentiation, differentiation.

—**Robert Goizueta, former Chairman,
Coca-Cola Company**

If you gave me $100 billion and said, "Take away the soft drink leadership of Coca-Cola in the world," I'd give it back to you and say, "It can't be done."

—**Warren Buffett, Chairman, Berkshire
Hathaway, and Coca-Cola's biggest shareholder**

OUTLINE

271

INTRODUCTION AND OBJECTIVES

A firm differentiates itself from its competitors "when it provides something unique that is valuable to buyers beyond simply offering a low price."[1] Differentiation advantage occurs when a firm is able to obtain from its differentiation a price premium in the market that exceeds the cost of providing the differentiation.

Every firm has opportunities for differentiating its offering to customers, although the range of differentiation opportunities depends on the characteristics of the product. An automobile or a restaurant offers greater potential for differentiation than standardized products such as cement, wheat, or computer memory chips. These latter products are called "commodities" precisely because they lack physical differentiation. Yet, even commodity products can be differentiated in ways that create customer value: "Anything can be turned into a value-added product or service for a well-defined or newly created market," claims Tom Peters.[2]

The personal computer has become a commodity item: the components are standardized and PCs are identified by their technical specifications rather than by their brand name. Yet, Dell Computer's direct sales model has allowed it to differentiate its PCs offerings by permitting customers to design their own computer system and offering complementary services such as online customer support, three-year on-site warranty, web hosting, installation and configuration of customers' hardware and software. Founded in 1984 by 19-year-old Michael Dell, Dell Computer has become the world's market leader in PCs and earned a return on equity that averaged 55 percent during 1998–2003. The lesson from Dell Computer is this: differentiation is not simply about offering different product features, it is about identifying and understanding every possible interaction between the firm and its customers, and asking how the these interactions can be enhanced or changed in order to deliver additional value to the customer.

Analyzing differentiation requires looking at both the firm (the supply side) and its customers (the demand side). While supply-side analysis identifies the firm's potential to create uniqueness, the critical issue is whether such differentiation creates value for customers, and whether the value created exceeds the cost of the differentiation. Hence, in this chapter we shall be concerned especially with the demand side of the market. By understanding what customers want, how they choose, and what motivates them, we can identify opportunities for profitable differentiation.

Differentiation strategies are not about pursuing uniqueness for the sake of being different. Differentiation is about understanding customers and how our product can meet their needs. To this extent, the quest for differentiation advantage takes us to the heart of business strategy. The fundamental issues of differentiation are also the fundamental issues of business strategy: Who are our customers? How do we create value for them? And how do we do it more effectively and efficiently than anyone else?

Because differentiation is about uniqueness, establishing differentiation advantage requires creativity – it cannot be achieved simply through applying standardized frameworks and techniques. This is not to say that differentiation advantage is not amenable to systematic analysis. As we have observed, there are two requirements for creating profitable differentiation. On the supply side, the firm must be aware of the resources and capabilities through which it can create uniqueness (and do it better than competitors). On the demand side, the key is insight into customers and their needs and preferences. These two sides form the major components of our analysis of differentiation.

By the time you have completed this chapter you will be able to:

- Understand what differentiation is, recognize its different forms, and appreciate its potential for creating competitive advantage.

- Analyze the sources of differentiation in terms of customers' preferences and characteristics, and of the firm's capacity for supplying differentiation.

- Formulate strategies that create differentiation advantage by linking the firm's differentiation capability to customers' demand for differentiation.

THE NATURE OF DIFFERENTIATION AND DIFFERENTIATION ADVANTAGE

Let us begin by exploring what differentiation is and why it is such an important basis for competitive advantage.

Differentiation Variables

The potential for differentiating a product or service is partly determined by its physical characteristics. For products that are technically simple (a pair of socks, a brick), that satisfy uncomplicated needs (a corkscrew, a nail), or must meet rigorous technical standards (a spark plug, a thermometer), differentiation opportunities are constrained by technical and market factors. Products that are technically complex (an airplane), that satisfy complex needs (an automobile, a vacation), or that do not need to conform to particular technical standards (wine, toys) offer much greater scope for differentiation.

Beyond these constraints, the potential in any product or service for differentiation is limited only by the boundaries of the human imagination. For seemingly simple products such as shampoo, toilet paper, and bottled water, the proliferation of brands on any supermarket's shelves is testimony both to the ingenuity of firms and the complexity of customer preferences. Differentiation extends beyond the physical characteristics of the product or service to encompass everything about the product or service that influences the value customers derive from it. This means that differentiation includes every aspect of the way in which a company relates to its customers. Thus, Levi Strauss's quest for differentiation advantage in the world market for jeans and casual clothing comprises not just the characteristics of its garments and the retail environments in which they are sold, but also the values it communicates to consumers including the care with which it treats the workers who manufacture its products in the third world, its concern for originality and authenticity, and its community involvement. Differentiation is not an activity specific to particular functions such as design and marketing; it infuses all activities within the organization and is built into the identity and culture of a company. As a result, companies that supply seemingly basic, no-frills offerings such as Volkswagen (with its Beetle), Southwest Airlines, and Wal-Mart may occupy market positions that are highly differentiated in terms of customers' perceptions.

Thus, differentiation strategy extends beyond product differentiation to embrace the totality of the relationship between a company and its customers. Ultimately, successful differentiation requires what Tom Peters calls "total customer responsiveness:"

> Every action, no matter how small, and no matter how far from the firing line a department may be, must be processed through the customer's eyes. Will this make it easier for the customer? Faster? Better? Less expensive? . . . Long-term profit equals revenue from continuously happy customer relationships minus cost.[3]

In analyzing differentiation opportunities, we can distinguish *tangible* and *intangible* dimensions of differentiation. Tangible differentiation is concerned with the observable characteristics of a product or service that are relevant to customers' preferences and choice processes. These include size, shape, color, weight, design, material, and technology. Tangible differentiation also includes the performance of the product or service in terms of reliability, consistency, taste, speed, durability, and safety.

Tangible differentiation extends to products and services that complement the product in question. There is little that is distinctive about Dell's computers. The differentiation lies in the speed with which they are delivered, the flexibility with which customers can configure their own systems, and after-sales services including technical support, on-line training courses, repair service, upgrading service, and customer discussion forum – to mention but a few. Opportunities for intangible differentiation arise because the value that customers perceive in a product or service does not depend exclusively on the tangible aspects of the offering. There are few products where customer choice is determined solely by observable product features or objective performance criteria. Social, emotional, psychological, and esthetic considerations are present in choices over all products and services. The desires for status, exclusivity, individuality, and security are powerful motivational forces in choices relating to most consumer goods. Where a product or service is meeting complex customer needs, differentiation choices involve the overall image of the firm's offering. Image differentiation are especially important for those products and services whose qualities and performance are difficult to ascertain at the time of purchase ("experience goods"). These include cosmetics, medical services, and education.

Differentiation and Segmentation

Differentiation is different from segmentation. Differentiation is concerned with *how* a firm competes – the ways in which it can offer uniqueness to customers. Such uniqueness might relate to consistency (McDonald's), reliability (Federal Express), status (American Express), quality (BMW), and innovation (Sony). Segmentation is concerned with *where* a firm competes in terms of customer groups, localities, and product types.

Whereas segmentation is a feature of market structure, differentiation is a strategic choice by a firm. A segmented market is one that can be partitioned according to the characteristics of customers and their demand. Differentiation is concerned with a firm's positioning within a market (or market segment) in relation to the product, service, and image characteristics that influence customer choice.[4] By locating within a segment, a firm does not necessarily differentiate itself from its competitors within the same segment. Ameritrade, E*Trade, and T.D. Waterhouse are all located within the online segment of the brokerage industry, yet these firms are not significantly differentiated from one another. At the same time, a company may pursue a differentiation strategy, but position itself within the mass market and span multiple segments. Dell Computer, Amazon, McDonald's, Ford Motor Company, and Starbucks Coffee all aim at well-defined positions of differentiation within their markets, while aiming at market share leadership.

However, differentiation decisions tend to be closely linked to choices over the segments in which a firm competes. By offering uniqueness in its offerings, a firm may inevitably target certain market niches. By selecting performance, engineering, and style as the basis on which BMW competes in the automobile industry, it inevitably appeals to different market segments than does VW. To the extent that differentiation is imitated by other companies, the result can be the creation of new market segments. In the beer industry innovative differentiation to offer light beer, high-alcohol beer, microbrews, and brewpubs have resulted in the emergence of new market segments.

The Sustainability of Differentiation Advantage

Although strategy analysis has traditionally emphasized cost advantage as the primary basis for competitive advantage, low cost offers a less secure basis for competitive advantage than does differentiation. The growth of international competition has revealed the fragility of seemingly well-established positions of domestic cost leadership. Across North America, Western Europe, and Japan, companies whose competitive advantage rested on cost leadership have been undercut by overseas competitors with lower labor costs. In the US textile industry, low-cost imports have driven leading producers such as Burlington Industries and Westpoint Stevens into Chapter 11. In steel, only government protection has allowed former giants such as USX (formerly US Steel) and Bethlehem Steel to survive the low-cost of competition from South Korea, Eastern Europe, and Latin America. Cost advantage is highly vulnerable to unpredictable external forces. The 50 percent rise of the euro against the US dollar in the two years up to January 2004 was devastating for the cost competitiveness of most European companies. Looking ahead to 2005 and 2006, it looked as though Airbus was doomed to fall behind Boeing once more. Despite a decade-long strategy that has resulted in Airbus wresting leadership of the world passenger jet market from Boeing and despite Boeing's catalog of strategic errors, currency market trends promised to restore Boeing's fortunes and market leadership.

Even within a domestic context, cost advantage may be vulnerable to new technology and strategic innovation. Thus, low-cost foreign competition is only partly to blame for the decline of the US integrated iron and steel producers. They have also lost ground to the minimill producers – Nucor, Chaparral Steel, Steel Dynamics, and a host of other newcomers. In retailing, former cost leaders such as Sears Roebuck and J. C. Penney were undermined by discount retailers such as Wal-Mart, Target, and Best Buy. In stockbroking, discount brokers such as Quick and Reilly, Brown & Company, Olde, and Seibert were undercut by online brokers such as Ameritrade and E*Trade.

Hence, sustained high profitability is associated more with differentiation than cost leadership. Table 9.1 shows that large companies earning the highest return on equity tend to be those that have pursued differentiation through quality, branding, and innovation.

ANALYZING DIFFERENTIATION: THE DEMAND SIDE

Successful differentiation involves matching customers' demand for differentiation with the firm's capacity to supply differentiation. Let's begin with the demand side. Analyzing customer demand enables us to determine which product characteristics have the potential to create value for customers, customers' willingness to pay for differentiation, and a company's optimal competitive positioning in terms of differentiation variables.

Analyzing demand begins with understanding why customers buy a product or service. What are the needs and requirements of a person who is purchasing a personal computer? What is motivating a company when it hires management consultants? Market research systematically explores customer preferences and customer perceptions of existing products. However, the key to successful differentiation is to understand customers. In gaining insight into customer requirements and preferences, simple, direct questions about the purpose of a product and its performance

TABLE 9.1 Companies Among the 300 Largest US Corporations with the Highest Return on Equity, 2002

	RETURN ON EQUITY %
Colgate Palmolive	367.8
Caremark Rx	303.2
American Standard	161.4
Yum Brands	98.1
Kellogg	80.5
Anheuser-Busch	63.4
Nextel Communications	58.3
Sara Lee	58.0
Altria Group	57.0
Wyeth	54.5
Gillette	53.8
H. J. Heinz	48.5
Pfizer	45.7
Dell Computer	43.0
TJX	41.3
Oracle	36.4
PepsiCo	35.6
3M	32.9
Eli Lilly	32.7
Sysco	31.9

Source: "The Fortune 500," *Fortune* (April 14, 2003).

attributes can often be far more illuminating than objective market research data obtained from large samples of actual and potential customers. Strategy Capsule 9.1 offers a striking example of the value of simplicity and directness in probing customer requirements.

Product Attributes and Positioning

Virtually all products and services serve multiple customer needs. As a result, understanding customer needs requires the analysis of multiple attributes. Market research has developed numerous techniques for analyzing customer preferences in relation to different product attributes. These techniques – including multidimensional scaling, conjoint analysis, and hedonic price analysis – can guide the positioning of new products, repositioning of existing products, and setting product prices.

Multidimensional Scaling

Multidimensional scaling (MDS) permits customers' perceptions of competing products' similarities and dissimilarities to be represented graphically and for the dimensions to be interpreted in terms of key product attributes.[5] For example, a survey of consumer ratings of competing pain relievers resulted in the mapping shown in

STRATEGY CAPSULE 9.1   Understanding What a Product Is About

Getting back to strategy means getting back to a deep understanding of what a product is about. Some time back, for example, a Japanese home appliance company was trying to develop a coffee percolator. Should it be a General Electric-type percolator, executives wondered? Should it be the same drip-type that Philips makes? Larger? Smaller? I urged them to ask a different kind of question: Why do people drink coffee? What are they looking for when they do? If your objective is to serve the customer better, then shouldn't you understand why that customer drinks coffee in the first place? Then you would know what kind of percolator to make.

The answer came back: good taste. Then I asked the company's engineers what they were doing to help the consumer enjoy good taste in a cup of coffee. They said they were trying to design a good percolator. I asked them what influences the taste in a cup of coffee. No one knew. That became the next question we had to answer. It turns out that lots of things can affect taste – the beans, the temperature, the water. We did our homework and discovered all the things that affect taste . . .

Of all the factors, water quality, we learned, made the greatest difference. The percolator in design at the time, however, didn't take water quality into account at all . . . We discovered next the grain distribution and the time between grinding the beans and pouring in the water were crucial. As a result we began to think about the product and its necessary features in a new way. It had to have a built-in dechlorinating function. It had to have a built-in grinder. All the customer should have to do is pour in water and beans . . .

To start you have to ask the right questions and set the right kinds of strategic goals. If your only concern is that General Electric has just brought out a percolator that brews coffee in ten minutes, you will get your engineers to design one that brews it in seven minutes. And if you stick to that logic, market research will tell you that instant coffee is the way to go . . . Conventional marketing approaches won't solve the problem. If you ask people whether they want their coffee in ten minutes or seven, they will say seven, of course. But it's still the wrong question. And you end up back where you started, trying the beat the competition at its own game. If your primary focus is on the competition, you will never step back and ask what the customers' inherent needs are, and what the product really is about.

Source: Kenichi Ohmae, "Getting Back to Strategy," *Harvard Business Review* (November–December 1988): 154. Copyright © 1988 by the President and Fellows of Harvard College; all rights reserved.

Figure 9.1. MDS has also been used to classify 109 single-malt Scotch whiskies according to the characteristics of their color, nose, palate, body, and finish.[6]

Conjoint Analysis

Conjoint analysis is a powerful means of analyzing the strength of customer preferences for different product attributes. The technique requires, first, an identification of the underlying attributes of a product and, second, market research to rank hypothetical products that contain alternative bundles of attributes. The results can then be used to estimate the proportion of customers who would prefer a hypothetical new product to competing products already available in the market.[7] A conjoint analysis undertaken by BCG of potential personal computer buyers identified price, manufacturer's reputation, portability, processing capability, memory capacity, word processing capability, and styling as critical attributes. The data were used to predict

FIGURE 9.1 Consumer perceptions of competing pain relievers: a multidimensional scaling mapping

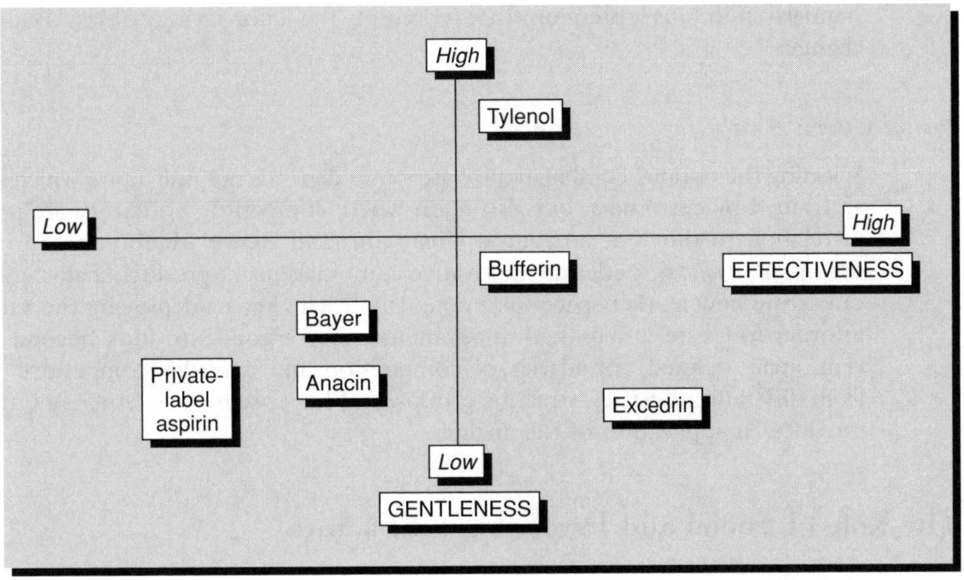

the share of customer preferences that forthcoming IBM and Apple new models would obtain, and to simulate the effects of changing the design features and prices.[8] Conjoint analysis has been used to design new products ranging from Marriott's Courtyard hotel chain[9] to nature tourism in the Amazon basin.[10]

Hedonic Price Analysis

The demand for a product may be viewed as the demand for the underlying attributes that the product provides.[11] The price at which a product can sell in the market is the aggregate of the values derived from each of these individual attributes. Hedonic price analysis observes price differences for competing products, relates these differences to the different combinations of attributes offered by each product, and calculates the implicit market price for each attribute. For example:

- For European automatic washing machines, price differences were related to differences in capacity, spin speed, energy consumption, number of programs, and reliability (as indicated by consumer organizations' data). Using estimates of the implicit price for each attribute, it is possible to determine the price premium that can be charged for additional units of a particular attribute. In Britain, for example, a machine that spins at 1000 rpm sells at about a $200 price premium to one that spins at 800 rpm.[12]

- In the case of spreadsheets, hedonic price analysis was used to value attributes such as compatibility with a Lotus platform, links to external databases, and LAN linkage.[13]

It may not be necessary to resort to hedonic price analysis to calculate the price advantage that differentiation will support. For example, if GE develops a new light bulb with twice the life of a standard bulb, this should sell at twice the price of the standard bulb plus a premium that represents the labor savings of less frequent bulb changes.

Value Curve Analysis

Selecting the optimal combination of attributes depends not only upon which attributes are valued by customers, but also upon where competitors' offerings are positioned in relation to different attributes. Chan Kim and Renee Mauborgne advocate the use of *value curves* to identify innovative combinations of product characteristics that can create new market space for a company.[14] The key to deploying the value curve in order to create differentiation advantage, they argue, is to look beyond the conventionally defined boundaries of competition and consider competitive offerings from different industries, strategic groups, and buyer segments. Strategy Capsule 9.2 provides an application of the analysis.

The Role of Social and Psychological Factors

The problem with analyzing product differentiation in terms of measurable performance attributes is that it does not delve very far into customers' underlying motivations. Very few goods or services are acquired to satisfy basic needs for survival: most buying reflects social goals and values in terms of the desire to find community with others, to establish one's own identity, and to make sense of what is happening in the world. Our discussion of goals in Chapter 2 referred to Maslow's hierarchy of needs: once basic needs for survival are satisfied, there is a progression from security needs, to belonging needs, to esteem needs, to self-actualization needs.[15] Most suppliers of branded goods recognize that their brand equities have much more to do with status and conformity than to survival or security. The disastrous introduction of "New Coke" in 1985 was the result of Coca-Cola giving precedence to tangible differentiation (taste preferences) over intangible differentiation (authenticity).[16] Harley-Davidson harbors no such illusions: It recognizes quite clearly that it is in the business of selling lifestyle, not transportation.

If the key customer needs that a product satisfies are self-identity and social affiliation, the implications for differentiation are far reaching. In particular, to understand customer demand and identify profitable differentiation opportunities requires that we analyze the product and its characteristics, but also customers, their lifestyles and aspirations, and the relationship of the product to these lifestyles and aspirations. Market research that looks behind the product and explores the demographic (age, sex, race, location), socioeconomic (income, education), and psychographic (lifestyle, personality type) characteristics of potential customers may be of some value. However, effective differentiation is likely to depend on an understanding of what customers want and how they behave rather than the results of statistical market

STRATEGY CAPSULE 9.2 Using the Value Curve to Establish Innovative Differentiation: Borders and Barnes and Noble

The value curve is drawn by plotting the performance characteristics of an offering along the different success factors that define competition within the market. Kim and Mauborgne suggest that all too often companies fail to see the scope for creating offerings with value curves that are radically different from those provided by market incumbents. During the late 1980s, the US market for books appeared stagnant. Borders and Barnes and Noble succeeded in reviving book retailing by developing a new model of bookselling that offered a very different value curve from that offered either by independent or chain book retailers.

Value curves for Borders and Barnes and Noble compared with conventional book retailers

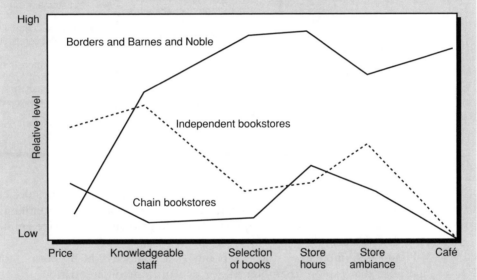

Source: Adapted from C. Kim and R. Mauborgne, "Creating New Market Space," *Harvard Business Review* (January–February 1999): 83–93.

research. While the phenomenon is complex, the answer, according to Tom Peters, is simple: business people need to listen to their customers:

> Good listeners get out from behind their desks to where the customers are . . . Further, good listeners construct settings so as to maximize "naive" listening, the undistorted sort . . . Finally, good listeners provide quick feedback and act on what they hear.[17]

In practice, understanding customer needs and preferences is likely to require more than listening. Typically, consumers cannot clearly articulate the motives that drive them and the emotions that different products trigger. Companies must observe their customers in order to understand their lives and their use of the product. The implication is that, for companies to understand their customers, they need to become

FIGURE 9.2 Identifying differentiation potential: the demand side

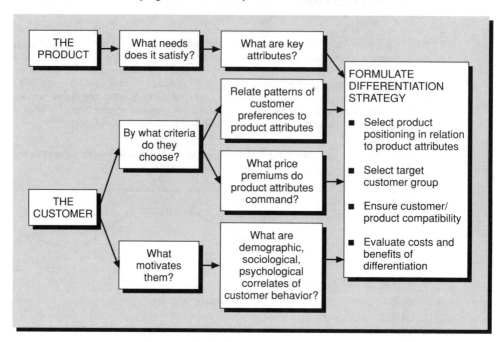

involved in them. Johansson and Nonaka show that Japanese companies emphasize intuition and relationships. Satisfying the customer is not about bundling together favored attributes, but is about going beyond functionality to provide emotional and esthetic satisfaction.[18]

Figure 9.2 summarizes the key points of this discussion by posing some basic questions that explore the potential for demand-side differentiation.

Broad-based versus Focused Differentiation

Differentiation, we have observed, may focus on a broad market appeal or on a specific market segment. The choice of market scope has important implications for demand analysis. Establishing broad-based differentiation advantage requires that a firm ascertains the general needs that the product satisfies and what different customers have in common in terms of their motivations and choice criteria. Establishing focused differentiation involves concentrating upon the factors that segment a market. To reconcile differentiation advantage with cost efficiency typically means that a company establishes uniqueness while still appealing to a broad range of customers:

■ McDonald's has extended its appeal across age groups, social groups, and national boundaries by emphasizing a few qualities with universal appeal: speed, consistency, value, hygiene, and family lifestyles.

- In food and apparel, the British retailer Marks & Spencer successfully established a reputation for product quality and fair dealing that extended across the traditional class divisions that segment British retailing.

- Honda has positioned itself within the US auto market to achieve a broad-based market appeal in contrast to most American and European brands, which target specific demographic and socioeconomic segments.

The challenge for broad-based differentiators is the tendency for focused differentiation to displace broad-based differentiation. In general, customers prefer a targeted product offering that matches their particular preferences to one that is designed to appeal to a broad range of tastes. The rapid decline of network broadcasting (NBC, ABC, CBS, and Fox in the US; BBC and ITV in the UK) reflects the inherent advantages of cable and satellite channels in targeting the specific interests of children, sports fans, movie watchers, music-video enthusiasts, sci-fi buffs, and home-shopping addicts.

At the same time, segment-focused approaches to differentiation run risks. Apart from the higher unit costs incurred in supplying a narrow rather than a broad market, there are dangers that market segments can change over time, or that a firm adopts an inappropriate segmentation in the first place. During the 1990s, General Motors' segmented marketing strategy that targeted each brand on a specific price bracket and particular socioeconomic category ran into increasing problems as US customers showed less and less identification with the segments GM had defined for them.

ANALYZING DIFFERENTIATION: THE SUPPLY SIDE

Demand analysis identifies customers' demands for differentiation and their willingness to pay for it, but creating differentiation advantage also depends on a firm's ability to offer differentiation. To identify the firm's potential to supply differentiation, we need to examine the activities the firm performs and the resources it has access to.

The Drivers of Uniqueness

Differentiation is concerned with the provision of uniqueness. A firm's opportunities for creating uniqueness in its offerings to customers are not located within a particular function or activity, but can arise in virtually everything that it does. Michael Porter identifies a number of drivers of uniqueness which are decision variables for the firm:

- Product features and product performance.

- Complementary services (e.g., credit, delivery, repair).

- Intensity of marketing activities (e.g., rate of advertising spending).

FIGURE 9.3 Differentiation of merchandise (hardware) and support (software)

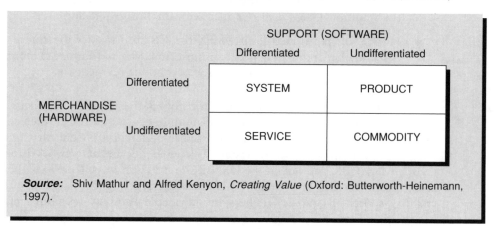

Source: Shiv Mathur and Alfred Kenyon, *Creating Value* (Oxford: Butterworth-Heinemann, 1997).

- Technology embodied in design and manufacture.

- The quality of purchased inputs.

- Procedures influencing the conduct of each activities (e.g., rigor of quality control, service procedures, frequency of sales visits to a customer).

- The skill and experience of employees.

- Location (e.g., with retail stores).

- The degree of vertical integration (which influences a firm's ability to control inputs and intermediate processes).[19]

Most transactions do not involve a single product or a single service, but are a combination of products and services. In analyzing the potential for differentiation, we can distinguish between differentiation of the product ("hardware") and ancillary services ("software"). On this basis, four transaction categories can be identified (see Figure 9.3).[20]

As markets mature, so systems comprising both hardware and software tend to "unbundle." Products become commoditized while complementary services become provided by specialized suppliers. However, as customer preferences become increasingly sophisticated and companies seek new opportunities for differentiation advantage, so hardware and software is repackaged into new systems. In the introduction I noted that, as the "Wintel"-standard has increasingly commoditized personal computers, so Dell Computer seeks new opportunities for bundling products with various support services.

A critical issue is whether such bundling really creates customer value. Thus, the offer of "one-stop shopping" by financial service companies through diversifying across personal banking, brokerage services, fund management, and insurance has had limited appeal to customers. The advent of internet-based electronic commerce has greatly reduced customers' transaction costs, allowing them easily to assemble their own bundles of goods and services at low cost. The declining fortunes of European tour operators that organize vacations comprising flights, hotel bookings, car hire, insurance, and other services is the result of the increasing consumer preference to use on-line information and reservations systems to create their own customized vacations.[21] The result, according to McKinsey consultants Hagel and Singer, is not just unbundling of products, but the unbundling of the corporation itself.[22]

Product Integrity

All companies face a range of differentiation opportunities. The primary issue is likely to be determining which forms of differentiation may be most successful in distinguishing the firm in the market and which are most valued by customers. However, such choices cannot be made on a piecemeal basis. Establishing a coherent and effective differentiation position requires that the firm assemble a complementary package of differentiation measures. If Beck's beer wishes to differentiate itself on the basis of the quality of its ingredients, then it must adopt production methods that are consistent with quality ingredients, and packaging, advertising, and distribution appropriate to a quality, premium-priced product.

Product integrity refers to the consistency of a firm's differentiation; it is the extent to which a product achieves:

> total balance of numerous product characteristics including basic functions, aesthetics, semantics, reliability, and economy . . . Product integrity has both internal and external dimensions. Internal integrity refers to consistency between the function and structure of the product – e.g., the parts fit well, components match and work well together, layout achieves maximum space efficiency. External integrity is a measure of how well a product's function, structure, and semantics fit the customer's objectives, values, production system, lifestyle, use pattern, and self-identity.[23]

In their study of product development in the car industry, Clark and Fujimoto argue that simultaneously achieving internal and external integrity is the most complex organizational challenge facing automakers, since it requires linking close cross-functional collaboration with intimate customer contact. The organizational changes among US and European automakers, including the growing role of product managers, have attempted to imitate the success of Toyota and Honda in achieving internal–external integration.[24]

Achieving combined internal and external product integrity is especially important to those supplying "lifestyle" products whose differentiation is based on customers' social and psychological needs. Here, the credibility of the image depends critically on the consistency of the image presented. A critical factor in such differentiation is the ability of employees and customers to identify with one another. Thus:

- Harley-Davidson's ability to develop its image of ruggedness, independence, and individuality is supported by a top management team that dons biking leathers and ride its "hogs" to owners' group rallies, and a management system that empowers shop-floor workers and fosters quality, initiative, and responsibility.

■ MTV's capacity to stay at the leading edge of popular culture and embody "coolness" for new generations of young people owes much to its internal culture and human resource management, which rely heavily on the ideas and enthusiasm of its youngest employees.[25]

Maintaining integrity of differentiation is ultimately dependent on a company's ability to live the values embodied in the images with which its products are associated (see Strategy Capsule 9.3).

STRATEGY CAPSULE 9.3   Body Shop: The Role of Values in Differentiation

---

Though Anita Roddick scorns businessmen and management principles, the success of Body Shop reveals an insightful and sophisticated approach to differentiation strategy. In some respects, Body Shop's strategy is consistent with other manufacturers of cosmetics and toiletries – success has always been associated with the establishment of a strong product image that requires consistency among the product, the packaging, the advertising and promotion, the retail environment, and the image of the company.

To this extent, Body Shop is not novel: its products are physically differentiated. This differentiation is carried through to the packaging and to the retail environment in which the products are sold. Indeed, Body Shop goes one step further than most competitors – it only sells its products within its own franchised stores. However, defining its image, Body Shop contradicted the industry's long-established conventions. Rather than peddle the allure of beauty, youth, and sexual attractiveness, Body Shop rejects this "magic" – "My products can only cleanse, moisten, and protect," says Roddick.

Body Shop emphasizes traditional notions of grooming, maintaining, and enhancing faces and bodies through the use of natural ingredients, many of them associated with the traditions of ethnic peoples throughout the world. This differentiation of the product is supported by a strong commitment to researching a wide range of natural products from oatmeal to quinoa oil.

Emphasis on the natural properties of its products is communicated by packaging that emphasizes simplicity, economy, and information and retail outlets that are open, non-ostentatious, and designed to encourage customers to look, read, sample, and interact with sales personnel.

Body Shop's values of honesty, simplicity, and fairness extend to its policies towards environmental and social responsibility. The primary medium for communication is Body Shop's employees and franchisees. Body Shop exerts special care in selecting its franchisees, rejecting those with prior business experience in favor of those with enthusiasm and commitment to Body Shop ideals. The result is that Body Shop is not simply supplying skin creams and shampoo, it is creating an identity with its customers built around the concepts of naturalness, global environmental responsibility, economic support for indigenous people through trade, and a rejection of traditional business methods (which it identifies with exploiting the weak and the natural environment).

The problems that Body Shop encountered in the late 1990s stem from allegations about Body Shop's ethical lapses, in terms of departures from "all natural" ingredients in its products, use of animal-tested ingredients, unfair treatment of franchisees and employees, and weaknesses of its community support and "fair trade" initiatives. Because Body Shop's values are fundamental to its image and relationships with customers, suppliers, franchisees, and employees these criticisms represent a fundamental threat to its competitive position.

Source: *Body Shop International*, Case 9-392-032 (Boston: Harvard Business School, 1992).

Signaling and Reputation

Differentiation is only effective if it is communicated to customers. But information about the qualities and characteristics of products is not always readily available to potential customers. The economics literature distinguishes between *search goods*, whose qualities and characteristics can be ascertained by inspection, and *experience goods*, whose qualities and characteristics are only recognized after consumption. This latter class of goods includes medical services, baldness treatments, frozen TV dinners, and wine. Even after purchase, performance attributes may be slow in revealing themselves – it took me almost ten years to reach the conclusion that my dentist was incompetent and my financial adviser was a charlatan.

In the terminology of game theory (see Chapter 4), the market for experience goods corresponds to a classic "prisoners' dilemma." The firm can offer a high-quality or a low-quality product. The customer can pay either a high or a low price. If quality cannot be detected, then equilibrium is established, with the customer offering a low price and the supplier offering a low-quality product, even though both would be better off with a high-quality product sold at a high price (see Figure 9.4).

The resolution of this dilemma is for producers to find some credible means of signaling quality to the customer. The most effective signals are those that change the payoffs in the prisoners' dilemma. Thus, an extended warranty is effective because providing such a warranty would be more expensive for a low-quality than a high-quality producer. Brand names, warranties, expensive packaging, money-back guarantees, sponsorship of sports and cultural events, and a carefully designed retail environment in which the product is sold are all signals of quality. Their effectiveness stems from the fact that they represent significant investments by the manufacturer that will be devalued if the product proves unsatisfactory to customers.

FIGURE 9.4 The problem of quality in experience goods: a "prisoners' dilemma"

		Producer's strategies	
		High quality	*Low quality*
Consumer's strategies	*High price*	7 / 7	10 / –5
	Low price	–5 / 10	3 / 3

Note: In each cell, the lower-left number is the payoff to the consumer and the upper-right number the payoff to the producer.

The need for signaling variables to complement performance variables in differentiation depends on the ease with which performance can be assessed by the potential buyer. The more difficult it is to ascertain performance prior to purchase, the more important signaling is.

- A perfume can be sampled prior to purchase and its fragrance assessed, but its ability to augment the identity of the wearer and attract attention remains uncertain. Hence, the key role of branding, packaging, advertising, and lavish promotional events in establishing an identity for the perfume in terms of the implied personality, lifestyle, and aspirations of the user.

- In financial services, the customer cannot easily assess the honesty, financial security, or competence of a broker, fund manager, or insurance company. Hence, financial service companies accord emphasis to symbols of security, stability, and competence – large, well-located head offices; conservative and tasteful office decor; smartly dressed, well-groomed employees; and stress on size and continuity over time.

Strategies for reputation building have been subjected to extensive theoretical analysis.[26] Some of the propositions that arise from this research include the following:

- Quality signaling is primarily important for products whose quality can only be ascertained after purchase ("experience goods").

- Expenditure on advertising is an effective means of signaling superior quality, since suppliers of low-quality products will not expect repeat buying, hence it is not profitable for them to spend money on advertising.

- A combination of premium pricing and advertising is likely to be superior in signaling quality than either price or advertising alone.

- The higher the sunk costs required for entry into a market and the greater the total investment of the firm, the greater the incentives for the firm not to cheat customers through providing low quality at high prices.

Brands

Brand names and the advertising that supports them are especially important as signals of quality and consistency – because a brand is a valuable asset, it acts as a disincentive to provide poor quality. For many consumer goods (and some producer goods) companies, their brand is their most important asset.

Brands fulfill multiple roles. Most importantly, a brand provides a guarantee by the producer to the consumer of the quality of the product. It does so in several ways. At its most basic, a brand identifies the producer of a product. This ensures that the producer is legally and morally accountable for the products supplied to market. Further, the brand represents an investment that provides an incentive to maintain quality and customer satisfaction. Hence, the brand represents a guarantee to the customer that reduces uncertainty and search costs. The more difficult it is to discern quality on inspection, and the greater the cost to the customer of purchasing a defective product, the greater the value of a brand. Thus, a well-known brand name is likely to be more important to us when we purchase a third-generation cellphone than when we buy a pair of socks.

The traditional role of the brand as a guarantor of reliability has become of particular significance in e-commerce. Internet transactions are characterized by the anonymity of buyers and sellers, lack of experience between most buyers and sellers, and lack of government regulation. As a result, well-established players in e-commerce – AOL, Amazon, Microsoft, eBay, and Yahoo! – carry substantial brand equity in terms of reducing buyers' perceived risk.

By contrast, the value conferred by leading consumer brands such as Coca-Cola, Harley-Davidson, Mercedes-Benz, Gucci, Virgin, and American Express is less a guarantee of reliability and more an embodiment of identity and lifestyle. For these brands advertising and promotion have long been the primary means of influencing and reinforcing customer perceptions. Increasingly, consumer goods companies are seeking new approaches to managing brand image. Guinness's "Storehouse" – a $50 million six-floor new building at its Dublin brewery – is a combined bar, restaurant, shop, museum, and conference center which offers a "brand experience" through which Guinness can operate as a "tribal hub" and reinvent itself for a new generation through "shared experience" and "emotional dialogue."[27]

The Costs of Differentiation

Differentiation adds cost. The direct costs of differentiation include higher-quality inputs, better-trained employees, higher advertising, and better after-sales service. The indirect costs of differentiation arise through the interaction of differentiation variables with cost variables. If differentiation narrows a firm's segment scope, it also limits the potential for exploiting scale economies. If differentiation requires continual product upgrading, it hampers the exploitation of experience curve economies.

One means of reconciling differentiation with cost efficiency is to postpone differentiation to later stages of the firm's value chain. Economies of scale and the cost advantages of standardization are frequently greatest in the manufacturing of basic components. Modular design with common components permits scale economies while maintaining considerable product variety. All the major automakers have reduced the number of platforms and engine types and increased the commonality of components across their model ranges, while offering customers a greater variety of colors, trim, and accessory options.

New manufacturing technology and the internet have redefined traditional trade-offs between efficiency and variety. Flexible manufacturing systems and just-in-time scheduling have increased the versatility of many plants, made model changeovers less costly, and made the goal of an "economic order quantity of one" increasingly realistic. More and more automobile, motorcycle, and domestic appliance plants are producing multiple models on a single assembly line.[28] Internet communication allows consumers to design their own products and quickly communicate their requirements to manufacturers. Pioneers of mass-customization include Capital One, which offers a unique package of credit facilities and interest rate charges to its credit card customers,[29] and Adidas, whose *mi adidas* program offers individually customized sports shoes through foot scanners installed in its retail stores.[30]

BRINGING IT ALL TOGETHER: THE VALUE CHAIN IN DIFFERENTIATION ANALYSIS

There is little point in identifying the product attributes that customers value most if the firm is incapable of supplying those attributes. Similarly, there is little purpose in identifying a firm's ability to supply certain elements of uniqueness if these are not valued by customers. The key to successful differentiation is matching the firm's capacity for creating differentiation to the attributes that customers value most. For this purpose, the value chain provides a particularly useful framework. Let's begin with the case of a producer good, i.e., one that is supplied by one firm to another.

Value Chain Analysis of Producer Goods

Using the value chain to identify opportunities for differentiation advantage involves four principal stages:

1. *Construct a value chain for the firm and the customer.* It may be useful to consider not just the immediate customer, but also firms further downstream in the value chain. If the firm supplies different types of customers – for example, a steel company may supply steel strip to automobile manufacturers and white goods producers – draw separate value chains for each of the main categories of customer.

2. *Identify the drivers of uniqueness in each activity.* Assess the firm's potential for differentiating its product by examining each activity in the firm's value chain and identifying the variables and actions through which the firm can achieve uniqueness in relation to competitors' offerings. Figure 9.5 identifies sources of differentiation within Porter's generic value chain.

3. *Select the most promising differentiation variables for the firm.* Among the numerous drivers of uniqueness that we can identify within the firm, which one should be selected as the primary basis for the firm's differentiation strategy? On the supply side, there are three important considerations.
   - First, we must establish where the firm has greater potential for differentiating from, or can differentiate at lower cost than, rivals. This requires some analysis of the firm's internal strengths in terms of resources and capabilities.

FIGURE 9.5 Using the value chain to identify differentiation potential on the supply side

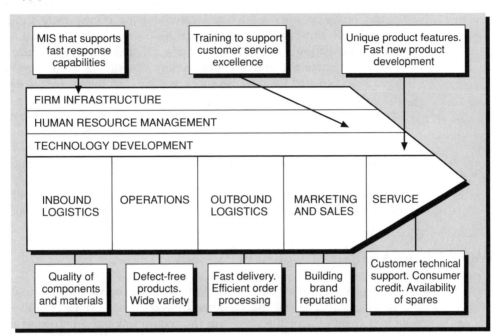

- Second, in order to identify the most promising aspects of differentiation, we also need to identify linkages among activities, since some differentiation variables may involve interaction among several activities. Thus, product reliability is likely to be the outcome of several linked activities: monitoring purchases of inputs from suppliers, the skill and motivation of production workers, and quality control and product testing.
- Third, the ease with which different types of uniqueness can be sustained must be considered. The more differentiation is based on resources specific to the firm or skills that involve the complex coordination of a large number of individuals, the more difficult it will be for a competitor to imitate the particular source of differentiation. Thus, offering business-class passengers wider seats and more legroom is an easily imitated source of differentiation. Achieving high levels of punctuality represents a more sustainable source of differentiation.

4. *Locate linkages between the value chain of the firm and that of the buyer.* The objective of differentiation is to yield a price premium for the firm. This requires that the firm's differentiation creates value for the customer. Creating value for customers requires either that the firm lowers customers' costs, or that customers' own product differentiation is facilitated. Thus, by reorganizing its product distribution around quick response technologies, Procter & Gamble

has radically reduced distribution time and increased delivery reliability. This permits retailers to reduce costs of inventory while simultaneously increasing their reliability to shoppers through lowering the risk of stockouts. To identify the means by which a firm can create value for its customers it must locate the linkages between differentiation of its own activities and cost reduction and differentiation within the customer's activities. Analysis of these linkages can also evaluate the potential profitability of differentiation. The value differentiation created for the customer represents the maximum price premium the customer will pay. If the provision of just-in-time delivery by a component supplier costs an additional $1,000 a month but saves an automobile company $6,000 a month in reduced inventory, warehousing, and handling costs, then it should be possible for the component manufacturer to obtain a price premium that easily exceeds the costs of the differentiation.

Strategy Capsule 9.4 demonstrates the use of value chain analysis in identifying differentiation opportunities available to a manufacturer of metal containers.

Value Chain Analysis of Consumer Goods

Value chain analysis of differentiation opportunities can also be applied to consumer goods. Few consumer goods are consumed directly; in most cases consumers are involved in a chain of activities involving the acquisition and purchase of the product. Hence, even when the customer is a consumer, it is still feasible to draw a value chain showing the activities that the consumer engages in when purchasing and consuming a product.

In the case of consumer durables, customers are involved in a long chain of activities from search, purchase, financing, acquiring accessories, operation, service and repair, and eventual disposal. Complex consumer value chains offer many potential linkages with the manufacturer's value chain, with considerable opportunity for innovative differentiation. Japanese producers of automobiles, consumer electronics, and domestic appliances have a long tradition of observing their customers' behavior in selecting and utilizing products, then using the information of customer usage and selection processes in planning product design and marketing. Harley-Davidson has been particularly effective at achieving differentiation advantage through careful examination of the activities that customers undertake in selecting, purchasing, using, and maintaining their motorcycles. Harley creates value for its customers through providing test ride facilities at its dealerships, financing, driving instruction, insurance, service and repair facilities, owners' club activities, and various sponsored events for Harley riders. Even nondurables involve the consumer in a chain of activities. Consider a frozen TV dinner: it must be purchased, taken home, removed from the package, heated, and served before it is consumed. After eating, the consumer must clean any used dishes, cutlery, or other utensils. A value chain analysis by a frozen foods producer would identify ways in which the product could be formulated, packaged, and distributed to assist the consumer in performing this chain of activities.

STRATEGY CAPSULE 9.4 Analyzing Differentiation Opportunities for a Manufacturer of Metal Containers

The metal container industry is a highly competitive, low-growth, low-profit industry. Cans lack much potential for differentiation and buyers (especially beverage and food canning companies) are very powerful. Clearly, cost efficiency is essential, but are there also opportunities for differentiation advantage? A value chain analysis can help a metal can manufacturer identify profitable opportunities for differentiation.

STAGE 1. Construct value chain for firm and customers. The principal activities of the can manufacturer and its customers are shown in the diagram below.

STAGE 2. Identify the drivers of uniqueness. For each of the can-making activities it is possible to suggest several possible differentiation variables. Examples are shown on the diagram.

STAGE 3. Select key variables. To select the most promising differentiation variables, the company's internal strengths must be considered. If the firm has strong technical capabilities, then it might design and manufacture products to meet difficult technical and design specifications, and provide sophisticated technical services to customers. If its logistics capabilities are strong it might offer fast and reliable delivery, possibly extended to electronic data interchange with customers.

STAGE 4. Identify linkages. To determine differentiation likely to create value for the customer, identify linkages between the can maker's potential for differentiation and the potential for reducing cost or enhancing differentiation within the customer's value chain. The diagram identifies five such linkages:

Identifying differentiation opportunities through linking the value chains of the firm and its customers: can manufacture

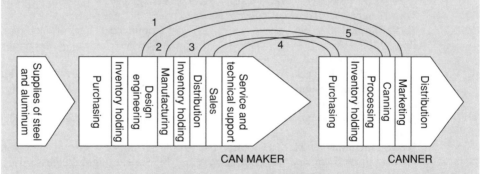

1. Distinctive can design can assist canners' marketing activities.

2. High manufacturing tolerances can avoid breakdowns in customer's canning lines.

3. Frequent, reliable delivery can permit canner to adopt JIT can supply.

4. Efficient order processing system can reduce customers' ordering costs.

5. Competent technical support can increase canner's efficiency of plant utilization.

SUMMARY

The attraction of differentiation over low cost as a basis for competitive advantage is its potential for sustainability. It is less vulnerable to being overturned by changes in the external environment, and it is more difficult to replicate.

The potential for differentiation in any business is vast. It may involve physical differentiation of the product, it may be through complementary services, it may be intangible. Differentiation extends beyond technology, design, and marketing to include all aspects of a firm's interactions with its customers.

The essence of differentiation advantage is to increase the perceived value of the offering to the customer either more effectively or at lower cost than do competitors. This requires that the firm match the requirements and preferences of customers with its own capacity for creating uniqueness.

The value chain provides a useful framework for analyzing differentiation advantage. By analyzing how value is created for customers and by systematically appraising the scope of each of the firm's activities for achieving differentiation, the value chain permits matching demand-side and supply-side sources of differentiation.

Successful differentiation requires a combination of astute analysis and creative imagination. The two are not antithetical. A systematic framework for the analysis of differentiation can act as a stimulus to creative ideas.

NOTES

[1] Michael E. Porter, *Competitive Advantage* (New York: Free Press, 1985): 120.

[2] Tom Peters, *Thriving on Chaos* (New York: Knopf, 1987): 56.

[3] Ibid.: 185.

[4] These distinctions are developed in more detail by Peter R. Dickson and James L. Ginter, "Market Segmentation, Product Differentiation and Marketing Strategy," *Journal of Marketing* 51 (April 1987): 1–10.

[5] See S. Schiffman, M. Reynolds, and F. Young, *Introduction to Multidimensional Scaling: Theory, Methods, and Applications* (Cambridge, MA: Academic Press, 1981).

[6] F.-J. Lapointe and P. Legendre, "A Classification of Pure Malt Scotch Whiskies," *Applied Statistics* 43 (1994): 237–57. On principles of MDS, see I. Borg and P. Groenen, *Modern Multidimensional Scaling: Theory and Application* (Springer Verlag, 1997).

[7] See P. Cattin and D. R. Wittink, "Commercial Use of Conjoint Analysis: A Survey," *Journal of Marketing* (Summer 1982): 44–53.

[8] Alan Rowe, Richard Mason, Karl Dickel, and Neil Snyder, *Strategic Management: A Methodological Approach*, 3rd edn (Reading, MA: Addison-Wesley, 1989): 127–8.

[9] J. Wind, P. Green, D. Shifflet, and M. Scarborough, "Courtyard by Marriott: Designing a Hotel Facility with Consumer-based Marketing Models," *Interfaces* 19, no. 1 (1989): 25–47.

[10] T. Holmes, C. Zinkhan, K. Alger, and E. Mercer, "Conjoint Analysis of Nature Tourism Values in Bahia, Brazil," FPEI Working Paper 57 (SE Center for Forest Economics Research, 1996).

11 Kelvin Lancaster, *Consumer Demand: A New Approach* (New York: Columbia University Press, 1971).

12 Phedon Nicolaides and Charles Baden Fuller, "Price Discrimination and Product Differentiation in the European Domestic Appliance Market," discussion paper (London: Center for Business Strategy, London Business School, 1987).

13 N. Gondal, "Hedonic price indexes for spreadsheets and an empirical test for network externalities," *Rand Journal of Economics* 25 (1994): 160–70.

14 C. Kim and R. Mauborgne, "Creating New Market Space," *Harvard Business Review* (January–February 1999): 83–93.

15 Abraham Maslow, "A Theory of Human Motivation," *Psychological Review* 50 (1943): 370–96.

16 Michael Bastedo and Angela Davis, "God, What a Blunder: The New Coke Story," December 17, 1993 (http://members. lycos.co.uk/thomassheils/newcoke.htm).

17 Tom Peters, op. cit.: 149.

18 Johny K. Johansson and Ikujiro Nonaka, *Relentless: The Japanese Way of Marketing* (New York: HarperBusiness, 1996).

19 Michael E. Porter, op. cit.: 124–5.

20 Shiv Mathur, "Competitive Industrial Marketing Strategies," *Long Range Planning* 17, no. 4 (1984): 102–9.

21 "Turbulent times for air charters," *Financial Times* (October 21, 2003): 21.

22 John Hagel and Marc Singer, "Unbundling the Corporation," *McKinsey Quarterly* no. 3 (2000).

23 Kim Clark and Takahiro Fujimoto, *Product Development Performance* (Boston: Harvard Business School Press, 1991): 29–30.

24 Ibid.: 247–85; K. B. Clark and T. Fujimoto, "The Power of Product Integrity," *Harvard Business Review* (November–December, 1990): 107–18.

25 John Seabrook, "Rocking in Shangri-La," *The New Yorker* (October 10, 1994): 64–78.

26 For a survey, see Keith Weigelt and Colin Camerer, "Reputation and Corporate Strategy: A Review of Recent Theory and Applications," *Strategic Management Journal* 9 (1988): 443–54.

27 "A Brand Day Out," *Financial Times Creative Business* (November 21, 2000): 14.

28 Richard J. Schonberger, *World Class Manufacturing Casebook: Implementing JIT and TQC* (New York: Free Press, 1987): 120–3; Joseph Pine, Bart Victor, Andrew Boynton, "Making Mass-customization Work," *Harvard Business Review* (September–October 1993): 108–16.

29 "Capital One Financial Corporation," Harvard Business School Case no. 7–900–124 (2000).

30 Ralf Seifert, "The *mi adidas* Mass Customization Initiative," IMD Case 159 (2002).

IV

Business Strategies in Different Industry Contexts

10

Industry Evolution

*No company ever stops changing . . . Each new genera-
tion must meet changes – in the automotive market,
in the general administration of the enterprise, and
in the involvement of the corporation in a changing
world. The work of creating goes on.*
—*Alfred P. Sloan Jr., President of General
Motors 1923–37, Chairman 1937–56*

OUTLINE

299

INTRODUCTION AND OBJECTIVES

The analysis of competitive advantage in Part III emphasized competition as a dynamic process in which firms vie to gain competitive advantage, only to see it eroded through imitation and innovation by rivals. The outcome of this process is an industry environment that is continually being reshaped by the forces of competition. This view of competition as a dynamic process contrasts with the static approach of the Porter Five Forces of Competition framework (see Chapter 3), which views industry structure as a stable determinant of the intensity of competition in an industry. In practice, industry structures continually evolve, driven externally by the forces of technology, demand, and economic growth, and internally by the competitive strategies of the firms within the industry. Firms that develop the capabilities and strategies suited to emerging industry circumstances prosper and grow; those that do not are eliminated. In this chapter we consider whether industry evolution can be anticipated. My central thesis is that, although every industry follows a unique development path, it is possible to detect some common patterns that are the result of common driving forces. Our task is to identify these patterns of industry evolution, the forces that drive them, and their implications for competition and competitive advantage.

We will examine the industry life cycle as a framework for viewing industry development and for classifying industries according to their stage of development. This raises two questions. First, is the industry life cycle a valid and useful description of how industries evolve? Second, does categorization of industries according to their stage of development (or on some other basis) serve any useful purpose? On this latter question, I argue that the purpose of classifying industries is not to ignore their unique features, but to help us recognize the key factors that determine the strategic character of an industry.

We study industry evolution to help us manage change. This requires that we predict future changes in the firm's external environment in order to *adapt* to change, but also that we identify opportunities to *shape* the firm's environment.

By the time you have completed this chapter, you will be able to:

- Recognize the different stages of industry development and understand the factors that drive the process of industry evolution.

- Identify the key success factors associated with industries at different stages of their development.

- Identify the strategies, organizational structures, and management systems appropriate to different stages of industry development.

- Use scenarios to explore industry futures.

- Appreciate the challenges of managing organizational change.

FIGURE 10.1 The industry life cycle

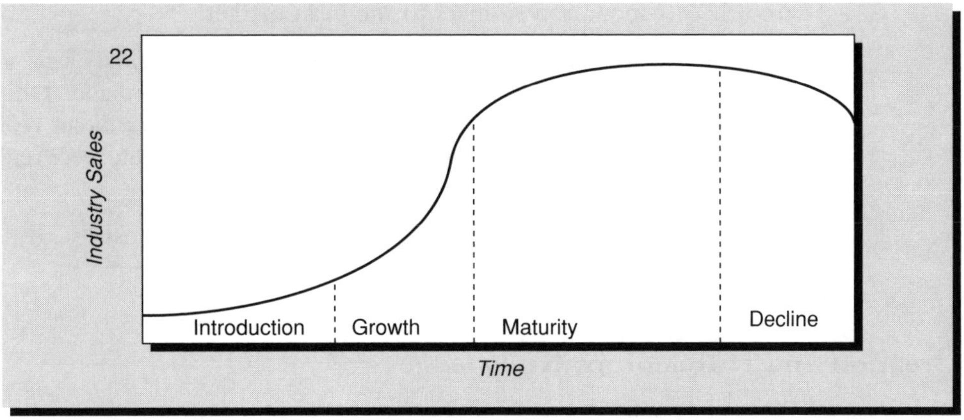

THE INDUSTRY LIFE CYCLE

One of the best-known and most enduring marketing concepts is the product life cycle.[1] Products are born, their sales grow, they reach maturity, they go into decline, and they ultimately die. If products have life cycles, so too do the industries that produce them. The industry life cycle is the supply-side equivalent of the product life cycle. To the extent that an industry produces a range and sequence of products, the industry life cycle is likely to be of longer duration than that of a single product. For example, though 128-bit video game consoles such as the PlayStation2, XBox, and Gamecube have a probable life cycle of a few years, the life cycle of the electronic games industry extends back to the release of the Atari 2600 in 1977.

The life cycle comprises four phases: *introduction* (or *emergence*), *growth*, *maturity*, and *decline* (see Figure 10.1). Before we examine the features of each of these stages, let us examine the forces that are driving industry evolution. Two factors are fundamental: demand growth and the production and diffusion of knowledge.

Demand Growth

The life cycle and the stages within it are defined primarily by changes in an industry's growth rate over time. The characteristic profile is an S-shaped growth curve.

- In the *introduction stage*, sales are small and the rate of market penetration is low because the industry's products are little known and customers are few. The novelty of the technology, small scale of production, and lack of experience means high costs and low quality. Customers for new products tend to be affluent, innovation-oriented, and risk-tolerant.

- The *growth stage* is characterized by accelerating market penetration as product technology becomes more standardized and prices fall. Ownership spreads from higher-income customers to the mass market.

- Increasing market saturation causes the onset of the *maturity stage* and slowing growth as new demand gives way to replacement demand. Once saturation is reached, demand is wholly for replacement, either direct replacement (customers replacing old products with new products) or indirect replacement (new customers replacing old customers).

- Finally, as the industry becomes challenged by new industries that produce technologically superior substitute products, the industry enters its *decline stage*.

Creation and Diffusion of Knowledge

The second driving force of the industry life cycle is knowledge. New knowledge in the form of product innovation is responsible for an industry's birth, and the dual processes of knowledge creation and knowledge diffusion exert a major influence on industry evolution.

In the introduction stage, product technology advances rapidly. There is no dominant product technology, and rival technologies compete for attention. Competition is primarily between alternative technologies and design configurations:

- The early years of the automobile industry featured competition between different power sources (steam vs. gasoline-powered internal combustion), transmission systems, cooling mode (air vs. water), and radically different steering and braking systems.

- The early years of the home computer industry saw competition between different data storage systems (audio tapes vs. floppy disks), visual displays (TV receivers vs. dedicated monitors), operating systems (CPM vs. DOS vs. Apple II), and microprocessors.

Dominant Designs and Technical Standards

The outcome of competition between rival designs and technologies is usually convergence by the industry around a *dominant design* – a product architecture that defines the look, functionality, and production method for the product and becomes accepted by the industry as a whole. Dominant designs have included the following:

- The IBM PC launched in 1981 established the basic design parameters of the personal computer as well as the key technical standard that was eventually to dominate the industry (the so-called "Wintel" standard).

- Leica's Ur-Leica 35mm camera developed by Oskar Barnack and launched in Germany in 1924 established what would become the dominant design for cameras, though it was not until Canon began mass-producing cameras based on the Leica design that the 35mm camera came to dominate still photography.[2]

■ When Ray Kroc opened his first McDonald's hamburger restaurant in Illinois in 1955, he established what would soon become a dominant design for the fast-food restaurant industry: a limited menu, no waiter service, eat-in and take-out options, roadside locations for motorized customers, and a franchise system of ownership and control.

A dominant design may or may not embody a technical standard. IBM's PC established the MS-DOS operating system and Intel x86 series of microprocessor as technical standards for personal computing. Conversely, the Boeing 707 was a dominant design for large passenger jets, but did not set industry standards in aerospace technology that would dominate subsequent generations of airplanes. Technical standards emerge where there are *network effects* – the need for users to connect in some way with one another. Where there are network effects, then each customer wants to choose the same technology as everyone else to avoid being stranded. A dominant design may confer certain network benefits – when all companies adopt a common architecture innovation gets quicker and suppliers to the industry can exploit economies of scale. However, unlike a proprietary technical standard, a firm that sets a dominant design does not gain any ownership stake in that design. Hence, except for some early-mover advantage, there is not necessarily any profit advantage from setting a dominant design.

Dominant designs are present in business models as well as products. In many new markets, competition is between rival *business models*. Such rivalry was especially evident in emerging e-commerce during the dot.com frenzy of 1998 to 2000. For example, the on-line grocery business was pioneered by dot.com start-ups such as Webvan and Peapod. However, they soon succumbed to competition form "bricks 'n' clicks" retailers such as Albertson's and Giant. A battle between rival business models is also developing in digital distribution of recorded music, where the record companies' own music download sites (such as Sony and Universal's Pressplay) compete with Apple's MusicStore, and with file-sharing services such as KaZaA.

From Product to Process Innovation

The emergence of a dominant design marks a critical juncture in an industry's evolution. Once the industry coalesces around a leading technology and design, there's a shift from radical to incremental product innovation. This transition may be necessary to inaugurate the industry's growth phase: greater standardization reduces risks to customers and encourages firms to invest in manufacturing. The shift in emphasis from design to manufacture typically involves increased attention to process innovation as firms seek to reduce costs and increase product reliability through large-scale production methods (see Figure 10.2). The combination of process improvements, design modifications, and scale economies results in falling costs and greater availability that drives rapidly increasing market penetration. Strategy Capsule 10.1 uses the history of the automobile industry to illustrate these patterns of development.

Knowledge diffusion is also important on the customer side. Over the course of the life cycle, customers become increasingly informed. As they become more knowledgeable about the performance attributes of rival manufacturers' products, so they are better able to judge value for money and become more price sensitive.

FIGURE 10.2 Product and process innovation over time

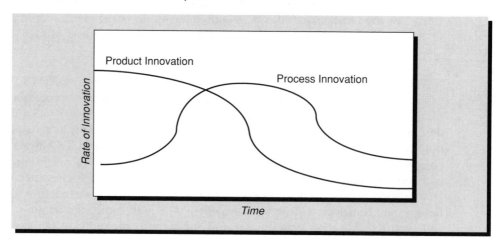

STRATEGY CAPSULE 10.1 Evolution of the Automobile Industry

The period 1890–1910 was one of rapid product innovation in the auto industry. After 1886 when Karl Benz received a patent on his three-wheel motor carriage, a flurry of technical advances occurred in Germany, France, the US, and Britain. Developments included:

- The first four-cylinder four-stroke engine (by Karl Benz in 1890).
- The honeycomb radiator (by Daimler in 1890).
- The speedometer (by Oldsmobile in 1901).
- Automatic transmission (by Packard in 1904).
- Electric headlamps (by General Motors in 1908).
- The all-steel body (adopted by General Motors in 1912).

Ford's Model T, introduced in 1908, with its front-mounted, water-cooled engine and transmission with a gearbox, wet clutch, and rearwheel drive, acted as a dominant design for the industry. During the remainder of the twentieth century automotive technology and design converged. A key indicator of this was the gradual elimination of nonconventional technologies and designs. Volkswagen's Beetle was the last mass-produced car with a rear-mounted, air-cooled engine. Citroën abandoned its distinctive suspension and braking systems. Four-stroke engines with four or six inline cylinders became dominant. Distinctive national differences eroded as American cars became smaller and Japanese and Italian cars became bigger. The fall of the Iron Curtain extinguished the last outposts of nonconformity: by the mid-1990s, East German two-stroke Wartburgs and Trabants were collectors' items. Increasing similarity between cars meant that by 2000, GM introduced a wireless telephone-activated device to help motorists locate their cars within car parks.

As product innovation slowed, so process innovation took off. In October 1913, Ford opened its Highland Park Assembly Plant with its revolutionary production methods based on interchangeable parts and a moving assembly line. In the space of one year, chassis assembly time was cut from 12 hours and 8 minutes to 1 hour and 33 minutes. The price of the Model T fell from $628 in 1908 to $260 in 1924. Between 1908 and 1927 over 15 million Model Ts had been produced.

STRATEGY CAPSULE 10.1 (cont'd)

The second revolutionary process innovation in automobile manufacturing was Toyota's system of "lean production," involving a tightly integrated "pull" system of production embodying just-in-time scheduling, team-based production, flexible manufacturing, and total quality management. During the 1970s and 1980s, lean production diffused throughout the world vehicle industry in the same way that Ford's mass-production system had transformed the industry half a century before.

Sources: www.daimlerchrysler.com; www.ford.com.

How General Is the Life Cycle Pattern?

To what extent do industries conform to this life cycle pattern? To begin with, the duration of the life cycle varies greatly from industry to industry:

■ The introduction phase of the US railroad industry extended from the building of the first railroad, the Baltimore and Ohio in 1827, to the growth phase of the 1870s. By the late 1950s, the industry was entering its decline phase.

■ The introduction stage of the US automobile industry lasted about 25 years, from the 1890s until growth took off in 1913–15. Maturity, in terms of slackening growth, set in during the mid-1950s.

■ In personal computers, the introduction phase lasted only about four years before growth took off in 1978. Between 1978 and 1983 a flood of new and established firms entered the industry. Toward the end of 1984, the first signs of maturity appeared: growth stalled, excess capacity emerged, and the industry began to consolidate around a few companies; however, it remained strong until the end of the 1990s.

■ Compact discs, introduced in 1984, passed almost immediately from introduction to growth phase. By 1988, they outsold conventional record albums in the United States. The market matured during the 1990s and went into decline in 2000 as direct downloading of digital music displaced CD sales.

The tendency over time has been for life cycles to become compressed. This is evident for all consumer electronic products, communication products, and also pharmaceuticals. In e-commerce, life cycles have become even more compressed. Businesses such as online gambling, business-to-business online auctions, and online travel services have gone from initial introduction to apparent maturity with a few years. Such time compression has required a radical rethink of strategies and management processes – "competing on internet time" is how Michael Cusumano and David Yoffie refer to the challenge.[3]

Patterns of evolution also differ. Industries supplying basic necessities such as residential construction, food processing, and clothing may never enter a decline phase

FIGURE 10.3 Innovation and renewal in the industry life cycle: retailing

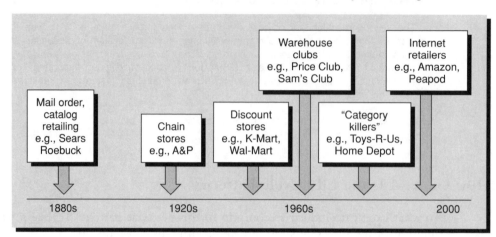

because obsolescence is unlikely for such needs. Some industries may experience a rejuvenation of their life cycle. In the 1960s, the world motorcycle industry, in decline in the US and Europe, re-entered its growth phase as the influx of new Japanese bikes stimulated the recreational use of motorcycles. Television manufacturing has experienced multiple revivals: maturity of the market for black and white sets was followed by the color TV boom, the demand for computer monitors and video games spurred another cycle, and flat-screen TVs created yet another growth phase during 2002–2004. Similar waves of innovation have revitalized retailing (see Figure 10.3). These rejuvenations of the product life cycle are not natural phenomena – they are typically the result of companies resisting the forces of maturity through breakthrough product innovations or developing new markets.

An industry is likely to be at different stages of its life cycle in different countries. Although the US auto market is in the early stages of its decline phase, markets in China, India, and Russia are in their growth phases. Multinational companies can exploit such differences: developing new products and introducing them into the advanced industrial countries, then shifting attention to other growth markets once maturity sets in. In the automobile and can-making industries, pursuing market growth phases is accompanied by shipping whole plants from North America and Western Europe to Latin America, Eastern Europe, and Asia.[4]

STRUCTURE, COMPETITION, AND SUCCESS FACTORS OVER THE LIFE CYCLE

Changes in demand growth and technology over the cycle have implications for industry structure, competition, and the sources of competitive advantage (key success factors). Table 10.1 summarizes the principal features of each stage of the industry life cycle.

TABLE 10.1 The Evolution of Industry Structure and Competition over the Life Cycle

	INTRODUCTION	GROWTH	MATURITY	DECLINE
Demand	Limited to early adopters: high-income, avant-garde.	Rapidly increasing market penetration.	Mass market, replacement/repeat buying. Customers knowledgeable and price sensitive.	Obsolescence.
Technology	Competing technologies. Rapid product innovation.	Standardization around dominant technology. Rapid process innovation.	Well-diffused technical know-how: quest for technological improvements.	Little product or process innovation.
Products	Poor quality. Wide variety of features and technologies. Frequent design changes.	Design and quality improve. Emergence of dominant design.	Trend to commoditization. Attempts to differentiate by branding, quality, bundling.	Commodities the norm: differentiation difficult and unprofitable.
Manufacturing and distribution	Short production runs. High-skilled labor content. Specialized distribution channels.	Capacity shortages Mass production. Competition for distribution.	Emergence of overcapacity. Deskilling of production. Long production runs. Distributors carry fewer lines.	Chronic overcapacity. Re-emergence of specialty channels.
Trade	Producers and consumers in advanced countries.	Exports from advanced countries to rest of world.	Production shifts to newly industrializing then developing countries.	Exports from countries with lowest labor costs.
Competition	Few companies.	Entry, mergers, and exits.	Shakeout. Price competition increases.	Price wars, exits.
Key success factors	Product innovation. Establishing credible image of firm and product.	Design for manufacture. Access to distribution. Building strong brand. Fast product development. Process innovation.	Cost efficiency through capital intensity, scale efficiency, and low input costs. High quality.	Low overheads. Buyer selection. Signaling commitment. Rationalizing capacity.

Product Differentiation

Emerging industries are characterized by a wide variety of product types that reflect the diversity of technologies and designs – and the lack of consensus over customer requirements. Standardization during growth and maturity phases increases product uniformity, with the result that a product may evolve toward commodity status unless producers are effective in developing new dimensions for differentiation, such as marketing variables, ancillary services (e.g., credit facilities, after-sales service), and product options.[5] A feature of the markets for personal computers, credit cards, securities broking, and internet access is their increasing commodity status in which buyers select primarily on price.

Organizational Demographics and Industry Structure

Industry evolution is associated with high rates of entry and exit and considerable changes in firm population. The field of *organizational ecology*, founded by Michael Hannan, John Freeman, and Glen Carroll, has examined the evolution of industries as a Darwinian process in which the size and composition of the population of firms in an industry are determined by the process through which firms are founded and the process of selection through which they compete for survival.[6] Some of the main findings of the organizational ecologists in relation to industry evolution are:

- The number of firms in an industry increases rapidly during the early stages of an industry's life. Initially an industry may be pioneered by a few firms. However, as these firms gain legitimacy, failure rates decline and the rate of new-firm foundings increases. New entrants have very different origins. Some are startup companies ("*de novo*" entrants); others are established firms diversifying from related industries ("*de alio*" entrants). The US automobile industry featured many hundreds of producers in the early years of the twentieth century,[7] while in TV receivers there were 92 companies in 1951.[8]

- With the beginnings of maturity, the number of firms begins to fall. Very often, industries go through one or more "shakeout" phases during which the rate of firm failure increases sharply. After this point, rates of entry and exit decline and the survival rate for incumbents increases substantially.[9] The shakeout phase of intensive acquisition, merger, and exit occurs, on average, 29 years into the life cycle and results in the number of producers being halved.[10] In the US tire industry, the number of players increased during the first 25 years, before waves of consolidation, typically triggered by technological and strategic changes within the industry.[11]

- As industries become increasingly concentrated and the leading firms focus upon the mass market, so a new phase of entry may take place as new firms take advantage of opportunities in peripheral regions of the market. An example of this "resource partitioning" is the US brewing industry: as the mass market became dominated by a handful of national brewers, so opportunities arose for new types of brewing companies – microbreweries and brew pubs – to establish themselves in specialist niches.[12]

However, generalization is dangerous. Scale economies and entry barriers play a key role in shaping the evolutionary paths of different industries. While in most industries, maturity is associated with increasing concentration – where technology becomes more accessible, capital intensive activities can be outsourced, or product differentiation declines – concentration may decline (as in credit cards, television broadcasting, and frozen foods). Some industries, especially where the first-mover achieves substantial patent protection, may start out as near-monopolies, then become increasingly competitive. Plain-paper copiers were initially monopolized by Xerox Corporation and it was not until the early 1980s that the industry was transformed by a wave of new entry. Winner-take-all industries, such as video game consoles, may remain near-monopolies or tight oligopolies throughout their life cycle.

Location and International Trade

The industry life cycle is associated with changes in the pattern of trade and direct investment that together result in international migration of production.[13] The life cycle theory of trade and direct investment is based on two assumptions. First, that demand for new products emerges first in the advanced industrialized countries of North America, western Europe, and Japan and then diffuses internationally. Second, that with maturity, products require fewer inputs of technology and sophisticated skills. The result is the following development pattern:

1. New industries begin in high-income countries (traditionally the United States, but increasingly in Japan and western Europe) because of the presence of a market and the availability of technical and scientific resources.

2. As demand grows in other markets, they are serviced initially by exports.

3. Continued growth of overseas markets and reduced need for inputs of technology and sophisticated labor skills make production attractive in newly industrialized countries. The advanced industrialized countries begin to import.

4. With maturity, a reduced need for skilled production workers, and an increased perception of the product as a commodity, the production activity shifts increasingly to developing countries in search of low-cost labor.

For example, consumer electronics were initially dominated by the United States and Germany. During the early 1960s, production shifted towards Japan. The 1980s saw the rise of Korea, Hong Kong, and Taiwan as leading exporters. By the mid-1990s, assembly had moved to lower-wage countries such as China, the

Philippines, Thailand, Mexico, and Brazil. We return to these issues of national-level competitiveness in Chapter 14.

The Nature and Intensity of Competition

Competition changes in two ways over the course of the industry life cycle. First, there is a shift from nonprice to price competition. Second, the intensity of competition grows, causing margins to narrow. During the introduction stage, competitors battle for technological leadership and competition focuses on technology and design. Gross margins can be high, but heavy investments in innovation and market development tend to depress return on capital. The growth phase is more conducive to profitability as market demand outstrips industry capacity – especially if incumbents are protected by barriers to entry. With the onset of maturity, increased product standardization stimulates price competition. How intense this is depends a great deal on the capacity/demand balance and the extent of international competition. In food retailing, airlines, motor vehicles, metals, oil refining, and insurance, maturity was associated with strong price competition and slender profitability. In household detergents, breakfast cereals, cosmetics, and investment banking, high levels of seller concentration and successful maintenance of product differentiation resulted in positive economic profits. The decline phase is almost always associated with strong price competition (and may degenerate into destructive price wars) and dismal profit performance. In many industries, excess capacity and the presence of overseas competitors are the main drivers of increasing price competition. However, there may be counteracting tendencies: industries may become more structured as established firms develop specializations and form stable alliances.[14] Changes in profitability over the industry life cycle are shown in Figure 10.4.

Key Success Factors and Industry Evolution

The changes in industry structure, demand, and technological requirements over the industry life cycle have important implications for the primary sources of competitive advantage at each stage of industry evolution:

■ During the introductory stage product innovation is the basis for initial entry and for subsequent success. Soon, however, knowledge alone is not enough. As the industry begins its evolution and technological competition intensifies, other requirements for success emerge. In moving from the first generation of products to subsequent generations, investment requirements tend to grow, and financial resources become increasingly important. Capabilities in product development soon need to be matched by capabilities in manufacturing, marketing, and distribution. Hence, in an emerging industry, firms need to support their innovation with a broad array of vertically integrated capabilities.

FIGURE 10.4 Return on invested capital at different stages of the industry life cycle

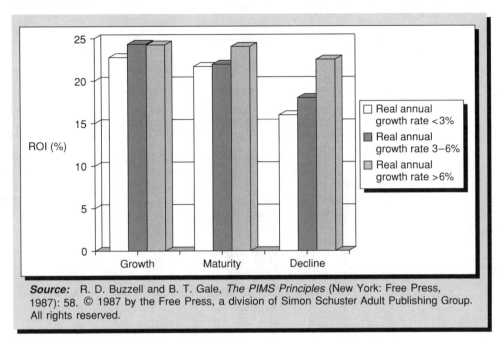

- Once the growth stage is reached, the key challenge is scaling up. As the market expands, the firm needs to adapt its product design and its manufacturing capability to large-scale production. As Figure 10.5 shows, investment in R&D, plant and equipment, and sales tends to be high during the growth phase. To utilize increased manufacturing capability, access to distribution becomes critical. At the same time, the tensions that organizational growth imposes create the need for internal administrative and strategic skills. We consider these issues in Chapter 11.

- With the maturity stage, competitive advantage is increasingly a quest for cost efficiency – or, at least, this is the case in those mature industries that tend toward commoditization. Cost efficiency through scale economies, low wages, and low overheads become the key success factors. Figure 10.5 shows that R&D, capital investment, and marketing are lower in maturity than during the growth phase.

- The transformation to the decline phase raises the potential for destructive price competition. Whether a firm has a competitive advantage is secondary to the importance of maintaining a stable industry environment. Hence, company strategies focus on encouraging the orderly exit of industry capacity and building a strong position in relation to residual market demand. We consider the strategic issues presented by mature and declining industries more fully in Chapter 12.

FIGURE 10.5 Differences in strategy and performance between businesses at different stages of the industry life cycle

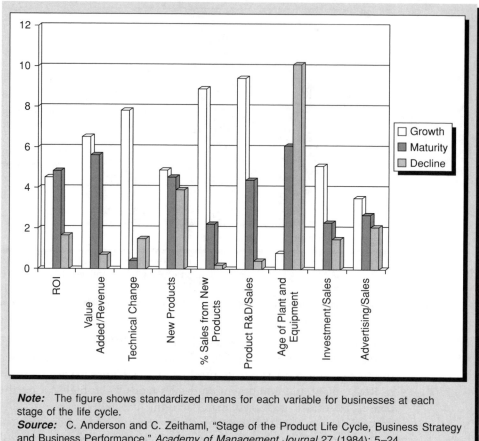

Note: The figure shows standardized means for each variable for businesses at each stage of the life cycle.

Source: C. Anderson and C. Zeithaml, "Stage of the Product Life Cycle, Business Strategy and Business Performance," *Academy of Management Journal* 27 (1984): 5–24.

ORGANIZATIONAL ADAPTATION AND CHANGE

In Chapter 1, I emphasized the importance of *fit*. For companies to be successful, their strategies and organizational structures need to be aligned with their industry environments. This concept of fit has its origin in *contingency* approaches to organization theory.[15] Industry evolution poses a huge challenge to managers: strategy and structure must adapt to keep pace with the rate of change in the external environment. As the pace of industry evolution accelerates, so the challenge of organizational change becomes more daunting.

Evolutionary Theory and Organizational Change

Theories of organizational evolution draw heavily upon biological theories of evolution. Organizations – like species – adapt to external change through *variation*, *selection*, and *retention*. The critical issue that divides organizational theorists is the level at which these evolutionary processes occur:

■ *Organizational ecologists* emphasize evolution at the industry level. Individual organizations are subject to *inertia* – the resistance to change that accompanies the processes of institutionalization.[16] Hence, evolutionary processes work at the level of the industry. The competitive process is a *selection mechanism*, in which organizations whose characteristics match the requirements of their environment survive, and organizations whose characteristics do not are eliminated through acquisition or liquidation. The implication is that industry evolution involves a changing population of companies. As we shall see, a number of empirical studies support this contention that industry evolution is achieved more by the changes in the composition of firms than by adaptation by companies in response to external change.[17]

■ *Evolutionary theorists* (such as Nelson and Winter) view evolution as occurring within individual organizations where the process of variation, selection, and retention takes place at the level of the *organizational routine*.[18] As we discussed in Chapter 5, these patterns of coordinated activity are the basis for organizational capability. While evolutionary theorists view firms as adapting to external change through the search for new routines, replication of successful routines, and abandonment of unsuccessful routines, such adaptation is neither fast nor costless. The search for new routines is triggered by declining performance; when companies are performing well there is little impetus for change. Hence, companies get caught in "*competency traps*"[19] where their "core capabilities become core rigidities."[20]

Although both these major schools of organizational evolution emphasize the barriers to organizational adaptation, companies can and do change. General Motors has led the world automobile industry since the mid-1920s. Siemens has been a leading player in the German telecommunications industry since the founding of Telegraphen-Bau-Anstalt von Siemens & Halske in 1847. Exxon (now Exxon Mobil) and Royal Dutch/Shell have dominated the petroleum industry for almost the whole of the twentieth century.

Yet these companies are exceptions. Of the companies forming the original Dow Jones Industrial Average in 1896, only General Electric remains in the Index today. Clearly, organizational change is difficult; it requires building new capabilities, it threatens existing power structures, and requires changes in top management teams.[21]

The ability of a firm to adapt to external change depends upon the nature of that change. Some features of an industry's evolution may follow a predictable life cycle pattern. However, changing key success factors may mean that firms that were successful in one phase of the industry's development may have to acquire quite different resources and capabilities in order to be successful in the subsequent phase of development. Markides and Geroski show that different companies typically lead different stages of an industry's development are usually undertaken by different companies – the "innovators" that pioneer the creation of a new industry are different companies from the "consolidators" that develop it:

> The fact that the firms that create new product and service markets are rarely the ones that scale them into mass markets has serious implications for the modern corporation. Our research points to a simple reason for this phenomenon: the skills, mind-sets, and competences needed for discovery and invention are not only different from those needed for commercialization; they conflict with the needed characteristics. This means that the firms good at invention are unlikely to be good at commercialization and vice-versa.[22]

Firms can adapt their capabilities to changes in their environment – especially if those capabilities are dynamic rather than static in nature (see Chapter 5). Some external changes may enhance a company's existing capabilities; others may be "competence destroying."[23] A critical factor determining a firm's ability to adapt to external change is whether the impact is at the "component" or the "architectural" level.[24] The demise of startups such as Webvan and Peapod in the on-line grocery business reflected the fact that the major impact of the internet on food retailing was at the component level – it created new opportunities for ordering and delivering grocery products rather than a completely new system of retailing. Hence, for established retailers such as Safeway, Albertson's, and Kroger, it was easy for them to bolt on online ordering and direct home delivery to their existing operations without the need for a complete reconfiguration of their value chains.

While some scholars identify the potential for companies to adapt through a series of discrete changes ("*logical incrementalism*"[25]), most evidence suggests that gradual, adaptive change is likely to encounter resistance from the forces of organizational inertia and, in any event, may be too slow to keep pace with change in the external environment. Elaine Romanelli and Michael Tushman identify a process of *punctuated equilibrium* in which organizational inertia produces a widening misalignment between the organization and its environment, which ultimately forces radical and comprehensive change on the company.[26] During the 1970s and 1980s, the oil majors maintained their top-heavy, vertically integrated structures despite increasing competition and market turbulence, but, by the mid-1980s, the fall in crude prices forced almost all of them to radical restructuring.[27]

Andy Grove of Intel has pointed to the necessity for top management to be alert to the need for radical strategic change. His experience at Intel suggests that continuous and adaptive change is effective only to a point. Then, at what Grove refers to as a *strategic inflection point*, a company must be willing to make a radical strategic shift. For Intel, such an inflection point occurred when it recognized that its future lay in microprocessors rather than its traditional business of designing and fabricating memory chips.[28]

The Challenge of Disruptive Technologies

New technologies present a particular challenge to established companies. *Disruptive technologies*, according to Clay Christensen, are those that offer a very different package of attributes from the existing technology. Thus, Sony's early transistor radios sacrificed sound fidelity but created a market for portable radios by offering a new and different package of attributes – small size, light weight, and portability.[29]

Established leaders in the older technology typically fail to make the transition to the new wave of technology:

- In steel, it was newcomer Nucor, using minimill technology, that became the most successful steelmaker while established giants US Steel and Bethlehem Steel sought government protection to stave off bankruptcy.

- In personal computers, not one of the leading minicomputer makers made a successful transition into PCs.

- In telecommunications equipment, it was newcomers Cisco Systems and Juniper Networks, rather than established leaders such as Lucent Technologies and Alcatel, that were most successful in exploiting the packet switching technologies associated with the internet.

The tendency for established industry leaders to succumb to stealth attacks by newcomers armed with disruptive technologies is not simply the result of complacency or inertia among incumbent firms. Based on detailed analysis of technological change in hard-disk drives, Christensen notes that the critical barriers to established companies developing a new technology are, first, customers don't want the new technology; second, the new technology doesn't perform as well as the existing technology. In hard disks, at every transition – from 14" to 8" to 5.25" to 3.5" drives – the established companies were on average two years behind newcomers in launching new generations products.[30]

Even when established companies recognize the potential of a new technology, the problem is that they can't develop the capabilities needed to be successful in adopting and developing it. The problem, according to Christensen and Overdorf, is that, as a company matures, so its capabilities become embedded in processes and values that tend to be inflexible. With regard to processes, Digital Equipment's failure in PCs stemmed from processes that were oriented toward internal development and sourcing of most major components, in contrast to the outsourcing model that dominated PC manufacture. With regard to values, Digital's belief that a 40 percent margin on its products was necessary in order to generate a reasonable return on capital meant that PCs were always a low strategic priority. The solution, according to Christensen and Overdorf, is for established companies to develop products and businesses that embody disruptive technologies in organizationally separate units.[31]

Despite the perils, there is evidence that a number of companies have been successful in riding the waves of disruptive technologies. Since the late nineteenth century, the typesetter industry has undergone three waves of disruptive, architectural changes in basic technology. Yet, although incumbents were at a disadvantage to new entrants in terms of new product development at each new wave of technology, with their ownership of key complementary resources – notably customer relationships, sales and service networks, and font libraries – many were able survive and prosper across different technological eras.[32]

Managing with Dual Strategies

Adapting to change requires that companies must compete simultaneously in two time periods. Strategy is about maximizing performance under today's circumstances; it is also about developing resources and capabilities for competing in the future. Whereas strategies for the present are primarily concerned with maximizing the effective deployment of current resources and capabilities, competing in the future is concerned with extending, augmenting, and redeploying resources and capabilities. Derek Abell identifies the pursuit of "dual strategies" – optimizing present performance while adapting to the future – as a critical strategic challenge.[33] Managing dual strategies requires dual planning systems:

- Short-term planning that focuses on strategic fit and performance over a one- or two-year period.

- Longer-term planning to develop vision, reshape the corporate portfolio, redefine and reposition individual businesses, develop new capabilities, and redesign organizational structures over periods of five years or more.

However, the challenge of managing dual strategies goes beyond establishing dual strategic planning systems. We have examined the arguments that new technologies, new capabilities, and new business should be developed in separate organizational units. Markides and Charitou show that 17 out of a sample of 67 companies were successful in pursing dual business models. They found that success had little to do with whether the new strategy was organizationally separated; the key was the ability of the new business model to access and deploy the company's existing resources and capabilities.[34]

Shaping the Future

A succession of management gurus from Tom Peters to Gary Hamel have argued that adapting to external change is a totally inadequate approach to competing in today's dynamic, unpredictable business environment. Companies that adapt to change are doomed to playing catch-up; competitive advantages accrue to those companies that act as leaders and initiators of change. Hamel and Prahalad argue that, for most companies, emphasis on competing in the present means that too much management energy is devoted to preserving the past and not enough to creating the future.[35] Their "new strategy paradigm" emphasizes the role of strategy as a

FIGURE 10.6 Competing for the future: Hamel and Prahalad's "new strategy paradigm"

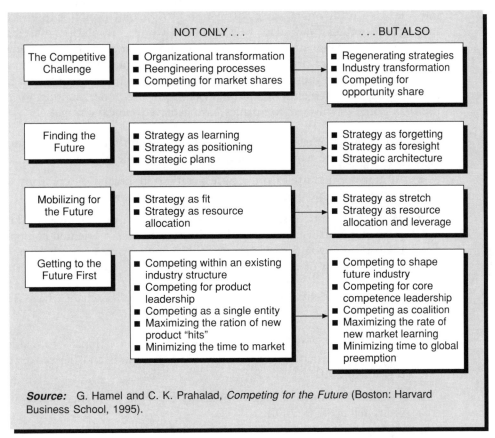

NOT ONLY . . .   . . . BUT ALSO

The Competitive Challenge
- Organizational transformation
- Reengineering processes
- Competing for market shares

→
- Regenerating strategies
- Industry transformation
- Competing for opportunity share

Finding the Future
- Strategy as learning
- Strategy as positioning
- Strategic plans

→
- Strategy as forgetting
- Strategy as foresight
- Strategic architecture

Mobilizing for the Future
- Strategy as fit
- Strategy as resource allocation

→
- Strategy as stretch
- Strategy as resource allocation and leverage

Getting to the Future First
- Competing within an existing industry structure
- Competing for product leadership
- Competing as a single entity
- Maximizing the ration of new product "hits"
- Minimizing the time to market

→
- Competing to shape future industry
- Competing for core competence leadership
- Competing as coalition
- Maximizing the rate of new market learning
- Minimizing time to global preemption

Source: G. Hamel and C. K. Prahalad, *Competing for the Future* (Boston: Harvard Business School, 1995).

systematic and concerted approach to redefining both the company and its industry environment in the future. This compares with the conventional, more static approach, which emphasizes the fit between the firm's strategy and, on the one hand, the industry environment and, on the other, the firm's resources and capabilities. Given that anticipating the future is not feasible given the unpredictability of the business environment, the challenge is to *create* the future. The main features of Hamel and Prahalad's paradigm are summarized in Figure 10.6.[36]

The idea that incremental change is an inadequate strategic response to the circumstances facing most companies is echoed by Michael Porter. He points to a tendency for companies to confuse incremental measures to promote efficiency and effectiveness with strategic decisions. Strategic decisions involve difficult-to-reverse choices over the allocation of the company's resources. The essence of strategy is choice. Achieving operational efficiency through cutting administrative staff, reducing inventories, pressing suppliers for lower prices, reengineering processes, and implementing TQM is important, but it is insufficient to save a company from a competitor's fundamental strategic innovation.[37]

According to Gary Hamel, in an age of revolution, "the company that is evolving slowly is already on its way to extinction."[38] The only option is to give up incremental improvement and adapt to a nonlinear world – revolution must be met by revolution. Achieving internal revolution requires changing the psychological and sociological aspects of organizations that restrict innovation among their members.

The problem with these appeals for revolutionary change among established companies is that they lack either empirical evidence or theoretical support for their rich rhetoric. Some established companies have achieved radical change:

- Nokia underwent a metamorphosis from a manufacturer of paper and rubber goods into the world's leading supplier of mobile phones.

- BP transformed itself from a bureaucratic state-owned oil company to one of the most flexible and innovative of the supermajors.

- Microsoft has successfully ridden a series of disruptive changes in the world's computer industry, including the transition to object-oriented computing, the networking revolution of the late 1990s, and is currently positioning itself for the conversion of computing, telecommunications, and home entertainment.

However, for most established companies, efforts at radical change have resulted in disaster:

- Enron's transformation from a utility and pipeline company to market-maker in energy, commodity, and communication futures and derivatives ended in disaster in 2001.

- Vivendi's multimedia empire built on the base of French water and waste utility fell apart in 2002.

- GEC's reincarnation as Marconi, a telecom equipment supplier, was swiftly followed by bankruptcy in 2002.

- When ICI, the former British chemical giant, attempted to reinvent itself as a specialty chemical company, the outcome was massive losses in employment and shareholder value.

- Kirch Gruppe's attempt to transform itself from a German publisher and film distributor into an international multimedia conglomerate came to grief in 2001 amongst debt and negative cash flows.

The perils of radical strategic change are not difficult to understand. We have noted that competitive advantage depends upon the deployment of superior organizational capabilities and these capabilities develop slowly. Strategic changes that take a company beyond its competence domain involve massive risks. Enron's failure has been viewed primarily in terms of individual wrong-doing. However, at the organizational level, is the problem that Enron had transformed itself from a natural gas company to a trader and market-maker in derivatives, but without building the higher level capabilities – particularly in risk management – that were essential to survive in investment banking.

Preparing for the Future: Scenario Analysis

Whether a company is seeking to adapt to external change or to shape industry evolution, a profound understanding of the forces driving industry change is critical. We cannot predict the future. "Only a fool would make predictions – especially about the future," remarked movie mogul Samuel Goldwyn. But although we cannot predict the future, we can think about what might happen. And we can do so in a systematic way that builds on what we know about current trends and signals to future developments. This is what *scenario analysis* does. Scenario analysis is not a forecasting technique, but a process for thinking and communicating about the future.

Herman Kahn, who pioneered their use first at the Rand Corporation and subsequently at the Hudson Institute, defined scenarios as "hypothetical sequences of events constructed for the purpose of focusing attention on causal process and decision points."[39] The multiple scenario approach constructs several – typically three or four – distinct and internally consistent views of how the future may look 5 to 25 years ahead (shorter in the case of fast-moving sectors). Its key value is in combining the interrelated impacts of a wide range of economic, technological, demographic, and political factors into a few distinct alternative stories of how the future might unfold. Scenario analysis can be either qualitative or quantitative – or involve some combination of the two. Quantitative scenario analysis models events and typically runs simulations in order to identify distinct and likely outcomes. Qualitative scenarios typically take the form of narratives and can be particularly useful in engaging the analytical abilities and imagination of decision makers.

For the purposes of strategy making, scenario analysis is used in companies to explore industry evolution, to examine developments in particular country markets, and to analyze the prospects for specific investment projects. Scenario analysis has been particularly useful in identifying possible threats and opportunities, generating flexibility of thinking by managers, and developing practical approaches to the management of risk. Applied to particular industries, scenarios can help clarify and develop alternative views of how changing customer requirements, emerging technologies, and new firm strategies may influence industry structure, and what the implications for competition and competitive advantage might be.

However, as with most strategy techniques, the value of scenario analysis is not in the results, but in the process. Scenario analysis is a powerful tool for knowledge management in terms of bringing together different ideas and insights about the business environment and building consensus about possible outcomes. Most importantly, however, scenarios can help evaluate alternative strategic options. By assessing how a strategy might perform under different scenarios, they can help a firm identify which strategies are most robust and can assist in contingency planning by forcing managers to address a series of "What if?" questions. Strategy Capsule 10.2 outlines the use of scenarios at Shell.

STRATEGY CAPSULE 10.2   Multiple Scenario Development at Shell

The Royal Dutch/Shell group of companies has pioneered the use of multiple scenario development as a basis for long-term strategic planning in an industry known for its high risks and very long-term investment projects. In 1967, a "Year 2000" study was inaugurated and scenario development soon became fundamental to Shell's planning process. Mike Pocock, Shell's former chairman, observed: "We believe in basing planning not on single forecasts, but on deep thought that identifies a coherent pattern of economic, political, and social development."

Shell views its scenarios as critical to its transition from planning toward strategic management, in which the role of the planning function is not so much to produce a plan, but to manage a process, the outcome of which is improved decision making by managers. This involves continually challenging current thinking within the group, encouraging a wider look at external influences on the business, promoting learning, and forging coordination among Shell's 200-odd subsidiaries.

Shell's global scenarios are prepared about every four years by its corporate-level planning staff. Economic, political, technological, and demographic trends are analyzed and two alternative scenarios are constructed for the development of the world economy over the following 20 years. Thus, Shell's 1984–2005 scenarios were:

■ *Next Wave*, which envisaged near-term crisis breaking down structural barriers to change and propelling the global economy into rapid technological progress and strong growth, but accompanied by increasing power of the oil-producing nations and stronger competition to oil from gas and electricity.

■ *Divided World*, in which the barriers to change – protectionism and regulation – stunt growth and technological progress, result in a divide between stagnation in Europe and the developing world and economic development in Asia-Pacific, and are accompanied by weak oil prices.

Once approved by top management, the scenarios are disseminated by reports, presentations, and workshops, where they form the basis for long-term strategy discussion by business sectors and operating companies.

Shell is adamant that its scenarios are not forecasts. They represent carefully thought-out stories of how the various forces shaping the global energy environment of the future might play out. Their value is in stimulating the social and cognitive processes through which managers think about the future. For example:

■ The formulation of scenarios involves bringing out the assumptions and mental models through which managers view their world. All too often these remain hidden and misunderstood – most importantly, by the individuals who hold them. This identification and sharing of implicit assumptions and theories is an important vehicle for mutual learning among different managers.

■ The scenario development process permits a deeper and broader understanding of the various forces driving change and how they interact. This can be assisted by sophisticated computer modeling, including simulation.

■ The incorporation of scenarios into the strategy formulation process encourages managers to build flexibility into their strategies by envisaging responses to hypothetical situations. Thus, in 1984, Shell had a scenario in which oil was $15 a barrel – which most viewed as inconceivable at a time when oil was $28 a barrel. When the price of oil fell precipitously to $10 in 1986, Shell was able to adjust more easily than most oil

STRATEGY CAPSULE 10.2 (*cont'd*)

majors because its managers had already considered their responses to dramatically lower prices. Arie De Geus sees scenarios as central to the role of strategic planning as a vehicle for institutional learning.

Sources: J. P. Leemhuis, "Using Scenarios to Develop Strategies," *Long Range Planning* 18 (April 1985): 30–37; Pierre Wack, "Scenarios: Uncharted Waters Ahead," *Harvard Business Review* (September–October 1985): 72 and "Scenarios: Shooting the Rapids," *Harvard Business Review* (November–December 1985): 139; Arie De Geus, "Planning as Learning," *Harvard Business Review* (March–April 1988): 70–4; Paul Schoemacher, "Multiple Scenario Development: Its Conceptual and Behavioral Foundation," *Strategic Management Journal* 14 (1993): 193–214.

Summary

Strategy is about establishing an identity and a direction for the development of a business into the future. How can we formulate a strategy for the future if the future is unknown and difficult to predict?

In this chapter we have learned that some regularities are evident in the evolutionary paths that industries follow. The life cycle model is a useful approach to exploring the impact of temporal processes of market saturation and technology development and dissemination and their impact on industry structure and the basis of competitive advantage. Classifying industries according to their stage of development can in itself be an insightful exercise:

- It acts as a shortcut in strategy analysis. Categorizing an industry according to its stage of development can alert us to the type of competition likely to emerge and the kinds of strategy likely to be effective.

- Classifying an industry encourages comparison with other industries. By highlighting similarities and differences with other industries, such comparisons can help us gain a deeper understanding of the strategic characteristics of an industry.

- It directs attention to the forces of change and direction of industry evolution, thereby helping us to anticipate and manage change.

Even if we can identify certain regularities in the pattern of industry evolution, adapting to change presents a huge challenge to companies. Organizational theories that emphasize inertia and conformity among organizations, suggest that industry adjustment may occur more through the birth of new firms and death of old ones, rather than through adaptation by established firms. This analysis is supported by empirical evidence that points to the limited success of established firms in dealing with industry evolution and disruptive technologies.

While various management consultants and commentators advocate radical and continuous change among established companies, there is little evidence that most companies have the capacity to manage such change. Certain tools and techniques – scenario analysis, in particular – may help managers understand and cope with change in the external environment, nevertheless, the fundamental truth is that, so long as developing new capabilities is slow and risky, a firm's capacity to successfully undergo radical change is inherently uncertain.

In the next two chapters, we discuss strategy formulation and strategy implementation in industries at different stages of their development: emerging industries, those characterized by technology-based competition, and mature industries.

APPENDIX: ALTERNATIVE APPROACHES TO INDUSTRY CLASSIFICATION

Industries can be classified in many ways: by type of customer (producer goods and consumer goods), by the principal resources used (capital-intensive, technology-intensive, and marketing-intensive), or by the geographic scope of the industry (local, national, global). The critical issue is whether a particular approach to industry classification can offer insight into the similarities and differences among industries for the purposes of formulating business strategies. Here are two useful approaches.

BCG's Strategic Environments Matrix

In the industry life cycle, the stage of maturity of an industry determines its key structural characteristics, which, in turn, determine the nature of competitive advantage. The Boston Consulting Group's strategic environments matrix reverses this direction: it is the nature of competitive advantage in an industry that determines strategies that are viable, which in turn determine the structure of the industry.

Two variables are used:

1. *The number of viable strategy approaches that are available.* This depends on the complexity of the industry in terms of the diversity of sources of competitive advantage. Complex products (automobiles, restaurants) offer more scope for differentiation than do commodities. Among commodities, the potential for competitive advantage depends on whether there are opportunities for cost advantage.

2. *The size of potential competitive advantage.* How big is the advantage available to the industry leader? This may derive from economies of scale, or brand leadership, or controlling the industry standard.

FIGURE 10.7 BCG's strategic environments matrix

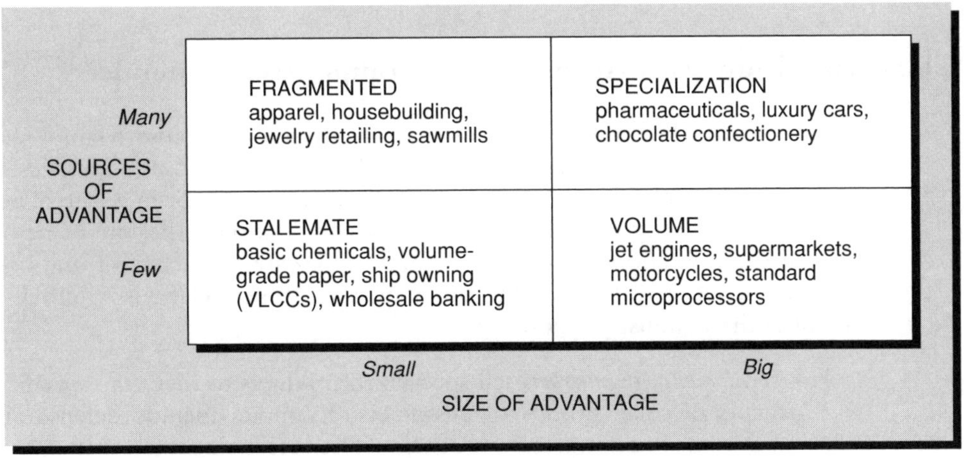

The two variables define four industry types (see Figure 10.7):

1. *Volume businesses* are those where the sources of advantage are few, but the size of advantage (typically resulting from scale economies) is considerable.

2. *Stalemate businesses* are those where the sources of advantage are few and the size of potential advantage is small. The result is a highly competitive industry where firms compete with similar strategies, but none is able to obtain significant advantage. Once a business is embroiled in a stalemate industry, survival and profitability require operational efficiency, low administrative overheads, and a cost-conscious corporate culture.

3. *Fragmented businesses* are those where the sources of competitive advantage are many, but the size of advantage is small. They typically supply differentiated products where brand loyalty is low, technology is well diffused, and scale economies are small. Success factors may include low costs through operational efficiency, focusing on an attractive market segment, responding quickly to change, and establishing novel forms of differentiation. Successful companies tend to be entrepreneurial. Franchising is one way of matching the advantages of size with those of flexibility and decentralization. An alternative strategy is to attempt to transform the business into a specialization or volume business. McDonald's transformed the fast-food industry from a fragmented industry into a specialized/volume industry. Starbucks is achieving a similar feat among gourmet coffee shops.

4. *Specialization businesses* are those where the sources of advantage are many and the size of the potential advantage is substantial. Specialization businesses feature varied customer needs, first-mover advantages, brand loyalty, scale economies, and few economies of scope (hence, there are no major advantages to firms with a broad market or product scope). Specialization businesses

require strategic differentiation – each firm focuses on a particular approach to product design, innovation, or branding.

Classifying Industries According to Competitive Dynamics

The extent to which different industries are affected by intense technological competition is not entirely a result of their level of maturity. Some industries are comparatively stable right through their life cycles, others seem to be in a state of permanent revolution. Focusing on dynamic aspects of competition – the rate of new product introduction, duration of product life cycles, the rate of decline of unit costs, geographical scope, and the stability of supplier–customer relations – Jeffrey Williams identifies three industry types:[40]

1. *Local monopoly markets* sell specialized products to meet the specific requirements of small groups of customers. Examples include defense and other government contractors, professional service companies that rely on close client contact (corporate law firms, private bankers), and exclusive consumer product companies (designer clothes, Rolls-Royces, and Ferraris). Product differentiation tends to be high: customers are resistant to standardization and elasticity of demand is low, reflecting customers' preference for specialty products. High-quality, low-volume production with lack of competition encourages craft-based production that is vertically integrated with little emphasis on economies of scale or experience.

2. *Traditional industrial markets* are large, not heavily segmented, and feature modest rates of product innovation. Competition is a quest for the benefits of size – economies of scale and brand leadership – but rival products are close substitutes and market domination is seldom achieved. The typical strategy is based on cost leadership, brand awareness, and product variety (e.g., Unilever, General Motors, Toyota, General Electric, Citigroup).

3. *Schumpeterian markets*, driven by a "gale of creative destruction," are "hypercompetitive" in nature (see Chapter 3). Product innovation is the dominant form of competition, with established products continually displaced by new products. Imitation means that speed in exploiting new products is essential. Product innovation must be supported by the manufacturing and marketing capabilities required to move quickly down the experience curve. Semiconductors, telecommunications, computers, consumer electronics, financial derivatives, recorded music, and some fashion goods are Schumpeterian in character. Annual reductions in real unit costs in excess of 8 percent are common for these products (see Table 10.2).

Some industries may be hybrids: thus, in the personal computer industry, components such as keyboards and power supplies are traditional industries, other components such as microprocessors are Schumpeterian industries, while some applications software and customer support are craft-based, sheltered industries. These hybrids pose considerable difficulties for strategy and organization.

TABLE 10.2 Classifying Industries According to Rate of Productivity Growth (as Indicated by Decline in Real Prices)

INDUSTRY	PERIOD	AVERAGE ANNUAL REAL CHANGE IN PRODUCER PRICE INDEX (%)
Local monopoly industries		
Surgical, orthopedic, and prosthetic appliances	1983–89	+4.9
Boot repair	1981–88	+2.8
General job printing	1982–89	+2.6
Musical instruments	1985–89	+2.6
Map, atlas, and globe cover printing	1982–89	+2.3
Entertainment	1980–87	+1.8
Highway construction	1970–88	+1.7
Burial caskets	1982–89	+1.7
Residential construction	1970–88	+1.6
Traditional manufacturing industries		
Passenger cars	1982–89	+0.3
Wheeled tractors	1982–89	0.0
Metal cans	1981–89	−0.1
Electric lamps	1983–89	−0.7
Gasoline engines (under 11hp)	1982–89	−0.8
Household refrigerators	1981–89	−0.9
Dynamic Schumpeterian industries		
Home electronic equipment	1982–89	−3.6
Microprocessors	1981–89	−4.6
Microwave cookers	1982–89	−4.6
Analog integrated circuits	1981–89	−4.8
Digital PBXs	1985–89	−4.9
Color TVs (more than 17-inch)	1980–89	−6.0
Memory-integrated circuits	1981–89	−6.0
Digital computers	1985–89	−10.3

NOTES

[1] For early work on the product life cycle, see Everett M. Rogers, *The Diffusion of Innovations* (New York: Free Press, 1962); and Theodore Levitt, "Exploit the Product Life Cycle," *Harvard Business Review* (November–December 1965): 81–94. For a contemporary discussion, see Philip Kotler, *Marketing Management*, 11th edn (Upper Saddle River, NJ: Prentice-Hall, 2002): Chapter 10.

[2] Thanks to Bob Edwards for information on the development of camera design.

[3] M. A. Cusumano and D. B. Yoffie, *Competing on Internet Time: Lessons From Netscape and Its Battle with Microsoft* (New York: Free Press, 1998).

[4] In metal containers, see: *Crown Cork and Seal and the Metal Container Industry* (Boston: Harvard Business School, 1978).

[5] In Shiv Mathur and Alfred Kenyon's "transaction cycle," differentiation re-emerges as products and service are recombined into new systems. See "Competitive System Dynamics," in *Creating*

Wealth: Shaping Tomorrow's Business (Oxford: Butterworth-Heinemann, 1997): Chapter 9.

6 G. Carroll and M. Hannan, *The Demography of Corporations and Industries* (Princeton: Princeton University Press, 2000). For a survey see: Joel Baum, "Organizational Ecology," in S. R. Clegg, C. Hardy, and W. R. Nord, *Handbook of Organizational Studies* (Thousand Oaks: Sage, 1996); and David Barron, "Evolutionary Theory," in D. O. Faulkner and A. Campbell (eds.), *The Oxford Handbook of Strategy* (Oxford: Oxford University Press, 2003) vol. 1: 74–97.

7 G. R. Carroll, L. S. Bigelow, M.-D. Seidel, and B. Tsai, "The Fates of *de novo* and *de alio* Producers in the American Automobile Industry, 1885–1981," *Strategic Management Journal* 17, Summer Special Issue (1996): 117–37.

8 S. Klepper and K. L. Simons, "Dominance by Birthright: Entry of Prior Radio Producers and Competitive Ramifications in the US Television Receiver Industry," *Strategic Management Journal* 17 (2000): 997–1016.

9 High rates of entry and exit may continue well into maturity. In US manufacturing industries in any given year, it was found that 39 percent of larger companies were not industry participants five years earlier and 40 percent would not be participants five years later. See T. Dunne, M. J. Roberts, and L. Samuelson, "Patterns of Firm Entry and Exit in US Manufacturing Industries," *Rand Journal of Economics* 19 (1988): 495–515.

10 S. Klepper and E. Grady, "The Evolution of New Industries and the Determinants of Industry Structure," *Rand Journal of Economics* (1990): 27–44.

11 S. Klepper and K. Simons, "The Making of an Oligopoly: Firm Survival and Technological Change in the Evolution of the US Tire Industry," *Journal of Political Economy* 108 (2000).

12 Glen Carroll and Anand Swaminathan, "Why the Microbrewery Movement? Organizational Dynamics of Resource Partitioning in the American Brewing Industry," *American Journal of Sociology* 106 (2000): 715–62.

13 R. Vernon, "International Investment and International Trade in the Product Cycle," *Quarterly Journal of Economics* 80 (1966): 190–207.

14 M. T. Hannan and G. R. Carroll, *Dynamics of Organizational Populations: Density, Legitimation, and Competition* (Oxford: Oxford University Press, 1992).

15 Contingency theory has its origins in P. R. Lawrence and J. W. Lorsch's book *Organization and Environment* (Boston: Harvard Business School, 1967). See also A. Ginsberg and N. Venkatraman, "Contingency Perspectives of Organizational Strategy," *Academy of Management Review* 10 (1985): 421–34.

16 Inertia is reinforced by social and psychological pressures for imitation resulting in the convergence of organizational forms (*isomorphism*). See: P. J. DiMaggio and W. W. Powell, "The Iron Cage Revisited: Institutional Isomorphism and Collective Rationality," in W. W. Powell and P. J. DiMaggio, *The New Institutionalism and Organizational Analysis* (Chicago: University of Chicago Press, 1991): 63–82.

17 For an introduction to organizational ecology, see: Michael T. Hannan and Glen R. Carroll, "An introduction to organizational ecology," in *Organizations in Industry* (Oxford: Oxford University Press, 1995): 17–31.

18 For a survey of evolutionary approaches, see: R. R. Nelson, "Recent Evolutionary Theorizing About Economic Change," *Journal of Economic Literature* 33 (March 1995): 48–90.

19 J. G. March, "Exploration and Exploitation in Organizational Learning," *Organizational Science* 2 (1991): 71–87.

20 D. Leonard-Barton, "Core Capabilities and Core Rigidities: A Paradox in Managing New Product Development," *Strategic Management Journal*, Summer Special Issue (1992): 111–25.

21 M. Wiersema and K. Bantel, "Top Management Team Turnover as an Adaptation

Mechanism," *Strategic Management Journal* 14 (1993): 485–504.

22 Costas Markides and Paul Geroski, "Colonizers and Consolidators: The Two Cultures of Corporate Strategy," *Strategy & Business* 32 (Fall 2003).

23 M. L. Tushman and P. Anderson, "Technological Discontinuities and Organizational Environments," *Administrative Science Quarterly* 31 (1986): 439–65.

24 R. M. Henderson and K. B. Clark, "Architectural Innovation: The Reconfiguration of Existing Systems and the Failure of Established Firms," *Administrative Science Quarterly* (1990): 9–30.

25 J. B. Quinn, "Strategic Change: Logical Incrementalism," *Sloan Management Review* 20 (Fall 1978): 7–21.

26 M. L. Tushman and E. Romanelli, "Organizational Evolution: A Metamorphosis Model of Convergence and Reorientation," in L. L. Cummins and B. M. Staw (eds), *Research in Organizational Behavior* 7 (1985): 171–26; E. Romanelli and M. L. Tushman, "Organizational Transformation as Punctuated Equilibrium: An Empirical Test," *Academy of Management Journal* 37 (1994): 1141–66.

27 R. Cibin and R. M. Grant, "Restructuring among the World's Leading Oil Companies," *British Journal of Management* 7 (1996): 283–308.

28 A. Grove, *Only the Paranoid Survive* (New York: Doubleday, 1996).

29 J. Bower and C. M. Christensen, "Disruptive Technologies: Catching the Wave," *Harvard Business Review* (January–February 1995): 43–53.

30 C. M. Christensen and J. L. Bower, "Customer Power, Strategic Investment, and the Failure of Leading Firms," *Strategic Management Journal* 17 (March 1996): 197–218.

31 C. M. Christensen and M. Overdorf, "Meeting the Challenge of Disruptive Change," *Harvard Business Review* (March–April 2000): 66–76.

32 Mary Tripsas, "Unravelling the Process of Creative Destruction: Complementary Assets and Incumbent Survival in the Typesetter Industry," *Strategic Management Journal* 18, Summer Special Issue (July 1997): 119–42.

33 Derek F. Abell, *Managing with Dual Strategies* (New York: Free Press, 1993).

34 C. Markides and C. D. Charitou, "Competing with Dual Strategies," SIM Working Paper 23 (London Business School, 2003).

35 Gary Hamel and C. K. Prahalad, *Competing for the Future* (Boston: Harvard Business School Press, 1995).

36 We shall return to Hamel and Prahalad's ideas about "competing for the future" when we discuss strategic innovation in mature businesses in Chapter 12.

37 Michael E. Porter, "What Is Strategy?," *Harvard Business Review* (November–December 1996): 61–80.

38 G. Hamel, *Leading the Revolution* (Boston: Harvard Business School Press, 2000): 5.

39 See C. A. R. NcNulty, "Scenario Development for Corporate Planning," *Futures* (April 1977). R. E. Linneman and H. E. Klein, "The Use of Multiple Scenarios by US Industrial Companies: A Comparison Study," *Long Range Planning* (December 1983): 94–101, found that over half of Fortune 500 companies were using multiple scenario analysis by the beginning of the 1980s. P. Malaska, "Multiple Scenario Approach and Strategic Behavior in European Companies," *Strategic Management Journal* 6 (1985): 339–55, found scenario analysis used most widely in the petroleum, transportation equipment, and electricity industries.

40 This section draws on several papers by Jeffrey R. Williams: "The Productivity Base of Industries," working paper 1983–84 (Graduate School of Industrial Administration, Carnegie-Mellon University, May 1984); "I Don't Think We're in Kansas Any More . . . : How Market Settings Influence CIM Strategies," *Long Range Planning* 23 (February 1990); "How Sustainable Is Your Competitive Advantage," *California Management Review* (Spring 1992).

11

Technology-based Industries and the Management of Innovation

Whereas a calculator on the ENIAC is equipped with 18,000 vacuum tubes and weighs 30 tons, computers in the future may have only 1,000 vacuum tubes and perhaps weigh only 1.5 tons.
—**Popular Mechanics,** *March 1949*

I can think of no conceivable reason why an individual should wish to have a computer in his own home.
—**Kenneth Olsen, Chairman, Digital Equipment Corporation, 1977**

OUTLINE

INTRODUCTION AND OBJECTIVES

Industries where competition centers on innovation and the application of technology provide some of the most fascinating and complex competitive environments in which to apply the concepts of strategy analysis. Consider the upheaval that wireless communication and internet protocols have caused in the telecom sector:

- In 1993, the world's three most valuable telecom companies were AT&T, Nippon Telephone and Telegraph (NTT), and British Telecom (BT), which accounted for 55 percent of the combined stock market value of the world's top 10 telecom companies. By the end of 2003, only NTT remained among the telecom top 10, a group now headed by newcomer Vodafone.

- A similar upheaval occurred on the manufacturing side of the telecom industry. In 1993, the world's leading producers of telecom equipment were AT&T, Alcatel, NEC, Siemens, GTE, and Motorola. By the end of 2003, three companies – Cisco Systems, Nokia, and Qualcomm – accounted for 78 percent of the stock market value of the world's top-10 telecom equipment producers.

There are few industries that have seen as much technological upheaval as has the telecom industry over the past ten years. At the same time, technological change has been a feature of almost every sector of the economy, not least because of the pervasive influence of microelectronics, digitization, new materials, and new forms of communication. In this chapter, we concentrate on the strategic management of innovation and technological change. Our focus is upon technology-intensive industries, which include both emerging industries (those in the introductory and growth phases of their life cycle) and well-established industries (such as pharmaceuticals, chemicals, telecommunications, and electronics) where technology continues to be the major driver of competition. The issues we examine, however, are also relevant to a much broader range of industries. Although industries such as food processing, fashion goods, domestic appliances, and financial services are not technology based to the same extent as consumer electronics or pharmaceuticals, innovation and the application of new technologies are important sources of competitive advantage.

In the last chapter, we saw how innovation is responsible for the creation of new industries, how innovation changes over the course of the industry life cycle, and the implications of this industry structure and competitive advantage. In this chapter we shall be looking at innovation and technology as weapons of competitive strategy. Our focus is the firm: how does the firm use technology and innovation in order to establish competitive advantage, to survive the brutal competition that characterizes so many technology-based industries and, ultimately, to earn superior profits over the long term?

By the time you have completed this chapter, you will be able to:

- Analyze how technology affects industry structure and competition.

- Identify the factors that determine the returns to innovation, and evaluate the potential for an innovation to establish competitive advantage.

- Formulate strategies for exploiting innovation and managing technology focusing in particular on:
  - the relative advantages of being a leader or a follower in innovation;
  - identifying and evaluating strategic options for exploiting innovation;
  - how to win standards battles;
  - how to manage risk.

- Design the organizational conditions needed to implement such strategies successfully.

This chapter is organized as follows. First, we examine the links among technology, industry structure, and competition in technology-intensive industries. Second, we explore the potential for innovation to establish sustainable competitive advantage. Third, we deal with key issues in designing technology strategies, including timing (to lead or to follow), alternative strategies for exploiting an innovation, setting industry standards, and managing risk. Finally, we examine the organizational conditions for the successful implementation of technology-based strategies.

COMPETITIVE ADVANTAGE IN TECHNOLOGY-INTENSIVE INDUSTRIES

Our focus is innovation. Innovation is responsible for industries coming into being, and innovation – if successful – creates competitive advantage. Let us begin by exploring the linkage between innovation and profitability.

The Innovation Process

Invention is the creation of new products and processes through the development of new knowledge or from new combinations of existing knowledge. Most inventions are the result of novel applications of existing knowledge. Samuel Morse's telegraph, patented in 1840, was based on several decades of research into electromagnetism from Ben Franklin to Orsted, Ampere, and Sturgion. The compact disc embodies knowledge about lasers developed several decades previously.

Innovation is the initial commercialization of invention by producing and marketing a new good or service or by using a new method of production. Once introduced, innovation diffuses: on the demand side, through customers purchasing the good or service; on the supply side, through imitation by competitors. An innovation may be the result of a single invention (most product innovations in chemicals and pharmaceuticals involve discoveries of new chemical compounds) or it may combine many inventions (the first automobile embodied a multitude of inventions, from the wheel, invented some 5,000 years previously, to the internal combustion engine). Not all invention progresses into innovation: among the patent portfolios of most technology-intensive firms are numerous inventions that have yet to find a viable commercial application. Many innovations may involve little or no new technology: the personal computer brought together existing components and technologies, but no fundamental scientific breakthroughs; most new types of packaging – including the vast array of anti-tamper packages – involve clever design but little in the way of new technology. Most business process patents are process innovations with little technological content.

Figure 11.1 shows the pattern of development from knowledge creation to invention and innovation. Historically, the lags between knowledge creation and innovation have been long:

FIGURE 11.1 The development of technology: from knowledge creation to diffusion

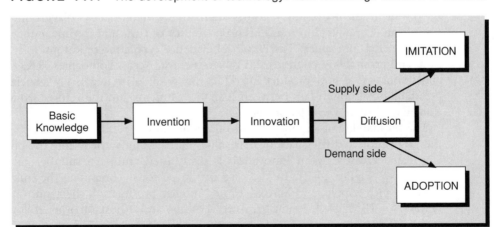

- Chester F. Carlson invented xerography in 1938 by combining established knowledge about electrostatics and printing. The first patents were awarded in 1940. Xerox purchased the patent rights and launched its first office copier in 1958. By 1974, the first competitive machines were introduced by IBM, Kodak, Ricoh, and Canon.

- The jet engine, employing Newtonian principles of forces, was patented by Frank Whittle in 1930. The first commercial jet airliner, the Comet, flew in 1957. Two years later, the Boeing 707 was introduced.

Recently, the innovation cycle has speeded up:

- The mathematics of *fuzzy logic* were developed by Lofti Zadeh at Berkeley during the 1960s. By the early 1980s, Dr. Takeshi Yamakawa of the Kyushu Institute of Technology had registered patents for integrated circuits embodying fuzzy logic, and in 1987, a series of fuzzy logic controllers for industrial machines was launched by Omron of Kyoto. By 1991, the world market for fuzzy logic controllers was estimated at $2 billion.[1]

- MP3, the audio file compression software, was developed at the Fraunhofer Institute in Germany in 1987; by the mid-1990s, the swapping of MP3 music files had taken off in US college campuses and in 1998 the first MP3 player, Diamond Multimedia's *Rio*, was launched. Despite the closure of Napster's file swapping service in 2001, the mushrooming of music piracy had caused CD sales to decline by 25 percent during 2002–2003.

The Profitability of Innovation

"If a man . . . make a better mousetrap than his neighbor, though he build his house in the woods, the world will make a beaten path to his door," claimed Emerson. Yet, the inventors of new mousetraps, and other gadgets too, are more likely to be found at the bankruptcy courts than in the millionaires' playgrounds of the Caribbean. Certainly, innovation is no guarantor of fame and fortune, either for individuals or for companies. The empirical evidence on technological intensity, innovation, and profitability confirms this mixed picture. Across companies, R&D intensity and frequency of new product introductions tend to be negatively associated with profitability, although lags between R&D investments and the returns from innovation may obscure the relationship.[2]

The profitability of an innovation to the innovator depends on the value created by the innovation and the share of that value that the innovator is able to appropriate. The value created by an innovation is distributed among a number of different parties (see Figure 11.2). In the case of the personal computer, the innovators – MITS, Tandy, Apple, and Xerox – earned modest profits from their innovation. The imitators – IBM, Dell, Compaq, Acer, Toshiba and a host of other followers into

FIGURE 11.2 Appropriation of value: who gets the benefits from innovation?

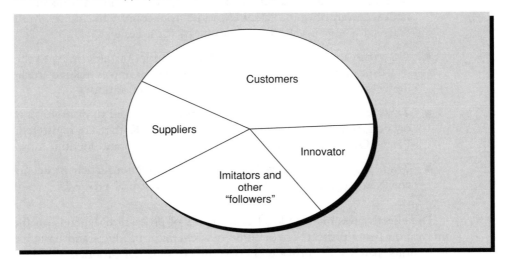

the PC industry earned rather more in total profits. Nevertheless, their returns were overshadowed by the huge profits earned by the suppliers to the industry: Intel in microprocessors, Seagate Technology and Quantum Corp. in disk drives, Sharp in flat-panel displays, and Microsoft in operating software. However, because of strong competition in the industry, the greatest part of the value created by the personal computer was appropriated by customers, who typically paid prices for their PCs that were far below the value that they derived.[3]

The term *regime of appropriability* is used to describe the conditions that influence the distribution of returns to innovation. In a strong regime of appropriability, the innovator is able to capture a substantial share of the value created: NutraSweet artificial sweetener (developed by Searle, subsequently acquired by Monsanto), Pfizer's Viagra, and Pilkington's float glass process generated huge profits for their owners. In a weak regime of appropriability, other parties derive most of the value: as in the case of personal computer industry described above. Four factors are critical in determining the extent to which innovators are able to appropriate the value of their innovation: property rights, the tacitness and complexity of the technology, lead-time and, complementary resources.

Property Rights in Innovation

Appropriating the returns to innovation depends, to a great extent, on the ability to establish property rights in the innovation. It was the desire to protect the returns to inventors that prompted the English Parliament to pass the 1623 Statute of Monopolies, which established the basis of patent law. Since then, the law has been extended to several areas of *intellectual property*, including:

- *Patents* are exclusive rights to a new and useful product, process, substance, or design. Obtaining a patent requires that the invention is novel, useful, and not excessively obvious. Patent law varies from country to country. In the United States, a patent is valid for 17 years (14 for a design).

- *Copyrights* are exclusive production, publication, or sales rights to the creators of artistic, literary, dramatic, or musical works. Examples include articles, books, drawings, maps, photographs, and musical compositions.

- *Trademarks* are words, symbols, or other marks used to distinguish the goods or services supplied by a firm. In the US and UK, they are registered with the Patent Office. Trademarks provide the basis for brand identification.

- *Trade secrets* offer less well-defined legal protection. Their protection relates chiefly to chemical formulae, recipes, and industrial processes.

The effectiveness of these legal instruments of protection depends on the type of innovation being protected. For some new chemical products and basic mechanical inventions, patents can provide effective protection. For products that involve new configurations of existing components or new manufacturing processes, patents may be less effective due to opportunities to innovate around the patent. Patents granted on dubious grounds may later be revoked or challenged in the courts. The US courts and Patent Office have continually broadened the scope of the patent laws. In 1980 patent law was extended to new plants created by biotechnology, in 1981 to software, and in 1998 to business processes. Thus, Dell Computer has 77 patents protecting its build-to-order system, while Amazon holds a patent on its "one-click-of-a-mouse" buying through a web site.[4] While patents and copyright establish property rights, their disadvantage (from the inventor's viewpoint) is that they make information public. Hence, companies may prefer secrecy to patenting as a means of protecting innovations.

Whatever the imperfections of patents and copyrights, companies have become increasingly attentive to the economic value of their intellectual property and, in the process, more careful about protecting and exploiting these knowledge assets. During the 1950s and 1960s, the leading companies in electronics research – RCA, IBM, and AT&T – pursued liberal patent licensing policies, almost to the point of giving away access to their patent portfolios.

When Texas Instruments began exploiting its patent portfolio as a revenue source during the 1980s, the technology sector as a whole woke up to the value of its knowledge assets. During the 1990s, TI's royalty income exceeded its operating income from other sources. An average of 167,000 patents were granted by the US Patent Office in each year between 2000 and 2003 – well over double the annual rate during the 1980s.

Tacitness and Complexity of the Technology

In the absence of effective legal protection through patents and copyrights, the extent to which an innovation can be imitated by a competitor depends upon the ease with which the technology can be comprehended and communicated. Two characteristics are especially important. The first is the extent to which the technical knowledge is tacit or codifiable. *Codifiable knowledge*, by definition, is that which can be written down. Hence, if it is not effectively protected by patents or copyright, diffusion is likely to be rapid and the competitive advantage not sustainable. Financial innovations such as mortgage-backed securities, zero-interest bonds, and new types of index options embody readily codifiable knowledge that can be copied very quickly. Similarly, Coca-Cola's recipe is codifiable and, in the absence of trade secret protection, is easily copied. Intel's designs for advanced microprocessors are codified and copyable; however, the processes for manufacturing these integrated circuits are based upon deeply tacit knowledge. Sharp was able to sustain its leadership in flat screen manufacture primarily because of the experiential knowledge required to make these difficult products.

The second characteristic is *complexity*. Most new toys, from the hula-hoop of 1958 to talking Gollom figures of 2003, and every new fashion, from the Mary Quant miniskirt of 1962 to Alexander McQueen's chiffon gowns of 2004, involve simple, easy-to-copy ideas. Airbus's A380 and Intel's 64-bit, Montecito microprocessor represent entirely different challenges for the would-be imitator.

Lead-Time

Tacitness and complexity do not provide lasting barriers to imitation, but they do offer the innovator *time*. The implication is that innovation offers a competitive advantage that is only temporary: it is a window of opportunity where the innovator can build on the initial advantage.

The innovator's *lead-time* is the time it will take followers to catch up. The challenge for the innovator is to use initial lead-time advantages to build the capabilities and market position to entrench industry leadership. Microsoft, Intel, and Cisco Systems were brilliant at exploiting lead-time to build advantages in efficient manufacture, quality, and market presence. By contrast, a number of innovative British companies have squandered their initial lead time advantage: DeHavilland with the Comet (the world's first jet airliner), EMI with its CT scanner, Clive Sinclair and the home computer, all failed to capitalize on their lead-time with large-scale investments in production, marketing, and continued product development.

A key advantage of lead-time is the ability to move down the learning curve ahead of followers. Despite AMD and Cyrix's successful cloning of Intel's microprocessors with very little time lag, Intel has used its time advantage and its 82 percent world market share to move quickly down its experience curve, cut prices, and so pressure the profit margins of its competitors. The ability to turn lead-time into cost advantage is thus a key aspect of the innovator's advantage.[5]

Complementary Resources[6]

Innovation brings new products and processes to market. This requires more than invention, it requires the diverse resources and capabilities needed to finance, produce, and market the innovation. These are referred to as *complementary resources*

FIGURE 11.3 Complementary resources

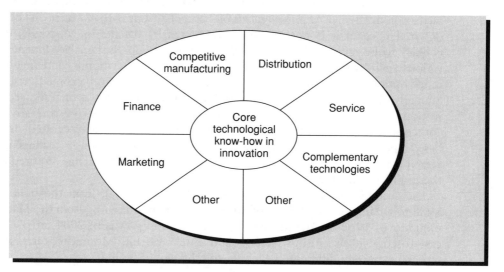

(see Figure 11.3). Chester Carlson invented xerography, but was unable for many years to bring his product to market because he lacked the complementary resources needed to develop, manufacture, market, distribute, and service his invention. Conversely, Searle (and its later parent, Monsanto) was able to provide almost all the development, manufacturing, marketing, and distribution resources needed to exploit its NutraSweet innovation. As a result, Carlson was able to appropriate only a tiny part of the value created by his invention of the plain-paper Xerox copier, while Searle/Monsanto was successful in appropriating a major part of the value created by its new artificial sweetener.

When an innovation and the complementary resources that support it are supplied by different firms, the division of value between them depends on their relative power. A key determinant of this is whether the complementary resources are *specialized* or *unspecialized*. Fuel cells, developed by Ballard AG and several other technological leaders, are likely to displace internal combustion engines in many of the world's automobiles. However, the problem for the developers of fuel cells is that their success depends upon automobile manufacturers making specialized investments in designing a whole new range of cars, oil companies providing specialized refueling facilities, and service and repair firms investing in training and new equipment. For fuel cells to be widely adopted will require that the benefits of the innovation are shared widely with the different providers of these complementary resources. Where complementary resources are generic, the innovator is in a much stronger position to capture value. Because Adobe Systems' Acrobat Portable Document Format (pdf) works with files created in almost any software application, Adobe is well positioned to capture most of the value created by its innovatory software product. However, there may be some strategic advantages from having co-specialized complementary resources to the extent that they raise barriers to imitation. Consider the threat that

Linux presents to Microsoft Window's dominance of PC operating systems. Because Intel has adapted its microprocessors to the needs of Windows and most applications software is written to run on Windows, the task for Linux – or any other operating systems – is that it is not enough to develop a workable operating system, it must also develop applications software and hardware that is compatible with the new operating system.

Which Mechanisms are Effective at Protecting Innovation?

How effective are these different mechanisms in protecting innovations? The principal conclusion from the evidence shown in Table 11.1 is, despite considerable variation across industries, patent protection is of limited effectiveness as compared with lead-time, secrecy, and complementary capabilities in manufacturing and in sales and service. Indeed, since the late 1980s, the effectiveness of patents appeared to have declined despite the strengthening of patent law. Although patents are effective in increasing the lead-time before competitors are able to bring imitative products to market, the lead-time gains tend to be small. The great majority of patented products and processes are duplicated within three years.[7]

Given the limited effectiveness of patents, why do firms continue to engage in patenting? As shown in Table 11.2, although protection from imitation is the principal motive, several others are also very important. In particular, much patenting

TABLE 11.1   The Effectiveness of Mechanisms for Protecting Innovation: Percentage of Innovations for which Different Mechanisms were Considered Effective

	PRODUCT INNOVATIONS					PROCESS INNOVATIONS				
	Secrecy (%)	Patents (%)	Lead time (%)	Sales/ service (%)	Manufacturing (%)	Secrecy (%)	Patents (%)	Lead time (%)	Sales/ service[1] (%)	Manufacturing[1] (%)
Food	59	18	53	40	51	56	16	42	30	47
Chemicals	53	37	49	45	41	54	20	27	28	42
Drugs	54	50	50	33	49	68	36	36	25	44
Computers	44	41	61	35	42	43	30	40	24	36
Electronic components	34	21	46	50	51	47	15	43	42	56
Telecom equipment	47	26	66	42	41	35	15	43	34	41
Medical equipment	51	55	58	52	49	49	34	45	32	50
All industries	51	35	53	43	46	51	23	38	31	43

[1] Shows the percentage of companies that reported that complementary capabilities in sales and service, and in manufacturing were effective in protecting their innovations.
Source: W. M. Cohen, R. R. Nelson, and J. P. Walsh, "Protecting Their Intellectual Assets: Appropriability Conditions and Why US Manufacturing Firms Patent (or Not)," NBER Working Paper No. W7552 (February 2000).

TABLE 11.2   Why do companies patent? (Responses by 674 US manufacturers)

	PRODUCT INNOVATIONS (%)	PROCESS INNOVATIONS (%)
To prevent copying	95	77
For licensing revenue	28	23
To prevent law suits	59	47
To block others	82	64
For use in negotiations	47	43
To enhance reputation	48	34
To measure performance	6	5

Source: W. M. Cohen, R. R. Nelson, and J. P. Walsh, "Protecting Their Intellectual Assets: Appropriability Conditions and Why US Manufacturing Firms Patent (or Not)," NBER Working Paper No. W7552 (February 2000).

activity appears to be strategic in intent – it is directed towards blocking the innovation efforts of other companies and establishing property rights in technologies that can then be used in bargaining with other companies in order to gain access to their proprietary technologies. In semiconductors and electronics, cross-licensing arrangements, where one company gives access to its patents across a field of technology in exchange for access to another company's patents, is critical in permitting "freedom to design:" the ability to design products that draw on technologies owned by different companies.[8]

Strategies to Exploit Innovation: How and When to Enter

Having established some of the key factors that determine the returns to innovation, let us consider some of the main questions concerning the formulation of strategies to manage technology and exploit innovation.

Alternative Strategies to Exploit Innovation

How should a firm maximize the returns to its innovation? A number of alternative strategies are available. Figure 11.4 orders them according to the size of the commitment of resources and capabilities that each requires. Thus, licensing requires little involvement by the innovator in subsequent commercialization, hence a limited investment. Internal commercialization – possibly through creating a new enterprise or business unit – involves a much greater investment of resources and capabilities. In between, there are various opportunities for collaboration with other companies. Joint ventures and strategic alliances typically involve substantial resource sharing between companies. On a more limited scale, specific activities may be outsourced to other companies.

FIGURE 11.4 Alternative strategies for exploiting innovation

	Licensing	Outsourcing certain functions	Strategic alliance	Joint venture	Internal commercialization
Risk and return	Very small investment risk, but small returns also limited (unless patent position very strong). Some legal risks	Limits capital investment, but may create dependence on suppliers/partners	Benefits of flexibility, risks of informal structure	Shares investment and risk. Risk of partner disagreement and culture clash	Biggest investment requirement and corresponding risks. Benefits of control
Resource requirements	Few	Permits external resources and capabilities to be accessed	Permits pooling of the resources and capabilities of more than one firm		Substantial requirements in terms of finance, production capability, marketing capability, distribution, etc.
Examples	Konica licensing its digital camera to Hewlett-Packard	Pixar's computer animated movies (e.g., *Toy Story*) marketed and distributed by Disney Co.	Apple and Sharp build the "Newton" PDA	Microsoft and NBC formed MSNBC	TI divestment of its Digital Signal Processing Chips

The choice of strategy mode depends on two main sets of factors: the characteristics of the innovation, and the resources and capabilities of the firm.

Characteristics of the Innovation

The extent to which a firm can establish clear property rights in an innovation is an important determinant of the number of strategy options that are feasible. Licensing is only viable where ownership in an innovation is clearly defined by patent or copyrights. Thus, in pharmaceuticals, licensing is widespread because patents are clear and defensible. Many biotech companies engage only in R&D and license their drug discoveries to large pharmaceutical companies that possess the necessary complementary resources. Similarly, Dolby Laboratories' main source of income is royalties from licensing its sound-reduction technologies. Conversely, Steve Jobs and Steve Wozniak, developers of the Apple I and Apple II computers, had little option other than to go into business themselves – the absence of proprietary technology ruled out licensing as an option.

The advantages of licensing are, first, that it relieves the company of the need to develop the full range of complementary resources and capabilities needed for commercialization, and second, that it can allow the innovation to be commercialized quickly. If the lead-time offered by the innovation is short, multiple licensing can allow for a fast global rollout. The problem, however, is that the success of the innovation in the market is totally dependent on the commitment and effectiveness of the licensees. When Raisio developed its innovative cholesterol-lowering margarine, Benecol, commercialization outside of Scandinavia was through a licensing arrangement with Johnson & Johnson. The slow rollout of the product and indecision over how to market Benecol in the US resulted in Raisio's losing much of its lead-time advantage; when the market launch finally occurred in the US, Unilever and other competitors were close behind.[9]

Resources and Capabilities of the Firm

As Figure 11.4 shows, the different strategic options require very different capabilities. Developing the innovation requires research, development, and creativity. Thus, a high proportion of major inventions are associated either with individuals or small organizations. Most of the major innovations of the twentieth century, were contributed by individual inventors – frequently working in their garage or garden shed.[10] Among 27 key inventions of the post-WWII period, only seven emerged from the R&D departments of established corporations.[11] Hence, the organizations that are best at innovation are often small firms and startup enterprises that do not possess the range of resources required for commercialization. These companies resort typically to licensing, outsourcing, or strategic alliances in order to access the complementary resources needed to take their innovation to market. Alternatively, they may seek to be bought out by a larger concern. In biotechnology and electronics, a two-stage model for innovation is common: the technology is developed initially by a small, technology-intensive startup, which then licenses to a larger concern.

Large, established corporations, which can draw on their wealth of resources and capabilities, are better placed for internal commercialization. Companies such as Sony, GE, Siemens, Hitachi, and IBM have traditionally developed innovations internally – yet, as technologies evolve, converge, and splinter, so these companies have increasingly resorted to joint ventures, strategic alliances, and outsourcing arrangements in order to access technical capabilities outside their corporate boundaries.

Timing Innovation: To Lead or to Follow?

To gain competitive advantage in emerging and technologically intensive industries, is it best to be a leader or a follower in innovation? As Table 11.3 shows, the evidence is mixed: in some products the leader has been the first to grab the prize, in others the leader has succumbed to the risks and costs of pioneering. Optimal timing of entry into an emerging industry and the introduction of new technology are complex issues. The extent of first-mover advantages (or disadvantages) associated with pioneering depends on the following factors:

1. *The extent to which innovation can be protected by property rights or lead-time advantages.* If an innovation is appropriable through patent or copyright protection or through a lead-time advantage such as learning, there is likely to be advantage in being an early mover. This is especially the case where patent

TABLE 11.3 Leaders, Followers, and Success in Emerging Industries

PRODUCT	INNOVATOR	FOLLOWER	THE WINNER
Jet airliner	De Haviland (Comet)	Boeing (707)	Follower
Float glass	Pilkington	Corning	Leader
X-ray scanner	EMI	General Electric	Follower
Office PC	Xerox	IBM	Follower
VCRs	Ampex/Sony	Matsushita	Follower
Diet cola	R. C. Cola	Coca-Cola	Follower
Instant camera	Polaroid	Kodak	Leader
Pocket calculator	Bowmar	Texas Instruments	Follower
Microwave oven	Raytheon	Samsung	Follower
Plain-paper copier	Xerox	Canon	Not clear
Fiber-optic cable	Corning	Many companies	Leader
Video games player	Atari	Nintendo/Sega	Followers
Disposable diaper	Procter & Gamble	Kimberley-Clark	Leader
Ink jet printer	IBM and Siemens	Hewlett Packard	Follower
Web browser	Netscape	Microsoft	Follower
MP3 music players	Diamond Multimedia	Apple (I-pod)	Follower
Operating systems for hand-held digital devices	Palm and Symbian	Microsoft (CE/Pocket PC)	Leaders

Source: Based in part on David Teece, *The Competitive Challenge: Strategies for Industrial Innovation and Renewal* (Cambridge, Ballinger, 1987): 186–8.

protection is important, as in pharmaceuticals. Here, competition can take the form of a patent race where the rewards are winner-takes-all.

2. *The importance of complementary resources.* The more important are complementary resources in exploiting an innovation, the greater the costs and risks of pioneering. Several firms have already failed in their attempts to develop and market an electric automobile. The problem of the pioneer, as General Motors is discovering, is that the development costs are huge, partly because of the need to orchestrate the development of a number of technologies (batteries and other power-storage devices, electric motors, and weight-reducing new materials), and partly because of the need to establish facilities for service and recharging. By 2003, it was clear that fuel cells rather than batteries would be the dominant technology for zero emission cars. Meanwhile, leadership in the market for environmentally friendly cars had been grabbed by Toyota and Honda with their hybrid gasoline/electrical powered cars. Followers are also favored by the fact that, as an industry develops, specialist firms emerge as suppliers of complementary resources. Thus, in pioneering the development of the British frozen foods industry, Unilever's Bird's Eye subsidiary had to set up an entire chain of cold stress and frozen distribution facilities. Later entrants were able to rely upon the services of public cold stores and refrigerated trucking companies.

3. *The potential to establish a standard.* As we shall see later in this chapter, markets vary as to whether they converge toward a technical standard or not. For the time being, let us simply note that the greater the importance of technical standards, the greater the advantages of being an early mover in order to influence those standards and gain the market momentum needed to establish leadership. Once a standard has been set, displacing it becomes exceptionally difficult. IBM had little success with its PS2 operating system against the entrenched position of Microsoft Windows. However, there is the risk of entering too early before the direction of technological development is clear. The brilliant British inventor, Sir Clive Sinclair, was first to market with an electronic calculator, a pocket TV set, and an electric-powered commuter tricycle. All these products were commercial failures – they were technologically underdeveloped because all were ahead of their time.

Optimal timing depends not only on the characteristics of the technology and the industry, but also on the resources and capabilities that the individual firm has at its disposal. Different companies have different *strategic windows* – periods in time when their resources and capabilities are aligned with the opportunities available in the market. A small, technology-based firm may have no choice but to pioneer the introduction of an innovation. Given its lack of complementary resources, its only chance of building sustainable competitive advantage is to grab first-mover advantage and use this to develop the necessary complementary resources before more powerful rivals appear. For the large, established firm with financial resources and strong production, marketing, and distribution capabilities, the strategic window is likely to be both longer and later. The risks of pioneering are greater for an established firm with a reputation and brands to protect, and to exploit its complementary resources effectively typically requires a more developed market. Consider the following examples:

■ In personal computers, Apple was a pioneer, IBM a follower. The timing of entry was probably optimal for each. Apple's resources were its imagination and its technology. Its strategic window occurred at the very beginning of the industry when these strengths could make the biggest impact. IBM had enormous strengths in manufacturing, distribution, and reputation. It could use these resources to establish competitive advantage even without a clear technological advantage. What was important for IBM was to delay its entry to the point when market and technological risks had been reduced and the industry had reached a stage of development where strengths in large-scale manufacturing, marketing, and distribution could be brought to bear.

■ In the browser war between Netscape and Microsoft, Microsoft had the luxury of being able to follow the pioneer, Netscape. Microsoft's huge product development, marketing, and distribution capabilities, and – most important – its vast installed base of the Windows operating system allowed it to overhaul Netscape's initial lead.

■ Although General Electric entered the market for CT scanners some four years after EMI, GE was able to overtake EMI within the space of three years because of its ability to apply vast technological, manufacturing, sales, and customer service capabilities within the field of medical electronics.

Managing Risks

Emerging industries are risky. There are two main sources of uncertainty:

■ *Technological uncertainty* arises from the unpredictability of technological evolution and the complex dynamics through which technical standards and dominant designs are selected. Hindsight is always 20/20, but ex ante it is difficult to predict how technologies and the industries that deploy them will evolve. At the beginning of 2004, for example, it was difficult to predict which would be the major new wireless communication applications during 2004–2006 or how the recorded music industry would evolve in response to the MP3.

■ *Market uncertainty* relates to the size and growth rates of the markets for new products. When Xerox introduced its first plain-paper copier in 1959, Apple its first personal computer in 1977, or Sony its Walkman in 1979, none had any idea of the size of the potential market. Forecasting demand for new products is hazardous since all forecasting is based on some form of extrapolation or modeling based on past data. One approach is to use analogies.[12] Another is to draw on the combined insight and experience of experts through the *Delphi technique*.[13]

If reliable forecasting is impossible, the keys to managing risk are alertness and responsiveness to emerging trends together with limiting vulnerability to mistakes through avoiding large-scale commitments. Useful strategies for limiting risk include the following:

■ *Cooperating with lead users.* During the early phases of industry development, careful monitoring of and response to market trends and customer requirements is essential to avoid major errors in technology and design. Von Hippel argues that lead users provide a vital source of market data for developing new products.[14] As well as providing an "early warning system" for emerging needs and technological trends, lead users can assist in the conception and development of new products and processes[15] and offer an early cash flow to offset development expenditures. In computer software, "beta versions" are released to computer enthusiasts for testing; in footwear, Nike test markets new product ideas with inner-city street gangs; in communications and aerospace, government defense contracts play a crucial role in developing new technologies.

■ *Limiting risk exposure.* The high level of risk in emerging industries requires that firms adopt financial practices that minimize their exposure to adversity. Uncertainties over development costs and the timing and amount of future cash flows require a strong balance sheet with limited debt financing. Restricting risk exposure also requires economizing on capital expenditure commitments and other sources of fixed cost. Smaller players in high-tech, high-risk industries from biotechnology to computer games typically concentrate on research and development and rely upon larger companies for manufacture, marketing and distribution. Even large companies are resorting increasingly to strategic alliances and joint ventures in developing major new initiatives.

■ *Flexibility.* The high level of uncertainty in emerging industries makes flexibility critical to long-term survival and success. Because technological and market changes are difficult to forecast, it is essential that top management closely monitor the environment and respond quickly to market signals. For Sichiro Honda, the founder of Honda Motor Company, a key aspect of flexibility was learning from failure: "Many people dream of success. To me success can only be achieved through repeated failure and introspection. In fact, success represents the 1 percent of your work that only comes from the 99 percent that is called failure."[16] Such flexibility and responsiveness were evident in Honda's initial entry into the US motorcycle market when, after its failure to attract interest in its bigger models, the Honda sales team recognized the market

STRATEGY CAPSULE 11.1 Keeping Your Options Open: Microsoft in Operating Systems

In 1988, as I wandered about the floor of Comdex, the computer industry's vast annual trade show, I could feel the anxiety among the participants. Since the birth of the IBM PC, six years earlier, Microsoft's Disk Operating System (DOS) had been the *de facto* standard for PCs. But DOS was now starting to age. Everyone wanted to know what would replace it.

Apple Computer, at the peak of its powers, had one of the largest booths showcasing the brilliantly graphical Macintosh operating system . . . Two different alliances of major companies, including AT&T, HP, and Sun Microsystems, offered graphical versions of Unix . . . And IBM was touting its new OS/2.

Amid the uncertainty, there was something very curious about the Microsoft booth . . . [which] resembled a Middle Eastern bazaar. In one corner, the company was previewing the second version of its highly criticized Windows system . . . In another, Microsoft touted its latest release of DOS. Elsewhere it was displaying OS/2, which it had developed with IBM. In addition, Microsoft was demonstrating new releases of Word and Excel that ran on Apple's Mac. Finally, in a distant corner, Microsoft displayed SCO Unix . . .

"What am I supposed to make of this?" grumbled a corporate buyer standing next to me. Columnists wrote that Microsoft was adrift, that its chairman and chief operating officer, Bill Gates, had no strategy.

Although the outcome of this story is now well known, to anyone standing on the Comdex floor in 1988 it wasn't obvious which operating system would win. In the face of this uncertainty, Microsoft followed the only robust strategy: betting on every horse.

Source: E. D. Beinhocker, "Robust Adaptive Strategies," *Sloan Management Review* (Spring 1999): 95–106.

potential of its 50cc Supercub.[17] Flexibility also means keeping options open and delaying commitment to a specific technology for as long as possible. Microsoft is well known for its strategy of investing in alternative technologies (see Strategy Capsule 11.1).

COMPETING FOR STANDARDS

In the previous chapter, I noted that the establishment of standards is a key event in industry evolution. The emergence of the digital, networked economy has made standards increasingly important and companies that own and influence industry standards are capable of earning returns that are unmatched by any other type of competitive advantage. The shareholder value generated by Microsoft and Intel from the "Wintel" PC standard, by Qualcomm from its CDMA digital wireless communications technology, and Cisco from its leadership role in setting protocol standards for the internet and packet switching are examples of this potential. Table 11.4 lists several companies whose success is closely associated with their control of standards within a particular product category.

TABLE 11.4 Examples of Companies that Control Industry Standards

COMPANY	PRODUCT CATEGORY	STANDARD
Microsoft	Personal computer operating systems	Windows
Intel	PC microprocessors	*86 series
Matsushita	Videocassette recorders	VHS system
Sony/Philips	Compact disks	CD-ROM format
Iomega	High capacity PC disk drives	Zip drives
Intuit	Software for on-line financial transactions	Quicken
Sun Microsystems	Programming language for web sites	Java
Rockwell and 3Com	56K modems	V90
Qualcomm	Digital cellular wireless communication	CDMA
Adobe Systems	Common file format for creating and viewing documents	Acrobat Portable Document Format

Types of Standard

A standard is a format, an interface or a system that allows interoperability. It is adherence to standards that allow us to browse millions of different web pages, that ensure the light bulbs made by any manufacture will fit any manufacturer's lamps, and that keep the traffic moving in Los Angeles (most of the time). Standards can be *public* or *private*.

- Public standards are those that do not involve any privately-owned intellectual property. Public standards tend to be set by government. They may be mandated – the Indian government decrees the standard that traffic shall drive on the left (though compliance is only partial); standards for London taxis require that they seat five or more persons, are wheelchair accessible, and have a turning circle of no more than 25 feet. Or they may be voluntary – the standards established by the American National Standards Institute (ASNSI), the British Standards Institute (BSI), and the International Standards Organization (ISO) involve voluntary compliance: however, their standards are often adopted by government where the public interest is involved (safety standards for children's toys). Not all public standards are implemented by public authorities: the QWERTY keyboard layout is non-proprietary but is the result of voluntary adoption.

- Private standards are those where the technologies and designs are owned by companies or individuals. Most private standards are *de facto* – they emerge from the individual choices of market participants. Thus, the pdf file format owned by Adobe Systems and the compact disc formats owned by Philips and Sony became standards through selection in the market. However, private standards may be established by public bodies. In 1953, the Federal Communications Commission selected RCA's color TV broadcasting format in preference to CBS's system.

Public and private standards may compete – the MP3 standard for compression of digital audio files is public (it was created by a working group of the ISO) but competes against the private Real Audio format.

A problem with *de facto* standards is that they may take a long time to emerge, resulting in duplication of investments and delayed development of the market. It was 40 years before a standard railroad gauge was agreed in the US.[18] One reason for the slow transition of wireless telecoms in the US from analog to digital technology was continuing competition between TDMA and CDMA standards. By contrast, Europe officially adopted GSM (a close relative of TDMA) in 1992.[19] Delayed emergence of a standard may kill the technology altogether. The failure of quadraphonic sound to displace stereophonic sound during the 1970s resulted from incompatible technical standards among manufacturers of audio equipment. The absence of a dominant standard discouraged record companies and consumers from investing in quadraphonic systems.[20] High-definition television (HDTV) may be going down the same road.[21]

A standard may be *open* or *closed*. Open standards are those where the details of the underlying technology are made available to third parties so that they can develop complementary products and services. Closed standards are those where the details are not made available outside the firm, or are made available only on a restricted basis. Thus, Microsoft Windows is a closed standard: although "developer packs" are issued to selected hardware and software companies, Microsoft does not make the source code publicly available.

Why Standards Appear: Network Externalities

Why do standards emerge in some product markets and not in others? Basically, standards emerge because suppliers and buyers want them. They want standards for those goods and services subject to *network externalities*.

A network externality exists whenever the value of a product to an individual customer depends on the number of other users of that product. The classic example of network externality is the telephone. Since there is little satisfaction to be gained from talking to oneself on the telephone, the value of a telephone to each user depends on the number of other users connected to the same telephone system. This is different from most products. When I pour myself a glass of Glenlivet after a couple of exhausting MBA classes, my enjoyment is independent of how many other people in the world are also drinking Glenlivet. Indeed, some products may have *negative* network externalities – the value of the product is less if many other people purchase the same product. If I spend $3,000 on an Armani silver-lamé tuxedo and find that half my colleagues at the faculty Christmas party are wearing the same jacket, my satisfaction is lessened. Figure 11.5 compares such "exclusivity" products with "network externality" products.

Network externalities do not require everyone to use the same product or even the same technology, but rather that the different products are *compatible* with one another through some form of common interface. In the case of wireless telephone service, it doesn't matter (as far as network externalities are concerned) whether we

FIGURE 11.5 Positive and negative network externalities

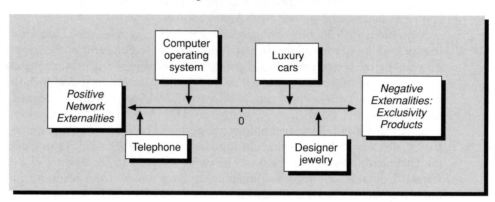

purchase service from AT&T, Nextel, or Sprint – the key issue is that each supplier's system is compatible to allow connectivity. Similarly with railroads, if I am transporting coal from Wyoming to New Orleans, my choice of railroad company is not critical since I know that, unlike during the 1870s, every railroad company now uses a standard gauge and is required to give "common carrier" access to other companies' rolling stock.

Network externalities arise from several sources:

- *Products where users are linked to a network.* Telephones, railroad systems, and e-mail instant messaging groups are networks where users are linked together. Applications software, whether spreadsheet programs or video games, also link users – they can share files and play games interactively. User-level externalities may also arise through social identification. I watch *Big Brother* and the Hollywood Oscar presentations on TV not because I enjoy them, but in order to engage in conversation with my colleagues on these subjects.

- *Availability of complementary products and services.* Where products are consumed as systems, the availability of complementary products and services depends on the number of customers for that system. The key problem for Apple Computer is that, because the Macintosh accounts for only 9 percent of the installed base of personal computers, fewer and fewer producers of applications software are writing Mac-based applications. I choose to drive a Ford Focus rather than a Ferrari Testarossa because I know that, should I break down 200 miles from Bismarck, North Dakota, spare parts and a repair service will be more readily available.

- *Economizing on switching costs.* By purchasing the product or system that is most widely used, there is less chance that I shall have to bear the costs of switching. By using Microsoft Office rather than Lotus SmartSuite, it is more likely that I will avoid the costs of retraining and file conversion when I become a visiting professor at another university.

The implication of network externalities is that they create *positive feedback*. The technology or system that has the largest installed base attracts the greatest proportion of new buyers because of the benefits of going with the market leader. Conversely, the more a technology is perceived to have a minority of the market, the more new and existing users will defect to the market leader. This process is called *tipping*: once a market leader begins to emerge, the leader will progressively gain market share at the expense of rivals. The result is a tendency toward a *winner-takes-all* market. The markets subject to significant network externalities tend to be dominated by a single supplier (Microsoft in the case of PC operating systems and office applications software, eBay in the case of internet auctions). Rival technologies may coexist for a time, but after one company appears to be gaining the upper hand, the market may then "tip" very quickly.

Once established, technical and design standards tend to be highly resilient. Standards are difficult to displace due to learning effects and collective lock-in. Learning effects cause the dominant technology and design to be continually improved and refined. A new technology, even though it may have the potential to overtake the existing standard, will initially be inferior. Such was the fate of the Wankel rotary engine. Continued refinement over 100 years has given the standard four-cycle engine a remarkable combination of efficiency, economy, and reliability. Although the Wankel rotary engine is believed by many to be potentially superior, the fact that it was only adopted by a single manufacturer (Mazda) meant that there has never been the continuous development needed to overcome its initial technical problems.

Even where the existing standard is inherently inferior, switching to a superior technology may not occur because of collective lock-in. The classic case is the QWERTY typewriter layout. Its 1873 design was based on the need to *slow* the speed of typing to prevent typewriter keys from jamming. Although the jamming problem was soon solved, the QWERTY layout has persisted, despite the patenting in 1932 of the faster and more efficient Dvorak Simplified Keyboard (DSK). The investments of millions of people in touch typing based on the QWERTY keyboard make it costly for individual keyboard users or keyboard manufacturers to switch.[22]

Winning Standards Wars

In markets subject to network externalities, control over standards is the basis of competitive advantage, and may be essential for survival. Apple Computer lost the standards war with IBM/Microsoft by the mid-1980s, since when it has been a marginal player in the computer industry. Other companies that lost standards wars with Microsoft – Lotus in spreadsheet software, Netscape in browers, WordPerfect in word processing software – no longer exist as independent companies. By identifying the extent and nature of network externalities in a particular market and the dynamics of how standards emerge, we can develop a strategy that can maximize our chances of setting the industry standard.

The single most important strategic issue in standards setting is recognition of the role of positive feedback: the technology that can establish early leadership will tend to attract new adopters. Building a "bigger bandwagon," according to Shapiro and Varian,[23] requires the following:

- *Before you go to war, assemble allies.* You'll need the support of consumers, suppliers of complements, even your competitors. Not even the strongest companies can afford to go it alone in a standards war.

- *Preempt the market* – enter early, achieve fast-cycle product development, make early deals with key customers, and adopt penetration pricing.

- *Manage expectations.* The key to managing positive feedback is to convince customers, suppliers, and the producers of complementary goods that you will emerge as the victor. These expectations become a self-fulfilling prophecy. The massive pre-launch promotion and publicity built up by Sony prior to the American and European launch of Playstation 2 in October 2000 was an effort to convince consumers, retailers, and game developers that the product would be the blockbuster consumer electronics product of the new decade, thereby stymieing Sega and Nintendo's efforts to establish their rival systems.

The lesson that has emerged from the classic standards battles of the past is that in order to create initial leadership and maximize positive feedback effects, a company must share the value created by the technology with other parties (customers, competitors, complementors, and suppliers). If a company attempts to appropriate too great a share of the value created, it may well fail to build a big enough bandwagon to gain market leadership (see Strategy Capsule 11.2). Thus, most of the standards battles being waged currently involve broad alliances, where the owner makes the standard open and offers attractive licensing terms to complementors and would-be competitors. For example, the battle being fought between Palm, Microsoft, and Symbian for leadership in operating systems for hand-held digital devices involves broad alliances including consumer electronics manufacturers, telecommunications hardware companies, software companies, and telecommunication suppliers. The alliances overlap: thus, Ericsson is a member of the Symbian alliance and has linked with Microsoft to include Microsoft software in its internet-accessing phones.[24]

Achieving compatibility with existing products is a critical issue in standards battles. Advantage typically goes to the competitor that adopts an *evolutionary strategy* (i.e., offers backward compatibility) rather than one that adopts a *revolutionary strategy.*[25] Microsoft Windows won the PC war against the Apple Macintosh for many reasons. Both companies offered an operating system with a graphical user interface. However, while Windows was designed for compatibility with the DOS operating system, the Apple Mac was incompatible both with DOS and the Apple II. Similarly, a key advantage of the Sony Playstation 2 over the Sega Dreamcast and Nintendo Cube was its compatibility with the Playstation 1.

What are the key resources needed to win a standards war? Shapiro and Varian emphasize the following:

- Control over an installed base of customers.

- Owning intellectual property rights in the new technology.

STRATEGY CAPSULE 11.2   Building a Bandwagon by Sharing Value: Lessons from VCRs and PCs

Profiting from standards requires two elements: first, setting the standard; second, retaining some proprietary interest in the standard in order to appropriate part of its value. There is a tradeoff between the two – the more value a company tries to appropriate, the greater the difficulty in building early support for its technology. Consider the standards wars in VCRs and PCs:

■ In VCRs, Matsushita's VHS format won against Sony's Betamax format not because of the technical superiority of VHS, but because Matsushita did not insist on such tight ownership of its technology and was more effective in gaining acceptability in the market. The key here was Matsushita's encouragement of adoption through licensing of the VHS system to Sharp, Philips, GE, RCA, and other competitors.

■ In personal computers, IBM was highly successful in setting the standard, partly because it did not restrict access to its technology. Its product specifications were openly available to "clone makers," and its suppliers (including Microsoft and Intel) were free to supply them with microprocessors and the MS-DOS operating system. IBM was remarkably successful at setting the standard, but failed to appropriate much value because it retained no significant proprietary interest in the standard – it was Intel and Microsoft that owned the key intellectual property. For Apple, the situation was the reverse. It kept tight control over its Macintosh operating system and product architecture, it earned high margins during the 1980s, but it forfeited the opportunity of setting the industry standard.

The tradeoff between market acceptance of a technology and appropriating the returns to a technology is shown below:

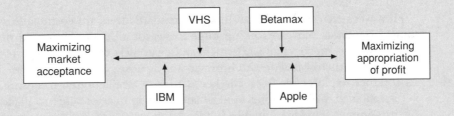

The innovator who enforces no ownership rights and gives away the innovation to anyone who wants it will probably maximize market penetration. On the other hand, the innovator who is most restrictive in enforcing ownership rights will maximize margins in the short run, but will probably have difficulty building a bandwagon big enough to establish market leadership. In recent battles over technical standards, the desire to gain market leadership has encouraged firms to be less and less restrictive over ownership in the interests of building their market bandwagon. Thus, in the battle for dominance of internet browser software, both Microsoft (Internet Explorer) and Netscape (Navigator) offered their products for free in the interests of wresting market leadership. When attacking an existing standard, there may be no alternative to giving the technology away: the only chance for Unix and Sun Microsystems' Java to establish themselves against Microsoft's Windows was by committing to an open standard.

STRATEGY CAPSULE 11.2 *(cont'd)*

Increasingly, companies are trying to reconcile market acceptance with value appropriation: Adobe gives away its Acrobat Reader in order to broaden the user base, but charges for the software needed to create pdf documents in Acrobat.

Where competition is weak, a company may be able to set the dominant standard while also appropriating most of the value: Nintendo in video games during the late 1980s and early 1990s is the classic example. However, once Nintendo met competition from Sega and Sony, its strategy backfired, as games developers and retailers welcomed competitors that offered a better deal.

Sources: *The World VCR Industry*, Case No. 9-387-098 (Boston: Harvard Business School, 1990); *Apple Computer – 1992*, Case No. 9-792-081 (Boston: Harvard Business School, 1994); *The Browser Wars, 1994–1998*, Case No. 9-798-094 (Boston: Harvard Business School, 1998); "The Video Game Industry," in R. M. Grant, *Cases in Contemporary Strategy Analysis*, 3rd edn (Oxford: Blackwell Publishers, 2001).

- The ability to innovate in order to extend and adapt the initial technological advance.

- First-mover advantage.

- Strength in complements, e.g., Intel has preserved its standard in microprocessors by promoting standards in buses, chipsets, graphics controllers, and interfaces between motherboards and CPUs.

- Reputation and brand name.[26]

However, even with such advantages, standards wars are costly and risky. A prolonged standards war can rack up huge losses for all contenders, and may result in giving away so much value to partners and customers that the returns to the winner are meager. Microsoft won the browser war against Netscape, but only by offering its Internet Explorer for free. The key is to give away enough to ensure rapid market acceptance, while keeping hold of sufficient sources of value to make ownership of the winning standard valuable. Thus, Adobe achieved rapid customer acceptance for its Acrobat pdf software by making the Acrobat Reader freely available, while charging a remunerative price for the full version of the software. The clearest trend in upcoming technological rivalries is for industry participants to collaborate in agreeing standards. Thus, in CDs, Philips and Sony avoided a standards war by pooling their CD patents and agreeing to a common standard.

IMPLEMENTING TECHNOLOGY STRATEGIES: CREATING THE CONDITIONS FOR INNOVATION

As we have noted previously, strategy formulation cannot be separated from its implementation. Nowhere is this more evident than in technology-intensive businesses.

Our analysis so far has taught us about the potential for generating competitive advantage from innovation and about the design of technology-based strategies, but has said little about the conditions under which innovation is achieved. The danger is that strategic analysis can tell us a great deal about making money out of innovation, but this isn't much use if we cannot generate innovation in the first place. If the essence of innovation is creativity and one of the key features of creativity is its resistance to planning, it is evident that strategy formulation must pay careful attention to the organizational processes through which innovations emerge and are commercialized. Because the features of new products and processes are unknown when resources are committed to R&D and there is no predetermined relationship between R&D expenditure and the output of innovations, the productivity of R&D depends heavily on the organizational conditions that foster innovation. Hence, the most crucial challenge facing firms in emerging and technology-based industries is: How does the firm create conditions that are conducive to innovation?

To answer this question, we must return to the critical distinction between invention and innovation. Invention is dependent on creativity. Creativity is not simply a matter of individual brilliance; it depends on the organizational conditions that foster ideas and imagination at the individual and group levels. Similarly, innovation is not just a matter of acquiring the resources necessary for commercialization; innovation is a cooperative activity that requires interaction and collaboration between technology development, manufacturing, marketing, and various other functional departments within the firm.

Managing Creativity

Invention is an act of creativity requiring knowledge and imagination. Companies' ability to improve their innovative performance has been hampered by limited understanding of the nature of creativity and lack of recognition of the individual traits and organizational conditions that generate creativity. The creativity that drives invention is typically an individual act that establishes a meaningful relationship between concepts or objects that had not previously been related. This reconceptualizing can be triggered by accidents: an apple falling on Isaac Newton's head or James Watt observing a kettle boiling. Creativity is associated with particular personality traits. Creative people tend to be curious, imaginative, adventurous, assertive, playful, self-confident, risk taking, reflective, and uninhibited.

The extent to which creative individuals are productive also depends on the organizational environment in which they work – this is as true for the researchers and engineers at Amgen and Microsoft as it was for the painters and sculptors of the Florentine and Venetian schools. Few great works of art or outstanding inventions are the products of solitary geniuses. There is a huge weight of empirical evidence to show that creativity is stimulated by human interaction. Michael Tushman's research into communication in R&D laboratories concluded that developing communication networks is one of the most important aspects of the management of R&D.[27] An important catalyst of interaction is *play*, which creates an environment of inquiry, liberates thought from conventional constraints, and provides the opportunity to establish new relationships by rearranging ideas and structures at a safe distance from reality. Apple Computer placed considerable emphasis on creating an atmosphere of playfulness:

> Almost every building had its own theme, so meeting and conference rooms . . . are named by employees who decide upon the theme of their building. In our "Land of Oz" building, the conference rooms are named "Dorothy" and "Toto." Our Management Information Systems Group has meeting rooms named "Greed," "Envy," "Sloth," "Lust," and the remaining deadly sins. It's not an accident that many of these are the symbols of childhood (popcorn included). William Blake believed that in growing up, people move from states of innocence to experience, and then, if they're fortunate, to "higher innocence" – the most creative state of all.[28]

But, what sort of interactions promote creativity, and between what types of individuals? The essence of play is that it permits unconstrained forms of experimentation. Stefan Thomke argues that experimentation is the basis for innovation and that experimentation needs to be managed in order to maximize learning, speed discovery, and avoid costly mistakes. In almost all fields, the costs of experimentation have fallen substantially with developments in computer modeling and simulation that permit prototyping and market research to be undertaken speedily and virtually.[29] Dorothy Leonard's research explores the composition and management of creative teams. She points to the merits of *creative abrasion* – fostering innovation through the interaction of different personalities and perspectives. Managers must resist the temptation to clone in favor of embracing diversity of cognitive and behavioral characteristics within work groups – creating what Leonard refers to as "*whole brain teams.*" Constructing such teams requires the use of cognitive and personality tests (such as Myers Briggs and the Hermann Brain Dominance Instrument) – it is particularly important that each individual recognizes his or her own personality and cognitive approach. Managing creative groups – whether in research, product development, marketing, or quality management – requires that conflict is constructive rather than destructive. The role of the manager is to clarify goals, make operating guidelines explicit, and depersonalize conflict.[30]

A central challenge is balancing the creative freedom of individuals with the need for direction, discipline and integration. As the *Economist* noted: "The two cultures – of the ponytail and the suit – are a world apart, and combustible together."[31] Anita Roddick of Body Shop cultivated a culture of "benevolent anarchy – encouraging questioning of established ways and going in the opposite direction to everyone else." All too often this whirlwind of creativity leads the company to the brink of anarchy.[32] However, for most companies the dangers are in the opposite direction – reluctance to allow creative freedom for those in research, development, design and new business ventures. In media companies, top management is notorious for its interference in creative processes. The success of HBO in producing TV shows (such as *Six Feet Under*) owes much to its ability to offer creative freedom to its content producers.

The most important discipline for ensuring that creativity is productive is to maintain linkage between creative processes and market need. Few important inventions have been the result of spontaneous creative activity by technologists; almost all have resulted from grappling with practical problems. James Watt's redesign of the steam engine was conceived while repairing an early Newcomen steam engine owned by Glasgow University. The basic inventions behind the Xerox copying process were the work of Chester Carlson, a patent attorney who became frustrated by the problems of accurately copying technical drawings. These observations reaffirm the notion that "necessity is the mother of invention," which explains why customers are such fertile sources of innovation – they are most acutely involved with matching existing products and services to their needs.[33] The relocation of R&D from corporate research departments to operating businesses is motivated by the desire to link technology development more closely with the needs of the business. It also permits the businesses to be better positioned to utilize the output of R&D units, so avoiding the fate of Xerox Corporation's PARC facility during the 1980s.[34]

Creativity requires management systems that are quite different from those appropriate to pursuing cost efficiency. In particular, creatively oriented people tend to be responsive to distinctive types of incentive. They desire to work in an egalitarian culture with enough space and resources to provide the opportunity to be spontaneous, experience freedom, and have fun in the performance of a task that, they feel, makes a difference to the strategic performance of the firm. Praise, recognition, and opportunities for education and professional growth are also more important than assuming managerial responsibilities.[35] Table 11.5 contrasts some characteristics of innovative organizations compared with those designed for operational efficiency.

TABLE 11.5 The Characteristics of "Operating" and "Innovating" Organizations

	OPERATING ORGANIZATION	INNOVATING ORGANIZATION
Structure	Bureaucratic. Specialization and division of labor. Hierarchical control.	Flat organization without hierarchical control. Task-oriented project teams.
Processes	Operating units controlled and coordinated by top management, which undertakes strategic planning, capital allocation, and operational planning.	Processes directed toward generation, selection, funding, and development of ideas. Strategic planning flexible, financial and operating controls loose.
Reward systems	Financial compensation, promotion up the hierarchy, power, and status symbols.	Autonomy, recognition, equity participation in new ventures.
People	Recruitment and selection based on the needs of the organization structure for specific skills: functional and staff specialists, general managers, and operatives.	Key need is for idea generators that combine required technical knowledge with creative personality traits. Managers must act as sponsors and orchestrators.

Source: Based on Jay R. Galbraith and Robert K. Kazanjian, *Strategy Implementation: Structure, Systems and Processes*, 2nd edn (St. Paul, MN: West, 1986).

From Invention to Innovation: The Challenge of Cross-functional Integration

The commercialization of new technology requires linking creativity and technological expertise, with capabilities in production, marketing, finance, distribution, and customer support. As we noted in Chapter 5, the challenge of new product development is that it draws upon every area of functional and technical expertise within the company. The organizational challenge is considerable: there are substantial differences between an organization that conceives and designs an innovative product and one that makes it and takes it to market. It is the classic dichotomy between knowledge generation (or *exploration*) and knowledge application (or *exploitation*).[36] Operating functions such as production and sales must be organized differently from technology and product development functions, giving rise to the need for differentiation and integration among departments.[37]

Tension between the operating and the innovating parts of organizations is inevitable. Innovation upsets established routines and threatens the status quo. The more stable the operating and administrative side of the organization, the greater the resistance to innovation. A classic example was the opposition by the US naval establishment to continuous-aim firing, a process that offered huge improvements in gunnery accuracy.[38]

The result has been an ongoing debate over the relative merits of large corporations and small, technology-based startups in fostering innovation and pioneering the development of new industries. Joseph Schumpeter, Alfred Chandler, and Charles Ferguson point to the benefits of large corporations in funding R&D efforts, developing *technological trajectories* that comprise streams of related innovations, and building links between innovation and the capabilities for manufacturing and marketing. The corporate model is exemplified by companies such as Canon, Hitachi, Samsung, Siemens, Philips, IBM, and Microsoft.[39] George Gilder and Annalee Saxenian, by contrast, identify the virtues of entrepreneurial capitalism as exemplified by the Silicon Valley model of technology-based startups – often spun off from more established companies, that finance through venture capital and IPOs, and rely upon networks of alliances to access the resources and capabilities needed for commercialization and development.[40]

Recent developments suggest that these two alternative models do not represent such sharp contrasts as suggested by the debate between Gilder and Ferguson. In particular, established corporations have increasingly attempted to counter bureaucracy and risk aversion and emulate the flexibility, creativity, and entrepreneurial spirit associated with technology-based startups. Among the organizational innovations being introduced by large corporations to improve new product development and the exploitation of new technologies are the following:

- *Cross-functional product development teams.* Cross-functional product development teams have proven to be highly effective mechanisms for integrating the different functional capabilities required to develop a new product, and for developing communication and cooperation across functional divisions.

STRATEGY CAPSULE 11.3   Product Development at Ford: From a
Sequential to a Team Approach

The Sequential Approach: Pre-Taurus

Designers designed a car on paper, then gave it to the engineers, who figured out how to make it. Their plans were passed on to the manufacturing and purchasing people . . . The next step in the process was the production plant. Then came marketing, the legal and service departments, and finally the customers. If a glitch developed, the car was bumped back to the design stage for changes. The farther along in the sequence, however, the more difficult it was to make changes.

The Team Approach: The Taurus

With Taurus . . . we brought all disciplines together, and did the whole process simultaneously as well as sequentially. The manufacturing people worked with the design people, engineering people, sales and purchasing, legal, service and marketing. In sales and marketing we had dealers come in and tell us what they wanted in a car to make it more user-friendly . . . We had insurance companies – Allstate, State Farm, American Road – tell us how to design a car so when accidents occur it would minimize the customer's expense in fixing it . . . We went to all stamping plants, assembly plants and put layouts on the walls. We asked them how to make it easier to build . . . It's amazing the dedication and commitment you can get from people.

Source: Taurus project leader, Veraldi, quoted by Mary Walton, *The Deming Management Method* (New York: Mead & Co., 1986): 130–1.

Japanese companies in automobiles, electronics, and construction equipment have been the most prominent pioneers of product development teams. Imai, Nonaka, and Takeuchi show how the structure of product development teams facilitates knowledge integration, learning, and swift development of innovative and defect-free new products.[41] The US auto producers have adopted many of these features in the redesigns of their own new model development processes. The Ford Taurus was one of Detroit's first team-based product development efforts (see Strategy Capsule 11.3). Clark and Fujimoto's study of new automobile development in Japan, the United States, and Europe provides fascinating insight into the organization of product development efforts and the advantages derived from "overlapping" the different stages of product development rather than simply sequencing them, and from providing strong leadership through "heavyweight" product managers.[42]

■   *Product champions* provide a means by which individual creativity and the desire to make a difference can be reconciled within organizational processes. The key is to permit the same individuals who are the creative forces behind an innovation or business idea also to be the leaders in commercializing those innovations. Companies that are consistently successful in innovation have the ability to capture and direct individuals' drive for achievement and success within their organizational processes; creating product champion roles is the most

STRATEGY CAPSULE 11.4   Innovation at 3M: The Role of the Product Champion

Start Little and Build

We don't look to the president, or the vice-president for R&D to say, all right, on Monday morning 3M is going to get into such-and-such a business. Rather, we prefer to see someone in one of our laboratories, or marketing or manufacturing units bring forward a new idea that he's been thinking about. Then, when he can convince people around him, including his supervisor, that he's got something interesting, we'll make him what we call a "project manager" with a small budget of money and talent, and let him run with it.

In short, we'd rather have the idea for a new business come from the bottom up than from the top down. Throughout all our 60 years of history here, that has been the mark of success. Did you develop a new business? The incentive? Money, of course. But that's not the key. The key . . . is becoming the general manager of a new business . . . having such a hot project that management just has to become involved whether it wants to or not. (Bob Adams, vice-president for R&D, 3M Corporation)

Scotchlite

Someone asked the question, "Why didn't 3M make glass beads, because glass beads were going to find increasing use on the highways?" . . . I had done a little working in the mineral department on trying to color glass beads we'd imported from Czechoslovakia and had learned a little about their reflecting properties. And, as a little extra-curricular activity, I'd been trying to make luminous house numbers – and maybe luminous signs as well – by developing luminous pigments.

Well, this question and my free-time lab project combined to stimulate me to search out where glass beads were being used on the highway. We found a place where beads had been sprinkled on the highway and we saw that they did provide a more visible line at night . . . From there, it was only natural for us to conclude that, since we were a coating company, and probably knew more than anyone else about putting particles onto a web, we ought to be able to coat glass beads very accurately on a piece of paper.

So, that's what we did. The first reflective tape we made was simply a double-coated tape – glass beads sprinkled on one side and an adhesive on the other. We took some out here in St. Paul and, with the cooperation of the highway department, put some down. After the first frost came, and then a thaw, we found we didn't know as much about adhesives under all weather conditions as we thought . . .

We looked around inside the company for skills in related areas. We tapped knowledge that existed in our sandpaper business on how to make waterproof sandpaper. We drew on the expertise of our roofing people who knew something about exposure. We reached into our adhesive and tape division to see how we could make the tape stick to the highway better.

The resulting product became known as "Scotchlite." Its principal application was in reflective signs; only later did 3M develop the market for highway marking. The originator of the product, Harry Heltzer, interested the head of the New Products Division in the product, and he encouraged Heltzer to go out and sell it. Scotchlite was a success and Heltzer became the general manager of the division set up to produce and market it. Heltzer later went on to become 3M's president.

Source: "The Technical Strategy of 3M: Start More Little Businesses and More Little Businesses," *Innovation* no. 5 (1969).

common means for achieving this. Given resistance to change within organizations and the need to forge cross-functional integration, leadership by committed individuals can help overcome vested interests in stability and functional separation. Schön's study of 15 major innovations concluded that: "the new idea either finds a champion or dies."[43] A British study of 43 matched pairs of successful and unsuccessful innovations similarly concluded that a key factor distinguishing successful innovation was the presence of a "business innovator" to exert entrepreneurial leadership.[44] 3M Corporation is exemplary in its use of product champions to develop new product ideas and grow them into new business units (see Strategy Capsule 11.4).

■ *Incubators.* During the 1990s, many large corporations established business development units whose role was to identify, fund, and foster new business opportunities. Such corporate venturing was driven primarily by innovations emerging from corporate R&D departments. Some of these initiatives have evolved into *corporate incubators* – corporate units designed to provide infrastructure and venture capital funding for new business ideas, both from within and outside the corporation. Ford's Consumer Connect was created to identify and develop new ways to leverage the company's capabilities, consumer base, and purchasing power in the new economy. British Telecom set up Brightstar in 2001 to create new businesses that would exploit BT's portfolio of over 14,000 patents.[45]

SUMMARY

In emerging industries and other industries where technology is the primary medium of competition, the nurturing and developing of innovation is the fundamental source of competitive advantage and the focus of strategy formulation. Does this mean that the principles of strategic management are fundamentally different in technology-based industries from other types of business environments? Many of the strategy issues we have discussed in this chapter are the same as those we covered in the previous chapters of the book. For example, the analysis of the determinants of the returns to innovation covered almost the same factors as our analysis of the returns to resources and capabilities: relevance to customer needs, barriers to imitation, and appropriability through well-established property rights.

At the same time, some aspects of strategic management in technology-based industries are distinctive. A common problem in technology-based industries is the speed of change and the difficulty of forecasting change. Conditions of Schumpeterian "creative destruction" (or, in Rich D'Aveni's terminology, *hypercompetition*) mean that traditional approaches to strategy formulation based on forecasting must be abandoned in favor of strategic management approaches that combine a clear sense of direction based on vision and mission, with the flexibility to respond to and take advantage of the unexpected.

Despite this turbulence and uncertainty, the principles of strategic analysis are critical in guiding the quest for competitive advantage in technology-intensive industries. Our analysis has been able to guide us on key issues such as:

- whether an innovation has the potential to confer sustainable competitive advantage;

- the relative merits of licensing, alliances, joint ventures, and internal development as alternative strategies for exploiting an innovation;

- the factors that determine the comparative advantages of being a leader or a follower in innovation.

This chapter also pointed to the central importance of strategy implementation in determining success. The key to successful innovation is not resource allocation decisions, but creating the structure, integration mechanisms, and organizational climate conducive to innovation. No other type of industry environment reveals so clearly the inseparability of strategy formulation and strategy implementation. Strategies aimed at the exploitation of innovation, choices of whether to be a leader or a follower, and the management of risk must take careful account of organizational characteristics.

Technology-based industries also reveal some of the dilemmas that are a critical feature of strategic management in complex organizations and complex business environments. For example, technology-based industries are unpredictable, yet some investments in technology have time horizons of a decade or more. Successful strategies must be responsive to changing market conditions, but successful strategies also require long-term commitment. The fundamental dilemma is that innovation is an unpredictable process that requires creating a nurturing organizational context, whereas strategy is about resource-allocation decisions. How can a company create the conditions for nurturing innovation while planning the course of its development? As John Scully of Apple has observed:

> Management and creativity might even be considered antithetical states. While management demands consensus, control, certainty, and the status quo, creativity thrives on the opposite: instinct, uncertainty, freedom, and iconoclasm.[46]

Fortunately, the experiences of companies such as 3M, Sony, Merck, Cisco Systems, and Canon point to solutions to these dilemmas. The need for innovation to reconcile individual creativity with coordination points toward the advantages of cross-functional team-based approaches over the isolation of R&D in a separate "creative" environment. Moreover, the need to reconcile innovation with efficiency points toward the advantage of parallel organizational structures where, in addition to the "formal" structure geared to the needs of existing businesses and products, an informal structure exists, which is the source of new products and businesses. The role of top management in balancing creativity with order and innovation with efficiency becomes critical. The success of companies in both Japan and Silicon Valley in managing technology (especially compared with the poor innovation performance of many large, diversified US and British corporations) points to the importance of technological knowledge among senior managers.

The increasing pace of technological change and intensifying international competition suggests that the advanced, industrialized countries will be forced to rely increasingly on their technological capabilities as the basis for international competitiveness. Strategies for promoting innovation and managing technology will become more important in the future.

NOTES

[1] "The Logic that Dares Not Speak its Name," *Economist* (April 16, 1994): 89–91. "Big Music Fights Back," *Economist* (June 14, 2001).

[2] R. D. Buzzell and B. T. Gale, *The PIMS Principles* (New York: Free Press, 1987): 274.

[3] The excess of the benefit received by the consumer over the price they paid is called *consumer surplus* in the economics literature (it is closely related to the term *delivered value* used in the marketing literature). See: D. Besanko, D. Dranove, and M. Shanley, *Economics of Strategy* (New York: Wiley, 1996): 442–3.

[4] "Knowledge Monopolies: Patent Wars," *Economist* (April 8, 2000): 95–9.

[5] We associate rapidly falling prices and costs primarily with electronics, although such a phenomenon is common with almost all new products. The ballpoint pen, invented by Ladislao Biro, is a classic example. At Christmas 1945, Biro pens sold at Gimbel's New York store for $12.50; by 1950, ballpoint pens were being sold for 15 cents. "Bic and the Heirs of Ball-Point Builder Are No Pen Pals," *Wall Street Journal* (May 27, 1988): 1, 27.

[6] This section draws upon: David J. Teece, "Profiting from Technological Innovation: Implications for Integration, Collaboration, Licensing and Public Policy," in *The Competitive Challenge: Strategies for Industrial Innovation and Renewal* (Cambridge, MA: Ballinger, 1987): 190.

[7] R. C. Levin, A. K. Klevorick, R. R. Nelson, and S. G. Winter, "Appropriating the Returns from Industrial Research and Development," *Brookings Papers on Economic Activity* 3 (1987).

[8] Peter Grindley and David Teece, "Managing Intellectual Capital: Licensing and Cross-Licensing in Semiconductors and Electronics," *California Management Review* 39 (Winter 1997).

[9] "Raisio," *Financial Times* (July 18, 1997): 13; "Raisio to Widen Benecol Range," *Financial Times* (December 6, 2000): 24.

[10] J. Jewkes, D. Sawyers, and R. Stillerman, *The Sources of Invention*, 2nd edn (London: Macmillan, 1969).

[11] D. Hamberg, *Essays in the Economics of Research and Development* (New York: John Wiley, 1966).

[12] For example, data on rates of market penetration and price decline for household appliances such as electric toothbrushes and compact disc players were used to forecast the market demand for high-definition TVs in the United States (B. L. Bayus, "High-Definition Television: Assessing Demand Forecasts for the Next

Generation Consumer Durable," *Management Science* 39 (1993): 1319–33.

13 See B. C. Twiss, *Managing Technological Innovation*, 2nd edn (New York: Longman, 1980).

14 Eric von Hippel, "Lead Users: A Source of Novel Product Concepts," *Management Science* 32 (July 1986).

15 In electronic instruments, customers' ideas initiated most of the successful new products introduced by manufacturers. See Eric Von Hippel, "Users as Innovators," *Technology Review* 5 (1976): 212–39.

16 Tom Peters, *Thriving on Chaos* (New York: Knopf, 1987): 259–66.

17 Richard T. Pascale, "Honda (B)," Case No. 384–050 (Boston: Harvard Business School): 5–6.

18 A. Friedlander, *The Growth of Railroads* (Arlington, VA: CNRI, 1995).

19 C. Shapiro and H. R. Varian, *Information Rules: A Strategic Guide to the Network Economy* (Boston: Harvard Business School Press, 1999): 264–7.

20 Steve Postrel, "Competing Networks and Proprietary Standards: The Case of Quadraphonic Sound," *Journal of Industrial Economics* 24 (December 1990): 169–86.

21 Robert Silva, "HDTV Progress Report, Fall 2002," *Home Theater* (http://hometheater.about.com/library/weekly/aadtvupdate3a.htm).

22 P. David, "Clio and the Economics of QWERTY," *American Economic Review* 75 (May 1985): 332–7; and Stephen Jay Gould, "The Panda's Thumb of Technology," *Natural History* 96 no. 1 (1986). For an alternative view see S. J. Leibowitz and S. Margolis, "The Fable of the Keys," *Journal of Law and Economics* 33 (1990): 1–26.

23 C. Shapiro and H. R. Varian, "The Art of Standards Wars," *California Management Review* 41 (Winter 1999): 8–32.

24 "If at First You Don't Succeed . . . ," *Business Week* (April 24, 2000): 62–5.

25 Shapiro and Varian, "The Art of Standards Wars," op. cit.: 15–16.

26 Ibid.: 16–18.

27 Michael L. Tushman, "Managing Communication Networks in R&D Laboratories," *Sloan Management Review* (Winter 1979): 37–49.

28 John Scully, *Odyssey* (Toronto: Fitzhenry and Whiteside, 1987): 187–8.

29 Stefan Thomke, "Enlightened Experimentation: The New Imperative for Innovation," *Harvard Business Review* (February 2001): 66–75.

30 Dorothy Leonard and Susan Straus, "Putting Your Company's Whole Brain to Work," *Harvard Business Review* (July–August 1997): 111–21; Dorothy Leonard and Peter Swap, *When Sparks Fly: Igniting Creativity in Groups* (Boston: Harvard Business School Press, 1999).

31 "How to Manage a Dream Factory," *Economist* (January 16, 2003).

32 L. Grundy, J. Kickel, and C. Prather, "Building the Creative Organization," *Organizational Dynamics* (Spring 1994): 22–37.

33 Eric Von Hippel, *The Sources of Innovation* (New York: Oxford University Press, 1988), provides strong evidence of the dominant role of users in the innovation process.

34 "The Lab That Ran Away from Xerox," *Fortune* (September 5, 1988); "Barefoot into PARC," *Economist* (July 10, 1993): 68.

35 Louis W. Fry and Borje O. Saxberg, "Homo Ludens: Playing Man and Creativity in Innovating Organizations," discussion paper (Department of Management and Organization, University of Washington, 1987).

36 J. March, "Exploration and Exploitation in Organizational Learning," *Organization Science* 2 (1991): 71–87.

37 P. Lawrence and S. Lorsch, *Organization and Environment: Managing Differentiation and Integration* (Cambridge, MA: Harvard University Press, 1967).

38 Elting Morrison, "Gunfire at Sea: A Case Study of Innovation," in Michael Tushman and William L. Moore (eds), *Readings in the Management of Innovation* (Cambridge, MA: Ballinger, 1988): 165–78.

[39] J. A. Schumpeter, *The Theory of Economic Development* (Cambridge, MA: Harvard University Press, 1934); Charles H. Ferguson, "From the People Who Brought You Voodoo Economics," *Harvard Business Review* (May–June 1988); A. D. Chandler, *Scale and Scope: The Dynamics of Industrial Capitalism* (Cambridge: Belknap Press, 1994).

[40] George Gilder, "The Revitalization of Everything: The Law of the Microcosm," *Harvard Business Review* (March–April 1988): 49–66; A. Saxenian, "Regional Networks and the Resurgence of Silicon Valley," *California Management Review* 33 (Fall 1990): 89–112.

[41] K. Imai, I. Nonaka, and H. Takeuchi, "Managing the New Product Development Process: How Japanese Companies Learn and Unlearn," in K. Clark, R. Hayes, and C. Lorenz (eds), *The Uneasy Alliance* (Boston: Harvard Business School Press, 1985).

[42] Kim Clark and Takahiro Fujimoto, *Product Development Performance: Strategy, Organization, and Management in the World Auto Industry* (Boston: Harvard Business School Press, 1991).

[43] D. A. Schön, "Champions for Radical New Inventions," *Harvard Business Review* (March–April, 1963): 84.

[44] R. Rothwell et al., "SAPPHO Updated – Project SAPPHO Phase II," *Research Policy* 3 (1974): 258–91.

[45] M. T. Hansen, H. W. Chesborough, N. Nohria, and D. N. Sull, "Networked Incubators: Hothouse of the New Economy," *Harvard Business Review* (September–October, 2000): 74–88; "How to Make the Most of a Brilliant Idea," *Financial Times* (December 6, 2000): 21.

[46] John Scully, op. cit.: 184.

12

Competitive Advantage in Mature Industries

We are a true "penny profit" business. That means that it takes hard work and attention to detail to be financially successful – it is far from being a sure thing. Our store managers must do two things well: control costs and increase sales. Cost control cannot be done by compromising product quality, customer service, or restaurant cleanliness, but rather by consistent monitoring of the "vital signs" of the business through observation, reports, and analysis. Portion control is a critical part of our business. For example, each Filet-O-Fish sandwich receives 1 fluid ounce of tartar sauce and 0.5 ounces of cheese. Our raw materials are fabricated to exacting tolerances, and our managers check them on an ongoing basis. Our written specification for lettuce is over two typewritten pages long. Our French fries must meet standards for potato type, solid and moisture content, and distribution of strand lengths.

—Edward H. Rensi, President and Chief Operating Officer, McDonald's U.S.A.[1]

OUTLINE

- INTRODUCTION AND OBJECTIVES
- COMPETITIVE ADVANTAGE IN MATURE INDUSTRIES
  Cost Advantage
  Segment and Customer Selection
  The Quest for Differentiation
  Innovation

364

INTRODUCTION AND OBJECTIVES

Although technology-based industries grab the attention of both business journalists and strategy researchers, if importance is measured by share of GDP rather than share of press coverage, mature industries – food, energy, construction, vehicles, financial services, and restaurants – retain their preeminence, even in the advanced industrialized nations.

Despite their heterogeneity – they range from massage parlors to steel – mature industries present several similarities from a strategic perspective. The purpose of this chapter is to explore the characteristics of mature industries, the strategies through which competitive advantage can be established within them, and the implications of these strategies for structure, systems, and leadership style. As we shall see, maturity does not imply lack of opportunity. Companies such as Hennes & Mauritz (fashion clothing), Ryanair (airlines), Starbucks (coffee shops), and Nucor (steel) have prospered on the basis of innovative strategies. Coca-Cola, Exxon Mobil, and General Electric were founded in the nineteenth century, yet, over the past decade, have achieved combinations of profitability and growth that would make most high-tech companies envious. Nor does maturity mean lack of innovation: as we shall see, many mature industries have been transformed by new technologies and new strategies.

By the time you have completed this chapter, you will be able to:

- ■ Recognize the principal strategic characteristics of mature industries.

- ■ Identify key success factors within mature industries and formulate strategies directed toward their exploitation.

- ■ Locate and analyze opportunities for strategic innovation in mature industries to establish competitive advantage.

- ■ Design organizational structures and management systems that can effectively implement such strategies.

COMPETITIVE ADVANTAGE IN MATURE INDUSTRIES

Our analysis of the industry life cycle (Chapter 10) suggests that maturity has two principal implications for competitive advantage: first, it tends to reduce the number of opportunities for establishing competitive advantage; second, it shifts these opportunities from differentiation-based factors to cost-based factors.

Diminishing opportunities for competitive advantage in mature industries stem from:

- Less scope for differentiation advantage resulting from increased buyer knowledge, product standardization, and less product innovation.

- Diffusion of process technology means that cost advantages based on superior processes or more advanced capital equipment methods are difficult to obtain and sustain.

- A highly developed industry infrastructure together with the presence of powerful distributors makes it easier to attack established firms that occupy particular strategic niches.

- The vulnerability of cost advantage to exchange rate movements and the emergence of low-cost overseas competitors.

Warren Buffett – "The Sage of Omaha" – observes this same process of deteriorating profit potential as enterprises transition from "franchises" into "businesses":

> An economic franchise arises from a product or service that (1) is needed or desired; (2) is thought by customers to have no close substitute; and (3) is not subject to price regulation. Franchises earn high rates of return on capital . . . [and] can tolerate mismanagement . . . In contrast, "a business" earns exceptional profits only if it is a low-cost operator or if supply of its product or service is tight. And a business, unlike a franchise, can be killed by poor management.[2]

Buffett observes that the profitability of the media business – newspapers, television, and magazines – "continues to erode as retailing patterns change and entertainment choices proliferate." The problem is that as the businesses have transformed from "franchises" into "businesses," consumers "enjoy greatly broadened choices as to where to find them." Unfortunately, demand can't expand in response to the new supply: "500 million American eyeballs and a 24-hour day are all that's available. The result is that competition has intensified, markets have fragmented, and the media industry has lost some – though far from all – of its franchise strength."

This trend toward deteriorating industry profitability is a constant threat in mature industries. As rivalry encourages overinvestment in capacity, international competition increases, and differentiation is undermined by commoditization, attaining a competitive advantage becomes essential to achieving positive economic profits.

Cost Advantage

If cost is the overwhelmingly important key success factor in most mature industries, what are the primary sources of low cost? Three cost drivers tend to be especially important:

- *Economies of scale.* In capital-intensive industries, or where advertising, distribution, or new product development is an important element of total cost, economies of scale are important sources of inter-firm cost differences. The increased standardization that accompanies maturity greatly assists the exploitation of such scale economies. The significance of scale economies in mature industries is indicated by the fact that the association between ROI and market share is stronger in mature industries than in emerging industries.[3]

- *Low-cost inputs.* Where small competitors are successful in undercutting the prices of market leaders in mature industries, it is frequently through their access to low-cost inputs. Established firms can become locked into high-cost positions through unionization of their workforces or through inertia. The decline in the market share of the US steel majors over the past three decades is partly the result of union agreements over wages, benefits, and working practices that guaranteed high-cost production. During the 1970s and 1980s they steadily lost ground to overseas suppliers and domestic minimills, both of which benefited from lower labor costs. New entrants into mature industries may gain cost advantages by acquiring plant and equipment at bargain-basement levels. During the 1990s, Tosco emerged as one of the largest and most profitable oil refiners in the United States: it acquired loss-making refineries from the majors at below-book prices then operated them with rigorous cost efficiency. Depressed stock markets can also allow assets to be acquired cheaply: during the Asian financial crisis of 1997–9, Citigroup and GE Capital acquired a number of Asian banks and finance companies at bargain-basement prices.

- *Low overheads.* During the early 1990s, some of the most profitable companies in mature industries tended to be those that had achieved the most substantial reductions in overhead costs. In discount retailing, Wal-Mart is famous for its parsimonious approach to overhead cost. Among the oil majors, Exxon is known for its rigorous control of overhead costs. Exxon's headquarters cost (relative to net worth) was estimated at less than one-quarter that of Mobil's.[4] When Exxon merged with Mobil, it was able to extract huge cost savings from Mobil. Excess overhead costs in mature firms can be pervasive and institutionalized and their elimination may require shock therapy. In the oil industry, the oil price collapse of 1986 triggered a wave of cost reduction and restructuring.[5] Among the Korean *chaebols*, the financial crisis of 1998 led to extensive reductions in overheads.

Cost efficiency in mature industries is rarely a basis for sustainable competitive advantage; it is typically a requirement for survival. Deteriorating performance among mature companies typically triggers the adoption of turnaround strategies. Research into successful turnaround strategies points to the critical role played by aggressive cost cutting. Hambrick and Schecter identified three successful approaches:

- *Asset and cost surgery* – aggressive cost reduction through reduction of excess capacity; halting of new investment in plant and equipment; and cutbacks in R&D, marketing expenditures, receivables and inventories.

- *Selective product and market pruning* – refocusing on segments that were most profitable or where the firm possessed distinctive strength.

- *Piecemeal productivity moves* – adjustments to current market position rather than comprehensive refocusing or reorganizing, including reductions in marketing and R&D expenditures, higher capacity utilization, and increased employee productivity.[6]

The importance of cost reduction in boosting profitability is confirmed by Grinyer, Mayes, and McKiernan's study of turnarounds among British companies (most of which were long-established companies in mature industries). The two factors that most frequently distinguished the "sharpbenders" from a control group of companies were, first, changes in top management and, second, intensive efforts to reduce production costs.[7]

Segment and Customer Selection

Sluggish demand growth, lack of product differentiation, and international competition tend to depress the profitability of mature industries. Yet, even unattractive industries may offer profitable niche markets. Not only do growth rates of demand vary between segments, but the structure of segments with regard to concentration, buyer power, and potential for differentiation varies considerably. As a result, segment selection can be a key determinant of differences in the performance of companies within the same industry. Wal-Mart's profitability was assisted by locating its stores in small and medium-sized towns where it faced little competition. In the auto industry, the eagerness of the major producers to enter higher-margin segments – luxury cars, light trucks, sport-utility vehicles (SUVs) and passenger vans – has resulted in deteriorating margins in these segments. In response, the automakers have sought to develop hybrid vehicles that span existing segments – Mercedes Grand Tourer Sport, Ford's Freestyle, and Nissan Murano – or create entirely new segments – such as DaimlerChrysler's super-micro Smart car. Opportunities for establishing new segments are often encouraged by the strategies of market leaders. The more that incumbents focus upon the mass market, the more likely it is that underserved niches will offer opportunities for new entrants willing to specialize in specific underserved niches.[8]

The logic of segment focus implies further disaggregation of markets – down to the level of the individual customer. Information technology permits new approaches to *customer relationship management* (CRM), making it possible to analyze individual characteristics and preferences, identify individual customers' profit contribution to the firm, and organize marketing around individualized, integrated approaches to customers. In the same way that Las Vegas casinos have long recognized that the major part of their profits derives from a tiny minority of customers – the "high rollers" – so banks, supermarkets, credit card companies, and hotels increasingly use transactions data to identify their most attractive customers, and those that are a drag on profitability.

The next stage in this process is to go beyond customer selection actively to target more attractive customers and transform less valuable customers into more valuable customers. Alan Grant and Leonard Schlesinger point to the need for companies to optimize their *value exchange* – the relationship between the investment a company makes in a customer relationship and the return that investment generates.[9] For example:

- Credit card issuer Capital One has long been a leader in using data warehousing, experimentation, simulation, and sophisticated statistical modeling to adjust the terms and features of its credit card offers to the preferences and characteristics of individual customers. At the heart of Capital One's information-based approach is an estimation of the life-time profitability of each customer and analysis of the four key events in the credit card life cycle: acquiring the customer, stimulating the customer's card use, retaining the customer, and managing default.[10]

- Amazon.com uses information on customers' prior transactions and comparisons with other customers making similar purchases to generate individualized purchase suggestions.

The Quest for Differentiation

Cost leadership, we noted in Chapter 9, is difficult to sustain, particularly in the face of international competition. Hence, differentiating to attain some insulation from the rigors of price competition is particularly attractive in mature industries. The problem is that the trend toward commoditization narrows the scope for differentiation and reduces customer willingness to pay a premium for differentiation:

- In tires and domestic appliances, companies' investments in differentiation through product innovation, quality, and brand advertising reputation have generated disappointing returns. Vigorous competition, price-sensitive customers and strong, aggressive retailers have limited the price premium that differentiation will support.

- In the deeply troubled airline sector, attempts to gain competitive advantage through offering more legroom, providing superior in-flight entertainment, and achieving superior punctuality have met little market response from consumers. The only effective differentiators appear to be frequent flier programs and services offered to first- and business-class travelers.

Standardization of the physical attributes of a product and convergence of consumer preferences constrains, but does not eliminate, opportunities for meaningful and profitable differentiation. Product standardization is frequently accompanied by increased differentiation of complementary services. In the auto industry, greater similarity among the competing models of different manufacturers has encouraged firms to compete on financing terms, leasing arrangements, warranties, after-sales services, and the like. In consumer goods, maturity is often associated with the focus of differentiation shifting from physical product characteristics to image. Entrenched consumer loyalties to specific brands of cola or cigarettes are a tribute to the capacity of brand promotion over long periods of time to create distinct images among near-identical products.

The intensely competitive retail sector produces particularly interesting examples of differentiation strategies. The dismal profitability earned by many retail chains (Kmart, J. C. Penny, and Federated Department Stores in the US; J. Sainsbury, Selfridges, and Storehouse in the UK) contrasts sharply with the sales growth and profitability of stores that have established clear differentiation through variety, style, and ambiance (The Gap, TJX, Bed, Bath and Beyond, Zara-Inditex, and Next). Table 12.1 shows financially successful and unsuccessful retailers as indicated by valuation ratio. A further lesson from highly competitive mature sectors such as retailing is that competitive advantage is difficult to sustain. Most of the outstandingly successful retailers of the previous decade – Toys-R-Us, Home Depot, Body Shop, and Marks & Spencer – have been displaced in the affections of consumers and investors by the rising stars of retail.

Innovation

We have characterized mature industries as industries where the pace of technical change is low. In many mature industries – steel, textiles, food processing, insurance, and hotels – R&D expenditure is below 1 percent of sales revenue, while in US manufacturing as a whole just three sectors – computers and electronics, pharmaceuticals, and aerospace – account for 65 percent of R&D spending.[11] In recent years, this conventional view of mature industries as lacking technological dynamism has come under attack. McGahan and Silverman show that, measured by patenting activity, mature industries are as innovative as emerging industries.[12] Certainly in mature products such as tires, brassieres, and fishing rods, continuing technological development is indicated by a steady flow of new patents (see Strategy Capsule 12.1). However, this finding may be strongly influenced by the inclusion of long-established but technologically dynamic sectors such as pharmaceuticals and computers as "mature."

What is clear is that the pressure of competition and the limited opportunities for technology-based advantage create impetus for innovation in other areas of competitive strategy. The strategic quest for new ways of doing business was referred to in Chapter 6. In relation to the innovation cycles identified by Abernathy and Utterback, it is possible that there is a third phase of innovation – *strategic innovation* – which

TABLE 12.1   Large Retailers with the Highest and Lowest Valuation Ratios, 2003

COMPANY	COUNTRY	VALUATION RATIO*	SALES ($, BILLIONS)
Top 15			
Amazon.com	US	n.a.	3.9
Caremark Rx	US	18.0	6.8
Expedia	US	16.6	0.6
Autozone	US	13.1	5.3
Hennes & Mauritz	Sweden	10.5	5.9
Next	UK	10.1	3.6
Bed, Bath & Beyond	US	8.5	3.7
Woolworth	Australia	8.0	16.0
Gap	US	4.1	14.5
TJX	US	6.9	12.0
Inditex	Spain	6.8	4.7
Wal-Mart	US	5.7	244.5
Radio Shack	US	5.6	4.6
Family Dollar Stores	US	5.1	4.2
Best Buy	US	5.0	20.9
Bottom 15			
Toys-R-Us	US	0.6	11.3
J. C. Penny	US	0.7	32.3
Federated Dept. Stores	US	1.1	15.4
J. Sainsbury	UK	1.1	29.8
Ito-Yokado	Japan	1.1	28.0
Ahold	Neth.	1.2	78.3
Safeway plc	UK	1.3	29.8
Pinault-Printemps-Redoute	France	1.4	32.2
Sears Roebuck	US	1.4	41.4
Dixons Group	UK	1.4	8.0
Albertson's	US	1.5	35.6
May Department Stores	US	1.7	11.9
Office Depot	US	1.7	11.4
CVS	US	1.9	24.2
Kingfisher	UK	2.0	17.6

*   Ratio of market value of equity to the book value of the company.
Source: *Business Week* Global 1000 (July 2003).

becomes most prominent once product and process innovation have begun to slacken (see Figure 12.1).

Because strategic innovation requires strategic initiatives that are new and unique, it is difficult to apply systematic, analytical approaches to their discovery and design. In Chapter 6, I showed how value chain analysis can assist the identification of "new game strategies" that reconfigure the sequence of activities undertaken by the firm.

Strategic innovation may also result from redefining markets and market segments.[13] This may involve:

STRATEGY CAPSULE 12.1   Innovation in Mature Industries: Brassiere Technology

The first patent for a "breast-supporting device" was issued in the United States in 1864. However the first patent relating to an undergarment named "brassiere" was issued to Mary Phelps Jacob in 1913. When the production of corsets was suspended in the US during the First World War (in order to conserve supplies of steel), the market for brassieres was assured. By 1940 over 550 US patents for brassieres and related breast supporters had been issued.

The technological quest for a better bra continued into the twenty-first century – spurred by the slow growth of sales in the advanced industrialized countries. The design innovations of recent years include:

- Wonderbra (owned by Sara Lee) introduced a "variable cleavage" bra equipped with a system of pulleys.

- The Airotic bra designed by Gossard (also owned by Sara Lee) features "twin air bags as standard" – these are inflatable by a "unique G-pump system."

- Charnos's Bioform bra replaces underwiring with soft molded polypropylene around a rigid ring – a design inspired by the Frisbee.

- The Ultimo bra, designed by Scottish model Michelle Mone assisted by a team of German scientists, is equipped with silicone gel pads.

- A number of new brassieres use "spacer fabric" which comprises "two outer textile layers separated by a ventilated inner layer of spacer yarns, to allow heat and moisture to escape. Various properties can be added to the fabrics, including anti-microbial, anti-mildew, anti-static, flame-retardant, absorptive, water-repellent and abrasion-resistant attributes . . ."

Sources: www.fashion-era.com/bras_after_1950.htm; "Bra Wars," *Economist* (December 2, 2000): 112.

FIGURE 12.1   Innovation over the life cycle: from technological to strategic innovation

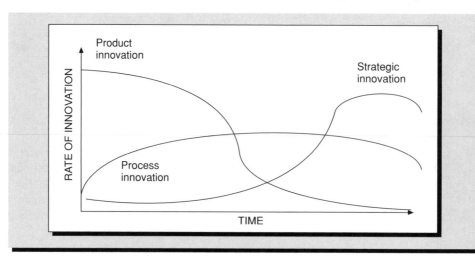

- *Embracing new customer groups.* In the same way that Henry Ford extended car ownership to ordinary families, AOL extended online information and entertainment to the mass market, and Sony have brought video games to new demographic segments.

- *Adding products and services that perform new but related functions.* In the US, Arco was an innovator in recreating the gas station as a convenience store. In book retailing, large stores such as Barnes and Noble as well as some small neighborhood bookstores have redefined book retailing by adding additional products and services. Many of these innovative forms of differentiation involve the creation of entirely new customer experiences – at restaurant chains such as Hard Rock Café and Planet Hollywood the food is a relatively minor contributor to the customer experience. Pine and Gilmore identify a progression of economic value that begins with commodities and leads through products and services before arriving at *experiences*. In the *experience economy*, companies go beyond providing a product or service that meets a clearly defined customer need and involve their customers in a process that engages them at the emotional, intellectual, even spiritual, level.[14]

Baden Fuller and Stopford's analysis of strategic innovation in mature businesses focuses on the reconciliation of multiple (often opposing) performance goals in order to create new options. Based on in-depth case analysis of successful mature companies, they conclude:

1. Maturity is a state of mind, not a state of the business; every enterprise has the potential for rejuvenation.

2. It is the firm that matters, not the industry. The industry sets a context, not a prison for the firm. Not only can the creative firm achieve success within a hostile industry environment, it can transform its industry environment. Look what Honda did to the motorcycle markets of North America and Europe during the 1960s.

3. Strategic innovation is the basis for competitive advantage in industries where the potential for competitive advantage seems limited. The essence of strategic innovation is reconciling alternatives: quality at low cost (Toyota), variety at low cost (Courtaulds), speed at low cost (Benetton), and so on.

4. Businesses should be selective in choosing their strategic territory. An island kingdom is more defensible than the Hapsburg Empire. The firm's market scope needs to be limited by its resources and capabilities.

5. The pursuit of strategic innovation requires an entrepreneurial organization with freedom to experiment and the capacity to learn.[15]

Rejuvenation represents as formidable a challenge to a mature enterprise as it does to an aging university professor. Indeed, change is likely to be even more difficult for organizations than for individuals. In Chapter 10, we noted the resistance to change caused by organizational inertia. Resistance to innovation and renewal also arises from the propensity for the managers of long-established firms to be trapped within their industry's conventional thinking about key success factors and business practices. Chapter 4 noted how established firms' responses to competitive threats may be limited by industry-wide systems of belief. J.-C. Spender refers to these common cognitive patterns as "industry recipes."[16] Studies of cognitive maps – the mental frameworks through which managers perceive and think about their environments and their companies – yield insights into why some firms are able to adapt better than others. A study of organizational renewal among railroad companies found that the ability of managers to learn in the form of changing their mental models of the business was critical to their capacity to renew themselves.[17]

The ability to break away from conventional wisdom and establish a unique positioning or novel form of differentiation may be critical in mature industries. Costas Markides identifies several examples of such contrarian thinking, including the following:

- Most US brokerage houses have embraced economies of scale, diversification, integration with investment banks, and new approaches to delivering services. Edward Jones has almost 2,000 offices, mostly in the US but also in Canada and the UK. Each office has just one investment adviser, there are no proprietary investment products, and no online investing. Edward Jones' strategy has been built on face-to-face relationships, motivating its office managers to develop their local business, and ambitious growth targets. Its business model is based more on McDonald's or Holiday Inns than on Goldman Sachs or Merrill Lynch. Between 1995 and 1999, its revenues doubled from $720 million to $1.8 billion.[18]

- Enterprise Rent-A-Car has adopted a location strategy that is quite different from its major competitors Hertz and Avis. Rather than concentrate on serving the business traveler through locating at airports and downtown, Enterprise concentrates on suburban locations, where it caters primarily to the consumer market.[19]

- The difficulty that established firms have in identifying and exploiting opportunities for strategic innovation is indicated by the fact that novel strategies in mature sectors are the work of newcomers. In long-established industries with well-entrenched incumbents – steel and autos, for example – it is only when challenged by new competitors – minimills in steel, Toyota and Honda in autos – that the established embark on change.[20]

How do companies break away from their traditional mindsets and achieve strategic innovation? According to Hamel, the role of strategy should be to foster revolution through reorganizing the strategy-making process. This means breaking top management's monopoly over strategy formulation, bringing in younger people from further down the organization, and gaining involvement from those on the periphery of the organization.[21] Companies also need to be aware of the process they are following to achieve innovation and change. Henk Volberda and Charles Baden Fuller conceive of sequences of managerial actions which they conceive of as "journeys of strategic renewal" and "trajectories of transformation."[22] Common to all these approaches is recognition that strategic innovation goes beyond rethinking strategies, it also requires new approaches to structuring and managing the mature business.

STRATEGY IMPLEMENTATION IN MATURE INDUSTRIES: STRUCTURE, SYSTEMS, AND STYLE

If the key to success in mature industries is achieving operational efficiency and reconciling this with innovation and customer responsiveness, achieving competitive advantage in mature businesses requires implementing structures, systems, and management styles that can mesh these multiple performance goals.

Efficiency through Bureaucracy

If maturity implies greater environmental stability, slower technological change, and an emphasis on cost efficiency, what types of organization and management approaches are called for? As we observed in Chapter 6, the conventional prescription for stable environments at the beginning of the 1960s came from Burns and Stalker, who argued that, whereas dynamic environments require organic organizational forms characterized by decentralization, loosely defined roles, and a high level of lateral communication, stable environments require a "mechanistic" organization characterized by centralization, well-defined roles, and predominantly vertical communication.[23] Henry Mintzberg describes this highly formalized type of organization dedicated to the pursuit of efficiency as the *machine bureaucracy*.[24] Efficiency is achieved through standardized routines, division of labor, and close management control based on bureaucratic principles. Such forms of organization were typical in mature industries with large-scale production and heavy reliance on Frederick Taylor's principles of scientific management. Division of labor extends to management as well as operatives. Mechanistic structures typically display high levels of vertical and horizontal specialization. Vertical specialization is reflected in the concentration of strategy formulation at the apex of the hierarchy, while middle and junior management supervise and administer through the application of standardized rules and procedures. Horizontal specialization in the company is organized around functional departments rather than product divisions.

The machine bureaucracy as described by Mintzberg is a caricature of actual organizations – probably the closest approximations are found in government departments performing highly routine administrative duties (e.g., the Internal Revenue Service or departments of motor vehicle licensing). However, in most mature industries, the features of mechanistic organizations are evident in highly routinized operations and application of highly detailed rules and procedures. McDonald's may not be a

TABLE 12.2 Strategy Implementation in Mature Industries: Conventional Features of Organization and Management

STRATEGY

Primary goal is cost advantage through economies of scale, capital-intensive production of standardized product/service. Dichotomization of strategy formulation (the preserve of top management) and strategy implementation (carried down the hierarchy).

STRUCTURE

Functional departments (e.g., production, marketing, customer service, distribution). Distinction between line and staff. Clearly defined job roles with strong vertical reporting/delegation relationships.

CONTROLS

Performance targets are primarily quantitative and short term and are elaborated for all members of the organization. Performance is closely monitored by well-established, centralized management information systems and formalized reporting requirements. Financial controls through budgets and profit targets particularly important.

INCENTIVES

Incentives are based on achievement of individual targets and are in the form of financial rewards and promotion up the hierarchy. Penalties exist for failure to attain quantitative targets, for failure to adhere to the rules, and for lack of conformity to company norms.

COMMUNICATION

Primarily vertical for the purposes of delegation and reporting. Lateral communication limited, often achieved through interdepartmental committees.

MANAGEMENT

Primary functions of top management: control and strategic decision making. Typical CEO: the administrator – who guides the organization through establishing and operating organizational systems and principles and building consensus (e.g., Alfred Sloan Jr. of General Motors); and the autocrat – whose primary role is decision making and who leads through aggressive use of power and sheer force of personality (Lee Iacocca of Chrysler and Al Dunlap of Sunbeam).

typical bureaucracy, but it certainly operates with highly standardized and refined operating procedures that govern virtually every aspect of how it does business (see the quotation that introduces this chapter). The characteristics of mechanistic organization and principles of bureaucracy are prominent among the large enterprises found in most mature industries, whether we are looking at DaimlerChrysler, Walt Disney Company, Exxon Mobil, or HSBC. The key features of these mature organizations are summarized in Table 12.2.

Beyond Bureaucracy

As was noted in Chapter 6, the past two decades have seen growing unpopularity of bureaucratic approaches to management, especially in mature industries. Factors contributing to this trend include:

- *Increased environmental turbulence.* Bureaucracy is conducive to efficiency in stable environments. However, the centralized, structured organization cannot readily adapt to change. Achieving flexibility to respond to external change requires greater decentralization, less specialization, and looser controls.

- *Increased emphasis on innovation.* The organizational structure, control systems, management style, and interpersonal relationships conducive to efficiency are likely to hinder innovation. As mature enterprises sought new opportunities for competitive advantage, so the disadvantages of formalized, efficiency-oriented organizations became increasingly apparent.

- *New process technology.* The efficiency advantages of bureaucratized organizations arise from the technical virtues of highly specialized, systematized production methods. The electronics revolution has changed the conditions for efficiency. Computer-integrated manufacturing processes permit cost efficiency with greater product variety, shorter runs, and greater flexibility. As automation displaces labor-intensive, assembly-line manufacturing techniques, there is less need for elaborate division of labor and greater need for job flexibility. Simultaneously, the electronic revolution in the office is displacing the administrative bureaucracy that control and information systems once required.

- *Alienation and conflict.* The dependence of bureaucracy on departmentalization, layering, and the control of some employees by others is conducive to alienation and conflict.

Companies in mature industries have undergone substantial adjustment over the past decade. Among large, long-established corporations management hierarchies have been pruned, decision making decentralized and accelerated, and more open communication and flexible collaboration fostered. The trend began in North America, spread to continental Europe, and is now evident in Japan and Korea. The changes are apparent in:

- Strategic decision processes that increase the role of business-level managers and reduce the role of corporate management; an emphasis on the strategy formulation process as more important than strategic plans *per se*.

- This shifting of decision-making power to the business level has been accompanied by shrinking corporate staffs.

- Less emphasis on economies of large-scale production and increased responsiveness to customer requirements together with greater flexibility in responding to changes in the marketplace.

- Increased emphasis on teamwork as a basis for organizing separate activities to improve interfunctional cooperation and responsiveness to external requirements.

- Wider use of profit incentives to motivate employees and less emphasis on controls and supervision.

These trends amount to a closer convergence between the organizational and managerial characteristics of firms in mature industries and those located in the newer, more technologically oriented industries. At the same time, the primary emphasis on cost efficiency remains. It is not that the goal of cost efficiency has been super-seded, rather that the conditions for cost efficiency have changed. The most powerful force for organizational change in mature industries has been the inability of highly structured, centralized organizations to maintain their cost efficiency in an increasingly turbulent business environment. As we observed in Chapter 9, the requirements for dynamic efficiency are different from the requirements for static efficiency. Dynamic efficiency requires flexibility, which necessitates higher levels of autonomy and nonhierarchical coordination. A feature of the revitalization efforts of Jack Welch at General Electric, Ferdinand Piech at Volkswagen, John Browne at British Petroleum, and Sandy Weill at Citigroup has been combining strong central direction with increased decision-making autonomy at the business level. By relying more on performance targets and less on approvals and committees, the old cor-porate empires have become more flexible and responsive while maintaining a strong focus on efficiency.

STRATEGIES FOR DECLINING INDUSTRIES

The transition from maturity to decline can be a result of technological substitution (typewriters, railroads), changes in consumer preferences (men's suits), demographic shifts (babyware in Italy), or foreign competition (cutlery in Sheffield, England). Shrinking market demand gives rise to acute strategic issues. Among the key features of declining industries are:

- Excess capacity.

- Lack of technical change (reflected in a lack of new product introduction and stability of process technology).

- A declining number of competitors, but some entry as new firms acquire the assets of exiting firms cheaply.

- High average age of both physical and human resources.

- Aggressive price competition.

Despite the inhospitable environment offered by declining industries, research by Kathryn Harrigan has uncovered declining industries where at least some participants earned surprisingly high profits. These included electronic vacuum tubes, cigars, and leather tanning. However, elsewhere – notably in prepared baby foods, rayon, and meat processing – decline was accompanied by aggressive price competition, com-pany failures, and instability.[25]

What determines whether or not a declining industry becomes a competitive blood-bath? Two factors are critical: the balance between capacity and output, and the nature of the demand for the product.

Adjusting Capacity to Declining Demand

The smooth adjustment of industry capacity to declining demand is the key to stability and profitability during the decline phase. In industries where capacity exits from the industry in an orderly fashion, decline can occur without trauma. Where substantial excess capacity persists, as has occurred in the steel industries of America and Europe, in the bakery industry, in gold mining, and in long-haul bus transportation, the potential exists for destructive competition. The ease with which capacity adjusts to declining demand depends on the following factors:

- *The predictability of decline.* If decline can be forecast, it is more likely that firms can plan for it. The problems of the steel industry, oil refining, and petrochemicals during the 1970s and 1980s were exacerbated by the unpredicted oil price shocks of 1974 and 1980. The more cyclical and volatile the demand, the more difficult it is for firms to perceive the trend of demand even after the onset of decline.

- *Barriers to exit.* Barriers to exit impede the exit of capacity from an industry. The major barriers are:
  - Durable and specialized assets. Just as capital requirements impose a barrier to entry into an industry, those same investments also discourage exit. The longer they last and the fewer the opportunities for using those assets in another industry, the more companies are tied to that particular industry. The intensity of price competition in steel, acetylene, and rayon during the 1970s was partly a consequence of the durability and lack of alternative uses for the capital equipment employed.
  - Costs incurred in plant closure. Apart from the accounting costs of writing off assets, substantial cash costs may be incurred in redundancy payments to employees, compensation for broken contacts with customers and suppliers, and dismantling and demolishing the plant.
  - Managerial commitment. In addition to financial considerations, firms may be reluctant to close plants for a variety of emotional and moral reasons. Resistance to plant closure and divestment arises from pride in company traditions and reputation, managers' unwillingness to accept failure, loyalties to employees and the local community, and the desire not to offend government.

- *The strategies of the surviving firms.* Smooth exit of capacity ultimately depends on the decisions of the industry players. The sooner companies recognize and address the problem, the more likely it is that independent and collective action can achieve capacity reduction. In the European petrochemical industry, for example, the problem of excess capacity was partially solved by a series of bilateral exchanges of plants and divisions – ICI swapped its polyethylene plants for BP's PVC plants, for example.[26] Stronger firms in the industry can facilitate the exit of weaker firms by offering to acquire their plants and take over their after-sales service commitments.

The Nature of Demand

Where a market is segmented, the general pattern of decline can obscure the existence of pockets of demand that are not only comparatively resilient, but also price inelastic. For example, despite the obsolescence of vacuum tubes after the adoption of transistors, Harrigan observed that GTE Sylvania and General Electric earned excellent profits supplying vacuum tubes to the replacement and military markets.[27] As late as 1994, the US air traffic control system depended on vacuum tubes supplied by a few specialist companies. In fountain pens, survivors in the quality pen segment such as Cross and Mont Blanc have achieved steady sales and high margins through appealing to high-income professionals and executives. Decline may be punctuated by periodic upswings of demand: during 1996–9, for instance, the quality cigar market was revived by a sudden return to fashion.

Strategies for Declining Industries

Conventional strategy recommendations for declining industries are either to divest or to harvest, i.e., to generate the maximum cash flow from existing investments without reinvesting. However, these strategies assume that declining industries are inherently unprofitable. If profit potential exists, then other strategies may be attractive. Harrigan and Porter[28] identify four strategies that can profitably be pursued either individually or sequentially in declining industries.

- *Leadership.* By gaining leadership, a firm is well placed to outstay competitors and play a dominant role in the final stages of the industry's life cycle. Once leadership is attained, the firm is in a good position to switch to a harvest strategy and enjoy a strong profit stream from its market position. Establishing leadership can be done by acquiring competitors, but a cheaper way is to encourage competitors to exit (and then acquire their plants). Inducements to competitors to exit may include showing commitment to the industry, helping to lower their exit costs, releasing pessimistic forecasts of the industry's future, and raising the stakes – e.g., by supporting more stringent environmental controls that make it costly for them to stay in business.

- *Niche.* Identify a segment that is likely to maintain a stable demand and other firms are unlikely to invade, then pursue a leadership strategy to establish dominance within the segment. The most attractive niches are those that offer the greatest prospects for stability and where demand is most inelastic.

- *Harvest.* By harvesting, a firm maximizes its cash flow from existing assets, while avoiding further investment. A harvesting strategy seek to boost margins wherever possible through raising prices and cutting costs by rationalizing the number of models, number of channels, and number of customers. Note, however, that a harvest strategy can be difficult to implement. In the face of strong competition, harvesting may accelerate decline, particularly if employee morale is adversely affected by a strategy that offers no long-term future for the business.

■ *Divest.* If the future looks bleak, the best strategy may be to divest the business in the early stages of decline before a consensus has developed as to the inevitability of decline. Once industry decline is well established, finding buyers may be extremely difficult.

Choosing the most appropriate strategy requires a careful assessment both of the profit potential of the industry and the competitive position of the firm. Harrigan and Porter pose four key questions:

■ Can the structure of the industry support a hospitable, potentially profitable decline phase?

■ What are the exit barriers that each significant competitor faces?

■ Do your company strengths fit the remaining pockets of demand?

■ What are your competitors' strengths in these pockets? How can their exit barriers be overcome?

Selecting an appropriate strategy requires matching the opportunities remaining in the industries to the company's competitive position. Figure 12.2 shows a simple framework for strategy choice.

FIGURE 12.2 Strategic alternatives for declining industries

COMPANY'S COMPETITIVE POSITION		Strengths in remaining demand pockets	Lacks strength in remaining demand pockets
INDUSTRY STRUCTURE	Favorable to decline	LEADERSHIP or NICHE	HARVEST or DIVEST
	Unfavorable to decline	NICHE or HARVEST	DIVEST QUICKLY

SUMMARY

Mature industries present challenging environments for the formulation and implementation of business strategies. Competition – price competition in particular – is usually strong and competitive advantage is often difficult to build and sustain: cost advantages are vulnerable to imitation, differentiation opportunities are limited by the trend to standardization. Stable positions of competitive advantage in mature industries are traditionally associated with cost advantage from economies of scale or experience, and differentiation advantage through brand loyalty. Such strategies are typically implemented through hierarchical organizations, with high levels of specialization and formalization, and centralized decision making directed toward maximizing static efficiency.

Increased dynamism of mature industries resulting from international competition, economic turbulence, and greater pressure for innovation has had two consequences. First, the conditions for cost efficiency have changed. In a dynamic environment, cost efficiency is less dependent on scale, specialization, and rigid control, and more on rapid adjustment to change. Second, as competition has become more intense, companies (especially those in the advanced industrialized countries) have been forced to seek new sources of competitive advantage through innovation and differentiation. Reconciling the pursuit of scale economies with the need for responsiveness and flexibility, and the requirements of cost efficiency with the growing need for innovation and differentiation, poses complex strategic and organizational challenges. Some of the most successful companies in mature industries – Wal-Mart in retailing, BP in oil and gas, Nike in shoes and sportswear, and Coca-Cola in beverages – are companies that have achieved flexibility through dismantling bureaucratic structures and procedures, exploited new technology to combine variety and flexibility with efficiency, encouraged high levels of employee commitment, and relentlessly pursued financial targets. We return to some of these challenges and firms' responses to them in Chapter 17.

NOTES

1 Edward H. Rensi, "Computers at McDonald's," in J. F. McLimore and L. Larwood (eds), *Strategies . . . Successes . . . Senior Executives Speak Out* (New York: Harper & Row, 1988): 159–60.

2 Letter to shareholders, *The 1991 Annual Report of Berkshire Hathaway Inc.*

3 Robert D. Buzzell and Bradley T. Gale, *The PIMS Principles* (New York: Free Press, 1987): 279.

4 T. Copeland, T. Koller, and J. Murrin, *Valuation: Measuring and Managing the Value of Companies*, 3rd edn (New York: Wiley, 2000): 305.

5 R. Cibin and Robert M. Grant, "Restructuring among the World's Leading Oil Companies," *British Journal of Management* 7 (December 1996): 283–308.

6 Donald C. Hambrick and Steven M. Schecter, "Turnaround Strategies for

Mature Industrial-Product Business Units," *Academy of Management Journal* 26, no. 2 (1983): 231–48.

[7] Peter H. Grinyer, D. G. Mayes, and P. McKiernan, *Sharpbenders* (Oxford: Basil Blackwell, 1988).

[8] G. R. Carroll and A. Swaminathan, "Why the Microbrewery Movement? Organizational Dynamics of Resource Partitioning in the American Brewing Industry," *American Journal of Sociology* 106 (2000): 715–62; C. Boone, G. R. Carroll, and A. van Witteloostuijn, "Resource Distributions and Market Partitioning: Dutch Daily Newspapers 1964–94," *American Sociological Review* 67 (2002): 408–31.

[9] A. W. H. Grant and L. A. Schlesinger, "Realize Your Customer's Full Profit Potential," *Harvard Business Review* (September–October 1995): 59–72.

[10] "Capital One Financial Corporation," Harvard Business School Case 9-700-124 (2000).

[11] National Science Foundation, *Survey of Industrial Research and Development* (Washington DC, 2000).

[12] A. M. McGahan and B. S. Silverman, "How Does Innovative Activity Change as Industries Mature?," *International Journal of Industrial Organization* 19, 7 (2001): 1141–60.

[13] Derek Abell, *Managing with Dual Strategies* (New York: Free Press, 1993): 75–8.

[14] B. J. Pine and J. Gilmore, "Welcome to the Experience Economy," *Harvard Business Review* (July–August 1998): 97–105.

[15] Charles Baden Fuller and J. Stopford, *Rejuvenating the Mature Business* (Boston: HBS Press, 1994): especially Chapters 3 and 4.

[16] J.-C. Spender, *Industry Recipes: The Nature and Sources of Managerial Judgment* (Oxford: Basil Blackwell, 1989). On a similar theme, see also Anne S. Huff, "Industry Influences on Strategy Reformulation," *Strategic Management Journal* 3 (1982): 119–31; and Gerry Johnson, "Strategic Frames and Formulae," *Strategic Management Journal* 8 (1987).

[17] P. S. Barr, J. L. Stimpert, and Anne S. Huff, "Cognitive Change, Strategic Action, and Organizational Renewal," *Strategic Management Journal* 13, Summer Special Issue (1992): 15–36.

[18] "A Lesson in Small Town Economics," *Financial Times* (November 30, 2000): 16.

[19] C. C. Markides, *All the Right Moves* (Boston: Harvard Business School Press, 1999).

[20] Paul R. Lawrence and Davis Dyer, *Renewing American Industry* (New York: Free Press, 1983): Chapter 2, "Autos: On the Thin Edge," and Chapter 3, "Steel: The Slumping Giant."

[21] G. Hamel, "Strategy as Revolution," *Harvard Business Review* 96 (July–August 1996): 69–82.

[22] Charles Baden Fuller and J. Stopford, op. cit.; Henk Volberda, "Toward the Flexible Form: How to Remain Vital in Hypercompetitive Environments," *Organization Science* 7 (July–August 1996): 359–87; Henk Volberda, Charles Baden Fuller and Frans van den Bosch, "Mastering Strategic Renewal," *Long Range Planning* 34 (April 2001): 159–78.

[23] T. Burns and G. M. Stalker (*The Management of Innovation*, London: Tavistock Institute, 1961) argued that dynamic environments required *organic* structures characterized by decentralization, loosely defined roles, and extensive lateral communication, while stable environments required *mechanistic* structures.

[24] Henry Mintzberg, *Structure in Fives: Designing Effective Organizations* (Englewood Cliffs, NJ: Prentice-Hall, 1983): Chapter 9.

[25] Kathryn R. Harrigan, *Strategies for Declining Businesses* (Lexington, MA: D. C. Heath, 1980).

[26] Joe Bower, *When Markets Quake* (Boston: Harvard Business School Press, 1986).

[27] Kathryn R. Harrigan, "Strategic Planning for Endgame," *Long Range Planning* 15 (1982): 45–8.

[28] Kathryn R. Harrigan and Michael E. Porter, "End-Game Strategies for Declining Industries," *Harvard Business Review* (July–August 1983): 111–20.

V

Corporate Strategy

13

Vertical Integration and the Scope of the Firm

The idea of vertical integration is an anathema to an increasing number of companies. Most of yesterday's highly integrated giants are working overtime at splitting into more manageable, more energetic units – i.e., de-integrating. Then they are turning around and re-integrating – not by acquisitions but via alliances with all sorts of partners of all shapes and sizes.

—Tom Peters, Liberation Management

OUTLINE

INTRODUCTION AND OBJECTIVES

Chapter 2 introduced the distinction between *corporate strategy* and *business strategy*. Corporate strategy is concerned primarily with the decisions over the *scope* of the firm's activities, including:

- *Product scope.* How specialized should the firm be in terms of the range of products it supplies? Coca-Cola (soft drinks), SAB Miller (beer), The Gap (fashion retailing), and Swiss Re (reinsurance) are specialized companies: they are engaged in a single industry sector. General Electric, Samsung, and Bertelsmann are diversified companies: each spans a number of different industries.

- *Geographical scope.* What is the optimal geographical spread of activities for the firm? In the restaurant business, most restaurants serve their local markets. McDonald's, by contrast, operates throughout the world.

- *Vertical scope.* What range of vertically linked activities should the firm encompass? Walt Disney Company is a vertically integrated company: it produces its own movies, distributes them itself to cinemas and through its own TV networks (ABC and Disney Channel), and uses the movies' characters in its retail stores and theme parks. Dell Computer is much more vertically specialized: it outsources many activities in its value chain, including components, assembly, logistics, and customer service to other companies.

Business strategy (also known as *competitive strategy*) is concerned with how a firm competes within a particular market. The distinction may be summarized as follows: corporate strategy is concerned with *where* a firm competes; business strategy is concerned with *how* a firm competes.[1] The major part of this book has been concerned with issues of business strategy. For the next four chapters, the emphasis is on corporate strategy: decisions that define the *scope of the firm*. I devote separate chapters to the different dimensions of scope – vertical scope (*vertical integration*), geographical scope (*multinationality*), and product scope (*diversification*). However, as we shall discover, the key underlying concepts for analyzing these different dimensions – economies of scope in resources and capabilities, transaction costs, and costs of corporate complexity – are common to all three.

In this chapter we begin by considering the scope of the form in general terms. We then focus specifically upon vertical integration since it takes us to the heart of many of the issues determining the optimal scope of the firm and, in particular, the role of transaction costs. Also, vertical integration has been a central issue in corporate strategy in recent years as outsourcing, alliances, and e-commerce have caused companies to rethink which parts of their value chains they wish to include within their organizational boundaries.

By the time you have completed this chapter, you will be able to:

■ Identify the relative efficiencies of firms and markets in organizing economic activity and apply the principles of *transaction cost economics* to explain why boundaries between firms and markets have shifted over the past two hundred years.

■ Assess the relative advantages of vertical integration and market transactions in organizing vertically related activities, understand the circumstances that influence these relative advantages, and advise a firm whether a particular vertical transaction should be integrated within the form or outsourced.

■ Identify alternative ways of organizing vertical transactions – including spot market transactions, long-term contracts, franchise agreements, and alliances – and advise a firm on the most advantageous transaction mode given the characteristics and circumstances of the transaction.

TRANSACTION COSTS AND THE SCOPE OF THE FIRM

In Chapter 6, we noted that firms came into existence because they were more efficient in organizing production than were market contracts between independent workers. Let us explore this issue and consider the determinants of firm boundaries.

Firms, Markets, and Transaction Costs

Although the capitalist economy is frequently referred to as a "market economy," in fact, it comprises two forms of economic organization. One is the *market mechanism*, where individuals and firms make independent decisions that are guided and coordinated by market prices. The other is the *administrative mechanism* of firms, where decisions over production, supply, and the purchases of inputs are made by managers and imposed through hierarchies. The market mechanism was characterized by Adam Smith, the eighteenth-century Scottish economist, as the "invisible hand" because its coordinating role does not require conscious planning. Alfred Chandler has referred to the administrative mechanism of company management as the "visible hand" because it is dependent on coordination through active planning.[2]

Why do institutions called "firms" exist in the first place? The firm is an organization that consists of a number of individuals bound by employment contracts with a central contracting authority. But firms are not essential for conducting complex economic activity. When I recently remodeled my basement, I contracted with a self-employed builder to undertake the work. He in turn subcontracted parts of the work to a plumber, an electrician, a joiner, a drywall installer, and a painter. Although

FIGURE 13.1 The scope of the firm: specialization versus integration

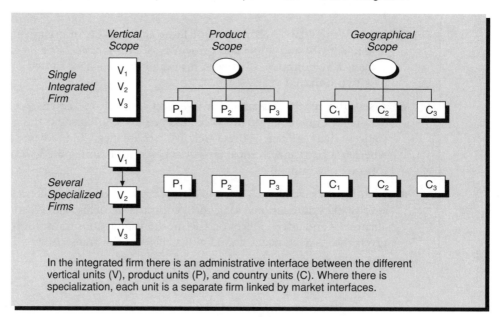

In the integrated firm there is an administrative interface between the different vertical units (V), product units (P), and country units (C). Where there is specialization, each unit is a separate firm linked by market interfaces.

the job involved the coordinated activity of several individuals, these self-employed specialists were not linked by employment relations but by market contracts ("$4,000 to install wiring, lights, and sockets").

What determines which activities are undertaken within a firm, or between individuals or firms coordinated by market contracts? Ronald Coase's answer was *relative cost*.[3] Markets are not costless: making a purchase or sale involves search costs, the costs of negotiating and drawing up a contract, the costs of monitoring to ensure that the other party's side of the contract is being fulfilled, and the enforcement costs of arbitration or litigation should a dispute arise. All these costs are types of *transaction costs*.[4] If the transaction costs associated with organizing across markets are greater than the *administrative costs* of organizing within firms, we can expect the coordination of productive activity to be internalized within firms.

This situation is illustrated in Figure 13.1. With regard to vertical scope, which is more efficient: three independent companies, one producing steel, the next rolling the steel into sheet, and the third producing steel cans, or having all three stages of production within a single company? In the case of geographical scope, which is more efficient: three independent companies producing cans in the US, UK, and Italy, or a single multinational company owning and operating the can-making plants in all three countries? In the case of product scope, should metal cans, plastic packaging, and domestic appliances be produced by three separate companies, or are there efficiencies to be gained by merging all three into a single company?

The Shifting Boundary between Firms and Markets

The answers to these questions have changed over time. During the nineteenth and for most of the twentieth century, companies grew in size and scope, absorbing transactions that had previously taken place across markets. As we observed in Chapter 6, companies that once were localized and specialized grew vertically, geographically, and across different industry sectors. This trend can be attributed to a fall in the administrative costs of the firm as compared with the transaction costs of markets. Two factors have greatly increased the efficiency of firms as organizing devices:

- *Technology.* The telegraph, telephone, and computer have played an important role in facilitating communications within firms and expanding the decision-making capacity of managers.

- *Management techniques.* Developments in the principles and techniques of management have greatly expanded the organizational and decision-making effectiveness of managers. Beginning with the dissemination of double-entry bookkeeping in the nineteenth century,[5] and the introduction of scientific management in the early twentieth century,[6] the past 50 years have seen rapid advances in all areas of management theory and methods.

Observing this growth in large corporations at the expense of markets, several leading economists of the late 1960s declared that the *market* economy had been replaced by a *corporate* economy. In 1969, J. K. Galbraith predicted that the inherent advantages of firms over markets in planning and resource allocation would result in increasing dominance of capitalist economies by a small number of giant corporations.[7]

During the 1980s and 1990s, these predictions were refuted by a sharp reversal of the trend toward increased corporate scope. Although large companies have continued to expand internationally, the dominant trends of the last 20 years have been "downsizing" and "refocusing," as large industrial companies reduced both their product scope through focusing on their core businesses, and their vertical scope through outsourcing. The result, as shown in Figure 13.2, was that aggregate concentration – the proportion of total output contributed by the largest companies – after increasing for most of the twentieth century, began to decline. These changes are associated with the more turbulent business environment that followed the oil shocks of 1973 and 1979, the end of fixed exchange rates (1972), the invention of the integrated circuit, and the upsurge of international competition. The implication seems to be that during periods of instability, the costs of administration within large, complex firms tend to rise as the need for flexibility and speed of response overwhelms traditional management systems.

Let us proceed by examining the relative efficiencies of firms and markets in organizing vertical transactions. We shall draw in particular upon Oliver Williamson's analysis of transaction costs, which forms the basis for a theory of economic organization that is particularly useful in designing vertical relationships.[8]

FIGURE 13.2 Changes in aggregate concentration over time: the 100 largest industrial companies' share of US industrial output

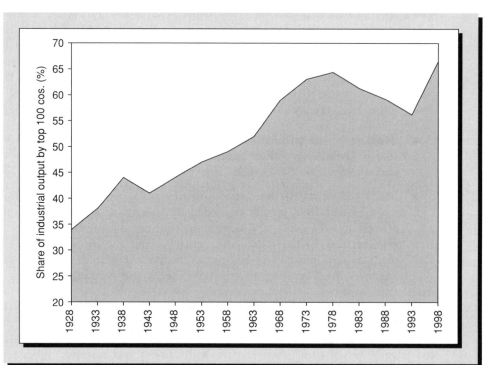

THE COSTS AND BENEFITS OF VERTICAL INTEGRATION

Changing ideas about the efficiency of large corporations as organizers of economic activity have exerted a strong influence on firms' vertical integration strategies. Thirty years ago the dominant belief was that vertical integration offered superior coordination as well as protection from the vagaries of the market. The prevailing wisdom today is that any benefits of vertical integration tend to be outweighed by the greater advantages of specializing in a narrow range of vertical activities. Such vertical specialization is conducive to flexibility and the development of core competencies. Moreover, most of the coordination associated with vertical integration benefits can be achieved through inter-firm collaboration. Let's explore some of these issues.

Defining Vertical Integration

Vertical integration refers to a firm's ownership of vertically related activities. The greater the firm's ownership and control over successive stages of the value chain for its product, the greater its degree of vertical integration. The extent of vertical integration is indicated by the ratio of a firm's value added to its sales revenue. Highly integrated companies – such as the major oil companies that own and control their value chain from exploring for oil down to the retailing of gasoline – tend to have low expenditures on bought-in goods and services relative to their sales.

Vertical integration can occur in two directions:

- *Backward integration* – where the firm takes over ownership and control of producing its own inputs (e.g., Henry Ford's upstream expansion from automobile assembly to the production of his own components, back to the production of basic materials including steel and rubber).

- *Forward integration* – where the firm takes over ownership and control of its own customers (e.g., Coca-Cola acquiring its local bottlers).

Vertical integration may also be *full* or *partial*:

- *Full integration* exists between two stages of production when all of the first stage's production is transferred to the second stage with no sales or purchases from third parties. Thus, before IBM entered PCs, all its microprocessors were produced in its own semiconductor plants and none was supplied to other customers.

- *Partial integration* exists when stages of production are not internally self-sufficient. Thus, in manufacturing TV receivers, Philips obtains cathode ray tubes (CRTs) both internally and from external suppliers of CRTs. Similarly, a major share of Philips' production of CRTs is sold to other TV manufacturers.[9] Partial integration is also typical of the oil and gas majors. "Crude-rich" companies (such as Statoil) produce more oil than they refine and are net sellers of crude oil; "crude-poor" companies (such as Exxon Mobil) have to supplement their own production with purchases of crude to keep their refineries supplied.

Technical Economies from the Physical Integration of Processes

Analysis of the benefits of vertical integration has traditionally emphasized the *technical economies* of vertical integration: cost savings that arise from the physical integration of processes. Thus, most steel sheet is produced by integrated producers in plants that first produce steel, then roll hot steel into sheet. Linking the two stages of production at a single location reduces transportation and energy costs. Similar technical economies arise in pulp and paper production and from linking oil refining with petrochemical production.

However, although these considerations explain the need for the co-location of plants, they do not explain why vertical integration in terms of *common ownership* is necessary. Why can't steel and steel sheet production or pulp and paper production be undertaken by separate firms owning facilities that are physically integrated with one another? To answer this question, we must look beyond technical economies and consider the implications of linked processes for *transaction costs*.

The Sources of Transaction Costs in Vertical Exchanges

Consider the value chain for steel cans, which extends from mining iron ore to delivering cans to food processing companies (see Figure 13.3). Between the production of steel and steel strip, most production is vertically integrated. Between the production of steel strip and steel cans, there is very little vertical integration: can producers such as Crown Holdings and Ball Corporation are specialist packaging companies that purchase steel strip from steel companies on contracts.[10]

The predominance of market contracts between steel strip production and can production is the result of low transaction costs in the market for steel strip: there are many buyers and sellers, information is readily available, and the switching costs for buyers and suppliers are low. The same is true for many other commodity products: few jewelry companies own gold mines; few flour-milling companies own wheat farms.

To understand why vertical integration predominates across steel production and steel strip production, let us see what would happen if the two stages were owned by separate companies. Because there are technical economies from hot-rolling steel as soon as it is poured from the furnace, steel makers and strip producers must invest in integrated facilities. A competitive market for bulk steel is impossible, each steel strip producer is tied to its adjacent steel producer. In other words, the market becomes a series of *bilateral monopolies*.

Why are these relationships between steel producers and strip producers problematic? To begin with, where a single supplier negotiates with a single buyer, there is no equilibrium price: it all depends on relative bargaining power. Such bargaining is likely to be costly: the mutual dependency of the two parties is likely to give rise to *opportunism* and *strategic misrepresentation* as each company seeks to both enhance and exploit its bargaining power at the expense of the other. Hence, once we move from a competitive market situation to one where individual buyers and sellers are locked together in close bilateral relationships, the efficiencies of the market system are lost.

FIGURE 13.3 The value chain for steel cans

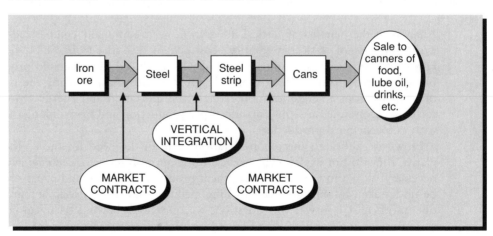

The culprits in this situation are *transaction-specific investments.* When a can maker buys steel strip, neither the steel strip producer nor the can maker needs to invest in equipment or technology that is specific to the needs of the other party. In the case of the steel producer and the steel roller, each company's plant is built to match the other party's plant. Once built, the plants have little value without the existence of the partner's complementary facilities. Once transaction-specific investments are significant then, even though there may be a number of suppliers and buyers in the market, it is no longer a competitive market: each seller is tied to a single buyer, which gives each the opportunity to "*hold up*" the other.

Hence, where a vertical relationship between companies requires one or both companies to make investments that are specific to the needs of the other party, a market contract will tend to be inefficient in coordinating the activities of the two parties. These inefficiencies arise from the negotiation and enforcement of contracts, including bargaining, monitoring, investing in activities whose only purpose is to improve bargaining power, and dispute resolution. These are key sources of transaction costs. The basic case for vertical integration is that by bringing both sides of the transaction into a single administrative structure, transaction costs may be avoided.

Empirical research gives considerable support to these arguments:

- In electricity generation, coal-fired power plants built adjacent to coal mines tend to be vertically integrated (i.e., the electricity utility also owns the coalmine).[11]

- In the automobile industry, components that are designed to meet the specific needs of a particular auto manufacturer are more likely to be manufactured in-house than low-tech, commodity items such as tires and spark plugs, where the components supplier did not need to make transaction-specific investments.[12]

- In aerospace, components that are designed specifically to meet the needs of an aerospace company are more likely to be produced in-house rather than purchased externally.[13]

- In the semiconductor industry, some companies specialize either in semiconductor design or in fabrication, while other companies are vertically integrated across both stages. Which is more efficient? Again, it depends on the characteristics of the transaction between the designer and the fabricator. The more technically complex the integrated circuit and, hence, the greater the need for the designer and fabricator to engage in technical collaboration, the better the relative performance of integrated producers.[14]

If companies recognize that transaction-specific investments give rise to opportunism, why don't they write a contract that takes account of these risks by fully specifying prices and terms of supply? The problem is uncertainty about the future. When the steel producer and the steel sheet roller are agreeing to build their integrated plant, it is impossible to anticipate all the circumstances that might arise over the 30-year life of the plant. Hence contracts are inevitably incomplete.

Administrative Costs of Internalization

Just because there are transaction costs in intermediate markets does not mean that vertical integration is necessarily an efficient solution. Vertical integration avoids the costs of using the market, but internalizing the transactions means that there are now costs of administration. The efficiency of the internal administration of vertical relations depends on several factors.

Differences in Optimal Scale between Different Stages of Production

Suppose that Federal Express requires delivery vans that are designed and manufactured to meet its particular needs. To the extent that the van manufacturer must make transaction-specific investments, there is an incentive for Federal Express to avoid the ensuing transaction costs by building its own vehicles. Would this be an efficient solution? Almost certainly not: the transaction costs avoided by Federal Express are likely to be trivial compared with the inefficiencies incurred in manufacturing its own vans. Federal Express purchases over 40,000 trucks and vans each year, well below the 200,000 minimum efficient scale of an assembly plant. (Ford produced two million commercial vehicles in 2002.)

The same logic explains why specialist brewers such as Anchor Brewing of San Francisco or Adnams of Suffolk are not backward integrated into cans and bottles like Anhauser Busch or SAB Miller. Dedicated can-making plants involve specific investments, creating problems of opportunism that vertical integration can avoid. However, small brewers simply do not possess the scale needed for scale efficiency in can manufacture.

Developing Distinctive Capabilities

A key advantage of a specialized company over one that is diversified across a number of vertically linked businesses is the specialized company's ability to develop distinctive capabilities. Even large, technology-based companies such as Xerox, Kodak, and Philips cannot maintain IT capabilities that match those of specialists such as EDS, IBM, and Accenture. The ability of a vertically-specialized company to work with many different customers stimulates learning and innovation. If General Motors' IT department only serves the in-house needs of GM, this does not encourage the rapid development of its IT capabilities.

However, this assumes that capabilities in different vertical activities are independent of one another. Where one capability builds on capabilities in adjacent activities, vertical integration may help develop distinctive capabilities. Thus, IBM's half-century of success in computers owes much to its technological leadership in semiconductors. In the semiconductor industry itself, producers of some of the world's most sophisticated integrated circuits – notably Intel – have resisted the trend towards de-integration of design and fabrication. Where new semiconductor designs require innovatory approaches to fabrication, complementarities exist between design and manufacturing that make vertical integration desirable.[15]

Managing Strategically Different Businesses

These problems of differences in optimal scale and developing distinctive capabilities may be viewed as part of a wider set of problems – that of managing vertically related businesses that are strategically very different. A major disadvantage to FedEx of owning a truck-manufacturing company is that the management systems and organizational capabilities required for truck manufacturing are very different from those required for express delivery. These considerations may explain the lack of vertical integration between manufacturing and retailing. Integrated design, manufacturing, and retailing companies such as Zara and Gucci are comparatively rare. Most of the world's leading retailers – Wal-Mart, The Gap, Carrefour – do not manufacture. Not only do manufacturing and retailing require very different organizational capabilities, they also require different strategic planning systems, different approaches to control and human resource management, and different top management styles and skills.

Strategic dissimilarities between businesses have encouraged a number of companies to vertically de-integrate. Marriott's decision to split into two separate companies, Marriott International and Host Marriott, was influenced by the belief that *owning* hotels is a strategically different business from *operating* hotels. Similarly, Britain's major brewing companies have all de-integrated: Whitbread plc divested its breweries and specialized in pubs, restaurants, and hotels; Scottish & Newcastle sold off most of its downstream assets and became a specialist brewer.

The Incentive Problem

Vertical integration changes the incentives between vertically related businesses. Where a market interface exists between a buyer and a seller profit incentives ensure that the buyer is motivated to secure the best possible deal and the seller is motivated to pursue efficiency and service in order to attract and retain the buyer. Thus, market contracts gives rise to what are termed *high-powered incentives*. Under vertical integration there is an internal supplier–customer relationship that is governed by corporate management systems rather than market incentives. Performance incentives exist, but these are *low-powered incentives* – if Shell's tanker fleet is inefficient and unreliable, then employees will lose their bonuses and the head of shipping may be fired. However, these consequences tend to be slow and undramatic.

One approach to creating stronger performance incentives within vertically integrated companies is to open internal divisions to external competition. As we shall examine more fully in Chapter 16, many large corporations have created *shared service organizations* where internal suppliers of corporate services such as IT, training, and engineering compete with external suppliers of the same services to serve internal operating divisions.

Competitive Effects of Vertical Integration

Monopolistic companies have used vertical integration as a means of extending their monopoly positions from one stage of the industry to another. The classic cases are

Standard Oil, which used its power in transportation and refining to foreclose markets to independent producers; and Alcoa, which used its monopoly position in aluminum production to squeeze independent fabricators of aluminum products in order to advantage its own fabrication subsidiaries. Such cases are rare. As economists have shown, once a company monopolizes one vertical chain of an industry, there is no further monopoly profit to be extracted by extending that monopoly position to adjacent vertical stages of the industry. A greater concern is that vertical integration may make independent suppliers and customers less willing to do business with the vertically integrated company, because it is now perceived as a competitor rather than as a supplier or customer. Such implications followed Disney's acquisition of ABC. Other studios (e.g., Dreamworks) became less interested in collaborating with ABC in developing new programming and shifted their advertising on new movies from ABC to other TV networks.

Flexibility

Both vertical integration and market transactions can claim advantage with regard to different types of flexibility. Where the required flexibility is rapid responsiveness to uncertain demand, there may be advantages in market transactions. The lack of vertical integration in the construction industry reflects, in part, the need for flexibility in adjusting both to cyclical patterns of demand and to the different requirements of each project. Vertical integration may also be disadvantageous in responding quickly to new product development opportunities that require new combinations of technical capabilities. Some of the most successful new electronic products of recent years – Apple's iPod, Microsoft's X-box, Dell's range of notebook computers – have been produced by contract manufacturers. Extensive outsourcing has been a key feature of fast-cycle product development throughout the electronics sector.

Yet, where system-wide flexibility is required, vertical integration may allow for speed and coordination in achieving simultaneous adjustment throughout the vertical chain. In fashion clothing, Zara has achieved unprecedented reductions in cycle time and increases in market responsiveness through a vertically-integrated approach that challenges the industry's dominant model of contract manufacture (see Strategy Capsule 13.1).

STRATEGY CAPSULE 13.1   Making Vertical Integration Work: Zara

---

Zara is the main division and brand of the Spanish clothing company, Inditex (Industria de Diseño Textil, S.A). Zara contributes 80 percent of Inditex's sales. Between 2000 and 2003, Inditex was one of the world's most successful fashion retailers growing at around 40 percent a year and with a net margin of 11 percent and a return on average equity of 30 percent – well ahead of Gap, H&M, or Mango. By the end of 2003, Zara operated over 1,400 stores in 40 countries.

Zara's success is based upon a business system that achieves a speed of response to market demand that is without precedent in the fast-moving fashion clothing sector. Zara's cycles of design, production, and distribution are substantially faster than any of its main competitors.

STRATEGY CAPSULE 13.1 *(cont'd)*

For most fashion retailers there is a gap of about six months between completing a new design and deliveries arriving at retail stores. Zara was capable of taking a new design from drawing board to retail store in as little as two weeks.

Products are designed in-house where Zara's designers occupy a building attached to the Inditex headquarters at La Coruna on the northwest tip of Spain. Over 40,000 garments are designed annually with about one-quarter entering production. Designs are sketched, committed to the CAD system, then a sample is handmade by skilled workers located within the design facility. Working alongside the designers are "market specialists" who deal with orders from Zara stores in a particular country or region, and "buyers" who handle procurement and production planning. The three groups coordinate closely and jointly decide which products are to go into production.

Half of Zara's products are manufactured within Zara's local network, which comprises Zara's own factories and subcontractors who undertake all sewing operations. The other half of production is outsourced to third-party manufacturers – most of whom are in Spain and Portugal, but some are as far away as Asia.

For its own production, 40 percent of fabric requirements are supplied by Comidex – a wholly-owned subsidiary of Inditex. Most fabric is supplied undyed. Postponing dying until later in the production process allows colors to be changed at short notice.

Finished products are ironed, labeled (including tags with prices in local currencies), bagged in boxes or on hangers ready for retail display, then transferred by monorail to the La Coruna distribution center. Each retail store submits its orders twice a week and receives shipments twice a week. Orders are dispatched within eight hours of receipt and are delivered within 24 hours in Europe, 48 hours in the US, and 72 hours in Japan.

Almost all of Zara's retail stores are owned and managed by Zara. This allows standardized layout and window displays and close communication and collaboration between store managers and designers, market specialists, and buyers at headquarters.

Zara's closely linked design-manufacture-distribution system with fast, frequent store deliveries allows quick response to market demand. At the beginning of each season only small numbers of each new item are produced (frequently, new items are placed initially in just a few lead stores). According to market response, Zara then adjusts production. Typically, Zara's products spend no more than two weeks in a retail store. Product market specialists provide a critical link between the market and production. They monitor sales of each item in each store and seek feedback from store managers. The resulting market information is used not just to adjust production, but also to make design or color modifications to existing items.

The close, informal information networks within Zara are critical to product design. Although designers begin working on new designs some nine months before each new season, the key feature of the design process is that constant adjustments to designs are made in response to new information on fashion trends and customer preferences. Designers and market specialists are encouraged to be alert to the new ranges released by the fashion houses of Milan, Paris, London, and New York; to the styles worn by trendsetters on TV, in popular music, and in the leading-edge clubs; and to feedback from store managers and other employees.

The speed at which Zara introduced new products resulted in Zara customers adjusting their retail buying behavior. Zara customers made more frequent visits to their local stores than was typical for other fashion retailers. They also tended to make faster purchase decisions in the knowledge that garments moved quickly and might not be restocked the following week.

During 2004, Zara margins were being squeezed by the rapid rise of the euro. However, international expansion continues unabated with new stores in China, Malaysia, and Russia.

Sources: www.hoovers.com; Kasra Ferdows, Jose Machuca, and Michael Lewis, "Zara" EECH Case Number 602-002-01, 2002.

TABLE 13.1 Vertical Integration (VI) versus Market Transactions: Some Relevant Considerations

CHARACTERISTICS OF THE VERTICAL RELATIONSHIP	IMPLICATION
How many firms are there in the vertically adjacent activity?	The fewer the number of firms, the greater are the bargaining costs of agreeing contracts
Do transaction-specific investments need to be made by either party?	The bigger is transaction-specific investment expenditure, the greater the advantages of vertical integration
How evenly distributed is information between the vertical stages?	The greater are information asymmetries, the more likely is opportunistic behavior and the greater the advantages of vertical integration
Are market transactions in intermediate products subject to taxes or regulations?	Taxes and regulations are a cost of market contracts that can be avoided with vertical integration
How uncertain are the circumstances of the transactions over the period of the relationship?	The greater are the uncertainties relating to costs, technologies and demand, the greater the difficulty of writing contracts, and the greater are the advantages of vertical integration in avoiding transaction costs
Are two stages similar in terms of the optimal scale of operation?	The greater the dissimilarity, the greater the advantages of market contracts as compared with VI
Are the two stages strategically similar (e.g., similar key success factors, common resources/capabilities)?	The greater the strategic dissimilarity, the greater the advantages of market contracts as compared with vertical integration
How great is the need for continual investment in upgrading and extending capabilities within individual activities?	The greater the need to invest in capability development, the greater the advantages of vertical specialization over vertical integration
How great is the need for entrepreneurial flexibility and drive in the separate vertical activities?	The greater the need for entrepreneurship and flexibility, the greater the advantages of high-powered incentives provided by market contracts, and the greater the administrative disadvantages of vertical integration
How uncertain is market demand?	The greater the unpredictability of demand, the more costly is vertical integration in terms of capacity adjustment costs
Does vertical integration compound risk, exposing the entire value chain risks affecting individual stages?	The heavier the investment requirements and the greater the independent risks at each stage, the more risky is vertical integration

Compounding Risk

To the extent that vertical integration ties a company to its internal suppliers, vertical integration represents a compounding of risk insofar as problems at any one stage of production threaten production and profitability at all other stages. When union workers at a General Motors brake plant went on strike in 1997, the company's US assembly plants were quickly brought to a halt. Such problems are particularly acute when technology or customer preferences are changing quickly. The problems caused by Ford's outmoded automobile designs during the late 1920s and early 1930s were exacerbated by Ford's high-level vertical integration.

Assessing the Pros and Cons of Vertical Integration

Is vertical integration a beneficial strategy for a firm to pursue? As with most questions of strategy – it all depends. We have observed that there are costs and benefits associated with both vertical integration and with market contracts between firms. The value of our analysis is that we are in a position to determine the factors that will determine the relative advantages of the two approaches to managing vertical relationships. Even within the same industry, different companies can be successful with very different degrees of vertical integration – depending upon the strategies they pursue and the resources and capabilities that they possess. Thus in low-end fashion clothing, Zara is much more vertically integrated than either Hennes & Mauritz or The Gap, while in designer clothing, Armani is more vertically integrated than Donna Karan. Table 13.1 summarizes some of these considerations.

DESIGNING VERTICAL RELATIONSHIPS

Our discussion so far has compared vertical integration with arm's-length relationships between buyers and sellers. In practice, there are a variety of relationships through which buyers and sellers can interact and coordinate their interests. Figure 13.4 shows

FIGURE 13.4 Different types of vertical relationship

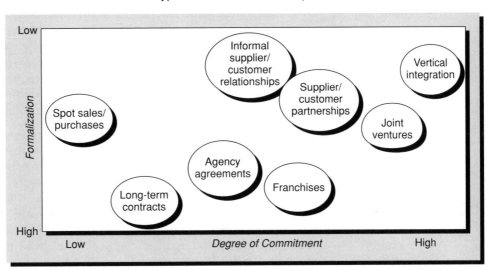

a number of different types of relationship between buyers and sellers. These relationships may be classified in relation to two characteristics. First, the extent to which the buyer and seller commit resources to the relationship: the arm's-length nature of spot contracts means that there is no significant commitment; vertical integration involves substantial investment. Second, the formalization of the relationship: long-term contracts and franchises typically involve complex written agreements, spot contracts may involve little or no documentation, but are bound by common law, collaborative agreements between buyers and sellers are by definition informal, while the formality of vertical integration is at the discretion of the firm's management.

Different Types of Vertical Relationship

Different types of vertical relationship offer different combinations of advantages and disadvantages. Consider for example the following:

- *Long-term contracts.* In the discussion so far, I have not distinguished been different types of market transactions. We can distinguish *spot contracts* – buying a cargo of crude oil on the Rotterdam petroleum market – from *long-term contracts* that involve a series of transactions over a period of time and specify the terms of sales and the responsibilities of each party. Spot transactions work well under competitive conditions – many buyers and sellers and a standard product – where there is no need for transaction-specific investments by either party. Where closer supplier–customer ties are needed – particularly when one or both parties need to make transaction-specific investments – then a longer-term contract may be needed both to avoid opportunism and to provide the security needed to make the necessary investment. However, long-term contracts introduce their own problems. In particular, they cannot anticipate all the possible circumstances that may arise during the life of the contract and run the risk either of being too restrictive or so loose that they give rise to opportunism and conflicting interpretation. The inflexibility problems of long-term contracts are particularly evident in IT outsourcing when the agreement may be for a period of 10 years or more. Thus, when Xerox signed a 10-year IT outsourcing deal in 1994, it could not take account of the financial difficulties and reorganization that it would undergo during 1999–2000.[16]

- *Vendor partnerships.* The greater the difficulties of specifying complete contracts for long-term supplier–customer deals, the more likely it is that vertical relationships will be based on trust and mutual understanding. Such relationships can provide the security needed for transaction-specific investments, the flexibility to meet changing circumstances, and the incentives to avoid opportunism.[17] Such arrangements may be entirely *relational contracts* with no written contract at all. The model for vendor partnerships has been the close collaborative relationships that many Japanese companies have with their suppliers. During the late 1980s, Toyota and Nissan directly produced about

20 to 23 percent of the value of their cars, whereas Ford accounted for 50 percent of its production value and GM for about 70 percent. Yet, as Jeff Dyer has shown, the Japanese automakers have been remarkably successful in achieving close collaboration in technology, quality control, design, and scheduling of production and deliveries.[18]

■ *Franchising.* Like other vertical forms that are intermediate between external market contracts and internal management hierarchy, franchising is an organizational form that aims to combine advantages of both. In particular, the franchising systems of companies such as McDonald's Restaurants, Domino's Pizza, Hilton Hotels, Blockbuster, and Seven-Eleven convenience stores are designed to facilitate the close coordination and investment in transaction-specific assets that vertical integration permits, with the high-powered incentives, flexibility, and cooperation between strategically dissimilar businesses that market contracts make possible. The key feature of multinational service chains in fast foods, hotels, and retailing is the strategic difference between managing brands, product development, and IT, and managing operations in local outlets. Franchising reconciles the need for large-scale management of brands, products, and IT, while leaving individual entrepreneurs to start up and manage individual outlets.

Choosing between Alternative Vertical Relationships

In selecting among different types of vertical relationships, all the advantages and disadvantages that we have discussed in relation to market contracts and vertical integration are relevant. Even within the same industry, what is best for one company will not make sense for another company whose strategy and capabilities are different. While most food and beverage chains have expanded through franchising, Starbucks, anxious to replicate precisely its unique "Starbucks experience," directly owns and manages its retail outlets.[19] While most banks have been outsourcing IT to companies such as IBM and EDS, Nick Morris, president of US credit card group Capital One, sees IT as a key source of competitive advantage: "IT is our central nervous system . . . if I outsourced tomorrow I might save a dollar or two on each account, but I would lose flexibility and value and service levels."[20]

In addition to the factors that we have already considered, the design of vertical relationships needs to take careful account of the following:

1. *Allocation of risk.* Any arrangement beyond a spot contract must cope with uncertainties over the course of the contract. A key feature of any contract is that its terms involve, often implicitly, an allocation of risks between the parties. How risk is shared is dependent partly on bargaining power and partly on efficiency considerations. In franchise agreements, the franchisee (as the weaker partner) bears most of the risk – it is the franchisee's capital that is at risk and the franchisee pays the franchiser a flat royalty based on sales revenues. In oil exploration, outsourcing agreements between the oil majors

(such as Chevron, Exxon Mobil, and ENI) and drilling companies (such as Schlumberger and Halliburton) have moved from fixed-price contracts to risk-sharing agreements where the driller often takes an equity stake in the project.

2. *Incentive structures.* For a contract to minimize transaction costs it must provide an appropriate set of incentives to the parties. Thus, unless a contract for the supply of ready-mixed concrete to construction projects specifies the proportions of cement, sand, and gravel, there is an incentive to supply substandard concrete. However, achieving completeness in the specification of contracts also bears a cost. The $400 toilet seats supplied to the US Navy may reflect the costs of meeting specifications that filled many sheets of paper. Very often, the most effective incentive is the promise of future business. Hence, in privatizing public services – such as passenger rail services or local refuse collection – the key incentive for service quality is a fixed-term operating contract with regular performance reviews and the prospect of competition at contract renewal time. Toyota and Marks & Spencer's vendor partnerships depend on the incentive that satisfactory performance will lead to a long-term business relationship.

Recent Trends

Decisions about vertical scope are no longer binary choices of "make or buy." There is a spectrum of vertical relationships that lie between the polar cases of pure market contracts and full vertical integration. Even within particular organizational modes, there are many different ways in which a vertical relationship is managed.

The main feature of recent years has been a growing diversity of intermediate vertical relationships that have attempted to reconcile the flexibility and incentives of market transactions with the close collaboration that is typical of vertical integration. Although collaborative vertical relationships are viewed as a recent phenomenon – associated with Silicon Valley and Japanese supplier networks – closely-linked value chains in which small, specialist enterprises collaborate are a long-time feature of craft industries in Europe, India, and elsewhere. These collaborative vertical relationships are evident in the industrial districts of northern Italy – notably in textiles,[21] packaging equipment,[22] and motorcycles.[23] The success of Japanese manufacturing companies with their close collaborative relationships with suppliers – including extensive knowledge sharing[24] – has exerted a powerful influence on American and European companies over the past two decades. There has been a massive shift from arm's-length supplier relationships to close vertical relationships with fewer suppliers. Long-term collaboration and single-supplier agreements have increasingly replaced competitive tendering and multiple sourcing. Most large manufacturers have drastically reduced their number of vendors and have introduced supplier certification programs as frameworks for quality management and technical collaboration.

The relationships of mutual dependence that result from close, long-term supplier–buyer relationships create vulnerability for both parties. While trust may alleviate some of the risks of opportunism, in many industries companies have sought to buttress their vertical relationships and create disincentives for opportunism through equity stakes and profit sharing arrangements. For example: Commonwealth Bank of Australia took an equity stake in its IT supplier, EDS Australia; pharmaceutical companies often acquire equity stakes in the biotech companies that undertake much of their R&D; and, as I have already noted, oilfield services companies are increasingly invited to take equity stakes in projects that they are contractors to.

However, in this world of closer vertical relationships, some trends have been in the opposite direction. The internet and growth of e-commerce has had a major impact on reducing the transaction costs of markets – particularly in pruning search costs. The result has been a revival in arm's-length competitive contracting through business-to-business e-commerce hubs such as Covisint (auto parts), Elemica (chemicals), and Rock and Dirt (construction equipment).[25]

While the form of vertical relationships has changed, the trend towards increasing outsourcing has continued. The result is that most companies have specialized in fewer activities within their value chains. Outsourcing has extended from components to a wide range of business services including payroll, IT, training, and customer service and support. Choosing which activities to specialize in requires an assessment of, first, which activities are most attractive in terms of profit potential and, second, in which activities the company possesses a competitive advantage. One of the dangers of vertical specialization is that firms can made poor decisions over which activities to concentrate upon. In fixed line telecoms, Global Crossing, Teligent and other companies came to grief because of their belief that the key to profitability lay in "owning the pipes." Under Jacques Nasser, Ford pursued a forward integration strategy in the belief that growth and profitability lay in finance and after-market services.

The extent of outsourcing and vertical de-integration has given rise to a new organizational form: the *virtual corporation*, where the primary function of the company is coordinating the activities of a network of suppliers.[26] Such extreme levels of outsourcing reduce the strategic role of the company to that of a systems integrator. The critical issue is whether a company that outsources most functions can retain *architectural capabilities* needed to manage the *component capabilities* of the various partners and contractors. The risk is that the virtual corporation may degenerate into a "hollow corporation" where it loses the capability to evolve and adapt to changing circumstances.[27] If, as Hamel and Prahalad argue, core competences are embodied in "core products" then the more these core products are outsourced, then the greater is the potential for the erosion of core competence.[28] Andre Prencipe's research into aero engines points to the complementarity between architectural capabilities and component capabilities. Thus, even when the aero engine manufacturers outsource key components, they typically retain ongoing R&D in those component technologies. In most cases, these are the components that embody critical technologies; without these skills the company would be reduced to a mere assembler and marketer, seriously jeopardizing the capacity to innovate and develop.[29]

SUMMARY

Deciding which parts of the value chain to engage in presents companies with one of their most difficult strategic decisions. The conventional analysis of vertical integration has looked simply at the efficiency of markets as compared to the efficiency of firms: if the cost of transacting through the market is greater than the cost of administering within the firm, then the company should vertically integrate across the stages. Transaction cost analysis does not, however, provide the complete answer. In the first place, vertical strategies are not simply make-or-buy choices – there is a wide variety of ways in which a company can structure vertical relationships. Secondly, the most critical long-run consideration is the development of organizational capability. If a company is to sustain competitive advantage, it must restrict itself to those activities where it possesses the capabilities that are superior to those of the other companies that perform those activities. If my company's data-processing capabilities are inferior to those of IBM and its logistics capabilities are inferior to those of Federal Express, I should consider outsourcing these activities. The most difficult issues arise where there are linkages between value chain activities. Even though a contract manufacturer may be able to manufacture my remote-controlled lawnmower more efficiently than I can internally, what would be the implications for my new product development capability if I no longer have in-house manufacturing?

Ultimately, vertical integration decisions revolve around two key questions. First, which activities will we undertake internally and which will we outsource? Second, how do we design our vertical arrangements with both external and internal suppliers and buyers? In the case of external relations, these may be conducted through spot contracts, long-term contracts, or some form of strategic alliance. Similar ranges of alternatives face the vertically integrated firm – including the option of arm's-length negotiated contracts. Both types of decision are critically dependent on the firm's competitive strategy and the capabilities it possesses. As we have already noted, the critical issue for the individual business is not to follow conventional wisdom but carefully to evaluate its strategic needs, its resources and capabilities at different stages in the value chain, the characteristics of the transactions involved, and the relative attractiveness of different stages of the value chain.

NOTES

[1] In practice, determining the boundary between business strategy and corporate strategy is blurred. When Dell Computer expanded from PCs into servers, was this diversification or simply product line extension within the same business? It all depends on where we draw industry boundaries.

[2] Alfred Chandler Jr., *Strategy and Structure* (Cambridge: MIT Press, 1962); Alfred Chandler Jr., *The Visible Hand: The Managerial Revolution in American Business* (Cambridge: MIT Press, 1977).

[3] R. H. Coase, "The Nature of the Firm," *Economica* 4 (1937): 386–405.

4 The term *interaction costs* has also been used to describe "the time and money expended whenever people and companies exchange goods, services or ideas." See J. Hagel and M. Singer, "Unbundling the Corporation," *Harvard Business Review* (March–April 1999): 133–44.

5 Although double-entry bookkeeping was invented in the fifteenth century, its use as a tool of management control did not become widespread until the nineteenth century (K. Hoskin and L. Zan, "A first *Discourso del Maneggio*: Accounting and the Production of Management Discourse at the Venice Arsenal," EIASM Working Paper 97–01 (1997)).

6 F. W. Taylor, *The Principles of Scientific Management* (Bulletin of the Taylor Society, 1916).

7 J. K. Galbraith, *The New Industrial State* (Harmondsworth: Penguin, 1969).

8 Oliver E. Williamson, *Markets and Hierarchies: Analysis and Antitrust Implications* (New York: Free Press, 1975); Oliver E. Williamson, *The Economic Institutions of Capitalism: Firms, Markets and Relational Contracting* (New York: Free Press, 1985).

9 R. Johnston and P. R. Lawrence, "Beyond Vertical Integration – The Rise of the Value-Adding Partnership," *Harvard Business Review* (July–August 1988): 94–101.

10 The situation is somewhat different in aluminum cans, where aluminum producers such as Alcoa and Pechiney and users such as Coca-Cola and Anheuser Busch are major producers of beverage cans.

11 P. Joskow, "Vertical Integration and Long-term Contracts: The Case of Coal-Burning Electricity Generating Plants," *Journal of Law, Economics, and Organization* 33 (Fall 1985): 32–80.

12 K. Monteverde and J. J. Teece, "Supplier Switching Costs and Vertical Integration in the Automobile Industry," *Bell Journal of Economics* 13 (Spring 1982): 206–13.

13 S. Masten, "The Organization of Production: Evidence from the Aerospace Industry," *Journal of Law and Economics* 27 (October 1984): 403–17.

14 J. Macher, "Vertical Disintegration and Process Innovation in Semiconductor Manufacturing Foundries vs. Integrated Producers," working paper (McDonough School of Business, Georgetown University, Washington DC, 2004).

15 K. Monteverde, "Technical Dialogue as an Incentive for Vertical Integration in the Semiconductor Industry," *Management Science* 41 (1995): 1624–38; Macher, op. cit. (2004).

16 L. Willcocks and C. Sauer, "High Risks and Hidden Costs in IT Outsourcing," *Financial Times*, Mastering Risk (May 23, 2000): 2–4.

17 These arrangements have been described as "value adding partnerships." See R. Johnston and P. R. Lawrence, op. cit.

18 J. H. Dyer, "Effective Interfirm Collaboration: How Firms Minimize Transaction Costs and Maximize Transaction Value," *Strategic Management Journal* 18 (1997): 535–56; J. H. Dyer, "Specialized Supplier Networks as a Source of Competitive Advantage: Evidence from the Auto Industry," *Strategic Management Journal* 17 (1996): 271–92.

19 M. Schilling and S. Kotha, "Starbucks Corporation (A)," in R. M. Grant and K. Neupert (eds), *Cases in Contemporary Strategy Analysis*, 2nd edn (Oxford: Blackwell, 1999): 218–43.

20 L. Willcocks and C. Sauer, "High Risks and Hidden Costs in IT Outsourcing," *Financial Times*, Mastering Risk (May 23, 2000): 3.

21 G. Lorenzoni, "Benetton," in C. Baden Fuller and M. Pitt (eds), *Strategic Innovation* (London: Routledge, 1996).

22 G. Lorenzoni and A. Lipparini, "The Leveraging of Interfirm Relationships as Distinctive Organizational Capabilities: A Longitudinal Study," *Strategic Management Journal* 20 (1999): 317–38.

23 G. Lorenzoni and A. Lipparini, "Relational Strategies and Learning by Interacting Mechanisms in the Italian Motorcycle Industry," paper presented at Strategic Management Society Conference, Barcelona (October 1997).

24 J. H. Dyer and K. Nobeoka, "Creating and Managing a High-performance Knowledge-Sharing Network: The Toyota Case," *Strategic Management Journal* 21 (2000): 345–68.

25 www.covisint.com; www.elemica.com; www.rockanddirt.com.

26 "The Virtual Corporation," *Business Week* (February 8, 1993): 98–104; W. H. Davidow and M. S. Malone, *The Virtual Corporation* (New York: HarperCollins, 1992).

27 H. W. Chesborough and D. J. Teece, "When is Virtual Virtuous? Organizing for Innovation," *Harvard Business Review* (May–June 1996): 68–79.

28 C. K. Prahalad and Gary Hamel, "The Core Competences of the Corporation," *Harvard Business Review* (May–June 1990): 79–91.

29 A. Prencipe, "Breadth and Depth of Technological Capabilities in Complex Product Systems: The Case of the Aircraft Engine Control System," *Research Policy* 27 (August 2000): 895–911.

14

Global Strategies and the Multinational Corporation

ABB is a company with no geographic center, no national ax to grind. We are a federation of national companies with a global coordination center. Are we a Swiss company? Our headquarters is in Zurich, but only 100 professionals work at headquarters and we will not increase that number. Are we a Swedish company? I'm the CEO, and I was born and educated in Sweden. But our headquarters is not in Sweden and only two of the eight members of our board of directors are Swedes. Perhaps we are an American company. We report our financial results in US dollars and English is ABB's official language. We conduct all high-level meetings in English. My point is that ABB is none of those things – and all of these things. We are not homeless. We are a company with many homes.
—**Percy Barnevik, CEO, Asea Brown Boveri**

The vast majority of our imports come from outside the country.

—*George Bush Jr.*

Outline

- Introduction and Objectives
- Implications of International Competition for Industry Analysis
    Patterns of Internationalization
    Implications for Competition
    Competition from Potential Entrants
    Rivalry among Existing Firms
    The Bargaining Power of Buyers

INTRODUCTION AND OBJECTIVES

Internationalization is the most important and pervasive force reshaping the competitive environment of business. It has opened national markets to new competitors and created new business opportunities for both large and small firms. Internationalization has occurred through two mechanisms: trade and direct investment. The growth of world trade has consistently outstripped the growth of world output, increasing export/sales and import penetration ratios for all countries and all industries. For the United States, the share of imports in sales of manufactured goods rose from less than 4 percent in 1960 to 28 percent in 2003. Trade in commercial services (transportation, communications, information, financial services, and the like) has grown even faster than merchandise trade. The second aspect of internationalization has been overseas direct investment by corporations. By 2003, the total stock of foreign direct investment by all companies was $7.8 trillion, compared with total US GDP of $11.1 trillion.[1]

The forces driving both trade and direct investment are, first, the quest to exploit market opportunities in other countries, and, second, the desire to exploit production opportunities by locating production activities wherever they can be conducted most efficiently. The resulting "globalization of business" has created networks of international transactions comprising merchandise trade, flows of services (including technology), flows of people (especially those with highly developed skills), flows of factor payments (interest, profits, and licensing and royalty income) and flows of capital.

The implications for competition and industry structure are far reaching. During the 1960s, local companies dominated most domestic markets. Internationalization has changed all that. In the US market for television sets, the leading domestic brands of yesteryear are still around, but all are owned by overseas companies: General Electric and RCA by the French company Thomson, Magnavox by Philips of the Netherlands, Zenith by LG of South Korea, while Motorola's television business is owned by Matsushita. However, most of the TV sets are manufactured elsewhere – in China, Mexico, Malaysia, and Brazil. Similarly with investment banking, London remains the world's biggest financial center, yet its leading investment banks are global giants based in New York, Frankfurt, and Zurich: Citigroup, Merrill Lynch, Goldman Sachs, Deutsche Bank, UBS and SBC. The venerable investment banks that once financed Britain's imperial might have now been absorbed by these international players: Warburg by UBC, Morgan Grenfell by Deutsche Bank, Barings by ING Group, Hambros by Société Generale, and Kleinwort-Benson by Dresner.

The ability to take advantage of international opportunities has been a key determinant of overall corporate success. The industry leadership of Citigroup in financial services, Honda in motorcycles, Vodafone in wireless communication, and Philip Morris in cigarettes owes much to these companies' ambitious global strategies. The risks are too great: for Saatchi & Saatchi in advertising, Daewoo in automobiles, and Marks & Spencer in retailing, overambitious internationalization marked the beginning of corporate decline.

For countries too, harnessing the forces of internationalization has been a prime determinant of relative economic performance. In 1950, Hong Kong's GDP per head of population lagged slightly behind that of the Philippines. By 2003, Hong Kong's development as a hub for international trade and commerce had given it a per capita GDP of $26,000, compared with $4,500 for the Philippines (at purchasing power parity rates of exchange). Within the European Union, Ireland's ability to take advantage of international trade and inward direct investment has resulted in real GDP doubling during 1993–2003; Italy's increased a mere 16 percent.

This chapter examines the implications of the internationalization of the business environment for the formulation and implementation of company strategy. In doing so, we extend our strategy framework to take account of the firm's national environment as a critical dimension of its competitive environment. By the time you have completed this chapter, you will be able to:

- Apply the tools of industry analysis to global industries, including identifying the impact of trade and direct investment on industry structure and competition and appraising the critical differences between national markets within the same industry.

- Analyze how the national environment of the firm influences its competitive advantage, in particular how the national context affects the resources and capabilities of the firm and the choice of strategies through which the firm can best exploit these national conditions.

- Formulate strategies for exploiting overseas business opportunities, including overseas entry strategies and overseas production strategies, and determine the appropriate degree of globalization or national differentiation.

- Design organizational structures and management systems appropriate to the pursuit of international strategies.

We begin by exploring the implications of international competition, first for industry analysis, and then for the analysis of competitive advantage.

IMPLICATIONS OF INTERNATIONAL COMPETITION FOR INDUSTRY ANALYSIS

Patterns of Internationalization

Internationalization occurs through trade and direct investment. On this basis we can identify different types of industry according to the extent and mode of their internationalization (see Figure 14.1):

- *Sheltered industries* are national, even local, in terms of firms' market scope. Most of the industries that were once sheltered from international competition by regulation, public ownership, or physical barriers to trade – banking, insurance, electricity generation, telecommunications, cement – are now well on the road to internationalization. Industries left in this category are primarily fragmented service industries (dry cleaning, hairdressing, auto repair), some small-scale manufacturing (handicrafts, homebuilding), and industries producing products that are nontradable because they are perishable (fresh milk, bread) or difficult to move (four-poster beds, garden sheds).

- *Trading industries* are those where internationalization occurs primarily through imports and exports. If a product is transportable, not nationally differentiated, and subject to substantial scale economies, exporting from a single location is the most efficient means to exploit overseas markets, which

FIGURE 14.1 Patterns of industry internationalization

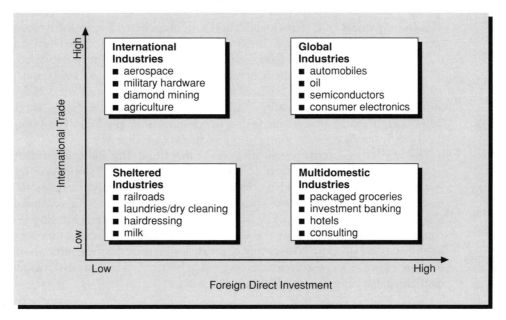

would apply for example with commercial aircraft, shipbuilding, and defense equipment. Trading industries also include products whose inputs are available only in a few locations: diamonds from South Africa, caviar from Iran and Azerbaijan.

■ *Multidomestic industries* are those that internationalize through direct investment – either because trade is not feasible (as in the case of service industries such as banking, consulting, or hotels) or because products are nationally differentiated (e.g., frozen dinners, recorded music).

■ *Global industries* are those in which both trade and direct investment are important. Most large-scale manufacturing industries tend to evolve towards global structures: in automobiles, consumer electronics, semiconductors, pharmaceuticals, and beer, levels of trade and direct investment are high.

By which route does internationalization typically occur? In the case of services and other nontradable products, there is no choice. The only way that Marriott, Starbucks, and Goldman Sachs can serve overseas markets is by creating subsidiaries (or acquiring companies) within these markets. In the case of manufacturing companies, internationalization typically begins with exports from the home base. Later a sales and distribution subsidiary is established in the overseas country. Eventually the company develops a more integrated overseas subsidiary that undertakes manufacturing and product development as well.

Implications for Competition

The consequences of internationalization for competition and industry attractiveness are mostly adverse. Although internationalization offers increased investment and marketing opportunities to companies, such opportunities mean increased intensity of competition. Consider the US markets for automobiles in 1970 and 2000. In 1970, the Big Three – GM, Ford, and Chrysler – dominated the US automobile industry, with American Motors and Volkswagen as minor producers. By the end of 2004 there were 11 companies with auto plants within the US.[2] The overall impact has been intensified price competition and lower profitability.

The impact of internationalization on competition and industry profitability can be analyzed within the context of Porter's Five Forces of Competition framework. For the purposes of our analysis, let us take our unit of analysis as national markets where the relevant "industry" comprises the firms supplying that national market. Hence, for the purposes of analyzing competition, the US auto industry includes all companies supplying autos to the US automobile market, whether they are domestic or overseas companies. Within this context, internationalization affects competition in three major ways: through reducing entry barriers, increasing rivalry, and enhancing the bargaining power of domestic buyers.

Competition from Potential Entrants

The growth of international trade indicates a substantial lowering of barriers to entry into national markets. Multilateral tariff reduction during successive GATT rounds, falling real costs of transportation, the removal of exchange controls, internationalization of standards, and convergence between customer preferences have made it much easier for producers in one country to supply customers in another. Many of the entry barriers that were effective against potential domestic entrants may be ineffective against potential entrants that are established producers in overseas countries.

Rivalry among Existing Firms

Internationalization increases internal rivalry within industries in four ways:

- *Lowering Seller Concentration.* International trade typically means that more suppliers are competing for each national market. Consider the US auto market. In 1970, GM, Ford, and Chrysler together held 84 percent of total sales, and there were just five manufacturers with market shares greater than 2 percent. By 2000, the combined share of the Big Three had fallen to 61 percent, and there were eight manufacturers with market shares greater than 2 percent. In European countries, the fall in market share of the national leaders (Fiat in Italy, Renault and Peugeot-Citroën in France, British Leyland in the United Kingdom, Seat in Spain) was even more dramatic. While internationalization decreases concentration in national markets, it increases concentration at the global level as competition forces smaller companies to either exit or merge.

■ *Increasing Diversity of Competitors.* Lower entry barriers and concentration ratios only partly explain the increasing intensity of competition between established firms. Equally important is the increasing diversity of competitors, which causes them to compete more vigorously while making cooperation more difficult. The cozy collusiveness observed in domestic oligopolies during the 1960s (e.g., in autos, steel, and banking) was possible because of the similarities among domestic companies in their costs, strategies, goals, and perceptions. The entry of overseas competitors into domestic markets upset these patterns of co-ordination – their different costs, goals, and strategies made tacit collusion much less likely.[3]

■ *Increasing Excess Capacity.* When internationalization occurs through direct investment, the result is likely to be increased capacity. To the extent that direct investment occurs through investment in new plants, industry capacity increases with no corresponding increase in market size. The automobile industry is a classic example of this – the investment by Japanese and Korean manufacturers in the US and Europe, and by US manufacturers in Latin America and Asia, added substantially to global excess capacity during the 1990s.

■ *Increasing the Bargaining Power of Buyers.* A further implication of the internationalization of business is that large customers can exercise their buying power far more effectively. Global sourcing provides a key tool for cost reduction by manufacturers. The growth of internet-based markets for components and materials enhances the power of industrial buyers.

ANALYZING COMPETITIVE ADVANTAGE IN AN INTERNATIONAL CONTEXT

The growth of international competition has been associated with some stunning reversals in the competitive positions of different companies. RCA in consumer electronics, and Xerox in office copiers, and International Harvester in agricultural equipment were leaders in their industries before being decimated by international competition. Conversely, the opening of international markets has made it possible for Honda in motorcycles, Microsoft in computer software, and IKEA in furniture retailing to achieve success that has exceeded their founders' wildest dreams.

To understand how internationalization has shifted the basis of competition, we need to extend our framework for analyzing competitive advantage to include the influence of firms' national environments. Competitive advantage, we have noted, is achieved when a firm matches its internal strengths in resources and capabilities to the key success factors of the industry. International industries differ from domestic industries in their sources of competitive advantage. When firms are located in different countries, their potential for achieving competitive advantage depends not

FIGURE 14.2 Competitive advantage in an international context

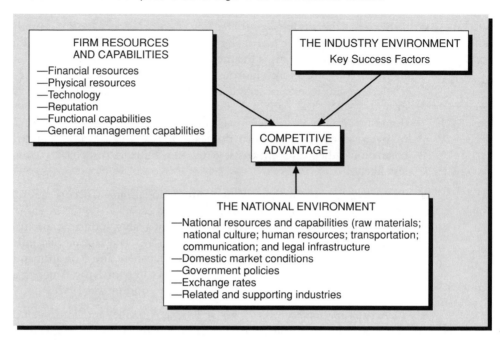

only on their internal stocks of resources and capabilities, but also on the conditions of their national environments – in particular, the resource availability within the countries where they do business. Figure 14.2 summarizes the implications of internationalization for our basic strategy model in terms of the impact both on industry conditions and firms' access to resources and capabilities.

National Influences on Competitiveness: Comparative Advantage

The role of national resource availability on international competitiveness is the subject of the *theory of comparative advantage*. The theory states that a country has a comparative advantage in those products that make intensive use of those resources available in abundance within that country. Thus, Bangladesh has an abundant supply of unskilled labor. The United States has an abundant supply of technological resources: trained scientists and engineers, research facilities, and universities. Bangladesh has a comparative advantage in products that make intensive use of unskilled labor, such as clothing, handicrafts, leather goods, and assembly of consumer electronic products. The United States has a comparative advantage in technology-intensive products, such as microprocessors, computer software, pharmaceuticals, medical diagnostic equipment, and management consulting services.

The term comparative advantage refers to the *relative* efficiencies of producing different products. So long as exchange rates are well behaved (they do not deviate far

TABLE 14.1 Indexes of Revealed Comparative Advantage for Certain Broad Product Categories

	USA	CANADA	GERMANY	ITALY	JAPAN
Food, drink, and tobacco	0.31	0.28	−0.36	−0.29	−0.85
Raw materials	0.43	0.51	−0.55	−0.30	−0.88
Oil and refined products	−0.64	0.34	−0.72	−0.74	−0.99
Chemicals	0.42	−0.16	0.20	−0.06	−0.58
Machinery and transportation equipment	0.12	−0.19	0.34	0.22	0.80
Other manufacturing	−0.68	−0.07	0.01	0.29	0.40

Note: Revealed comparative advantage for each product group is measured as: (Exports less Imports)/Domestic Production.
Source: OECD.

from their purchasing power parity levels), then comparative advantage is translated into competitive advantage. Hence, comparative advantages are revealed in trade performance: Bangladesh has a positive balance of trade in leather goods and clothing; the US has a positive trade balance in microprocessors and pharmaceuticals. Table 14.1 shows revealed comparative advantages for several product groups and several countries. Positive values show comparative advantage, negative values show comparative disadvantage. Thus, Japan has a strong comparative advantage in machinery and transportation equipment, and a strong disadvantage in oil and refined products.

Trade theory has traditionally emphasized the role of natural resource endowments, labor supply, and capital stock in determining comparative advantage. However, empirical research points to the central role played by "home-grown" resources, of which the most important is knowledge (including technology, human skills, and management capability) and the resources needed to commercialize knowledge (capital markets, communications facilities, and a legal system).[4] The remarkable economic development of the "tiger economies" of South Korea, Taiwan, Hong Kong, Malaysia, and Singapore demonstrates how disadvantages in endowments of natural resources are far outweighed by concerted development of capital, education, technology, and communications and transportation infrastructure.[5]

The ability to exploit comparative advantages based upon large investments in technology and infrastructure requires the availability of sufficient market demand. Hence, in most capital- and technology-intensive industries, large countries (such as the US) are at an advantage over small countries.[6] A similar logic motivates the creation of free trade areas such as the European Union, Mercosur, and NAFTA.

Porter's National Diamond

Michael Porter's study of patterns of comparative advantage among 13 industrialized nations offers striking insight into the role of dynamic, endogenous national conditions on firms' international competitive advantage.[7] Porter's analysis is built on two main principles:

FIGURE 14.3   Porter's national diamond framework

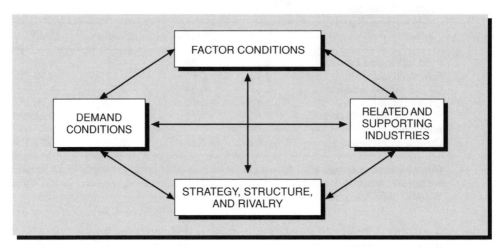

1. To analyze national competitiveness we need to focus upon *firm performance*. The role of the national environment is providing a context within which firms develop their identity, resources, capabilities, and managerial styles.[8]

2. For a country to sustain a competitive advantage in a particular industry sector requires *dynamic* advantage: firms must broaden and extend the basis of their competitive advantage by *innovation* and *upgrading*. The *dynamic conditions* that influence innovation and the upgrading are far more important than initial resource endowments in determining national patterns of competitiveness.

Porter's analysis is summarized in his national diamond framework (see Figure 14.3).[9]

Factor Conditions

Whereas the conventional advantage of comparative analysis focuses on endowments of broad categories of resource, Porter's analysis emphasizes, first, "home-grown" resources and, second, the role of highly specialized resources. For example, in analyzing Hollywood's preeminence in film production, Porter points to the local concentration of skilled labor, including the roles of UCLA and USC schools of film. Also, resource constraints may encourage the development of substitute capabilities: in Japan, lack of raw materials has spurred miniaturization and low-defect manufacturing; in Italy, restrictive labor laws have stimulated automation.

Related and Supporting Industries

For many industries, a critical resource is the presence of related and supporting industries. One of the most striking of Porter's empirical findings is that national competitive strengths tend to be associated with "clusters" of industries. One such cluster is US strength in semiconductors, computers, and computer software. For each of these industries, critical resources are the other related industries. In Germany, a mutually supporting cluster exists around chemicals, synthetic dyes, textiles, and textile machinery.

Demand Conditions

Demand conditions in the domestic market provide the primary driver of innovation and quality improvement. For example:

- The preeminence of Swiss and Belgian chocolate makers may be attributed to their highly discerning domestic customers.

- The dominance of the world market for cameras by Japanese companies owes much to Japanese consumers' enthusiasm for amateur photography and their eager adoption of innovation in cameras.

- German companies' (Mercedes, BMW, Porsche) dominance of the high-performance segment of the world automobile industry, as compared to their much weaker position in mass-produced autos, may be linked to German motorists' love of quality engineering and their irrepressible urge to drive on autobahns at terrifying speeds.

Strategy, Structure, and Rivalry

National competitive performance in particular sectors is inevitably related to the strategies and structures of firms in those industries. Porter puts particular emphasis on the role of competition between domestic companies in driving innovation and the upgrading of competitive advantage. Domestic competition is usually more direct and personal than that between companies from different countries. As a result, the maintenance of strong competition within domestic markets is likely to provide a powerful stimulus to innovation and efficiency. The most striking feature of the Japanese auto industry is the presence of nine companies, all of which compete fiercely within the domestic market. The same can be said for cameras, consumer electronic products, and facsimile machines. Conversely, lack of domestic competition may explain why the efforts of European governments to create "national champions" in so many industries have been so unsuccessful.

Consistency between Strategy and National Conditions

Establishing competitive advantage in global industries requires congruence between business strategy and the pattern of the country's comparative advantage. For example, in the British cutlery industry, competition from South Korean manufacturers benefiting from low wage and low steel costs meant that it was virtually impossible for companies such as J. Billam to survive in the mass market for stainless steel cutlery. The only firms to prosper, or even survive, were those that relied on technology (such as Richardson in kitchen knives), or focused on the high-quality silverware segment. In stereo systems and other audio products, US and European companies (such as Bose and Bang & Olufsen) have survived by focusing on skill-intensive and design-intensive products; Sony, Matsushita, and other Japanese producers compete on the basis of their strengths in microelectronics and process technologies, the low end of the market (e.g., retailers' own brands) is supplied by companies in Thailand, Malaysia, and China.

The linkage between the firm's competitive advantage and its national environment also includes the relationship between firms' organizational capabilities and the national culture and social structure. Stimulated by Max Weber's analysis of the impact of religion on enterprise,[10] national culture has been shown to exert a powerful influence on management practices in general and on the capability profiles of firms in particular. The capabilities of Japanese companies in integrating diverse technologies into innovative new products (electronic musical instruments, color copying machines), and in quality enhancement through continuous improvement, owes much to Japanese traditions of assimilating outside ideas and cooperative social behavior. Similarly, the excellence of US firms in financial management and pioneering new industries through entrepreneurship may link with US traditions of individualism and quest for material wealth. We shall return to the implications of national cultures for strategic management later in this chapter.

APPLYING THE FRAMEWORK: INTERNATIONAL LOCATION OF PRODUCTION

To examine how national resource conditions influence international strategies, we look at two types of strategic decision in international business: first, the decision of where to locate production activities and, second, the decision of how to enter a foreign market.

So far, our discussion of the linkage between the competitive advantage of the firm and its national environment has assumed, implicitly, that each firm is based within its home country. In fact, a primary motivation of multinational strategies is to access the resources and capabilities available in other countries. Whether a firm markets its product in many countries or only in its domestic market, it must decide where it is to produce it. Some firms market globally but concentrate production in their home country (e.g. Boeing, Microsoft, and E & J Gallo). Others establish country subsidiaries, where each produces for its own national market (e.g. the tobacco company BAT and food service company Sodexho). Other companies market mainly in their home country but produce all over the world (e.g. Eni S.p.A produces oil and gas in over 20 countries but most of its sales of oil products and gas are in Italy.

Determinants of Geographical Location

The decision of where to manufacture requires consideration of three sets of factors:

TABLE 14.2 Hourly Compensation Costs in US Dollars for Production Workers in Manufacturing

	1975	1980	1985	1990	1995	2000	2002
United States	6.36	9.87	13.01	14.91	17.19	19.76	21.33
Mexico	1.47	2.21	1.59	1.58	1.51	2.08	2.38
Australia	5.62	8.47	8.20	13.07	15.27	14.47	15.55
Hong Kong	0.76	1.51	1.73	3.20	4.82	5.63	5.83
Israel	2.25	3.79	4.06	8.55	10.54	12.86	12.14
Japan	3.00	5.52	6.34	12.80	23.82	22.27	18.83
Korea	0.32	0.96	1.23	3.71	7.29	8.19	9.16
Taiwan	0.40	1.00	1.50	3.93	5.94	5.85	5.41
Denmark	6.28	10.83	8.13	18.04	24.07	21.49	24.23
France	4.52	8.94	7.52	15.49	20.01	15.70	17.42
Germany (former West)	6.31	12.25	9.53	21.88	31.58	24.42	26.14
Italy	4.67	8.15	7.63	17.45	16.22	14.01	14.91
Spain	2.53	5.89	4.66	11.38	12.88	10.78	12.03
Sweden	7.18	12.51	9.66	20.93	21.44	20.14	20.10
Switzerland	6.09	11.09	9.66	20.86	29.30	21.24	24.10
United Kingdom	3.37	7.56	6.27	12.70	13.67	16.45	17.40

Source: US Department of Labor, Bureau of Labor Statistics, January 2004.

- *National resource availability.* Where key resources differ between countries in their availability or cost, then firms should manufacture in countries where resource supplies are favorable. For the oil industry this means exploring in Kazakhstan, Angola, and Venezuela. For Nike and Reebok, it means locating shoe assembly where labor costs are low: China, Thailand, India, and the Philippines. (Table 14.2 shows differences in employment costs between countries.) For semiconductor and computer companies, it means establishing R&D facilities in California's Silicon Valley in order to exploit US microelectronics expertise.[11]

- *Firm-specific competitive advantages.* For firms whose competitive advantage is based on internal resources and capabilities, location depends on where those resources and capabilities can best be deployed. The competitive advantages of Toyota, Nissan, and Honda rest primarily on their own technical, manufacturing, and product development capabilities. Traditionally, these companies concentrated production within Japan where they could exploit scale economies. During the 1980s, they demonstrated the ability to transfer these competitive advantages to overseas locations.

- *Tradability.* The ability to locate production away from markets depends on the transportability of the product. Production within the local market is favored when transportation costs are high, local customers have differentiated preferences, and governments create barriers to trade.

Location and the Value Chain

Location decisions must take account of the fact that the production of any good or service is composed of a vertical chain of activities and that the input requirements of each stage vary considerably. The result is that different countries are likely to offer differential advantage at each stage of the value chain. Table 14.3 shows the pattern of international specialization within textiles and apparel and consumer electronics. In textiles and apparel, the resource requirements for the different production stages are very different. Fiber production is concentrated in the countries with comparative advantage in agricultural production (for cotton and wool) and chemicals (for synthetic fibers). The production of yarn and cloth is capital intensive and occurs in both newly industrialized and mature countries. Apparel is labor intensive – here

TABLE 14.3 Comparative Advantage in Textiles and Consumer Electronics by Stage of Processing

INDUSTRY	COUNTRY	STAGE OF PROCESSING	INDEX OF REVEALED COMPARATIVE ADVANTAGE
Textiles and apparel	Hong Kong	1	−0.96
		2	−0.81
		3	−0.41
		4	+0.75
	Italy	1	−0.54
		2	+0.18
		3	+0.14
		4	+0.72
	Japan	1	−0.36
		2	+0.48
		3	+0.78
		4	−0.48
	USA	1	+0.96
		2	+0.64
		3	+0.22
		4	−0.73
Consumer electronic products	Brazil	1	−0.62
		2	+0.55
	Hong Kong	1	−0.41
		2	+0.28
	Japan	1	+0.53
		2	+0.97
	S. Korea	1	−0.01
		2	+0.73
	USA	1	+0.02
		2	−0.65

Notes: Revealed comparative advantage is measured as: (Exports − Imports)/(Exports + Imports). For textiles and apparel, the stages of processing are: 1. fiber (natural and manmade), 2. spun yarn, 3. textiles, 4. apparel. For consumer electronics, the stages of processing are: 1. components, 2. finished products.
Source: United Nations.

the developing countries have a clear comparative advantage. Similarly with consumer electronics: component production is research and capital intensive and is concentrated in the US, Japan, Korea, and Malaysia; assembly is labor intensive and is concentrated in China, Thailand, and Latin America.

In principle, a firm can identify the resources required by each stage of the value chain, then determine which country offers these resources at the lowest cost.[12] For example, Nike locates R&D and design in the US; the production of fabric, rubber, and plastic shoe components in Korea, Taiwan, and China; and assembly in India, China, the Philippines, and Indonesia.[13]

However, these benefits from fragmenting the value chain must be traded off against the added costs of coordinating globally dispersed activities. Transportation costs are one consideration. Another is increased inventory cost. Where learning curves are steep, the time costs of shipping components can be great: semiconductors can lose 5 percent of their value while being shipped from Asia to the United States. Just-in-time scheduling often necessitates that production activities are carried out in close proximity to one another. Although the labor cost of building an automobile in Mexico is only 20 percent of the labor cost in the US, this cost advantage of Mexican production is almost entirely offset by higher costs of components. The importance of close linkages through geographical proximity depends on the strategy of the company. Companies that compete on speed and reliability of delivery (e.g. Zara and Dell Computer) typically forsake the cost advantages of a globally dispersed value chain in favor of integrated operations with fast access to the final market.

Figure 14.4 summarizes the relevant criteria in location decisions.

FIGURE 14.4 Determining the optimal location of value chain activities

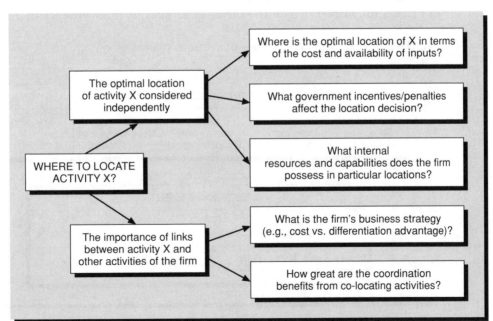

APPLYING THE FRAMEWORK: FOREIGN ENTRY STRATEGIES

Many of the considerations relevant to locating production activities also apply to choosing the mode of foreign market entry. A firm enters an overseas market because it believes that it will be profitable. This assumes not only that the overseas market is attractive – that its structure is conducive to profitability – but also that the firm can establish a competitive advantage *vis-à-vis* local producers and other multinational corporations (MNCs). We discussed the analysis of industry and market profitability in Chapters 3 and 4. Our focus here is on how the firm can best establish competitive advantage in a foreign market.

In exploiting an overseas market opportunity, a firm has a range of options with regard to mode of entry. These correspond closely to the firm's strategic alternatives with regard to exploiting innovation (see Chapter 11). The basic distinction is between market entry by means of *transactions* and market entry by means of *direct investment*. Figure 14.5 shows a spectrum of market entry options arranged according to the degree of commitment by the firm. Thus, at one extreme there is exporting through individual spot-market transactions; at the other, there is the establishment of a fully owned subsidiary that undertakes a full range of functions.

How does a firm weigh the merits of different market entry modes? Five sets of consideration are critical.

1. Is the firm's competitive advantage based on firm-specific or country-specific resources?

If the firm's competitive advantage is country based, the firm must exploit an overseas market by exporting. Thus, to the extent that Hyundai's competitive advantage in the US car market is its low Korean wage rates, it must produce in Korea and

FIGURE 14.5 Alternative modes of overseas market entry

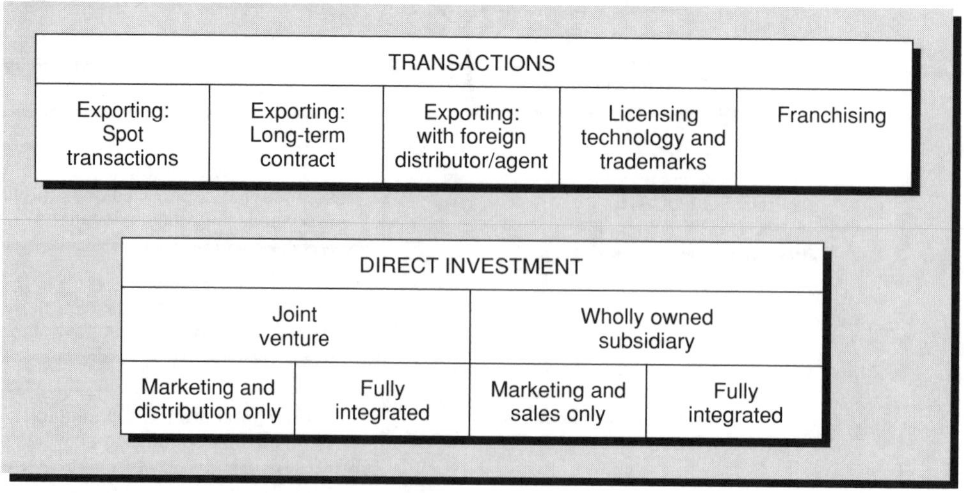

TRANSACTIONS				
Exporting: Spot transactions	Exporting: Long-term contract	Exporting: with foreign distributor/agent	Licensing technology and trademarks	Franchising

DIRECT INVESTMENT			
Joint venture		Wholly owned subsidiary	
Marketing and distribution only	Fully integrated	Marketing and sales only	Fully integrated

export to the United States. If Toyota's competitive advantage is company specific, then assuming that advantage is transferable within the company, Toyota can exploit the US market either by exports or by direct investment in US production facilities.[14]

2. Is the product tradable and what are the barriers to trade?

If the product is not tradable because of transportation costs or import restrictions, then accessing that market requires entry either by investing in overseas production facilities or by licensing the use of key resources to local companies within the overseas market.

3. Does the firm possess the full range of resources and capabilities for establishing a competitive advantage in the overseas market?

Competing in an overseas market is likely to require that the firm acquire additional resources and capabilities, particularly those related to marketing and distributing in an unfamiliar market. Accessing such country-specific resources is most easily achieved by establishing a relationship with firms in the overseas market. The form of relationship depends, in part, on the resources and capabilities required. If a firm needs marketing and distribution, it might appoint a distributor or agent with exclusive territorial rights. If a wide range of manufacturing and marketing capabilities is needed, the firm might license its product and/or its technology to a local manufacturer. In technology-based industries, firms frequently exploit their innovations internationally by licensing their technology to local companies. In marketing-intensive industries, firms may offer their brands to local companies through trademark licensing. Alternatively, a joint venture might be sought with a local manufacturing company. The difficulties that US companies faced when entering the Japanese market encouraged many to form joint ventures with local companies (e.g., Fuji-Xerox, Caterpillar-Mitsubishi). Typically, such joint ventures combined the technology and brand names of the overseas partner with the local market knowledge and manufacturing and distribution facilities of the local partner.

4. Can the firm directly appropriate the returns to its resources?

Whether a firm licenses the use of its proprietary resources or chooses to exploit them directly (either through exporting or direct investment) depends partly on appropriability considerations. In chemicals and pharmaceuticals, the patents protecting product innovations tend to offer strong legal protection, in which case patent licenses to local producers can be an effective means of appropriating their returns. In computer software and computer equipment, the protection offered by patents and copyrights is looser, which encourages exporting rather than licensing as a means of exploiting overseas markets.

With all licensing arrangements, key considerations are the capabilities and reliability of the local licensee. This is particularly important in licensing brand names, where the licenser must carefully protect the brand's reputation. Thus, Cadbury-Schweppes licenses to Hershey the trademarks and product recipes for its Cadbury's range of chocolate bars for sale in the United States. This arrangement reflects the fact that Hershey has production and distribution facilities in the US that Cadbury cannot match, and that Cadbury views Hershey as a reliable business partner. The need to exert close control over the use of one's trademarks, technologies, and trade secrets is reflected in the design of international franchising systems.

5. What transaction costs are involved?

A key issue that arises in the licensing of a firm's trademarks or technology concerns the transaction costs of negotiating, monitoring, and enforcing the terms of such agreements as compared with internationalization through a fully owned subsidiary. In expanding overseas, Starbucks owns and operates its coffee houses while McDonald's franchises its burger restaurants. McDonald's competitive advantage depends primarily upon the franchisee faithfully replicating the McDonald's system. This can be enforced effectively by means of franchise contracts. Starbucks believes that its success is achieved through creating the "Starbucks experience" which is as much about ambiance as it is about coffee. It is difficult to articulate the ingredients of this experience, let alone write it into a contract.

Issues of transaction costs are fundamental to the choices between alternative market entry modes. Barriers to exporting in the form of transport costs and tariffs are forms of transaction costs; other costs include exchange rate risk and information costs. Transaction cost analysis has been central to theories of the existence of multinational corporations. In the absence of transaction costs in the markets either for goods or for resources, companies exploit overseas markets either by exporting their goods and services or by selling the use of their resources to local firms in the overseas markets.[15] Thus, multinationals tend to predominate in industries where:

- firm-specific intangible resources such as brands and technology are important (transaction costs in licensing the use of these resources favor direct investment);

- exporting is subject to transaction costs (e.g., through tariffs or import restrictions);

- customer preferences are reasonably similar between countries.

Strategy Alternatives for Overseas Production

This analysis has examined alternative strategies for exploring overseas *market* opportunities. The same type of analysis can be performed by analyzing overseas *production* opportunities. A firm can access the resources and capabilities available for producing in an overseas country either by *transactions* (e.g., importing) or by *direct investment*. Thus, Exxon Mobil accesses the crude oil production of the North Sea by purchasing oil both on long-term contracts with Statoil, BP, and other producers, and on spot contracts through the London and Rotterdam oil markets. At the same time, Exxon Mobil also has production facilities in the North Sea – some of which are wholly owned, and some of which are joint ventures with Shell and other companies. Nike's production of shoes in Asia is entirely through long-term contracts with local production companies.

Multinational companies have traditionally been interested in overseas production for two main reasons: to access raw materials and cheap labor, and to provide local production to overseas markets. Increasingly, however, direct investment by multinational firms is driven not only by the quest for overseas markets, raw materials, and lower-cost labor, but also by the desire to access technology. Kenichi Ohmae's view that multinational firms need to be based in all three of the world's leading industrial centers – North America, Japan, and Europe – in order to be "where the action is" is supported by evidence that a key role of the foreign subsidiaries of multinational corporations is gaining access to locally available technological knowledge.[16]

International Alliances and Joint Ventures

During the last decade and a half, one of the most striking features of the development of international business has been the upsurge in the numbers of joint ventures and other forms of strategic alliance across national borders. Consider for example the US and Japanese automobile companies: despite the intense competition between them – which extends from the marketplace into government policies and international relations – there has been a remarkable growth in collaborative arrangements between them. Figure 14.6 shows GM's network of alliances with other automakers.

FIGURE 14.6 General Motors Alliances with Competitors

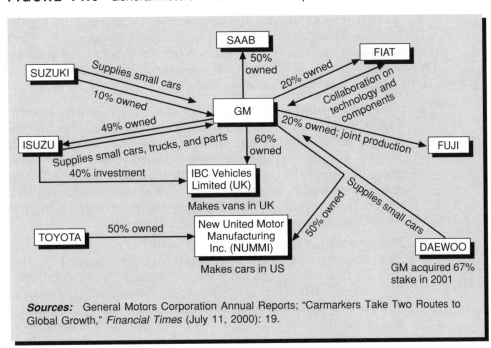

Sources: General Motors Corporation Annual Reports; "Carmakers Take Two Routes to Global Growth," *Financial Times* (July 11, 2000): 19.

The traditional reason for cross-border alliances and joint ventures was the desire by multinational companies to access the market knowledge and distribution capabilities of a local company, together with the desire by local companies to access the technology, brands, and product development of the multinationals. Such arrangements were supported by the policies of the host government in China, India, and other countries, where foreign companies were obliged to take a local partner. In technology-based industries – computers, semiconductors, telecom equipment, pharmaceuticals, and aerospace – the rapid growth of international collaboration reflects companies' desire to access other companies' different technological capabilities. Local partners can also facilitate the rapid global rollout of new products and technologies.

The success of international joint ventures and other forms of strategic alliance has been mixed. There are plenty of examples of international joint ventures that have been spectacular failures. Joint ventures that share management responsibility are far more likely to fail than those with a dominant parent or with independent management.[17] The greatest problems arise between firms that are also competitors: reconciling cooperation with competition requires a tolerance for ambiguity that has proved particularly difficult for some North American companies.

Disagreements over the sharing of the contributions to and returns from an alliance are a frequent source of break-up. In several of the alliances between Japanese and western firms, the Japanese partner was better at appropriating the benefits of the alliance.[18] However, in long-term partnerships there is the potential for the benefits to flow in both directions. Thus, during the early years of Xerox's joint venture with Fuji to manufacture and sell copiers in Asia, the flow of technology was mainly from Xerox. When Xerox Corporation ran into problems during the 1990s, it was saved by technology, product designs, and management techniques from Fuji-Xerox.[19]

The effective strategic management of international alliances, argue Hamel, Doz, and Prahalad, depends on a clear recognition that collaboration is competition in a different form.[20] Though both partners must benefit if the alliance is to continue, sharing benefits depends on three key factors:

- *The strategic intent of the partners.* Japanese companies have entered partnerships with the clear intent of gaining global dominance, and in this respect strategic partnerships are just one step on the road to global expansion. By contrast, western companies have often entered partnerships with the goal of giving up manufacturing to more efficient Japanese producers. The willingness of western companies to yield major items of value added to former competitors limits their ability to learn from their partners and is likely to lead to a cumulative abandonment of activities and capabilities.

- *Appropriability of the contribution.* The ability of each partner to capture and appropriate the skills of the other depends on the nature of each firm's skills and resources. Where skills and resources are tangible or explicit, they can easily be acquired. Where they are tacit and people embodied, they are more difficult to acquire. To avoid the unintended transfer of know-how to partners, Hamel et al. argue the need for a "gatekeeper" to monitor and administer contacts with strategic partners.

- *Receptivity of the company.* The more receptive a company is in terms of its ability to identify what it wants from the partner, to obtain the required knowledge or skills, and to assimilate and adapt them, the more it will gain from the partnership. In management terms, this requires the setting of performance goals for what the partnership is to achieve for the company and managing the relationship to ensure that the company is deriving maximum learning from the collaboration.[21]

MULTINATIONAL STRATEGIES: GLOBALIZATION VERSUS NATIONAL DIFFERENTIATION

So far, we have viewed international expansion, whether by export or by direct investment, as a means by which a company can exploit its competitive advantages not just in its home market but also in foreign markets. However, there is more to internationalization than simply extending the geographical boundaries of a company's market. International scope may also be a source of competitive advantage over nationally based competitors. In this section, we explore whether, and under what conditions, firms that operate on an international basis, either by exporting or by direct investment, are able to gain a competitive advantage over nationally focused firms. If such "global strategies" have potential for creating competitive advantage, in what types of industry are they likely to be most effective? And how should they be designed and deployed in order to maximize their potential?

The Benefits of a Global Strategy

A global strategy is one that views the world as a single, if segmented, market. Theodore Levitt of Harvard Business School has argued that companies that compete on a national basis are highly vulnerable to companies that compete on a global basis.[22] The superiority of global strategies rests on two assumptions:

- *Globalization of customer preferences.* National and regional preferences are disappearing in the face of the homogenizing forces of technology, communication, and travel. "Everywhere everything gets more and more like everything else as the world's preference structure is relentlessly homogenized," observes Levitt. Nor is this trend restricted to technology-based products such as pharmaceuticals and computers; it is just as prevalent in branded consumer goods such as Corona beer, Adidas sportswear, and McDonald's hamburgers.

- *Scale economies.* Firms that produce standardized products for the global market can access scale economies in product development, manufacturing, and marketing that offer efficiency advantages that nationally based competitors cannot match. In automobiles, consumer electronics, investment banking, and many other industries, domestic firms have increasingly lost ground to global competitors.

Subsequent contributions by George Yip and others to the analysis of global strategies have shown that the benefits of pursuing a global strategy extend well beyond the scale economies that Levitt concentrated upon.[23] There are four major benefits from a global strategy:

Economies of Scale and Economies of Replication

As we noted in Chapter 8, the most important source of scale economy in most industries is product development. Over time, scale economies in manufacturing have become less important (in few industries do companies need to expand internationally in order to exploit scale economies at the plant level), while the scale economies associated with new product development have become more important as the costs of developing new products have soared.

However, there is a further source of scale economy that is especially important to international expansion. That is economies in the replication of knowledge-based assets – including organizational capabilities. When a company has created a knowledge-based asset or product – whether a recipe, or a piece of software, or an organizational system – creating the original knowledge was costly but, once created, subsequent replication is typically cheap. Thus, once Disney has built Disneyland, Anaheim and Walt Disney World in Florida, a Disneyland theme park in Paris or Hong Kong can be built at a fraction of the cost. Similarly with McDonald's: its business system was built in the US over several decades. Once created it can be replicated in additional countries at a fraction of the cost.

Economies from International Production

Global strategy does not necessarily involve production in one location and then distributing globally. Global strategies also involve exploiting the efficiencies from locating different activities in different places. As we have seen, companies internationalize not just in search of market opportunities but also in search of resource opportunities. Traditionally this has meant a quest for raw materials and low-cost labor. Increasingly it means a quest for knowledge. For example, in the semiconductor industry, overseas subsidiaries are set up primarily to access knowledge in the host country rather than to exploit their existing knowledge.[24]

Economies of Learning

If competitive advantage involves innovation and the constant deepening and widening of capabilities, then learning plays a central role in developing and sustaining competitive advantage. If learning involves communicating and interacting with one's proximate environment, then multinationals have the advantage of working within multiple national environments. The critical requirement is that the company possesses some form of global infrastructure for communication and knowledge transfer that permits new experiences, new ideas, and new practices to be transferred and integrated. A growing stream of research suggests that the most important advantage of multinationals over domestic companies is their ability to access knowledge in multiple locations, to synthesize that knowledge, and to transfer it efficiently across national borders.[25]

Competing Strategically

Through their presence in multiple national markets, multinational companies possess a key strategic advantage over their nationally focused competitors: multinationals can fight aggressive competitive battles in individual national markets using their cash flows from other national markets. This *cross-subsidization* of competitive initiatives in one market using profits from other markets has conventionally been identified with predatory pricing – cutting prices to a level that drives competitors out of business. Such pricing practices are likely to contravene both the World Trade Organization's antidumping rules and national antitrust laws. In practice, most cross-subsidization involves expenditures on advertising, sales promotion, and dealer support that are financed by cash flows from other markets.[26]

Faced with aggressive competition from the local subsidiary of a foreign MNC, the domestic competitor is in a weak position: it has no overseas revenues to finance aggressive competition in its home market. Such was the position US television manufacturers faced against strong Japanese competition in the 1970s. The most effective response to competition in one's home market may be to retaliate in the foreign MNC's own home market. Thus, when Kodak was attacked by Fuji in the US market – an attack that was symbolized by Fuji's sponsorship of the 1984 Olympic Games in Los Angeles – Kodak responded by attacking Fuji in Japan.[27] To effectively exploit such opportunities for national leveraging, some overall global coordination of competitive strategies in individual national markets is required.

In industries that are dominated by MNCs – automobiles, oil and gas, semiconductors and investment banking – the trend of the past two decades has been for companies to seek to position themselves in all three of the world's major industrial centers: North America, Europe, and Japan. Thus, in automobiles Daimler-Benz merged with Chrysler in the US and acquired Mitsubishi in Japan. Ford and GM have augmented their strong positions in the US and Europe with major acquisitions in the Far East (Ford acquired Mazda; GM acquired Daewoo and an equity stake in Suzuki). The head of McKinsey & Co.'s Tokyo office, Kenichi Ohmae, argues the case for *triad power* – that the need to access technology, developing customer preferences, and scale economies requires global players to become true insiders within all of the world's major markets: the United States, Europe, and Japan.[28]

The Need for National Differentiation

For all the advantages of global strategy, the evidence of the past decade is that national differences in customer preferences continue to exert a powerful influence in most markets: products that are designed to meet the needs of the "global customer" often fail to be popular in any market. Ford's first world car, the Mondeo/Contour, is an example of this. Moreover, costs of national differentiation can be surprisingly low if common basic designs and common major components are used. Flexible manufacturing systems have reduced the costs of customizing products to meet the preferences of particular customer groups.

Domestic appliances provide an interesting test of the globalization hypothesis. In washing machines, Levitt pointed to the success of Italian companies' mass-produced standardized products over Hoover's nationally differentiated washing machines. Subsequent analysis has shown that national preferences have remained remarkably durable: French and US washing machines are primarily top loading, elsewhere in Europe they are mainly front loading; the Germans prefer higher spin speeds than the Italians, US machines feature agitators rather than revolving drums, and Japanese machines are small. The result is that some nationally focused companies (such as Hotpoint in the UK) were more profitable than the pioneers of globalization, Electrolux and Whirlpool.[29]

The forces for national differentiation are not just customer preferences. There are a number of sources of national market differences that MNCs must be attentive to:

- *Laws and government regulations.* Governments are the most important players in building obstacles to globalization. National sovereignty means that each country imposes different rules and regulations that relate, not just to the design and performance characteristics of products, but to the ways of doing business as well. Cars sold in Britain have the steering wheel on "the wrong side" because traffic laws mandate driving on "the wrong side." The world market for pharmaceuticals is fragmented by the requirement that drugs must undergo separate approvals in each country.

- *Distribution channels.* Differences between the distribution systems of different countries are among the biggest barriers to global marketing strategies. Procter & Gamble must adapt its marketing, promotion, and distribution of toiletries and household products to take account of the fact that, in the US, a few chains account for a major share of its US sales; in southern Europe, most sales are through small, independent retailers; while in Japan, P&G must sell through a multi-tiered hierarchy of distributors.

- *Presence of lead countries.* Countries differ in their levels of sophistication and acceptance of innovation on a product-by-product basis. For consumer products Japan is the lead market; for computer hardware and software and fast food, the US is the lead market; for automobile technology and design, Europe tends to lead; for mobile telecommunications, Japan, Europe and South Korea share lead market status. These differences in market progressiveness encourage a sequential approach to global strategy in which products are introduced first in the lead market, followed by a global rollout. This sequential approach to competing internationally can increase the returns to a global strategy since it offers the opportunity to learn from experiences in the lead market then adapt products and marketing approaches to maximize their chances of success in subsequent country launches.

As a result, even the most ardent exponents of globalization must take account of local preferences and customs if they are to be internationally successful.

McDonald's Big Mac is a global, standardized product. But McDonald's also offers McChicken Korma Nan in Britain, CroquMcDo (a grilled ham and cheese sandwich) in France, teriyaki chicken burgers in Japan, noodles in Korea, cappuccino in Italy, and beer in Germany.[30] The key to successful globalization lies in ensuring uniformity in components and activities where important scale economies are present, while catering to cultural and language differences that do not impede scale efficiency. Thus, the 2001 Honda Accord is a global car, but one whose dimensions, accessories, trim, and paintwork are adapted to meet different national preferences. Ultimately, companies must find ways to reconcile the benefits of globalization with the need to address the specifics of local markets in terms of regulation, competition, distribution, and customer preferences – what Sony's former chairman described as "global localization."[31]

The Cultural Dimension

Adapting strategy to take account of different national environments is not simply about adapting to local market differences. Strategy – and the structures and systems through which it is implemented – needs to be consistent with national cultures. Many of the problems encountered in international expansion have arisen from replicating overseas strategies, structures and management approaches that were developed within the home country. Difficulties in recognizing and managing cultural differences represent one of the most complex and fragile areas of international management. The ongoing problems of Paris Disneyland, the troubled aftermath of the DaimlerChrysler merger, and the difficulties experienced by British retailer Marks & Spencer in Europe and North America are evidence that even experienced and highly sophisticated companies find cross-cultural management fraught with difficulty.

Adapting to differences in national cultures begins with recognition and analysis. Several attempts have been made to characterize and classify national cultures on the basis of a few key variables. Geert Hofstede has used two cultural dimensions: *individualist versus collectivist* and *egalitarian versus hierarchical*. Countries with high levels of both individualism and egalitarianism include the US and Australia. Countries with high levels of collectivism and acceptance of hierarchy include India, China, and Venezuela. Countries with high levels of both individualism and hierarchy include France and South Africa, while Costa Rica combines collectivism with egalitarianism.[32]

STRATEGY AND ORGANIZATION WITHIN THE MULTINATIONAL CORPORATION

The Evolution of Multinational Strategies and Structures

Balancing the benefits of globalization against those of adaptation to national market conditions is a central issue not only for the strategy of multinational firms but also for their organizational structures. As we have already observed, strategy and

FIGURE 14.7   The development of the multinational corporation: alternative parent–subsidiaries relations

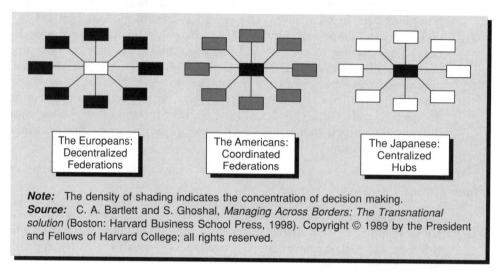

The Europeans:
Decentralized
Federations

The Americans:
Coordinated
Federations

The Japanese:
Centralized
Hubs

Note: The density of shading indicates the concentration of decision making.
Source: C. A. Bartlett and S. Ghoshal, *Managing Across Borders: The Transnational solution* (Boston: Harvard Business School Press, 1998). Copyright © 1989 by the President and Fellows of Harvard College; all rights reserved.

structure are not easily changed in the short or medium term and the strategy-structure configurations adopted by today's MNCs tend to reflect the choices made by the companies at the time of their international expansion. Because of their size and international spread, MNCs are likely to find fundamental changes in their organizational structure especially difficult: once an international distribution of func-tions, operations, and decision-making authority has been determined, reorganization can be difficult and costly, particularly when host governments become involved. Bartlett and Ghoshal emphasize that this "administrative heritage" of an MNC – its con-figuration of assets and capabilities, its distribution of managerial responsibilities, and its ongoing set of relationships – determine and constrain its ability to build new strategic capabilities.[33] The result is that early choices with regard to strategy and structure have a lasting impact on the development of organizational capability.

Hence, the starting point for analyzing the strategic challenges facing an MNC today is consideration of the circumstances and strategic choices that the company made during its initial phase of international expansion. Bartlett and Ghoshal identify three phases in the development of the MNC, each associated with different choices regard-ing the balance between globalization and national differentiation and between cen-tralization and decentralization. Figure 14.7 illustrates these three phases.

Pre-WWI: The Era of the European Multinationals

During the early decades of the twentieth century, European multinationals – companies such as Unilever, Royal Dutch/Shell, ICI, and Philips – were pioneers of multinational expansion. These companies are described by Bartlett and Ghoshal as *multinational federations*: each national subsidiary was accorded operational autonomy and parental control was limited to the appointment of senior managers to the subsidiaries, authorization of major capital expenditures, and receipt of dividends from subsidiaries. National subsidiaries typically undertook their own product development, manufacturing, and marketing.[34] The "hands-off" approach of the corporate head office to its overseas subsidiaries was a response to conditions at the time of internationalization: international transportation and communication were slow, costly, and unreliable, and national markets were highly differentiated.

Post-WWII: The Era of the American Multinationals

The emergence of the United States as the world's dominant industrial nation at the end of World War II was followed by the preeminence of US multinationals such as GM, Ford, IBM, Coca-Cola, Caterpillar, Gillette, and Procter & Gamble in their respective industries. Although the subsidiaries of these US multinationals typically operated with substantial independence in terms of product introduction, manufacturing, and marketing, the US parent companies occupied a dominant position within these groups. As a result, the US base acted as the source of capital, new product and process technology, and management capabilities. The primary competitive advantage of overseas national subsidiaries was their access to the resources and capabilities of their parents.

The 1970s and 1980s: The Japanese Challenge

During the 1970s, Japanese companies emerged as leading global players across a number of manufacturing industries, from steel and shipbuilding to automobiles and consumer electronics. A distinguishing feature of the Japanese multinationals was their pursuit of global strategies from centralized domestic bases. Companies like Honda, Toyota, Matsushita, and NEC concentrated R&D and manufacturing in Japan, while overseas subsidiaries were initially for sales, distribution, and customer support. By offering globally standardized products manufactured in large-scale plants, Japanese companies were able to exploit substantial scale and experience advantages. Over time, Japanese MNCs have dispersed their manufacturing and, in many cases, their R&D as well. However, most have retained a strong global integration.

Matching Global Strategies and Structures to Industry Conditions

Although global preeminence in manufacturing industries passed from European to American to Japanese companies between 1920 and 1980, it is not possible to point to any particular strategy/structure combination as uniquely successful for MNCs. The strength of European multinationals was their adaptation to the conditions and requirements of individual national markets. The strength of the US multinationals was their ability to transfer technology and proven new products from their domestic strongholds to their national subsidiaries. That of the Japanese global corporations was the efficiency advantages derived from global integration.

The relative merits of each configuration depend on market and competitive conditions – and hence the key success factors – in different industries. In semiconductors, electronics, and motorcycles, the importance of scale economies and the lack of national differences in customer requirements underscore the benefits of global strategies and structures. Where scale economies are more modest relative to the size of national markets and where national market differences are important – such as in processed foods, recorded music, beer, children's clothing, and furniture – responsiveness to national customer preferences takes precedence. In a number of industries, there are considerable benefits from global integration, and also the need to respond to differentiated national requirements. Capital- and technology-intensive products (such as telecommunications equipment, military hardware, and power-generating equipment) supplied to public authorities in different countries are typical examples. Strategy Capsule 14.1 shows how different strategy/structure configurations have had differential success in three different industry environments.

The Transnational Corporation

As I have observed in previous chapters, increasing international competition has meant that companies have had to exploit multiple sources of competitive advantage and develop both breadth and depth of organizational capability. For MNCs this has meant reconciling the advantages of global integration with those of national differentiation. Escalating costs of research and new product development have made global strategies with global product platforms a prerequisite for viability in many manufacturing and service markets. At the same time, the resilience of national market differences and the need for swift response to local circumstances has required greater decentralization. Accelerating technological change further exacerbates these contradictory forces: despite the cost and "critical mass" benefits of centralizing research and new product development, innovation occurs at multiple locations within the MNC and requires nurturing of creativity and initiative throughout the organization. A key tradeoff is the decentralization conducive to generating innovation, and the global centralization needed to efficiently exploit these innovations – the familiar *exploration versus exploitation* dilemma once again. Thus, Philips, with its decentralized, nationally responsive organization structure, was extremely successful in encouraging company-wide innovation. In its TV business, its Canadian subsidiary developed its first color TV, its Australian subsidiary developed its first stereo sound TV, and its British subsidiary developed teletext TVs. However, lack of global integration has constrained its ability successfully to exploit its innovation on a global scale. During the 1980s and 1990s, Philips was on the losing side of a number of key standards battles: its V2000 VCR system lost out to Matsushita's VHS system and its digital audio tape lost out to other digital recording formats.

Developing the organizational capability to pursue both responsiveness to national markets and global coordination simultaneously requires, according to Christopher Bartlett, "a very different kind of internal management process than existed in the relatively simple multinational or global organizations. This is the 'transnational organization.' "[35] The distinguishing characteristic of the *transnational* is that it becomes an integrated network of distributed and interdependent resources and

STRATEGY CAPSULE 14.1   Matching Multinational Strategy to Industry Characteristics

Consumer Electronics

During the 1980s, Matsushita was highly globally integrated, Philips was the most multinational in terms of international spread and responsiveness of national subsidiaries to local require- ments, whereas GE was primarily US-based and oriented toward the requirements of the North American market. During the 1980s, customer preferences for consumer electronic products were highly uniform across countries, and competitive advantage was strongly determined by the ability of companies to access global economies in product development and manufacturing, and coordinate the global marketing of new products and new models. By the end of the 1980s, Matsushita was the clear winner, Philips was still hanging on (despite dismal profitability), and GE had exited from the industry.

Branded, Packaged Consumer Goods

In branded, packaged consumer goods, national differences remained strong during the 1980s. Unilever, with its locally responsive multinational spread, and Procter & Gamble, despite its strong US and European bases, increased their global leadership. Meanwhile Kao, the lead- ing Japanese soaps and personal hygiene products supplier, largely failed in its attempts to penetrate international markets.

Telecommunications Equipment

In contrast to electronics and branded, packaged consumer goods, telecommunications equip- ment is subject to substantial global scale economies in R&D and manufacturing, *and* requires responsiveness to the specific requirements of national telecommunication companies. ITT, the most international of the major players, was increasingly unable to achieve the integra- tion necessary to leverage its global position. NEC, despite its technological capabilities and dominant position in Japan, has so far failed to develop a strong position in Europe or North America. One of the most successful companies has been Ericsson, which, despite its small domestic market, has effectively combined global integration with national responsiveness (see Figure 14.8).

FIGURE 14.8

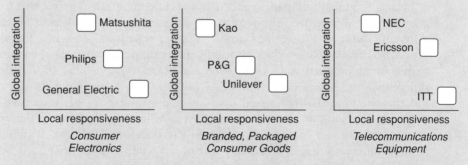

Sources: Adapted from C. A. Bartlett and S. Ghoshal, *Managing Across Borders: The Transnational Solution* (Boston: Harvard Business School Press, 1989) and S. Ghoshal, Presentation at IAFE, Castelgandolfo, 1990.

FIGURE 14.9 The transnational corporation

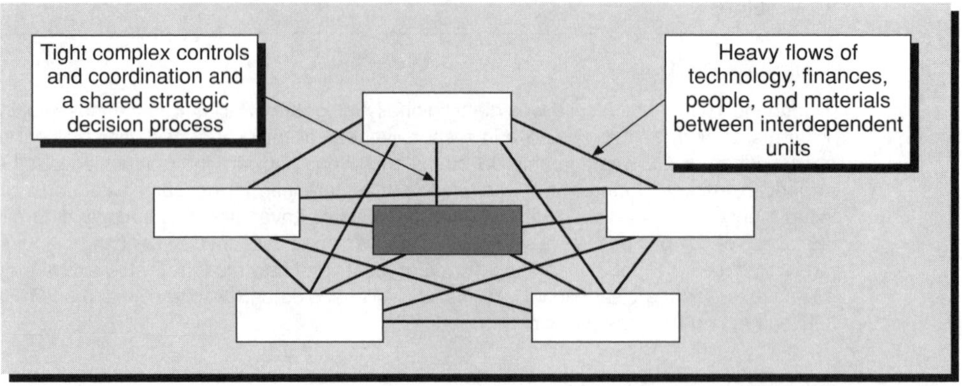

capabilities (see Figure 14.9). Features of the transnational corporation include the following:

- Each national unit is a source of ideas, skills, and capabilities that can be harnessed for the benefit of the total organization.

- National units achieve global scale economies by designating them the company's world source for a particular product, component, or activity.

- The center must establish a new, highly complex managing role that coordinates relationships among units but does so in a highly flexible way. The key is to focus less on managing activities directly and more on creating an organizational context that is conducive to the coordination and resolution of differences. Creating the right organizational context involves "establishing clear corporate objectives, developing managers with broadly based perspectives and relationships, and fostering supportive organizational norms and values."[36]

Balancing global integration and national differentiation requires that a company adapts to the differential requirements of different products, different functions, and different countries. Procter & Gamble adopts global standardization for some of its products (Pringles potato chips and high-end perfumes for example), while for others (hair coloring products and laundry detergent, for example) it allows significant national differentiation. Across countries, P&G organizes global product divisions to serve most of the industrialized world because of the similarities between their markets, while for emerging market countries (such as China and India) it operates through country subsidiaries in order to adapt to the distinctive features of these markets. Among functions, R&D is globally integrated while sales is organized by national units that are differentiated to meet local market characteristics.

The transnational form is more of a direction of development than a distinct organizational archetype. It represents a convergence of the different strategy configurations of MNCs. Thus, traditional "decentralized federations" such as Philips and Royal Dutch/Shell have reorganized to achieve greater integration within their far-flung empires of national subsidiaries, whereas Japanese global corporations such as Toyota and Matsushita are drastically reducing the role of their Japanese headquarters and increasing the roles of their national subsidiaries. Meanwhile, American multinationals such as Ford and GM are moving in two directions: while they reduce the role of their US bases they are simultaneously increasing integration among their different national subsidiaries.

A critical task for the top managers of MNCs is to establish structures and systems that allow local adaptation and initiative while maintaining the close linkages that diffuse innovations and best practices and integrate the knowledge generated in different locations. Where overseas subsidiaries have the autonomy and the leadership to take the initiative in product development and new investment proposals, they can make an important contribution to the competitive advantage of the MNC.[37] The distinctive capabilities that individual subsidiaries develop are likely to be strongly influenced by the national resources and markets within their host countries. Among multinational semiconductor companies, the development of capabilities reflects the international patterns of competitive advantage in customer industries – European subsidiaries have developed strong capabilities in integrated circuits for digital wireless communication, Japanese subsidiaries have developed strength in the microprocessors and memory chips required by the consumer electronics industry, US subsidiaries have been lead developers of computer chips. The implication is that the national subsidiaries of MNCs need to be assigned global mandates that are determined by the internal resources and capabilities that they possess and by the opportunities available in the country where they are based.

Firms need to establish the organizational structures and management systems that permit decentralization while creating the tight linkages to diffuse innovations and best practices and integrate the different types of knowledge generated in different locations.[38]

Strategy Capsule 14.2 discusses the move toward the integrated, global network form at Ford and Unilever.

STRATEGY CAPSULE 14.2   Building the Transnational Corporation: Unilever and Ford

---

Unilever

Unilever was formed in 1930 from the merger of the Dutch company Margarine Unie, and the British soap company Lever Brothers. Over the following seven decades, the company evolved through a process of trial and error into a global food, cleaning products, and toiletries group. A key aspect of this evolution was the changing relationship between the parent company and the national subsidiaries. During the 1940s and 1950s, each national subsidiary became locally managed with a high degree of autonomy. This decentralization was balanced by heavy investment in management education and development designed not only to train managers, but also to create a common culture. In 1955, the Four Acres management training center near London was opened. Unilever seeks the best and brightest university graduates who are

STRATEGY CAPSULE 14.2 (cont'd)

trained in groups of 25 to 30 for similar managerial positions. This shared experience creates an informal network of equals who continue to meet and exchange information and ideas across different companies and countries. Coherence and coordination is further enhanced by an extensive system of attachments whereby a manager is placed for a short or long period of time at the head office or in another subsidiary. These cross-postings help build managers' worldwide informal networks, and establish unity and a common sense of purpose across national cultures. Managers' personal networks are an important mechanism for the transfer of ideas.

Unilever is organized primarily on a geographical basis with subsidiaries in each country responsible for a particular business. Thus, in Britain, Lever Brothers Ltd supplies soaps and household detergents, Walls Ice Cream Ltd supplies ice cream, and Birds Eye Foods Ltd produces and distributes frozen foods. In addition there are worldwide product groups. Thus, food products are divided into five strategic groups: edible fats, ice cream, beverages, meals and meal components, and professional markets. The balance between centralized require-ments and local adaptability varies by function and product. Thus, in the food category there are *global fast foods* (hamburgers, fried chicken, soft drinks), *international foods* (Indian, Chinese, and Italian foods sold in many national markets), and *national foods* (steak and kidney pies in Britain).

According to CEO Floris Maljers, flexibility in a matrix organization is essential for it to operate as a transnational: "I like to use an analogy with a dance called the quadrille. This is an old-fashioned dance in which four people change places regularly. This is also how a good matrix should work, with sometimes the regional partner, sometimes the product partner, sometimes the functional partner, and sometimes the labor-relations partner taking the lead. Flexibility rather than hierarchy should always be a transnational's motto – today and in the future."

Ford

In 1970, Ford was an archetypal US multinational with a dominant North American core and more-or-less stand-alone subsidiaries in Britain, Germany, Australia, and elsewhere, each of which designed, manufactured, and marketed its own line of autos. For example, in Britain, Ford's most popular car was the British-made Cortina, in Germany it was the German-built Taunus.

The quest for scale economies in engineering and design and component manufacture encouraged increasing international integration. This began with the formation of Ford of Europe, and continued with the consolidation and integration of new product development and manu-facturing. Small car design was located primarily in Ford of Europe and in Mazda in Japan; large car design was centered in Dearborn. Ford's smallest car, the Festiva/Fiesta, is manufactured in South Korea and Spain; its Escort is manufactured in Michigan, Mexico, Britain, and Germany; the Mercury Capri is made in Australia. Similar global specialization occurred in engines and other major subassemblies.

Under chairman Alex Trotman, the Ford 2000 initiative aimed at greatly increasing the extent of international integration. The Mondeo/Contour was Ford's first serious attempt at developing a world car. The primary challenge of Ford 2000 was to develop global models of automobile faster and at a much lower cost than the $6 billion that the Mondeo/Contour had cost.

Sources: Floris A. Maljers, "Inside Unilever: The Evolving Transnational Company," *Harvard Business Review* (September–October 1992): 46–51; Maryann Keller, *Collision: GM, Toyota, Volkswagen and the Race to Own the 21st Century* (New York: Doubleday, 1993); Ford Motor Company Annual Reports.

SUMMARY

Moving from a national to an international business environment represents a quantum leap in complexity. In an international environment, a firm's potential for competitive advantage is determined, not just by its own resources and capabilities, but also by the conditions of the national environment in which it operates, including input prices, exchange rates, and a host of other factors. The extent to which a firm is positioned in a single market or multiple national markets also influences its competitive position.

Our approach in this chapter is to simplify the complexities of international strategy by applying the same basic tools of strategy analysis that we developed in earlier chapters. For example, in analyzing international expansion, the critical issue in determining whether a firm should enter an overseas market is an analysis of the profit implications of such an entry. This requires an analysis of (a) the attractiveness of the overseas market using the familiar tools of industry analysis; and (b) the potential of the firm to establish competitive advantage in that overseas market, which requires consideration of whether the firm can transfer its resources and capabilities from its home base to that overseas market, and whether these resources and capabilities can yield a competitive advantage in the same way as they did at home.

However, establishing the potential for a firm to create value from internationalization is only a beginning. Subsequent analysis needs to design an international strategy: Do we enter an overseas market by exporting, licensing, or direct investment? If the latter, should we set up a wholly owned subsidiary or a joint venture? Once the strategy has been established, then a suitable organizational structure needs to be designed.

The fact that so many companies that have been outstandingly successful in their home market have failed so miserably in their overseas expansion demonstrates the complexity of international management. In some cases, the companies have failed to recognize that the resources and capabilities that underpinned their competitive advantages in their home market could not be readily transferred or replicated in overseas markets. In others, the problems were in designing the structures and systems that could effectively implement the international strategy.

As the lessons of success and failure from international business become recognized and distilled into better theories and analytical frameworks, so we advance our understanding of how to design and implement strategies for competing globally. We are at the stage where we recognize the issues and the key determinants of competitive advantage in an international environment. However, there is much that we do not fully understand. Designing strategies and organizational structures that can reconcile critical tradeoffs between global scale economies versus local differentiation, decentralized learning and innovation versus worldwide diffusion and replication, and localized flexibilities versus international standardization remain key challenges for senior managers.

NOTES

[1] UNCTAD, *World Investment Report 2003* (New York: United Nations, 2003).

[2] GM, Ford, DaimlerChrysler, Honda, Toyota, Nissan, Suzuki, Mitsubishi, BMW, Fuji (Subaru), and Isuzu.

[3] Collusion in international industries is not unknown. During the 1930s, Standard Oil of New Jersey (now Exxon) and the Royal Dutch/Shell Group effectively regulated competition in the international oil industry. The world cigarette industry for much of the twentieth century was neatly divided between American Tobacco and the Imperial Tobacco Group of Britain. American Tobacco agreed not to compete within the former British Empire; Imperial agreed to keep outside the Americas, while exports to other countries were handled by a jointly owned subsidiary British American Tobacco (BAT). See M. Corina, *Trust in Tobacco* (London: Michael Joseph, 1975).

[4] A key finding was that *human capital* (knowledge and skills) was more important than *physical capital* in explaining the pattern of US trade – the so-called *Leontief Paradox*. See W. W. Leontief, "Domestic Production and Foreign Trade," in Richard Caves and H. Johnson (eds), *Readings in International Economics* (Homewood, IL: Irwin, 1968).

[5] L. C. Thurow, *Building Wealth: The New Rules for Individuals, Companies and Nations* (New York: HarperCollins, 1999).

[6] Paul Krugman, "Increasing Returns, Monopolistic Competition, and International Trade," *Journal of International Economics* 9 (November 1979): 469–79.

[7] Michael E. Porter, *The Competitive Advantage of Nations* (New York: Free Press, 1990).

[8] Porter's view differs sharply from those observers who point to the emergence of the "stateless corporation" (ABB's Percy Barnevik among them). Although the national market is comparatively unimportant to a number of MNCs (ABB, Nestlé, Royal Dutch/Shell Group, Philips, and Hoffman-La Roche) that is not to say that their capabilities, strategy, and management style are not influenced by their national home base. See "The Stateless Corporation," *Business Week* (May 14, 1990): 98–106.

[9] For a review of the Porter analysis, see Robert M. Grant, "Porter's *Competitive Advantage of Nations*: An Assessment," *Strategic Management Journal* 12 (1991): 535–48.

[10] Max Weber, *The Protestant Ethic and the Spirit of Capitalism* (London: Unwin University Books, 1930).

[11] P. Almeida, "Knowledge Sourcing by Foreign Multinationals: Patent Citation Analysis in the US Semiconductor Industry," *Strategic Management Journal* 17 (December 1996): 155–65.

[12] The linking of value-added chains to national comparative advantages is explained in B. Kogut, "Designing Global Strategies and Competitive Value-Added Chains," *Sloan Management Review* (Summer 1985): 15–38.

[13] "Nike: International Context," HBS Case Services Case 9-385-328 (Boston: Harvard Business School, 1985); and "Nike in China," HBS Case Services Case 9-386-037 (Boston: Harvard Business School, 1985).

[14] The role of firm-specific assets in explaining the multinational expansion is analyzed in Richard Caves, "International Corporations: The Industrial Economics of Foreign Investment," *Economica* 38 (1971): 1–27.

[15] The role of transactions cost is explained in D. J. Teece, "Transactions Cost Economics and Multinational Enterprise," *Journal of Economic Behavior and Organization* 7 (1986): 21–45. See also "Creatures of Imperfection," in "Multinationals: A Survey," *Economist* (March 27, 1993): 8–10.

[16] Kenichi Ohmae, *Triad Power: The Coming Shape of Global Competition* (New York: Free Press, 1985).

17 J. Peter Killing, "How to Make a Global Joint Venture Work," *Harvard Business Review* (May–June 1982): 120–7.

18 See Robert Reich and Eric Mankin, "Joint Ventures with Japan Give Away our Future," *Harvard Business Review* (March–April 1986).

19 "Xerox and Fuji Xerox," Case 9-391-156 (Boston: Harvard Business School, 1992).

20 Gary Hamel, Yves Doz, and C. K. Prahalad, "Collaborate with Your Competitors – and Win," *Harvard Business Review* (January–February 1989): 133–9.

21 Ibid.

22 Theodore Levitt, "The Globalization of Markets," *Harvard Business Review* (May–June 1983): 92–102.

23 G. S. Yip, *Total Global Strategy II* (Upper Saddle River, NJ: Prentice Hall, 2003); Charles Baden Fuller and John Stopford, "Globalization Frustrated," *Strategic Management Journal* 12 (1991): 493–507; "Rough and Tumble Industry," *Financial Times* (July 2, 1997): 13.

24 Paul Almeida, "Knowledge Sourcing by Foreign Multinationals: Patent Citation Analysis in the US Semiconductor Industry," *Strategic Management Journal* 17, Winter Special Issue (1996): 155–65. See McDonald's individual country web sites, e.g., www.mcdonalds.com (US), www.mcdonalds.co.uk (UK), www.mcdonalds.fr (France).

25 A. K. Gupta and P. Govindarajan, "Knowledge Flows within Multinational Corporations," *Strategic Management Journal* 21 (April 2000): 473–96; P. Almeida, J. Song, and R. M. Grant, "Are Firms Superior to Alliances and Markets? An Empirical Test of Cross-Border Knowledge Building," *Organization Science* 13 (March–April 2002): 147–61.

26 Gary Hamel and C. K. Prahalad, "Do You Really Have a Global Strategy?," *Harvard Business Review* (July–August 1985): 139–48.

27 R. C. Christopher, *Second to None: American Companies in Japan* (New York: Crown, 1986).

28 Kenichi Ohmae, *Triad Power: The Coming Shape of Global Competition* (New York: Free Press, 1985).

29 Charles Baden Fuller and John Stopford, "Globalization Frustrated," *Strategic Management Journal* 12 (1991): 493–507.

30 See McDonald's individual country web sites, e.g., www.mcdonals.com (US), www.mcdonalds.co.uk (UK), www.mcdonalds.fr (France).

31 A. Morita, "Global Localization," in *Genryn* (Tokyo: Sony, 1996): Chapter 8.

32 G. H. Hofstede, *Cultures and Organizations: Software of the Mind* (New York: McGraw-Hill, 1997).

33 Christopher A. Bartlett and Sumantra Ghoshal, *Managing Across Borders: The Transnational Solution*, 2nd edn (Boston: Harvard Business School Press, 1998).

34 Ibid.

35 Christopher Bartlett, "Building and Managing the Transnational: The New Organizational Challenge," in Michael E. Porter (ed.), *Competition in Global Industries* (Boston: Harvard Business School Press, 1986): 377.

36 Ibid.: 388.

37 J. Birkinshaw, N. Hood, and S. Jonsson, "Building Firm-specific Advantages in Multinational Corporations: The Role of Subsidiary Initiative," *Strategic Management Journal* 19 (1998): 221–42.

38 Jay R. Galbraith, *Designing the Global Corporation* (San Francisco: Jossey-Bass, 2000).

15

Diversification Strategy

Telephones, hotels, insurance – it's all the same. If you know the numbers inside out, you know the company inside out.
—Harold Sydney Geneen, Chairman of ITT, 1959–78, and instigator of 275 company takeovers

OUTLINE

INTRODUCTION AND OBJECTIVES

Deciding "What business are we in?" is the starting point of strategy and is fundamental to the firm's very identity. Many companies use mission statements to make this identity explicit. Xerox defines itself as "The Document Company," Eastman Kodak as a "picture company," while Shell is a "global group of energy and petrochemical companies."

A company's conceptualization of its business scope may change over time. Many companies have dramatically reduced their range of business interests. Hanson, the Anglo-American conglomerate, with businesses stretching from cigarettes and retailing to chemicals and coal, is now a supplier of building materials. Philips has pruned its business portfolio to emerge as a global supplier of electronics, lighting, and small appliances. Other companies have moved in the opposite direction. Microsoft began as a supplier of microcomputer operating software, expanded into application and networking software, and is now a broad-based supplier of computer software, information services, and entertainment systems. Other companies have totally transformed their businesses. Nokia, once a supplier of paper and rubber goods, emerged as the world's biggest manufacturer of mobile phones during the mid-1990s.

Corporate strategy decisions can be the basis on which a company transcends its industry life cycle and secures long-term growth and prosperity. Thus, PepsiCo broken out of the confines of cola drinks to become one of the world's most successful suppliers of drinks, snacks, and breakfast cereals, while developing then spinning off its restaurant business (Taco Bell, Pizza Hut, and Kentucky Fried Chicken). Over its 100-year history, 3M has maintained its vigor and prosperity through continually creating, acquiring, and divesting businesses.

Alternatively, misconceived corporate strategies can destroy jobs and shareholder value with frightening speed. AT&T's corporate strategy since the 1984 break-up of the Bell system has been an almost unmitigated disaster. Its expansion into computers, wireless communication, broadband, and cable TV was achieved through the acquisitions of NCR, McCaw Cellular, Media One, and TCI. These businesses were subsequently sold off – usually at a massive loss. In 1989, AT&T was America's 4th most valuable company; by 2003 it had fallen to 134th.

Our goal in this chapter is to establish the basis upon which companies can make corporate strategy decisions that create rather than destroy value. This goal is ambitious since at first glance, diversification decisions appear impossibly complex. Which is a better strategy for a soft drinks company: to be specialized like Coca-Cola, or diversified, like PepsiCo or Cadbury-Schweppes? How is it possible for Microsoft to weigh the advantages and disadvantages of entering the market for video games consoles?

In practice, we make these types of decision every day in our personal lives. If my car doesn't start in the morning, should I try to fix it myself or have it towed directly to the garage? There are two considerations. First, is repairing a car an attractive activity to undertake? If the garage charges $75 an hour, but I can earn $500 an hour consulting, then car repair is not attractive to me. Second, am I any good at car repair? If I am likely to take twice as long as a skilled mechanic, then I possess no competitive advantage in car repair.

Diversification decisions by firms involve the same two issues:

- How attractive is the industry to be entered?

- Can the firm establish a competitive advantage within the new industry?

These are the very same factors we identified in Chapter 1 (see Figure 1.3) as determining a firm's profit potential. Hence, no new analytic framework is needed for appraising diversification decisions: diversification may be justified either by the superior profit potential of the industry to be entered, or by the ability of the firm to create competitive advantage in the new industry. The first issue draws on the industry analysis developed in Chapter 3; the second draws on the analysis of competitive advantage developed in Chapters 5 and 7.

Our primary focus is on the latter question: under what conditions does operating multiple businesses assist a firm in gaining a competitive advantage in each? This leads into exploring linkages between different businesses within the diversified firm, what has often been referred to as "synergy."

By the time you have completed this chapter, you will be able to:

- Appreciate the factors that have influenced diversification in the past and the recent trend toward "refocusing."

- Identify the conditions under which diversification creates value for shareholders and, in particular, to evaluate the potential for sharing and transferring resources and capabilities within the diversified firm.

- Determine the relative merits of diversification and strategic alliances in exploiting the linkages between different businesses.

- Recognize the organizational and managerial issues to which diversification gives rise and why diversification so often fails to realize its anticipated benefits.

TRENDS IN DIVERSIFICATION OVER TIME

As a background to our analysis of diversification decisions, let's begin by examining the factors that have influenced diversification strategies in the past.

Post-War Diversification

In Chapter 13, we saw how the development of the modern corporation since the mid-nineteenth century had involved an expansion in their geographical, vertical, and

TABLE 15.1 Changes in the Diversification Strategies of the Fortune 500, 1949–74

	1949 (%)	1954 (%)	1959 (%)	1964 (%)	1969 (%)	1974 (%)
Single-business companies	42.0	34.1	22.8	21.5	14.8	14.4
Vertically integrated companies	12.8	12.2	12.5	14.0	12.3	12.4
Dominant-business companies	15.4	17.4	18.4	18.4	12.8	10.2
Related-business companies	25.7	31.6	38.6	37.3	41.4	42.3
Unrelated-business companies	4.1	4.7	7.3	8.7	18.7	20.7
	100.0	100.0	100.0	100.0	100.0	100.0

Note: Single-business companies have more than 95 percent of their sales within their main business. Vertically integrated companies have more than 70 percent of their sales in vertically related businesses. Dominant-business companies have between 70 and 95 percent of their sales within their main business. Related-business companies have more than 70 percent of their sales in businesses that are related to one another. Unrelated-business companies have less than 70 percent of their sales in related businesses.
Source: Richard P. Rumelt, "Diversification Strategy and Profitability," *Strategic Management Journal*, 3 (1982): 359–70. Reproduced by permission of John Wiley & Sons Limited.

product scope. During the period 1950 to 1980, diversification – the expansion of companies across different product markets – was an especially important source of corporate growth. Research at the Harvard Business School documented the diversification trend among large US corporations.[1] Over time, the number of single-business companies among the ranks of the Fortune 500 declined steadily, whereas the most diversified companies – both related business and unrelated business – increased in number (see Table 15.1). Similar trends occurred in Europe (see Table 15.2) and also in Japan.[2] The 1960s and 1970s saw the height of the diversification boom with a flurry of mergers and acquisitions between unrelated companies and the emergence of a new form of corporate entity – the conglomerate – represented in the US by ITT, Textron, and Allied-Signal, and in the UK by Hanson, Slater-Walker, and BTR.

Diversification during the 1960s and 1970s was a consequence of several factors. Chapter 13 pointed to the developments in management techniques and organizational forms that reduced the costs of internal administration compared to the transaction costs of markets. Foremost among these developments was the multidivisional structure, which allowed companies to add divisions without overloading corporate management. Infatuation with the "science of management" encouraged the view that chief executives no longer needed industry-specific experience and, so long as companies adopted suitable structures, systems, and decision making techniques, companies were unconstrained by industry boundaries. Professional managers could run widely diversified corporations through applying the common tools of financial controls, investment appraisal techniques, incentive systems, and techniques of business portfolio analysis.[3]

Corporate goals were also important. From the 1950s to the early 1980s, growth rather than profitability was the primary quest of large corporations. In the benign

TABLE 15.2 Changes in the Diversification Strategies of Large European
Companies, 1950–93

	1950 (%)	1960 (%)	1970 (%)	1983 (%)	1993 (%)
France					
Single business	45	35	20	24	20
Dominant business	18	22	27	11	15
Related business	31	36	41	53	52
Unrelated business	5	5	9	12	14
Germany					
Single business	37	27	27	18	13
Dominant business	22	24	15	17	8
Related business	31	38	38	40	48
Unrelated business	9	11	19	25	32
UK					
Single business	24	18	6	7	5
Dominant business	50	36	32	16	10
Related business	27	48	57	67	62
Unrelated business	–	–	6	11	24

Notes:
1. Some column totals do not equal 100 due to rounding.
2. The categorization of firms by strategies is consistent for each country over time, but is not consistent between countries.

Sources: R. Whittington, M. Mayer, and F. Curto, "Chandlerism in Post-war Europe: Strategic and Structural Change in France, Germany and the UK, 1950–1993," *Industrial and Corporate Change* 8 (1999): 519–50. Updating earlier research by data in D. Channon, *The Strategy and Structure of British Enterprise* (Cambridge: Harvard University Press, 1973) and G. Dyas and H. Thanheiser, *The Emerging European Enterprise* (London: Macmillan, 1976).

post-war economic environment, profits were easy and shareholders quiescent, encouraging many corporate CEOs to become rampant empire builders.

Post-1980s Refocusing

The early 1980s saw the beginnings of a sharp reversal in the trend toward diversification. Between 1980 and 1990, the average index of diversification for the Fortune 500 declined from 1.00 to 0.67.[4] Unprofitable "non-core" businesses were increasingly divested during the later 1980s, and a number of diversified companies fell prey to leveraged buyouts.[5] Despite the fact that acquisition activity was extremely heavy during the 1980s – some $1.3 trillion in assets were acquired, including 113 members of the Fortune 500 – only 4.5 percent of acquisitions during the 1980s represented unrelated diversification.[6] Moreover, acquisitions by the Fortune 500 were outnumbered by dispositions. Divesting of unrelated businesses was typically accompanied by restructuring around a small number of closely related businesses.[7]

This trend towards specialization is the result of three principal factors: management's emphasis on shareholder value rather than growth, increased turbulence in the business environment, and new ideas about corporate strategy and the nature of the firm.

Emphasis on Shareholder Value

The forces causing companies to narrow their corporate scope were reviewed in Chapter 13. In relation to product scope, the overwhelmingly important factor driving the retreat from diversification and the refocusing around core businesses was the reordering of corporate goals from growth to profitability. The new emphasis on profitability was the result of several factors. The economic downturns and interest-rate spikes of the mid-1970s, the early 1980s, and 1989–90 revealed the inadequate profitability of many large, diversified corporations. A second factor was increased pressure on incumbent management from shareholders and financial markets. Shareholder activism has been led by institutional shareholders, especially by pension funds such as California's Public Employees Retirement System. The result of such pressure has been to increase the influence of independent members of boards of directors and to unseat incumbent management. The increasing insecurity of top management positions is indicated by rising CEO turnover. During 2000, 39 of the top-200 US companies replaced their CEO (up from 23 in 1999). Ousted CEOs have included Douglas Ivester at Coca-Cola, Michael Hawley at Gillette, Durk Jager at Procter & Gamble, and Jacques Nasser at Ford.[8]

The surge in leveraged buyouts during the 1980s was a key ingredient in a more active market for corporate control. Where an incumbent management team had destroyed shareholder value, corporate raiders saw the opportunity to use debt financing to mount a takeover bid, and then to oust existing management in favor of a team that would embark on aggressive restructuring. Kohlberg Kravis Roberts' $25 billion takeover of the tobacco and food giant RJR Nabisco in 1989 demonstrated that even the largest US companies were not safe from acquisition.[9] The result was a rush by poorly performing corporate giants to restructure before leveraged buyout specialists did it for them. Leading the trend to spin off diversified businesses or even break up completely, have been ITT, AT&T, Tenneco and General Mills in the US, and Hanson, Philips, BTR, ICI, and Metallgesellschaft in Europe. Added incentive to divest non-core businesses was provided by the stock market – the "conglomerate premium" of the 1970s was replaced by a "conglomerate discount" – the market valuation of the whole was less than the sum of the parts.

Turbulence and Transaction Costs

In Chapter 13, we observed that the relative costs of organizing transactions within firms and across markets depend upon the conditions in the external environment. Administrative hierarchies are very efficient in processing routine transactions, but in turbulent conditions the pressure of decision making on top management results in stress, inefficiency and lags. In responding to dynamic market conditions, specialized companies are likely to be more agile than large diversified corporations where strategic changes and investment proposals require approval at divisional and corporate levels. The greater the speed of change in external markets, the greater the strains on the corporate planning and capital budgeting systems of diversified corporations. At the same time, external factor markets have become increasingly efficient. The tendency for some diversified companies to spin off their growth businesses has been influenced by the belief that these businesses could better exploit their growth opportunities by drawing directly on external markets for finance, human resources, and technology.

The refocusing trend is less evident in Asia and Latin America than in North America and Europe. In these regions, large conglomerates continue to dominate their national economies – Samsung and Hyundai in South Korea, Tata Group in India, Charoen Pokphand in Thailand, Swire Pacific and Hutchinson Whampoa in Hong Kong, Lippo in Indonesia, and Keppel Group in Singapore. One reason for the continued dominance of large conglomerates in emerging market countries may be higher transaction costs associated with less developed markets for finance, information, and labor that offer diversified companies advantages over their more specialized competitors.[10]

Trends in Management Thinking

New ideas about corporate strategy have also influenced patterns of corporate evolution. There is less confidence over the applicability of a common set of management principles and techniques to many different businesses, and greater emphasis on the role of resources and capabilities in building competitive advantage. This has encouraged firms to focus on their major strengths in resources and capabilities and avoid the risks of spreading themselves too thinly. If deploying core resources and capabilities requires diversification into new product markets, this has occured increasingly through collaborative arrangements with other companies rather than through internal diversification or outright acquisition.

This is not to imply that ideas concerning synergies from operating in multiple product markets are dead. Indeed, recent years have seen continuing interest in economies of scope and the transferability of resources and capabilities across industry boundaries. The major change is that strategic analysis has become much more precise about the circumstances in which diversification can create value from multi-business activity. Mere linkages between businesses are not enough: the key to creating value is the ability of the diversified firm to share resources and transfer capabilities more efficiently than alternative institutional arrangements, where the additional costs of management do not outweigh the value created. Figure 15.1 summarizes some of the key developments in diversification strategy over the past 40 years.

MOTIVES FOR DIVERSIFICATION

Diversification has been driven by three major goals: growth, risk reduction, and profitability. As we shall see, although growth and risk reduction have been prominent motives for diversification, they tend to be inconsistent with the creation of shareholder value.

FIGURE 15.1 Diversification: the evolution of management thinking and management practice

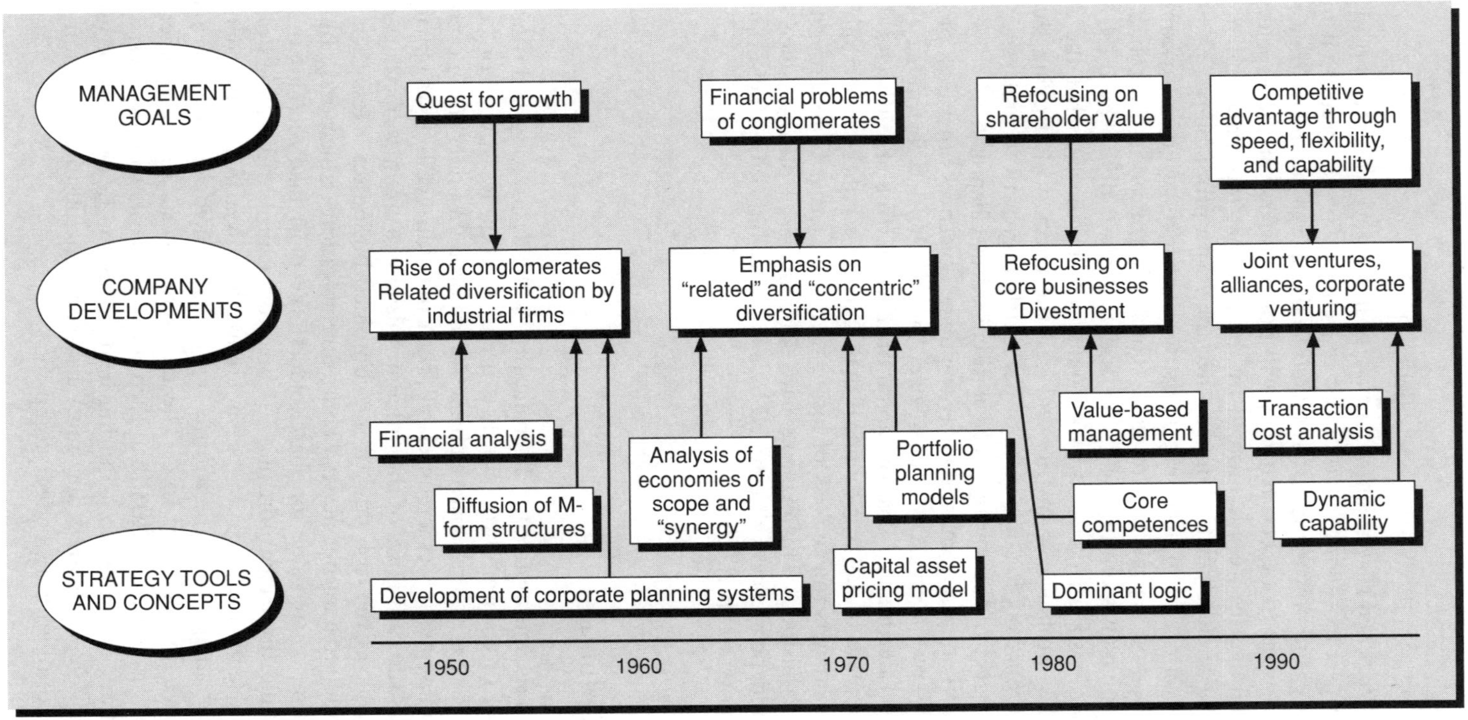

Growth

We noted that an important factor in the reversal of the postwar diversification trend was a reordering of corporate objectives. To the extent that managers' status, security, and power are closely linked to the size of enterprise they control, there are good reasons to expect that they will pursue *growth* at the expense of profitability. Such tendencies were reinforced by the fact that top management salaries are correlated more closely with company size than with profitability.

For firms in declining industries, managers' aversion to contraction makes diversification especially attractive. Thus, diversification by tobacco companies and oil companies during the 1970s and 1980s was driven by the fear of declining sales in domestic markets, and was undeterred by the fact that the diversification was into less profitable industries and had the effect of destroying shareholder value.[11] The propensity for managers to pursue their growth in preference to profitability is one aspect of the *agency problem* discussed in Chapter 6.

Top management's ability to pursue objectives other than profitability is constrained by two main factors. First, over the long term a firm must earn a return on capital greater than its cost of capital or it will not be able to raise the capital necessary to replace its assets. Second, if management sacrifices profitability for other objectives, managers run the risk of losing their jobs, either from a shareholders' revolt or from acquisition. This explains why companies sell off diversified businesses when their independence is threatened by a takeover bid or by a fall in profitability that attracts potential predators.[12]

Risk Reduction

A second motive for diversification is the desire to spread risks. To isolate the effects of diversification on risk it is useful to consider "pure" or "conglomerate" diversification, where separate businesses are brought under common ownership but, because these businesses are unrelated, their individual cash flows remain unchanged. So long as the cash flows of the different businesses are imperfectly correlated, then the variance of the cash flow of the combined businesses is less than the average of that of the separate businesses. Thus, diversification reduces risk. But does this risk reduction create value for shareholders? We must take account of the fact that investors hold diversified portfolios. If investors can hold diversified portfolios what possible advantage can there be in companies diversifying for them? The only possible advantage could be if firms can diversify at lower cost than individual investors. In fact the reverse is true: The transaction costs to shareholders of diversifying their portfolios are far less than the transaction costs to firms diversifying through acquisition. Not only do acquiring firms incur the heavy costs of using investment banks and legal advisers, they must also pay an acquisition premium in order to gain control of an independent company.

The *capital asset pricing model* (CAPM) formalizes this argument. The theory postulates that the risk that is relevant to determining the price of a security is not the overall risk (variance) of the security's return, but *systematic risk*: that part of the variance of the return that is correlated with overall market risk. Systematic risk is measured by the security's *beta coefficient*. Corporate diversification does not reduce systematic risk: if three separate companies are brought under common ownership, in the absence of any other changes, the beta coefficient of the combined company is simply the weighted average of the beta coefficients of the constituent companies. Hence, the simple act of bringing different businesses under common ownership does not create shareholder value through risk reduction.[13]

Empirical studies are generally supportive of the absence of shareholder benefit from diversification that simply combines independent businesses. Studies of conglomerates in the United States have shown that their risk-adjusted returns to shareholders are typically no better than those offered by mutual funds or by matched portfolios of specialized companies.[14] Another study found that unrelated diversification failed to lower either systematic or unsystematic risk, though moderate, closely related diversification did reduce both.[15]

Hence, so long as securities markets are efficient, diversification whose sole purpose is to spread risk will not benefit shareholders. However, risk spreading through diversification may benefit other stakeholders. If cyclicality in the firm's profits is accompanied by cyclicality in employment, then so long as employees are transferable between the separate businesses of the firm, there may be benefits to employees from diversification's ability to smooth output fluctuations. Managers appear to be especially enthusiastic about the risk-spreading benefits of diversification. Their risk adversity is motivated by their desire to protect their independence and their jobs. Downturns in profit, even if only temporary, can stimulate concern among shareholders and stock analysts. Downturns may make the company temporarily dependent on financial markets for borrowing and may encourage takeover bids.

Special issues arise once we consider the risk of bankruptcy. For a marginally profitable firm, diversification can help avoid cyclical fluctuations of profits that can push it into insolvency. It has been shown, however, that diversification that reduces the risk of bankruptcy is beneficial to the holders of corporate debt rather than to equity holders. The reduction in risk that bondholders derive from diversification is the *coinsurance effect*.[16] Managers and other employees are also likely to have strong interests in any strategy that reduces the risk of bankruptcy.

Are there circumstances where reductions in unsystematic risk can create shareholder value? If there are economies to the firm from financing investments internally rather than resorting to external capital markets, the stability in the firm's cash flow that results from diversification may reinforce independence from external capital markets. For Exxon Mobil, BP and the other major oil companies one of the benefits of extending across upstream (exploration and production), downstream (refining and marketing), and chemicals is that the negative correlation of the returns from these businesses increases the overall stability of the companies' cash flows. This in turn increases their capacity to undertake huge risky investments in offshore oil production, transcontinental pipelines, and natural gas liquefaction.

Profitability

If we return to the assumption that corporate strategy should be directed toward the interests of shareholders, what are the implications for diversification strategy? We have already revisited our two sources of superior profitability: industry attractiveness and competitive advantage. For firms contemplating diversification, Michael Porter proposes three "essential tests" to be applied in deciding whether diversification will truly create shareholder value:

1. *The attractiveness test.* The industries chosen for diversification must be structurally attractive or capable of being made attractive.

2. *The cost-of-entry test.* The cost of entry must not capitalize all the future profits.

3. *The better-off test.* Either the new unit must gain competitive advantage from its link with the corporation, or vice versa.[17]

The Attractiveness and Cost-of-entry Tests

A critical realization in Porter's "essential tests" is that industry attractiveness is insufficient on its own. Although diversification is a means by which the firm can access more attractive investment opportunities than are available in its own industry, it faces the problem of entering the new industry. The second test, *cost of entry*, recognizes that the attractiveness of an industry to a firm already established in an industry may be different from its attractiveness to a firm seeking to enter the industry. Industries such as pharmaceuticals, management consulting, or investment banking offer above-average profitability – but this occurs because they are protected by barriers to entry. Firms seeking to enter investment banking or pharmaceuticals have a choice. They may enter by acquiring an established player, in which case not only does the market price of the target firm reflect the superior profit prospects of the industry, but the diversifying firm must also offer an acquisition premium of around 25 to 50 percent over the market price to gain control.[18] Alternatively, entry may occur through establishing a new corporate venture. In this case, the diversifying firm must directly confront the barriers to entry protecting that industry. This typically involves high risk and low returns over a long period.[19]

The "Better-off" Test

Porter's third criterion for successful diversification – *the better-off test* – addresses the basic issue of competitive advantage: If two businesses producing different products are brought together under the ownership and control of a single enterprise, is there any reason why they should become any more profitable? Diversification has the potential to enhance the competitive advantage of the diversified business, the original core business, or both businesses. Combining the different businesses in separate, but related product areas can enhance the competitive advantages of the businesses of both the acquired company and the acquiree. For example:

- In acquiring Quaker Oats, PepsiCo believed that combining its FritoLay snack foods business with Quaker Oats' breakfast cereals and convenience foods businesses would exploit operating economies, enhance marketing capability, and offer greater distribution clout with supermarkets. Combining Pepsi's Pepsi-Cola and Tropicana drinks businesses with Quaker's Gatorade would offer economies in distribution as well as enhanced brand management.

- J.P. Morgan's acquisition of Bank One was intended to strengthen the competitive advantage of both. Morgan's investment banking activities would now have access to Bank One's retail network, while Bank One could gain business from Morgan's wealthy individual and corporate customers. In addition, combining corporate head offices would create substantial cost savings.

Yet, although the potential for value creation from exploiting linkages between the different businesses may be considerable, the practical difficulties of exploiting such opportunities have made diversification a corporate minefield. Let us examine the issues systematically.

COMPETITIVE ADVANTAGE FROM DIVERSIFICATION

If the primary source of value creation from diversification is exploiting linkages between different businesses, what are the linkages and how are they exploited? As we shall see, the primary means by which diversification creates competitive advantage is through the sharing of resources and capabilities across different businesses. Before addressing this issue, let us look first at the potential for diversification to enhance a firm's market power.

Market Power

The potential for diversification to enhance profitability by increasing a firm's market power has interested antitrust authorities in the United States and Europe for several decades. It has been claimed that large diversified companies can exercise market power through four mechanisms:

- *Predatory pricing.* Just as global corporations derive strength from their ability to finance competitive battles in individual markets through cross-subsidization, so multibusiness companies can use their size and diversity to discipline or even drive out specialized competitors in particular product markets through predatory pricing – cutting prices to below the level of rivals' costs. In December 2003, AOL France accused France Telecom of predatory pricing in ISP services through its subsidiary Wanadoo.[20]

- *Bundling.* A more direct way in which a diversified firm can extend its monopoly in one market into a related market is by bundling the two products together. The US Justice Department's case against Microsoft is that Microsoft abused its monopoly power in PC operating systems by bundling its Explorer web browser with Windows, thereby overcoming Netscape's initial leadership in this market.[21]

■ *Reciprocal buying.* A diversified company can leverage its market share across its businesses by reciprocal buying arrangements with customers. This means giving preference in purchasing to firms that become loyal customers for another of the conglomerate's businesses. Although reciprocal buying arrangements have been seen as a risk in several mergers,[22] the potential is greatest in those emerging market countries whose business sectors are dominated by a few large conglomerates.

■ *Mutual forbearance.* Corwin Edwards argued that:

> When one large conglomerate enterprise competes with another, the two are likely to encounter each other in a considerable number of markets. The multiplicity of their contacts may blunt the edge of their competition. A prospect of advantage in one market from vigorous competition may be weighed against the danger of retaliatory forays by the competitor in other markets. Each conglomerate may adopt a live-and-let-live policy designed to stabilize the whole structure of the competitive relationship.[23]

Through modeling *multimarket competition* among diversified firms, game theory has permitted more rigorous analysis of mutual forbearance. In repeated games involving players that meet in multiple markets, companies are likely to refrain from aggressive action in any one market for fear of triggering more generalized warfare.[24] Such behavior is most likely among companies that meet in multiple geographical markets for the same product or service – the airline industry, for example[25] – though such tendencies may also exist where diversified companies meet in multiple product markets.[26]

Economies of Scope

The most general argument concerning the benefits of diversification focuses on the presence of *economies of scope* in common resources:

> Economies of scope exist whenever there are cost savings from using a resource in multiple activities carried out in combination rather than carrying out those activities independently.[27]

Economies of scope exist for similar reasons as economies of scale. The key difference is that the economies of scale relate to cost economies from increasing the scale of production for a single product; economies of scope are cost economies from producing increasing output across multiple products. The nature of economies of scope varies between different types of resources and capabilities.

Tangible Resources

Tangible resources – such as distribution networks, information technology systems, sales forces, and research laboratories – offer economies of scope by eliminating duplication between businesses through creating a single shared facility. The greater the fixed costs of these items, the greater the associated economies of scope are likely to be. Entry by cable TV companies into telephone services, and telephone companies into cable TV, are motivated by the desire to spread the costs of networks and billing systems over as great a volume of business as possible. Since privatization, British Gas, a former monopoly supplier of gas, has diversified into supplying electricity, fixed-line telephone services, mobile telephone services, broadband internet connections, home security systems, home insurance, and home appliance repair.

Economies of scope also arise from the centralized provision of administrative and support services by the corporate center to the different businesses of the corporation. Among diversified companies, accounting, legal services, government relations, and information technology tend to be centralized – often through *shared service organizations* that supply common administrative and technical services to the operating businesses. Similar economies arise from centralizing research activities in a corporate R&D lab. In aerospace, the ability of leading US companies such as Boeing, Honeywell, and United Technologies to spread research expenditures over both military and civilian products has given these companies an advantage over overseas competitors with more limited access to large defense contracts.[28]

Economies of scope can also arise in finance. By combining an industrial company with a financial services company, General Electric lowers its cost of capital to both sides of the company.

Intangible Resources

Intangible resources such as brands, corporate reputation, and technology offer economies of scope primarily due to the ability to transfer them from one business area to another at low marginal cost.[29] When a company has built a strong brand reputation around a particular product, there is a strong incentive to introduce related products that can exploit the same brand equity. Starbucks has used its brand strength to introduce Starbucks ice creams, Starbucks Frappacino and DoubleShot bottle drinks, and Starbucks Barista home espresso machines.

Organizational Capabilities

Organizational capabilities can also be transferred within the diversified company. For example:

- LVMH is the world's biggest and most diversified supplier of branded luxury goods. Its distinctive capability is the management of luxury brands. This capability comprises market analysis, advertising, promotion, retail management, and quality assurance. These capabilities are deployed across Louis Vuitton (accessories and leather goods); Hennessey (cognac); Moet et Chandon, Dom Perignon, Verve Cliquot, and Krug (champagne); Celine, Givenchy, Kenzo, Dior, Guerlain, and Donna Karan (fashion clothing and perfumes); TAG Heuler and Chaumet (watches); Sephora and La Samaritaine (retailing); and some 25 other branded businesses.

■ Sharp Corporation – originally established to manufacture metal products and the Ever Sharp Pencil – developed capabilities in the miniaturization of electronic products that it has deployed to develop and introduce a stream of innovative products, beginning with the world's first transistor calculator (1964), the first LCD pocket calculator (1973), LCD color TVs, personal organizers (beginning with the ill-fated Apple Newton in 1993), internet view-cams, ultraportable notebook computers, and 3G mobile telephones.

Some of the most important capabilities in influencing the performance of diversified corporations are general management capabilities located at the corporate level. Consider the case of General Electric. In an era when conglomerates are being dismantled, GE has remarkably consistent financial performance. Although it possesses strong technological and operational capabilities at business level, its core capabilities lie at the corporate level. These include its ability to motivate and develop its managers, its outstanding strategic and financial management that reconciles decentralized decision making with strong centralized control, and its international management capability. Similar observations could be made about 3M. While 3M's capabilities in technical know-how, new product development, and international marketing reside within the individual businesses, it is the corporate management capabilities and the systems through which they are exercised that maintain, nourish, coordinate, and upgrade these competitive advantages.[30]

Economies from Internalizing Transactions

Although economies of scope provide cost savings from sharing and transferring resources and capabilities, does a firm have to diversify across these different businesses in order to exploit those economies? The answer is no. Economies of scope in resources and capabilities can be exploited simply by selling or licensing the use of the resource or capability to another company. In Chapter 11, we observed that a firm can exploit proprietary technology by licensing it to other firms. In Chapter 14, we noted how technology and trademarks are licensed across national frontiers as an alternative to direct investment. The same can be done to exploit resources across different industries. Harley-Davidson exploits its brand name across many products. However, it sticks to manufacturing motorcycles and licenses its brand name to the manufacturers of T-shirts, clothing, key rings, cigarettes, and studded leather underwear. Walt Disney exploits the enormous value of its trademarks, copyrights, and characters partly through diversification into theme parks, live theater, cruise ships, and hotels; and partly through licensing the use of these assets to producers of clothing, toys, music, comics, food, and drinks, as well as to the franchisees of Disney's retail stores. Disney's income from licensing fees and royalties was over $2 billion in 2003.

Even tangible resources can be shared across different businesses through market transactions. Airport and railroad station owners exploit economies of scope in their facilities not by diversifying into catering and retailing, but by leasing out space to specialist retailers and restaurants. Caterpillar exploits economies of scope in its parts distribution network not by diversifying into the supply of a wider range of parts, but by distributing parts for Chrysler, Hyundai, Hewlett-Packard, and Siemens.[31]

What determines whether economies of scope are better exploited internally within the firm through diversification, or externally through market contracts with independent companies? The key issue is relative efficiency: what are the transaction costs of market contracts, as compared with the costs of managing economies of scope within the diversified enterprise? Transaction costs include the costs involved in drafting, negotiating, monitoring, and enforcing a contract. The costs of internalization consist of the management costs of establishing and coordinating the diversified business.[32]

Let's return to the Walt Disney Company. Why does Disney choose to license Donald Duck trademarks to a manufacturer of orange juice rather than set up its own orange juice company? Why does it own and operate its own Disneyland and Disney World theme parks rather than license its trademarks to independent theme park companies? And why, in the case of Tokyo Disneyland, did it choose a licensing arrangement with the Oriental Land Company, which owns and operates Tokyo Disneyland?

These issues are complex. Much depends on the characteristics of the resource or capabilities. Though the returns to patents and brand names can often be appropriated efficiently through licensing, complex general management capabilities may be near impossible to exploit through market contracts. There is little scope for Sony to deploy its new product development capabilities other than within its own business. A similar situation occurs with Berkshire Hathaway and its skills in identifying attractive acquisition candidates then nurturing the management of these companies. The more deeply embedded a firm's capabilities within the management systems and the culture of the organization, the greater the likelihood that these capabilities can only be deployed internally within the firm. Even with simpler resources, market contracts may not be effective in protecting the value of the resources in question. Texaco chose to exploit its coal gasification technology internally by developing its own power-generation plants rather than license the technology, for fear that licensing would not adequately safeguard its proprietary interests.

The Diversified Firm as an Internal Market

We see that economies of scope on their own do not provide an adequate rationale for diversification – they must be supported by the presence of transaction costs. However, the presence of transaction costs in any nonspecialized resource can offer efficiency gains from diversification, even where no economies of scope are present.

Consider the case of financial capital. Where significant costs are incurred in using external capital markets (the margin between borrowing and lending rates, and the underwriting costs of issuing securities), diversified companies can benefit from lower costs of capital by building a balanced portfolio of cash-generating and cash-absorbing businesses. A central role of the corporate head office in diversified corporations is to allocate capital among the different businesses according to the profit prospects of the different investment opportunities. In this respect, the diversified corporation represents an internal capital market in which the different businesses compete for investment funds.

Some companies operate highly sophisticated internal financial markets. Since 1985, British Petroleum Finance International has managed the financing of BP's 50+ operating companies, undertaken standard accounting functions, traded in foreign exchange, managed leasing, and offered 24-hour trading in short-term instruments through offices in London, New York, and Melbourne.[33] Although internal capital markets are free from the myriad regulations that raise the costs of using external financial institutions,[34] in general, the internal capital markets of diversified firms have difficulty in emulating the efficiency associated with competitive, highly developed external capital markets.[35]

Efficiencies also arise from the ability of diversified companies to transfer employees – especially managers and technical specialists – between their divisions, and to rely less on hiring and firing. As companies develop and encounter new circumstances, so different management skills are required. The costs associated with hiring include advertising, the time spent in interviewing and selection, and the costs of "head-hunting" agencies. The costs of dismissing employees can be very high where severance payments must be offered. A diversified corporation has a pool of employees and can respond to the specific needs of any one business through transfer from elsewhere within the corporation. Not only are such internal transfers less costly than external transfers, they are also much less risky because of the superior information the firm possesses on internal job candidates. The broader set of opportunities available in the diversified corporation as a result of internal transfer may also result in attracting a higher caliber of employee. Graduating students compete intensely for entry-level positions with diversified corporations such as Matsushita, General Electric, Unilever, and Nestlé in the belief that these companies can offer richer career development than more specialized companies.

Information Advantages of the Diversified Corporation

An important benefit of internal capital and labor markets within the diversified corporation is that the corporate head office of the diversified corporation has better access to information than is available to external capital and labor markets. As a result, the diversified corporation may be more efficient in reallocating labor and capital among its divisions than are external capital and labor markets in allotting labor and capital among independent businesses. In the case of capital, these information advantages may be especially great for new ventures. Despite a well-developed market for venture capital in the United States and Europe, the risks associated with such ventures are compounded by the limited information available to potential lenders and investors. A diversified company such as 3M or Hewlett-Packard has full access to the information on performance and prospects for each of its business units.

These information advantages may be even greater in the case of labor. A key problem of hiring from the external labor market is not just cost but limited information. A resumé, references, and a day of interviews are a poor indicator of how an otherwise unknown person will perform in a specific job. The diversified firm that is engaged in transferring employees between business units and divisions has access to much more detailed information on the abilities, characteristics, and past performance of each of its employees. This informational advantage exists not only for individual employees but also for groups of individuals working together as teams. As a result, in diversifying into a new activity, the established firm is at an advantage over the new firm, which must assemble a team from scratch with poor information on individual capabilities and almost no information on how effective the group will be at working together. As a result, in an economy where new industries are constantly arising, there are reasons to expect that diversification by established firms offers some advantages over exploiting new opportunities compared with entirely new ventures.[36]

DIVERSIFICATION AND PERFORMANCE

We have established that diversification has the potential to create value for shareholders in certain circumstances: where it exploits economies of scope and where transaction costs in the markets for resources make it inefficient to exploit these economies of scope through market contracts. Diversification that seeks to reduce risk or achieve growth is likely to destroy shareholder value. How do these predictions work in practice?

The Findings of Empirical Research

Empirical research into diversification has concentrated on two major issues: first, how do diversified firms perform relative to specialized firms and, second, does related diversification outperform unrelated diversification?

The Performance of Diversified and Specialized Firms

To the extent that diversified companies face a wider range of investment opportunities and can readily shift resources from less attractive to more attractive industries, they should be able to achieve higher profitability and higher growth than specialized firms. On the other hand, the ability of specialized firms to focus on building excellence across a narrow range of capabilities may give them a competitive advantage over diversified companies.

Despite a large number of empirical studies over three decades, no consistent, systematic relationships have emerged between performance and the degree of diversification. However, there is some evidence that, beyond a certain point, high levels of diversification are associated with deteriorating profitability – possibly because of the problems of complexity that diversification creates. Among British companies, diversification was associated with increased profitability up to a point, after which further diversification was associated with declining profitability. Other studies have also detected a curvilinear relationship between diversification and profitability.[37] As with most studies seeking to link strategy to performance, a key problem is distinguishing *association* from *causation*. If diversified companies are generally more profitable than specialized firms, is it because diversification increases profitability or because profitable firms channel their cash flows into diversifying investments?

It is also likely that the performance effects of diversification depend on the mode of diversification. There is a mass of evidence pointing to the poor performance of mergers and acquisitions in general – for acquiring firms, the stock market returns to acquisition are unequivocally negative.[38] Among these, mergers and acquisitions involving companies in different industries appear to perform especially poorly.

Some of the most powerful evidence concerning the relationship between diversification and performance relates to the refocusing initiatives by a large number of North American and European companies. The evidence, ranging from conglomerates such as ITT and Hanson, to the oil majors, tobacco companies, and engineering companies such as Daimler-Benz, is that narrowing business scope leads to increased profitability and higher stock market valuation. Markides provides systematic evidence of the performance gains to diversified companies from divesting noncore activities.[39] This may reflect a changing relationship between diversification and profitability over time: the growing turbulence of the business environment may have increased the costs of managing complex, diversified corporations. As already noted, the stock market's verdict on diversification has certainly shifted over time with highly diversified firms having their earnings valued at a deficit rather than a premium to the overall market and takeover announcements being greeted by share price reductions for bidding firms.[40] As a result, diversified companies have fallen prey to leveraged buyout specialists seeking to add value through dismembering these companies.

Related and Unrelated Diversification

Given the importance of economies of scope in shared resources and capabilities, it seems likely that diversification into *related* industries should be more profitable than diversification into *unrelated* industries. Empirical research initially supported this prediction. Rumelt discovered that companies that diversified into businesses closely related to their core activities were significantly more profitable than those that pursued unrelated diversification.[41] By 1982, Tom Peters and Robert Waterman were able to conclude: "virtually every academic study has concluded that unchanneled diversification is a losing proposition."[42] This observation provided the basis for one of Peters and Waterman's "golden rules of excellence" – *Stick to the Knitting*.

Our principal finding is clear and simple. Organizations that do branch out but stick very close to their knitting outperform the others. The most successful are those diversified around a single skill, the coating and bonding technology at 3M for example. The second group in descending order, comprise those companies that branch out into related fields, the leap from electric power generation turbines to jet engines from GE for example. Least successful, as a general rule, are those companies that diversify into a wide variety of fields. Acquisitions especially among this group tend to wither on the vine.[43]

However, other evidence shattered this consistent picture. The apparent superiority of related diversifiers could be explained by the impact of risk and industry influences.[44] Some studies even found unrelated diversification to be more profitable than related.[45]

The lack of clear performance differences between related and unrelated diversification is troubling. Two factors may help explain the confused picture. First, related diversification may offer greater potential benefits, but may also pose more difficult management problems for companies such that the potential benefits are not realized. The issues concerning the management of the diversified corporation are addressed in Chapter 16. Suffice it to say at this point that economies of scope from sharing and transferring resources and capabilities among different businesses within the diversified corporation need to be managed and such management is not costless. Second, the distinction between "related" and "unrelated" diversification is confused in some studies. Relatedness refers to common resources and capabilities, not similarities of products and technologies. Thus, champagne and luggage are not obviously related industries: however, it is clear that LVMH has pursued closely related diversification. Let us consider this issue further.

The Meaning of Relatedness in Diversification

If relatedness refers to the potential for sharing and transferring resources and capabilities between businesses, there are no unambiguous criteria to determine whether two industries are related – it all depends upon the company undertaking the diversification. Empirical studies have defined relatedness in terms of similarities between industries in technologies and markets. These similarities emphasize relatedness at the *operational* level – in manufacturing, marketing, and distribution – typically activities where economies from resource sharing are small and achieving them is costly in management terms. Conversely, some of the most important sources of value creation within the diversified firm are the ability to apply common general management capabilities, strategic management systems, and resource allocation processes to different businesses. Such economies depend on the existence of *strategic* rather than *operational* commonalities among the different businesses within the diversified corporation.[46]

- Berkshire Hathaway is involved in insurance, candy stores, furniture, kitchen knives, jewelry, and footwear. Despite this diversity, all these businesses have been selected on the basis of their ability to benefit from the unique style of

TABLE 15.3 The Determinants of Strategic Relatedness between Businesses

CORPORATE MANAGEMENT TASKS	DETERMINANTS OF STRATEGIC SIMILARITY
Resource allocation	Similar sizes of capital investment projects Similar time spans of investment projects Similar sources of risk Similar general management skills required for business unit managers
Strategy formulation	Similar key success factors Similar stages of the industry life cycle Similar competitive positions occupied by each business within its industry
Performance management and control	Targets defined in terms of similar performance variables Similar time horizons for performance targets

Source: R. M. Grant, "On Dominant Logic, Relatedness, and the Link Between Diversity and Performance," *Strategic Management Journal*, 9 (1988): 641. Reproduced by permission of John Wiley & Sons Limited.

corporate management established by chairman Warren Buffett and CEO Charles Munger.

■ Richard Branson's Virgin Group covers a huge array of businesses from airlines to bridal stores. Yet, they share certain strategic similarities: almost all are startup companies that benefit from Branson's entrepreneurial zeal and expertise; almost all sell to final consumers and are in sectors that offer opportunities for innovative approaches to differentiation.

The essence of such strategic-level linkages is the ability to apply similar strategies, resource allocation procedures, and control systems across the different businesses within the corporate portfolio. Table 15.3 lists some of the strategic factors that determine similarities among businesses in relation to corporate management activities.[47]

Unlike operational relatedness, where the benefits of exploiting economies of scope in joint inputs are comparatively easy to forecast, and even to quantify, relatedness at the strategic level may be much more difficult to appraise.

Diversification decisions are determined more by perceived relatedness than by actual relatedness. Prahalad and Bettis use the term *dominant logic* to refer to managers' cognition of the rationale that links their different business activities.[48] Certainly, a dominant logic in the form of a common view within the company as to its identity and rationale is a critical precondition for effective integration across different businesses. (This issue is discussed further in Chapter 16.) There is a danger, however, that dominant logic may not be underpinned by any true economic synergies. In the same way that Allegis Corporation attempted to diversify around serving the needs of the traveler, so General Mills diversified into toys, fashion clothing, specialty retailing, and restaurants on the basis of "understanding the needs and wants of the homemaker."

SUMMARY

Diversification is like sex: its attractions are obvious, often irresistible. Yet, the experience is often disappointing. For top management it is a minefield. The diversification experiences of large corporations are littered with expensive mistakes: Exxon's attempt to build Exxon Office Systems as a rival to Xerox and IBM, Vivendi's diversification from water and environmental services into media, entertainment and telecoms, AT&T's entry into computers with its acquisition of NCR. Despite so many costly failures, the urge to diversify continues to captivate senior managers. Part of the problem is the divergence between managerial and shareholder goals. While diversification has offered meager rewards to shareholders, it is the fastest route to building vast corporate empires. A further problem is hubris. A company's success in one line of business tends to result in the top management team becoming overconfident of its ability to achieve similar success in other businesses.

Nevertheless, if companies are to survive and prosper over the long term they must change, and this change inevitably involves redefining the businesses in which the company operates. Hewlett-Packard and IBM are among the longest-established companies in the fast-paced US electronics industry. The success and longevity of both have been based on their ability to adapt their product lines to changing market opportunities. While HP has shifted from measuring instruments to computers and printers, to cameras and other imaging products, IBM has moved from typewriters to computers to consulting services. New entrepreneurial startups will typically pioneer the development of new industries, at the same time the sophisticated organizational capabilities of large, long-established corporations offer the potential for these companies to create value in other industries when their core businesses are in decline. The histories of 3M, Canon, Samsung, and Du Pont show that diversification is a central theme in the process by which large companies successfully evolve. In most examples of successful long-term evolution, diversification did not represent a discontinuity, it was typically a logical step in which existing resources and capabilities were deployed outside of the existing portfolio of businesses.

If companies are to use diversification as part of their long-term adaptation and avoid the many errors that corporate executives have made in the past, then better strategic analysis of diversification decisions is essential. The objectives of diversification need to be clear and explicit. Shareholder value creation has provided a demanding and illuminating criterion with which to appraise investment in new business opportunities. Rigorous analysis may also counter the tendency for diversification to be a diversion, a form of escapism resulting from the unwillingness of top management to come to terms with difficult competitive circumstances in the firm's core businesses.

The analytic tools at our disposal for evaluating diversification decisions have developed greatly in recent years. Twenty years ago, diversification decisions were based on vague concepts of synergy that involved the identification of linkages between different industries. More specific analysis of the nature and extent of economies of scope in resources and capabilities has given greater precision to our analysis of synergy. At the same time, we recognize that economies of scope are insufficient to ensure that diversification creates value. A critical issue is the optimal organizational form for exploiting these economies. The transaction costs of markets must be compared against the management costs of the diversified corporation. These management costs depend heavily on the top management capabilities and management systems of the particular company. This type of analysis has caused many companies to realize that economies of scope often can be exploited more efficiently and with less risk through collaborative relationships with other companies rather than through diversification.

NOTES

1   A. D. Chandler Jr., *Strategy and Structure: Chapters in the History of the Industrial Enterprise* (Cambridge, MA: MIT Press, 1962); L. Wrigley, "Divisional Autonomy and Diversification," doctoral dissertation (Boston, Harvard Business School, 1970); R. P. Rumelt, *Strategy, Structure and Economic Performance* (Cambridge, MA: Harvard University Press, 1974).

2   H. Itami, T. Kagono, H. Yoshihara, and S. Sakuma, "Diversification Strategies and Economic Performance," *Japanese Economic Studies* 11, no. 1 (1982): 78–110.

3   Michael Goold and Kathleen Luchs, "Why Diversify? Four Decades of Management Thinking," *Academy of Management Executive* 7, no. 3 (August 1993): 7–25.

4   G. F. Davis, K. A. Diekman, and C. F. Tinsley, "The Decline and Fall of the Conglomerate Firm in the 1980s: A Study in the De-Institutionalization of an Organizational Form" (Evanston, IL: Northwestern University, September 1993).

5   For a discussion of restructuring of diversified companies, see R. E. Hoskisson and M. A. Hitt, *Downscoping: How to Tame the Diversified Firm* (New York: Oxford University Press, 1994).

6   A. Shleifer and R. W. Vishny, "The Takeover Wave of the 1980s," *Science* 248 (July–September 1990): 747–9.

7   J. R. Williams, B. L. Paez, and L. Sanders, "Conglomerates Revisited," *Strategic Management Journal* 9 (1988): 403–14.

8   "The CEO Trap," *Business Week* (December 11, 2000): 44–9. The impact of CEO replacement is examined in Margarethe Wiersema, "Holes In the Top: Why CEO Firings Backfire," *Harvard Business Review* (December 2002): 98–109.

9   B. Burrough, *Barbarians at the Gate: The Fall of RJR Nabisco* (New York: Harper & Row, 1990).

10   T. Khanna and K. Palepu, "Why Focused Strategies May Be Wrong for Emerging Markets," *Harvard Business Review* (July–August 1997): 41–51; T. Khanna and K. Palepu, "The Right Way to Restructure Conglomerates in Emerging Markets," *Harvard Business Review* (July–August 1999): 47–57.

11   R. M. Grant and R. Cibin, "Strategy, Structure and Market Turbulence: The International Oil Majors, 1970–1991," *Scandinavian Journal of Management* 12, no. 2 (1996): 165–88.

12   David A. Ravenscraft and F. M. Scherer, "Divisional Selloff: A Hazard Analysis," in *Mergers, Selloffs and Economic Efficiency* (Washington, DC: Brookings Institute, 1987); and Michael E. Porter, "From Competitive Advantage to Corporate Strategy,"

Harvard Business Review (May–June 1987): 43–59.

13 These principles are outlined in any standard corporate finance text. See, for example, R. A. Brealey and S. Myers, *Principles of Corporate Finance*, 6th edn (McGraw-Hill, 2000): Chapter 8.

14 See, for example, H. Levy and M. Sarnat, "Diversification, Portfolio Analysis and the Uneasy Case for Conglomerate Mergers," *Journal of Finance* 25 (1970): 795–802; R. H. Mason and M. B. Goudzwaard, "Performance of Conglomerate Firms: A Portfolio Approach," *Journal of Finance* 31 (1976): 39–48; F. W. Melicher and D. F. Rush, "The Performance of Conglomerate Firms: Recent Risk and Return Experience," *Journal of Finance* 28 (1973): 381–8; J. F. Weston, K. V. Smith, and R. E. Shrieves, "Conglomerate Performance Using the Capital Asset Pricing Model," *Review of Economics and Statistics* 54 (1972): 357–63.

15 M. Lubatkin and S. Chetterjee, "Extending Modern Portfolio Theory into the Domain of Corporate Strategy: Does It Apply?," *Academy of Management Journal* 37 (1994): 109–36.

16 S. A. Ross and R. W. Westerfield, *Corporate Finance* (St. Louis: Times Mirror/Mosby College, 1988): 681.

17 Michael E. Porter, "From Competitive Advantage to Corporate Strategy," *Harvard Business Review* (May–June 1987): 46.

18 The history of diversification is littered with companies that overpaid in order to gain a position in a seemingly attractive industry. During the 1980s, the eagerness for movie studios resulted in Sony, Matsushita, and Viacom paying excessive acquisition prices for Columbia Pictures, MCA, and Paramount. During the 1990s, the commercial banks acquired investment banks at hugely inflated prices.

19 A study of 68 diversifying ventures by established companies found that, on average, breakeven was not attained until the seventh and eighth years of operation: R. Biggadike, "The Risky Business of

Diversification," *Harvard Business Review* (May–June 1979).

20 www.theregister.co.uk/content/22/3449.html.

21 "Plaintiffs Joint Proposed Findings of Fact – Revised," *US vs. Microsoft* Civil Action No. 98-1232 (TPJ) (www.usdoj.gov/atr/cases/3361_pdf-toc.htm).

22 See, for example, E. Blackstone, "Monopsony Power, Reciprocal Buying and Government Contracts: The General Dynamics Case," *Antitrust Bulletin* 17 (Summer 1972): 445–62.

23 US Senate, Subcommittee on Antitrust and Monopoly Hearings, *Economic Concentration*, Part 1, Congress, 1st session (1965): 45.

24 B. D. Bernheim and M. D. Whinston, "Multimarket Contact and Collusive Behavior," *Rand Journal of Economics* 2 (1990): 1–26.

25 In the US airline industry, extensive multimarket contact resulted in a reluctance to compete on routes dominated by one or other of the airlines. See J. A. C. Baum and H. J. Korn, "Competitive Dynamics of Interfirm Rivalry," *Academy of Management Review* 39 (1996): 255–91.

26 H. J. Korn and J. A. C. Baum, "Chance, Imitative and Strategic Antecedents to Multimarket Contact," *Academy of Management Journal* 42 (1999): 171–93.

27 The formal definition of economies of scope is in terms of "sub-additivity." Economies of scope exist in the production of goods $x_1, x_2, \ldots, x_n$, if $C(X) < \Sigma_i C_i(x_i)$

where: $X = \Sigma_i(x_i)$
$C(X)$ is the cost of producing all n goods within a single firm
$\Sigma_i C_i(x_i)$ is the cost of producing the goods in n specialized firms.

See W. J. Baumol, John C. Panzar, and Robert D. Willig, *Contestable Markets and the Theory of Industry Structure* (New York: Harcourt Brace Jovanovich, 1982): 71–2.

28 More generally, research intensity is strongly associated with diversification.

For the US, see C. H. Berry, *Corporate Growth and Diversification* (Princeton: Princeton University Press, 1975); for the UK, see Robert M. Grant, "Determinants of the Interindustry Pattern of Diversification by U.K. Manufacturing Companies," *Bulletin of Economic Research* 29 (1977): 84–95.

[29] Among service companies, the ability to transfer corporate reputation across different markets was found to be an important influence on the profitability of diversification. See P. R. Nayyar, "Performance Effects of Information Asymmetry and Economies of Scope in Diversified Service Firms," *Academy of Management Journal* 36 (1993): 28–57.

[30] The role of capabilities in diversification is discussed in C. C. Markides and P. J. Williamson, "Related Diversification, Core Competencies and Corporate Performance," *Strategic Management Journal* 15 (Special Issue, 1994): 149–65.

[31] "A Moving Story of Spare Parts," *Financial Times* (August 29, 1997): 7.

[32] This issue is examined more fully in David Teece, "Towards an Economic Theory of the Multiproduct Firm," *Journal of Economic Behavior and Organization* 3 (1982): 39–63.

[33] "Inside the New In-House Banks," *Euromoney* (February 1986): 24–34.

[34] Robert K. Ankrom, "The Corporate Bank," *Sloan Management Review* (Winter 1994): 63–72.

[35] Julia P. Liebeskind, "Internal Capital Markets: Benefits, Costs and Organizational Arrangements," *Organization Science* 11 (2000): 58–76.

[36] A. A. Alchian and H. Demsetz, "Production, Information Costs, and Economic Organization," *American Economic Review* 62 (1972): 777–95, argue that the collection and processing of information is the basic role of management and provides the primary rationale for the existence of the firm.

[37] R. M. Grant, A. P. Jammine, and H. Thomas, "Diversity, Diversification and Performance in British Manufacturing Industry," *Academy of Management Journal* 31 (1988): 771–801; L. E. Palich, L. B. Cardinal, and C. C. Miller, "Curvilinearity in the Diversification-Performance Linkage: An Examination of over Three Decades of Research," *Strategic Management Journal* 22 (2000): 155–74.

[38] G. Andrade, M. Mitchell, and Erik Stafford, "New Evidence and Perspectives on Mergers," *Journal of Economic Perspectives* 5, no. 3 (2001): 103–120.

[39] C. C. Markides, "Consequences of Corporate Refocusing: Ex Ante Evidence," *Academy of Management Journal* 35 (1992): 398–412; C. C. Markides, "Diversification, Restructuring and Economic Performance," *Strategic Management Journal* 16 (1995): 101–18.

[40] G. A. Jarrell, J. A. Brickly, and J. M. Netter, "The Market for Corporate Control: Empirical Evidence Since 1980," *Journal of Economic Perspectives* 2, no. 1 (Winter 1988): 49–68.

[41] R. P. Rumelt, *Strategy, Structure and Economic Performance* (Cambridge, MA: Harvard University Press, 1974).

[42] Tom Peters and Robert Waterman, *In Search of Excellence* (New York: Harper & Row, 1982): 294.

[43] Ibid.

[44] H. K. Christensen and C. A. Montgomery, "Corporate Economic Performance: Diversification Strategy versus Market Structure," *Strategic Management Journal* 2 (1981): 327–43; R. A. Bettis, "Performance Differences in Related and Unrelated Diversified Firms," *Strategic Management Journal* 2 (1981): 379–83.

[45] See, for example, A. Michel and I. Shaked, "Does Business Diversification Affect Performance?," *Financial Management* 13, no. 4 (1984): 18–24; G. A. Luffman and R. Reed, *The Strategy and Performance of British Industry, 1970–80* (London: Macmillan, 1984).

[46] For a discussion of relatedness in diversification, see J. Robins and M. F. Wiersema, "A Resource-Based Approach to the Multibusiness Firm: Empirical Analysis of Portfolio Interrelationships and Corporate

Financial Performance," *Strategic Management Journal* 16 (1995): 277–300; and J. Robins and M. F. Wiersema, "Measurement of Related Diversification: Are the Measures Valid for the Concepts?," discussion paper (Graduate School of Management, Irvine, CA: University of California, November 1997).

47 For a discussion of the role of strategic linkages between businesses in affecting the success of diversification, see Robert M. Grant, "On Dominant Logic, Relatedness, and the Link Between Diversity and Performance," *Strategic Management Journal* 9 (1988): 639–42.

48 C. K. Prahalad and R. A. Bettis, "The Dominant Logic: A New Linkage Between Diversity and Performance," *Strategic Management Journal* 7 (1986): 485–502.

16

Managing the Multibusiness Corporation

Some have argued that single-product businesses have a focus that gives them an advantage over multibusiness companies like our own – and perhaps they would have, but only if we neglect our own overriding advantage: the ability to share the ideas that are the result of wide and rich input from a multitude of global sources.

GE businesses share technology, design, compensation and personnel evaluation systems, manufacturing practices, and customer and country knowledge. Gas Turbines shares manufacturing technology with Aircraft Engines; Motors and Transportation Systems work together on new propulsion systems; Lighting and Medical Systems collaborate to improve x-ray tube processes; and GE Capital provides innovative financing packages that help all our businesses around the globe. Supporting all this is a management system that fosters and rewards this sharing and teamwork, and, increasingly, a culture that makes it reflexive and natural at every level and corner of our Company.

—**Jack Welch, Chairman, General Electric Company, 1981–2001**

Outline

- Introduction and Objectives
- The Structure of the Multibusiness Company
  The Theory of the M-Form Corporation
  The Divisionalized Firm in Practice
- The Role of Corporate Management

- Managing the Corporate Portfolio
    - GE and the Development of Strategic Planning Techniques
    - Portfolio Planning: The GE/McKinsey Matrix
    - Portfolio Planning: BCG's Growth-Share Matrix
    - Value Creation Through Corporate Restructuring
- Managing Individual Businesses
    - Business Strategy Formulation
    - Performance Control and the Budgeting Process
    - Strategic Management Styles
    - Using PIMS in Strategy Formulation and Performance Appraisal
- Managing Internal Linkages
    - Common Corporate Services
    - Business Linkages and Porter's Corporate Strategy Types
    - The Corporate Role in Managing Linkages
- Recent Trends in the Management of Multibusiness Corporations
    - Corporate Managers as Drivers of Organizational Change
- Summary
- Notes

Introduction and Objectives

In the last chapter, we argued that the case for diversification rests ultimately on the ability of the diversified corporation to exploit sources of value from operating across multiple businesses more effectively than can specialized firms linked by markets. Chapters 13 and 14 arrived at the same conclusion in relation to vertical integration and multinational operations. Hence, multibusiness companies[1] – whether vertically integrated, multinational, or diversified across multiple products – face two critical issues. First, can value be created through the relationships between businesses that span different activities or different markets? Second, how should a company be structured and managed to exploit these sources of value? Chapters 13, 14, and 15 addressed the first question in relation to vertical, multinational, and multiproduct scope. This chapter addresses the second question.

Multibusiness corporations face the challenge of managing multiple activities in multiple markets. Their common characteristic is that they are *multidivisional*: they comprise a number of divisions or subsidiaries, and these divisions and subsidiaries are typically divided into a number of separate business units. The separate parts of the company are coordinated and controlled by a corporate headquarters. Our emphasis here is on the organizational structures, management systems, and leadership styles through which strategy is *formulated* and *implemented* within these multibusiness companies. As we will see, corporate strategy is not simply a matter of answering the question: "What businesses should we be in?" Some of the most difficult issues of corporate strategy pertain to the roles and activities of the corporate head office and the relationships between the businesses and the corporate center. We are concerned with five main areas of corporate-level strategic management:

1. The composition of the company's portfolio of businesses (decisions about diversification, acquisition, and divestment).

2. Resource allocation among the company's different businesses.

3. The role of head office in the formulation of business unit strategies.

4. Controlling business unit performance.

5. Coordinating business units and creating overall cohesiveness and direction for the company.

By the time you have completed this chapter you will be able to:

- Recognize the central issues of formulating and implementing corporate strategy.

- Deploy the concepts and techniques necessary for making judgments about these issues.

- Recommend an appropriate organization structure, management system, and leadership style for a multibusiness corporation.

THE STRUCTURE OF THE MULTIBUSINESS COMPANY

Chapter 1 introduced the distinction between business strategy and corporate strategy and observed that, within the multibusiness company, corporate management takes primary responsibility for corporate strategy, and divisional management takes primary responsibility for business strategy. This corporate/divisional distinction is the basis feature of the multibusiness corporation. Whether we are referring to a multiproduct company (such as Viacom), a multinational company (such as SABMiller), or a vertically integrated corporation (such as Alcoa), almost all multibusiness companies are organized as multidivisional structures where business decisions are located at the business level and the corporate center exercises overall coordination and control. As we noted in Chapter 6, the emergence of the multidivisional structure during the early twentieth century was one of the key innovations in the history of management since it facilitated the development of the large diversified, multi-national corporations.

The allocation of decision making between corporate and divisional levels has shifted over time. The initial rationale for the multidivisional firm was the separation of strategic and operational decision making. During recent decades, more strategic decision making has been devolved to the divisional and business unit levels, while corporate headquarters have taken responsibility for corporate strategy and the management of overall corporate performance. Our primary focus is to analyze and understand the role of the corporate center in managing the multibusiness company.

The Theory of the M-form Corporation

Once Alfred Chandler had documented the origin and diffusion of the multi-divisional form, it was left to Oliver Williamson to theorize about its efficiency advantages.[2] Williamson identified four key features of the divisionalized firm (or, in his terminology, the *M-form*) that are the basis of its superiority as an organizational form:

1. *Adaptation to bounded rationality.* Managers are limited in their cognitive, information-processing, and decision-making capabilities. Thus, the top management team cannot be responsible for all coordination and decision making within a complex organization, and the multidivisional corporation permits management responsibilities to be decentralized.

2. *Allocation of decision making.* Decision-making responsibilities should be separated according to the frequency with which different types of decisions are made. Thus, decisions that are made with high frequency (e.g., operating decisions) need to be separated from decisions that are made infrequently (e.g., strategic decisions).

3. *Minimizing coordination costs.* In the functional organization, decisions concerning a particular product or business area must pass up to the top of the company where all the relevant information and expertise can be brought to bear. In the divisionalized firm, so long as close coordination between different business areas is not necessary, most decisions concerning a particular business can be made at the divisional level. This eases the information and decision-making burden on top management.

4. *Global rather than local optimization.* In functional organizations, senior managers tend to emphasize functional goals over those of the organization as a whole. In multidivisional companies, divisional heads, as general managers, are more likely to identify with the performance goals of the company as a whole.

These features result in the multidivisional firm offering possible solutions to two key problems of the large, managerially controlled corporation:

- *Allocation of resources.* Resource allocation within any administrative structure is a political process in which power, status, and influence can triumph over purely commercial considerations.[3] To the extent that the multidivisional company can create a competitive internal capital market in which capital is allocated according to financial and strategic criteria, it can avoid much of the politicization inherent in purely hierarchical systems. The multidivisional company can achieve this through operating an internal capital market where budgets are linked to past and projected divisional profitability, and individual projects are subject to a standardized appraisal and approval process. The efficiency of this process is enhanced by the extent and quality of information that is available within the divisionalized company.

- *Resolution of agency problems.* A second shortcoming of the modern corporation is the tendency for salaried top managers to pursue personal goals that conflict with the wealth-maximizing goals of owners. To the extent that the multibusiness, multidivisional company places a layer of corporate management between the shareholders and operating management, this organizational form might be expected to exacerbate the agency problem. However, Williamson argues to the contrary that, given the limited power of shareholders to discipline and replace managers, and the tendency for top management to dominate the board of directors, the multidivisional form may act as a partial remedy to the agency problem. The rationale is as follows: The corporate management of the multidivisional company acts as an interface between the stockholders and the divisional managers and can ensure adherence to profit goals. Because divisions and business units are typically profit centers, financial performance can readily be monitored by the head office, and divisional managers can be held responsible for performance failures. The multidivisional corporation thus creates the discipline of the capital market within the diversified corporation. So long as corporate management is focused on shareholder goals, the informational and control advantages of the multidivisional company can provide a particularly powerful system for enforcing profit maximization at the divisional level. The key tools are corporate management's ability to allocate funds, threaten divestiture, and reward or fire divisional presidents. General Electric under Jack Welch, Hanson under Lord Hanson, Emerson Electric under Charles Knight, and British Petroleum under John Browne are all companies where the multidivisional structure proved to be highly effective in imposing a strong profit motivation among business-level managers.

Oliver Williamson explains these merits of the multidivisional corporation as follows:

> The M-form conglomerate can be thought of as substituting an administrative interface between an operating division and the stockholders where a market interface had existed previously. Subject to the condition that the conglomerate does not diversify to excess, in the sense that it cannot competently evaluate and allocate funds among the diverse activities in which it is engaged, the substitution of internal organization can have beneficial effects in goal pursuit, monitoring, staffing, and resource allocation respects. The

goal-pursuit advantage is that which accrues to M-form organizations in general: since the general management of an M-form conglomerate is disengaged from operating matters, a presumption that the general office favors profits over functional goals is warranted. Relatedly, the general office can be regarded as an agent of the stockholders whose purpose is to monitor the operations of the constituent parts. Monitoring benefits are realized in the degree to which internal monitors enjoy advantages over external monitors in access to information – which they arguably do. The differential ease with which the general office can change managers and reassign duties where performance failures or distortions are detected is responsible for the staffing advantage. Resource allocation benefits are realized because cash flows no longer return automatically to their origins but instead revert to the center, thereafter to be allocated among competing uses in accordance with prospective yields.[4]

The assumption that the corporate management of diversified, multidivisional companies is better able to allocate capital efficiently and more likely to operate their companies in the interests of shareholders is not wholly consistent with the evidence. Some of the most notorious examples of chief executives operating their companies as personal fiefdoms are found among diversified, divisionalized corporations. Armand Hammer at Occidental Petroleum, Russ Johnson at RJR Nabisco, Howard Hughes at Hughes Corporation, and Jean-Marie Messier at Vivendi Universal all pursued empire building at the expense of shareholder return.[5] Corporate executives of diversified companies may be less emotionally committed to particular businesses, but this does not necessarily mean that they are more predisposed to shareholder return than to Napoleonic personal grandeur.

The proposition that the multidivisional structure is more efficient for the management of diversified firms has been tested in a number of studies. Most studies have found that among diversified firms, those with multidivisional structures have outperformed both looser holding companies and more centralized unitary forms.[6]

The Divisionalized Firm in Practice

Despite the theoretical arguments in favor of the divisionalized corporation and empirical evidence of its efficacy, close observation reveals that its reconciling the benefits of decentralization with those of coordination Is an ongoing problem for multibusiness companies. Henry Mintzberg points to two important rigidities of divisional structures that limit decentralization and divisional adaptability:[7]

- *Constraints on decentralization.* Although operational authority in the M-form firm is dispersed to the divisional level, the individual divisions often feature highly centralized power that is partly a reflection of the divisional president's personal accountability to the head office. In addition, the operational freedom of the divisional management exists only so long as the corporate head office is satisfied with divisional performance. Monthly financial reviews typically mean that variances in divisional performance precipitate speedy corporate intervention.

- *Standardization of divisional management.* In principle, the divisional form permits divisional management to be differentiated by their business needs.

In practice, there are powerful forces for standardization across divisions through common control systems, common management development processes, common corporate culture, and the tendency of the corporate center to promote similar types of managers to top divisional positions. The imposition by Exxon of its standard financial control systems and hierarchical culture on its entrepreneurial IT subsidiary, Exxon Office Systems, was a key factor in the venture's eventual failure. The problems of coexisting with different internal cultures and management systems also arise from mergers and acquisitions. Daimler Benz's merger with Chrysler and American Express's acquisition of Shearson and Lehman point to the difficulties of reconciling conflicting corporate cultures.

THE ROLE OF CORPORATE MANAGEMENT

How does the corporate center manage value creation? The multibusiness corporation brings together a number of separate businesses that are placed under the control of a corporate headquarters. If this arrangement is to add value, then the additional profits generated within the different businesses must exceed the costs of the corporate headquarters. To explore the potential for corporate management to add value, we must consider the role and functions of corporate managers. Clearly, the corporate center is responsible for formulating corporate strategy, which includes decisions concerning diversification, international expansion, acquisition, divestment, and the allocation of resources between businesses.

However, the functions and responsibilities of corporate management extend much further. In addition to defining and shaping the business portfolio, corporate managers have administrative and leadership roles with regard to implementing corporate strategy, participating in divisional strategy formulation, coordinating the different divisions, and fostering overall cohesion, identity, and direction within the company. These functions extend beyond what is normally thought of as "corporate strategy." For this reason, Goold, Campbell, and Alexander refer to the role of the corporate headquarters in the multibusiness company as "corporate parenting."[8]

If the purpose of corporate management in the multibusiness company is to add value to the businesses it manages, there are three main areas where this can occur:

- Managing the corporate portfolio, including acquisitions, divestments, and resource allocation.

- Exercising guidance and control over individual businesses, including influencing business strategy formulation and managing financial performance.

- Managing linkages among businesses by sharing and transferring resources and capabilities.

Let us consider each of these corporate management activities and establish the conditions under which they can create value.

MANAGING THE CORPORATE PORTFOLIO

The fundamental question we posed in Chapter 1 in order to identify corporate strategy was: "What business are we in?" This question points us directly to the composition and balance of a company's portfolio of businesses. The key issues are extensions of the portfolio (acquisitions, mergers, new ventures, and market entries), deletions from the portfolio (divestments), and changes in the balance of the portfolio through the allocation and reallocation of capital expenditures and other resources. While additions to and deletions from the corporate portfolio are typically major but infrequent strategic decisions, resource allocation among businesses is an ongoing strategic responsibility of corporate management. Although the resource allocation process focuses on capital budgeting, the assignment and transfer of senior divisional managers are also vital corporate management activities, as is reassignment of responsibilities and "strategic mandates" between business units. These portfolio management roles of the corporate center have been closely associated in the strategic management literature with the development and deployment of *portfolio planning models* and, more recently, with restructuring strategies based on shareholder value analysis. Let's consider both these sets of tools.

GE and the Development of Strategic Planning Techniques

The development of portfolio planning techniques for multibusiness corporations is closely associated with General Electric. Indeed, General Electric has been a leading source of corporate strategy concepts and innovations and a pioneer of corporate management techniques. GE has been among the top five members of *Fortune* magazine's "America's Most Admired Corporations" since the listings began. Peer admiration for GE is linked primarily to its highly effective and constantly evolving system of corporate management. As one executive remarked, "When Japanese managers come to visit us, they don't ask to see our research centers or manufacturing facilities. All they want to know is about our management system."[9]

At the end of the 1960s, GE comprised 46 divisions and over 190 businesses. In response to the challenges of managing this sprawling industrial empire, GE launched a series of initiatives aimed at developing a more effective system of corporate planning backed by better analytic techniques. Working with the Boston Consulting Group, McKinsey & Co., Arthur D. Little, and the Harvard Business School, GE spawned three innovations that were to transform the corporate strategy formulation in multibusiness companies:

- *Portfolio planning models* – two-dimensional, matrix-based frameworks to evaluate business unit performance, formulate business unit strategies, and assess the overall balance of the corporate portfolio.
- *The strategic business unit (SBU)* – the basic organizational unit for which it is meaningful to formulate a separate competitive strategy. Typically, an SBU is a business consisting of a number of closely related products and for which

most costs are not shared with other businesses. McKinsey recommended the reorganization of GE into SBUs for formulating and monitoring business strategies.

- *The PIMS database* – an internal database that comprises strategic, market, and performance data on each of GE's businesses for assisting strategy formulation by providing analysis of the impact of market structure and strategy variables on profitability.[10]

Portfolio Planning: The GE/McKinsey Matrix

The best-known products of GE's corporate planning initiatives of 1969–72 are the portfolio planning models developed by McKinsey, BCG, and A. D. Little. The basic idea is to represent the businesses of the diversified company within a simple graphical framework that can be used to assist strategy analysis in four areas:

1. *Allocating resources.* Portfolio analysis examines the position of a business unit in relation to the two primary sources of profitability: industry attractiveness and the competitive advantage of the firm. These indicate the attractiveness of the business for future investment.

2. *Formulating business unit strategy.* The current positioning of the business in relation to industry attractiveness and potential competitive advantage indicates the strategic approach that should be taken with regard to capital investment and can point to opportunities for repositioning the business.

3. *Analyzing portfolio balance.* The primary usefulness of a single diagrammatic representation of the company's different businesses is the ability of corporate management to take an overall view of the company. This permits planning the overall balance of:
   - *cash flows*: by balancing cash-generating businesses against cash-absorbing businesses, the diversified company can achieve independence from external capital markets;
   - *growth*: by balancing a mix of businesses in different stages of their life cycles, the diversified company can stabilize its growth rate and achieve continuity over time.

4. *Setting performance targets.* To the extent that positioning with regard to industry attractiveness and competitive position determine profit potential, portfolio-planning matrices can assist in setting performance targets for individual businesses.

The two axes of the GE/McKinsey matrix (see Figure 16.1) are the familiar sources of superior profitability for a firm: *industry attractiveness* and *competitive advantage*. Industry attractiveness is computed on the basis of the following factors:

- Market size.

- Market growth (real growth rate over 10 years).

FIGURE 16.1 The GE/McKinsey portfolio planning matrix

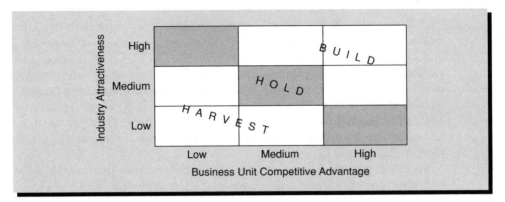

- Industry profitability (three-year average return on sales of the business and its competitors).

- Cyclicality (average annual percentage trend deviation of sales).

- Inflation recovery (ability to cover cost increases by higher productivity and increased prices).

- Importance of overseas markets (ratio of international to US market).

Business unit competitive advantage is computed on the basis of the following variables:

- Market position (as indicated by share of the US market, share of world market, and market share relative to that of leading competitors).

- Competitive position (superior, equal, or inferior to competitors) with regard to quality, technology, manufacturing, distribution, marketing, and cost.

- Return on sales relative to that of leading competitors.

Strategy recommendations are shown by three regions of Figure 16.1:

- Business units that rank high on both dimensions have excellent profit potential and should be *grown*.

- Those that rank low on both dimensions have poor prospects and should be *harvested* (managed to maximize cash flow with little or no new investment).

- In-between businesses are candidates for a *hold* strategy.

The value of this technique is its simplicity. For a complex company such as General Electric, with its 43 SBUs, it permits a single overview of all the company's businesses and their relative strategic positioning.

Portfolio Planning: BCG's Growth-Share Matrix

The Boston Consulting Group's matrix is similar: it also uses industry attractiveness and competitive position to compare the strategic positions of different businesses and draw strategy inferences. However, unlike the McKinsey matrix, it uses single variables for each axis: industry attractiveness is measured by *rate of market growth*, competitive advantage by *relative market share* (the business unit's market share relative to that of its largest competitor).

The four quadrants of the BCG matrix predict patterns of profits and cash flow and offer strategy recommendations as to appropriate strategies. These are summarized in Figure 16.2.

The BCG growth-share matrix is even more elementary than the McKinsey matrix, but again, in providing a first-cut analysis, there are virtues in simplicity:

- Because information on only two variables is required, the analysis can be prepared easily and quickly.

- It assists senior managers in cutting through the vast quantities of detailed information on individual businesses to reveal some key differences in their positioning.

- The analysis is versatile – it can be applied not only to business units, but also to analyzing the positioning and performance potential of different products, brands, distribution channels, and customers.

FIGURE 16.2   The BCG growth–share matrix

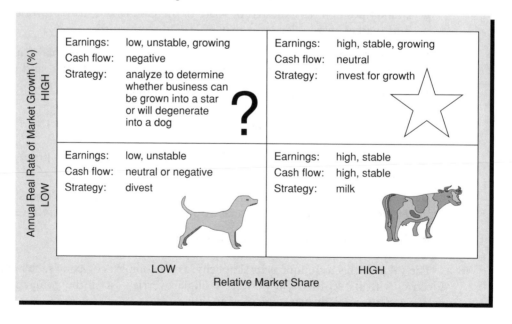

FIGURE 16.3 Applying the BCG matrix to Time Warner Inc.

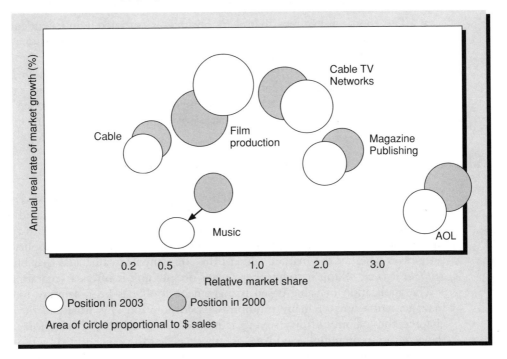

- It provides a useful point of departure for more detailed analysis and discussion of the competitive positions and strategies of individual business units.

The value of combining several elements of strategically useful information in a single graphical display is illustrated by the application of the BCG matrix to Time Warner (see Figure 16.3). Not only does the display show the positioning of the business units with regard to market growth and relative market share, it also indicates the relative sales revenues of the units, their patterns of distribution, and movements in their strategic position over time.

Since the 1980s, portfolio planning matrices (including those of BCG and McKinsey) have lost their popularity as analytic tools. Among their weaknesses are the following:

- Both are gross oversimplifications of the factors that determine industry attractiveness and competitive advantage. This is especially true of the BCG matrix, which uses just two variables: market share is not a good indicator of competitive advantage; market growth is a poor proxy for market profit potential.

- The positioning of businesses within the matrix is highly susceptible to measurement choices. For example, relative market share in the BCG matrix depends critically on how markets are defined. Is BMW's North American auto business a "dog" because it holds about 2 percent of the total auto market, or a cash cow because BMW is market leader in the luxury car segment?

■ The approach assumes that every business is completely independent. Where linkages exist between business units, viewing each as a standalone business inevitably leads to suboptimal strategy choices. In terms of market growth and relative market share, Disney's theatrical productions (such as *Lion King* and *Beauty and the Beast*) represent a "dog" business. However, to the extent that Disney's theatrical productions utilize themes and characters developed for other media, they contribute to the success of Disney's creative content in general.

Value Creation Through Corporate Restructuring[11]

If portfolio analysis was a key framework for strategy analysis during the diversification era of the 1970s, the refocusing of the 1990s has been closely associated with the application of shareholder value analysis to corporate strategy decisions. In appraising the business portfolio of a company, the fundamental criterion to be applied to each business is whether the market value of the company is greater *with* that business or *without* it (i.e., selling it to another owner or spinning it off as a separate entity).

The application of value-based management tools has been salutary for the top management teams of many multibusiness corporations. As noted in the previous chapter, the majority of diversifying acquisitions have destroyed shareholder wealth: the acquisition premiums paid have greatly exceeded the value added by the acquired businesses. Conversely, stock market valuations have responded positively to divestments, or even to the anticipation of divestment.

Applying the techniques of shareholder value analysis outlined in Chapter 2, McKinsey & Co. has proposed a systematic framework for increasing the market value of multibusiness companies through corporate restructuring. McKinsey's *Pentagon Framework* consists of a five-stage process, illustrated in Figure 16.4. The five stages of the analysis are:

1. *The current market value of the company.* The starting point of the analysis is the current market value of the company, which comprises the value of equity plus the value of debt. (As we know from Chapter 2, this equals the net present value of the anticipated cash flow to the company.)

2. *The value of the company as is.* Even without any changes to strategy or operations, it may be possible to value simply by managing external perceptions of a company's future prospects. Over the past ten years, companies have devoted increasing attention to managing investor expectations by increasing the flow of information to shareholders and investment analysts and establishing departments of investor relations.

3. *The potential value of the company with internal improvements.* As we shall see in the next section, the corporate head office of a company has opportunities for increasing the overall value of the company by making strategic and operational improvements to individual businesses that increase their cash flows.

FIGURE 16.4 The McKinsey restructuring pentagon

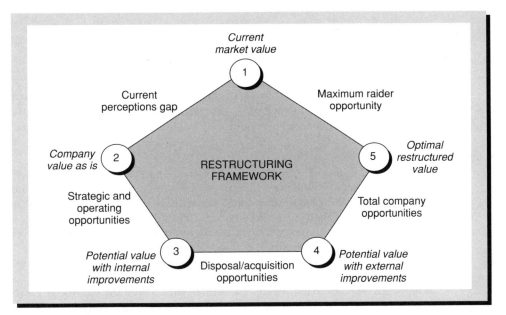

Strategic opportunities include exploring growth opportunities such as investing in global expansion, repositioning a business in relation to customers and competitors, or strategic outsourcing. Operating improvements would include cost-cutting opportunities and taking advantage of the potential to raise prices.

4. *The potential value of the company with external improvements.* Once top management has determined the value of its constituent businesses and of the company as a whole, it is in a position to determine whether changes in the business portfolio will increase overall company value. The key issue is whether an individual business, even after strategic and operating improvements have been made, could be sold for a price that is greater than its potential value to the company.

5. *The optimum restructured value of the company.* This is the maximum value of a company once all the potential gains from changing investor perceptions, making internal improvements, and taking advantage of external opportunities have been exploited. The difference between the maximum restructured value and the current market value represents the profit potential available to a corporate raider from taking advantage of the restructuring opportunities.

This type of analysis has been traditionally associated with leveraged buyout specialists and other corporate raiders. However, faced with the increasing threat of acquisitions, such analysis is increasingly being undertaken by corporate senior managers themselves. The restructuring measures undertaken by the oil majors during 1986–92 exemplify this process: increasing the value of existing businesses through cost cutting, while taking advantage of external opportunities for trading assets and selling businesses.[12]

MANAGING INDIVIDUAL BUSINESSES

Despite the emphasis given to economies of scope and other types of linkage among the businesses within the multibusiness firm, some of the most important opportunities for corporate headquarters to create value arise from what Goold, Campbell, and Alexander call "standalone influence." This relates to the corporate parent's ability to:

> . . . appoint the general manager of each business and influence management development and succession planning within the businesses. It can approve or reject budgets, strategic plans, and capital expenditure proposals and it can influence the shape and implementation of these plans and proposals. It can provide advice and policy guidance to the businesses. The parent also influences the businesses by the hints and pressures passed on through both formal and informal line management meetings and contacts, and, more indirectly, through the corporate culture.[13]

There are two primary means by which the corporate headquarters can exert control over the different businesses of the corporation. It can control decisions, through requiring that particular categories of decision – typically those involving significant resource commitments – are referred upward for corporate approval. Thus, a company may require that all capital expenditure decisions involving a commitment of funds of over $20 million are approved by the executive committee. Alternatively, corporate may seek to control businesses through controlling performance targets, backed by incentives and penalties to motivate the attainment of these targets. The distinction is between *input* and *output* controls: the company can control the inputs into the process (i.e., the decisions) or it can control the outputs (the performance). Although most companies use a combination of input and output controls, there is an unavoidable trade-off between the two: more of one implies less of the other. If a company exerts tight control over divisional decisions, it must accept the performance outcomes that arise from those decisions. If the company exerts rigorous controls relating to performance in terms of annual profit targets, it must give divisional managers the freedom to make the decisions necessary to achieve these targets. Here, we concentrate on two aspects of corporate influence: influence over business strategy formulation, and financial control.

Business Strategy Formulation

In Chapter 1, I identified corporate strategy as being set at the corporate level and business strategy as set at the business level. In reality, business strategies are formulated jointly by corporate and divisional managers. In most diversified, divisionalized companies, business strategies are initiated by divisional managers and the role of corporate managers is to probe, appraise, amend, and approve divisional strategy proposals. The critical issue for corporate management is to create a strategy-making process that reconciles the decentralized decision making essential to fostering flexibility, responsiveness, and a sense of ownership at the business level, with the ability of the corporate level to bring to bear its knowledge, perspective, and responsibility for the shareholder interest. Achieving an optimal blend of business-level initiative and corporate-level guidance and discipline is a difficult challenge for the multibusiness corporation. Common to the success of General Electric, Exxon Mobil, Samsung, and Unilever is a system of strategic management that has managed this difficult tradeoff between business initiative and corporate control. Strategy Capsule 16.1 describes key elements of the strategic planning process at Exxon.

STRATEGY CAPSULE 16.1   Strategic Planning at Exxon

In terms of profitability and shareholder return, Exxon is the most successful of the oil and gas majors as well as being one of the world's largest and most international companies. Exxon's strategic planning system has been highly effective at reconciling the critical dilemmas facing large multibusiness corporations: notably the conflict between long-term strategic planning and rigorous, short-term financial control; and between strong centralized direction and flexible, responsive, business-level decision making. Exxon's strategic planning process follows an annual cycle that is similar to the "generic" strategic planning process outlined in Chapter 6 (see Figure 6.7).

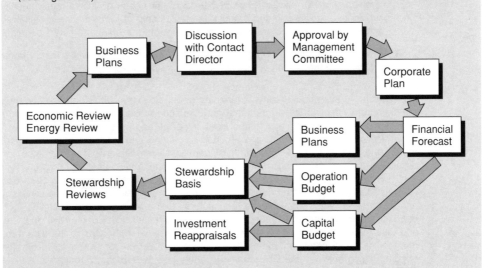

The principal stages of the planning cycle are as follows:

1. *Economic Review and Energy Review* are forecasts of the economy and energy markets prepared in spring by the Corporate Planning Department to provide a basis for strategic planning.

2. *Business Plans* are developed during the spring and summer by individual businesses and are aggregated and refined at the divisional level. Their time horizon is ten years for upstream, five years for downstream and chemicals. Prior to discussion,

STRATEGY CAPSULE 16.1 *(cont'd)*

negotiation, and approval by the Management Committee, the plans are discussed with each division's Contact Director and evaluated by Corporate Planning Department (during October).

3. *The Corporate Plan* results from the aggregation of individual business plans. The approved business and corporate plans then provide the basis for the financial and performance plans (formulated during November).

4. *The Financial Forecast* comprises forecasts of revenues, operating costs, capital expenditures, interest and other expenses, income, and cash flow for divisions and for the company as a whole over a two-year period.

5. *The Operating and Capital Budgets* are set for the upcoming year (the first year of the plans).

6. *The Stewardship Basis* is a statement of annual targets against which the next year's performance by each division will be judged. The objectives include financial objectives, operating targets (e.g., wells drilled, contracts signed, capacity utilization, throughput), safety and environmental objectives, and strategy mileposts. A key aspect of the stewardship process is to identify performance measures that reflect *controllable* aspects of the business. Thus, profit performance targets are set such that they can be adjusted for unforecasted price and exchange rate movements.

7. *Stewardship Reviews.* In February of each year, each division's performance for the previous year is evaluated against its stewardship objectives. These reviews involve presentations by the divisional top management to the Management Committee.

8. *Investment Reappraisals* occur in August and September and involve the divisions reporting back on the outcomes of specific investment projects.

In addition to this annual strategic planning cycle, *Strategic Studies* are *ad hoc* projects by the Corporate Planning Department that address specific issues such as country and product studies and responses to major market, technological, and political changes.

In terms of the ability to link and reconcile expertise and influence at both the corporate and business level, Exxon's strategic management system features clearly defined corporate, divisional, and business unit responsibilities (with matching accountability), together with close communication and coordination between these levels. Thus, despite the clear division of responsibilities between corporate strategy and corporate performance and business strategy and performance – the former is the responsibility of the Management Committee (composed of Exxon's executive board members), the latter is the responsibility of the Divisional Presidents and their management teams – close linkage exists between the two, to the extent that each member of the Management Committee is "Contact Director" for two or three divisions. The ongoing dialog between the Divisional Presidents and the Contact Directors is a mechanism for knowledge sharing and initiating strategic changes that adds flexibility to the formal strategic planning process. The result is a system of strategy formulation and performance management that is simultaneously top down and bottom up – strategy is a result both of top-down priorities and guidelines and bottom-up decision making from those closest to the individual businesses.

Strategy formulation and financial control are linked by the close integration of budgeting and performance management with strategic planning. This is reinforced by Exxon's emphasis on *stewardship* – a doctrine of managerial responsibility and accountability that makes each executive personally responsible to the corporation and its shareholders.

Performance Control and the Budgeting Process

Most multidivisional companies operate a dual planning process: strategic planning concentrates on the medium and long term, financial planning controls short-term performance. Typically, the first year of the strategic plan includes the performance plan for the upcoming year in terms of an operating budget, a capital expenditure budget, and strategy targets relating to market share, output and employment levels, and specific strategic milestones. Annual performance plans are agreed between senior business-level and corporate-level managers. They are monitored on a monthly or quarterly basis, and are reviewed more extensively in meetings between business and corporate management after the end of each financial year.

The corporate head office is responsible for setting, monitoring, and enforcing performance targets for the individual divisions. Performance targets may be financial (return on invested capital, gross margin, growth of sales revenue), strategic (market share, rate of new product introduction, market penetration, quality), or both. Performance targets are primarily annual, but also longer term – most companies set targets for between two and five years. However, the monitoring of these targets to detect deviations from annual performance targets results in considerable weight being placed on monthly and quarterly performance data.

Incentives for achieving target performance include financial returns (salary, bonuses, stock options), promotion, and intangible rewards that enhance organizational status and self-image (e.g., praise, recognition). Sanctions include blame and loss of reputation, demotion, and, ultimately, dismissal. Some diversified companies have proved to be highly effective in using performance monitoring and a combination of incentives and sanctions to create an intensely motivating environment for divisional managers. At ITT, Geneen's obsession with highly detailed performance monitoring, ruthless interrogation of divisional executives, and generous rewards for success developed a highly motivated, strongly capable group of young, senior executives who were willing to work unremittingly long hours. They demanded as high a standard of performance from their subordinates as Geneen did of them.[14] The existence of precise, quantitative performance targets that can be monitored on a short-term (monthly or quarterly) basis can provide an intensely competitive internal environment that is highly effective in motivating a business unit and divisional managers. PepsiCo's obsession with monthly market share results nourishes an intense and aggressive, marketing-oriented culture. As one PepsiCo executive explained, "The place is full of guys with sparks coming out of their asses."[15] Even in businesses where interdependence is high and investment gestation periods are long, as in oil and gas, short- or medium-term performance targets can be highly effective. Under Chairman and CEO John Browne, British Petroleum developed a strong performance-oriented culture in which the traditional strategic planning system was largely replaced by a system of performance contracts in which each business unit general manager agreed a set of financial, strategic, and operational targets with Chairman Browne.

As I discussed in Chapter 2, reconciling short-term financial targets with longer-term strategic goals represents a dilemma for many companies. For example, in technology-based industries, financial targets may stunt innovation. The *balanced scorecard* (discussed in Chapter 2) represents one solution to this problem. Another approach to reconciling long-term strategic goals with on-going performance control is to establish a series of *milestones* that set dates for achieving specific stages in the development of products, projects, or the business as a whole. Milestones might include the signing of particular contracts, the production of a product prototype, the market launch of a new product, achieving a particular level of market penetration, or reducing costs by a specific level. Larry Bossidy and Ram Charan emphasize the key role of milestones in bringing reality to strategic plans by translating long-term objectives into specific short-term actions.[16] High-tech companies may also achieve high levels of financial awareness and responsibility, not through tight formal control, but though a culture that emphasizes commitment to profitability and fiscal prudence. AOL is a company that has continuously made big financial bets and been willing to forgo short-term profitability for longer-term strategic goals, yet maintains a strong financial discipline primarily through a culture that emphasizes financial returns and disciplined investment decisions.

Implementing performance management typically means the introduction of performance-related pay. Over time, top management compensation has become increasingly closely tied to company performance. This has occurred through the growing size of performance-related annual bonuses as a percentage of salary, and the increasing role of stock options. Moreover, performance bonuses and options packages are being extended down corporate hierarchies to increasing numbers of employees. In the UK, salary comprised 54 percent of total executive compensation as compared with bonuses 24 percent, and options and long-term incentive plans 22 percent.[17]

Strategic Management Styles

One implication of the tradeoff between *input control* (controlling decisions) and *output control* (controlling performance) is that companies must choose how far to emphasize strategic planning relative to financial planning as their primary control system. A study of corporate strategy by Michael Goold and Andrew Campbell found that large, British, multibusiness companies could be classified according to whether their management systems emphasized strategy or finance as the basis of planning and control.[18] Their research identifies two strategic management styles:

- *Strategic planning* was associated with substantial involvement by corporate headquarters in business-level planning. Strategies emphasized strategic objectives (market share, innovation, quality leadership) over financial objectives, and the long term over the short term. Strong corporate involvement in business-level planning limits the independence of divisional top management, thereby undermining their initiative and sense of ownership. This may also slow strategic decision making and limit responsiveness to new circumstances and opportunities. Strong corporate influence may also impose a unitary view of the world. A strategic planning style is appropriate for companies whose businesses are small in number, do not span too wide a range of products and industries, and with strong linkages between them. The style is more appropriate to companies that compete in international and technology-intensive markets where longer-term strategic goals are more important than short-term profit targets.

- *Financial control* implied limited involvement by corporate management in business strategy formulation, which was the responsibility of divisional and business unit managers. The primary influence of headquarters was through short-term budgetary control. By setting profit targets that were ambitious, short term, and easily measured, managers were strongly motivated to increase efficiency and expand business into profitable areas. Careful monitoring of performance by headquarters – with rigorous questioning of managers responsible for deviations from target – maintained constant pressure on divisional management and created a challenging working environment. The benefits of the financial control style were in the autonomy it gave to business units, including the sense of ownership and personal commitment it engendered among divisional managers.[19] This autonomy also encouraged managers to break away from ineffective strategies at an early stage. The key drawbacks of financial control arose from the tendency to neglect long-term strategic development and difficulties in managing cooperation between different divisions. Hence, the financial control style is suited to companies characterized by broad business diversity, with investment projects that are mainly short and medium term in fruition, and in low-tech industries with limited international competition.

Table 16.1 summarizes key features of the two styles.

Using PIMS in Strategy Formulation and Performance Appraisal

The PIMS program grew out of General Electric's internal database and was subsequently extended and developed by the Strategic Planning Institute, which conducts research and provides advisory services to the member companies. The PIMS database comprises information on over 5,000 business units that is used to estimate the impact of strategy and market structure on business-level profitability. Table 16.2 shows an estimated PIMS equation.

PIMS data are used by multibusiness companies to assist in three areas of corporate management:

- *Setting performance targets for business units.* Using the regression coefficients in the PIMS profitability equations, it is possible to plug into the PIMS regression the actual levels of the strategic and industry variables for a particular business and thereby calculate its "Par ROI" – the level of ROI that would be expected for the business given its profile of strategic and industry characteristics if its performance were typical of the sample as a whole. "Par ROI" represents a benchmark that can be used as the basis for profitability targets or for evaluating actual profitability.

TABLE 16.1   Characteristics of Different Strategic Management Styles

	STRATEGIC PLANNING	FINANCIAL CONTROL
Business Strategy Formulation	Business units and corporate center jointly formulate strategy. Center responsible for coordination of strategies among business units.	Strategy formulated at business unit level. Corporate HQ largely reactive, offering little coordination.
Controlling Performance	Primarily strategic goals with medium- to long-term horizon.	Financial budgets set annual targets for ROI and other financial variables with monthly and quarterly monitoring.
Advantages	Can exploit linkages among businesses. Can give appropriate weight to innovation and longer-term competitive positioning.	Business units given autonomy and initiative. Business units can respond quickly to change. Encourages development of business unit managers. Highly motivating.
Disadvantages	Loss of divisional autonomy and initiative. Conducive to unitary view. Resistance to abandoning failed strategy.	Short-term focus discourages innovation, building longer-term competitive position, and sharing resources and skills among businesses. Businesses may be willing to give ground to determined competitors.
Style suited to:		
Portfolio Structure	Small number of businesses across narrow range of sectors with close interrelations.	Many businesses across wide range of industries. Linkages ideally few.
Type of Investment	Large projects with long-term paybacks.	Small capital investments with short payback periods.
Environmental Features	Industries with strong technological and global competition.	Mature industries (technical change modest or slow). Stable industry environment without strong international competition.
UK Examples	BP, BOC, Cadbury-Schweppes, Lex Group, STC, United Biscuits.	Hanson, BTR, General Electric Company, Ferranti, Tarmac

Source: Based on M. Goold and A. Campbell, *Strategies and Styles* (Oxford: Blackwell, 1987).

- *Formulating business unit strategy.* Because the PIMS regression equations estimate the impact of different strategy variables on ROI, these estimates can indicate how a business can adjust its strategy in order to increase its profit performance.

- *Allocating investment funds between businesses.* Past profitability of business units is a poor indicator of the return on new investment. PIMS' "Strategic Attractiveness Scan" indicates investment attractiveness based on (a) estimated future real growth rate of the market, and (b) the "Par ROI" of the business.

TABLE 16.2 The PIMS Multiple Regression Equations: The Impact of Industry and Strategy on Profitability

PROFIT INFLUENCES	IMPACT ON:	
	ROI	ROS
Real market growth rate	0.18	0.04
Rate of price inflation	0.22	0.08
Purchase concentration	0.02	N.S.
Unionization (%)	−0.07	−0.03
Low purchase amount:		
low importance	6.06	1.63
high importance	5.42	2.10
High purchase amount:		
low importance	−6.96	−2.58
high importance	−3.84	−1.11
Exports−Imports (%)	0.06	0.05
Customized products	−2.44	−1.77
Market share	0.34	0.14
Relative quality	0.11	0.05
New products (%)	−0.12	−0.15
Marketing, percentage of sales	−0.52	−0.32
R&D, percentage of sales	−0.36	−0.22
Inventory, percentage of sales	−0.49	−0.09
Fixed capital intensity	−0.55	−0.10
Plant newness	0.07	0.05
Capital utilization	0.31	0.10
Employee productivity	0.13	0.06
Vertical integration	0.26	0.18
FIFO inventory valuation	1.30	0.62
R^2	0.39	0.31
F	58.3	45.1
Number of cases	2,314	2,314

Note: For example, if Real Market Growth Rate of a business was to increase by one percentage point, the equation predicts that its ROI (return on investment) would rise by 0.18% and ROS (return on sales by 0.04%).
Source: Robert D. Buzzell and Bradley T. Gale, *The PIMS Principles: Linking Strategy to Performance* (New York: Free Press, 1987): 274. © 1987 by the Free Press, a division of Simon Schuster Adult Publishing Group. All rights reserved.

The analysis offers predictions as to the "strategic attractiveness" of investment in the business, and the cash flow that can be expected from it.

MANAGING INTERNAL LINKAGES

As we saw in the previous chapter, the main opportunities for creating value in the multibusiness company arise from sharing resources and transferring capabilities among the different businesses within the company. This sharing occurs both through the centralization of common services at the corporate level and through direct linkages between the businesses.

Common Corporate Services

The simplest form of resource sharing in the multidivisional company is the centralized provision of common services and functions. These include corporate management functions such as strategic planning, financial control, cash and risk management, internal audit, taxation, government relations, and shareholder relations. They also include services that are more efficiently provided on a centralized basis, such as research, engineering, human resources management, legal services, management development, purchasing, and any other administrative services subject to economies of scale or learning. By 2000, shared corporate services accounted for 43 percent of headquarters staff among large UK corporations.[20]

In practice, the benefits of centralized provision of common services tend to be smaller than many corporate managers anticipate. Although there is little doubt that centralized provision can avoid costs of duplication, the key problem tends to be a lack of incentive among corporate headquarters staff and specialized corporate units to exploit cost efficiencies or to meet the needs of their business-level customers. During the 1960s and 1970s, many companies found that their corporate staffs tended to grow under their own momentum with few obvious economies from central provision and no obvious benefits to the businesses in terms of superior services.

As a result, many companies separated their corporate headquarters into two groups: a *corporate management unit* responsible for supporting the corporate management team in core support activities such as strategic planning, finance, and legal, and a *shared services organization* responsible for supplying common services such as research, engineering, training, and information technology to the businesses. The tendency has been to create market incentives for these shared service organizations by requiring them to supply services on an arm's-length basis to internal operating units, frequently in competition with independent suppliers of the same services. For example, prior to its merger with British Petroleum, Amoco split its head office between a Corporate Roles group – comprising the Controller, Treasurer, Financial Operations, Corporate Planning, Corporate Secretary, and Quality Management – and a Shared Services Organization, including Human Resources, IT, Government Relations, Public and Government Affairs, Purchasing, Facilities and Services, Business Processing, Analytical Services, Environment-Health-Safety, Supply, Engineering and Construction, Tax, Auditing, and Legal Services. These 14 service groups initially had a three-year "monopoly" on supplying services to the business groups, after which the businesses were free to obtain services from inside or outside the Amoco group. The Royal Dutch/Shell Group has also separated its corporate services organization, which supplies training, legal, contracting and procurement, security, IT, and intellectual property services, from its corporate center, which provides planning, finance, HR, and legal support to the top management team.[21]

Business Linkages and Porter's Corporate Strategy Types

Exploiting economies of scope doesn't necessarily mean centralizing resources at the corporate level. Resources and capabilities can also be shared between the businesses.

Michael Porter has argued that the way in which a company manages these linkages determines its potential to create value for shareholders.[22] He identifies four corporate strategy types.

- *Portfolio management.* The most limited form of resource sharing is where the parent company simply acquires a portfolio of attractive, soundly managed companies, allows them to operate autonomously, and links them through an efficient internal capital market. The typical organizational structure for portfolio management is the *holding company* – a parent company that owns controlling stakes in a number of (typically unrelated) subsidiaries, but, beyond appointing the boards of the subsidiary companies, does not exert significant management control. Investor AB of Sweden (managed and controlled by the Wallenberg family), Koor Industries of Israel, and Berkshire Hathaway of the US (headed by legendary investor Warren Buffett) are leading examples of this organizational form. Value is created by acquiring companies at favorable prices, closely monitoring their financial performance, and operating an effective internal capital market.

- *Restructuring.* British conglomerates BTR and the former Hanson, and US leveraged buyout operators such as KKR, have created value by restructuring: acquiring poorly managed companies, then intervening to dispose of under-performing businesses and assets, restructure liabilities, and change management and reduce costs in ongoing businesses. The voluntary breakup of Hanson during the late 1990s reflected Lord Hanson's belief that increasing capital market efficiency meant that profitable opportunities for corporate restructuring had largely disappeared.

- *Transferring skills.* Organizational capabilities can be transferred between business units. Altria transfers brand management and distribution capabilities among its Philip Morris cigarettes and its Kraft-General Foods businesses. Sharp transfers its optoelectronics and miniaturization capabilities across a number of consumer, electronic, and office equipment products. Creating value by sharing skills requires that the same capabilities are applicable to the different businesses, and also that mechanisms are established to transfer these skills through personnel exchange and best practice transfer.

- *Sharing activities.* Porter argues that the most important source of value arises from exploiting economies of scope in common resources and activities. For these economies to be realized, corporate management must play a key coordinating role, including involvement in formulating business unit strategies and intervention in operational matters to ensure that opportunities for sharing R&D, advertising, distribution systems, and service networks are fully exploited. Such sharing is facilitated by:
  - a strong sense of corporate identity;
  - a corporate mission statement that emphasizes the integration of business-level strategies;
  - an incentive for cooperation among businesses;
  - inter-business task forces and other vehicles for cooperation.

The Corporate Role in Managing Linkages

The closer the linkages among businesses, the greater the opportunities for creating value from sharing resources and transferring capabilities, and the greater the need for corporate headquarters to manage the coordination of divisional strategies and activities. In the conglomerate, the independence of each business limits the opportunities for managing linkages. The coordinating role of the head office is restricted to managing the budgetary process and establishing "framework conditions" for divisional planning in the form of economic forecasts, scenarios, and a common format for strategic plans.

In more closely related companies such as the highly vertically integrated oil companies, or companies with close market or technological links (such as IBM, Procter & Gamble, American Express, and Alcoa), corporate management is likely to play a much greater coordinating role. This is likely to involve not only coordination of strategies but also operational coordination in order to exploit the economies of scope and transferable skills discussed in Chapter 15. One indicator of the impact of divisional interrelationships on the coordinating role of corporate management is the size of the corporate headquarters in different types of companies. Berkshire Hathaway, which has almost no linkages among its businesses, has a corporate staff of about 50. Hewlett-Packard, with about the same sales but much closer linkages between its divisions, has close to 3,000 employees at its Palo Alto head office. Goold and Campbell note that the companies that are closely involved with creating value in their businesses through "*value-added corporate parenting*" tend to have significant numbers of headquarters staff involved in developing key technical and functional capabilities. Thus, Pfizer and Corning have strong corporate R&D groups; Dow has a strong corporate manufacturing function; and Virgin's corporate team plays a key role in managing the Virgin brand.[23]

The need to marry decentralized decision making with multiple dimensions of coordination gives rise to complex issues of organizational design within the multibusiness company. Virtually all multibusiness companies are organized around some form of matrix; even companies that are based on product divisions tend to have a geographical organization through country managers who coordinate government relations, taxation, and legal affairs within each country, and functional heads responsible for coordination and best practice transfer in manufacturing, marketing, and other functions across the corporation.

Opportunities for sharing and transferring resources and capabilities may also be accessed through various types of *ad hoc* organizational arrangements such as *cross-divisional task forces*. Such task forces might be formed for the introduction and dissemination of total quality management, to reengineer financial management practices, to promote fast-cycle new product development, to coordinate business development in Vietnam, and so on.

Corporate management may also encourage divisional managers to exploit interbusiness linkages through exhortations to divisional managers. A key aspect of the top-down aspect of corporate planning is for the CEO to identify company-wide issues for divisional managers to take account of in their strategies and operating decisions. The annual planning cycle typically begins with the CEO issuing corporate priorities and performance targets, which might include cross-divisional issues such as expansion into China, increasing inventory turnover, integrating IT networks, and the like. In many companies, the periodic launching of company-wide initiatives provides a key mechanism for disseminating strategic changes, best practices, and management innovations.[24] At General Electric, Jack Welch was an especially effective exponent of corporate initiatives as a means of driving organizational change. These were built around communicable and compelling slogans such as "GE's growth engine," "boundarylessness," "six-sigma quality," and "destroy-your-business-dot-com."

Exploiting linkages between businesses requires careful management, and this imposes costs. Though Porter may be right that the *potential* for value creation increases as a company moves from a loose, "portfolio management" strategy toward the more integrated, "shared activity" strategy, it is not apparent that this potential is always realized. For example, most attempts at exploiting the potential for cross-selling across different businesses have yielded disappointing results, especially in financial services.[25] A study by Lorsch and Allen offers insight into the corporate management implications of exploiting close linkages between businesses. They compared three conglomerates with three vertically integrated paper companies.[26] The coordination requirements of the paper companies resulted in greater involvement of head office staff in divisional operations, larger head office staffs, more complex planning and control devices, and lower responsiveness to change in the external environment. By contrast, the conglomerates made little attempt to exploit linkages even if they were present:

> The conglomerate firms we had studied seemed to be achieving appreciable degrees of financial and managerial synergy but little or no operating synergy. Some of the firms saw little immediate payoff in this operating synergy; others met with little success in attempting to achieve it.[27]

The success with which the corporate headquarters manages linkages between businesses depends on top management's understanding the commonalities among its different businesses. As we noted in the last chapter, the mindset and underlying rationale that give cohesiveness to the diversified company have been defined by C. K. Prahalad and Richard Bettis as the dominant logic of the enterprise.[28] They define *dominant logic* as "the way in which managers conceptualize the business and make critical resource allocation decisions." For a diversified business to be successful, they argue, there must be sufficient strategic similarity among the different businesses so that top management can administer the corporation with a single dominant logic. For example:

- Emerson Electric comprises a number of different businesses (electric motors, air conditioning, electrical appliances, control instruments), but the common goal of being a low-cost producer in each of its businesses provides a unifying thread.[29]

- Unilever's dominant logic is that it is an international manufacturer and marketer of branded, packaged consumer goods. Pursuing this logic has encouraged Unilever to exit animal feeds, transportation, packaging, and chemicals, and build on its core businesses of processed foods, household detergents and cleaning supplies, and toiletries.

- Jack Welch's restructuring of GE's business portfolio was preceded by his conceptualizing of GE as three intersecting circles, each containing 15 businesses. One circle was GE's core businesses (such as lighting, appliances, and turbines); the second was high-technology businesses (such as aerospace, medical equipment, and electronics); the third was service businesses (such as financial and information services).[30]

These strategic similarities can promote learning across the company, as strategies that prove successful in one business can be applied in others. At the same time, the tendency for headquarters to encourage uniformity in the strategies applied in different businesses can cause a failure to fit strategy to the circumstances of the individual business. Although Altria (then Philip Morris) successfully transferred its marketing capabilities from its cigarette business to Miller Brewing, the deployment of these same capabilities and approaches at its Seven-Up soft drink subsidiary was a costly failure.[31]

RECENT TRENDS IN THE MANAGEMENT OF MULTIBUSINESS CORPORATIONS

The past decade and a half has seen major changes in our thinking about the multibusiness corporation and the role played by its corporate center. At the basis of this shift has been a focus on value creation. As a result, corporate strategy has been seen less in terms of the effective control of vast corporate empires and much more about identifying the means by which the corporate center can create value for the individual businesses. The discussion of corporate management styles in terms of "parenting roles" as compared to "systems of corporate control" reflects this shift of thinking. Key elements of the current approach include:

- A view of corporate headquarters less as the apex of a hierarchy and more as a support service for the businesses.

- Less emphasis on formal management systems, and more on relationships and informal coordination.

- Decentralization of both operational and strategic decisions from corporate to divisional levels.

- Emphasis on the role of headquarters, and the CEO in particular, as a catalyst and driver of organizational change.

Many of these changes in multibusiness management have been closely associated with the developments at General Electric during the past two decades. In the same way that General Electric pioneered the development of formal approaches to corporate strategy and control, it has also been a prime mover in the dismantling of these formal controls in favor of a more flexible, informal, and dynamic approach to corporate strategy. The effectiveness of GE's system of corporate management in promoting adaptability and high performance has resulted in GE becoming a model for many other large, multibusiness corporations – not just in North America, but in Europe and Asia too. Strategy Capsule 16.2 describes the key developments at GE.

STRATEGY CAPSULE 16.2   General Electric: Welch's Reinvention of Corporate Management

---

The "reinventing" of GE has been closely associated with the role of CEO Jack Welch, who took over in 1981 and retired in 2001. Welch's tenure began with an intensive period of restructuring, which transformed the composition of GE's business portfolio through acquisitions and disposals and extended the conglomerate's global reach. Toward the mid-1980s, Welch's attention shifted from the business portfolio to the structure, systems, and style of GE. Among the changes he initiated were the following.

1. *Delayering.* Welch's fundamental criticism of GE's management was that it was slow and unresponsive. A precondition for a more nimble enterprise was fewer levels of management. Welch eliminated GE's sector level of organization (which combined a number of businesses) and within each business pressed for the flattening of management pyramids through reducing the layers of hierarchy from nine or ten to four or five:

   > We used to have things like department managers, subsection managers, unit managers, supervisors. We're driving those titles out . . . We used to go from the CEO to sectors, to groups, to businesses. We now go from the CEO to businesses. Nothing else.[1]

2. *Changing the Strategic Planning System.* During the 1970s, GE had developed a systematic and formalized approach to strategy formulation and appraisal. Welch believed that not only was the system slow and inefficient, it also stifled innovation and opportunism. A Harvard case study outlines the changes:

   > Nowhere was the change more striking than in the area of strategic planning and operational reviews. Although the basic processes were retained, the old staff-led, document-driven process of the 1970s was largely replaced by more personal, less formal, but very-intensive face-to-face discussions and small meetings. To cut through the bureaucracy Welch asked each of his 13 business heads to reduce the complex, multivolume planning documents to a slim "playbook" that summarized key strategic issues and actions. On each page, they provided concise answers to questions about their global, market dynamics, key competitive activity, major competitive risks, and proposed GE business responses. These documents became the basis for a half-day shirtsleeve review in mid-summer. Business heads and their key people (usually from three to ten in total) met with the Office of the CEO members and their key staff in an open dialogue on core plans and strategies.[2]

3. *Redefining the Role of Headquarters.* The changes in the strategic planning system are indicative of a broader set of changes in the role of the corporate headquarters. Welch viewed headquarters as interfering too much in the businesses, generating too much unnecessary paper, and failing to add value. His objective was to "turn their role 180 degrees from checker, inquisitor, and authority figure to facilitator, helper, and supporter of the 13 businesses. Ideas, initiatives, and decisions could now move quickly." Welch explained his view of corporate HQ as follows:

STRATEGY CAPSULE 16.2 *(cont'd)*

What we do here at headquarters . . . is to multiply the resources we have, the human resources, the financial resources, and the best practices . . . Our job is to help, it's to assist, it's to make these businesses stronger, to help them grow and be more powerful.[3]

4. *The Coordinating Role of Corporate.* Placing increased emphasis on informal aspects of corporate–business relations increased the role of corporate in facilitating coordination across GE's businesses. The Corporate Executive Council was reconstituted to include the leaders of GE's 13 businesses and several key corporate executives. It met two days each quarter to discuss common problems and issues. The Council became an important vehicle for identifying and exploiting synergies. By 1990, Welch had formulated his notions of coordination and integration within his view of the "boundaryless company." A key element of this concept was a blurring of internal divisions so that people could work together across functional and business boundaries. Welch aimed at "integrated diversity" – the ability to transfer the best ideas, most developed knowledge, and most valuable people freely and easily between businesses.

Boundaryless behavior is the soul of today's GE . . . Simply put, people seem compelled to build layers and walls between themselves and others, and that human tendency tends to be magnified in large, old institutions like ours. These walls cramp people, inhibit creativity, waste time, restrict vision, smother dreams and, above all, slow things down . . . Boundaryless behavior shows up in the actions of a woman from our Appliances business in Hong Kong helping NBC with contacts needed to develop satellite television service in Asia . . . And finally, boundaryless behavior means exploiting one of the unmatchable advantages a multibusiness GE has over almost any other company in the world. Boundaryless behavior combines 12 huge global businesses – each number one or number two in its markets – into a vast laboratory whose principal product is new ideas, coupled with a common commitment to spread them throughout the Company.[4]

Notes

[1] "GE Chief Hopes to Shape Agile Giant," *Los Angeles Times* (June 1, 1988): D1.

[2] General Electric: Jack Welch's Second Wave (A), Case 9-391-248 (Boston: Harvard Business School, 1991).

[3] Jack Welch, "GE Growth Engine," speech to employees (1988).

[4] "Letter to Share Owners," General Electric Company 1993 Annual Report (Fairfield, CT, 1994): 2.

Corporate Managers as Drivers of Organizational Change

Devolution of decision-making authority from corporate to business level does not imply a passive role for the corporate HQ. In many respects, corporate management has become more interventionist in attempting to influence business operations. A critical role for corporate management is in driving large-scale organizational change. This has required new organizational structures. For example, GE's "Work-Out" initiative set up forums where employees could speak their minds about management and propose changes in business structures and operating practices. Work-Out was a vehicle for cultural change in which the relationship between manager and subordinate was redefined and the creativity of employees was unleashed.

Achieving large-scale organizational change requires chief executives whose primary role is that of change maker. In the oil sector, Lucio Noto at Mobil, James Kinnear at Texaco, John Browne and David Simon at BP, Serge Tchuruk at Total, and Franco Bernabe at ENI were all pioneers of fundamental organizational change that embraced strategy, structure, and culture.[32] Intel's former CEO, Andy Grove, has emphasized the important role of chief executives in identifying and responding to *strategic inflection points* – instances where seismic shifts in a firm's competitive environment require a fundamental redirection of strategy.[33] At Intel, such inflection points included the transition from DRAM chips to microprocessors, the decision to focus on its x86 series of microprocessors in favor of RISC architecture, and the decision to replace its faulty Pentium chips.[34]

The role of corporate management in the large, multibusiness company has been shaped by the challenges that these corporate executives have faced. These include the overriding need to establish competitive advantage within each of the business areas in which the firm competes, the need for responsiveness to external change, the need to foster innovation, and the need for cost efficiency. The problem for top management is that these challenges require conflicting adjustments. For example:

- Rigorous financial controls are conducive to cost efficiency and autonomy; flexible controls are conducive to responsiveness and innovation.

- Multibusiness companies have typically been based on the advantages of exploiting existing resources and capabilities across different markets, yet competitive advantage in the future is dependent on the creation of new resources and capabilities.

- Active portfolio management based on the maximization of shareholder value is best achieved with independent businesses; the creation of competitive advantage increasingly requires the management of business interdependencies.

The common dilemma is this: how can the resource advantages of the large company be exploited, while achieving the responsiveness and creativity associated with small companies? The key is to reconcile the flexibility of decentralized decision making with high levels of coordination that can harness the resources, capabilities, and learning potential of the large organization. In Chapter 14, we noted how conflicting pressures for globalization and local adaptability were resolved by multinationals moving toward a "transnational" structure. Similar tendencies are observable in managing the tensions within diversified corporations. At IBM, CEO Lou Gerstner resisted stock market pressures to break up the company in favor of internal changes that would transform its performance and adapt it to a new era of networked IT. The changes involved:

- Aggressive cost cutting and employee reduction.

- Encouraging responsiveness and flexibility through greater autonomy, while more effectively exploiting internal resources and capabilities through internal coordination.

- A breaking down of corporate boundaries and an increased willingness to learn from other companies and to collaborate with other companies in strategic alliances.

Achieving coordination in terms of sharing capabilities, transferring capabilities, harmonizing market initiatives in different countries, and collaborating to develop new products and exploit new technologies requires horizontal communication and cooperation rather than hierarchically designated initiatives. For such coordination to be effective in creating value in the multibusiness company requires that divisions are identified not only with their particular businesses, but also with a corporate identity. Just as the single-business company needs clarity of purpose to provide its strategy with direction and its employees with commitment, so the diversified firm typically needs an identity and a rationale that give meaning to its strategy beyond the composition of its portfolio. Hence, key roles of corporate management in coordinating the diversified company are providing *leadership*, defining *mission*, and establishing a set of values and beliefs that create a unifying *corporate culture*.

Strategic similarities and *dominant logic* across the different businesses may not be adequate as an integrating force – especially in developing the loyalty and commitment needed to mobilize the talents and creativity of employees. At the same time, the very diversity of the multibusiness corporation may make it difficult to establish a common culture that unifies the various businesses and their different employees. LVMH, the French producer of Moët & Chandon champagne, Hennessy cognac, Dior and Givenchy perfumes, and Louis Vuitton luggage is a company that has made great efforts to establish a unifying set of values and traditions:

> The common cultural trunk is based on the permanent search for quality of the products and the management, human relations based on responsibility and initiative, and rewarding competences and services.[35]

A major theme in American Express's "one enterprise" program aimed at integrating its various financial service companies was the development of a common set of values oriented around quality, outstanding customer service, and marketing excellence.

Based on their observations of Procter & Gamble, 3M, Matsushita, Corning Glass, Komatsu, and other companies, Bartlett and Ghoshal argue that combining flexible responsiveness with integration and innovation requires rethinking the role of management and the distribution of management roles within the company.[36] They identify three central management processes: the *entrepreneurial process* (decisions about the opportunities to exploit and the allocation of resources), the *integration process* (how organizational capabilities are built and deployed), and the *renewal process* (the shaping of organizational purpose and the initiation of change). Conventionally, all three processes have been concentrated within the corporate HQ. Bartlett and Ghoshal propose a distribution of these functions between three levels of the firm: corporate ("top management"), the business and geographical sector coordinators ("middle management"), and the business units ("front-line management"). The critical features of the relationships between these management levels and between the individual organizational members form a social structure based on cooperation and learning. Figure 16.5 illustrates their framework.

FIGURE 16.5 Management processes and levels of management

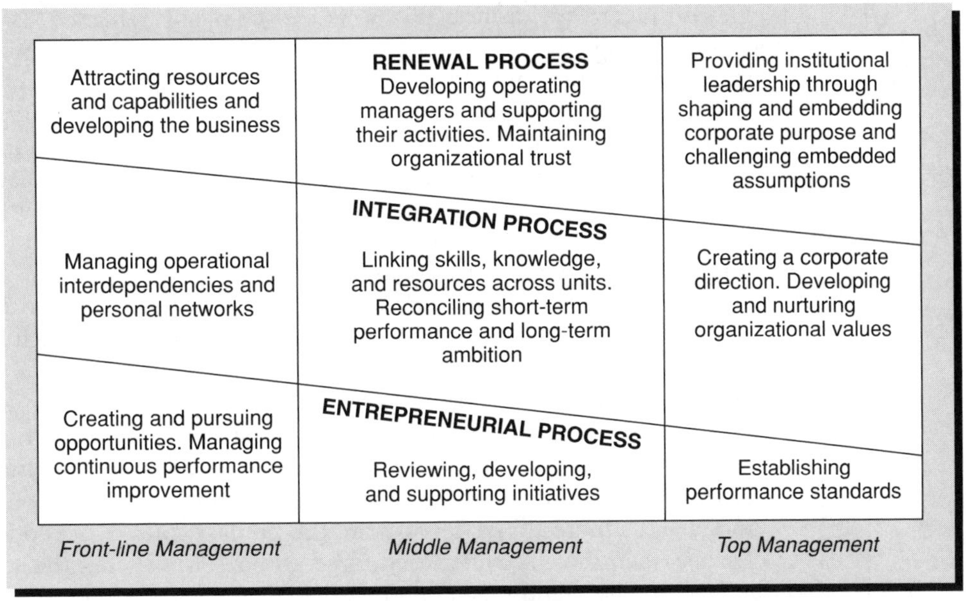

	RENEWAL PROCESS	
Attracting resources and capabilities and developing the business	Developing operating managers and supporting their activities. Maintaining organizational trust	Providing institutional leadership through shaping and embedding corporate purpose and challenging embedded assumptions
	INTEGRATION PROCESS	
Managing operational interdependencies and personal networks	Linking skills, knowledge, and resources across units. Reconciling short-term performance and long-term ambition	Creating a corporate direction. Developing and nurturing organizational values
	ENTREPRENEURIAL PROCESS	
Creating and pursuing opportunities. Managing continuous performance improvement	Reviewing, developing, and supporting initiatives	Establishing performance standards
Front-line Management	*Middle Management*	*Top Management*

SUMMARY

The formulation and implementation of corporate strategy present top management with a tangle of issues of almost impenetrable complexity. Increasing globalization of multiproduct companies adds further layers of complexity. It is almost impossible to establish generic recommendations for how multibusiness companies should implement their corporate strategies: each firm possesses a unique portfolio of products and markets; each owns a unique set of resources and capabilities; each has developed a distinct administrative structure, management style, and corporate culture. As might be expected, empirical research offers little clear guidance as to the correlates of superior performance – close relationships between businesses may or may not lead to higher profitability, sharing resources and capabilities offers economies but also imposes management costs, and there are no consistent relationships between a company's performance and the characteristics of its structure, control system, or leadership style.

Designing the appropriate organizational structure, management systems, and leadership style of a multibusiness corporation depends critically on *fit* with the corporate strategy of the company. Fundamental to this fit is the *rationale* for the firm. Diversification – both across product markets and across geographical markets – can create value in different ways. Each source of gain from diversification is likely to imply a quite different approach to managing the firm. For a conglomerate firm, value can be created through the strategic judgment of the CEO with regard to business prospects and company valuation, and the ability to operate a highly efficient internal capital market. Hence, organization and management systems should be oriented toward a clear separation of business levels on corporate decisions and a highly effective system for budgetary control and project evaluation. For a technology-based diversified corporation, value is created through the transfer and integration of knowledge, ideas, and expertise. The company must be organized in order to facilitate the transfer and application of knowledge. Corporate HQ is likely to play a critical role in technological guidance and in divisional integration.

At a more detailed level, the design of structure and systems, and the allocation of decision-making responsibilities, depends on specific issues such as:

- *The characteristics of the resources and capabilities that are being exploited within the multibusiness corporation.* If capital is the primary common resource, then the corporate system must be established to ensure its efficient allocation. If common corporate services such as information technology and administrative services are the primary sources of economies of scope, then these activities need to be grouped together at the corporate level. If the brand marketing capability is the key common resource, then systems need to be established that facilitate the transfer of marketing capabilities between businesses.

- *The characteristics of the businesses.* If the businesses are highly diverse in terms of their industry characteristics and competitive positions, then a high degree of divisional autonomy is required, as well as the establishment of corporate systems that are sufficiently flexible to accommodate that flexibility. If the businesses are more similar (e.g., P&G's diversification across branded, packaged consumer goods), then a greater uniformity of systems and style is desirable.

Ultimately, finding the appropriate structure, systems, and style with which to manage a multibusiness corporation is dependent on establishing an identity for the company. The failure of most of the conglomerates of the 1960s and early 1970s came about either because they did not establish a clear identity, or because their identity was so closely linked with a single person (e.g., Geneen at ITT) that the companies found difficulty surviving the demise of that person. In other cases, the rationale on which the identity was based was found to be flawed (e.g., Allegis Corp.). Conversely, the success of diversified corporations such as General Electric, Matsushita, British Petroleum, Canon, and Emerson Electric reflects a cohesiveness between the businesses of the company, the strategies being pursued, the structure of the organization, and its management style. This permits a sense of identity and clarity of vision with regard to the fundamental strategic question: *"What kind of company are we seeking to become?"*

NOTES

1. I use the term *multibusiness company* to refer to a company that comprises multiple business units. These may comprise different vertical activities, different geographical units, or different product sectors.

2. This section draws on Oliver E. Williamson, *Markets and Hierarchies: Analysis and Antitrust Implications* (New York: Free Press, 1975); and Oliver E. Williamson, "The Modern Corporation: Origins, Evolution, Attributes," *Journal of Economic Literature* 19 (1981): 1537–68.

3. J. L. Bower, *Managing the Resource Allocation Process* (Boston: Harvard Business School Press, 1986).

4. Williamson, "The Modern Corporation," op. cit.

5. E. J. Epstein, *Dossier: The Secret History of Armand Hammer* (New York: Carroll & Graf, 1999); B. Burrough, *Barbarians at the Gate: The Fall of RJR Nabisco* (New York: Harper & Row, 1990).

6. See, for example, Peter Steer and John Cable, "Internal Organization and Profit: An Empirical Analysis of Large UK Companies," *Journal of Industrial Economics* 21 (September 1978): 13–30; Henry Armour and David Teece, "Organizational Structure and Economic Performance: A Test of the Multidivisional Hypothesis," *Bell Journal of Economics* 9 (1978): 106–22; and David Teece, "Internal Organization and Economic Performance," *Journal of Industrial Economics* 30 (1981): 173–99.

7. Henry Mintzberg, *Structure in Fives: Designing Effective Organizations* (Englewood Cliffs, NJ: Prentice-Hall, 1983): Chapter 11.

8. M. Goold, A. Campbell, and M. Alexander, *Corporate-Level Strategy: Creating Value in the Multibusiness Company* (New York: Wiley, 1994).

9. "General Electric: Strategic Position – 1981," Case 381–174 (Boston: Harvard Business School, 1981): 1.

10. The PIMS database is referred to extensively in Chapter 3.

11. This section draws on T. Copeland, T. Koller, and J. Murrin, *Valuation: Measuring and Managing the Value of Companies*, 3rd edn (New York: Wiley, 2000).

12. R. Cibin and R. M. Grant, "Restructuring Among the World's Largest Oil Companies," *British Journal of Management* 7 (December 1996): 411–28.

13. Goold, Campbell, and Alexander, op. cit.: 90.

14. Geneen's style of management is discussed in Chapter 3 of Richard T. Pascale and Anthony G. Athos, *The Art of Japanese Management* (New York: Warner Books, 1982).

15. "Those Highflying PepsiCo Managers," *Fortune* (April 10, 1989): 79.

16. Larry Bossidy and Ram Charan, *Execution: The Discipline of Getting Things Done* (New York: Crown Business, 2002): 197–201.

17. M. J. Conyon, S. I. Peck, L. E. Read, and G. V. Sadler, "The Structure of Executive Compensation Contracts: The UK Evidence," *Long Range Planning* 33 (August 2000): 478–503.

18. M. Goold and A. Campbell, *Strategies and Styles* (Oxford: Blackwell, 1987).

19. J. Roberts points to the role of the "psychological contract" between divisional and corporate management as a key motivating device. See "Strategy and Accounting in a U.K. Conglomerate," *Accounting, Organizations and Society* 15 (1990): 107–26.

20. M. Goold, D. Pettifer, and D. Young, "Redesigning the Corporate Center," *European Mangement Review* 19, no. 1 (2001): 83–91.

21. "Organizational Restructuring within the Royal Dutch/Shell Group," in R. M. Grant, *Cases in Contemporary Strategy Analysis*, 3rd edn (Oxford: Blackwell, 2003).

22. Michael E. Porter, "From Competitive Advantage to Corporate Strategy," *Harvard Business Review* (May–June 1987): 46.

23 M. Goold, D. Pettifer, and D. Young, op cit.

24 J. Darragh and A. Campbell, "Why Corporate Initiatives Get Stuck," *Long Range Planning* 34 (January 2001): 33–52.

25 "Cross-selling's Elusive Charms," *Financial Times* (November 16, 1998): 21.

26 Jay W. Lorsch and Stephen A. Allen III, *Managing Diversity and Interdependence: An Organizational Study of Multidivisional Firms* (Boston: Harvard Business School Press, 1973).

27 Ibid.: 168.

28 C. K. Prahalad and R. Bettis, "The Dominant Logic: A New Linkage Between Diversity and Performance," *Strategic Management Journal* 7 (1986): 485–502.

29 "Shades of Geneen at Emerson Electric," *Fortune* (May 22, 1989): 39.

30 "General Electric – Going with the Winners," *Fortune* (March 26, 1984): 106.

31 "The Seven-Up Division of Philip Morris Inc.," Case 9-385-321 (Boston: Harvard Business School, 1989).

32 R. M. Grant, "The Chief Executive as Change Agent," *Planning Review* 24, no. 1 (December 1995): 9–11.

33 A. S. Grove, *Only the Paranoid Survive: How to Exploit the Crisis Points that Challenge Every Company* (New York: Bantam, 1999).

34 R. A. Burgelman and A. Grove, "Strategic Dissonance," *California Management Review* 38 (Winter 1996): 8–28.

35 Roland Calori, "How Successful Companies Manage Diverse Businesses," *Long Range Planning* 21 (June 1988): 85; "LVMH Tries to Adjust After a Life of Luxury," *Financial Times* (June 11, 1993): 26.

36 C. A. Bartlett and S. Ghoshal, "Beyond the M-Form: Toward a Managerial Theory of the Firm," *Strategic Management Journal* 14, Winter Special Issue (1993): 23–46; C. A. Bartlett and S. Ghoshal, "The Myth of the General Manager: New Personal Competencies for New Management Roles," *California Management Review* 40 (Fall 1997): 92–116; and "Beyond Structure to Process," *Harvard Business Review* (January–February 1995).

17

Current Trends in Strategic Management

I sometimes feel like I'm behind the wheel of a race car . . . One of the biggest challenges is that there are no road signs to help navigate. And, in fact, no one has yet determined which side of the road we're supposed to be on.

—*Stephen M. Case, Chairman,*
AOL Time Warner[1]

OUTLINE

505

INTRODUCTION

Let us cast our minds back to January 1, 2000. Despite all the hoopla surrounding the beginning of a New Millennium – for most people the transition from the twentieth to the twenty-first century had little real significance.

What a difference four years can make! In retrospect it is clear that the beginning of the new millennium marked a watershed – both for business and for the world. On March 10, 2000, the NASDAQ hit its all-time high of 5,132. Over the next two years it lost 62 percent of its value. In the vanguard of the stock market decline was the meltdown of the high-flying internet stocks. As the dot.com bubble rapidly deflated, a new category of stocks emerged – the Ninety-Five Percent Club – those that had lost more than 95 percent of their value. The declining stock market was closely linked to developments in the real economy. During the latter half of 2000, growth, productivity and profits all went into decline. On January 3, 2001, the Fed announced the first in a sequence of interest rate cuts. Faith in the wonders of the "New Economy" soon dissipated. Opinion became divided between those who viewed the period of IT-led productivity growth as over and those who claimed that the New Economy had been a mirage from the start.

The economic rumblings of 2000 were soon overshadowed by events on a larger scale. The September 11, 2001 destruction of the World Trade Center inaugurated a new era in world history. During the next two years, US-led invasions of Afghanistan and Iraq established new governments in both countries. Meanwhile, the institutions that had dominated international relations for over half a century – NATO and the United Nations – were relegated to a back seat in world affairs.

The fall-out for the business world was considerable. In addition to plunging most of the world into recession, the US government's "war on terrorism" and increasing unilateralism reversed many of the trends towards closer integration of the world economy. New security measures made international shipment of goods slower and more costly; international financial transactions became subject to increasing scrutiny and regulation; and the collapse of the Doha round of multilateral trade talks and growing trade tensions between the US and EU and US and China were seen as harbingers of a new era of protectionism.

In this chapter we shall review some of the major current trends in the external environment of business and consider their implications for strategic management. Unlike the other chapters of this book, this chapter will not equip you with tools and frameworks that you can deploy directly in your own companies or in case analysis. My approach is exploratory. My goal is to introduce you to some of the ideas that are reshaping our thinking about business strategy and to stimulate your thinking about the kinds of strategies that are likely to be effective during this era of uncertainty and rapid change and the types of organization suited to implementing such strategies.

TRENDS IN THE EXTERNAL ENVIRONMENT OF BUSINESS

Whatever Happened to the New Economy?

The period of intense economic and technological change beginning in the latter part of the 1990s has been described as the "third industrial revolution" – following the first industrial revolution that began in Britain at the end of the eighteenth century and involved the mechanization of production, and the second industrial revolution that began in the US at the end of the nineteenth century and saw the rise of the modern corporation and the introduction of telephones, automobiles, and electrical power. The "New Economy" of the late 1990s was driven by digital technologies and new communications media – notably wireless telephony and the internet. It was fueled too by the worldwide trends towards privatization, deregulation, and free trade. However, its glories were short-lived – by 2003, many of the pioneers of the New Economy (WorldCom and Global Crossing in telecom, Marconi in telecom equipment, WebVan and Value America.com in e-retailing) had met ignominious ends.

While the bubble economy of the late 1990s was inflated by irrational exuberance, the technological changes of the past 10 years, and the productivity gains that they have produced, are real. At the root of the New Economy phenomenon is the shift from an industrial to a knowledge economy where software rather than hardware is the primary source of value. Stanford economist, Paul Romer argues that the critical feature of software – whether it is a movie, a book, a computer program, or a business system – is that its initial cost of creation is very high, but subsequent copies cost much less. Economies of replication together with the complementary relationships between different types of knowledge permit unprecedented levels of productivity growth (see Figure 17.1). Digital technologies reinforce these increasing returns by reducing costs of replication to near zero and allowing instantaneous global distribution.[1]

Looking beyond 2004, the potential for digital technologies to generate continuing productivity gains and revolutionize manufacturing and service industries appears undiminished. The capacity for advanced digital technologies to radically increase the functionality and decrease the price of a wide range of products is indicated by Intel's heavy investments developing new chips for internet wireless access, digital signal processing, high-definition LYCOS displays, and home entertainment systems.[2] The availability of the internet as a communication device and a global distribution channel allows new industries to be created and destroyed at unprecedented speed. During 2003, two Scandinavian entrepreneurs, Niklas Zennstrom and Janus Friis, inflicted massive damage upon the world music industry through their KaZaa file-sharing system and threatened the world telecom industry with a similar fate with their SkyPe voice-over-internet system.[3] The potential for information and communication technologies to transform administrative and decision-making processes within companies remains huge – most corporations have far to go in achieving paperless processes and real-time decision making.

FIGURE 17.1 US labor productivity: changes in nonfarm output per hour worked from year-ago quarter, 1995–2003

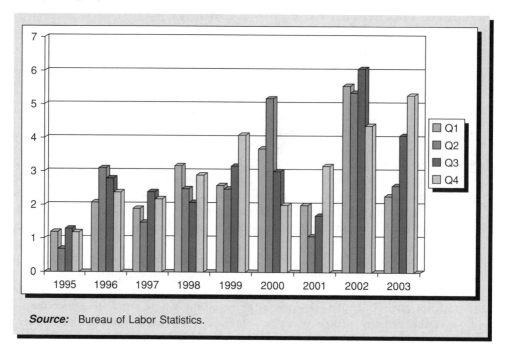

Source: Bureau of Labor Statistics.

Competition and Turbulence

The euphoria of the late 1990s owes much to the upsurge in corporate profitability during these years. In retrospect, this profit boom appears to be an aberration from the downward trend of real return on capital since the early 1960s. From mid-2000 until early 2003, industrial profitability in the US declined sharply before picking up again during late 2003. Outside the US, the situation was worse: in Japan and most of western Europe, the great majority of large corporations failed to cover their cost of capital during 2000–2003. Rather than being a source of untold riches, the main impact of digital technologies and the internet has been to increase competition and narrow profit margins across a broad range of business sectors. Not only did e-commerce reduce entry barriers, it also widened the geographical span of markets and increased price transparency. Digital technologies, combined with network effects, established winner-take-all markets where rivalry for market leadership intensified price competition. Figure 17.2 shows US industrial profitability between 1990 and 2003.

Intensifying competition is one source of increased turbulence in the business environment – it is not the only one. Accelerating technological change was a major source of unpredictability. The rise and fall of Palm, the rise of Nokia and decline of Motorola in mobile telephones, and the riches-to-rags sagas of Lucent, Nortel,

FIGURE 17.2 Return on equity of US manufacturing corporations, 1990–2003

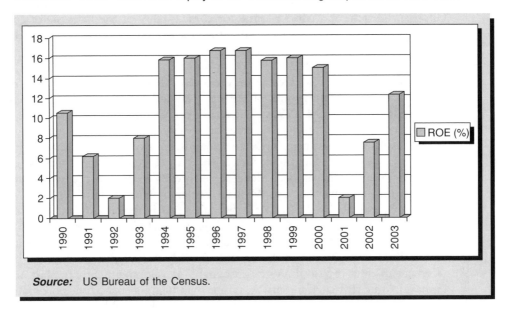

Source: US Bureau of the Census.

and Alcatel are all evidence of the ruthless forces of creative destruction. Economic turbulence is evident too in the volatile price levels in a number of markets. Consider the following:

■ In April 2002, falling world steel prices resulted in the Bush administration imposing a surcharge on steel imports. In December 2003 the tariff was lifted amidst a booming steel market. Between March 2003 and March 2004 the price of hot-rolled steel in the US had increased from $240 to $410 per ton.

■ The euro was born on January 1st 1999 with a value of US$1.12. By Spring 2002, its value had sunk to 86 cents. However, during the next two years it rose more than 50 percent against the dollar to a high of $1.30.

■ Memory chip prices have been on a roller coaster for most of the new decade. On the Asian spot market, 128-megbyte DRAMs were selling for a little over $1 in January 2002. By March prices were up to $4.38 before dropping to $2.09 in May. Only three months later prices had climbed to over $10.

Societal Pressures

In Chapter 1, I discussed the concept of *strategy as fit* – the notion that a successful strategy is one that is adapted to meet the characteristics of the firm's environment and its internal resources and capabilities. In analyzing the external environment we have emphasized the industry environment and the sources of profit within it. But firms' strategies also need to take account of the social environment. Organizational ecologists have emphasized the role of *legitimacy* in organizational survival,[4] while Ghoshal, Bartlett, and Moran argue for compatibility of the interests of companies and interests of society and stressed that the goal of value creation extends well beyond shareholder value.[5]

The events of 2001–2004 have done much to validate these ideas and discredit the doctrine of shareholder value maximization that was ascendant for most of the 1990s. It is notable that some of the most lauded exponents of shareholder value maximization during the 1990s – Enron, WorldCom, Tyco International, Vivendi, and Marconi – were the most spectacular casualties of the new decade.

The result has been an upsurge in demands for an increased social responsibility by corporate leaders. The most vocal criticism has been directed against executive compensation, which has been deemed overgenerous to the point of obscenity in the cases of executives such as Michael Eisner of Disney, Jack Welch of GE, and Richard Grasso of the NYSE. At a broader level it fueled expectations that companies should broaden their responsibilities to include the interest of local communities, the natural environment, and third world economic development. By the end of 2003, the majority of the *Fortune Global 500* had instituted formal programs of environmental responsibility or sustainable development. Stuart Hart and C. K. Prahalad argue that such initiatives, rather than being a cost to the corporation, may be routes to innovation, growth, and, ultimately, shareholder value.[6]

Expectations concerning the societal role of corporations have important implications for the relationships between employees and the companies that they work for. In the past, employment was regarded primarily as a source of economic security and material reward. Increasingly in the advanced industrial economies, individuals are looking beyond financial gain to seek identity, fellowship, and meaning. This transition has important implications not just for human resource management but, more broadly, for strategy, the role of management, and corporate identity.[7]

NEW DIRECTIONS IN STRATEGIC THINKING

Beyond Downsizing and Shareholder Value

The 1990s were a phenomenal period for corporate profitability and shareholder returns. The business environment was largely benign – low interest rates, subdued inflation, buoyant consumer demand, deregulation and privatization, and rampant technological advance provided uniquely favorable conditions for new investment. Profitability was also boosted by the dominant credo of shareholder value maximization. The resulting drive to cut costs, refocus, outsource, reengineer and delayer offered a massive boost to the bottom lines of most large corporations.

By the early years of the new decade the need for a change in firms' strategy priorities was evident. Two key problems faced senior managers. First, the gains from cost cutting and corporate restructuring – the low-hanging fruit on the tree of profit – had been picked. Second, the unremitting quest for shareholder value had unforeseen and undesired consequences for many companies. Rather than maximize the flow of profits upon which stock market valuation depended, some companies had gone further and had attempted to directly manage their stock market valuations through influencing investors' perceptions and market expectations, by smoothing fluctuations in reported earnings and, in some cases, artificially manipulating financial statements – "creative accounting."

The responses to these problems – in terms of strategic management – were twofold: first, a "back to basics" movement in which companies have refocused their strategies upon the fundamental sources of profitability; second, an emphasis on accessing more complex and difficult to reach sources of competitive advantage.

Back to Basics

The bursting of the dot.com bubble and the collapse of profitability in telecoms after a decade of overinvestment has been followed by a wave of healthy skepticism over New Economy management alchemy. The new cynicism that has greeted most new management ideas is reflected in the declining sales of business books and the declining revenues of many strategic management consultants.

In its place, numerous firms have adopted a "back-to-basics" approach in reformulating their strategies. For many companies, such strategies have involved rejecting the late-1990s' themes of e-commerce and permanent revolution in favor of return to the trends of the early 1990s – refocusing, process reengineering, and cost cutting. Thus, many electric utilities have exited their energy trading and merchant power production activities. Among commercial and retail banks disenchantment with investment banking, bancassurance, and on-line banking has encouraged a similar refocusing upon core activities and established products.

However, for many companies, back-to-basics has been less reactive and more innovative. The essence of a back-to-basics approach to strategy is a focus on the fundamentals of profitability. In essence, these mean deploying the tools of strategy analysis outlined in this book to probe and access the sources of profitability arising from deploying internal resources and capabilities to exploit opportunities in the external environment.

Central to such a back-to-basics approach is avoiding management fads and strategy bandwagons in favor of unique, customized strategies that exploit idiosyncratic advantages. A classic example of a back-to-basics strategy is Austrian Airlines' repositioning during 2002–2003. In contrast to nearby Swissair which was forced into reorganization after a disastrous strategy of acquisition and international expansion in which it attempted to emulate the strategies of its larger competitors, Austrian Airlines has pursued a strategy that has been carefully tailored to the realities of the airline industry and to its specific strengths in resources and capabilities (see Strategy Capsule 17.1).

A further aspect of the "new fundamentalism" has been the old-fashioned quest for market power. Across a large number of market sectors, depressed profitability has triggered a scramble for consolidation through mergers and acquisitions. While business leaders sing the praises of entrepreneurship and the vibrant cut-and-thrust of "creative destruction," the strategic responses to the harsh realities of competition

STRATEGY CAPSULE 17.1   Back to Basics at Austrian Airlines

After a disastrous 2001 in which Austrian Airlines' economic profit (earnings before interest and tax *less* cost of capital) sank to negative 224 million euros, the company embarked upon a total strategic reorientation. Early in 2002, Austrian announced:

> . . . its new Group strategy, the central requirement of which is the absolute value orientation of all activities. The Austrian Airlines Group will make active and consistent use of its market opportunities following the correction of structural deficits . . . Working from its highly favorable market position, the Group will concentrate on achieving drastic cost reduction and developing two quite specific market niches. These are West–East transfer, in which the company already enjoys a leading position, and the expansion of profitable flights from and to Austria itself. This will be supported by membership of the Star Alliance, the efficiency of the Vienna hub and a clear allocation of competences through the Production Company Concept. (Annual Report 2002)

The new strategic plan was a classic example of a company tailoring strategy to the requirements of its market environment and to the strengths and weaknesses of its resources and capabilities.

Beginning with cost cutting, Austrian systematically assessed all its activities and eliminated 10 percent of its employees. Acknowledging its small size (relative to Lufthansa, BA, and Air France) it adopted a niche strategy in which it set the goal of dominating its domestic market (with the target of 65 percent of the traffic from Vienna airport) while exploiting the opportunities of Vienna's traditional position as gateway between east and west Europe – a positioning that became increasingly attractive with the proposed eastwards expansion of the EU. To mitigate the disadvantages of small size and a limited domestic market, Austrian forged closer cooperation with other airlines – notably with the Star Alliance, Lufthansa, and ANA – to provide the network linkages that would substitute for Austrian's lack of critical mass at the international level.

In pursuing its niche strategy, Austrian engaged in aggressive expansion of its route structure during 2002 – a period when most airlines were pruning their routes. During 2002 and 2003, Austrian added additional flights to central and eastern European destinations including Pozan (Poland), Chisinau (Moldavia), Riga (Latvia), Skopje (Macedonia), Minsk (Belarus), Sarajevo (Bosnia), and Baku (Azerbaijan). In addition, Austrian added a number of western European destinations and several long-haul destinations (including Beijing, Osaka, Dubai, Delhi, Libya, and Montreal/Toronto). By the end of 2003, Austrian was flying to more destinations than any other European airline and had succeeded in establishing Vienna as a thriving hub for east–west travel within Europe and beyond.

By 2003, the new strategy was showing bottom line results: for 2003, earnings before interest and tax were 53 percent higher than the previous year.

have often been defensive. In many instances the professed goals of merging with competitors are cost efficiencies from scale and improved cost control. Across several industries, however, the extent and international scope of consolidation points to the primary benefit being less competition. The returns to less competition are not only monopoly rent. As British economist J. R. Hicks observed: "The best of all monopoly profits is a quiet life." While concentration in most global industries was on a downward trend from 1950 to 1990,[8] in recent years global concentration has increased sharply in several mature sectors. In particular:

- The world cement industry has been transformed by mergers and acquisitions from a fragmented industry populated by local producers to one dominated by four global groups: Lafarge (France), Holcim (Switzerland), Cemex (Mexico), and Heidelberg (Germany).

- In oil and gas, a wave of mergers, triggered by BP's merger with Amoco in 1997, has resulted in a small group of "supermajors:" Exxon Mobil, Royal Dutch/Shell, BP-Amoco-Arco, Total-Fina-Elf, ChevronTexaco, and Conoco-Philips.

- Investment banking has become dominated by a small group of "bulge bracket" players led by Citigroup, Goldman Sachs, Morgan Stanley Dean Witter, Merrill Lynch, and UBS.

- In aluminum the leading groups – Alcan (US), RusAl (Russia), Alcan (Canada), Norsk Hydro (Norway), and Pechiney (France) – seem poised for yet more consolidation.

- Consolidation in alcoholic drinks has resulted in distilled sprits consolidating around three leading players – Diageo, Pernod-Ricard, and Allied Domecq – and the beer sector featuring four massive global players – Anheuser Busch, Interbrew, SAB Miller, and Heineken.

Seeking More Complex Sources of Competitive Advantage

Focus on strategy fundamentals does not necessarily lead to simple strategies. In many industries increasing pressure of competition and the entry of firms with unassailable cost advantages requires that established players access new sources of profitability. As we observed in Chapter 7, there are few competitive advantages that are sustainable over a significant period of time in today's dynamic business environment. Ultimately, the only sustainable competitive advantage is the ability to create new sources of competitive advantage. A key fear of companies that have maintained both profitability and market share over periods of many years is their capacity to build layers of competitive advantage – Toyota, Wal-Mart, 3M, Canon, Dell, and L'Oreal. These companies have meshed the diverse performance goals of cost efficiency, differentiation, innovation, responsiveness, and global learning. As we shall see, reconciling the different requirements of different performance dimensions imposes highly complex organizational challenges that are pushing companies to fundamental rethinking of the structures and management systems.

The Quest for a New Model of the Corporation

The spectacular success of the corporate sector in generating shareholder value during the 1990s and the resurgence of US business over this same period owes much to a model of the firm built on shareholder sovereignty, resolution of agency problems through financial incentives and individual insecurity, and performance-based management built around an integrated system of metrics. By the late 1990s, the shareholder-based model of capitalism had spread from its Anglo-Saxon heartland to influence corporate governance and management practices in continental Europe (Germany in particular), Japan, and South Korea.

Widespread disillusion with the materialist bias, personal greed, and financial skullduggery associated with the quest for shareholder value has undermined the credibility of shareholder capitalism while failing to offer a viable alternative. Certainly, there is little evidence of any return to the managerial models of yesteryear – the US managerial capitalism of the 1960s and 1970s, the German system of stakeholder corporatism, or the Japanese corporate model based upon collaboration, lifetime employment, and continuous improvement.

If we accept that the major features of today's business world are greater dynamism and increased complexity, it seems unlikely that emerging models of management will be based upon mechanistic approaches of administrative science or the simple economic rationality of shareholder value approaches. If organizations are to achieve more effective reconciliation of the contradictions between short-run vs. long-run optimization, individual initiative vs. coordinated response, cost efficiency vs. innovation, and global integration vs. local responsiveness, models of the firm that embody a richer set of human relationships are called for.

Several approaches to the nature of the business enterprise view the firm not just as a legal and social institution, but also as a social organism that develops over time. Peter Senge regards the firm as a *learning organization* – a social organism centered on a knowledge system.[9] Arie de Geus extends this concept of the firm as a living organism to examine the processes of adaptation among the world's longest-living companies (including Stora, a Swedish paper company founded in the thirteenth century, Japan's 400-year old Sumitomo, 195-year old Du Pont, and Pilkington, the British glass maker founded in the 1820s).[10] De Geus observes that longevity is associated with *financial conservatism, sensitivity* to the external environment, and *cohesion* from a sense of identity infused through a strong corporate culture, yet with significant *tolerance* for individuality.

Moving beyond biological analogies to the elucidation of principles that relate strategy, structure and management systems to organizational performance under conditions of complexity and unpredictability requires a major leap in the theoretical analysis that we deploy within strategic management. Fortunately, there are indications that help is at hand. Let us examine two areas of theoretical advance: complexity and real options.

Complexity Theory

Across a number of different fields of study it has been shown that complex systems – open systems in which a large number of independent agents interact – are subject to common patterns of behavior. Such complex systems may be natural (weather patterns, seismic activity, or sub-atomic particles), biological (the evolution of species, the behavior of ant colonies or flocks of birds), or social (crowd behavior, group dynamics). Complexity theory relates the behavior of these complex systems.

Some of the common features of complex adaptive systems are:

- *Unpredictability.* The behavior of complex adaptive systems cannot be predicted in any precise sense. There is no tendency to stable equilibria, cascades of change are constantly interacting and reshaping competitive landscapes. Exogenous changes are subject to a *power-law distribution* whereby small changes typically result in small consequences but may also trigger major movements. The typical example is dropping grains of sand onto a sand pile where small sand movements are interspersed by major landslides.[11]

- *Self-organization.* A key feature of biological and social systems is their capacity for self-organization. As with other living organisms – bee colonies and shoals of fish – companies have the capacity to self-organize, adapt to change, and create new structures and systems in the absence of formal authority. Computer simulations of synchronized behavior show that, with just a few simple rules, sophisticated patterns of coordination emerge at the system level. For human organizations there are three main requirements for self-organization:
  - *Identity.* Organizations need to be founded on an intent that drives the sense-making process within the organization.
  - *Information.* Information provides the medium through which an organization relates to its environment and through which the individuals within the organization know how to react to external changes.
  - *Relationships.* Relationships are the pathways through which information is transformed into intelligent, coordinated action. The more access individuals have to one another, the greater the possibilities for organized activity. Responsiveness to a wide range of external circumstances necessitates every individual having a wide range of connections to other individuals, with the potential for unplanned connections.[12]

- *Inertia and chaos.* Evolutionary processes can produce three types of outcome: an orderly outcome where change is so limited that the system suffers inertia, disorder where changes produce chaotic outcomes, and an intermediate region where small changes that result in a power-law distribution result in small and large shifts and this achieves the most rapid evolutionary adaptation. These results point to the advantages of systems that evolve to the *edge of chaos* – they are capable of small, localized adaptations, but also have the potential to make larger leaps toward higher *fitness peaks* while avoiding tumbling off the fitness edge into chaos.[13]

The implications of these ideas for strategic management are radical and far-reaching. If business is a complex system, then it is inherently unpredictable – not only is it impossible to forecast the business environment, but managers cannot predict what the outcomes of their actions will be. The concept of the CEO as the peak decision maker and strategy architect is not only unrealistic, it is undesirable. Managers must rely upon the self-organizing properties of their companies. The critical issues are how can they select the structures, systems and management styles that will allow these self-organizing properties to generate the best outcomes? A key framework has been Kaufman's concept of a *fitness landscape*.[14] The challenge for managers is to design organizational systems that allow self-organization the best chance of attaining the highest level of performance (*"fitness"*). Drawing upon the contributions of Brown, Eisenhardt, McKelvey, and Levinthal, the following recommendations have been made as to how companies can best scale the performance peaks associated with locating at the edge of chaos:[15]

- *Establish simple rules.* If the complex coordinated behaviors of complex systems with no centralized authority (the flying formations of birds) can be simulated with a few simple rules, it seems feasible that such rules play a similar role in reconciling individual initiative and overall coordination within companies. Some companies do not plan strategy in any formal sense, but craft simple rules that can help locate the company where the opportunities are richest. These include rules of thumb in screening opportunities (*"boundary rules"*). Thus, Cisco's acquisitions strategy is guided by the rule that it will acquire companies with fewer than 75 employees of which 75 percent are engineers. Second, rules can designate a common approach to how the company will exploit opportunities (*"how-to rules"*). Thus, Yahoo has a few rules regarding the look and functionality of new web pages, but then gives freedom to developers to design new additions. Third, companies have rules to determine priorities in resource allocation (*"priority rules"*). Thus, Intel allocates manufacturing capacity according to each product's gross margin. It was this role that allowed it to evolve from a memory chip company to a microprocessor company even before such a transition had been determined by top management.[16] Many of Jack Welch's initiatives at GE fulfilled a similar role. Rather than offer specific direction to business-level chief executives he introduced periodically key corporate initiatives: "Be #1 or #2 in your industry," "Six-sigma," "Destroy your business dot.com." These stimulated and focused decentralized initiatives, but did not directly manage them.[17]

- *Establish conditions for both incremental and radical change.* If achieving the highest level of adaptive performance requires a combination of frequent small changes with occasional radical leaps, management systems can be designed to encourage these outcomes. Consider for example the reorientation of many companies' strategic planning systems from agreeing strategy inputs towards agreeing performance outputs. One of the merits of performance-based planning (at BP, for example) is that it provides strong incentives for cost reduction and continuous improvement, while establishing a framework where serious performance shortfalls trigger corporate intervention which will usually involve major strategic changes.

- *Accelerate evolution through flexible organizational structure.* Organizational structures tend to ossify over time as power centers build and interactions become institutionalized. Periodic large-scale corporate reorganizations are not enough: to exploit innovation and entrepreneurial initiative, flexibility in organizational structure is essential. Eisenhardt and Brown use the term "patching" to describe a process in which new organizational units are continually being created, merged, and redefined to foster initiative.[18] Achieving flexibility may require leaving structures only partially defined. This may be especially effective in assisting collaboration between different business units within a company. Rather than attempt to manage business unit linkages from the corporate level, it may be better for corporate to create a context within which businesses can co-evolve. The key elements of such a context are, first, linking rewards to individual business performance rather than to reward collaborative efforts; second, maintaining porous boundaries to each business such that a multiplicity of voluntary collaborations can thrive between individuals across the businesses. Walt Disney Company exemplifies co-evolution between different internal divisions. Disney's *Lion King* movie spawned videos, theme park attractions, a stage musical, and over 150 kinds of merchandise. These spin-offs were not planned by corporate strategists, they occurred through voluntary cooperation across Disney's different divisions.[19]

■ *Use adaptive tension to position at the edge of chaos.* Given the tendency for too little tension to produce inertia and too much to create chaos, the challenge for top management is to create a level of adaptive tension that optimizes the pace of organizational change and innovation. Bill McKelvey shows how Jack Welch's management style may be interpreted from a complexity viewpoint as imposing a set of rules and powerful incentives that established levels of adaptive tension between the 1st and 2nd critical values. The rule of "Be #1 or #2 in your industry" combined with powerful incentives for individual managers established conditions highly conducive to rapid adaptation.[20]

Applications of complexity theory to strategy management promise to add analytic support to the argument of Mintzberg and others in favor of *emergent* rather than *planned* approaches to strategy making. Mintzberg's critique of the "planning" and "design" schools of strategy making was based on the argument that intuition and decentralized processes were better ways to make strategy than rational frameworks and systematic decision processes.[21] However, by establishing a body of theory that shows how self-organization and localized adaptation can take an organization toward the edge of chaos, complexity theory provides a sound intellectual basis for Mintzberg's intuition. Many of the changes that have taken place in the strategic planning systems of large companies in recent years – reduced formality, emphasis on performance goals, focus upon direction rather than content – are consistent with the tenets of complexity theory.[22]

Real Options

We noted in Chapter 2 that there are two sources of value for individual projects or entire firms: cash flows and options. In recent years considerable progress has been made in developing principles and techniques for the valuation of real option values. Most of this analysis has been developed for valuing individual investment projects, though the same principles can be extended to valuing entire companies. However, despite these developments, our techniques of strategy analysis rest heavily upon the first component of firm value – cash flows to the firm. Thus, our analyses of industries and of resources and capabilities are primarily directed towards identifying the potential for profits.

As the business environment becomes increasingly volatile and unpredictable, the value of both projects and firms becomes increasingly dependent upon option values. Under these circumstances, the principles of real option valuation become important not just to the appraisal of investment projects, but to the formulation of firm strategy. From an options viewpoint, strategy is concerned with creating and managing options.

Analysis of strategy in terms of option-creation has focused upon particular types of strategic decisions – for example, R&D decisions,[23] acquisitions,[24] and alliance formation.[25] However, application of real options thinking to strategic analysis at a broader level has been limited to broad generalizations such as the value of flexibility. If we are to take on board options thinking more widely, then we need to reconsider most of our core strategy models and strategy techniques. For example:

- Industry analysis has taken the view that decisions about industry attractiveness depend upon profit potential. However, if industry structure becomes so unstable that forecasting industry profitability is no longer viable, it is likely that industry attractiveness will depend much more on option value. From an options perspective, an attractive industry is one that is rich in options – for example an industry that produces a number of different products, is comprised of multiple segments, has many strategic groups, utilizes a diversity of alternative technologies and raw materials and where internal mobility barriers tend to be low. Thus, consumer electronics, semiconductors, packaging, and investment banking would seem to be more attractive in terms of options than electricity or steel or car rental.

- An options approach also had major implications for the analysis of resources and capabilities. An attractive resource is one that offers opportunies for deployment in multiple businesses and to support alternative strategies. A Scottish island is likely to offer greater option value than a North Sea oilfield. Similarly with capabilities: highly specialized capabilities such as expertise in the design of petrochemical plants offers less option potential than expertise in the marketing of fast-moving consumer goods.

Some of these ideas concerning option value of capabilities have been addressed in the literature on *dynamic capabilities*. According to David Teece and colleagues, dynamic capabilities are "the firm's ability to integrate, build, and reconfigure internal and external competences to address rapidly changing environments."[26] Eisenhardt and Martin emphasize this capacity for reconfiguring their competencies: "Dynamic capabilities are the organizational and strategic routines by which firms achieve new resource combinations as markets emerge, collide, split, evolve, and die."[27] While it is easy to identify adaptable companies that, presumably, possess such dynamic capabilities – HP, Sony, 3M, and Virgin, for example – specifying in precise terms what dynamic capabilities are, where they are located, and what their internal architecture comprises represents a formidable challenge. Eisenhardt and Martin suggest that the critical feature is a process that allows the firm to alter its resource base.

REDESIGNING THE ORGANIZATION

As business environments become more complex, more competitive, and less predict-able, survival requires that companies perform at a higher level with a broader reper-toire of capabilities. Building multiple capabilities and achieving excellence across multiple performance dimensions requires managing dilemmas that cannot be resolved as sim-ple tradeoffs. A company must be efficient today, while also adapting for tomorrow; it must produce at low cost, while also innovating; it must deploy the massed resources of a large corporation, while showing the entrepreneurial flair of a small startup; it must achieve high levels of reliability and consistency, while also being flexible in adapting to change. Reconciling these conflicts within a single organization presents huge management challenges. We know how to devise structures and incentive systems that drive cost efficiency, we also know the organizational conditions conducive to innovation. But how on earth do we do both simultaneously?

Among the multiplicity of innovations and new developments in organizational design, two major trends may be discerned. The first is the design of organizations to facilitate the development and deployment of organizational capability. The second is the design of organizations to permit rapid adaptability.

Capability-based Structures

In Chapter 6, we noted that organizational design has been dominated by the require-ments of cooperation rather than coordination. As a result, hierarchical structures have emphasized control and the need for unitary lines of command. Once we acknow-ledge that building outstanding capabilities is the primary goal of organizational design, then the emphasis shifts to the need to achieve effective coordination. If we accept that most enterprises need to deploy multiple capabilities and the coordina-tion needs of different capabilities vary, it follows that our organizational structure must encompass different patterns of interaction. Hence, most business enterprises are unlikely to be successful with a unitary structure and will need to encompass multiple structures.

Beyond Unitary Structures

The principles of knowledge management offer one approach to understanding how different capabilities require different types of structure. Knowledge management dis-tinguishes between activities directed toward building the firm's stock of knowledge and those directed toward deploying the existing stock of knowledge. James March refers to the former as *exploration* and the latter as *exploitation*.[28] The observation that exploratory capabilities (R&D and market research, for example) need to be organized differently from knowledge-exploiting capabilities (operations and finance, for example) is well known. A more difficult challenge is the fact that the same people undertake both exploratory and exploitation activities as part of their same jobs. Thus, a plant manager may be primarily engaged in knowledge exploitation, but when she is involved in training activities, new product development, and benchmarking studies, her emphasis is exploration.

The solution is the simultaneous deployment of different structures for different tasks.[29] Thus, the primary structure of the firm is established for the basic tasks of knowledge exploitation – purchasing, producing, selling, distributing. However, exploratory activities, such as new product development, typically require interacting with different people within a different type of collaborative relationship. Here, a multifunctional product development team is more conducive to developing and applying product development capability. Similarly, for identifying and transferring manufacturing best practices, an informal cooperative group comprising different plant managers is likely to be most effective.

Separate structures for pursuing the exploratory activities required for developing and adapting the organization have been described as *parallel learning structures*.[30] While operational tasks typically require high levels of specialization and coordination through rules and routines, activities oriented toward innovation and adaptation require lower levels of specialization and coordination through planning and mutual adjustment, both of which are likely to be communication intensive. Examples of parallel structures include:

- At 3M, the formal structure exists in terms of business units, and divisions within which individuals have clearly defined job tasks. In addition, there is an informal structure for the purpose of new product development whereby individuals are permitted, indeed encouraged, to "bootleg" time, materials, and use of facilities to work on new product ideas. If new products that emerge from the informal structure are deemed promising, they are taken within the formal structure to be launched, and ultimately may form the basis for a business unit within the formal structure.

- Total quality management is a tool for changing work practices in order to eliminate defects and improve performance. Implementation of TQM is typically through the creation of a parallel structure of quality circles, often coordinated by quality management committees and task forces. Thus, Texaco's "Star Quality" program created a hierarchy of quality management groups extending up to the corporate-level quality team chaired by the CEO.

- GE's "Work-Out" program was a classic example of a parallel structure effecting change within the formal structure. Work-Out sessions took the form of meetings held away from GE's offices where the norms that governed the formal organization were suspended, and free interchange of ideas was encouraged. The outcome was a powerful device for initiating change within the formal structure.

- Business process reengineering and other radical change initiatives are typically initiated and implemented by task forces operating outside the formal structure. Thus, Chevron's "breakthrough teams" were formed from multiple functions and multiple vertical levels in the company and were challenged to devise ways of finding substantial reductions in costs. The result was a series of far-reaching proposals for reorganizing and outsourcing information technology, restructuring the corporate head office, and reducing operating costs.

Where the purpose of the new structures is to develop capabilities, they may be almost entirely informal. In the appendix to Chapter 5, I discussed informal knowledge-sharing networks called *communities of practice*.[31] Within the Royal Dutch/Shell Group of companies over 100 communities of practice have emerged. These have been merged into about 20 Global Networks that are focused around areas of technology such as the Wells Global Network and the Subsurface Knowledge Sharing Network, and around commercial activities such as Competitor Intelligence and Procurement. During the past eight years, communities of practice have emerged as important innovations at organizations ranging from Hewlett-Packard to the World Bank.[32]

Team-based, Project-based, and Process-based Structures

Creating structures that foster organizational capabilities may require different patterns of interaction than are typical of conventional structures. Increased reliance upon teams reflects the recognition that routines require patterns of interaction that are spontaneous and poorly understood – hence, they cannot be "managed" in any directive sense. Flexible, team-based structures can achieve the kinds of adaptable integration that are the basis of dynamic capabilities, yet, beyond some very basic requirements of team structure, we know little about the dynamics of team interaction.[33]

More companies are organizing their activities less around functions and continuous operations and more around time-designated projects where a team is assigned to a specific project with a clearly defined outcome and a specified completion date. While construction companies and consulting firms have always been structured around projects, project-based organizations, featuring temporary cross-functional teams with specific objectives, are increasingly viewed as models achieving innovation, adaptability, and rapid learning in more traditional organizations. A radical experiment in project-based organization was initiated by Oticon A/S, the Danish manufacturer of hearing aids. CEO Lars Kolind abolished Oticon's formal organization and introduced a project-based company in which over 100 self-directed projects competed to attract employees. A ten-person top management team acted as project owners, but with few decision-making responsibilities other than to enforce basic rules such as "no paper-based communication."[34]

The desire to improve coordination across multiple, linked capabilities has encouraged companies to align their structures more closely with their internal *processes*. While business process reengineering directs attention to the microstructure of processes, interest in organizational capabilities has fostered a more integrated view of processes that focuses on how individual processes fit together in sequences and networks of complementary activities. For example, a company's order fulfillment process would span the whole chain of activities, from supplying information to potential customers, to customer selection and ordering, to manufacturing, through to distribution. Similarly, the customer relations process embraces the entirety of a company's interactions with its customers through marketing and after-sales services. In many cases, these macro processes extend beyond the company. Thus, supply-chain management involves linking internal logistics with those of suppliers and suppliers'

suppliers. Volvo's reorganization of its "order fulfillment process" with the goal of a 14-day cycle between customer order and customer receipt of a customized automobile involved reorganizing and reintegrating the order process, the production planning process, supply chains, the distribution process, and dealer relations.[35]

Organizing for Adaptability

One of the implications we drew from our brief review of complexity theory was the idea that, in order to cope with a complex environment, an enterprise might have to resort to simple rules. A similar implication may be drawn in relation to internal organization. To the extent that organizations are required to perform tasks whose complexity and variety require structures and systems that we cannot design for the simple reason that we do not have the knowledge, then the optimal response may be to simplify the formal structure to allow the individuals within the organization to self-organize. Loosening the structure may be a critical step toward building the *ambidextrous organization* – one that can combine multiple capabilities and accommodate both gradual, evolutionary change and occasional revolutionary leaps.[36]

The paradox of simplicity is that reducing complexity at the formal level can foster greater variety and sophisticated coordination at the informal level. At GE, Jack Welch's system of management emphasized the "3Ss" – "Speed, Simplicity, Self-confidence." His quest for simplicity has involved a minimalist approach to formal control systems augmented with periodic corporate initiatives ("growth," "boundarylessness," and "Six-Sigma"). Yet, paradoxically, this paring down of formal systems permitted more complex patterns of coordination and collaboration within GE. Recognizing the limits of formal controls, Welch guided GE by influencing attitudes, expectations, values, and behaviors.[37]

This focus upon organizational context rather than organizational structure is a discernible trend across many companies. Thus, most companies have given more attention to organizational culture, values and modes of behavior, while relying more upon coordination occurring voluntarily and spontaneously. Three concepts have proven practically useful in this: *identity*, *modularity*, and *networks*.

Identity

To manage the organizational context includes influencing social and behavioral norms, but these depend upon some shared cognition of what the organization is and an emotional attachment towards what the organizational represents. These ideas are components of what has been termed *organizational identity* – a collective understanding of what is presumed core, distinctive, and enduring about the character of an organization.[38] A strong consensus around organizational identity provides a powerful focus for flexible, coordinated action, but to the extent that identity is rooted in a past that is not longer relevant to the present, identity can represent an impediment to strategic change. To this extent companies may need to manage their external image in order to achieve a change in identity. Thus, IBM's identity as a vertically integrated supplier of mainframe computers hampered its development as a supplier of PCs, peripherals, and IT services. Changing its identity required considerable investment in projecting images that allowed the reorientation of its identity.

Modularity

If the essence of dynamic capability is in building over time strong capabilities in technologies and specific functions, and in reconfiguring these to meet the requirements of a changing environment, what kind of structure can achieve such a combination of continuity and flexibility? In Chapter 6, we examined the argument that hierarchical structures based on loosely coupled, semi-autonomous modules possessed considerable adaptation advantages over more tightly integrated structures. Such modular structures may be particularly useful in reconciling the need for close collaboration at the small group level with the benefits of critical mass.[39] Thus, the key to Microsoft's success in designing huge software programs such as Windows NT, Internet Explorer, and Microsoft Office, which require the coordinated efforts of close to 500 software developers, is to modularize these programs using its "synch and stabilize" system.[40]

Networks

A key feature of the changes in strategy, structure, and management systems has been less distinction between what happens within the firm and what happens outside it. Organization theory emphasizes the distinction between the organization and its environment, while economics distinguishes between markets and hierarchies as alternate organizational mechanisms. The growth of inter-firm collaboration and the development of the "contingent workforce" – people who work for companies but who are not covered by long-term employment contracts – has blurred this distinction, and theory has recognized a continuum of organizational forms and a multiplicity of contractual forms that make it clear that spot markets and unitary firms are just two specific organizational forms. As "command and control" modes of management give way to less formal patterns of coordination, so internal relationships within the firm are less differentiated from external relationships. The immediate implication is that the boundaries of the firm are less distinct and more permeable. If cooperation across individuals and small enterprises can achieve the close coordination conventionally associated with corporations, the large, integrated company may disappear as the dominant organizational form in many industries. We have already noted how in the Italian clothing industry networks of small firms simultaneously achieve integration, flexibility, and innovation. The potential for networks of small firms to emulate the advantages of large corporations is evident in the Italian motorcycle industry, where small companies such as Aprilia, Italjet, and Ducati have integrated networks of suppliers to take market share from the dominant Japanese manufacturers through innovation, design, and proliferation of models.[41]

Internet technology plays a critical role in increasing the efficiency of communication and coordination within inter-firm networks. Intranets that link together internal units of the enterprise with outside suppliers, customers and partners have had a major influence in blurring corporate boundaries. At Cisco Systems, internet systems not only link customers and suppliers for the purposes of ordering and invoicing, but also provide common systems for managing technology and joint product development and extend budgeting and strategic planning systems to its partners.[42] The internet and intranets also allow the geographical expansion of networks. Some of the most remarkable and successful network forms are the open-source software communities that have created highly successful computer software such as Linux and Apache.

Inter-firm networks facilitate the design and production of complex products that require a wide range of technical and commercial capabilities in sectors subject to rapid change. In automobiles, fashion clothing, aerospace, machine tools, and telecom equipment, networks allow each firm to specialize in a few capabilities while providing the close linkages needed to integrate these different capabilities. The flexibility of these linkages offers the potential for the capabilities resident within an inter-firm network to be reconfigured in order to adapt quickly to external change.[43]

NEW MODES OF LEADERSHIP

New organizational structures and strategic priorities point to new models of leadership. The era of restructuring and shareholder focus has been associated with "change-masters"[44] – highly visible, individualistic, often hard-driving management styles of CEOs such as Lee Iacocca at Chrysler, John Browne at BP, Michael Eisner at Disney, and Rupert Murdoch at News International. These leaders have been, first and foremost, strategic decision makers, charting the direction and redirection of their companies, and making key decisions over acquisitions, divestments, new products and cost cutting.

The responses that have been suggested to the problems of complex business environments in terms of both strategy formulation and organizational design imply a very different role for the chief executive than the "buck-stops-here" peak decision-making role traditionally associated with corporate leadership. The guidelines for strategy and organization design that we have discussed so far point to management leadership as directed more toward the creation and maintenance of the organizational environment rather than decision making *per se*.

If the foundation of strategy is a sense of organizational identity, then a key role of top management is to clarify and communicate that identity. James Collins and Jerry Porras, in their influential study of successful companies *Built to Last*, emphasize the critical and complementary roles of *core values*, *core purpose*, and an *envisioned future*.[45]

The role of values and purpose is not just to provide a foundation for strategy, but also to unify and inspire the efforts of organizational members. To this end, the purpose and values of the enterprise must be consistent with those of its employees. To the extent that our lives are a search for meaning, the satisfaction that our work offers will depend critically on the congruence between organizational purpose and our own aspirations. British Petroleum's 2000 rebranding included the theme "beyond petroleum," an attempt to communicate a more meaningful and resonant image to its stakeholders than the production of petroleum products. Ultimately, creating a common identity between the organization and those who work within it may require the organization to recognize the existence of human emotion and, ultimately, the human soul.[46]

What do these considerations imply about the job of the chief executive and the top management team? The emphasis has shifted away from "the CEO as decision maker" towards "the CEO leader of organizational culture, climate, identity, and processes responsible for clarifying shared vision; enriching the culture; aligning vision, strategy, organizational design, and human resources; and promoting understanding of events."

These roles are likely to require different types of management skills:

> The balance has clearly shifted from attributes traditionally thought of as masculine (strong decision-making, leading the troops, driving strategy, waging competitive battle) to more feminine qualities (listening, relationship-building, and nurturing). The model today is not so much "take it on your shoulders" as it is to "create the environment that will enable others to carry part of the burden." The focus is on unlocking the organization's human asset potential.[47]

Research into the psychological and demographic characteristics of successful leaders has identified few consistent or robust relationships – successful leaders come in all shapes, sizes and personality types. However, a recent stream of research has pointed to the role of a set of personality attributes that have been referred to as *emotional intelligence*. These comprise:

- *Self-awareness* in terms of the ability to read and understand one's emotions and assess one's strengths and weaknesses, underlain by the confidence that stems from positive self-worth.

- *Self-management* in terms of control, integrity, conscientiousness, initiative, and achievement orientation.

- *Social awareness* in relation to sensing others' emotions (empathy), reading the organization (organizational awareness), and recognizing customers' needs (service orientation).

- *Social skills* in relation to influencing and inspiring others: communicating, collaborating, and building relationships with others; and managing change and conflict.[48]

Daniel Goleman argues that these attributes positively associated with superior performance across all leadership styles and over a wide range of management situations.

Jim Collins' studies of companies that have achieved sustained success over long periods of time also claims to have identified some common characteristics of outstandingly successful companies. What he terms "Level 5 Leadership" involves a paradoxical combination of personal humility – often shyness – and intense resolve within the organization.[49] Transformational leaders such as Philip Morris's Joseph Cullman, Kimberly-Clark's Darwin Smith and Nucor's Ken Iversen have combined these characteristics with a number of specific management practices:

- Giving priority to building the right team over creating the right strategy.

- Willingness to confront reality while maintaining faith in the future.

- Building organizational momentum.

- Possessing depth of knowledge concerning the fundamental economics of the business, what the company is best at, and how to ignite the passions of its people.

- Pioneering a few carefully selected technologies while maintaining skepticism over technology bandwagons.

- Maintaining discipline of thought, action, and people.

SUMMARY

While the future remains unknowable, its roots are in the present and the past. From what we observe today, we can identify many of the key developments of the next few years. The trends that we discern in science and technology, economic development, government policies, social structure, demographics, and lifestyles will shape the business environment for the remainder of the decade. We have reviewed some of the sources of competitive advantage in the emerging business environment and the capabilities that companies will need to develop and deploy.

Some of the most critical, and difficult, issues concern the structures, systems, and styles needed to build and exercise these capabilities. The configurations that were so successful during the last two decades of the twentieth century are unlikely to serve enterprises so well in this first decade of the twenty-first.

Emerging theories of complexity, self-organization, knowledge management, and leadership can augment our existing standard tools of strategic management. Even more encouraging is the fact that experimentation and innovation at the coal-face of managerial practice offer lessons that are yielding solutions capable of wider application and the seeds of new principles and frameworks. AES's "honeycomb" structures, Sun Microsystems' networks of alliances, Kao Corporation's system of "biological self-control," Yahoo!'s strategy of "structured emergence," and Oticon's "spaghetti organization" suggest novel approaches to managing within complex, high-velocity environments.

Strategic management remains highly dependent on concepts and theories drawn from the basic disciplines of economics, sociology, psychology, biology, and systems theory. However, the encouraging feature of the past few years has been greater synthesis across these disciplines and between theory and practice. One indicator of progress is that strategic management is less obviously a net importer of ideas and findings from its contributing disciplines. In areas such as the analysis of competition, determinants of long-run profitability, organizational design, and the management of technology, it is strategic management scholars who are breaking new ground and influencing thinking in the underlying disciplines.

Formidable challenges lie ahead. As the opportunities for creating value from downsizing, refocusing, restructuring, and reengineering have become mined out, so managers have been forced to explore new territory seeking new sources of competitive advantage. In the aftermath of the late-1990s' technology, it is apparent that new sources of value are elusive. While our basic tools of strategy analysis – industry analysis and the analysis of resource and capabilities – remain valid and robust, it is clear that we shall need to continually develop our concepts and frameworks to meet the circumstances of tomorrow. The challenge is to apply what we know, recognize what we don't know, and engage in reflective observation in order to extend our domain of understanding.

NOTES

1 Paul Romer, "The Soft Revolution," *Journal of Applied Corporate Finance* (Summer 1998); Carl Shapiro and Hal Varian, *Information Rules* (Boston: Harvard University Press, 1998).

2 "Intel: What is CEO Craig Barrett up to?," *Business Week* (March 8, 2004).

3 "Catch Us if You Can," *Fortune* (February 9, 2004): 64–74.

4 D. N. Barron, "Evolutionary Theory," in D. O. Faulkner and A. Campbell, *Oxford Handbook of Strategy*, vol. 1 (Oxford: Oxford University Press, 2003): 90–1.

5 S. Ghoshal, C. A. Bartlett, and P. Moran, "A New Manifesto for Management," *Sloan Management Review* (Spring 1999): 9–20.

6 S. L. Hart and M. B. Milstein, "Creating Sustainable Value," *Academy of Management Executive* 17 (May 2003): 56–67; C. K. Prahalad and Allen Hammond, "Serving the World's Poor, Profitably," *Harvard Business Review* (September 2002): 68–77.

7 Lynda Gratton, *Living Strategy: Putting People at the Heart of Corporate Purpose* (FT/Prentice Hall, 2000).

8 P. Ghemawat and F. Ghadar, "The Dubious Logic of Global Megamergers," *Harvard Business Review* (July–August 2000): 64–74.

9 Peter Senge, *The Fifth Discipline* (London: Century, 1990); Peter Senge, A. A. Kleiner, Charlotte Roberts, Richard Ross, George Roth, and Bryan Smith, *The Dance of Change: The Challenges to Sustaining Momentum in Learning Organizations* (New York: Doubleday, 1999).

10 A. de Geus, *The Living Company* (Boston: Harvard Business School Press, 1997). See also "How to Live Long and Prosper," *Economist* (May 10, 1997): 59.

11 P. Bak, *How Nature Works: The Science of Self-organized Criticality* (New York: Copernicus, 1996).

12 M. J. Wheatley and M. Kellner Rogers, *A Simpler Way* (Berrett-Koehler, 1996); M. J. Wheatley and M. Kellner Rogers, "Self-Organization: The Irresistible Future of Organizing," *Strategy and Leadership* 24 (July–August 1996): 18–25.

13 For a review of the development of complexity theory and its applications to management, see P. Anderson, "Complexity Theory and Organizational Science," *Organization Science* 10 (1999): 216–32.

14 S. A. Kaufman, *The Origins of Order: Self Organization and Selection In Evolution* (New York: Oxford University Press, 1993).

15 S. L. Brown and K. M. Eisenhardt, *Competing on the Edge: Strategy as Structured Chaos* (Boston: Harvard Business School Press, 1998); W. McKelvey, "Energizing

Order-creating Networks of Distributed Intelligence: Improving the Corporate Brain," *International Journal of Innovation Management* 5 (June 2001): 132–54; D. A. Levinthal, "Adaptation on a Rugged Landscape," *Management Science* 43 (1997): 934–50.

16 For discussion of the role of rules in strategy making, see K. M. Eisenhardt and D. Sull, "Strategy as Simple Rules," *Harvard Business Review* (January–February 2001): 107–16.

17 Bill McKelvey, "A Simple Rule Approach to CEO Leadership in the 21st Century" (Paper presented at the ISUFI Conference, Ostuni, Italy, September 11–13, 2003).

18 K. M. Eisenhardt and S. L. Brown, "Patching: Restitching Business Portfolios in Dynamic Markets," *Harvard Business Review* (May–June 1999): 72–84.

19 K. M. Eisenhardt and D. C. Galunic, "Coevolving: At Last, a Way to Make Synergies Work," *Harvard Business Review* (January–February 2000): 91–101.

20 Bill McKelvey, "A Simple Rule Approach to CEO Leadership," op cit.

21 H. Mintzberg, *The Rise and Fall of Strategic Planning* (New York: Free Press, 1994); H. Mintzberg, B. Ahlstrand, and J. Lampel, *Strategy Safari: A Guided Tour through the Wilds of Strategic Management* (New York: Free Press, 1998).

22 R. M. Grant, "Strategic Planning In a Turbulent Environment: Evidence from the Oil Majors," *Strategic Management Journal* 24 (2003): 491–518.

23 R. G. McGrath, "A Real Option Logic for Initiating Technology Positioning Investment," *Academy of Management Review* 22 (1997): 974–96.

24 H. T. J. Smit, "Acquisition Strategies as Option Games," *Journal of Applied Corporate Finance* (2001): 79–89.

25 M. J. Leiblein and D. D. Miller, "An Empirical Examination of the Effect of Uncertainty and Firm Strategy on the Vertical Boundaries of the Firm," *Strategic Management Journal* 24 (2003): 839–60.

26 D. J. Teece, G. Pisano, and A. Shuen, "Dynamic Capabilities and Strategic Management," *Strategic Management Journal* 18 (1997): 509–33.

27 K. M. Eisenhardt and J. A. Martin, "Dynamic Capabilities: What are They?," *Strategic Management Journal* 21 (2000): 1105–21.

28 J. G. March, "Exploration and Exploitation in Organizational Learning," *Organization Science* 2 (1991): 71–8.

29 J. Ridderstråle, "Business Moves Beyond Bureaucracy," *Financial Times*, Mastering Management (November 6, 2000): 14–15.

30 G. Bushe and A. B. Shani, *Parallel Learning Structures* (Reading, MA: Addison-Wesley, 1991).

31 J. S. Brown and P. Duguid, "Organizational Learning and Communities of Practice," *Organizational Science* 2 (1991): 40–57.

32 E. C. Wenger and W. M. Snyder, "Communities of Practice: The Organizational Frontier," *Harvard Business Review* (January–February 2000).

33 J. R. Katzenbach and D. K. Smith, "The Discipline of Teams," *Harvard Business Review* (March–April 1993): 111–20.

34 For description and analysis of the Oticon experiment, see "This Organization Is Disorganization," *Fast Company* (April 1997): 77–83; and N. J. Foss, "Internal Disaggregation in Oticon: An Organizational Economics Interpretation of the Rise and Decline of the Spaghetti Organization" (Department of Industrial Economics and Strategy, Copenhagen Business School, October 2000).

35 S. Hertz, J. K. Johansson, and F. de Jager, "Customer-focused Cost Cutting: Process Management at Volvo," *Journal of Supply Chain Management* 6, no. 3 (2001): 128–41.

36 M. L. Tushman and C. A. O'Reilly III, "The Ambidextrous Organization: Managing Evolutionary and Revolutionary Change," *California Management Review* 38, no. 4 (Summer 1996): 8–30.

37 "General Electric: End of the Welch Era," in R. M. Grant, *Cases in Contemporary Strategy Analysis*, 3rd edn (Oxford: Blackwell, 2002).

38 D. A. Gioia, M. Schultz, and K. G. Corley, "Organizational Identity, Image and Adaptive Instability," *Academy of Management Review* 25 (2000): 63–81.

39 R. Sanchez and T. Mahoney, "Modularity, Flexibility and Knowledge Management in Product and Organization Design," *Strategic Management Journal* 17, Winter Special Issue (1996): 63–76; M. A. Schilling, "Toward a General Modular Systems Theory and its Application to Inter-firm Product Modularity," *Academy of Management Review* 25 (2000): 312–34.

40 M. A. Cusumano, "How Microsoft Makes Large Teams Work Like Small Teams," *Sloan Management Review* (Fall 1997): 9–20.

41 G. Lorenzoni, A. Lipparini, and M. Zollo, "Dual Network Strategies: Managing Knowledge-based and Efficiency-based Networks in the Italian Motorcycle Industry," Discussion paper (2001).

42 P. J. Brews, "The Challenge of the Web-Enabled Business," *Financial Times*, Mastering Management (November 27, 2000): 4–7. See also D. Tapscott, D. Ticoll, and A. Lowry, *Digital Capital: Harnessing the Power of Business Webs* (Boston: Harvard Business School Press, 2000).

43 R. Gulati, N. Nohria, and A. Zaheer, "Strategic Networks," *Strategic Management Journal* 21 (2000): 203–15, reviews recent research into inter-firm networks.

44 R. M. Kanter, *The Change Masters* (New York: Simon & Schuster, 1983).

45 J. C. Collins and J. I. Porras, *Built to Last* (New York: Harper Business, 1996).

46 L. Grattan, "Building Companies Founded on People," *Financial Times* Mastering Management (November 27, 2000): 14–15; L. Grattan, *Living Strategy: Putting People at the Heart of Corporate Purpose* (London: Prentice Hall, 2000).

47 Ruth L. Williams and Joseph P. Cothrel, "Building Tomorrow's Leaders Today," *Strategy and Leadership* 26 (September–October 1997): 17–23.

48 D. Goleman, "What Makes a Leader?," *Harvard Business Review* (November–December 1998): 93–102.

49 J. Collins, "Level 5 Leadership: The Triumph of Humility and Fierce Resolve," *Harvard Business Review* (January 2001): 67–76.

Index